Handbook of Communication in the Legal Sphere

Handbooks of
Applied Linguistics

Communication Competence
Language and Communication Problems
Practical Solutions

Edited by
Karlfried Knapp
Daniel Perrin
Marjolijn Verspoor

Volume 14

Handbook of Communication in the Legal Sphere

Edited by
Jacqueline Visconti

With the collaboration of Monika Rathert

ISBN 978-1-5015-1092-2
e-ISBN (PDF) 978-1-61451-466-4
e-ISBN (EPUB) 978-1-5015-0110-4

Library of Congress Cataloging-in-Publication Data
Names: Visconti, Jacqueline, 1966- editor.
Title: Handbook of communication in the legal sphere / edited
 by/Herausgegeben von Jacqueline Visconti.
Description: Berlin ; Boston : De Gruyter Mouton, 2018. | Series:
Handbooks
 of applied linguistics ; 14 | Includes bibliographical references and
 index.
Identifiers: LCCN 2018017457 (print) | LCCN 2018021142 (ebook) | ISBN
 9781614516699 (hardback) | ISBN 9781501510922 | ISBN 9781501501104 (e-book
 epub)
Subjects: LCSH: Law--Language. | Forensic linguistics. | BISAC: LANGUAGE ARTS
 & DISCIPLINES / Linguistics / General. | LAW / General.
Classification: LCC K213 (ebook) | LCC K213 .H359 2018 (print) | DDC
 340/.14--dc23
LC record available at https://lccn.loc.gov/2018017457

Bibliographic information published by the Deutsche Nationalbibliothek
The Deutsche Nationalbibliothek lists this publication in the Deutsche Nationalbibliografie;
detailed bibliographic data are available in the Internet at http://dnb.dnb.de.

© 2024 Walter de Gruyter Inc., Boston/Berlin
This volume is text- and page-identical with the hardback published in 2018.
Typesetting: Integra Software Services Pvt. Ltd.
Printing and binding: CPI books GmbH, Leck

www.degruyter.com

Preface

The present handbook constitutes Volume 14 of the De Gruyter Mouton *Handbooks of Applied Linguistics*. This series is based on an understanding of Applied Linguistics as an inter- and transdisciplinary field of academic enquiry. The Handbooks of Applied Linguistics provide a state-of-the-art description of established and emerging areas of Applied Linguistics. Each volume gives an overview of the field, identifies most important traditions and their findings, identifies the gaps in current research, and gives perspectives for future directions.

In the late 1990s when the handbook series was planned by its Founding Editors Gerd Antos and Karlfried Knapp, intensive debates were going on as to whether Applied Linguistics should be restricted to applying methods and findings from linguistics only or whether it should be regarded as a field of interdisciplinary synthesis drawing on psychology, sociology, ethnology and similar disciplines that are also dealing with aspects of language and communication. Should it be limited to foreign language teaching or should it widen its scope to language-related issues in general? Thus, what *Applied Linguistics* means and what an Applied Linguist does was highly controversial at the time.

Against this backdrop, Gerd Antos and Karlfried Knapp felt that a series of Handbooks of Applied Linguistics could not simply be an accidental selection of descriptions of research findings and practical activities that were or could be published in books and articles labeled as "applied linguistic". Rather, for them such a series had to be based on an epistemological concept that frames the status and scope of the concept of Applied Linguistics. Departing from contemporary Philosophy of Science, which sees academic disciplines under the pressure to successfully solve practical everyday problems encountered by the societies which aliment them, the founding editors emphasized the view that was only emerging at that time – the programmatic view that Applied Linguistics means the solving of real world problems with language and communication. This concept has become mainstream since.

In line with the conviction that Applied Linguistics is for problem solving, we developed a series of handbooks to give representative descriptions of the ability of this field of academic inquiry and to provide accounts, analyses, explanations and, where possible, solutions of everyday problems with language and communication. Each volume of the Handbook of Applied Linguistics series is unique in its explicit focus on topics in language and communication as areas of everyday problems and in pointing out the relevance of Applied Linguistics in dealing with them.

This series has been well received in the academic community and among practitioners. In fact, its success has even triggered competitive handbook series by other publishers. Moreover, we recognized further challenges with language and communication and distinguished colleagues keep on approaching us with proposals to edit further volumes in this handbook series. This motivates both De Gruyter Mouton publishers and the series editors to further develop the *Handbooks of Applied Linguistics*.

Karlfried Knapp (Erfurt), Founding Editor
Daniel Perrin (Zürich), Editor
Marjolijn Verspoor (Groningen), Editor

Contents

List of Figures —— IX

Jacqueline Visconti
Introduction —— 1

Part I: The foundations of legal language

Christopher Williams
1 **Legal drafting** —— 13

Lawrence M. Solan
2 **The interpretation of laws** —— 36

Janny HC Leung
3 **Language rights** —— 54

Richard Powell
4 **Language planning and legal systems** —— 83

Tommaso Agnoloni and Giulia Venturi
5 **Semantic processing of legal texts** —— 109

Part II: Forensic linguistics and court setting

Barbara Pasa and Lucia Morra
6 **Implicit legal norms** —— 141

Sabine Ehrhardt
7 **Authorship attribution analysis** —— 169

Georgina Heydon
8 **Topic management in police-suspect interviewing** —— 201

Michael Jessen
9 **Forensic voice comparison** —— 219

Chris Heffer
10 Narrative practices and voice in court —— 256

Part III: Legal language outside of court

Alan Durant and Jennifer Davis
11 Linguistic analysis in trade mark law: current approaches and new challenges —— 287

Roger W. Shuy
12 Defamation, language and linguistics —— 321

Peter Robson
13 Future directions in law and popular culture: a British perspective —— 339

Part IV: International legal settings

Silvia Ferreri
14 Multilingual interpretation of European Union law —— 373

Marina Timoteo
15 Contemporary Chinese law: a linguistic perspective —— 402

Roberta Aluffi
16 Unity and varieties of Arabic as a legal language: practices of interpretation and translation —— 423

Domenico Francavilla
17 Law, language and communication in the Indian context —— 435

Andrea Ortolani
18 The many languages of Japanese legal language —— 450

Biographical notes —— 479

Index —— 485

List of Figures

Figure 5.1	LRI-Core layers: foundational and legal core share *anchors* (high level concepts typical for law) (Breuker and Hoekstra 2004) —— 116
Figure 5.2	Ontology Learning Layer Cake (Buitelaar, Cimiano and Magnini 2005) —— 118
Figure 5.3	T2K^2 workflow —— 127
Figure 5.4	A screenshot of the knowledge graph extracted from the collection of Italian European directives on consumer protection —— 129
Figure 5.5	Extract of the DALOS Knowledge Base —— 132
Figure 9.1	Abstract representation of different combinations of intra-individual and inter-individual variation —— 221
Figure 9.2	Histogram of articulation rate in a population of 100 male adult speakers of German —— 223
Figure 9.3	The odds form of Bayes' theorem applied to FVC —— 233
Figure 9.4	Schematic illustration of LR-calculation in a case with high similarity and low typicality —— 235
Figure 9.5	Schematic illustration of LR-calculation in a case with high similarity and high typicality —— 236
Figure 9.6	Schematic illustration of Gaussian Mixture Models for suspect data and the background model —— 239
Figure 9.7	Same illustration as in Figure 9.6, now supplied with Evidence —— 240
Figure 9.8	Likelihood ratio concept used with the Direct Method of Forensic Automatic Speaker Recognition —— 241
Figure 9.9	Example of a Tippett plot —— 246
Figure 10.1	The Voice Projection framework —— 269

Jacqueline Visconti
Introduction

The study of legal communication has become increasingly interdisciplinary over the past fifty years. Besides fields traditionally interested in legal language, such as philosophy and, more recently, linguistics, this study has attracted an array of other disciplines, such as economics, sociology, psychology and anthropology. Communication within the realms of law and administration of justice is indeed a multifaceted phenomenon, facing problems presented by globalization, migration and increasing multilingualism in the legal domain, and involving crucial equality issues in access to justice in more complex, multicultural societies.

The obscurity of legal language, in particular, has been criticized in most, if not all, legal traditions. An impulse towards improving transparency and clarity has been provided by the plain language movement, which has mainly addressed the language of the law and contracts (cf. Williams 2011 for an update). In the past few decades, the issue has been raised also in relation to judicial texts: as pointed out by Lord Neuberger in a speech on open justice (March 2011), judges should avoid making judgments that are "readable by few, comprehensible by fewer still" (see also e.g. Kimble 2006). Such initiatives have also recently been extended to civil law settings (cf. e.g. the Italian *Ministero della Giustizia* 2016 and Montolío 2012 for a similar initiative by the Spanish Government).

Yet, obscurity need not be a feature of legal writing. As Italian lawyer and politician Vittorio Scialoja wrote, law is the art of tracing limits, and a limit does not exist unless it is clear.[1] As is well known in both the linguistic and the legal world, the reconstruction of the meaning of a text, i.e. its interpretation, is a complex operation, involving parameters of a linguistic, situational, inter-textual, cognitive, cultural and ideological nature. The fascination with the performative, "magical", character of legal language, as a language to "do things with words", was already perceived by philosophers such as Leonhardus Lessius in the XVII century or Karl Olivecrona in the XX century, and it is still thriving today (cf. Visconti 2009: 394–395).

The complex set of relations between language and law has been the topic of many recent monographs, collected volumes on the pragmatics of legal language, conferences and Handbooks (suffice it to mention, looking at the past few years only, Capone and Poggi 2016–2017; Coulthard and Johnson 2010; Giltrow and Stein 2017; Kurzon and Kryk-Kastovsky 2018; Solan and Tiersma 2012).

---

[1] "*Il diritto è arte di tracciare limiti, e un limite non esiste se non in quanto sia chiaro*" (Scialoja 1911: 942) [my translation].

Jacqueline Visconti, DIRAAS, University of Genova, Honorary Fellow (University of Birmingham)

https://doi.org/10.1515/9781614514664-001

So, why yet another handbook on the topic? The novelty of the present handbook, besides the striking interdisciplinary span of its contributions, is twofold: while most research on legal language is conducted by linguists and philosophers, this one sees a dominant share of contributions from lawyers; this signals a welcome and needed innovation in an interdisciplinary field that (with few exceptions) has seen until recently a lukewarm response by legal experts, and allows us to get a new view on the many facets of the relationship between language and law.

Secondly, while most handbooks focus on the Anglo-Saxon and European legal traditions, this one includes chapters dedicated to Arabic, Chinese, Indian, and Japanese legal language; in such traditions the interface between language and law takes forms that may be unexpected in our most familiar legal settings.

The topics addressed in this volume range from foundational issues, such as legal drafting and interpretation, language rights, language planning, artificial intelligence modeling of legal reasoning (Part I), to essential updates in forensic linguistics and court settings, such as authorship attribution, forensic speaker comparison, narrative practices in court, implicit aspects of meaning, and police suspect interviewing (Part II), recent trends in trade mark law, defamation, and less widely discussed topics, such as the relation of law with popular culture, film and television (Part III), as well as the above-mentioned lesser-known international settings (Part IV).

In the remainder of this section, a description of the contributions will provide further insights into the amplitude and interest of the debated topics.

Part I: The foundations of legal language

Chapter 1, by Chris Williams, focuses on legal drafting, a highly formal and complex style of writing that has evolved over the centuries where extreme precision and detail are usually required. Some of the key features of legal drafting are analyzed, in particular the characteristics distinguishing legislative drafting from contract drafting. Some of the similarities and differences are outlined between the drafting style of the civil law system – which is based on Roman law – and that of the common law system operating in most English-speaking countries. The way legal drafting has developed in the English-speaking world is assessed, in relation to the pressure exerted by proponents of 'plain language'. Finally, possible developments for the future of legal drafting are outlined, with particular reference to the impact of information technology on how legal drafters write and how their work is increasingly under scrutiny by experts and non-experts.

Legal interpretation, in particular the tension between fidelity to the language of the law and fidelity to the communicative intent of the lawmaker, is the focus of Chapter 2, by Lawrence Solan. In both civil law systems and common law systems, the law privileges a statute's language as the most important factor in interpretation when a dispute arises. In an ideal world, the language of the law would always convey the intention of the legislature. When it fails to do so, Lawrence Solan argues, the problem is most often a matter attempting to apply the law to borderline cases of the meanings of individual words within the law, i.e., vagueness. On other occasions, the problem stems from pragmatic inference. Far less frequently are the problems of statutory interpretation a function of linguistic semantics, or the aspects of meaning that derive from the syntactic structure of the sentences that a statute contains. Using chiefly examples from the U.S., but also examples from other legal systems, this chapter attempts to describe which aspects of our linguistic capacity are most in tune with the values of a legal system heavily dependent upon language, and where the goals of the legal system and language work at cross-purposes.

Chapter 3, by Janny Leung, addresses language rights, a less widely discussed and yet distinct intersection between language and law, which views law as a protector of language. The topic is more macroscopic than topics usually investigated by linguistic or legal analysis alone, and crosses disciplinary boundaries between linguistics, law, policy, education and politics. The chapter describes the historical, political and legal context of language rights, outlines relevant international human rights instruments and national law, and examines the theoretical foundations and conceptual definitions involved in what has now become an established "language rights paradigm" before offering a detailed critique and outlining challenges facing the field.

Combining research on language planning, examination of legislation and judicial resources, observations of court proceedings, and interviews with lawyers and law lecturers, Chapter 4 by Ric Powell discusses how and why language planning is applied to the legal domain, how this affects legal practice, and what its implications are for access to justice. Except in cases of legal revolution or transplant, language reform in legal domains proceeds cautiously. In the common law tradition, manipulation of language status, corpus and acquisition has been initiated in a dozen or so postcolonial polities to introduce national languages or languages of wider communication into systems that hitherto functioned predominantly in English. In most cases the result of planning has not gone much beyond predominantly oral use of an additional language, alongside the existing medium, at lower court level. However, there have been more extensive effects in Canada, Hong Kong, Malaysia and the Subcontinent, while Myanmar has replaced English by Burmese in all areas except legal education. The question therefore arises of why language-in-law reform is rarely extensive, and what circumstances have impelled it in those polities where it has proceeded furthest. In addition to examining the motivations for and mechanisms of language planning this chapter considers how it affects those who work in the legal domain. The result of reform is invariably legal bilingualism, involving the use of at least two languages in courtrooms, law offices and law schools, and the burdens and benefits of this bilingualism fall primarily on practitioners mediating between professionals using one language or register and lay participants using another. The chapter concludes by reflecting on whether reforming the medium of law is likely to enhance access to justice. This raises the important question of what else changes in law when the medium in which it is administered changes.

Chapter 5 by Tommaso Agnoloni and Giulia Venturi provides an overview of the field of semantic processing of legal texts, combining views and perspectives from the computational linguistic and Artificial Intelligence and Law (AI & Law) communities. How to connect the computational models to tasks that attorneys, judges, and law students actually perform and texts they actually use has been and is still today the main goal of the AI & Law community. A number of studies have been carried out so far devoted to access and model the semantics of legal discourse implicitly encoded in legal documents. At the same time, it has always been well-known that modeling what a lawyer does is more complex than modeling experts in technical/scientific domains. This is due on the one hand to the fact that the language of legal documents is highly convoluted and "unnatural", and on the other hand to the fact that making a computer able to perform legal reasoning entails that it would be able to represent and reason about [...] situations using a great deal of commonsense knowledge as well as technical knowledge. In this context, it is of paramount importance the use of Natural Language Processing (NLP) techniques and tools that, when complemented with tools for knowledge management, enable computers to process the content (the semantics) of a large amount of documents by relying on the underlying linguistic structure. It is shown how the two research communities can benefit from the interaction of these two approaches: the legal artificial intelligence community can gain insight into the advantages offered by state-of-the-art linguistic technologies, and computational linguists can take advantage of the already existing legal resources (corpora as well as lexicons and ontologies) for training, adapting and evaluating state-of-the-art NLP technologies to the specificity of the legal domain.

Part II: Forensic linguistics and court setting

Chapter 6 by Barbara Pasa and Lucia Morra aims to provide further insight into implicit legal norms, building on previous studies from both the legal and the linguistics domain (Sacco's 'cryptotypes' and Grice's 'implicatures'). The chapter proposes and discusses a functional taxonomy, illustrating how different types of implicit legal norms can be identified. This may be of particular interest to judges and lawyers: as interpreters of the law, they are involved in a strategic, non-cooperative game with the legislature and cannot ignore the fact that a legal text will imply more that it says. The empirical cases provide focus on gender discrimination analysed in a comparative perspective (for instance, a judgment made on the implicit assumption that marriage is naturally linked to a heterosexual paradigm as enshrined in a Constitution, or a statute based on the implicit assumption that the parent and child relationship requires a biological relation between them); they constitute the basis of an illustrative corpus of study which may contribute to future research in this promising field.

The written language of letters, e-mails, text messages etc. becomes the object of forensic analyses when it is used to commit a criminal offence and when it is relevant as a trace to an offender. For obvious reasons, offenders send their writings anonymously, and for similarly obvious reasons, law enforcement procedures are aimed at revoking this anonymity by either socio-linguistically profiling the authors of anonymous texts or by conducting comparative analyses. The linguistic discipline which focuses on the inference of author-specific characteristics from the characteristics of a text is commonly denoted as authorship attribution, which is part of the multifaceted field of forensic linguistics. Chapter 7 by Sabine Ehrhardt provides a broad overview of the field with an explicit emphasis on the specific conditions that prevail in a forensic context. First of all, it is devoted to the objectives of forensic linguistic analyses, including the notion of idiolect as basic assumption, the scope of forensic linguistic analyses and the specific tasks that are requested by mandating parties or authorities. Moving from the objectives to the methods of authorship analyses, it discusses qualitative, statistical and automatic approaches. Finally, the objects of forensic linguistic analyses, i.e. texts as offences and in the context of offences, are looked at in detail focusing on a corpus of forensic text samples that have been analysed and collected in a law enforcement authority over a period of 10 years.

Chapter 8 on police-suspect interviewing by Georgina Heydon examines the interactional priorities of police interviews with suspects and discusses the utilization of linguistic theory to enhance the interview model. Although the international research supporting interviewing has been dominated over the past two decades by the discipline of psychology, recently a number of studies focussing on the language of police interviewing have demonstrated the valuable contributions to be made by forensic linguists. Initially, this chapter will provide an overview of linguistic contributions to the field of police interviewing research. Following this, three main features of police interviews will be discussed, each of which relates to the institutional goals of police-suspect interviews: voluntariness, narrative accounts, and the right to silence. Each of these features will be analysed using linguistic methods, primarily drawn from Conversation Analysis, including turn-taking structures, preference and topic management. The results will be applied to the cognitive interviewing model in order to explain the relevance of linguistic perspectives to the practice of police interviewing. Finally, the chapter will discuss the opportunities and challenges around introducing linguistic insights to police officers during their interviewing training courses.

Forensic Voice Comparison (FVC), also known as Forensic Speaker Comparison, is one of the most widely used applications in the field of forensic speech and audio analysis, and is the subject of Chapter 9 by Michael Jessen.

The court or another mandating authority is interested to know whether for any given pair of audio recordings, the same speaker or two different speakers occur in these two recordings. There are different established methodological approaches to address the FVC task and there are some general principles that are common to all approaches. At the beginning of this chapter, these general principles are explained, focusing on the notions of speaker-discriminatory power (the ability to effectively distinguish between speakers), intra- vs. inter-individual variation, similarity and typicality, and the multidimensionality and (in)dependence of different speaker-discriminatory features. The classification of different approaches that is used in this chapter is one that distinguishes between the auditory-acoustic approach on the one hand and the automatic and semiautomatic approach on the other hand. What defines these approaches and what the stronger and weaker aspects of them are is shown in subsequent sections and summarised in a conclusion.

Chapter 10 by Chris Heffer is centred on narrative practices in court. Understanding forensic narrative helps us to understand better both the nature of the legal process and the nature of narrative. Since legal cases fundamentally concern disputed stories of wrongdoing, narrative remains highly significant to the legal process in general and the trial context in particular. However, the institutional and evidential complexity of a trial, along with its anti-narrative legal constraints, challenge our literary- and conversation-based conceptions of narrative. To understand the narrativity of the trial, then, we need to consider not just the textual product (narrative text, however that is defined) but also the discursive practices that lead to the construction of the forensic narrative. Considering forensic narrative in the broader context of legal communication can give us a deeper understanding of how narrators might lose voice in court. For example, the discursive asymmetry of witness examination, with the lawyer in firm interactional control, is far less significant than broader issues of authority, power and ideology that determine the conditions for, and uptake of, narrative practices in court. The final section of the chapter considers how differences in narrative practices might be consequential to trial outcomes and reflects critically on one or two possible reforms.

Part III: Legal language outside of court

Chapter 11, by Alan Durant and Jennifer Davis, focuses on current approaches and new challenges in trade mark law. Trade mark law is prominent among areas considered of special interest to scholars concerned with language use in the legal sphere. This chapter describes the interaction that has taken place between law and linguistics on the subject. It begins with a summary of the main legal measures governing verbal signs used as marks, taking European Union trade mark law as its main point of reference but introducing US law where appropriate. The chapter describes how courts address language-related questions associated with trade marks, and asks how compatible the kinds of understanding of communication relied on in trade mark law are with accounts developed in linguistics. Highlighting both commonality and contrast, the contribution made to trade mark law by linguists in two major traditions is discussed: an applied linguistic tradition of expert evidence and an interdisciplinary tradition of efforts to understand how trade marks work in semiotic terms. The chapter then considers several 'intermediate' studies between linguistics and trade mark law: studies which mobilise linguistic scholarship in support of arguments for specific changes in the law. Examples of such interdisciplinary work are all concerned with US law. But, although it is largely US scholars who have paid most attention to linguistic issues in trade mark law, the insights and difficulties of such work can also illuminate approaches taken by the European courts and the challenges they face. The chapter concludes with a discussion of how linguistic contributions to trade mark law might be developed through further collaboration between lawyers and linguists.

Chapter 12 by Roger W. Shuy deals with defamation. It begins with definitions of defamation in American law, noting certain differences that apply in the laws of British, German, and other jurisdictions. Defamation includes both slander (spoken language) and libel (written language). Next is a brief description of how American laws of defamation developed over time and exist today, followed by an overview of the theory and tools used by linguists whose assistance is called upon by retaining lawyers in defamation cases. These linguistic tools include brief descriptions of pragmatics, speech acts, grammatical referencing, discourse analysis of the text, and discourse framing found in the language evidence. To illustrate the specific ways these linguistic tools are used, six actual American defamation cases in which the author either consulted or testified at trial are reviewed. Such lawsuits illustrate how the felicity conditions of speech acts such as accusing, opining, reporting, requesting, and apologizing provided salient evidence for determining whether or not defamation could be proved. The cases also helped untangle grammatical references, provided clues to the possible intentions of the speakers and writers, revealed the uses of visual and discourse framing, and addressed the knotty issue of conveyed meaning.

Chapter 13 by Peter Robson is about future directions in law and popular culture. This essay notes the emergence of a thriving literature on law and popular culture over the past 20 years focusing principally on film but also looking at television. Law and film has had a much closer connection with how and law and justice are presented to audiences today. This scholarship started with a practical concern as to how accurate the portrayal of the legal system was. The work has developed to look at the impact on political and social issues of films on the justice system. The nature of the link between the narrative structure of the courtroom and the drama of the film has important implications for legal practice. This has given law and film a relevance beyond the academy. Equally important has been the work to assess the impact of the art form on the behaviour of the people. The initial assumption that there must be some kind of causal link has been addressed to a limited extent with empirical studies. The chapter also looks at the limited scholarship on television with its focus on policing rather than lawyering. Whilst examining the expansion of this work and the continued appeal of law and film, it goes on to pose questions about the methodology of much of the law and popular culture scholarship. The chapter asks how films are deemed important and how their analysis can get beyond demonstrating a connection with a purported *Zeitgeist*. Other approaches with their strengths and weakness are noted. The essay concludes with an attempt to go beyond the critical and provide a constructive approach to a specific issue on British television in the form of how judges have been portrayed.

Part IV: International legal settings

Chapter 14 by Silvia Ferreri concerns multilingual interpretation of European Union law. The policy implemented within the EEC by Regulation N. 1/1958 to guarantee the citizens' linguistic rights provides that all the official languages of the Member states have the same status. The European Court of Justice (ECJ) has repeatedly confirmed the equal value of all the linguistic versions. This ambitious choice has created a real challenge for the drafters of legislation and interpreters alike. Very few similar experiences exist in contemporary times, perhaps only South Africa has a similar variety of official languages. The reaction of many observers has often been tainted of skepticism: the least that can generally be said is that judges will hardly be able to effectively consider all the (now) 24 versions of any piece of relevant legislation. The most likely situation is that an interpreter will seek confirmation of his/her reading of a disputed provision in the languages most similar to one's own (or in a foreign language that for historical reasons is widely known in a certain territory). Within the ECJ case law one of the most evident consequences is the prevailing inclination toward a purposive interpretation: only having regard to the aims of a regulation or a directive announced in the opening recitals and in the preparatory works can an ambiguous rule be clarified if more than one texts are equally equivalent and none of them has the standing of "authentic" text.

Chapter 15 by Marina Timoteo focuses on Chinese law and language. Modern Chinese legal language is largely a translated language, as a result of an extensive process of modernization through legal transplants in various law fields, which is intimately connected with the creation of new law taxonomies. These legal transplants have posed several relevant problems in language and law concerning the nature of language, legal translations and cultural transplants. The first part of the chapter introduces this process and the related problems. Examples of the development of some key legal concepts through the different stages of the Chinese legal modernization between the XIX and XXI centuries are provided. The second part presents some critical aspects of contemporary Chinese legal language. Specific focus is on problems of linguistic uncertainty that, according to several prominent scholars working on the topic of Chinese law and language, is one the main marking points of both written and spoken legal Chinese. Sources and features of uncertainty are analyzed and described, also in the perspective of legal translations. In the third part the growing complexity emerging in contemporary Chinese law and language will be discussed. In particular, the following issues are analyzed: the increasing influence on China of legal models from common law, whose models and concepts have been inserted within a taxonomy traditionally based on civil law models; the coexistence of different legal Chinese languages, in particular in Mainland China and in the Hong Kong Special Administrative Region; the emergence of China as a global actor and the increasing globalization of its legal system.

Chapter 16 by Roberta Aluffi is on Arabic as a legal language. Arabic is, at the same time, unitary and diverse. This is specifically true for the legal sphere. Arabic is the language of the Qur'an, hence of the *fiqh*, the Islamic legal doctrine. The vocabulary of *fiqh* was developed by legal scholars over centuries, but retains its importance in the religious field to this day. Building on the linguistic heritage of the Islamic legal doctrine, modern national states shape their official legal languages. Moreover, Arabic is an international legal language, officially adopted by a number of international organization (United Nations, African Union etc.). Arabic is not always the only language used for legal purposes in an Arab state. Although other languages compete with it, both in the legislature or in the courtrooms; multilingualism is rarely officially recognized. Multilingualism requires the interpreter to engage in translation practices, which are also necessary in dealing with conflicts of laws questions, where multiculturalism increases the difficulties of the task.

Chapter 17 by Domenico Francavilla analyses the problem of the language of the law in India, by considering the complex multilingual situation in this area, constitutional rules concerning official languages, the persistent use of English as the language of the law, particularly in the Supreme Court, and some issues concerning Hindi legal language. Through this analysis, the chapter aims to show that the usual identification of Indian law and English language hides a picture that is much more complex. Several languages continuously interact in the legal sphere, with deep implications in terms of the relations between different parts of India, and of attitudes towards the legacy of common law in the contemporary Indian legal system. Dealing with these complex underlying issues, Indian policy and practices appear to search for a dynamic balance in trying to take into account the several components of India's diversity.

Chapter 18 by Andrea Ortolani concerns the birth and evolution of Japanese legal language. Modern Japanese law can be considered as a complex structure made of multilingual and multicultural layers. The first part of the chapter introduces the main features of the Japanese language, the problems related to the reception of the Chinese writing system, and modern language policy. By 1898, Japan had enacted a

Constitution, a civil code and several statutes in all fields of law. This achievement was the result of the effort of the intellectuals of the time, who studied the Western legal systems, created a new Japanese legal lexicon and translated the laws and the legal literature of foreign countries, thus introducing Western law in the Archipelago. The second part of the chapter presents the characteristics of the Japanese legal language, the role played by language in the evolution of legal doctrines and problems of translation of Japanese law. Some recurring patterns underlying the Japanese reception of foreign law are outlined, which had and still have an impact in shaping the modern legal system.

Acknowledgment: The project was initiated with Prof. Monika Rathert, who had to step down at the onset.

References

Capone, Alessandro & Francesca Poggi (eds.). 2016–2017. *Pragmatics and law: philosophical perspectives*. Berlin: Springer.

Coulthard, Malcolm & Alison Johnson (eds.). 2010. *The Routledge handbook of forensic linguistics*. London: Routledge.

Giltrow, Janet & Dieter Stein (eds.). 2017. The pragmatic turn in law. Inference and interpretation in legal discourse. Berlin: De Gruyter Mouton.

Kimble, Joseph. 2006. *Lifting the fog of legalese: essays on plain language*. Carolina Academic Press.

Kurzon, Dennis & Barbara Kryk-Kastovsky (eds.). 2018. *Legal pragmatics*. Amsterdam: John Benjamins.

Ministero della Giustizia. 2016. *Gruppo di lavoro sulla sinteticità degli atti processuali*. Relazione al Ministro. 1 December 2016 https://www.personaedanno.it/dA/6351a6a7bf/allegato/Sinteticita%20atti%20-%20II%20relazione%20161201.pdf

Montolío, Estrella. 2012. La modernización del discurso jurídico español impulsada por el Ministerio de Justicia. Presentación y principales aportaciones del Informe sobre el lenguaje escrito. *Revista de Llengua i Dret* 57. 95–121.

Scialoja, Vittorio. 1911. Diritto pratico e diritto teorico. *Rivista del diritto commerciale* I. 942.

Solan, Lawrence & Peter M. Tiersma (eds.). 2012. *The Oxford handbook of language and the law*. Oxford: Oxford University Press.

Visconti, Jacqueline. 2009. Speech acts in legal language. *Journal of Pragmatics* 41. 393–400.

Williams, Christopher. 2011. Legal English and plain language: an update. *ESP across Cultures* 8. 139–151.

Part I: **The foundations of legal language**

Christopher Williams
1 Legal drafting

1 Introduction

The history of legal drafting is as old as the history of written law itself, stretching back to at least 3000 BC in the case of Ancient Egyptian law. The Codex Hammurabi in Babylonia dates back to approximately 1760 BC. Ancient India and China also had flourishing legal systems centuries before the Roman Empire developed the system known today as Roman law (which in turn was heavily influenced by the Greek model), while Islamic law evolved from the early Middle Ages. The common law system is generally considered to have originated in the twelfth century.

The Western traditions of legal drafting largely evolved in the ecclesiastical, royal, feudal, and municipal chanceries and law courts of medieval Europe when the so-called 'chancery style' was forged. This style was characterized by many features which make legal documents hard for laypersons to understand. Reactions against the difficulties of reading legal documents are long-standing (especially during the Enlightenment period in German-speaking lands as far as legislative texts are concerned). However, some chancery-style features still linger in various countries such as the excessive length of texts, the complexity and excessive length of sentences, and the persistence of ritual features and archaisms (and Latin) in the vocabulary. For further details on the history of legal drafting see, e.g., Mellinkoff (1963) or Tiersma (2012).[1]

According to *Black's Law Dictionary* (2004: 531), legal drafting refers to the "practice, technique, or skill involved in preparing legal documents – such as statutes, rules, regulations, contracts, and wills – that set forth the rights, duties, liabilities, and entitlements of persons and legal entities." We are therefore dealing with a highly formal and complex style of writing that has developed over the centuries where extreme precision and detail are usually required, also because the text has to withstand critical scrutiny from legal practitioners, notably lawyers and judges. As Mellinkoff (1983: 15) observed: "Some day someone will read what you have written, trying to find something wrong with it. This is the special burden of legal writing, and the special incentive to be as precise as you can." On the other hand, the text needs to be sufficiently flexible so as to apply to all manner of situations that may arise (Mattila 2013). Hence the recourse not merely to technical 'terms of art' which generally have a very specific meaning – even if such terms in actual fact "make up a negligible portion of legal documents" (Bivin 2008: 12) – but also to so-called 'vague terms' (Endicott 2011), particularly adjectives such as 'reasonable', 'reckless', 'prompt' or 'fair', or the abundant use in contracts of 'any' and 'or' (Adams 2008: 195–210; Burnham 2003:

---

[1] I am indebted to Heikki Mattila for his observations on an earlier draft of this chapter.

https://doi.org/10.1515/9781614514664-002

Chapter 7.4.2; Burnham 2009: 258; Coulthard and Johnson 2007: 40). Finding the right balance between the need for precision and flexibility is no easy matter: in contract drafting, for example, Barton, Haapio and Borisova (2015: 8) affirm that "[t]he wrong sort of flexibility in a contract may lead to higher costs and frustration; the right sort of flexibility may enable better commercial relationships."

In Section 2 of this chapter I analyse in more detail some of the key features of legal drafting: in particular I examine some of the characteristics distinguishing legislative drafting from contract drafting.

In Section 3 I briefly outline some of the similarities and differences between the drafting style of the civil law system – which is based on Roman law – and that of the common law system which operates in most of the English-speaking world. For reasons of space other major legal systems such as Islamic law are not taken into consideration.

In Section 4 I examine the way legal drafting has evolved in the English-speaking world, largely as a result of the pressure exerted by proponents of the phenomenon known as 'plain language' which has impacted in many ways on how legal texts tend to be written these days. The case of legal drafting in the English-speaking world is especially interesting precisely because the style has changed noticeably over the last few decades, with a shift away from old-fashioned 'legalese' towards a more modern style based on standard formal English, whereas the change in drafting style in civil law countries (which includes most European nations) has, on the whole, tended to be less noticeable, arguably because the question of modernizing the legal language of civil law-based countries is perceived as being less urgent than it is in common law countries.

I also point out that within the sphere of legal drafting in the English-speaking world progress has not been uniform. For example, the precepts of plain language have generally affected legislative drafting to a greater degree than they have in the field of contracts (Williams 2011: 146). Moreover, within the realm of legislative drafting, it would appear that international bodies such as the European Union or the United Nations tend to adopt a rather more conservative drafting policy than individual nations, partly because of the complexities involved in drafting texts in a multilingual environment which may well encourage a more cautious approach among legal drafters (Williams 2011: 149).

In Section 5 I briefly analyse possible developments for the future of legal drafting, with particular reference to the impact of information technology on the way legal drafters write and how their work is increasingly under the scrutiny of growing numbers of experts and non-experts alike. I also draw my overall conclusions concerning legal drafting.

In the Appendix I attempt to identify some of the major strands in the vast literature on legal drafting which I have classified into five groups, namely, works dealing with

1) legal drafting in general;
2) legislative drafting;
3) contract drafting;

4) geographically-specific works on legal drafting (i.e. relating to a particular country or organization);
5) legal drafting and plain language.

Clearly, many works cut across more than one category, but I have tried to identify the aspect I deem to be key to each work.

2 What legal drafting is about

The expression 'legal drafting' comes within the broader category of legal writing which in turn comes within the realm of specialized forms of written communication. Legal writing tends to be split into two categories: legal analysis and legal drafting. The former includes certain types of law-related documents such as memoranda (which may serve a variety of purposes, for example, as records of research carried out on a given legal question) or letters to clients, as well as more 'persuasive' forms of communication such as appellate briefs or negotiation letters written on behalf of clients in their defence. This type of legal analysis tends to be the variety of written communication most extensively taught in American law schools and is primarily carried out by (practising or would-be) lawyers.[2] Legal drafting, on the other hand, is concerned with preparing texts which are drawn up to be legally binding by establishing sets of rules or laws designed to govern or regulate the conduct of a given group of individuals or community or, for example in the case of a contract, between two or more parties. Such texts may be enforced by a controlling authority, e.g. a court of law.

Another important distinction between legal drafting and legal writing is that "drafting has to be able to stand the test of time because drafting is a future-oriented endeavor whereas most legal writing deals with past events" (Espenschied and Luna 2013: 544).

Those actively involved in the legal drafting process are not only lawyers (generally the persons responsible for drawing up contracts or wills), but also professional drafters, especially in the preparation of legislative texts. If we include the preparation of court rulings within the category of legal drafting, given that a court decision is legally binding and needs to be written down, then to that extent judges may also be considered as carrying out the role of legal drafters. It should be borne in mind that in a common law jurisdiction such as that of England and Wales, as Bates (2009: 2) observes, "[j]udicial decisions may be the basis of significant areas of law, either solely or in conjunction with subsequent legislation. Judicial decisions are also often an important, although not

---

[2] In this chapter the blanket term 'lawyer' is adopted since other terms are culture-specific, e.g. 'attorney' (the US), 'solicitor', 'barrister' (England and Wales, Australia, Canada), or 'advocate' (Scotland). The more generic term 'counsel' is used sparingly as it may often be used to refer to a team of lawyers rather than an individual lawyer.

necessarily exclusive, legal basis for the general principles applied in the interpretation of legislation, and they determine the interpretation of specific legislative provisions."

Other definitions relating to legal drafting may differ with respect to the basic outline given above. For example, Xanthaki (2013c: 57) argues that "[l]egislative drafting must be distinguished from legal drafting, which involves the construction of a text used in the judicial process." However, she later qualifies that statement by affirming (Xanthaki 2013c: 57–58) that "of course this does not mean to say that drafting is completely foreign to the legislative process. In fact, the drafting process is part of the legislative process, which in turn is part of the policy process."

The exceptionally formal and often highly complex style of legal drafting has evolved over time. It requires special training and a combination of skills which, as mentioned above, include an attention to detail but also ensuring that the text may be valid in all foreseeable circumstances. These skills and the prestige attached to the profession have long been acknowledged, as is highlighted in this memorable quote from Mayer (1966: 50–51):

> Intellectually, the draftsman's skills are the highest in the practice of law. Judges at bottom need merely reach decisions [...]; negotiators and advocates need understand only as much of a situation as will gain a victory for their clients; counselors can be bags of wind. [...] But the documents survive, and to draw them up well requires an extraordinary understanding of everything they are supposed to accomplish. [...] Probably the greatest compliment a lawyer can receive from his profession (a compliment never publicized) is an assignment to draft a major law.

A less idyllic view of the context in which the legislative drafter operates has been expressed recently by Widiss (2015: 96) who reiterates the famous simile attributed to Otto von Bismarck: "For well over a century, we have been warned that because laws are like sausages, it is better not to see them being made. The contemporary Congress – notorious for its gridlock and dysfunction – might seem to argue this approach all the more strongly." And in contract drafting, Adams (2008: xxv) argues that "lawyers are coming to be seen as impediments to business rather than facilitators" given that a business contract "will almost certainly be cluttered with deficient usages that, collectively, turn prose into 'legalese'".

There is also an ongoing debate as whether legal drafting should be viewed as an art, a science, or a craft, and whether or not a drafter should be seen as essentially an expert 'technician' or as something more – see, for example, Adams (2007: 20); Bowman (2005); Haggard and Kuney (2007: 125); Markman (2001) – but a detailed analysis of this debate is beyond the scope of this chapter.

2.1 Comparing legislative drafting and contract drafting

If legal drafting as a whole is concerned with writing texts that are legally binding and future-oriented, there are, however, some major differences in the professional contexts in which the various types of drafters operate. We can make a rough-and-ready distinction between legislative drafters on the one hand and contract drafters on the other. The precise duties and professional role of a legislative drafter tend to vary considerably between one country or organization and another, reflecting the specific legal culture and tradition of that country or organization. In the UK, for example, the legislative drafter is a civil servant working for the Office of the Parliamentary Counsel. Bates (2009: 5) points out that most legislative drafters began their careers as lawyers:

> The drafters are traditionally recruited after some years in private practice. There is no formal induction course for new recruits and the drafters acquire their knowledge on an "apprenticeship" system. Drafting is most commonly undertaken in teams of two drafters, with a junior drafter and a more senior experienced drafter; and drafters do not specialise in substantive areas of law but are allocated instructions as they are received.

Seen from a worldwide perspective, however, not all legislative drafters come from a legal background. For example, Ehrenberg-Sundin notes (2004) that in Sweden legislative drafting is carried out by language experts and lawyers working as a team in the Division for Legal and Linguistic Draft Revision in the Ministry of Justice:

> There are five language experts and five legal revisers checking the quality of texts from all the ministries. This final revision one or two weeks before the Government decides on the text is an important checkpoint. [...] this team has a key role in legislative drafting in the ministries. The legal revisers check the constitutional and formal quality of the texts, and the language experts ensure that the proposed new or amended draft Acts and Ordinances are as easy as possible to read and understand.

Swedish legislative drafting is also described in Swedish Ministry of Justice (2005).

The situation of the European Union is also unique in that, in an organization with 24 official languages, the drafters are lawyer-linguists, i.e. experts in both the law and with a knowledge of at least two of these official languages. Moreover, in this multilingual environment it is often the case that EU drafters may be writing in a language that is not their mother tongue (Robertson 2010: 147–148). The EU also constitutes a special case insofar as it was originally set up in 1957 by six civil law countries with French predominating as the lingua franca in the drafting sphere. However, Felici (2015: 126) points out that "[f]ollowing the accession of Sweden and Finland and, more recently, the Eastern European countries, English has become the current *de facto* administrative *lingua franca* shifting the balance from French to English." It is calculated that the vast majority of legislative texts in the EU today begin their life in English, even if native English-speaking drafters constitute only around 13 per cent of the overall total (Robertson 2010: 149; Williams 2011: 148).[3]

---

[3] This situation is unlikely to change in the foreseeable future even after the referendum held in the United Kingdom on 23 June 2016 where a majority of voters expressed their desire to leave the European Union.

Another special case in the legislative drafting world is Canada where the "bijural nature of the Canadian legal system, along with the obligations that derive from bilingualism, has an unquestionable impact on the drafting of federal legislation. In that respect, federal legislation needs to speak to Canadian citizens in a language that acknowledges, in both English and French, the common law and civil law legal traditions" (Canada Department of Justice 2015a). Indeed, bijuralism in Canada has witnessed a gradual redress in favour of civil law which was once threatened by the "assimilation of civil law by common law" (Canada Department of Justice 2015b). An exhaustive comparison of the specificities of legislative drafters throughout the world is clearly beyond the scope of this chapter.

Contract drafters, by contrast, are usually lawyers either working individually or for a law firm or for a company or corporation (in-house counsel). In some cases the drafting of contracts may be undertaken by a paralegal, i.e. someone who cannot give legal advice or represent clients in a lawsuit but can draft legal documents, albeit under the supervision of a lawyer. The precise status of a paralegal in the English-speaking world changes from one jurisdiction to another. However, it is principally lawyers who will be required to draft other legally binding documents that fall outside the realms of legislative drafting and contract drafting such as preparing a will, or a property transaction, or drawing up a charter or code of conduct, for example, regulating a sports club.

A first yardstick of comparison between legislative drafting and contract drafting concerns the drafter's perspective vis-à-vis the text that has to be written and the readership the drafter has in mind. Bellis (2011: 14) sums up the role of the legislative drafter (with specific reference to the United States) as follows:

> Like the classic Puritan, the legislative counsel must be in this world, that is the world of politics, and yet not of it, in order to be effective. The legislative counsel must also focus on the needs of the ultimate users of a text, mostly the judges but sometimes the public or others, in order to meet both the needs of the legislative counsel's immediate clients, the politicians, and the needs of the legislative counsel's ultimate clients, the public. So the legislative counsel is outside of the political process, and as scrupulously neutral as humanly possible, yet acutely aware of the political concerns of the politicians the legislative counsel works with.

Contract drafters, on the other hand, will also be very much aware that the text they are preparing may be read one day by a judge, but not by the general public. Indeed, as Adams (2008: xxix) points out, "until such time as a problem arises, a contract's only readers may well be the lawyers who drafted it and, to a varying degree, their clients."

Closely connected to the above point is the fact that legislative drafting is usually a collaborative activity involving a multiplicity of people – often including politicians or other elected representatives such as local councillors who may have no specific legal training – all of whom contribute, to varying degrees, to the final draft of the text, whereas the number of people involved in drafting a contract is usually very small.

Another major difference between legislative drafting and contract drafting lies in the way a legislative text, as opposed to a contract, is structured and produced.

Drafting a contract may often be a relatively mechanical exercise, as Hill (2001: 59) points out: "Not surprisingly, lawyers have come up with a production process by which each lawyer can access the accumulated wisdom of many: the 'form.' The form is typically not a form in the 'fill-in-the-blanks' sense; rather, it is an actual contract the lawyer or someone she works with has used in one or more previous transactions." In this respect drafting a piece of legislation does not generally allow for the possibility of using the time-saving 'cut-and-paste' technique.

Finally, the mind-frame of legislative drafters may sometimes differ with respect to that of contract drafters concerning the overall length of the text, though neither type of drafter is renowned for prioritizing brevity. Indeed, exhaustiveness is a key criterion for all types of drafters when preparing legally binding texts: the difference lies in whether this attention to detail is the result of ingrained custom or of necessity. For example, the common law contract drafter may well be inclined towards prolixity simply because of the widespread perception that there is nothing to be gained from being more concise, as Hill (2001: 76) observes: "Deletions generally must meet a high threshold of justification: omitting a provision because it doesn't do much, but does clutter up the form, rarely suffices. But inclusion of new boilerplate that doesn't seem to help but couldn't hurt requires much less justification. Contracts get progressively longer and more cumbersome, and usually not to any positive end." We will return to the question of the notorious length of contracts in the common law system in Sections 4 and 5. The legislative drafter, on the other hand, has no incentive to make the text longer than it need be. Having said that, the complexity of certain topics requiring regulation, such as the UK's *Companies Act* 2009 (where the list of contents alone occupies 59 pages), *Equality Act* 2010 or *Finance (No. 2) Act* 2015, will often lead to the drafting of a text that stretches to hundreds of pages.

3 Differences between the civil law system and the common law system and their effect on legal drafting styles

As was mentioned in Section 2, a well-known difference in drafting styles between the civil law system which operates in most of continental Europe and the common law system in force in most English-speaking nations concerns the average length of a contract. In the common law system contracts tends to be far wordier than their civil law counterparts (Hill 2001; Hill and King 2004; Mattila 2013; Williams 2010: 218–219). An illustration of this distinction between common law drafting and civil law drafting – and this applies to both contracts and to legislation – is the rationale behind providing lists or catalogues. Common law drafters are inclined to provide exhaustive lists covering all possible hypotheses whereas a catalogue in the civil law system "is not aimed at all the circumstances the legislator may wish to cover, but rather at providing mere illustrations of possible situations being covered [...] which [...] can be extended by the courts to further appropriate situations and circumstances" (Steiner 2010: 19).

The codified nature of the law in civil law systems inevitably shapes the way legislation is drafted. In her comparison between the legislative drafting styles in France and England, Steiner (2010: 14–24) outlines the differences between the principles of conciseness, generality and simplicity underlying the civil law system with respect to the detailed particularity and complexity of common law legislative texts, even if the differences would seem to be less marked today. There are certain areas such as French tax law "where a large number of provisions have become increasingly verbose, extremely technical and overly detailed" (Steiner 2010: 20). However, tax law may be treated as a special case: as we will see in Section 5, rewriting cumbersome tax laws has also been undertaken in a number of common law countries.

However, the civil law / common law divide should not be exaggerated. As Xanthaki (2014: 211) affirms, "[a]t the end of the day, what drafters pursue across the divide is legislative quality." She also points to the gradual whittling down of the dissimilarities between drafting styles (Xanthaki 2014: 211):

> At least in Europe, there is a noted convergence between common and civil law legislative drafting extending from conceptual approaches to actual drafting conventions. The comparative analysis of (statutory) interpretation, the modern application of precedent, and drafting rules and conventions in the common and civil laws of Europe paint a clear picture of approximation and convergence, to the point where the sacred civil versus common law dividing wall is now critically shaken.

Other scholars have pointed to the steady encroachment of common law drafting at the expense of civil law drafting, notably in the sphere of international contracts, but also at a national level, as Steadman and Sprague (2015) argue: "Nowadays common law drafting techniques are increasingly dominating international contracts practice. Even civil law legal practitioners rely on them for structuring international agreements and, increasingly more frequently, when drafting 'national' contracts too."

It could be argued, then, that while in legislative drafting we would appear to be heading towards a gradual – albeit only partial – convergence between the two systems in a spirit of 'hatchet-burying' (Xanthaki 2012b), contract drafting, at least at an international level, would seem to be slowly evolving towards a predominance of the common law style over that of civil law. A detailed analysis of this fascinating topic, however, lies outside the scope of this chapter.

4 The influence of plain language on legal drafting

Undoubtedly, one of the most influential and visible factors affecting recent changes in the way legally binding texts are written, particularly in the English-speaking world, has been the impact of what is generally known as the Plain language movement. The word 'movement' is essentially a misnomer in that interest in plain language has been manifested in various countries and has taken various guises, often responding to the specific needs and situations of a given legal system.

Today the principles of plain language in legislative drafting are well-established and widely accepted, so it is hard to appreciate that, for example, only four decades ago the findings of the Renton Committee on the Preparation of Legislation, set up in 1973 "[w]ith a view to achieving greater simplicity and clarity in statute law" (cited in Simon of Glaisdale 1985: 133), were greeted with great enthusiasm but in practice were not followed up in any significant way in the UK until 1996 with the creation of the Tax Law Rewrite Project (Williams 2007: 104–109). The Project terminated its mandate in 2010 (Seely 2010) by which time the Office of the Parliamentary Counsel had decided to apply modern drafting rules to all legislative texts, following the examples of the Offices of the Parliamentary Counsel in Australia and New Zealand which had already started experimenting on a wide scale with modern drafting techniques from the late 1980s and early 1990s (Williams 2011: 141).

These days a number of pan-national organizations devoted to plain language exist, international conferences on plain language in law are held regularly, and information and ideas are exchanged via journals, blogs and other online forms of communication (see, for example, Clarity, Good law initiative, PLAIN, plainlanguage.gov: the websites are listed at the end of this chapter). Moreover, many of the websites run by the Offices of the Parliamentary Counsel (e.g. Australia, New Zealand, the UK) openly endorse plain language and practically all drafting manuals these days devote considerable importance to ways of ensuring the highest degree of clarity and comprehensibility when drafting legislative texts. Indeed, the UK's Office of the Parliamentary Counsel (2013: 3) asserts that "Parliamentary Counsel has adopted a plain English style which would have been unrecognisable to their 1970s predecessors, as well as a culture of innovation over precedent."

Here is a typical piece of modern legislative prose, taken from Section 13 of the UK *Consumer Rights Act* 2015:

Goods to match a sample
(1) This section applies to a contract to supply goods by reference to a sample of the goods that is seen or examined by the consumer before the contract is made.
(2) Every contract to which this section applies is to be treated as including a term that – (a) the goods will match the sample except to the extent that any differences between the sample and the goods are brought to the consumer's attention before the contract is made, and (b) the goods will be free from any defect that makes their quality unsatisfactory and that would not be apparent on a reasonable examination of the sample.[4]

---

4 http://www.legislation.gov.uk/ukpga/2015/15/pdfs/ukpga_20150015_en.pdf (accessed 27 November 2015).

Some of the innovative traits that distinguish this type of prose from the more traditional style of 'legalese' include the absence of old-fashioned adverbials such as *hereto* or *whereof* (as, on the contrary, can be found in the brief extract from the contract agreement cited below); the absence of the controversial modal auxiliary *shall* (on *shall* in legal texts see, for example, Williams 2009) and its replacement by the simple present (e.g. *This section applies* ...) or the *is to* construction (e.g. *is to be treated* ...). In general, the style corresponds to a type of modern formal English that can be found in any formal context in English, and hence it will strike the non-expert reader as being less alien than the antiquated prose common to legislative texts years ago.

As was outlined in the previous section, the rationale behind the common law system, with its emphasis on precedent, has tended over time to lead to a more conservative, antiquated drafting style with respect to that of the civil law system. And we have observed that the wordy, old-fashioned style of drafting discernible in the language of contracts still prevails in much of the English-speaking world, despite the efforts of plain language exponents. Below is a typical example of what could be labelled as 'legalese' taken from a recent contract: "The parties hereto may waive any of their rights under this Grant agreement unless such waiver is contrary to law, provided that any such waiver shall be in writing and signed by the party making such waiver." The text in question begins with one of the classic formulaic expressions of contractual legalese: "IN WITNESS WHEREOF, the parties hereto have executed this Agreement as of the day and year above written."[5]

Clearly, despite the numerous success stories of recent years in legislative drafting, the 'mission' of the Plain language movement is far from over.

5 The future of legal drafting and concluding remarks

In this overview of legal drafting I have attempted to outline some of its major features, many of which have become consolidated and, in some cases, fossilized over time, though others have developed in the direction of enhanced clarity and comprehensibility. We have observed that, taken as a whole, legislative drafting has evolved more noticeably, particularly in recent decades and above all in common law systems, with respect to contract drafting which has proved to be more resistant to change.

The impact of information technology and the Internet on legal drafting should not be underestimated, both in national settings as well as in international settings

---

[5] Grant Agreement between State of California, Board of State and Community Corrections and Mendocino County 2015: http://www.co.mendocino.ca.us/bos/meetings/MG39930/AS39972/AS39975/AS39996/AI40405/DO40516/1.PDF (accessed 27 November 2015).

such as the European Union or the United Nations which have dedicated websites containing a wealth of information, much of it law-related. Computer-assisted legislative drafting and knowledge management systems for legislative drafting (Boer, Winkels, Hoestra & van Engers 2003), through the development of appropriate software, may well be the key to the future in multilingual drafting bodies. However, also contract drafting is becoming increasingly influenced by the Internet and IT, as can be seen by the burgeoning number of online resources making freely available model forms and agreements, often of an interactive kind. Adams (2011) hypothesizes that

> [d]ocument-assembly software is likely to play a significant role in the future of contract drafting. To draft a contract using document-assembly software, you answer an online logic-driven questionnaire, supplying party names and other information and selecting deal terms from among the alternatives offered. The system then pulls together in a Word document, or a PDF, the relevant preloaded contract language, as supplemented by information provided by the user. You can start each transaction afresh, without being limited by choices made for previous transactions.

Not only has technology helped enormously in facilitating the work of legal drafters, but the ubiquity and popularity of the Internet has encouraged governments to invest in finding user-friendly ways of conveying information concerning legislation, and has led to a widening of the readership of legislative texts to interested laypersons who, before the advent of the Internet, would probably not have taken the trouble to search for a paper copy of a law, say, in the local public library. The awareness on the part of legislative drafters that the end product they are preparing may well be scrutinized by a potentially much larger number of experts and non-experts alike than in the past will arguably have a long-term effect on the style drafters use in the direction of enhanced comprehensibility. The impact of technology and the web on readers' expectations in the legal sphere is succinctly expressed by the Good law initiative:

> Law has a wider readership than ever before. The web has made it possible for people to find sources of law more easily. Once there, they tend to find the experience confusing. Reading legislation is not intuitive. One part of a statute often needs to be read alongside another; the last dated version is not the complete story; regulations have to be read alongside Acts of Parliament, and sometimes case law as well.
>
> The digital age brings new opportunities as well: tools for publishing and arranging law, and techniques for diagnosing and predicting how law is used. So this is an exciting time for re-thinking how legislation can be made easier for users.[6]

Pulling in the opposite direction, however, is the fact that many laws are concerned with highly specialized and technical matters, such as stamp duty, deep sea mining, leasehold reform, or equitable life payments, and may therefore be of little interest to, or beyond the comprehension of most laypersons.

---

6 https://www.gov.uk/guidance/good-law.

Nevertheless, in purely stylistic terms, it is unimaginable that in the English-speaking world there will be a return to the old way of drafting laws. The precepts of plain language would appear to be widely accepted and are promoted by the vast majority of drafters these days.

The future of contract drafting is harder to predict. As we have seen, in most of the English-speaking world, despite the vociferous calls for reform from the Plain language movement, the legal profession has generally gone its own way and preserved the archaic, convoluted style of 'legalese'. However, it could be hypothesized that, sooner or later, the economic advantages to be gained from using a simplified style of contract drafting, particularly in international trade where the majority of traders are non-native speakers of English, may prevail over the lawyer's traditional wariness of innovation.

Appendix: The literature on legal drafting

In this Appendix I have included a number of bibliographical references for the benefit of leaders who may wish to pursue the subject of legal drafting further. However, the list of references is far from being exhaustive, and I make no claim to have mentioned all of the major scholars who have written on the subject over the years. Moreover, for reasons of space I have not included a list of legal drafting manuals, although I may occasionally refer to such manuals for illustrative purposes.

Law and jurisprudence have long enjoyed considerable prestige as branches of knowledge, and laws affect people's lives in a number of ways. It is therefore unsurprising that the literature on legal drafting is dauntingly vast. For reasons of space the list of bibliographical references is restricted to works written in English, the majority of which refer to the phenomenon of legal drafting in the English-speaking world. However, a number of works referring to legal drafting in the non-English-speaking world are also included.

The literature on legal drafting ranges from scholarly studies favouring a more theoretical approach to the topic to the works of writers whose aims are more practical, either in terms of suggesting how to improve a given legal drafting style or how to acquire the skills required to draft a legally binding document. Furthermore, within the sphere of legal studies, legal drafting cuts across a number of disciplines and, unlike areas such as the law of torts or employment law, it has attracted the attention not only of scholars well versed in the law but also of linguists, some of whom may have received no legal training but who nevertheless may be able to offer valuable insights about legal drafting. This is particularly the case as regards the adoption of plain language in the legal sphere.

For ease of reference, I have listed the references in alphabetical order. Each reference in this Section is only included once in one of the five categories, according to the element that I consider as being key for each one. Inevitably, there are numerous references which comfortably belong to at least two categories: the line of demarcation between works on legislative drafting and works on legal drafting and plain language is particularly fuzzy. The classifications I have adopted are thus by no means perfect, but it is hoped that, for all their shortcomings, they may serve as a useful guide in this introductory chapter on legal drafting.

A.1 Works on legal drafting in general or on law-related matters

As has been outlined above, the expression 'legal drafting' is an umbrella term. The following are works which tend to focus primarily on legal drafting as a whole. However, I have also included in this category a few references on law-related topics that did not fit into any of the other categories: Allen (1957); *Black's Law Dictionary* (2004); Brightman (2002); Brody, Rutherford, Vietzen & Dembach (1994); Child (1992); Cook (1951); Coulthard & Johnson (2007); Darmstadter (2008); Dick (1972); Dickerson (1986); Emmet (2012); Endicott (2011); Ferreri (2013); Haggard & Kuney (2007); Hillman (2015); Imhanobe (2010); Lebovits (2015); Mattila (2013); Mayer (1966); Murawski (1999); Piesse (1995); Raysman (2009); Rideout & Ramsfield (1994); Rylance (2012); Salembier (2009); Schauer (2015); Swisher (1981); Tiersma (1999); Trevor (2015); Van Blerk (1998); Williams (2005).

A.2 Works on legislative drafting

As we have seen, legislative drafting occupies a major role within legal drafting and is the central concern of the following: Bates (2009), (2010); Bellis (2011); Bergsten (2009); Berry (2010); Boer, Winkels, Hoestra & van Engers (2003); Bowman (2005), (2012); Bridge (1981); Clinton (2012a), (2012b); Cormacain (2013a), (2013b); Crabbe (1994), (1998), (2000), (2010); Dale (1977); Debaene, van Kuyck & Van Buggenhout (1999); Dickerson (1958); Greenberg (2006), (2008), (2010); Kellermann, Ciavarini Azzi, Jacobs & Deighton-Smith (1998); Langenfeld (2014); Lortie & Bergeron (2007); Lupo & Scaffardi (2014); Markman (2010), (2011); McLeod (2009); McCluskie (2004); Moran (2010); Nampoothiry (2010); Nzerem (2010); Petersson (1999); Rosenbaum (2007); Rynearson (2013); Seidman (2001); Simon of Glaisdale (1985); Spencer (2008); Stefanou (2011); Stefanou & Xanthaki (2008); Thuronyi (1998); Turnbull (1997); Voermans (2009), (2011); Webster (2010); Widiss (2015); Williams (2008); Xanthaki (2001), (2012a), (2012b), 2013a), (2013b), (2013c), (2014); Zammit (2011).

A.3 Works on contract drafting

Contract drafting is the other major area that comes within legal drafting and is the major focus of the following: Adams (2001), (2007), (2011), (2013), (2014); Adams &

Scherr (2015); Barton, Haapio & Borisova (2015); Burnham (2003), (2009); Espenschied (2010); Espenschied & Luna (2013); Hill (2001); Hill & King (2004); Sapiro, Frisby & Rodich (2015); Siviglia (2009); Stark (2013); Steadman & Sprague (2015); Torbert (2012); Williams (2010).

A.4 Geographically-specific works on legal drafting

The following are works in which one particular country, group of countries, or international organization such as the European Union is the core interest in relation to legal drafting: Bekink & Botha (2007); Böckenförde & Wiesner (2009); Burger (2002); Canada Department of Justice (2015a), (2015b); Hewagama (2010); Ilahi (2014); Jamieson (2007); Magketla & Seidman (1987); Murphy (2006); Muzuji (2014); O'Keeffe (1996); Peralta (2011); Robertson (2010); Steiner (2010); Torbert (2007).

A.5 Works on legal drafting and plain language

In recent decades plain language has become a central concern in legal drafting, both in legislative drafting as well as contract drafting. The following is a small selection of the works available on the subject: Adler (2007); Asprey (2010); Assy (2011); Barnes (2006); Bivins (2008); Butt (2002); Butt & Castle (2013); Charrow & Erhardt (1986); Coshott (2014); Cutts (2001); (2002); (2003); Dickerson (1954); Eagleson (1990); Ehrenberg-Sundin (2004); European Union (2010); Felici (2015); Garner (1995), (2002), (2006), (2015); Horn (2011), Hunt (2002), (2003); Kimble (1994), (2006a), (2006b), (2008–2009); Martineau (1991); Martineau & Martineau (2012); Martineau & Salerno (2005); Mellinkoff (1983); Office of the Parliamentary Counsel (UK) (2013); Osbeck (2012); Penman (1993); Pennisi (2014); Redish (1991); Robinson (2014); Roebuck (2014); Schiess (2007), (2008); Seely (2010); Steadman (2013); Sullivan (2001); Swedish Ministry of Justice (2005); Tanner (2004); Tiersma (2006); Timm & Oswald (1985); Turfler (2015); Wagner & Cacciaguidi-Fahy (2008); Williams (2007), (2009), (2011), (2013a), (2013b); Wydick (2005).

References

Adams, Kenneth A. 2001. *Legal usage in drafting corporate agreements*. Westport, CT: Greenwood Publishing Group.
Adams, Kenneth A. 2007. The craft of contract drafting: An interview with Kenneth Adams. *The Lawyers Weekly* December 14, 2007: 20. http://www.adamsdrafting.com/downloads/TLW_Dec14_p20.pdf (accessed 19 November 2015).

Adams, Kenneth A. 2011. The new associate and the future of contract drafting. *New York Law Journal* April 1, 2011. http://www.adamsdrafting.com/wp/wp-content/uploads/2014/01/NYLJ-New-Assoc-Future-of-Contract-Drafting-Directors-Cut.pdf (accessed 27 November 2015).

Adams, Kenneth A. 2013 [2008]. *A manual of style for contract drafting*, 3rd edn. Chicago: American Bar Association.

Adams, Kenneth A. 2014. Banishing *shall* from business contracts: throwing the baby out with the bathwater. *The Australian Corporate Lawyer* September 24(3). 12–13. http://www.adamsdrafting.com/wp/wp-content/uploads/2014/09/Banishing-Shall-from-Business-Contracts-ACLA.pdf (accessed 15 November 2015).

Adams, Kenneth A. & René Mario Scherr. 2015. Top ten tips in drafting and negotiating international contracts. Associate of Corporate Counsel. http://www.acc.com/legalresources/publications/topten/drafting-and-negotiating-intl-contracts.cfm?makepdf=1 (accessed 15 November 2015).

Adler, Mark. 2007. *Clarity for lawyers: The use of plain English in legal writing*, 2nd edn. London: Law Society.

Allen, Layman E. 1957. Symbolic logic: a razor-edged tool for drafting and interpreting legal documents. *Yale Law Journal* 66(2). 833–879. http://digitalcommons.law.yale.edu/cgi/viewcontent.cgi?article=5523&context=fss_papers (accessed 15 November 2015).

Asprey, Michèle M. 2010. *Plain language for lawyers*, 4th edn. Sydney: Federation Press.

Assy, Rabeaa. 2011. Can the law speak directly to its subjects? The limitations of plain language. *Journal of Law and Society* 38(3). 376–404.

Barnes, Jeffrey. 2006. The continuing debate about 'plain language legislation': a law reform conundrum. *Statute Law Review* 27(2). 83–132.

Barton, Thomas D., Helena Haapio & Tatiana Borisova. 2015. Flexibility and stability in contracts. *Lapland Law Review* 2 (Special issue on *Flexibility in contracting* edited by Nystén-Haarala Soili, Thomas D. Barton & Jaakko Kujala). 8–28. https://www.ulapland.fi/loader.aspx?id=3b5ebc2d-34df-44c3-aba5-bf679e23847d (accessed 22 November 2015).

Bates, St. John. 2009. Different approaches to legislative drafting in the EU member states. Workshop paper delivered in Tiblisi, Georgia, 14 December 2009. http://www.sigmaweb.org/publicationsdocuments/44577527.pdf (accessed 21 November 2015).

Bates, St. John. 2010. Drafting by more than words: the use of graphics, labels and formulae in legislation. *Commonwealth Law Bulletin* 36(1) (Special issue on legislative drafting). 107–116.

Bekink, Bernard & Christo Botha. 2007. Aspects of legislative drafting: Some South African realities (or plain language is not always plain sailing). *Statute Law Review* 28(1). 34–67.

Bellis, Douglass. 2011. The role and efficacy of legislative drafting in the United States: An update on the American drafting process. *The Loophole* November 2011. 13–27. http://www.opc.gov.au/calc/docs/Loophole/Loophole_Nov11.pdf (accessed 15 November 2015).

Bergsten, Eric. 2009. Methodological problems in the drafting of the CISG. In André Janssen and Olaf Meyer (eds.), *CISG Methodology* 5–32. Munich: Sellier European Law Publishers.

Berry, Duncan. 2010. Keeping the statute book up to date: a personal view. *Commonwealth Law Bulletin* 36(1) (Special issue on legislative drafting). 79–105.

Bivins, Peggy Gale. 2008. *Implementing plain language into legal documents: The technical communicator's role*. PhD thesis submitted at the University of Central Florida, Orlando, Florida. http://etd.fcla.edu/CF/CFE0002022/Bivins_Peggy_G_200805_MA.pdf (accessed 19 November 2015).

Black's Law Dictionary 2004. 8th edn. Edited by Bryan A. Garner. St. Paul, MN: West Group Publisher. http://www.scribd.com/doc/199691370/Black-s-Law-Dictionary-8th-Edition#scribd (accessed 19 November 2015).

Böckenförde, Markus & Verena Wiesner. 2009. *Max Planck manual on legislative drafting on the national level of Southern Sudan*. Heidelberg: Max Planck Institute for Comparative Public

Law and International Law. https://www.mpil.de/shared/data/pdf/national_manual_legal_drafting(c).pdf (accessed 15 November 2015).

Boer, Alexander, Radboud Winkels, Rinke Hoestra & Tom M. van Engers. 2003. Knowledge management for legislative drafting in an international setting. In Danièle Bourcier (ed.), *Knowledge management and information systems* (JURIX 2003 Sixteenth Annual Conference), 91–100. Amsterdam: IOS Press.

Bowman, Geoffrey. 2005. The art of legislative drafting. *European Journal of Law Reform* 7(1–2). 3–17. A slightly revised version is available at http://webarchive.nationalarchives.gov.uk/+/http:/www.cabinetoffice.gov.uk/media/190031/dale.pdf (accessed 15 November 2015).

Bowman, Geoffrey. 2012. Public and private drafting: objectives, problems, styles and approaches. Statute Law Society joint event with Clarity, 15 October 2012. 1–9. http://www.statute-lawsociety.co.uk/wp-content/uploads/2014/01/GBowman_notes.pdf (accessed 15 November 2015).

Bridge, John. 1981. National legal tradition and Community Law: legislative drafting and judicial interpretation in England and the European Community. *Journal of Common Market Studies* 19(4). 351–376.

Brightman, Rt Hon the Lord. 2002. Drafting quagmires. *Statute Law Review* 23(1). 1–11.

Brody, Susan L., Jane Rutherford, Laurel A. Vietzen & John C. Dembach. 1994. *Legal drafting*. New York: Aspen Publishers.

Burger, Andrew J. 2002. *A guide to legislative drafting in South Africa*. Claremont, South Africa: Juta Law.

Burnham, Scott J. 2003. *Drafting and analyzing contracts: A guide to the practical application of the principles of contract law*, 3rd edn. LexisNexis.

Burnham, Scott J. 2009. Transactional skills training: Contract drafting – beyond the basics. *The Tennessee Journal of Business Law*. 253–295.

Butt, Peter. 2002. Modern legal drafting. *Statute Law Review* 23(1).12–23.

Butt, Peter & Richard Castle. 2013 [2001]. *Modern legal drafting: A guide to using clearer language*, 3rd edn. Cambridge: Cambridge University Press.

Canada Department of Justice. 2015a. About bijuralism. http://www.justice.gc.ca/eng/csj-sjc/harmonization/bijurilex/aboutb-aproposb.html (accessed 22 November 2015).

Canada Department of Justice. 2015b. The Supreme Court of Canada and its impact on the expression of bijuralism. http://www.justice.gc.ca/eng/rp-pr/csj-sjc/harmonization/hfl-hlf/b3-f3/bf3b.html (accessed 22 November 2015).

Charrow, Veda R. & Myra K. Erhardt. 1986. *Clear and effective legal writing*. Boston: Little, Brown & Company.

Child, Barbara. 1992. *Drafting legal documents*, 2nd edn. St. Paul, MN: Thomson West.

Clinton, Jaja Tonye. 2012a. *Legislative drafting: An introduction to theories and principles*. Oisterwijk, The Netherlands: Wolf Legal Publishers.

Clinton, Jaja Tonye. 2012b. Teaching legislative drafting: the necessity for clinical legal education. *NIALS International Journal of Legislative Drafting* 1(1). 74–87. http://www.nials-nigeria.org/journals/legdraftTonye%20Clinton%20Jaja.pdf (accessed 15 November 2015).

Cook, Robert Nevin. 1951. *Legal drafting*. New York: Foundation Press.

Cormacain, Ronan. 2013a. An empirical study of the usefulness of legislative drafting manuals. *The Theory and Practice of Legislation* 1(2). 205–225.

Cormacain, Ronan. 2013b. Have the Renton Committee's recommendations on electronic access to legislation been fulfilled? *European Journal of Current Legal Issues* 19(3). 1–18. http://webjcli.org/rt/printerFriendly/264/361 (accessed 15 November 2015).

Coshott, Derwent. 2014. Living in the past: the critics of plain language. *European Journal of Law Reform* 16(3). 541–552.

Coulthard, Malcolm and Alison Johnson. 2007. *An introduction to forensic linguistics*. London: Routledge.
Crabbe, Vincent Cyril Richard Arthur Charles. 1994. *Legislative drafting volume 1*. Abingdon, UK: Routledge.
Crabbe, Vincent Cyril Richard Arthur Charles. 1998. Teaching legislative drafting: the Commonwealth experience. *Statue Law Review* 19(2). 113–128.
Crabbe, Vincent Cyril Richard Arthur Charles .2000. The role of Parliamentary Counsel in legislative drafting. Paper written following a UNITAR Sub-Regional Workshop on Legislative Drafting for African Lawyers (Kampala, Uganda 20 to 31 March 2000). Geneva: United Nations Institute for Training and Research (UNITAR). http://www.agora-parl.org/sites/default/files/UNITAR%20%20The%20role%20of%20the%20Parliamentary%20Counsel%20in%20Legislative%20Drafting%20-%202000%20-%20EN%20-%20PI.pdf (accessed 15 November 2015).
Crabbe, Vincent Cyril Richard Arthur Charles. 2010. The ethics of legislative drafting. *Commonwealth Law Bulletin* 36/1 (Special issue on legislative drafting). 11–24.
Cutts, Martin. 2000. *Lucid law*. High Peak, Derbyshire UK: Plain Language Commission. http://www.clearest.co.uk/pages/publications/books/lucidlaw (accessed 15 November 2015).
Cutts, Martin. 2001. *Clarifying Eurolaw*. High Peak, Derbyshire UK: Plain Language Commission.
Cutts, Martin. 2002. *Clarifying EC Regulations*. High Peak, Derbyshire UK: Plain Language Commission. http://www.clearest.co.uk/pages/publications/books/clarifyingecregulations (accessed 15 November 2015).
Dale, Sir William. 1977. *Legislative drafting: A new approach. A comparative study of methods in France, Germany, Sweden and the United Kingdom*. London: Butterworths.
Darmstadter, Howard. 2008. *Hereof, thereof, and everywhereof: A contrarian guide to legal drafting*. Chicago: American Bar Association.
Debaene, Stijn, Raf van Kuyck & Bea Van Buggenhout. 1999. Legislative technique as basis of a legislative drafting system. *Jurix*. 23–35.
Dick, Robert C. 1972. *Legal drafting*. Toronto: Carswell Co.
Dickerson, Reed. 1954. Legislative drafting: A challenge to the legal profession. *Articles by Maurer Faculty*. Paper 1494. 635–637. http://www.repository.law.indiana.edu/cgi/viewcontent.cgi?article=2495&context=facpub (accessed 19 November 2015).
Dickerson, Reed. 1958. Legislative drafting: American and British practices compared. *Articles by Maurer Faculty*. Paper 1498. 865–908. http://www.repository.law.indiana.edu/facpub/1498?utm_source=www.repository.law.indiana.edu%2Ffacpub%2F1498&utm_medium=PDF&utm_campaign=PDFCoverPages (accessed 19 November 2015).
Dickerson, Reed. 1986. *The fundamentals of legal writing*, 2nd edn. Boston: Little, Brown & Company.
Eagleson, Robert D. 1990. *Writing in plain English*. Canberra: AGPS Press.
Ehrenberg-Sundin, Barbara. 2004. Plain language in Sweden, the result after 30 years. Speech given at the plain language conference *Lenguaje ciudadano* on 5 October 2004. http://www.plainlanguage.gov/usingPL/world/world-sweden.cfm (accessed 21 November 2015).
Emmet, David. 2012. *Drafting*, 16th edn. Oxford: Oxford University Press.
Endicott, Timothy. 2011. *Vagueness in law*, 2nd edn. Oxford: Oxford University Press.
Espenschied, Lenné Eidson. 2010. *Contract drafting: Powerful prose in transactional practice*. Chicago: American Bar Association.
Espenschied, Lenné & Bruce G. Luna. 2013. More on doctrinal courses: integrating transactional skills. *The Tennessee Journal of Business Law*. 535–568.
European Union. 2010. *Clear writing throughout Europe*. Proceedings of the Conference organized by the European Commission in Brussels, 26 November 2010. http://nellip.pixel-online.org/files/publications_PLL/10_Clear%20writing%20throughout%20Europe.pdf (accessed 15 November 2015).

Felici, Annarita. 2015. Translating EU legislation from a *lingua franca*: Advantages and disadvantages. In Susan Šarčević (ed.), *Language and culture in EU law: Multidisciplinary perspectives*, 123–140. Farnham, UK: Ashgate Publishers.

Ferreri, Silvia (ed.). 2013. *Document quality control in public administrations and international organisations*. Studies on translation and multilingualism (2)2013. Luxembourg: Publications Office of the European Union. https://www.google.it/webhp?sourceid=chrome-instant&ion=1&espv=2&ie=UTF8#q=Ferrari+Silvia+(ed.)+2013.+Document+Quality+Control+in+Public+Administrations+and+International+Organisations.+European+Commission (accessed 15 November 2015). The bibliography is available at http://ec.europa.eu/dgs/translation/publications/studies/document_quality_control_study_bibliography_en.pdf (accessed 15 November 2015).

Garner, Bryan A. 1995. *Guidelines for drafting and editing court rules*. Washington, DC: Administrative Office of the US Courts.

Garner, Bryan A. 2002. *The elements of legal style*. Oxford: Oxford University Press.

Garner, Bryan A. 2006. *The Redbook: A manual on legal style*, 2nd edn. St. Paul, MN: Thomson West.

Garner, Bryan A. 2015. On prohibitions, pains and penalties. Lawmakers should work toward adopting strong, standardized language in criminal statutes. *ABA Journal* July 1, 2015. http://www.abajournal.com/mobile/mag_article/lawmakers_should_work_toward_adopting_strong_standardized_language/ (accessed 15 November 2015).

Greenberg, Daniel. 2006. The nature of legislative intention and its implications for legislative drafting. *Statute Law Review* 27(1). 15–28.

Greenberg, Daniel. 2008. *Drafting of legislation: New Oxford companion to law*. Oxford: Oxford University Press.

Greenberg, Daniel. 2011. *Laying down the law*. London: Sweet & Maxwell.

Haggard, Thomas R. & George W. Kuney. 2007 [1996]. *Legal drafting in a nutshell*, 2nd edn. St. Paul, MN: Thomson West.

Hewagama, Ranjit. 2010. The challenges of legislative drafting in small Commonwealth jurisdictions. *Commonwealth Law Bulletin* 36(1) (Special issue on legislative drafting). 117–123.

Hill, Claire A. 2001. Why contracts are written in legalese. *Chicago-Kent Law Review* 77. 59–85.

Hill, Claire A. & Christopher King. 2004. How do German contracts do as much with fewer words? *Chicago-Kent Law Review* 79. 889–926. http://scholarship.kentlaw.iit.edu/cklawreview/vol79/iss3/23 (last accessed 19 November 2015).

Hillman, William C. 2015 [2002]. *Documenting secured transactions: Effective drafting and litigation*, 2nd edn. New York: Practising Law Institute.

Horn, Nick. 2011. Legislative section headings: drafting techniques, plain language, and redundancy. *Statute Law Review* 32(3). 186–208.

Hunt, Brian. 2002. Plain language in legislative drafting: is it really the answer? *Statute Law Review* 23(1). 24–46.

Hunt, Brian. 2003. Plain language in legislative drafting: an achievable objective or a laudable ideal? *Statute Law Review* 24(2). 112–124.

Ilahi, Mazhar. 2014. Legislative drafting in plain Urdu language for the Islamic Republic of Pakistan. A question of complex intricacies. *European Journal of Law Reform* 16(3). 59–76.

Imhanobe, Sylvester O. 2010. *Legal drafting and conveyancing with precedents*. Abuja, Nigeria: Temple Legal Consult.

Jamieson, Nigel. 2007. The Scots Statute: Style and substance. *Statute Law Review* 28(3). 182–198.

Kellermann, Alfred, Giuseppe Ciavarini Azzi, Scott H. Jacobs & Rex Deighton-Smith (eds.). 1998. *Improving the quality of legislation in Europe*. The Hague: Asser Instituut, Kluwer Law International.

Kimble, Joseph. 1994. Answering the critics of plain language. *The Scribes Journal of Legal Writing*: 51–85. http://www.plainlanguagenetwork.org/kimble/Answering2.pdf (accessed 15 November 2015).

Kimble, Joseph. 2006a. *Lifting the fog on legalese: Essays on plain language*. Durham, NC: Carolina Academic Press.
Kimble, Joseph. 2006b. A crack at federal drafting. *The Scribes Journal of Legal Writing* 10. 67–78.
Kimble, Joseph. 2008–2009. Lessons in drafting from the new Federal Rules of Civil Procedure. 12 *Scribes Journal of Legal Writing*. 25–88.
Langenfeld, Amy. 2014. Capitol drafting: legislative drafting manuals in the law school classroom. *Perspectives: Teaching Legal Research and Writing* 22(2). 141–146.
Lebovits, Gerald. 2015. Drafting New York civil litigation documents: Part XLII – In Limine, trial and post-trial motions continued. *New York State Bar Association Journal* 87(5). 57–60. http://papers.ssrn.com/sol3/papers.cfm?abstract_id=2625742 (accessed 15 November 2015).
Lortie, Serge & Robert C. Bergeron. 2007. Legislative drafting and language in Canada. *Statute Law Review* 28(2). 83–118.
Lupo, Nicola & Lucia Scaffardi (eds.). 2014. *Comparative law in legislative drafting: The increasing importance of dialogue amongst parliaments*. The Hague: Eleven International Publishing.
Magketla, Neva & Robert B. Seidman. 1987. Legal drafting and the defeat of development policy: the experience of Anglophonic Southern Africa. *Journal of Law and Religion* 5(2). 421–472.
Markman, Sandra C. 2010. Training of Legislative Counsel: learning to draft without Nellie. *Commonwealth Law Bulletin* 36(1) (Special issue on legislative drafting). 25–39.
Markman, Sandra C. 2011. Legislative drafting: art, science or discipline? *The Loophole* November 2011: 5–12. http://www.opc.gov.au/calc/docs/Loophole/Loophole_Nov11.pdf (accessed 15 November 2015).
Martineau, Robert J. 1991. *Drafting legislation and rules in plain English*. Eagan, MN: West Publishing Company.
Martineau, Robert J. & Robert J. Martineau Jr. 2012. *Plain English for drafting rules and statutes*. LexisNexis (Matthew Bender & Co.).
Martineau, Robert J. & Michael B. Salerno. 2005. *Legal, legislative and rule drafting in plain English*. St. Paul, MN: West Academic Publishing.
Mattila, Heikki E.S. 2013. *Comparative legal linguistics*, 2nd edn. Farnham, UK. Ashgate.
Mayer, Martin. 1966. *The lawyers*. New York: Harper & Row.
McLeod, Ian. 2009. *Principles of legislative and regulatory drafting*. Oxford: Hart Publishing.
McCluskie, John. 2004. New approaches to UK legislative drafting: The view from Scotland. *Statute Law Review* 25(2). 13–6143.
Mellinkoff, David. 1983. *Legal writing: sense and nonsense*. St. Paul, MN: West Group Publishers.
Moran, Eamonn. 2010. Foreword. *Commonwealth Law Bulletin* 36(1) (Special issue on legislative drafting). 1–6.
Murawski, Thomas. 1999. *Writing readable regulations*. Durham, NC: Carolina Academic Press.
Murphy, Gavin. 2006. How legislation is drafted and enacted in Bangladesh. *Statute Law Review* 27(3). 133–149.
Muzuji, Jamil Ddamulira. 2014. The expungement of criminal records in South Africa: the drafting history of the law, the unresolved issues, and how they could be resolved. *Statute Law Review* 35(3). 278–303.
Nampoothiry, N.K. 2010. The role of Parliamentary Counsel in legislative drafting. *Commonwealth Law Bulletin* 36(1) (Special issue on legislative drafting). 57–65.
Nzerem, Richard C. 2010. Prioritising legislative proposals in the legislative process. *Commonwealth Law Bulletin* 36(1) (Special issue on legislative drafting). 67–77.
Office of the Parliamentary Counsel (UK). 2013. When laws become too complex. https://www.gov.uk/government/uploads/system/uploads/attachment_data/file/187015/GoodLaw_report_8April_AP.pdf (accessed 27 November 2015).
O'Keeffe, Peter. 1996. Amending legislation in the Australian Senate. *Statute Law Review* 17(3). 229–240.

Osbeck, Mark. 2012. What is 'good legal writing' and why does it matter? *Drexel Law Review* 4(2). 417–467.

Penman, Robyn. 1993. Unspeakable acts and other deeds: A critique of plain legal language. *Information Design Journal* 7(2). 121–131.

Pennisi, Giulia Adriana. 2014. Editorial: Plain language. Improving legal communication. *European Journal of Law Reform* 16(3). 533–540.

Peralta, Paul. 2011. Emerging from the shadow: legislative drafting in Gibraltar. *The Loophole* November 2011: 28–40. http://www.opc.gov.au/calc/docs/Loophole/Loophole_Nov11.pdf (accessed 15 November 2015).

Petersson, Sandra. 1999. Gender-neutral drafting: recent Commonwealth developments. *Statute Law Review* 20(1). 35–65.

Piesse, Edmond Leolin. 1995 [1946]. *The elements of drafting*, 9th edn revised by James K. Aitken & Peter Butt. Sydney: Law Book Company.

Raysman, Richard. 2009 [1984]. *Computer law: drafting and negotiating forms and agreements*. New York: Law Journal Press.

Redish, Janice. 1991. *How to write regulations and other documents in clear English*. Washington, DC: American Institutes for Research.

Rideout J. Christopher & Jill J. Ramsfield. 1994. Legal writing: A revised view. *Washington Law Review* 69. 35–99.

Robertson, Colin. 2010. Legislative drafting in English for non-native speakers: some do's and don'ts (with reference to EU legislation). *ESP Across Cultures* 10 (Special issue on Legal English across cultures edited by Maurizio Gotti & Christopher Williams). 147–167.

Robinson, William. 2014. Making EU legislation clearer. *European Journal of Law Reform* 16(3). 610–632. http://icclearclarity.com/wpcontent/uploads/2014/12/EJLR_2014_16_03_006.MakingEULegislationClearer.WilliamRobinson.pdf (accessed 15 November 2015).

Roebuck, Derek. 2014. Plain, clear, and something more? Criteria for communication in legal language. *European Journal of Law Reform* 16(3). 633–650.

Rosenbaum, Kenneth L. 2007. Legislative drafting guide: A practitioner's view. *FAO Legal Papers Online* 64, February 2004.

Rylance, Paul. 2012. *Writing and drafting in legal practice*. Oxford: Oxford University Press.

Rynearson, Arthur J. 2013. *Legislative drafting step by step*. Washington DC: International Law Institute, and Durham NC: Carolina Academic Press.

Salembier, J. Paul. 2009. *Legal and legislative drafting*. Canada: LexisNexis.

Sapiro, Jerome Jr., April E. Frisby & Norman J. Rodich. 2015. When deals go bad: Drafting contracts with litigation in mind. Paper presented on 9 October 2015 at the 88th Meeting of the Litigation and Business Law Sections of the State Bar of California. The State Bar of California. 1–25.

Schauer, Frederick. 2015. Is law a technical language? *San Diego Law Review* 52: 501–513. http://papers.ssrn.com/sol3/papers.cfm?abstract_id=2689788 (accessed 15 November 2015).

Schiess, Wayne. 2007. The art of consumer drafting. *The Scribes Journal of Legal Writing* 11. 1–23. http://papers.ssrn.com/sol3/papers.cfm?abstract_id=1329038 (accessed 15 November 2015).

Schiess, Wayne. 2008. *Preparing legal documents nonlawyers can read and understand*. Chicago: American Bar Association.

Seely, Antony. 2010. Tax law rewrite: the final bills. House of Commons Library 21 April 2010. http://researchbriefings.parliament.uk/ResearchBriefing/Summary/SN05239 (accessed 28 November 2015).

Seidman, Ann Wilcox. 2001. *Legislative drafting for democratic social change*. London: Kluwer Law International.

Simon of Glaisdale, Lord. 1985. The Renton Report: Ten years on. *Statue Law Review* 6(1). 133–138.

Siviglia, Peter. 2009. Designs for courses on drafting contracts. *The Scribes Journal of Legal Writing*. 89–97.

Spencer, John R. 2008. The drafting of criminal legislation: need it be so impenetrable? *Cambridge Law Journal* 67(3). 585–605.

Stark, Tina L. 2013 [2007]. *Drafting contracts: How and why lawyers do what they do*, 2nd edn. New York: Aspen Publishers.

Steadman, Barbara J. 2013. *Drafting legal documents in plain English*. Milan: Giuffré Editore.

Steadman, Jean & Steven Sprague. 2015. *Common law contract law. A practical guide for the civil law lawyer*. IPSOA Wolters Kluwer.

Stefanou, Constantin. 2011. Is legislative drafting a form of communication? *Commonwealth Law Bulletin* 37(3). 407–416.

Stefanou, Constantin & Helen Xanthaki (eds). 2008. *Drafting legislation: A modern approach – in memoriam of Sir William Dale*. Aldershot, UK: Ashgate-Dartmouth.

Steiner, Eva. 2010. *French law: a comparative approach*. Oxford: Oxford University Press.

Sullivan, Ruth. 2001. Some implications of plain language drafting. *Statute Law Review* 22(3). 145–180.

Swedish Ministry of Justice 2005. The Swedish Government promotes clear drafting. Stockholm: Ministry of Justice. http://elibrary.lt/resursai/Uzsienio%20leidiniai/Countries/Sweden/Justice/2005/mj2005_05.pdf (accessed 15 November 2015).

Swisher, Peter N. 1981. Techniques of legal drafting: a survival manual. *15 University of Richmond Law Review* 873 (1981), reprinted in *31 Law Review Digest 4* (1982). 873–893. http://scholarship.richmond.edu/cgi/viewcontent.cgi?article=1022&context=law-faculty-publications (accessed 15 November 2015).

Tanner, Edwin. 2004. Clear, simple and precise legislative drafting: Australian guidelines explicated using an EC directive. *Statute Law Review* 25(3). 223–250.

Thuronyi, Victor (ed.). 1998. *Tax law design and drafting* (2 volumes). Washington, DC: International Monetary Fund.

Tiersma, Peter. 1999. *Legal language*. Chicago: University of Chicago Press.

Tiersma, Peter. 2006. Communicating with juries: how to write more understandable jury instructions. *The Scribes Journal of Legal Writing* 10: 1–53. Also available with minor changes in the version published by National Center for State Courts, Williamsburg, VA, at http://courts.oregon.gov/Multnomah/docs/Judges/Wilson/JudgeWilson_CommunicationgWithJurors.pdf (accessed 15 November 2015).

Tiersma, Peter. 2010. *Parchment, paper, pixels: law and the technologies of communication*. Chicago: University of Chicago Press.

Tiersma, Peter. 2012. A history of the language of the law. In Lawrence M. Solan & Peter Tiersma (eds.), *The Oxford handbook of language and law*, 13–26. Oxford: Oxford University Press.

Timm, Paul R. & Daniel Oswald. 1985. Plain English laws. Symbolic or real? *Journal of Business Communication* 22. 31–38.

Torbert, Preston M. 2007. Globalizing legal drafting: What the Chinese can teach us about *Ejusdem Generis* and all that'. *The Scribes Journal of Legal Writing* 11. 41–50. http://www.princeton.edu/~piirs/programs/PTIC/Docs/globalizing%20legal%20drafting.pdf (accessed 15 November 2015).

Torbert, Preston M. 2012. Contract drafting: a Socratic manifesto. *The Scribes Journal of Legal Writing* 14: 93–119. www.koncision.com/wp-content/uploads/2012/09/Contract-Drafting-A-Socratic-Manifesto.pdf (accessed 15 November 2015).

Trevor, Mary B. 2015. The care and feeding of the twenty-first-century developing legal writer: A primer for the supervising practitioner. *Legal Communication & Rhetoric JALWD* 12: 219–246. http://papers.ssrn.com/sol3/papers.cfm?abstract_id=2680490 (accessed 15 November 2015).

Turfler, Soha. 2015. Language ideology and the plain-language movement: how straight-talkers sell linguistic myths. *Legal Communication & Rhetoric JALWD* 12. 195–218.

Turnbull Ian. 1997. Legislative drafting in plain language and statements of general principle. *Statute Law Review* 18(1). 21–31.

Van Blerk, Peter. 1998. *Legal drafting: civil proceedings*. Claremont, South Africa: Juta & Company.

Voermans, Wim. 2009. Concern about the quality of EU legislation: what kind of problem, by what kind of standards? *Erasmus Law Review* 2/1. 59–95. http://www.erasmuslawreview.nl/files/ELR_issue6_004.pdf (accessed 15 November 2015).

Voermans, Wim. 2011. Styles of legislation and their effects. *Statute Law Review* 32(1). 38–53.

Wagner, Anne & Sophie Cacciaguidi-Fahy (eds.). 2008. *Obscurity and clarity in the law*. Aldershot, UK: Ashgate Publishers.

Webster, Robin. 2010. Teaching legislative drafting: reflections on the Commonwealth Secretariat Short Course. *Commonwealth Law Bulletin* 36(1) (Special issue on legislative drafting): 41–56.

Widiss, Deborah A. 2015. Making sausage: what, why and how to teach about legislative process in a legislation or leg-reg course. *Journal of Legal Education* 65(1). 96–120. http://papers.ssrn.com/sol3/papers.cfm?abstract_id=2685236 (accessed 15 November 2015).

Williams, Christopher. 2005. *Tradition and change in legal English: Verbal constructions in prescriptive texts*. Bern: Peter Lang.

Williams, Christopher. 2007. Crossovers in legal cultures in Westminster and Edinburgh: Some recent changes in the language of the law. *ESP Across Cultures* 4. 101–118.

Williams, Christopher. 2008. The end of the "masculine rule"? Gender-neutral legislative drafting in the United Kingdom and Ireland. *Statute Law Review* 29(3). 139–153.

Williams, Christopher. 2009. Legal English and the 'modal revolution'. In Raphael Salkie, Pierre Busuttil & Johan van der Auwera (eds.), *Modality in English: Theory and description,* 199–210. Berlin: Mouton de Gruyter.

Williams, Christopher. 2010. Functional or dysfunctional? The language of business contracts in English. *Rassegna Italiana di Linguistica Applicata* 3. 217–227.

Williams, Christopher. 2011. Legal English and plain language: an update. *ESP Across Cultures* 11. 139–151.

Williams, Christopher. 2013a. Is legal English 'going European'? The case of the simple present. *Canadian Journal of Linguistics* 58(1). 105–126.

Williams, Christopher. 2013b. Changes in the verb phrase in legislative language in English. In Bas Aarts, Joanne Close, Geoffrey Leech & Sean Wallis (eds.), *The verb phrase in English: Investigating recent language change with corpora*, 353–371. Cambridge. Cambridge University Press.

Wydick, Robert C. 2005. *Plain English for lawyers*, 5th edn. Durham, NC: Carolina Academic Press.

Xanthaki, Helen. 2001. The problem of quality in EU legislation: what on earth is really wrong? *Common Market Law Review* 38. 651–676.

Xanthaki, Helen. 2012a. Technical considerations in harmonization and approximation: legislative drafting techniques for full transposition. In Mads Andenas (ed.), *Theory and practice of harmonization*, 536–550. London: Edward Elgar Publishing.

Xanthaki, Helen. 2012b. Editorial: Burying the hatchet between common and civil law drafting styles in Europe. *Legisprudence* 6(2). 133–148.

Xanthaki, Helen. 2013a. *Thornton's legislative drafting*, 5th edn. London: Bloomsbury.

Xanthaki, Helen. 2013b. The regulatory reform agenda and modern innovations in drafting style. In Luzius Mader & Sergey Kabyshev (eds.), *Regulatory reform. Implementation and compliance*, 128–141. Baden-Baden: Nomos.

Xanthaki, Helen. 2013c. Legislative drafting: a new sub-discipline of law is born. *IALS Student Law Review* 1(1). 57–70.

Xanthaki, Helen. 2014. *Drafting legislation: art and technology of rules for regulation*. Oxford: Hart Publishing.
Zammit, Borda Aldo (ed.). 2011. *Legislative drafting*. Abingdon, UK: Routledge.

Websites focusing on legal drafting and related topics

Australian Government Office of Parliamentary Counsel. https://opc.gov.au/ (accessed 27 November 2015).
centerforplainlanguage. http://centerforplainlanguage.org/ (accessed 27 November 2015).
Clarity: an international association promoting plain language. http://www.clarity-international.net/ (accessed 27 November 2015).
Good law initiative. https://www.gov.uk/guidance/good-law (accessed 27 November 2015).
legislation.gov.uk. http://www.legislation.gov.uk/ (accessed 27 November 2015).
New Zealand Parliamentary Counsel Office. http://www.legislation.govt.nz/ (accessed 27 November 2015).
PLAIN (Plain Language Association International). http://plainlanguagenetwork.org/ (accessed 27 November 2015).
plainlanguage.gov. http://www.plainlanguage.gov/ (accessed 27 November 2015).
UK Office of the Parliamentary Counsel. https://www.gov.uk/government/organisations/office-of-the-parliamentary-counsel (accessed 27 November 2015).
US House of Representatives Office of the Legislative Counsel. https://legcounsel.house.gov/HOLC/Drafting_Legislation/Drafting_Guide.html (accessed 27 November 2015).
US Senate Office of the Legislative Counsel. http://www.slc.senate.gov/Drafting/drafting.htm (accessed 27 November 2015).

Lawrence M. Solan
2 The interpretation of laws

1 Introduction: Why must we interpret laws?

Statutory interpretation becomes necessary because of a gap between our desire to govern ourselves under a rule of law based heavily on language, and the design of our language faculty. Much of the problem is more conceptual than linguistic. Should a notebook that contains a calendar be considered a "diary" for purposes of the customs laws?[1] Would people have called an airplane a vehicle in 1919?[2] Concepts generally have fuzzy boundaries, but the law is an all-or-nothing affair, so we cannot shrug our shoulders at such questions when they occur in legal concepts. Borderline cases like these are examples of vagueness in law. At the same time, laws can be ambiguous in the sense that they have more than one distinct meaning. When a law refers to categories of workers engaged in interstate commerce, does it refer to those workers considered to be engaged in interstate commerce at the time the law was enacted, or does it refer to an open class of workers, whose status may change with the law over time?[3] As Ralf Poscher (2012) points out, moreover, some laws can be both vague and ambiguous at the same time. Furthermore, language is underspecified as a means of communication, requiring us to draw inferences as to why people say what they do. U.S. Supreme Court Justice Stephen Breyer notes, when he asks his wife, "is there any butter," he is talking about their refrigerator, but does not need to say so, because they both understand the context well enough.[4]

In resolving such linguistic uncertainties, courts attempt to further a number of legal values, which sometimes mutually reinforce each other, but which are other times in tension. The principal value is fidelity to the legislative will, which reinforces democratic values (see Eskridge 2016). However, other values, including interpreting disputed laws in a manner consistent with other code provisions (called the "whole act rule" or "whole code rule" in U.S. jurisprudence), fair notice to those accused of crimes, fidelity to constitutional values, and consistency among judicial decisions all have their place.

Courts have different ways of accomplishing these goals. As for fidelity to the legislative will, one is to focus on the ordinary meaning of the language, on the assumption that the legislature most likely intended the law to be understood in its ordinary sense (Eskridge 2016, Slocum 2015, Scalia and Garner 2012, Solan 2010).

---

1 United States v. Mead Corp., 533 U.S. 218 (2001).
2 McBoyle v. United States, 283 U.S. 25 (1931).
3 Circuit City Stores, Inc. v. Adams, 532 U.S. 105 (2001).
4 Ali v. Federal Bureau of Prisons, 552 U.S. 214 (2008).

A second is to focus on the statute's purpose and to resolve disputes accordingly. A third is to attempt to glean more specifically from context what the legislature intended, often inferred from looking at the historical record surrounding the law's enactment.

Legal systems sometimes choose among these methods of interpretation, but most employ all of them to one degree or another, with judges exercising discretion as to which approach to interpretation fits a given problem. For example, the Spanish Civil Code contains the following provision:

> Rules shall be construed according to the proper meaning of their wording and in connection with the context, with their historical and legislative background and with the social reality of the time in which they are to be applied, mainly attending to their spirit and purpose.[5]

In this short passage, textual language is given priority, followed by context, legislative background, the need to construe codes dynamically (see Eskridge 1994 for the importance of this value in the interpretation of statutes in the U.S.), and according to the legislature's purpose in enacting the law (teleology in the Roman law tradition).

Below I discuss both linguistic and non-linguistic considerations used in resolving disputes over the application of laws. I focus primarily on U.S. cases, but also make reference to Civil Law jurisprudence. First, though, I introduce a thorny problem: where does language end and inferences about the world begin?

2 Language or pragmatic inference?

Most of us live most of our lives with a pretty good understanding of what is expected of us and what we may expect from others. If I teach a class that meets on Tuesdays from 11:00 until 12:00, I know perfectly well where I should be during that period, and what I should be doing when I am there. Some of my knowledge involves understanding the English language, which is my native language. I know what all the words mean when I receive my teaching schedule, and I know how they relate to each other. That is what one knows when one knows a language.

At least that is part of what one knows when one knows a language. One also must know enough about the culture in which the language is used to make appropriate decisions to resolve uncertainty when the words are not clear. When it comes to the language of time, even clear words are not as clear as they might seem to be at

---

[5] *Spanish Civil Code, Article 3*. WORLD INTELLECTUAL PROPERTY ORGANIZATION, (2009), English translation available at http://www.wipo.int/wipolex/en/text.jsp?file_id=221319. For further discussion of European perspective, see Section 4.1 below, and references cited therein.

first glance. When I teach from 11:00 until 12:00, my class really begins at 11:00 and it really ends at 12:00. If someone invites me for dinner at 7:00, in contrast, it would be rude to get there early, unless I have a close and casual relationship with the host. It is also rude to arrive more than a little later than the time of the invitation, especially if the host is preparing a meal. So there is a culturally-determined window of time implicit in a dinner invitation, even though "come to dinner at 7:00" and "class begins at 11:00" seem to share a great deal of vocabulary and syntax.

Many linguists explain such facts by distinguishing between lexical and sentence semantics on the one hand, and pragmatic inference on the other. At some point, our construction of language is less about the words that were uttered than it is about why someone would say such a thing in the particular circumstances of the utterance. This is certainly true when it comes to the conventions concerning time. Grice (1975) distinguished between what is "said" and what is "implied." The former, Grice argues, is more or less associated with the "conventional meaning" of the language in question. "Please come for dinner at 7:00" implies that the guest should not be early, and should not be too late, at least in my own social culture. But what is said is exactly what is on the page: come at 7:00.

The two examples are both directives. One is from the administration of my law school, the other from a hypothetical friend. Each has given me an instruction – a plan.[6] In the case of the teaching schedule, once I commit to any particular schedule, the implied understanding of what it means to be prompt enters the scene. The same holds true for the dinner invitation. The difference between the two is that the norms of promptness are not the same in the classroom and the home in connection with social engagements. It is surely not the case that 11:00 is construed tightly in English, whereas 7:00 is construed more loosely in some general sense.

When judges and others interpret laws, they must achieve the right balance of attention to the language itself and attention to the context-sensitive pragmatic considerations that are part of everyday understanding of language. By "right balance" I mean the balance that best advances fidelity to the intention of the legislature (a democratic value) and fidelity to the rule of law as a value in its own right (perhaps through coherent interpretation across a code). As we shall see, these considerations sometimes reinforce each other, but at other times are in tension.

Judge Richard A. Posner (2010) illustrates this point by imagining a trial for possession of child pornography. No one would think that the prosecutor or judge has violated the law by handling the evidence that is the subject of the trial. Significantly, the law need not carve out such situations as exceptions. The system permits such reasonable pragmatic inferences to be drawn.

---

6 For excellent discussion of laws as plans, see Shapiro (2013).

3 Relying on the law's language

3.1 Finding ordinary meaning

This eclectic approach to the interpretation of laws works fine when the various approaches lead to the same conclusion, and the application of the criteria is straightforward. However, this is not always the case. For example, when a court gives special deference to the ordinary meaning of the words used in a law, how do we know which meaning is the ordinary one? Furthermore, the reason to defer to the law's ordinary meaning is that we assume that such deference will best reflect the legislature's intention. This leaves open the question of how defeasible this approach should be when there exists independent evidence that the legislature intended a meaning either broader or narrower than an expression's ordinary usage. This section discusses difficulties in determining which of an expression's meanings is the "ordinary" one. The next section addresses the extent to which the ordinary meaning may yield to other interpretations.

3.1.1 Native speaker intuition

Traditionally, judges have determined ordinary meaning the way we all do it every day: they rely on their knowledge of the language as native speakers. Consider this entertaining case: *62 Cases of Jam v. United States*.[7] A federal law, the Food, Drugs and Cosmetics Act, requires that foods be labeled accurately. Misbranded foods are to be taken off the market. Regulations set legal standards for various types of food sold. One such food type is jam. Regulations set the proportion of fruit and other ingredients that must be present for a seller to call its product jam. Section 403 of the statute requires that products that resemble regulated food categories but fail to meet the legal standards be clearly labeled as "imitation" products. The product in question in this case looked and tasted like jam, but was indeed labeled as "imitation" jam since it failed to meet the legal standards for being labeled jam. In holding that the product was not misbranded, the Supreme Court straightforwardly relied on the ordinary meaning of the law's language:

> In ordinary speech there can be no doubt that the product which the United States here seeks to condemn is an "imitation" jam. It looks and tastes like jam; it is unequivocally labeled "imitation jam." The Government does not argue that its label in any way falls short of the requirements of § 403 (c). Its distribution in interstate commerce would therefore clearly seem to be authorized by that section.[8]

---

[7] 350 U.S. 593 (1951).
[8] 350 U.S. at 599–600.

How did the Court determine the ordinary sense of the statute's language? It did not say, and seems never to have considered that an issue. After all, the statute really is clear on its face, and the manufacturer clearly complied with it. This case represents the traditional approach to ordinary meaning: we know it when we hear or see it.

"Ordinary meaning" is a distributional concept. It is an estimate of the relative frequency of one meaning over others. While judges may have solid intuitions about word meaning, their sense of how meaning is distributed may not reflect the actual facts of which meaning is the more common one. Studies show that both lay people and judges are subject to what has been called the "false consensus bias" when it comes to the meanings of words. We tend to overestimate the extent to which our understanding of language reflects the norm. In Solan, Rosenblatt and Osherson (2008), participants were given a story about a workplace injury in which an individual was sickened when he inhaled sand particles used in a sandblasting operation. Participants then had to say whether this was a "pollution" injury, a question that relates to insurance coverage. The scenario was selected because the courts are not in accord about the resolution of this issue. About 40 percent of the participants said it was pollution, 40 percent said it was not, and 20 percent said they could not tell. They were then told that 100 people like them were being asked the same question and were asked how many of these people they thought would be in agreement with them. People generally believed that a substantial majority would be in agreement with them (between 60 and 65 percent) even though this was not the case. A similar set of questions was asked with respect to a different scenario in which the term in dispute was "earth movement." The results were similar. The study was further tested on a group of judges attending a conference. The judges also overestimated the extent to which their understanding reflected the norm.

3.1.2 Replacing the judge with the dictionary

All of this suggests that when the issue is a distribution of how an expression is understood our intuitions may not be accurate. The legal system understands this fragility. Because of it, judges have turned to a different source of information about ordinary meaning: the dictionary. Reference to dictionaries by the U.S. Supreme Court has increased exponentially over the Court's history. Through the 1860s, there were fewer than ten references per decade to the dictionary in Supreme Court cases. Then, from 1870, continuing for the next 100 years, citations numbered between 24 and 69 per decade. Finally, since the 1980s, citations increased to 100 for the 1980s, and 193 and 192 for the most recent two decades.[9]

---

9 See Solan (2003: 276), updated here to include the decade from 2000–2009.

The Supreme Court's extensive use of dictionaries has received a great deal of attention in the scholarly literature, almost all of it negative (see, e.g., Aprill 1998; Mouritsen 2010; Brudney and Baum 2013). Among the problems with reliance on dictionaries to determine ordinary meaning are the fact that dictionaries vary in how they order definitions, some historically, others in order of prevalence; the fact that among definitions they do not draw a line between what is ordinary and what is unusual, having no theory about how to made such a determination; and the fact that the interpretive issues that arise in court cases are often either different from or more subtle than the decisions made by lexicographers in crafting definitions. That is, dictionaries are often inadequately contextualized to suit judicial purposes.[10] Making matters worse, judges have taken to finding definitions that reinforce the positions they wish to support, and bickering with one another over which dictionary is the best one for the task at hand.

Consider the Supreme Court's 1994 decision in *MCI Telecommunications Corp. v. American Telephone and Telegraph Company* ("AT&T").[11] For decades, AT&T held a virtual monopoly on telephone service in the United States. Then, in the 1970s, given the development of new technology that made competition possible, AT&T was broken up into a number of smaller companies, and competitors entered the market. MCI was one of the new telephone companies.

AT&T was required to publish its tariffs on a regular basis by filing them with the Federal Communications Commission ("FCC"). In fact, the federal Communications Act requires that all carriers make such filings. However, the statute also permits the FCC to modify this requirement through the issuance of regulations:

> (2) The Commission may, in its discretion and for good cause shown, modify any requirement made by or under the authority of this section either in particular instances or by general order applicable to special circumstances or conditions except that the Commission may not re-quire the notice period specified in para-graph (1) to be more than one hundred and twenty days.[12]

Because this filing requirement is burdensome, the FCC decided to "modify" the requirement by making it inapplicable to "nondominant" carriers, on the theory that the requirement would tend to suppress the very development of competition from newcomers that the law was intended to encourage. The question in the case before the Supreme Court was whether the term "modify" in the statute should be construed to permit the elimination of the filing requirement altogether for this subset of carriers.

Writing for a majority of five (there were three dissenters), Justice Scalia focused on dictionary definitions of "modify." Most of the definitions indicated changing something in a modest or minor way. *Webster's Third New International Dictionary*

---

10 See Costello v. United States (Posner, J.)(
11 512 U.S. 218 (1994).
12 47 U.S.C. § 203(b)(2).

(a leading unabridged dictionary of American usage), however, also included "to make a basic or important change in" among the definitions. MCI Telecommunications relied on this definition, arguing that the term is ambiguous as to how substantial a change may be for it to still be considered a modification. Under U.S. administrative law principles, courts are to defer agencies' interpretation of statutes in which the legislature grants authority to the agency.[13] Yet Justice Scalia did not accept the argument that the broad definition found in *Webster's Third* was sufficient to establish an ambiguity. Unlike other cases in which different definitions established ambiguity, this case involved "one dictionary whose suggested meaning contradicts virtually all others."[14] Thus, *Webster's Third* was dubbed a rogue dictionary.

My analysis of the linguistic issue is that *modification* comfortably incorporates situations in which a rule remains constant, but an adjustment is made in identifying the population to whom the rule applies. A high school that has a rule requiring all students to take their lunch on the campus can modify this rule by creating an exclusion for seniors (see Solan 2010 for further discussion). Here, however, where the rule was changed to apply only to one company, the case is a close one. If I am right, the battle over the dictionaries is irrelevant in this case.

3.1.3 Turning to the corpus

One way to avoid both the risk of idiosyncratic interpretation and dictionary shopping is for judges and legal scholars to rely on large corpora of language, essentially becoming their own lexicographers. This has begun to happen. In essence, the judge acquires all of the lexicographer's "file cards" and makes an independent decision about the distribution of different senses of the word. If the corpus is constructed to include examples from many different genres and walks of life, the distributional facts are likely to identify both prototypical and outlying senses.

The U.S. Supreme Court engaged in a corpus analysis in 1998. In *Muscarello v. United States*,[15] the question was whether a person who has drugs in one part of his car and a gun in another as he drives to a drug deal has "carried a firearm" "during and in relation to a drug trafficking crime." All nine justices agreed that the ordinary meaning should prevail, but they split 5–4 on what that meaning is. Much of the discussing involved a childish-sounding argument about which dictionary is the most authoritative and which allusions to literature and the Bible the most convincing. However, in his majority opinion, Justice Breyer also reported a search of news articles from Westlaw and Lexis, in which he found that about one third of the occurrences of

---

13 Chevron U.S.A., Inc. v. Natural Resources Defense Council, Inc., 467 U.S. 837 (1984).
14 512 U.S.at 226.
15 524 U.S. 125 (1998).

"carry" in close proximity to "weapon" involved transporting the weapon in a vehicle of some sort. The dissenting judges took the position that the normal way to carry a gun is to carry it on one's person, and the statute should have been so construed.

Who was right? The dissent probably had the better of the linguistic argument. While it is true that it is not unusual to speak of carrying a weapon in a vehicle, absent the modifier "in a vehicle" the normal implication is that if someone is said to carry a gun, in all likelihood that individual is said to carry a gun on his or her person. Linguists refer to the default reading as the "unmarked case." Mouritsen (2010) conducted a corpus analysis of the language using the Corpus of Contemporary American English ("COCA") developed by linguists at Brigham Young University, and found a large predominance of the expression being used to convey carrying on one's person.

Significantly, the statute has no modifier that expresses the means by which the firearm must be conveyed. That can mean either that the legislature had in mind the unmarked case, or it could mean that the legislature left open the conviction of those who carry a firearm to a drug crime, no matter how they got it there. We cannot know which of these understandings the Congress had in mind when it enacted the statute. A principle of law – the rule of lenity – requires that such indeterminacy be resolved in favor of the defendant, as the dissenting justices pointed out.

But the majority had a good argument as well. The broad reading of the statute is probably less preferred, but is by no means entirely unnatural. That reading, although harsher, appears to do a better job furthering the statute's purpose: to separate guns from commerce in illegal drugs. It should not be surprising, then, that the dissenting opinion in *Muscarello* was written by the most textualist member of the Supreme Court at that time – Justice Antonin Scalia. To him, the case was about the more natural textual reading trumping a purposive (i.e., teleological) approach to interpreting statutes.

Judges have occasionally enlisted the assistance of corpora since then. Judge Posner, in *United States v. Costello*,[16] was confronted with determining whether a woman whose boyfriend – an undocumented immigrant – moved in with her – had violated a statute making it a crime to "harbor" such undocumented people. Posner first criticized the lower court for relying on dictionaries to determine the scope of the statute. He then conducted a Google News search, and found that "harbor" is used predominantly in circumstances describing efforts to hide the individual being harbored. Harboring is used with such groups as Jews, refugees, enemies, fugitives and Quakers, but not with guests or victims. Posner concluded that having one's boyfriend live with her openly does not qualify as "harboring" him.

Two state supreme courts have engaged in corpus analysis in an effort to determine a law's ordinary meaning. The Supreme Court of Utah, in *Rasabout v State*,[17]

---

[16] 666 F.3d 1040 (7th Cir. 2012).
[17] 267 P.3d 912, 918 (Utah 2011).

confronted the issue of whether a gang member who issued twelve shots from a semi-automatic weapon "discharged" the gun once or discharged the gun twelve separate times. The difference affected his sentence: Either he committed twelve separate, consecutive crimes, or a single crime of emptying the weapon. The majority opinion looked up "discharge" in several dictionaries and determined that twelve separate offenses had been committed. In his concurring opinion, Associate Chief Justice Lee, like Judge Posner before him, criticized reliance on dictionaries as insufficiently sensitive to context. Lee, instead, turned to COCA, , with which he was familiar, having been a member of Brigham Young's law faculty prior to joining the Supreme Court of Utah.[18] The search demonstrated that the majority had it right: "Discharge" is typically used to describe each single shot from a weapon, although it can also be used to speak of emptying a weapon of its ammunition.

Finally, in 2016, the Supreme Court of Michigan decided *People v. Harris*,[19] in which both the majority and dissenting opinions relied on a corpus analysis (using COCA), but disagreed about how the analysis should be conducted. Three Detroit police officers had been subjected to disciplinary proceedings when one of them assaulted a driver who had been stopped, while the others watched and did nothing to help. Police departmental rules require that the officers testify at such proceedings. This, in principle, could jeopardize their constitutional privilege against being forced to incriminate themselves, except that a Michigan law declares statements made at such disciplinary proceedings inadmissible at any subsequent criminal proceedings brought against police officers. The statute says:

> An involuntary statement made by a law enforcement officer, and any information derived from that involuntary statement, shall not be used against the law enforcement officer in a criminal procedure.[20]

A video of the incident showed that the three officers had lied in their testimony in the disciplinary proceeding. They were subsequently prosecuted for assault and battery, and for obstruction of justice. The obstruction charge was based on their false testimony. The linguistic question was whether such false statements should be considered "information" for purposes of construing the Michigan statute. The majority said that a statement need not be accurate to count as information, citing numerous references to "false information" and "inaccurate information" in the corpus. Thus, the majority decided that the statute immunizes false statements as well as true ones from use in subsequent criminal proceedings against law enforcement officers. The dissenting justices focused on occurrences of "information" in the corpus without modifiers that go to the accuracy of the statement, and found that the unmodified noun is almost

---

18 Justice Lee continues to teach at Brigham Young, but is no longer a full-time member of the faculty.
19 No. 149872, decided June 22, 2016.
20 MCL 15.593.

always used to express truthful statements. As in *Muscarello*, we cannot tell whether the legislature intended the term to generalize to all modifiers, or to be construed in its "unmarked" version, which would include only truthful statements.

The case thus illustrates an important limitation in the use of corpus linguistics in legal analysis. A corpus is itself nothing more than a large data set, searchable using various tools. The corpus does not tell legal analysts what questions to ask about the data. Having a corpus at hand is more or less a sophisticated version of having a lexicographer's file cards available. Each file card has an example of the word's usage, but that says nothing about how to sort the cards, and what principles to use in writing the definitions. These observations do not suggest that linguistic corpora are useless in legal settings. Rather, they serve as a reminder that a corpus and its accompanying software together constitute a tool, and a tool is only good at helping to answer questions when it is clear what questions to ask.

3.2 Deciding that the most ordinary meaning is not the intended meaning

Legal systems generally recognize that laws are created in particular contexts, and that it is often necessary to understand the relevant context in order to apply the law faithfully. Sometimes this inquiry into context reveals that the legislature intended a meaning that is narrower than the full range of ordinary meaning. In other instances, context suggests that a broader than ordinary understanding was intended. This problem is not new: Aristotle recognized it in the Nicomachean Ethics:

> [E]very law is laid down in general terms, while there are matters about which it is impossible to speak correctly in general terms. Where it is necessary to speak in general terms but impossible to do so correctly, the legislator lays down that which holds good for the majority of cases, being quite aware that it does not hold good for all. The law, indeed, is none the less correctly laid down because of this defect; for the defect lies not in the law, nor in the lawgiver, but in the nature of the subject matter, being necessarily involved in the very conditions of human action.[21]

These issues do not arise from careless drafting, Aristotle rightly comments. The real problem is that it is not clear how broadly the laws should be construed in individual cases. An "ordinary meaning" approach is not adequate to handle all cases precisely because a law written in general terms "does not hold good for all."

As for a narrower-than-ordinary-meaning interpretation (the need for which was Aristotle's principal concern), consider the U.S. Supreme Court's 2015 decision

---

21 Aristotle, *Nicomachean Ethics*, bk. 5, ch. 10 (F. H. Peters trans., 5th ed. 1893) (c. 384 B.C.E.). For discussion, see Schauer (2003: 42–48).

in *Yates v. United States*.²² Following corporate financial scandals in the first years of this century, Congress enacted the Sarbanes-Oxley Act, whose goal was to hold corporate executives, lawyers and accountants responsible for actions conducted in the name of the company. Of special concern was the fact that Arthur Andersen, the accounting firm of Enron Corporation, which had been manipulating prices in the energy sector of the economy, had destroyed documents and electronically-stored information on the eve of a government investigation into the accounting firm's role. The accounting firm was initially convicted of obstructing justice, but that conviction was reversed because the firm had not yet been subpoenaed, and claimed that it was under no legal obligation to maintain the records.²³ Soon thereafter, in 2002, Congress made it clear that the destruction of documents in anticipation of a federal investigation would be a criminal act going forward. The relevant portion of the Sarbanes-Oxley Act provides:

> Whoever knowingly alters, destroys, mutilates, conceals, covers up, falsifies, or makes a false entry in any record, document or tangible object with the intent to impede, obstruct, or influence the investigation or proper administration of any matter within the jurisdiction of any department or agency of the United States ... shall be fined under this title, imprisoned not more than 20 years, or both.²⁴

Yates did not obstruct justice by destroying documents or electronic storage devices. Yates was the captain of a fishing boat operating off the coast of Florida. He and his comrades had been catching grouper that were under the legal minimum length for keeping the fish. A government vessel approached and officers commenced boarding the fishing boat. While onboard, the agents identified a large number of undersized fish, which they had the crew segregate in crates. Yates and his crew then threw the undersized fish overboard and substituted larger fish for the ones that the government officials had identified. The legal question that made its way to the Supreme Court was whether Yates had "knowingly ... destroyed ... a tangible object ... with the intent to impede [or] obstruct ... the investigation ... of a matter within the jurisdiction of an agency of the United States."

A majority (five) of the Supreme Court Justices found that Yates did not violate the statute even though the fish that were destroyed clearly can be considered tangible objects. Writing for the majority, Justice Ginsburg noted: "Whether a statutory term is unambiguous, however, does not turn solely on dictionary definitions of its component words. Rather, "[t]he plainness or ambiguity of statutory language is determined [not only] by reference to the language itself, [but as well by] the specific context in which that language is used, and the broader context of the statute as a

---

22 574 U.S.___ (2015).
23 Arthur Andersen LLP v. United States, 544 U.S. 696 (2005).
24 18 U.S.C. § 1519.

whole."²⁵ Indeed there is a canon of construction, *noscitur a sociis*, which says that words should be construed in association with the words that surround them. Moreover, the title of the provision, "Destruction, Alteration, or Falsification of Records in Federal Investigations and Bankruptcy" suggests that the law was intended to deal with documents and the like – not fish.

The dissenting opinion, written by Justice Kagan, opened with the ordinary meaning rule: "When Congress has not supplied a definition, we generally give a statutory term its ordinary meaning." ²⁶ No doubt those in the majority would agree with this statement. The issue is whether the ordinary meaning rule is defeasible, and if so, how defeasible it is. *Yates* demonstrates that when a law – especially a criminal law – can be construed to include a category that goes way beyond its intended scope – at least some of the time courts are unwilling to construe the law broadly, notwithstanding the ordinary meaning of the terms.

Now let us consider a case in which the legislature most likely intended a meaning broader than the ordinary meaning of the law's terms would suggest. Congress enacted the Voting Rights Act in 1965, as one of a number of civil rights statutes passed in the mid-1960s. In *Chisom v. Roemer*,²⁷ decided in 1991, the Supreme Court decided that the Act applies not only to the election of legislators, but also to the election of state court judges in states that hold such elections. African-American voters in Louisiana alleged that the districts for elections of members of the state supreme court were structured in such a way as to decrease the voting power of a district in which a majority of voters were members of minority groups, by combining that district with three other districts in which white voters predominated. If true, this voting scheme at least arguably would violate the Voting Rights Act, which was concerned with voting schemes in southern states that had the effect of reducing the likelihood of a black person being elected. However, as a threshold issue, the relevant section of the Voting Rights Act applies to elections of "representatives" and it is not clear that state supreme court justices should be considered representatives. The statute prohibits electoral practices in which minority voters "have less opportunity than other members of the electorate to participate in the political process and to elect representatives of their choice."

A majority held that notwithstanding the fact that it is unusual to consider a supreme court justice a "representative," the better interpretation of the statute includes judicial elections. Looking at the purpose of the law and the legislative history, it did not seem plausible that the legislature would enact a civil rights law that left a safe harbor for racist election practices for judges. Consequently, the ordinary meaning of the statute's terms yielded to a more expansive reading that took the law's purpose and enactment history into account.

---

25 574 U.S. at ___, slip op. at 14.
26 574 U.S. at ___ (Kagan, J., dissenting), slip op. at 2.
27 501 U.S. 380 (1991).

These cases illustrate not only the limits of the ordinary meaning approach to statutory interpretation, but also the need to combine pragmatic inference with construal of the words themselves.

3.3 Ordinary meaning and fair notice

People accused of wrongdoing are entitled to know what it is that the law has prohibited them from doing.

In a famous 1931 Supreme Court decision, *McBoyle, v. United States*,[28] Justice Oliver Wendell Holmes stated the principle. McBoyle had flown a stolen airplane from one state to another. A federal law made it a crime to transport a motor vehicle, knowing it to have been stolen, across state lines. The statute defined "motor vehicle" as follows: "the term 'motor vehicle' shall include an automobile, automobile truck, automobile wagon, motor cycle, or any other self-propelled vehicle not designed for running on rails." After concluding that the term "motor vehicle" did not adduce in the mind an image of an airplane, Holmes noted:

> Although it is not likely that a criminal will carefully consider the text of a law before he murders or steals, it is reasonable that a fair warning should be given to the world in language that the common world will understand, of what the law intends to do if a certain line is passed. To make the warning fair, so far as possible the line should be clear. When a rule of conduct is laid down in words that evoke in the common mind only the picture of vehicles moving on land, the statute should not be extended to aircraft, simply because it might seem to us that a similar policy applies, or upon the speculation that, if the legislature had thought of it, very likely broader words would be used.

Note that Holmes calls for reliance on ordinary language for reasons other than adherence to the will of the legislature (see Eskridge 2016). In fact, it may well be that the legislature intended a broader meaning than the ordinary understanding would allow. Rather, the reason for concern about fair notice is to ensure that the courts do not stretch the fair understanding of what has been enacted, thus becoming legislators in their own right, and undermining the importance of the legislative process, which is constitutionally mandated.

3.4 Resolving vagueness

Reliance on language also leaves open the question of how to deal with laws that become vague at the margin. Philosophers distinguish vagueness from ambiguity in

---

[28] 283 U.S. 25 (1931).

that the former concerns borderline instances of a concept, while the latter concerns a clash between two distinct meanings or structures. As has been long-recognized (see Rosch 1975), concepts often have fuzzy boundaries, and it is not always an easy task to decide when one concept ends and another begins.

To take a classic example from U.S. law,[29] if a statute prohibits "using a gun" in a drug trafficking crime, has a person who traded his gun for cocaine "used" the gun within the meaning of the law? In a sense, he did use it. But he only used it as an object of value, not as a weapon. Should this count? A majority in the U.S. Supreme Court said it should, with a strong dissenting opinion from the left by the usually conservative justice, the late Antonin Scalia. The case is interesting because what the defendant did was surely within the bounds of what it means to "use" something, but remote from what it ordinarily means to "use a gun." Philosophers of language refer to this as the "pet fish problem" (Fodor and Lepore 1996). At least in U.S. culture, the most prototypical pet is a dog about the size of an Irish setter, and the prototypical fish is a trout or salmon, or another fish of about that size and shape. But the prototypical pet fish is not half dog/half fish. Nor is it the size of a salmon. Rather, it is a small fish – a guppy or a gold fish. If terms become vague once they stray far enough from prototypical usage, we must recognize in advance that the term in question is a phrase, and that the prototype of the phrase does not equal the sum of the prototypes of the words that constitute the phrase. Rather, the phrase has its own prototype. The Supreme Court erred in not recognizing this fact about ordinary meaning.

Yet many classic cases of statutory interpretation are about resolving vagueness, and they do not all involve pet fish problems. The ordinary meaning approach is the principal way to resolve such cases: default to the more typical interpretation. That is what many of the dictionary battles are intended to accomplish (i.e., the ordinary meaning of "modify"), although the dictionary does so poorly for reasons discussed above.

4 Relying on non-linguistic legal values

Because this Handbook is focused on the communicative aspects of law and legal analysis, this chapter has focused thus far on language-centric issues in statutory interpretation. It must be recognized, however, that there are competing values in law. Here, I will touch briefly on a few of them.

---

29 Smith v. United States, 508 U.S. 223 (1993). The same statute prohibits carrying a firearm in a drug trafficking crime, and was the law in issue in *Muscarello*, discussed above.

4.1 Coherence within the code

One earmark of the rule of law is consistency. Like things should be treated alike. Legal theorists from both common law and Roman law perspectives make this point (see, e.g, Dworkin 1988; Zippelius 2006/2008; Shapiro 2013; Greenawalt 2013). It is possible to reduce this value to the value of adhering to the legislative will on the assumption that the legislature presumptively has in mind the relationship between particular code provisions and the larger statutory scheme. Indeed, U.S. judges make this argument. Consider this statement by Justice Scalia:

> The meaning of terms on the statute books ought to be determined, not on the basis of which meaning can be shown to have been understood by a larger handful of the Members of Congress; but rather on the basis of which meaning is (1) most in accord with context and ordinary usage, and thus most likely to have been understood by the whole Congress which voted on the words of the statute (not to mention the citizens subject to it), and (2) most compatible with the surrounding body of law into which the provision must be integrated – a compatibility which, by a benign fiction, we can assume Congress always has in mind.[30]

Scalia thus adds coherence with the code to ordinary meaning as means for promoting the legislative will.

But this move sells short the value of coherence in its own right. Justice Scalia, somewhat contrary to the statement quoted above, put it this way in determining that a civil rights law entitling a winning plaintiff to recover "a reasonable attorney's fee" did not include the cost of expert witness testimony:

> Where a statutory term presented to us for the first time is ambiguous, we construe it to contain that permissible meaning which fits most logically and comfortably into the body of both previously and subsequently enacted law. We do so not because that precise accommodative meaning is what the lawmakers must have had in mind (how could an earlier Congress know what a later Congress would enact?), but because it is our role to make sense rather than nonsense out of the *corpus juris*.[31]

This statement sounds a great deal like Ronald Dworkin, who advocated judges ruling in a manner that would make the law as good as it could be. It is further an expression of Savigny's (1840) systematic approach to statutory interpretation, still influential in Roman law jurisprudence (see Maxeiner 2013; Zippelius 2008; Zimmermann 1997).[32] The motivation is not fidelity to the legislative will. It is rather a recognition that the rule of law is enhanced when courts value coherent construction of the code.

---

[30] Green v. Bock Laundry Machine Co., Inc., 490 U.S. 504, 528 (Scalia, J., concurring)(1989).
[31] West Virginia Univ. Hosps. v. Casey, 499 U.S. 83, 100–01 (1991) (internal citations omitted).
[32] Savigny (1840: 172) identified four "elements" of interpretation: the grammatical, the logical, the historical and the systematic. The systematic element deals with coherence among code provisions, the logical with coherence within a code provision. Often, scholars add purpose or teleology to this list.

4.2 Consistent precedent

Common law and Roman law systems differ with respect to the role of precedent in statutory cases. Precedent is binding only in the former. The difference, however, is often more formal than substantive. All legal systems value consistency in decision making. Once a high court makes a series of decisions about either a particular code provision or a cluster of code provisions, that court will have to come to terms with its earlier decisions in making subsequent ones. The value of such consistency lies not in fidelity to the legislative will, but rather in respect for a basic rule of law value in its own right. To take an example from U.S. law, the Supreme Court has been aggressive for decades in supporting the obligation to arbitrate certain claims, rather than going to court. In deciding new cases, the Supreme Court routinely refers to its own earlier decisions as reason to continue in the tradition of enforcing arbitration clauses in contracts.[33] Thus, "making sense rather than nonsense of the corpus juris" incorporates a broad understanding of "corpus juris" to include the body of interpretive legal decisions by the courts themselves, independent of judgments about legislative intent (see Eskridge 2016, Solan 2016 for discussion).

4.3 Fidelity to constitutional and other basic norms

A canon of construction holds that if there is more than one reasonable interpretation of a law, an interpretation that complies with constitutional requirements should be given priority over one that does not. However, controversy continues over what it means to comply with the Constitution. Does it refer to a direct conflict between the Constitution and an interpretation in connection with the case at hand, or does it refer to a concern that sooner or later one interpretation is more likely to lead to constitutional issues than another? Over time, the Supreme Court has expanded the doctrine, moving from the former to the latter approach. Thus, despite no strong textual support, the Supreme Court has held that the National Labor Relations Act, which establishes the right of workers to join labor unions, does not apply to teachers at Catholic schools, because at some point, work rules established through collective bargaining may conflict with the right of the Church to set religiously-based educational practices in Catholic schools.[34] The majority based its decision on the presumption that Congress would not have intended to impede such religious liberty, although, as the dissent pointed out, there was no evidence that Congress had any intention of exempting religious schools from the right of workers to organize. Perhaps a better

---

33 See, e.g., AT&T Mobility LLC v. Concepcion, 563 U.S. 333 (2011); Circuit City Stores, Inc. v. Adams, 532 U.S. 105 (2001) (both enforcing arbitration clauses in contested situations).
34 National Labor Relations Board v. Catholic Bishop of Chicago, 440 U.S. 490 (1979).

explanation for the decision was the majority's judgment that statutory disputes should be resolved in favor of promoting constitutional values, regardless of what the legislature had in mind (see Solan 2010 for further discussion).

5 Conclusion

Legal interpretation is highly situational. Although the tools applied to the construction of laws are not many, their weights and applicability from one case to another is not fixed. Moreover, debates about how defeasible interpretive principles are further impede efforts to create a formal science of statutory interpretation. The overall picture is far from chaotic, but it can never be fully determinative, given the gaps between how our linguistic faculties are designed, and the goal of living under a language-based rule of law.

Much of the debate over the proper way to engage in statutory interpretation can be seen as a struggle between a rule-based approach, in which the ordinary meaning of a law's words and a limited number of specific canons of construction are deemed sufficient to determine a statute's application in a particular case (see, e.g., Scalia and Garner 2012), and a more eclectic approach, in which the statutory interpreter considers information specific to the enactment of the legislation, including reference to its purpose, which is gleaned from examining the circumstances underlying its enactment (see, e.g., Eskridge 2016). The purposive approach is standard procedure in Roman law jurisdictions, which favor teleological inquiry.

Most interpreters of laws appear to consider evidence of meaning that goes well beyond the ordinary meaning and the canons of construction, while at the same time respecting the language of the legislation as primary. It will never be possible to specify where lines should be drawn so that respect for the formal nature of the legislative process on the one hand, and respect for what the legislature attempted to accomplish on the other, are guaranteed equal respect. Even so, the issues to be confronted are relatively clear, and courts do appear to operate within a limited range of freedom to resolve disputes over the meanings of laws.

References

Aprill, Ellen. 1998. The law of the word: dictionary shopping in the Supreme Court. *Arizona State Law Journal* 30. 275–336.
Brudney, James J. and Laurence Baum. 2013. Oasis or mirage: The Supreme Court's thirst for dictionaries in the Rehnquist and Roberts eras. *William & Mary Law Review* 55. 483–580.
Dworkin, Ronald. 1981. *Law's empire*. Cambridge, MA: Harvard University Press.
Eskridge, William N., Jr. 1994. *Dynamic statutory interpretation*. Cambridge, MA: Harvard University Press.

Eskridge, William N., Jr. 2016. *Interpreting law: a primer on how to read statutes and the constitution.* St. Paul, MN: Foundation Press.

Fodor, Jerry and Ernest Lepore. 1996. The red herring and the pet fish: why concepts still can't be prototypes. *Cognition* 58. 253–270.

Greenawalt, Kent. 2013. *Statutory and common law interpretation.* Oxford: Oxford University Press.

Grice, H.P. 1975. Logic and conversation. In Peter Cole and Jerry E. Morgan (eds.), *Syntax and semantics, vol. 3: speech acts,* 41–58. New York: Academic Press.

Maxeiner, James. 2013. Scalia & Garner's reading law: a civil law for the age of statutes? *Journal of Civil Law Studies* 6. 1–35.

Mouritsen, Stephen C. 2010. The dictionary is not a fortress: definitional fallacies and a corpus-based approach to plain meaning. *Brigham Young Law Review* 2010. 1915–1980.

Peczenik, Aleksander. 2008. *On law and reason.* Dordrecht: Kluwer Academic Publishers.

Poscher, Ralf. 2012. Ambiguity and vagueness in legal interpretation. In Peter M. Tiersma and Lawrence M. Solan (eds.), *The Oxford handbook of language and law.* Oxford: Oxford University Press.

Posner, Richard A. 2010. *How judges think.* Cambridge, MA: Harvard University Press.

Rosch, Eleanor. 1975. Cognitive representations of semantic categories. *Journal of Experimental Psychology: General* 104(3). 192–233.

Savigny, Friedrich Carl von. 1840/1979. *System of the modern Roman law, volume 1* (translated by William Holloway). Westport, CT: Hyperion Press.

Scalia, Antonin and Bryan Garner. (2012) *Reading law: the interpretation of legal texts.* St. Paul, MN: Thomson/West.

Schauer, Frederick. 2003. *Profiles, probabilities and stereotypes.* Cambridge, MA: Harvard University Press.

Slocum, Brian G. 2015. *Ordinary meaning: a theory of the most fundamental principle of legal interpretation.* Chicago: University of Chicago Press.

Shapiro, Scott. 2013. *Legality.* Cambridge, MA: Harvard University Press.

Solan, Lawrence. 2016. Precedent in statutory interpretation. *North Carolina Law Review* 94. 1165–1234.

Solan, Lawrence M. 2010. *The language of statutes: laws and their interpretation.* Chicago: University of Chicago Press.

Solan, Lawrence. 2003. Finding ordinary meaning in the dictionary. In Marlyn Robinson (ed.), *Language and the law: proceedings of a conference,* 255–278. Buffalo, NY: William S. Hein & Co.

Solan, Lawrence M., Terri Rosenblatt and Daniel Osherson. 2008. False consensus bias in contract interpretation. *Columbia Law Review* 108. 1268–1300.

Zimmermann, Reinhard. 1997. Statuta sunt stricte interpretanda? Statutes and the common law: a continental perspective. *Cambridge Law Journal* 56. 315–328.

Zippelius, Reinhold. 2006/2008. Introduction to German legal methods (translated by Kirk W. Junker and P. Matthew Roy). Durham, NC: Carolina Academic Press.

Janny HC Leung
3 Language rights

1 Introduction

Most current work in the interdisciplinary field of language and law focuses on a cluster of interrelated topics: the language of the law; language in legal processes; language as evidence; and the legal regulation of language use. *Language rights* is a less widely discussed and yet distinct intersection between language and law, which views law as a protector of language.[1] The topic is more macroscopic than topics usually investigated by linguistic or legal analysis alone, and crosses disciplinary boundaries between linguistics, law, policy, education and politics. The chapter describes the historical, political and legal context of language rights, outlines relevant international human rights instruments and national law, and examines the theoretical foundations and conceptual definitions involved in what has now become an established "language rights paradigm" before offering a detailed critique and outlining challenges facing the field.

2 History and origin

To understand language rights today, it is necessary to trace the field's history and politics. Firstly, it is important to note that language rights are often concerned with, and mostly examined in relation to, linguistic minorities rather than whole populations. Such minorities are often the creation of a kind of nationalist politics that emerged from late 18C in Europe, promulgating the idea that people who share a single "root" and "culture" should form a political unit. Language is the principal expression (as well as means of expression) of such a sense of common identity, and the concept of *national languages* took hold. The resulting "one nation, one language" ideology, however, scarcely reflected the social reality of most societies in the world, which are predominantly multilingual. In France, for example, when the revolution broke out in 1789 – a moment now viewed as defining in French national history – less than half of the population spoke French. Far from being a descriptive term denoting an existing referent, the concept of *national language* is something constructed and imposed.

What constitutes a national language is usually a standardized variety with a written form and formal register that together make the variety suitable for official use. Since a national language will by default be the language of public life (often

---

[1] As we shall see below, the terms *law* and *language* both require qualifications in this context.

including education), competence in that language becomes a prerequisite for civil participation, access to resources, and upward social mobility. Speakers of other languages are put under pressure to speak that national language, which will generally be considered to be associated with modernity and progress (May 2006). Other, co-existing languages are "minoritized", and come to be seen as a threat to national unity; younger generations often see little or no value in learning them. There is then a close link between patterns of language use, on the one hand, and social status and opportunity, on the other. Minority groups who lose their language are almost always those who are socially and politically subordinated (ibid).

Considering that there are 7,000 plus languages in the world (according to ethnologue.com; estimates vary), and only 193 sovereign states[2] which are currently members of the United Nations, if the "one-nation-one-language" concept worked efficiently and if each nation were to become a state, then there would either be over 7,000 states or fewer than 193 languages in the world. (Note here that some nations in different parts of the world share the same common language as a consequence of colonization.) Although neither scenario has been (or easily could be) fulfilled, many minority languages have been displaced, and some have disappeared altogether. Challenging such a threat to the existence of established languages, a range of separatist movements (some of them a bi-product of homogenizing policies that backfired) formed among national minorities during the twentieth century, mostly with the ultimate political goal of state-formation.

Nationalism takes many forms. One common facet, however, is a belief that one's own nation is superior to others. Such a sentiment, coupled with economic pressures and the expansion of capitalism, underpinned European imperialist conquests in many parts of the world during the period from late fifteenth to early nineteenth century, especially in Africa. The national or dominant language of the relevant colonial empire was imposed on its colonies to a varying extent, leading to linguistic hierarchies that typically saw the coloniser's language occupy a more prestigious position and the native languages degraded or even actively suppressed (e.g., school children were punished for speaking native languages, for instance by being compelled to wash their mouths out with soap; see Crystal 2000: 84–86).

The significance of national languages has gradually changed, however, as a different climate of linguistic nationalism has spread across the world, especially during and following the major historical period of decolonization (usually considered to be from the 1940s onwards). Many postcolonial African territories found themselves in

---

2 *Nation*, *states*, and the compound noun *nation-states*, are confusing terms, and more so because of the frequency at which they are used interchangeably (many states who are members of the United Nations are not *nations*). *Nation* is typically defined culturally and *states* a politically sovereign entity; the two do not necessarily overlap – there are stateless nations (e.g., Quebec in Canada, Wales in the United Kingdom and Catalonia in Spain) and multinational states (e.g., Belgium and Canada).

need of a language to unify their multiethnic populations in a nation-building project. Even though the language of the expelled colonial power in no sense represented the identity of the native people, it could fill the role of a *lingua franca* in an otherwise fragmented, newly formed state. Decades later in many cases, the former colonial language continues to compete for status with native languages and more often than not wins out, constituting what has been called a kind of linguistic re-colonisation or neo-colonialism. In former settler colonies indigenous populations remain marginalized; and in a large number of them (for example in Canada, Australia, New Zealand, and the United States) indigenous people live in a state of internal colonialism even after the departure of imperialist powers.

Although nationalist ideologies have dwindled in many regions, and been transformed in response to a wide range of both local and international pressures, sovereign states remain the dominant form of contemporary political organization.[3] Some of them have adopted a more tolerant attitude towards minorities, in line with increased recognition of minority rights and a celebration of multiculturalism and diversity in recent decades by regional and international bodies such as UNESCO (see below for details of relevant international human rights instruments). How far such increased awareness assists with continued survival of minority languages is unclear, nevertheless. In some circumstances there are undoubtedly additional motives behind glorification of tradition and culture, which may ultimately not contribute to that outcome. Heller and Duchêne (2012), for example, note that in the neoliberal economic environment, minority identities are often commodified (e.g., in forms of "authentic" tourist experiences, language schools, etc.) and used to construct a niche market. For example, French Canadian identity has been used in the branding of products, including cheese and soaps.

A further, and growing, source of pressure on minority languages is globalization. Desire to participate in the global economy drives the learning and adoption of international languages (e.g., French, Spanish and especially English), as well as regional lingua francas. Such languages are seen as a key to social and economic opportunities, and, in some cases, a ticket to migration to places offering further opportunities.

In an inevitably fast-forward way, the above brief summary describes the main historical and sociopolitical forces that have brought about language shift in minority communities. In addition to these forces, particular technological advances including the invention of print in the fifteenth century (itself linked to the spread of nationalism; see Anderson 1992) and the emergence of digital media in late twentieth century, as well as language standardization and a belief that monolingualism facilitates efficient management and economic growth, also play a part in explaining the extensively documented historical reduction in linguistic diversity.

---

3 Despite the fact that their sovereignty appears to be increasingly curtailed by developments in regional and international legal order, and their political control partially overtaken by globalizing forces.

Before moving to more direct consideration of language rights, it is worth pausing to take stock. Several points stand out from the history. Firstly, it is not a coincidence that language rights are almost always focused on social minorities. Historically, minority language rights originated as reactions to government interventions concerned with language use in particular societies, interventions that may have been motivated by various, context-dependent factors. In other words, the sovereign states have been considered the greatest threat to minorities, rather than being agents for their protection. Secondly, some contemporary pressures on minority language groups do not derive from the state but come from other forces and actors. Even national languages, especially those belonging to smaller nations, may be recognized as being under threat (see the Swedish example in Heller and Duchêne 2012).

Modern advocacy for language rights is not only prompted by concerns for minority rights but is also viewed as a means of securing, or at least stabilizing, linguistic diversity. Anthropologists and linguists have been documenting languages for more than a century; although language "death" has always occurred, it has been observed that languages are now disappearing at a rate unprecedented in the history of mankind (Crystal 2000), to the extent that this process has been described as "linguistic genocide" (Skutnabb-Kangas 2000). Perhaps the most striking warning in relation to language loss at the global level was provided by Krauss (1992), in a speech at an Endangered Languages Symposium taking place as part of the 1991 Linguistic Society of America conference. Using overall numbers, intergenerational transfer, and official status as parameters, he estimated that only 10% of all languages in the world could be considered "safe"; the rest were either "moribund" or "in danger". Since 1991, there have been divergent estimates and reports. Harmon and Koh (2010), for example, report that between 1975 and 2005 global linguistic diversity declined by 20%. Another recent account shows that language endangerment is unevenly distributed across the world: 75% of the languages in use in Australia, Canada and the United States in 1950 are now extinct or moribund; but less than 10% of languages have become "extinct" or "moribund" in sub-Saharan Africa (Simons and Lewis 2013). The same analysis suggests that 19% of living languages are no longer being learnt by children.

Both this study and Krauss's report rely on data from Ethnologue.com (in its 18th edition at the time of writing), a research project started in 1951 which seeks to catalogue all of the world's living languages. UNESCO also keeps track of the world's languages in danger and publishes reports periodically (in 1996, 2001 and 2010). On compelling evidence provided by such data, many concerned sociolinguists have become involved in current advocacy for language rights. A non-profit organization called Terralingua, for example, has expressed linguistic diversity in ecological terms, as a kind of "biocultural" diversity that deserves protection. Drawing on arguments associated with linguistic relativism, the biological metaphor (languages as "species", as in "endangered" languages and language "death") has undoubted rhetorical strength (Errington 2003); at the same time, it has limited accuracy (for two different kinds of critique, see Blommaert 2001 and May 2004) and invites further, less figurative analysis.

3 Evolution in international and regional human rights instruments

As a major component of minority protection, language-related rights in systems of national law and in international treaties predate by more than a century the contemporary notion of human rights that developed between the two world wars and became institutionalized after World War II (Braën 1987; Tierney 2006).[4] With the maturing of human rights regimes the concept of human rights gradually took hold of the popular imagination, and as new threats to human rights have emerged the scope of the rights being formulated has expanded (Freeman 2011). One (albeit controversial) way of capturing this process is to categorize rights into three generations: the first generation focused on civil and political rights; the second on economic and social rights; and the third on cultural or identity rights which concern the collective development of social groups. Rights related to language can be found in all three generations of human rights (De Varennes 1999). But cutting across the three historical emphases, the evolution of language rights, as fueled by historical events, is as much about language as it is about the exercise, subversion, and maintenance of power.

To ensure political stability among minorities created by newly demarcated states following the First World War (whose claim to self-determination in many cases had not been satisfied), the League of Nations devised a scheme of minority protection that extended to racial, linguistic and religious minorities (Henrard 2000). The thinking of the Permanent Court of International Justice, predecessor to the International Court of Justice, in that period (as expressed in their opinion on minority schools in Albania) remains influential today: it demands the prohibition of discrimination and special measures "to ensure for the minority elements suitable means for the preservation of their racial peculiarities, their traditions and their national characteristics" (Henrard 2000:10), justifying such measures on the principle of equality rather than by privilege.

Emphasis on minority protection was soon superseded, however, by a new focus: focus on individual human rights, as the League was replaced by the United Nations (UN) following the Second World War. Language-related rights formulated in the UN were conceived in terms of civil and political participation, and emphasized non-discrimination and freedom of expression. For example Article 1(3) of the United Nations Charter 1945 provides for "fundamental freedom for all without distinction as to race, sex, language, or religion". This provision is then expanded in Article 2 of the Universal Declaration of Human Rights (UDHR) 1948:

---

[4] See the Final Act of the Congress of Vienna 1815, a multilateral treaty signed by seven European countries that offered protection of linguistic minorities.

> Everyone is entitled to all the rights and freedoms set forth in this Declaration, without distinction of any kind, such as race, colour, sex, language, religion, political or other opinion, national or social origin, property, birth or other status. (...)

Although UN declarations are not legally binding on member states, the UDHR has become in effect the foundation of international human rights law and of the UN. Articles 2, 4, 24 and 26 of the later International Covenant on Civil and Political Rights (ICCPR) 1966 reiterate UDHR's stance and prohibit discrimination based on language. Effective from 1976, the ICCPR is a binding treaty that has been signed and ratified by most states in the world. Article 14, concerned with the right to a fair trial, engages language use in a criminal context. Anyone facing a criminal charge should have the right "to be informed promptly and in detail in a language which he understands of the nature and cause of the charge against him", and the right "to have the free assistance of an interpreter if he cannot understand or speak the language used in court" (s.3). Article 27 contains a specific provision for linguistic minorities, but only guarantees them the right to use their own language in the private domain. This Article nevertheless remains the most important statement of minority rights in international law. Debate has continued as to whether the Article imposes a negative or a positive right (see discussion in May 2012: 198–201), because of its ambiguous formulation:

> In those States in which ethnic, religious or linguistic minorities exist, persons belonging to such minorities shall not be denied the right, in community with the other members of their group, to enjoy their own culture, to profess and practice their own religion, or to use their own language.

Wider expectation of more affirmative action by state actors began only later, in the 1990s. The United Nations Declaration of the Rights of Persons Belonging to National or Ethnic, Religious and Linguistic Minorities (UNDM) 1992 may nevertheless be considered an extension of Article 27 ICCPR. Article 1(1) requires that states "shall protect the existence and the national or ethnic, cultural, religious and linguistic identity of minorities within their respective territories and shall encourage conditions for the promotion of that identity". Article 2.1 extends the right to use a minority language to public domains, by stipulating that persons belonging to national or ethnic, religious and linguistic minorities "have the right to enjoy their own culture, to profess and practise their own religion, and to use their own language, in private and in public, freely and without interference or any form of discrimination." Article 4, in particular, encourages states to take positive measures to protect linguistic minorities:

1. States shall take measures where required to ensure that persons belonging to minorities may exercise fully and effectively all their human rights and fundamental freedoms without any discrimination and in full equality before the law.
2. States shall take measures to create favourable conditions to enable persons belonging to minorities to express their characteristics and to develop their culture, language, religion, traditions and customs, except where specific practices are in violation of national law and contrary to international standards.

3. States should take appropriate measures so that, wherever possible, persons belonging to minorities may have adequate opportunities to learn their mother tongue or to have instruction in their mother tongue.
4. States should, where appropriate, take measures in the field of education, in order to encourage knowledge of the history, traditions, language and culture of the minorities existing within their territory. Persons belonging to minorities should have adequate opportunities to gain knowledge of the society as a whole.
5. States should consider appropriate measures so that persons belonging to minorities may participate fully in the economic progress and development in their country.

Some regional instruments which came into effect about the same time as ICCPR have gone further and framed language rights as a class of human rights. The European Charter for Regional or Minority Languages (ECRML) 1992, a convention which at the time of writing has been ratified by 25 states and signed by 8 states without ratification, considers that "the right to use a regional or minority language in private and public life is an inalienable right". For the purpose of ECRML, "regional or minority languages" are languages "traditionally used within a given territory of a State by nationals of that State who form a group numerically smaller than the rest of the State's population; and different from the official language(s) of that State" (Article 1). Article 1 also explicitly excludes dialects of the official language(s) of the State, and the languages of migrants. "(A)ccording to the situation of each of these languages", parties to the Charter shall make education (Article 8), court proceedings (Article 9) and public services (Article 10) available in regional or minority languages. The Framework Convention for the Protection of National Minorities (FCNM) 1995, ratified by 39 states and signed by 4 states without ratification at the time of writing, applies specifically to "national minorities"; but it does not define what a national minority is. FCNM recognizes that "every person belonging to a national minority has the right to learn his or her minority language" and requires parties to the Convention to ensure, as far as possible, "adequate opportunities for being taught the minority language or for receiving instruction in this language" (Article 14). Both the Charter and the Framework Convention create binding obligations on parties, who are required to submit a periodic report. But the obligations are not enforceable by individual petition (Dunbar 2001).

A number of international instruments adopted since the millennium also touch on language rights. The UNESCO Universal Declaration on Cultural Diversity 2002 considers multilingualism an aspect of cultural diversity. Among the goals articulated in its action plan are safeguarding "the linguistic heritage of humanity and giving support to expression, creation and dissemination in the greatest possible number of languages" and encouraging "linguistic diversity – while respecting the mother tongue – at all levels of education, wherever possible, and fostering the learning of several languages from the earliest age." The Declaration promotes the value of cultural diversity, but without imposing obligations on member states.

The United Nations Declaration on Rights of Indigenous Peoples (UNDRIP) 2007 recognizes the right for indigenous peoples to

> revitalize, use, develop and transmit to future generations their histories, languages, oral traditions, philosophies, writing systems and literatures, and to designate and retain their own names for communities, places and persons.
>
> Article 13(1)

and

> establish and control their educational systems and institutions providing education in their own languages, in a manner appropriate to their cultural methods of teaching and learning.
>
> Article 14(1)

As with the provisions of earlier instruments, these are negative rights, essentially securing freedom to pursue one's interests without interference from others. A positive right is created by Article 14(3), however, which provides that

> States shall, in conjunction with indigenous peoples, take effective measures, in order for indigenous individuals, particularly children, including those living outside their communities, to have access, when possible, to an education in their own culture and provided in their own language.

Similarly the Organization for Security and Co-operation in Europe (OSCE) has made a number of recommendations on linguistic rights, most notably the Hague Recommendations Regarding the Education Rights of National Minorities in 1996 and the Oslo Recommendations Regarding the Linguistic Rights of National Minorities in 1998.

Although these international and regional instruments, considered together, have taken increasingly bold steps in demanding positive action from states and in conferring rights on linguistic minorities, there remains a considerable amount of hedging in the language they use: there are many instances of "where appropriate", "wherever possible", "according to the situation of each of these languages", "if there is sufficient demand", or "as far as possible" where obligations are imposed on states, making it impossible in practice for individuals to lodge complaints. Lack of definition in the Framework Convention also allows states simply to declare that they have no minorities. In short, there has been increased recognition of a right to language, culture and identity, but no legally binding international instrument that unreservedly compels states to take proactive measures to protect minority languages. International and regional communities formulating such instruments are perceived by some to be "wanting to be *seen* as doing something rather than in fact committing themselves fully" (Skunabb-Kangas and Phillipson 1994: 5).

4 Recognition at national level

An overall tendency in the formulations outlined above, noted by Skunabb-Kangas (2000), is that protection to linguistic minorities is given in the weakest terms in international human rights instruments; regional instruments offer moderately restrictive provisions; and the strongest protection is to be found at national level (in constitutions or specific legislation). Skunabb-Kangas's observation in this respect is broadly consistent with common understanding that human rights set minimal standards for the conduct of individual governments.

Rights conferred in national law are by their nature different from human rights, which are primarily moral rights. By contrast, legal and constitutional rights are considered civil rights (Donnelly 2013). Human rights are mainly only claimed when rights are not protected, either on paper or in practice, by national governments. Language rights can take the form either of civil rights, or human rights, or both. Much of the controversy surrounding language rights, in fact, lies in how far they are positioned as possible candidates to be human rights.

National law is more likely than abstract international and moral principles to be influenced by regional or international developments. The African Union (AU), through its Language Plan of Action for Africa (2006), requires its 54 member states (i.e., all African states except Morocco) to develop language legislation that protects language rights (Chumbow 2012). Even though this requirement is not strictly enforced, and implementation has been slow, the policy shows that pan-African leaders see a need to protect indigenous languages through legal measures. The Plan focuses on "revitalizing", "revalorizing", "instrumentalising" and "intellectualizing" African languages (ibid, 7).

Faingold (2004) offers an overview of language rights provisions at national level by studying 187 constitutions around the world. In his account, 85 nations give constitutional protection to language rights for all citizens, while some other nations offer, or also offer, constitutional protection for specific language groups. Although it is helpful to gain a sense in this way of the extent to which states show regard for language rights in their constitutional law, Faingold's study gives no details of the kinds of language right offered in each constitution. A different and arguably more useful perspective may however be gained by looking more closely at the constitutional protection offered in two particular countries that are relatively advanced in their language rights provision.

Consider Canada first. English and French are official languages which enjoy equal status (Section 133 of the Constitutional Act 1867; and Section 16 of the Canadian Charter of Rights and Freedoms). The Charter, a bill of rights entrenched in the Canadian Constitution, sanctions both individual and collective rights; and language rights in particular are granted to officially recognized minority communities. Article 23 of the Charter confers educational rights supported by public funds on the English or French linguistic minority population wherever the number of children of citizens in a province is sufficient to warrant primary and secondary education in their mother tongue. The Canadian Supreme Court has ruled that language rights are basic rights, although this ruling can be interpreted only in the context of Canadian democracy and does not extend to all languages present in Canadian territory (e.g., indigenous languages and migrant languages).

Now compare Canada with South Africa, another country stipulating advanced provision in the language field. Article 6 of the 1996 South African Constitution guarantees one of the most elaborate language rights provisions available at national level. It assigns official status to eleven languages, recognizes the historically diminished use and status of indigenous languages, and commits to taking measures to advance the use of these languages in public services and through creation of the Pan South African Language Board. But in practice, English and Afrikaans remain by far the dominant languages; and complaints abound about the huge gulf between law in books and law in action (Strydom 2012).

5 Definitions

It may seem odd that definitions of essential terms related to language rights have not been given earlier in the chapter. But this is deliberate. In the author's view, it is impossible to understand language rights without reviewing their origins and legal development at both national and international levels. This is largely because the history of language rights continues to surface in varying ways in current perceptions of them and in opinions, including informed opinions, about them. In particular, although language-related provisions have been incorporated into international instruments and into national law for a long time, the idea that language rights could form a standalone concept is relatively recent. The complicated historical emergence of the concept may accordingly, at least in part, explain why conferring language rights is even now not fully accepted as a coherent proposition.

Generally speaking, the phrase *language rights* in recent standalone conceptualizations refers to updated formulations of language-related rights which now go beyond freedom of expression and rights based on fair trial and non-discrimination to focus in addition on rights to identity, mother tongue education, and use of one's own language in the public sphere. Much of the advocacy related to such expanded language rights is concerned with minority language speakers, and varies in the degree of affirmative action and commitment required of the state. Beyond generic formulation of this kind, however, there is little consistency in the literature as to what language rights entail. Moreover, while it is possible to document what language rights *include*, relatively little attempt has been made to define what language rights *are*. The resulting divergent content that the concept has been made to carry means that reaching a coherent definition is likely to remain a challenge for some time to come.

By way of clarification, a few dichotomies commonly present in the literature should be noted:

- *Individual vs. Collective Rights*: It is possible to conceive of language rights as individual and/or as collective rights. Individual rights are enjoyed by any person; collective rights are held by a group such as an indigenous population. Some arrangements for group-based minority rights protection were included in the League of Nations between the World Wars; but after World War Two the UN focused more on individual rather than collective rights. Collective rights became controversial because they could be exploited by authoritarian regimes to privilege certain groups over others (e.g., by the Nazi regime and then much later by the Apartheid regime in South Africa) (Sanders 1991); there was also a widely held belief that human rights are the rights of individuals (Freeman 2011). From the 1990s onwards, however, collective rights for minorities have regained acceptance. It has been argued for example that the collective nature of language (i.e., language as something used with and in relation to other people) requires that language rights should be conceptualized at least in part as collective rights (Skunabb-Kangas 2012). Kymlicka (1995), on the other hand, argues that group-based rights can be thought of as individual rights accorded to individual members of a larger group.
- *Territoriality vs. Personality Principles*: Language rights may be claimed by people living in a particular territory or alternatively by speakers of a particular language. For example, in Switzerland rights to services in German or Italian depend on which canton a person is in. On the other hand, a deaf person is generally entitled to interpretation services in sign language regardless of his/her location. Some states (such as India) also grant language rights to individuals where there are a sufficient number of speakers of the same language in a political or regional grouping. In real-world situations the two apparently contrasting principles often overlap: in Canada for example, personally based linguistic rights are circumscribed by territorial considerations (Bastarache 2012).
- *Positive vs. negative rights*: Negative rights generally refer to freedom from interference; positive rights require affirmative actions to be taken by others, typically states. Effectively the same contrast is made using the terms "promotion-oriented rights" or "tolerance-oriented rights" (Kloss 1971). Most controversies related to the language rights paradigm concern positive rights.

To illustrate in more detail how language rights have been created, it is useful to look more closely at three articulations of particular sets of language rights.

5.1 Universal Declaration of Linguistic Rights (UDLR)

The Declaration is a product of the World Conference on Linguistic Rights organized in 1996 through a collaboration between the International PEN Club (an international association of writers) and the non-profit group CIEMEN (Escarre International Center for Ethnic Minorities and the Nations). Although the title of the resulting document – Universal Declaration of Linguistic Rights – resembles an international human rights instrument, the document is in fact only a set of draft recommendations; that draft was submitted to UNESCO in 1996 but has never received official endorsement.

The original document contains 52 Articles. Article 1 distinguishes between "language communities" and "language groups", the former referring to "any human society established historically in a particular territorial space, whether this space be recognized or not, which identifies itself as a people and has developed a common language as a natural means of communication and cultural cohesion among its members", and the latter "any group of persons sharing the same language which is established in the territorial space of another language community but which does not possess historical antecedents equivalent to those of that community" (such as immigrants, refugees, deported persons and members of diasporas). By using the term "language communities", UDLR avoids associating language rights with minority or regional language, a decision that follows from treating such languages as being on equal footing with official or majority languages (Article 5). The distinction between "language communities" and "language groups" corresponds to the rights set out in Article 3, which confers fewer rights to the latter than to the former.

Articles 12 and 15 further provide that all language communities have the right to use their language in official settings. More specifically, such languages must be used in communication with public authorities (Article 16), as well as in official documents (Article 17), in the language of the law and legal proceedings (Article 18 & 19), in political assemblies (Article 20), and for public records (Article 21 & 22). Articles 23–30 focus on education but do not provide explicitly for mother tongue education. Article 25, for example, stipulates that all language communities are entitled to "have at their disposal all the human and material resources necessary to ensure that their language is present to the extent they desire at all levels of education within their territory", without specifying where such resources should come from. Article 26 states that "(a)ll language communities are entitled to an education which will enable their members to acquire a full command of their own language, including the different abilities relating to all the usual spheres of use, as well as the most extensive possible command of any other language they may wish to know." It is unclear, however, whether this Article is intended to oblige states to offer instruction in any language that a person belonging to a particular language community may wish to know, which would be a grave burden (e.g., if someone from Kazakhstan happens to wish to learn Malagasy). Notwithstanding a characteristic reluctance in UDLR to name a duty-bearer, Article 30 implies, somewhat erratically, that universities have a positive obligation: "language and culture of all language communities must be the subject of study and research at university level".

5.2 Linguistic Human Rights (LHRs)

Prompted by an awareness that existing conceptions of language rights are too broad and incoherent to be realistically adopted, Skunabb-Kangas and Phillipson (1994; also in Kontra et al. 1999) have put forward the concept of *linguistic human rights* (LHRs). Posited as a sub-type of the broader category of language rights, LHRs would be inalienable, fundamental human rights. Skunabb-Kangas and Phillipson express the hope that such LHRs will ultimately be enshrined in a legally binding international human rights instrument, as enforceable rights.

As regards detailed working, Skunabb-Kangas and Phillipson propose that LHRs exist at two levels. First, at an individual level LHRs offer people the right to "identify positively with their mother tongue, and have that identification respected by others, irrespective of whether their mother tongue is a minority language or a majority language" (1994: 2). This aspect of LHRs includes the right to learn the mother tongue and receive at least basic education through the medium of the mother tongue, the right to use it in official situations, and the right to learn at least one of the official languages of one's country of residence. Secondly, at a collective level LHRs confer the right of minority groups to exist, to enjoy and develop their language, and the right to establish, maintain and have control over schools and other training and educational institutions. LHRs should also guarantee political representation in state affairs, and autonomy to administer internal matters.

Skutnabb-Kangas (2000) elaborates further on her thinking as regards how individual LHRs can be realized in education. Everybody should have the right, she argues, to learn the mother tongue(s) fully and to be educated through the medium of one's mother tongue (i.e., not only learning it as a subject) in a state-financed education system, and the right to use the mother tongue in most official situations (including schools, healthcare, courts and government offices). Where the minority language is not an official language, the linguistic minority should have the right to become bilingual in their mother tongue and at least one official language. This is clearly an ambitious proposal, since it imposes positive duties on the state and confers a right to receive state-financed mother tongue education to "everyone", without further qualification (e.g., as regards status or speech community size).

5.3 Minority language rights (MLR)

Another notable framework in the language rights movement is Minority Language Rights. This framework focuses on group-differentiated rather than universally applied basic rights, both in national and in international law. The paradigm was initially situated within a surge of attention given to minority rights during the political turmoil in Eastern Europe that followed the collapse of communism. It challenges the privileging of majority languages in public policy and aims to redress longstanding disadvantages that minority language speakers have faced.

May (2005) sees MLR as a broader, more inclusive term than LHR (the latter may be considered a particular version of MLR). LHR and MLR advocates both ascribe a key role to educational rights (May 2012), but may also address language use in other public domains such as media and courtrooms. MLR provided the underlying rationale for instruments including ECRML, FCNM, UNDM and UNDRIP; such instruments do not cover all minority languages equally and are more preoccupied with specific (e.g., territorial-based) categories of linguistic minorities.

6 Contested issues

Although the goals of language rights paradigms are clearly commendable, various contested issues have plagued their development. A number of these are now examined.

6.1 Theoretical basis: why should language rights be human rights?

The most fundamental and possibly most difficult question related to the development of language rights is this: what is their precise theoretical basis? Many language rights proposals simply proclaim that language is a right, with whatever accompanying reasoning reading more like conclusion than argument. Language rights are of course not alone in facing a philosophical challenge in justifying their existence; in fact, the wider human rights discourse itself is also sometimes said to be self-fulfilling and somewhat tautological. Human rights may be considered rights that one has simply by being human, derived from 'the inherent dignity' of the human person (e.g., in UDHR). What leads from human dignity into human rights may nevertheless be obscure. Some argue that human rights can be justified on the basis of international consensus; however, as Freeman (2011) points out apparent consensus is "neither complete nor sincere" (68); in any case, even if consensus is reached this is a fact rather than an argument. Another source of justification comes from natural law theory, based ultimately on metaphysical claims; natural law theory posits that there are objective goods which are essential to the flourishing of humans, and human rights are components of that common good. In such a rationale there is again little agreement as to what such common good consists of, however.

Adopting such lines of arguments selectively, language rights discourse tends to argue that such rights are essential for a life of dignity, and that linguistic diversity contributes to biodiversity by encoding knowledge about it (see Skutnabb-Kangas 2012); such an extensive knowledge resource embedded in languages is presumed to constitute a common good. Other arguments derive from a "difference-aware" notion of equality (Dunbar 2001), postulating minority language rights as for example a means of redressing the unequal treatment minorities have received.

Despite these sorts of difficulty, it is worth remembering that relative lack of theoretical foundations for human rights has not prevented significant practical successes. Support for human rights has been garnered on a range of varying and sometimes pragmatic grounds. This observation is nevertheless of limited value in relation to language rights. By contrast with human rights more generally, advocacy on language rights as a human right has so far met with little success, if lack of UN endorsement and even a single polity as signatory to UDLR are taken as indicators. The burden is accordingly on campaigners to supply compelling arguments as to why the language rights they propose should be considered to be human rights.

A number of serious challenges face such language rights advocacy and are worth considering. The first issue to note goes back to the problem of definition. It is difficult to see, for example, how a coherent theoretical *basis* for language rights can be found without uniform understanding of what language rights *mean*. Secondly, implementation of human rights (e.g., ensuring a fair trial) requires resources. Where such rights apply, they trump other claims in being considered basic; such competition for resources with other social goods poses a particular difficulty in relation to rights that impose a positive duty on states to act. Given the emphasis in much language rights advocacy on affirmative action, in the form of language planning and support across different public sectors, campaigning for such rights must justify why states should be morally and financially responsible for them. For example, what exactly is the moral value of improving the chance of a particular language surviving? Thirdly, MLR proposals in particular are often claimed to correct linguistic imbalances and historical inequalities. But the selective attention given to minorities in such approaches begs the question of whether such means of redress are best formulated as "rights", rather than in some other way. As Donnelly (2013: 19) has succinctly put the matter: "Not everything that *is* right is something to which anyone *has* a right", and conversely, "many things to which people have rights are not right". A sound argument for language rights needs to show a strong connection from "I want to" to "I am entitled to": from the first sense of *right* (good and desirable) to the word's second sense (entitlement).

Another major area of challenge concerns the wider climate in which language rights advocacy takes place. Such campaigning has coincided with an explosion of a rights culture which expanded during the 1990s and which has developed a tendency to turn every problem arising from social injustice or bad governance into a human rights claim (e.g., a right to affordable internet access or a right to higher education); such multiplication of rights inevitably puts additional pressure on the international human rights system overall. This tendency in contemporary rights thinking has led to concern about "rights inflation" and a consequent devaluation of the currency of human rights. Ignatieff (2014), for example, criticizes the failure of the UN High Commissioner for Human Rights to contain people's urge to codify aspirations in economic, social and cultural spheres into rights terminology. An excessive reach of human rights, it can be argued, might hollow out the power of human rights discourse and make conflicts between rights more frequent and perhaps even inevitable.

6.2 Conceptual clarity: who are the right holder and the duty bearer?

Rights are used to create relationships between people and things. Donnelly (2013) illustrates this using a paradigmatic statement of a right: "A has a right to x with respect to B". Language rights discussions tend to focus on what value the variable x may have, but are inconsistent in the value they assign to A; and B is often neglected altogether.

A signifies the right holder. Two types of candidate appear as potential right holders in language rights discourse: language and language speakers. Concern related to the loss of linguistic diversity is often a major driver behind language rights advocacy (e.g., in the preamble to UDLR), so it is commonly languages that such advocacy seeks to protect. Emphasis on education, with the aim of ensuring that languages can be passed on to the next generation, reflects such motivation. Such prioritization has implications, however, that are not always taken into account as regards the theoretical basis for language rights: is an educational right, for example, an effective means of saving languages (similar to preserving the environment or heritage), with linguistic diversity the ultimate goal? Although traditionally minority groups are the main target of protection, putting languages at the centre of protection is not unprecedented (as can be seen in ECRML, which – despite not having any legal force – seeks to protect regional and minority languages as a cultural asset).

Alternatively, language rights campaigning can focus on language speakers. Such discourse may be framed in terms of resistance to forced assimilation through language, or in terms of benefits that follow from mother tongue education (which linguistic majorities typically enjoy but not minorities, thus raising an equality issue). This general line of argument does not sit easily, however, with the way some language rights proposals and relevant instruments are selective as regards which language speakers should enjoy such rights (a topic discussed in more detail in the next section). Clarifying exactly who and what is protected is crucial, especially because protection of language can even turn out to be at odds with the interests of the speakers of minority languages themselves (Dunbar 2001).

What of the specific language speakers who are the presumed holders of language rights? Typically, they are speakers[5] of indigenous, regional or minority languages;

---

5 *Speaker* is in itself a problematic term. Does a speaker of a minority language have to speak it as a "mother tongue", or is a certain level of proficiency expected? Or is it group membership that matters

that is why they are considered vulnerable to language-related shifts and decline. But consider the names of existing rights instruments (with emphasis added): European Charter for *Regional or Minority Languages;* the UN Declaration of the Rights of *Persons* Belonging to National or Ethnic, Religious and *Linguistic Minorities;* the Framework Convention for the Protection of *National Minorities;* the UN Declaration on Rights of *Indigenous Peoples*). In UDLR language users are called "language communities", as opposed to "language groups" and in contrast with terms such as "persons", "peoples", "minorities", "populations", "community" and "group", which all have special significance in international law. Some but not all of the terms in question have already established connections with the right to self-determination, for instance in Article 1(2) of the UN Charter where self-determination is a right assigned to "peoples" (a term associated with colonialism) but not "minorities" or "populations" (Thornberry 1989).

B is the duty bearer. Rights are meaningless without corresponding duty bearers. Skutnabb-Kangas proposes unequivocally that everyone has a right to receive basic education in their mother tongue in state-financed education. By contrast, the consistency with which UDLR avoids naming any duty bearer seems to suggest that such omissions are strategic. But it is difficult to see any benefit that accrues from this strategy. Article 8.2 and Article 25 state that all language communities are entitled "to have at their disposal whatever means are necessary" to ensure the transmission and continuity of their language and to "have at their disposal all the human and material resources necessary" so that their language is present in education. But where such "means" and "human and material resources necessary" are to come from (from the communities themselves or from the state?) is left open. In other words, the relevant provisions are ambiguous between imposing a negative or a positive duty on the state. If such presumably intentional ambiguity was expected to serve as a means to attract endorsement by states, it has not achieved its purpose.

6.3 Precise scope: who has language rights?

Selectivity as regards exactly who the holders of language rights should be poses a further, fundamental challenge in securing a solid basis for such rights. If language rights are essential to human dignity, then why are they denied to some? Scholars have observed that the appeal to universality has practical limitations, as aptly described in the following quote:

(thus including younger generations in the group who might instead "speak" a dominant language)? Such criterion of speakers can affect whether a group may be considered "minority".

Its very attraction – namely, that its standards apply universally to all individuals regardless of history, numbers, or nationhood – is precisely its weakness .... Even if we agree that there are such universal linguistic human rights, they are unable to address the real policy questions that are at the heart of linguistic conflict around the world, which invariably centre around more extensive rights-claims, by both minorities and majorities, that are conditional on size, history, and national self-determination.

(Patten and Kymlicka 2003: 35)

Does it make more sense that language rights should be conceptualized as universal human rights (cf., the LHR model) or as group-differentiated rights (cf., MLR and to some extent UDLR)? While the former kind of right must be applied uniformly across individuals, the latter kind can be justified in terms of the extra safeguard offered to disadvantaged or weak minority groups, as a way of achieving social equality (Council of Europe 2012).

A number of other key terms and concepts are also problematic in language rights discourses, in ways that raise similar issues. Those issues are simultaneously theoretical and, if language rights are legally adopted, also acutely practical.

6.3.1 Minority

No generally accepted definition of *minority* exists (Henrard 2000). UNDM does not provide a definition, but the name of the declaration suggests two categories of minority: national minorities, and ethnic, religious and linguistic minorities. Both categories are to be understood in relation to a sovereign state. The concept of *national minority* may be used to restrict the wider meaning of *minority* by implying a strong tie to the nation; such minorities will include regional majorities which form a minority in relation to the nation as a whole. An often cited reason for distinguishing national minorities, including indigenous peoples, from other ethnic minorities (such as immigrants and refugees), is that the former are potentially self-governing societies which already had a societal culture when they were incorporated into the larger polity (Kymlicka 1995).

The concept of minority is usually ascribed both objective and subjective components. The objective aspect foregrounds quantitative difference (i.e., less than half of the population). The size of the relevant population does seem in some contexts to play a role in determining people's language rights. For example, Canada and Peru offer protection of certain language rights on a "where numbers warrant" basis. The subjective dimension of *minority* involves some sense of community, unity, or historical continuity (Bastarache et al. 1987), as well as possession of ethnic, religious or linguistic qualities which distinguish the group in question from the majority population. Non-dominance is also held to be a factor. It has been argued, for example, that inequality arises mostly from unequal power relationships between dominant vs. non-dominant groups, rather than as a difference based on absolute numbers (Paulston 1997). On the other hand, there are also communities without any dominant groups; for example, the form of cultural diversity that exists in Papua New Guinea has resulted in no single group being able to dominate the political landscape (Department of Education 2015).

6.3.2 Dialectal rights?

The issue of *dialect* has been constantly marginalized, sometimes completely ignored, in minority or language rights discourses. This neglect may be prompted by the inevitably fuzzy boundary between language and dialect (the two concepts are both categorically and gradually vague; see Leung 2012). As a result of the fuzzy boundary between these two concepts, an arbitrary legal distinction between the two can contain state commitments to language support within limits (e.g., in terms of which language varieties are distinctive enough to be used in public services and education). Some relevant international instruments have specifically excluded 'dialects of official languages' from the scope of protection (e.g., Article 1 of ECRML).

Given, however, that there is no principled distinction between language and dialect, other than as a reflection of political boundaries or influence, lack of attention to dialect remains a major lacuna in any language-related law. In Sabah, a Malaysian state, Rungus people resist receiving their "mother-tongue" education in Kadazandusuns, because that variety feels foreign to them even though the Rungus language has been officially categorized as a dialect of Kadazandusuns (Stephen and Atin 2004). Or consider the case of Romansh in Switzerland, one of four national languages (Romansh, plus German, French and Italian). Romansh has gained semi-official status but consists of five idioms (i.e., language varieties, or dialects) which are not always mutually comprehensible. To minimize cost in providing public services and education, the Swiss government adopted a standardized version of the language called Romansh Grischun (RG), which, so it was envisaged, would displace the idioms. The strategy of standardization in the name of supporting a minority language prompted considerable anger and frustration among Romansh speakers. For them, RG is a language that nobody speaks. As a consequence of the policy intervention the question arises whether, since RG is a form of Romansh and Romansh is used in schools and public services, there can be any room left for making a "language right" argument in favour of idiom speakers.

Consider a contrasting, much larger-scale example. China is in the process of Mandarinizing the entire country. This aim is codified in the 2001 Law on the Standard Spoken and Written Chinese Language of the People's Republic of China, which promulgates Putonghua as the standard dialect and stipulates that Putonghua must be used by all state organs, schools and educational institutions ("except where otherwise provided for in laws"), as well as in broadcasting and TV stations, service industry, etc. Echoing Smen Egerod's entry on Sino-Tibetan Languages in the *New Encyclopedia Britannica*, which says that "Chinese as the name of a language is a misnomer", sinologist Victor Mair has argued that "the Chinese language" is better represented as the Sinitic Language Family, which consists of many mutually unintelligible languages (e.g., Mair 1991). Viewed from this perspective, language rights issues can appear to be nullified simply by re-branding languages as dialects.

6.3.3 Dominated majorities

There are some populations missing from language rights discourses. Overwhelming focus on "minorities" begs a crucial question: do majority language speakers enjoy equivalent language rights? Many language rights proposals assume they already have them, so there is no need to specify those rights. Skunabb-Kangas and Phillipson (1994) state that it is "only speakers of official languages who enjoy all linguistic human rights" (2).

History might however be thought to show that numerical majorities have also been subject to domination, for example in colonial and postcolonial situations. In fact, what is sometimes called neo-imperialism or neo-colonialism (Phillipson 2006) has created situations in which numerical majorities have to adopt a language foreign to them. Despite having very few fluent speakers of English in the country, for example, South Sudan recently adopted English as its sole official language. Edward Mokole, Ministry of Higher Education, told a BBC reporter,

> English will make us different and modern. From now on all our laws, textbooks and official documents have to be written in that language. Schools, the police, retail and the media must all operate in English.
>
> (BBC, 8 October 2011)

6.3.4 Immigrants and refugees

An *immigrant group* is "every linguistic minority a majority of whose adult members are foreign born or the children of foreign born" (Kloss 1971: 253); *refugee* refers to anyone outside their country of origin because his or her life or freedom is threatened in their country of nationality "for reasons of race, religion, nationality, membership of a particular social group or political opinion" (1951 Refugee Convention Article 1(A)2). Immigrants and refugees are often excluded from treatment as minorities.

Kloss (1971) summarises four "shallow" reasons (255) used to justify why immigrants should give up their languages: 1) doing so is part of the tacit agreement involved in their immigration, 2) they are better off in the host country, so giving up their language and culture is a worthwhile sacrifice, 3) they should not be locked into a cultural ghetto, and 4) it is their duty to assimilate linguistically in order to preserve the host nation's unity. The idea that traditional immigrant minorities should enjoy a greater right to ethnic identity than recently arrived immigrant groups, however, has been challenged (e.g., in Keller 1998).

If language rights are understood as basic and inalienable human rights (as contrasted with group-differentiated rights), such rights cannot be denied to them. It has been argued that immigrants should enjoy tolerance-based language rights (Kloss 1971). On the other hand, if language rights that include a positive duty (such as state-funded mother-tongue education) are extended to immigrants and refugees (as in Skutnabb-Kangas's proposal), the burden imposed on states comes into question, and such rights could have the unintended consequence of discouraging states from accepting immigrants and refugees.

6.4 Idealized assumptions: is language rights discourse "empirically grounded"?

The language rights paradigm has been criticized by some sociolinguists for not being sufficiently grounded in contemporary knowledge of sociolinguistics. An important debate on this topic took place between Blommaert, on one side, and Skunabb-Kangas, Phillipson and Kontra on the other in the pages of the *Journal of Sociolinguistics* in 2001. For present purposes, the significance of the debate lies in how far it shows that division between the protagonists did not lie so much in their understanding of language as in their ideological stance (especially divergence between a focus on relativism and on universalism).

In the course of this virtual debate, Blommaert (2001, as well as later, in 2005) criticises language rights advocacy for relying on an idealized view of language. He contends that terms such as "English" or "Dutch" ignore internal differences among speakers and varieties, and neglect inequalities created by differential access to intra-language status varieties (*note*: such varieties are to be distinguished from dialect discussed above). Displaying his own idealism, Blommaert argues that "the aim should be to make available the power varieties of languages – any language so chosen – to all citizens" (136). In contrast, Skunabb-Kangas et al. (2001) argue that their aim is to situate LHRs in international law, and to be successful in doing so the terminology of that field must be adopted. Terms such as *sociolects* and *varieties* do not make much sense to international lawyers, and, unlike "languages", are not categories already associated with rights. Kontra (in Skunabb-Kangas et al. 2001) adds that there is room for intra-language discrimination studies to complement inter-language discrimination studies, noting however that the former topic has not been well researched. Blommaert (2001) also expresses doubt about the choice of the state as the appropriate battleground, noting that, for example in Africa, many states are largely powerless. Skunabb-Kangas et al. (2001) respond that states are the political units which negotiate human rights conventions and sometimes ratify them; as such, they are the duty bearers of language rights. In the same way as perspectives on language rights need to "stand the test of ethnographic analysis" (Blommaert 2001: 136), linguistic critiques of language rights, it can be argued, need to comprehend the multidisciplinary context in which such discourse takes place.

Applying his theoretical points, Blommaert (2001) suggests that linguistic issues in education can be put on hold until "more pupils have opportunities to study beyond primary education" (139). This comment echoes a common reaction to language rights advocacy, given that the UN is struggling to meet its millennium goal of universal primary education: namely that language rights are something peripheral that must give way. Kontra (in Skunabb-Kangas et al. 2001) counters such thinking by pointing out that education inevitably takes place in one medium or another; so postponing worries about the medium of instruction may leave the issue too late for some groups, because non-L1 education "can mean no formal education" (150). Citing Williams (1998), Skunabb-Kangas and Phillipson add that mother tongue education is even more important where resources are scarce, since it offers greater prospects for social success to people in need.

Other criticisms center on monolithic constructs in rights discourse, for example the liberal and also postmodern rejection of a presumed linkage between language, ethnicity and identity. Identity is irreducibly multiple, constantly changing, and subject to negotiation and renegotiation (Stroud 2001). Charges of an embedded essentialism have however been rebutted in May (2004); he argues that the dichotomy between essentialist and anti-essentialist is a false one and that language being contingent to identity does not imply insignificance. The language rights paradigm has also been criticized for ignoring the geographic mobility of minorities (Blommaert 2004), for presuming linguistic purity (Darnell 2004), and for assuming a singular "mother tongue" (Freeland 2004). While local variation and other complexities are always a feature of languages, whether criticisms in these terms negate the language rights paradigm seems a different question; as Heller (2004: 286) puts it, linguists should be "free to decide to set aside complexity in the interests of strategic simplification, or else, on the contrary, to argue for a complex understanding when everyone pushes for a simple one".

Finally, one may also ask: are language rights, as presently conceptualized, what people want or need, or is this a notion of justice imposed on people who may feel differently? The question is particularly tricky, given how much attention in language rights advocacy is given to the education of young children, who are not in a position to decide the medium of their own education. Many minority parents, especially in marginalized communities, want their children to learn powerful languages so they can live a better life than their parents have. Paulston and Heidemann (2006) report that the black population in South Africa prefers their children to be educated in English rather than in their various mother tongues. Although language rights are rights which people do not have to exercise unless they wish to, advocates often take a clear stance in favour of mother-tongue education and language maintenance. In her fieldwork with native communities in Canada, anthropologist Darnell (2004) found communities committed to retaining their Aboriginal identities nevertheless not showing interest in maintaining their traditional language in an idealized, pristine form; rather, English was creatively adapted to expressing traditional purposes. Similarly, implementation of mother-tongue education in the Coastal region of Nicaragua in the 1990s became highly politically charged among Creole English communities, with the result that many parents opted to put their children in monolingual Spanish schools where English was taught as a foreign language (Freeland 2004).

6.5 Grounding in reality: are language rights practicable?

One of the most commonly heard criticisms of the language rights paradigm is its idealism. Even Skutnabb-Kangas, who is clearly sympathetic to the cause, calls UDLR "completely unrealistic" (2000: 545). The first UNESCO meeting to discuss UDLR exposed the practical, economical and political impossibility of realizing the proposed rights in most African, Asian and Latin American countries (Skutnabb-Kangas 2000: 548).

Skutnabb-Kangas (2006) argues, on the other hand, that her own formulation of LHRs is economically viable. Her exemplar was Papua New Guinea, based on Klaus's (2003) survey of the success of that small country (population 7.5 million), with the highest linguistic diversity in the world (over 850 indigenous languages), in adopting about half of its indigenous languages for use in elementary education. A closer look at Klaus's report, however, reveals that mother-tongue education reform received "enormous financial and technical assistance from Australia" and from the World Bank to a far lesser extent (5). Further, the reforms turned out to be short-lived and had been phased out. From 2013 onwards, government policy has been to use English at elementary levels; and the Department of Education's current focus is to improve English proficiency among elementary teachers (Department of Education 2015).

Another way of considering whether language rights are practicable assesses the likelihood that states will sign and ratify an instrument containing such rights, if values underlying such rights are perceived as in conflict with state interests. Traditional thinking in sovereign states is wary of nations divided by languages, fearing that such division may ultimately lead to political fragmentation. Although a homogenizing policy can cause conflict and disintegration, states view minorities as a threat to national unity and prefer them to be assimilated. Although human rights are supposed to be above politics, the organizational structure for human rights remains deeply entrenched in the domestic politics of sovereign states.

Despite these obstacles, the immediate goal of language rights advocacy is incorporation of formulations of language rights into human rights instruments. But from one perspective, language rights seekers are trying to get themselves onto a sinking boat. Not only are obstacles to the enforcement of human rights well documented, but human rights as a site of political hopes seems to have waned (Pupavac 2012); and the purposes served by such rights have become "obscured in ever more declarations, treaties and diplomatic lunches" (Douzinas 2000: 380). Even as efforts are made to incorporate human rights to international law, questions surround how far human rights do lead to emancipation (questions articulated in detail in Perugini and Gordon 2015, who argue that the human rights regime actually perpetuates domination).

7 Conclusion

Despite the obscure relationship between morality and linguistic diversity, few have challenged the general desirability of linguistic diversity. In fact, the need to protect minority languages has been acknowledged in international human rights instruments, although their implementation has been largely dependent on the will of particular states. Contemporary language rights advocacy calls for a greater burden to be borne by states. Despite academic interest generated by the topic, the language rights paradigm has had limited effect in its target arena of international law, and seems likely to remain aspirational. Even if the UN does adopt a version of language rights proposals, it remains to be seen how far such an instrument will redress inequality.

Implicit in the language rights paradigm discussed in this chapter is an ideology of what a perfect society looks like. It is pluralinguistic, in that all native languages (except those of immigrants, refugees and tourists) function as official languages (Stage 6 of Churchill 1986's policy response to addressing the educational needs of minorities, cited in May 2012: 178). It is as yet unclear, however, whether official linguistic equality (for a survey, see Leung forthcoming) does promote language survival. Fishman (1968) suggests that bilingualism without diglossia tends to be transitional, because the dominant language eventually replaces the weaker language; but separate roles played by different speech varieties can ensure that none become superfluous. The key to stable bilingualism, accordingly, seems to lie in functional separation of speech varieties rather than in functional equality. In contrast, Judt & Lacorne (2004:4) argue that stability of institutional bilingualism or multilingualism depends on geographical compartmentalisation: "The cases of institutionalized bilingualism or multilingualism are rare and not very durable, except in countries where the linguistic minorities are associated with a clearly identified territory."

Brown (1995) writes somewhat brutally of rights discourse as a whole, "If rights are what historically subjugated peoples most need, rights may also be one of the cruelest social objects of desire dangled above those who lack them." (128). This is because human rights discourse assigns a passive role to the rights holder, changing him or her from an agent engaged in political struggle into a petitioner to established authority. As described by Donnelly (2013: 20): "Human rights is the language of victims and the dispossessed"; and Pupavac (2012) contends that language rights advocacy subjects oppressed communities to more external governance rather than offering more freedom; it unwittingly contributes to an expansion of global governance and legal imperialism which is antithetical to humanist emancipatory politics.

In the context of such severe criticisms, it is necessary to ask whether there are alternative or supplementary means of language maintenance and minority empowerment that do not reduce human agency and autonomy in such ways. More successful language revitalization efforts might for instance be carried out 'not by the majority government but by the minority itself' (Paulston & Heidemann 2006: 303). States themselves may not be the most effective protector or promoter of languages, especially in a globalised world where there is external pressure to use regional and international languages. Ireland pumps about €11 million each year into promoting and supporting the use of the Irish language (Department of Community, Rural and Gaeltacht Affairs 2010), the first official language of the country, only to see its first Irish Language Commissioner resigning in 2014 as a protest against government failure to protect Irish. On the other hand, it is unclear what the alternatives are.

International law does not restrict states from designating one or more languages as official language(s) and then treating them differently from non-official languages, so long as the policy respects freedom of expression and non-discrimination. To the extent that linguistic minorities are a creation of sovereign states, a number of authors have queried whether empowerment of minority linguistic communities may require more radical changes than inscribing language rights as human rights. Significant improvement to linguistic minority rights may require a re-imagining of sovereign states away from the current direction of political nationalism (May 2012).

In a manner resembling the distinction between procedural and substantive justice, the legitimacy of a language policy does not derive only from its content or outcomes but also from how the policy is arrived at (its process). Which language practices are acceptable in the public sphere of a particular community is at least partly dependent on opportunities to participate in public decision-making. Increasing political participation by minorities requires direct confrontation with local politics, which language rights paradigms largely avoid (e.g., few advocates have challenged the legitimacy of established national or official languages). Concerned that the language rights movements could lead to greater ethnolinguistic division by selecting disadvantaged groups for special treatment, Stroud (2001) advocates defusing a traditional "nation-state approach" to language issues and reformulating the concept of citizenship in a more participatory approach (which he calls "linguistic citizenship", whereby speakers themselves exercise control over their language).

A realistic assessment of the implications of proclaiming language rights as human rights (including the potential achievements, collateral effects, and limitations of doing so) is urgently needed. While language rights may empower some communities, incorporating a native language into educational or public institutions typically leads to language standardization, which can have the effect of reducing dialectal diversity. Rights discourse may be one instrument for emancipation, but it can suppress alternative voices urging justice, discourage political activism, and distract local efforts which might be more effective in bringing about attitudinal shifts. Rights discourse itself is also unlikely to mitigate use of soft power as a means of ideological control, for example in slogans commonly found in schools in China such as "speak Mandarin, write standardised characters, be a civilised person" or "no dialects, no foul words, be a good little citizen". Moreover, state promotion of minority rights can also be used as a means of legitimizing control over minority groups (Schiaffini 2004). How such considerations should weigh against the risk of linguistic marginalization is far from a settled question.

References

Anderson, Benedict. 1992. *Imagined communities: reflections on the origin and spread of nationalism*. London and New York: Verso.
Bastarache, Michel, Braën, André, Didier, Emmanuel and Foucher, Pierre. 1987. *Language rights in Canada*. Québec: Les Éditions Yvon Blais Inc.
Bastarache, Michel. 2012. Bilingual interpretation rules as a component of language rights in Canada. In Peter Tiersma and Lawrence Solan (eds.), *The Oxford handbook of language and law*. Oxford: Oxford University Press. 159–174.
BBC, 8 October 2011, South Sudan adopts the language of Shakespeare. Available at http://www.bbc.co.uk/news/magazine-15216524
Blommaert, Jan. 2001. The Asmara Declaration as a sociolinguistic problem: Reflections on scholarship and linguistic rights. *Journal of Sociolinguistics* 5(1). 131–155.
Blommaert, Jan. 2004. Rights in places: comments on linguistic rights and wrongs. In Jane Freeland and Donna Patrick (eds.), *Language rights and language survival*, 55–65. Manchester: St. Jerome.
Blommaert, Jan. 2005. Situating language rights: English and Swahili in Tanzania revisited. *Journal of Sociolinguistics* 9(3). 390–417.
Braën, André. 1987. Language rights. In Michel Bastarache (ed.), *Language rights in Canada*, 3–67. Montréal: Les Éditions Yvon Blais Inc.
Brown, Wendy. 1995. *States of injury: power and freedom in late modernity*. Princeton, NJ: Princeton University Press.
Council of Europe. 2012. *Shaping language rights – Commentary on the European Charter for Regional or Minority Languages in light of the committee of experts evaluation (Regional or Minority Languages, No.9)*.
Crystal, David. 2000. *Language death*. Cambridge: Cambridge University Press.
Chumbow, Beban Sammy. 2012. Towards a legal framework for language charters in Africa. In Claudine Brohy, Theodorus de Plessis, Joseph-G. Turi and José Woehrling (eds), *Law, language and the multilingual state*, 1–26. Bloemfontein: SUN MeDIA.
Darnell, Regna. 2004. Revitalization and retention of First Nation languages in Southwestern Ontario. In Jane Freeland and Donna Patrick (eds.), *Language rights and language survival*, 87–102. Manchester: St. Jerome.
De Varennes, Fernand. 1999. The existing rights of minorities in international law. In Miklós Kontra, Robert Phillipson, Tove Skutnabb-Kangas and Tibor Várady (eds.), *Language: a right and a resource*. Budapest: Central European University Press.

Department of Community, Rural and Gaeltacht Affairs. June 2010. *Annual Output Statement Vote 27*.
Department of Education. 2015. Education for All 2015 National Review Report: Papua New Guinea. Available at http://unesdoc.unesco.org/images/0023/002316/231679e.pdf
Donnelly, Jack. 2013. *International human rights (4th edn.)*. Boulder, CO: Westview Press.
Douzinas, Costas. 2000. *The end of human rights*. Oxford: Hart Publishing.
Dunbar, Robert. 2001. Minority language rights in international law. *International and Comparative Law Quarterly* 50(1). 90–120.
Errington, Joseph. 2003. Getting language rights: the rhetorics of language endangerment and loss. *American Anthropologist* 105(4). 723–732.
Faingold, Eduardo D. 2004. Language rights and language justice in the constitutions of the world. *Language Problems and Language Planning* 28(1). 11–24.
Fishman, Joshua. 1968. Societal bilingualism: stable and transitional. In Joshua Fishman, *Language in sociocultural change*, 135–152. California: Stanford University Press.
Fishman, Joshua. 1994. On the limits of ethnolinguistic democracy. In Tove Skutnabb-Kangas and Robert Phillipson, (eds., in collaboration with Mart Rannut), *Linguistic human rights: overcoming linguistic discrimination*, 49–62. Berlin: Mouton de Gruyter.
Fishman, Joshua. 2006. Language policy and language shift. In Thomas Ricento (ed.), *An introduction to language policy: theory and method*, 311–328. Malden, MA: Blackwell.
Freeland, Jane. 2004. Linguistic rights and language survival in a Creole space. In Jane Freeland and Donna Patrick (eds.), *Language rights and language survival*, 103–138. Manchester: St. Jerome.
Freeman, Michael. 2011. *Human rights* (2nd edn.). Cambridge: Polity.
Harmon, David and Jonathan Koh. 2010. The index of linguistic diversity: a new quantitative measure of trends in the status of the world's languages. *Language Documentation and Conservation* 4. 97–151.
Heller, Monica. 2004. Analysis and stance regarding language and social justice. In Jane Freeland and Donna Patrick (eds.), *Language rights and language survival*, 283–286. Manchester: St. Jerome.
Heller, Monica and Alexandre Duchêne. 2012. Pride and profit: changing discourses of language, capital and nation-state. In Alexandre Duchêne and Monica Heller (eds.), *Language in late capitalism: pride and profit*. New York: Routledge.
Henrard, Kristin. 2000. *Devising an adequate system of minority protection: individual human rights, minority rights and the right to self-determination*. The Hague: Kluwer Law International.
Ignatieff, Michael. 2014. Rights inflation and role conflict in the office of The High Commissioner for Human Rights. Felice. D. Gaer and Christen L. Broecker (eds.), *The United Nations High Commissioner for Human Rights: Conscience for the world*, 35–45. Leiden: Martinus Nijhoff.
Judt, Tony and Denis Lacorne. 2004. The politics of language. In Judt and Lacorne (eds.), *Language, nation, and state: identity politics in a multilingual age*, 1–16. New York: Palgrave Macmillan.
Keller, Perry. 1998. Re-thinking ethnic and cultural rights in Europe. *Oxford Journal of Legal Studies* 18(1). 29–59.
Klaus, David. 2003. The use of indigenous languages in early basic education in Papua New Guinea: A model for elsewhere? *Language and Education* 17(2). 105–11.
Kloss, Heinz. 1971. Language rights of immigrant groups. *International Migration Review* 5(2). 250–268.
Kontra, M., R. Philipson, T. Skutnabb-Kangas and T. Várady (eds.). 1999. *Language: a right and a resource. Approaching linguistic human rights*. Budapest: Central European University Press.
Krauss, Michael. 1992. The world's languages in crisis. *Language* 68(1). 4–10.
Kymlicka, Will. 1995. *Multicultural citizenship: a liberal theory of minority rights*. Oxford: Clarendon Press.

Leung, HC Janny. 2012. On the edge of reason: law and borderline cases. In M. Wan (ed.), *The legal case: cross currents between law and the humanities*. Oxon and New York: Routledge.

Leung, HC Janny. forthcoming. *Shallow Equality and Symbolic Jurisprudence in Multilingual Legal Orders*. Oxford and New York: Oxford University Press.

Mair, Victor. 1991. What Is a Chinese "dialect/topolect"? Reflections on some key Sino-English linguistic terms. *Sino-Platonic Papers* 29. Available on http://sino-platonic.org

May, Stephen. 2004. Rethinking linguistic human rights: answering questions of identity, essentialism and mobility. In Jane Freeland and Donna Patrick (eds.), *Language rights and language survival*, 35–54. Manchester: St. Jerome.

May, Stephen. 2005. Language rights: Moving the debate forward. *Journal of Sociolinguistics* 9(3). 319–347.

May, Stephen. 2006. Language policy and minority rights. In Thomas Ricento (ed.), *An introduction to language policy: theory and method*, 255–272. Malden, MA: Blackwell.

May, Stephen. 2012. *Language and minority rights: ethnicity, nationalism and the politics of language* (2nd ed.). New York and London: Routledge.

Paulston, Christina Bratt and Heidemann, Kai. 2006. Language policies and the education of linguistic minorities. In Thomas Ricento (ed.), *An introduction to language policy: theory and method*. Malden, MA: Blackwell. 292–310.

Patten, Alan and Kymlicka, Will. 2003. Introduction: language rights and political theory. In Will Kymlicka and Alan Patten (eds.), *Language rights and political theory*. Oxford: Oxford University Press.

Perugini, Nicola and Gordon Neve. 2015. *The human right to dominate*. New York: Oxford University Press.

Phillipson, Robert. 2006. Language policy and linguistic imperialism. In Thomas Ricento (ed.), *An introduction to language policy: theory and method*, 346–361. Malden, MA: Blackwell.

Pupavac, Vanessa. 2012. *Language rights: from free speech to linguistic governance*. Basingstoke: Palgrave Macmillan.

Ruiz, Richard. 1984. Orientations in language planning. *The Journal for the National Association for Bilingual Education* 8(2). 15–34.

Sanders, Douglas.1991. Collective rights. *Human Rights Quarterly* 13. 368–386.

Schiaffini, Patricia. 2004. The language divide: identity and literary choice in modern Tibet. *Journal of International Affairs* 57: 81–98.s

Simons, Gary F. and Lewis, M. Paul. 2013. The world's languages in crisis: A 20-year update. In Elena Mihas, Bernard Perley, Gabriel Rei-Doval and Kathleen Wheatley (eds.) *Responses to language endangerment. In honor of Mickey Noonan*, 3–19. Amsterdam: John Benjamins.

Skutnabb-Kangas, Tove and Robert Phillipson, (eds., in collaboration with Mart Rannut). 1994. *Linguistic human rights: overcoming linguistic discrimination*. Berlin: Mouton de Gruyter.

Skutnabb-Kangas, Tove. 2000. *Linguistic genocide in education – or worldwide diversity and human rights?* Mahwah, NJ: Lawrence Erlbaum Associates.

Skutnabb-Kangas, Tove, Robert Philipson and Mikloás Kontra. 2001. Reflections on scholarship and linguistic rights: a rejoinder to Jan Blommaert. *Journal of Sociolinguistics* 5(1). 143–155.

Skutnabb-Kangas, Tove. 2006. Language policy and linguistic human rights. In Thomas Ricento (ed.), *An introduction to language policy: theory and method*, 273–291. Malden, MA: Blackwell.

Stephen, Jeannet and Veronica Petrus Atin. 2004. Language and intergroup perception in Sabah. In Jane Freeland and Donna Patrick (eds.), *Language rights and language survival*, 151–169. Manchester: St. Jerome.

Stroud, Christopher. 2001. African Mother-tongue programmes and the politics of language: linguistic citizenship versus linguistic human rights. *Journal of Multilingual and Multicultural Development* 22(4). 339-355.

Strydom, Hennie. 2012. Obstacles in the way of a multilingual South African State. In Claudine Brohy, Theodorus de Plessis, Joseph-G. Turi and José Woehrling (eds.), *Law, language and the multilingual state*, 31-44. Bloemfontein: SUN MeDIA.

Thornberry, Patrick. 1989. Self-determination, minorities, human rights: a review of international instruments. *The International and Comparative Law Quarterly* 38(4). 867-889.

Tierney, Stephen. 2006. Reflections on the evolution of language rights. In André Braën, Pierre Foucher and Yves Le Bouthillier (eds.), *Languages, constitutionalism and minorities*. Markham, Ontario: LexisNexis Canada.

Turi, Joseph-G. 1994. Typology of language legislation. In Tove Skutnabb-Kangas and Robert Phillipson (eds., in collaboration with Mart Rannut) *Linguistic human rights: overcoming linguistic discrimination*, 111-119. Berlin: Mouton de Gruyter.

Williams, E. 1998. *Investigating bilingual literacy: evidence from Malawi and Zambia*. Education Research No. 24. London: Department for International Development.

Richard Powell
4 Language planning and legal systems

1 Introduction

In contrast to interpreting, which strives case by case to give individuals deficient in the legal medium the same access to justice as the proficient, language planning seeks to adapt the language of a legal system itself to the needs of communities who use a different language. Adaptation may involve giving legal standing to more than one language within the same jurisdiction and sometimes within the same set of proceedings. There may also be an aim of phasing one language into the legal domain and another out. To accord legal equivalence to different languages rules must be devised about which medium is to be used when. If one of the languages has not previously been used in formal legal communication there will be a need for linguistic modification and the generation of lexical and textual resources. Hence complex, sustained activity on a large scale is implied. Many factors outside the immediate communicative needs of specific legal events come into play, and the motivation behind language planning itself is often primarily political or cultural rather than technical.

The following three controversies serve as illustrations of the range of ways in which language planning for the administration of justice may invoke macro-level sociocultural and political agendas that go beyond the resolution of legal or linguistic ambiguity.

(1) A year before the 1997 transfer of Hong Kong's sovereignty to China a local fishmonger was successfully prosecuted for infringing a by-law compelling shopkeepers to obtain planning permission for any "alteration or addition" extending out in front of their premises (*R v Tam Yuk-ha*, 1996). After the implementation of the Basic Law agreed with Beijing, Tam exercised her prerogative to have her appeal heard in Chinese. Justice Yeung concluded that no one would consider the metal trays Tam displayed fish on to constitute the 'building of constructions' (增建工程) as specified in the Chinese text of the by-law. He consequently ruled in her favour. Subsequently reversed, but with recurrences warded off by rewording of the English and Chinese texts of the relevant ordinance, the case was touted as an example of someone being convicted in English but acquitted in Chinese and it fueled an ongoing debate about Hong Kong's cultural identity and the future of its English-based legal system.

(2) In October 2009 Malaysia's de facto Opposition leader Anwar Ibrahim filed a memorandum of appeal in a defamation suit against former premier Mahathir Mohamad. The appeal was dismissed on the grounds that the memorandum was written in English. The National Language Act and the Rules of Court require documents to be filed in Malay except in urgent cases. In his ruling judge Abdul Malek condemned the failure to use the national language as an "injustice to the respondent"

and "a pure and simple abuse of the process of the court" (Hafiz Yatim, 2009.12.09). Anwar's lawyer, the late political leader Karpal Singh, subsequently commented that it was curious the judges had chosen to deliver this ruling in English. On appeal their right to do so was upheld, but few doubted that the key issue at stake was symbolic and ideological rather than legal or communicative.

(3) While conducting interviews about language issues in commercial law in 2012, I was given an account by a Colombo lawyer (Powell, 2012) of how he had been approached for an opinion on possible discrepancies between the English and Sinhalese texts of Sri Lanka's Companies Act. Confirming his client's suspicions, he had concluded that the English wording left greater scope for the range of distributions payable from company proceeds. Moreover the narrower Sinhalese wording appeared to result from mistranslation of the Canadian and New Zealand texts on which the Sri Lankan law was modelled. He had nevertheless advised his client against relying on any leeway in the English version. Sri Lankan law gives authority to Sinhalese texts in the event of conflicts regarding new legislation and it would be politically as well as legally unwise to label them 'mistranslations'. The position of Sinhala as the national language, then, outweighed any suggestion that the intention of the lawmakers might have been misinterpreted.

While the above examples, and many of those cited below, concern English in relation to postcolonial official languages, wherever the admissibility or authority of languages in legal disputes is in question it is likely that macro-level factors beyond individual courtrooms or law offices will come into play. Thus the choice between Portuguese and Tetum in Timor Leste courtrooms is bound up not only with the linguistic competences of relevant parties and the legal lexicon and discourses available to each language, but also with the internal and external sociopolitical agendas of the Fretelin authorities who framed language policy. Similarly, the decision to relegate Indonesian (the language most Timorese citizens, including lawyers, were educated in) to the status of 'working language' was based primarily on politics, not language or law. But this does not mean that language-in-law policies ignore access to justice. The latter is often a key motivation for them. Rather, they invoke conceptions of justice that are not confined to the needs of the litigants and defendants in particular cases but touch on justice for the nation, justice for linguistic majorities and minorities, and even justice for languages themselves.

In addition to the complex motivations behind language planning, the complexity of linguistic ecology makes it difficult to target specific changes at particular areas of language use in isolation from other sociolinguistic and sociological behaviour. In the case of law, for example, introducing a new medium may affect legal education, recruitment to the legal and judicial professions, and public perceptions of the justice system.

When we consider what language planning entails, it is hardly surprising that so many minority and colonial languages survive as legal media, that monolingual law predominates in highly multilingual societies, and that polities like Belgium and

Cameroon that sustain the principle of multilingual law at a national level tend to manage it through parallel monolingual streams. Language planning may nevertheless be a plausible and appropriate means of reducing language disadvantage, particularly where a linguistic majority or a small number of large minorities, is targeted. In many jurisdictions where law had once been conducted exclusively in a colonial medium planning has enhanced legal access and transparency for citizens speaking a language of wider communication.

In the following section (2) I will review language planning as both an administrative practice and an object of academic analysis. I will then (3) consider the conceptual implications for administrators and researchers of applying language planning to the law before discussing (4) the motivations that typically underlie it. There follows an account of language planning implementation through three analytical lenses typically associated with the field: (5) status reform, or the manipulation of language use through rules; (6) corpus reform, or the preparation of languages for legal use through the development of lexis and corpora; (7) and acquisition planning, or the training of lawyers, law-related professionals and lay participants with regard to lexicogrammatical innovations and texts in languages hitherto little used for law.

The chapter will then go on to discuss (8) some of the outcomes of language planning in legal practice and identify common patterns according to the way multilingualism is managed and the degree to which language shift has occurred in legal domains. The chapter concludes (9) with an appraisal of the potential of language planning to improve access to justice.

The eminence and gravitas associated with particular languages is clearly of great relevance to the legal domain, where choosing the appropriate register is paramount for practitioners, and this led Haarmann (1990) to view 'prestige planning' as an independent variable. Here, however, prestige concerns are taken as a strategic dimension of status-, corpus-, and acquisition-planning. Discourse planning, or the promotion of ideologies and arguments in support of certain languages, is a relatively new addition to the field (Lo Bianco, 2009) and of considerable relevance to research on legal language because of the law's symbolic power. For reasons of space it has not been given separate treatment here but in the concluding remarks the performative and legitimising functions of legal texts are discussed.

2 Language planning as an activity and object of analysis

While concerted, systematic and self-conscious language planning may have a relatively short history, large-scale manipulation of code- and style-choice is not a recent phenomenon. From thirteenth century Vietnam we have the development of the Chinese-based *Nom* script, followed by its gradual replacement four centuries later with romanised *Quốc Ngữ*, reforms reflecting respectively the contemporary influence of Chinese scholarship and Christian missionary activity while nonetheless nurturing indigenous literature (Lo Bianco 2001: 168–170). In Europe we find lexical standardisation with a view to reconstituting national identity undertaken in sixteenth-century Italy by the Accademia della Crusca (Nencioni 1986: 111), with Richelieu's Académie Française (Cooper 1989: 3–11) and Leibnitz's *Sprachpflege* (Leibnitz 1683/1916: 19) driven by similar nationalising agendas the following century.

However, it was perhaps not until the era of postcolonial nationalisation that language planning emerged as a self-conscious academic, as well as an administrative, activity. The Bangla Academy was established in 1955 as part of resistance in East Pakistan to the pro-Urdu policies and political dominance of Karachi (Bangla Academy 2014). A year later, just ahead of independence from Britain, Malaya set up *Balai Pustaka* (later *Dewan Bahasa dan Pustaka*, or DBP) to identify the boundaries of Malay, equip it for national education, and recruit teachers (Kamarul et al 2003: 1–9). The optimism of developing nations was matched by that of linguists from the developed world who saw opportunities to put their training to work in the interest of social development (Wright 2003: 9; Rubdy 2008: 212; Hill 2010: 45). Funding for large-scale projects by bodies such as the Ford Foundation (Hornberger 2006: 26) and engagement with real-world issues encouraged conceptualisation while honing technical and managerial skills (Lo Bianco 2010: 150). It is fair to say that the seminal years of language planning were focused primarily on problems of socioeconomic development in postcolonial multilingual polities, and this agenda is also present in most of the planning that has been applied to law. With decolonisation a large number of countries found themselves with both educational and legal systems shaped by colonial powers and functioning in colonial languages. Often, the colonial language was poorly understood by a majority of citizens.

What, then, do language planners do, and what do language planning researchers study? A number of terms, including 'language engineering' (Springer 1956), predate the use of 'language planning' by Haugen (1966, adopting Ulrich Weinrich's coinage), and equivalents in many different languages have emerged, including *planification linguistique* and *intervention sur la langue* in French (Calvet 2002: 16), *Sprachplanung* in German (Ammon et al. 2006) and *perancangan bahasa* in Malay (Abdullah Hassan 1987). All refer to deliberate and extended efforts to influence language use and most cover two main activities: revising the form of a language through orthography, spelling or lexicogrammatical standardisation and innovation; and establishing rules about which language, or language variety, is to be used in any particular domain. There are inconsistencies in descriptions of linkage between language planning and language policy, partly because of the recursive quality of the relationship, but the latter tends to be treated as the goal (Cooper 1989: 30) or result (Tollefson 2008: 3) of the former. Language planning is also sometimes taken to include unplanned (Kaplan and Baldauf 1997: 297–299) and circumstantial (Corson 1989: 141) outcomes. We should note that even in the absence of explicit policies, no educational or legal system gives official recognition to all the languages spoken by participants. Choices made systematically often reveal underlying language ideologies, and these result in what Ali Rahman and Mohammad Faravardin (2009: 53) have dubbed "language policy with the manager left out".

While most of the planning targeted by researchers is large-scale and often conducted at government level or authorised by government departments, a local turn can be seen in Kaplan and Baldauf's (1997: 52) attention to meso- and micro-level planning and Nekvapil's (2006: 3) treatment of institutions independent of governments such as commercial enterprises (Nekvapil, 2006: 12). We are therefore entitled to see not only rules about language for entire jurisdictions, but also the management of language within a single courtroom or legal practice, as within the purvey of language planning.

3 Implications of applying language planning to legal domains

A majority of language planning studies target educational policy and practice. In Malaysia, for example, where some 146 languages are spoken (Ethnologue, 2014), one level of research focuses on the politics and economics of government policies that incorporate Malay, Mandarin, Tamil and English into state education (Asmah 2007; Gill 2005; Kua 2005). Another considers the challenges such policies pose for particular language communities (Ting 2010; Kärchner-Ober, Mukherjee & David 2011). A third analyses engagement with national policy at the scale of specific educational cohorts (Abdullah Hassan 1994: 113) or individual schools (Lim and Presweg 2010).

Again prioritising examples from education, another research genre evaluates planning through the prism of language rights, with Tollefson (2002: 3) arguing that language-in-education policies merely reproduce inequalities and serve dominant groups, a stance Lo Bianco (2009: 114) largely agrees with while pointing out that policies have nonetheless helped postcolonial polities to assert and extend cultural autonomy. Language-in-education policy provides indispensable context for examinations of language-in-law policy on two levels: it sheds light on political agendas, something that cannot be ignored when dealing with national institutions such as the law; and it helps explain the language repertoires and preferences of the professional and lay participants in legal systems.

Some discussions of language rights make reference to constitutional provisions (Asmah 1979: 11) or international human rights conventions (Phillipson 1992: 93), but language use within the legal domain is seldom the subject of language planning as an administrative activity or object of linguistic analysis. We can, however, draw on at least three bodies of research to help clarify issues within the ambit of language planning for law: descriptions of legalese and the sociology of legal language; studies of legal translation and interpreting; and analyses of bilingual communication.

3.1 Legalese and the sociology of legal language

While there is general agreement among linguists, lawyers and lay observers about the peculiar nature of legal language, as Gibbons (1999:1) remarks, it is easier to recognise than define. A series of attempts to do so have revealed some of its complexity. With regard to English legalese, Mellinkoff (1963) described its retention of Law French, Latin and English archaisms. Tiersma (1999: 100) elaborated on these multilingual influences and the tendency of legalese to retain features abandoned in other domains, but also saw capacity for innovation.

As far as the characteristics of legal writing are concerned, Bhatia (1993), Tiersma (1999) and Gibbons (2003) highlight long sentences, lexical density and complexity, repetition in preference to anaphoric devices, passive constructions and impersonal nouns, features which according to Bhatia (1993) are marshalled in the service of producing autonomous, authoritative texts. Similar features have also been highlighted in Swedish (Lundquist 1995), Spanish (Orts Llopis 2007) and Turkish (Altay 2002). As for oral legalese, often considered to be "at the written end of the continuum" (Gibbons 2003:33), many studies show how it ranges from extreme formality to calculated informality (Fuller 1993) and involves a number of overlapping discourse types (Maley 1994). Genre analysis as pioneered by Bhatia (1993) has been productive in showing how oral features are linked to writing processes, each stage of each event shaped by its main communicative purpose but all of them interconnected within the wider purposes of professional culture.

Analysis of the complexity of legalese, of interest to anyone working in the general field of language and law, is crucial to language planning because shifting the law into languages hitherto absent from the legal domain entails the generation not only of lexical equivalents but also of entire texts and rhetorical practices that seek to replicate the discursive features of those they are augmenting or replacing. Indeed if legal professions are to maintain their sense of integrity in the wake of language reform, the sociological dimensions of legal language must also be considered.

Far from a "neutral instrument of purposes peculiar to the internal development of legal regulation", Goodrich (1984: 173) saw law as a "specific, sociolinguistically defined speech community". However, Maley et al (1994) have highlighted the variety of tasks and roles lawyers perform as bridges between the law and lay participation. More recently, Bhatia (2011) argues that the generic hybridity many legal texts exhibit reveals considerable interdiscursivity and heterogeneity within legal practice as a whole, with practitioners routinely pulled between different jurisdictional, professional and cultural loyalties.

I would argue that one of the reasons language shift in legal systems tends to be limited is that language planners perennially underestimate the complexity of legal language, concentrating on lexical innovation without giving due consideration to the implications of introducing new lexis into legal texts and professional practices. Lawyers, on the other hand, instinctively know that changing the language of law, regardless of whether it changes decision-making itself, has an important impact on the practice of law, even when formal institutions and procedures are retained. This helps explain the resistance of some of them to language planning. Legalese may represent a specific professional speech community but it is not sealed off from the culture of the wider community. As Ng (2009: 6) has argued in the case of Hong Kong, English and Cantonese trials are "trials that take place in two different worlds".

3.2 Legal translation and interpreting

Legal translation and interpreting are the converse of legal language planning inasmuch as they aim to enable the language-disadvantaged to participate in monolingual legal systems, or at least for these systems to accommodate input from the language-disadvantaged. Language planning, on the other hand, attempts to accommodate the legal system itself to the language needs of communities – especially majority communities – by amending the medium of the law. Hence it allows trials to take place in Sri Lanka without the use of interpreters or written translations by authorising them in Sinhala or Tamil. Having said that, in the absence of comprehensive legal transplant it is impossible to envisage any change in the language of the law that does not rely heavily on translation from an existing legal medium to a new one. Hong Kong's widespread use of Cantonese in its lower courts is founded upon the comprehensive translation of laws and ordinances from English into Chinese that was undertaken between 1989 and 1994; interpreters remain important there as many participants speak English or other languages and will continue to do so for the foreseeable future.

Studies of legal translation are also instructive for language planning since, as Šarčevič (1997: 70–71) explains, in order to understand the legal effect of texts translators need effectively to translate entire legal systems. Working with Turkish and English, Altay (2002) goes further in expecting translators to understand the historical dimensions of texts in order to achieve pragmatic equivalence. If this is the scope and depth required of those who translate utterances and texts, how much greater is the challenge for those planning language shift for entire legal systems.

Language planning and legal translation are overlapping subjects for a number of studies. Zaiton and Ramlah (1994: 116) examined innovations in the Malay legal lexicon from a translator's point of view and concluded that it would take considerable time for Malay to emulate the registers, style and authority of English legalese. Zubaidah's (2002) comprehensive survey of Malaysia's court-based interpreters is framed by a review of the socio-historical relationship between English and Malay and an account of language planning measures that have enabled the latter to be used extensively in court, though not to the exclusion of interpreting.

3.3 Bilingual legal communication

While concerted or circumstantial language planning has resulted in routine use of more than one language in a number of legal systems, many of them restrict any particular proceeding to a particular language. Hong Kong still frowns upon 'mixed language' trials (Ng 2009: 121). Sri Lanka requires Sinhala or Tamil for the subordinate courts and forbids English except in the higher courts (Government of Sri Lanka, 2011). Switzerland assigns the official language of the canton in which a case begins to subsequent proceedings right up to Federal Tribunal Level (Castillo [personal communication] 2015). In practice, however, code-mixing, code-switching and code-shifting are common in legal discourse, especially when law is surrounded by a society in which language alternation is endemic. It has been reported in Hong Kong (Leung 2012), Kenya (Powell and David 2011), Malaysia (David 1993, 2003), Sri Lanka (Powell 2008b), Tanzania (Rwezaura 1994) and Botswana (Thekiso 2001).

Analyses of bilingual discourse shed light on planned language shift by revealing some of the motivations that underlie language choice. Sometimes motivation may be obscure, and where bilingual proficiency is common, it may be subconscious and perhaps even random, but when it can be linked to a change in topic or legal task or courtroom interlocutor it adds to our knowledge about the sociocultural associations, as well as lexicogrammatical limitations, of specific languages and may thus help explain why some languages are favoured over others for particular kinds of legal communication.

Language shift will always involve a transitional period, and evidence from Malaysia and Sri Lanka, where legal language planning began more than 40 years ago, suggests that this period may be indefinite, so just as language planning depends on translation, it also requires bilingual practitioners. The way lawyers and judges switch languages in court has been examined in many of the studies mentioned above, but the literature on bilingual legal discourse is conspicuously lacking in accounts of how legal practitioners, many of whom bring personal bilingualism to their profession, study and practise law in more than one language. A recent study conducted in a Malaysian faculty of law (UM Baseline Study 2014) suggests that language choice is institutionally constrained rather than individually exercised and involves a large variety of factors, including national language policies for education and for law; medium of study and research materials; geographical location of worksite; legal specialisation; and the demands of the employment market and associated financial incentives.

4 Motivations behind language planning in legal domains

While researchers (e.g. Jernudd & Das Gupta 1971: 211) have long acknowledged the highly politicised nature of language planning, some (Cooper 1989: 34; Tollefson

2002:6) go further in arguing that it makes use of language conflicts for political ends. It would be naïve to expect legal systems, as nationally established authority-conferring institutions, to be isolated from politics. I would argue that the *primary* aim of language planning in them is rarely legal reform, at least in the sense of improving access to justice and the transparency of legal communication, even though both of these play their part as genuine incentives, as well as strategic pretexts.

One of the clearer illustrations of the political dimensions of language-in-law policy comes from Myanmar. At first sight its comprehensive shift to Burmese, making it one of the few jurisdictions in the common law tradition (Tun Shin 2013: 2.10) to have effectively replaced English, appears a rational response to the communicative needs of a society where no more than 5% are proficient in the colonial medium (Bolton 2008). However, there is a close correlation between the phasing out of legal English and a policy of isolating the country from Commonwealth influence while reducing the independence of a legal profession with a record of opposing the military regime (Aung Thoo [personal communication] 2005/2012). The ebb and flow of language policy is more ideological than pragmatic. Hence a Translation Committee for Technical Terms was established in the 1960s without an attempt to translate the All Burma Codes or legal authorities – indeed the citation of precedents was subsequently discouraged (Myint Zan [personal communication] 2013). While Cheesman (2011: 824) sees some pragmatism behind the reinstatement of Anglo-Indian statutes in the 1970s, which may well help to explain the unexpected return to English legal education in the 1980s, the anomalous insistence on English in law schools seems anything but pragmatic: lawyers are unlikely to need the language in practice and many law students are reported to be incapable of passing exams in it without memorising answers to leaked questions (Myint Zan 2008: 17–20).

Sri Lankan language planning also evinces the dominance of political considerations beyond the legal system. The 1961 Language of the Courts Act may have helped address the linguistic needs of Sinhalese-speaking litigants and witnesses by substituting Sinhala for English, but it came on a wave of Sinhalese nationalism and rode roughshod over the needs of the minority Tamil community, which felt more threatened by official Sinhalese than it had by official English. The 1966 Tamil Language (Special Provisions) Regulation, which authorised Tamil for courts in the north and east, was not enough to forestall decades of communal conflict (Coperahewa 2011: 2009–10).

Malaysia's first prime minister announced the 1967 National Language Act with rhetoric that combined pragmatism with nationalism. Partial retention of English for the courts was to allow the wheels of justice to go round under a legal profession weak in Malay, yet those who did not speak the national language were warned to learn it in order to avoid questions about their patriotism (*The Straits Times* 1967). The legislation left considerable leeway to choose between English and Malay, but subsequent interpretations in favour of more Malay, supported by legislation and court rules, show the key imperatives to have been political rather than linguistic. After an initial focus on the technical details and difficulties of extending legal Malay (*Utusan Malaysia* 1983; 1990), editorials in government-controlled newspapers focused more on nationalist ideology than communicative problems (Rashid Darham 1990; *Utusan Online* 1998). Mead (1988: 11–16) contends that a push for more Malay in the 1980s was motivated largely by the ruling party's need to curb political disaffection among key Malay constituents.

Another example of underlying political imperatives comes from Tonga. All legislation is gazetted in Tongan (Crown Law Tonga 2013) as well as English, the former having authority in the event of a dispute over criminal, though not civil, law (*Police vs Sikuea* 1996), and all proceedings in the police courts are conducted in it (personal observation 2014). Rather than the communicative needs of litigants, however, the main reason for bilingual legislation appears to be the preference of parliament, where debates are conducted in Tongan. In practice the lower courts hardly refer to legislation and produce no legal records, while higher court proceedings are officially and exclusively in English.

Wherever there is language planning we find the hand of politics. Official Irish is undoubtedly pragmatic in the thinly populated *Gaeltacht* (Ó Flatharta [personal communication] 2012/2013), but its occasional use at the very highest judicial level (e.g. *The State (Mac Fhearraigh) v. Mac Gamhna* 1983; *Ó Beoláin v. Fahy* 2011) tends to be triggered by constitutional and rights issues more often than by concern for communicative need, and its status as first official language gives it more currency in proceedings than Welsh, which has more habitual speakers yet is rarely considered a practical medium of jury trials in Wales (Davies 2011). Without the 1997 change in sovereignty it is doubtful Chinese would have expanded as it has in Hong Kong courts, given that the L1 of 95% of the population was hitherto largely ignored, except by interpreters. The political importance of Portuguese in Timor Leste, outstripping its communicative importance, has already been mentioned. Even in Canada–where the small number of francophones in some provinces is used to excuse monolingualism in the judiciary (Levesque 2012), evade obligations to assemble francophone juries (Bastarache 2012) and overlook the equal authority of French and English legislative texts (Cleroux 2011.9.19)–politics has tended to override pragmatism in favour of official bilingualism whenever governments feel worried about the stability of the federation. It is hardly a coincidence that the Official Languages Act, enshrining the right to be heard in court and to read legislation in French as well as English, was passed at a time when calls for Quebec sovereignty were soaring

The complex calculations entailed in language planning for authoritative national institutions such as law inevitably go beyond immediate communicative needs and involve political interests, but this by no means disqualifies planning as a means of reducing language-based disadvantage. By reviewing the components of planning in the next three sections we will see that where planning retains sight of the communicative needs of participants it may compliment and improve on interpreting and translation as a support for linguistically disadvantaged legal participants.

5 Status planning

Since language planning invariably touches on the relationship between two or more languages, some means of regulating that relationship is generally involved. The most authoritative regulations are statutory, but other legal and professional mechanisms also play their part.

In many polities where there is little dispute over language authority the constitution fails to specify an official language (e.g. Germany's *Grundgesätz*, Mexico's *Constitución Política*). Burmese was declared authoritative in Myanmar's 1974 constitution and again, as 'Myanmar language' in the general provisions of its 2008 replacement, but the language for the legal system is not specifically mentioned. But in some highly multilingual societies and especially in postcolonial polities that have moved away from a colonial medium we find constitutional provisions extending to legal language.

The Indian Constitution (Art. 348) authorises English for the Supreme Court and High Court until parliament provides otherwise, but in the latter proceedings may be in Hindi or official state languages with presidential approval. Sri Lanka's 1978 Constitution (Art.24) installs Sinhala for subordinate courts, or Tamil in areas where it is the language of administration, but the minister of justice may authorise English for proceedings and records. Under the 1982 Constitution Act (Art.9.1) Canadian citizens may use either English or French in any court and in *Charlebois v City of St John* (2005) the Supreme Court ruled that provincial authorities do not have discretion to modify this right. The Malaysian Constitution (Art. 152) instated Malay as the national language while originally making provision for the continued use of English in court but was later amended to incorporate the National Language Act, which restricts the use of English.

The second tier of status planning is standard legislation. Sri Lanka's 1956 Official Language Act and 1961 Language of the Courts Act, for example, instated Sinhala for law, with the 1966 Tamil Language (Special Provisions) Regulation authorising Tamil in some regions. In neighbouring India the Civil Procedure Code (s.137) and Criminal Procedure Code (s.558) allow states to determine the language(s) of the court (Jayaram and Rajyashree, 2000:138–139). Kenya's 1967 Civil Procedure Act authorises English for the superior courts and English and Kiswahili for the subordinate courts. In Hong Kong the 1974 Official Languages Ordinance made Chinese official alongside English (Cheung, 1997:318) and was amended in 1995 (Government of Hong Kong Department of Justice, 2007) to allow both languages for court proceedings. Language legislation may also address legal drafting. Bangladesh's 1987 Bengali Language Implementation Act requires bilingual drafting of legislation. Malaysia's 1967 National Language Act makes English authoritative for prior statutes, Malay for subsequent ones.

A third influence on status planning is case law, which is particularly influential in common law jurisdictions. Interpreting or filling in lacunae in constitutional and statutory, there have been rulings on a wide range of language disputes, including the admissibility of Hindi at high court level in India provided English translations are supplied (*High Court of Uttarakhand* 2010); the obligation in Malaysia to use the national language when filing motions (*Zainun Dahan* 1997) and show proficiency in it for bar admission (*Utusan Malaysia* 1984.6.02); and the constitutionality of excluding jurors on the grounds that they understand the language of witnesses and may pay more attention to it than English translations (*Hernandez v. New York* 1991).

While constitutions, statutes and judgments may come to mind first when considering legal language rules, the sharpest tools of status planning are professional regulations and orders. These depend on enabling legislation for their authority, but whereas constitutional and statutory provisions are often drafted widely, court rules and legal directions are narrowly drafted in order to regulate systematic and consistent procedure on the ground. Pakistan's Supreme Court Rules allow for documentary submissions (Ord. V, 26) and accompanying translations (Ord VII, 2) in Urdu. A 1985 amendment of Tanzania's Court of Appeal Rules allows Kiswahili to be used in court and specifically authorises it for the hearing of testimony in the High Court (Rwezaura 1994: 115). Philippines Supreme Court Rules are somewhat vague in requiring a "language known to the accused" to be used for arraignments and "an official language" for judgments (Martin 2012: 16), but a 2010 Supreme Court administrative circular was rather more specific in yielding to resistance from judges and stenographers in Bulacan to the use of Filipino there, declaring its use merely optional (Martin 2012: 8). Most of Malaysia's legislation on legal language allows considerable discretion for judges, but when the government has seen a need for greater use of Malay, specific implementation has generally come in the form of practice directions (*New Straits Times* 1981) or judicial (*Utusan Malaysia* 1981) and registrar (*Utusan Malaysia* 1983) circulars. Orders from the police may also influence language practice: in 2005 India's Director General of Police ordered first information reports to be written in English or vernacular Hindi in order to clamp down on use of an Urduised legalese that few understand (Siwach and Rohatki 2012).

Planning may take more subtle forms but still be influential. The fact that Tanzania has a Kiswahili version of its constitution, whereas Kenya does not, gives some indication of the higher expectations attached to the language there, where it is also used for the Government Gazette. Judicial and bar websites may also give cues, with the secondary use of Urdu in Pakistan's Supreme Court portal perhaps guiding, as much as reflecting, the secondary use of the language in the legal system there. Where justices have discretion, courtroom practice itself is persuasive. Under the law Malaysian advocates must seek permission to use English in court, but in practice most of them simply take their lead from the presiding judge's practices and preferences (Powell 2008a: 39).

6 Corpus planning

Corpus planning, described as the modification and innovation of language forms by Cooper (1989: 31) and *actions sur la langue* by Calvet (1987: 282), may intertwine closely with status planning (the allocation of language functions, or *actions sur les langues*), and for Kaplan and Baldauf (1997: 29) both involve manipulation of form and function. Corpus planning is likely to involve linguists and often follows on from status planning, which is done primarily by policy-makers, but their relationship is typically recursive. As far as the legal domain is concerned, there are two main kinds of activity: lexical and sometimes lexicogrammatical innovation to equip languages for legal communication; and the production of legal corpora in the language in question that draw on these innovations and establish their currency in legal discourses. As with status planning, corpus planning has important sociopolitical dimensions. As Bourdieu put it succinctly (1982: 18): "En fait il n'y a pas de mots neutres".

Lack of terminology is the most frequently heard excuse for failing to use in legal contexts languages that support large speech communities in other domains. In the early days of independence Malaysia's justice minister was pessimistic about translating sufficient terms into Malay from English given that the latter itself relied heavily on Latin and French (*The Singapore Free Press* 1960). A quarter of a century later a shortage of Malay terms was thought to be disadvantaging non-English-speakers in labour disputes (*Utusan Malaysia* 1984). Only recently a former Chief Justice (Koshy 2013) acknowledged the continuing limitations of the Malay legal lexicon. Perry (2000) reported confusion among Sri Lankan lawyers over the meaning of Sinhala terms. Harms (2012) claims no indigenous African language has sufficient terms for legal practice and Moeketsi (1999) cites lexical deficiencies at the most basic level of legal discourse there. Thekiso's (2001: 207) examples of Setswana in Botswanan courts are heavily laced with English. On a visit to Dhaka International University's law department in 2014 I was told that code-mixing was inevitable given the lack of Bangla terms, while in discussions at Tonga's Attorney General's Office the same year I learnt that lack of lexis was the biggest hurdle facing legal translators.

In fact comprehensively framed government-funded legal lexicology goes back at least six decades. In the early 1950s Sri Lanka's Legal Drafting Department started work on a Sinhala, and later a Tamil, legal lexicon (Coperahewa 2011: 214). In 1963 Malaysia's DBP set up a committee for legal terms and brought out the first Malay legal terminology seven years later (Dewan Bahasa 1986: xi). Each Indian state administration has a Language Cell dealing with lexicography; in many states these are also responsible for legislative drafting (Jayaram and Rajyashree 2000: 67). Funding appears to be inadequate for the enormity of the task (Jayaram and Rajyashree 2000: 27), although it should also be noted that even in Malaysia, where there seem to be adequate resources to build new court complexes, establish e-filing systems and sponsor law students to study overseas, the 3000 legal terms produced by DBP in 1980 have scarcely been added to. DBP is the authorised but not the only lexical source, and alternatives include judicial portals. But many practitioners confess (Powell 2012) to turning to Google Translate when drafting in Malay. Tanzania issued a slim Kiswahili legal dictionary in the 1960s (Rwezaura 1994: 112), but few lawyers seem to be aware of it (Maosa [personal communication] 2013).

Given that it took English law six centuries to move from Latin and Law French into English (Mellinkoff 1963), perhaps six decades is too short for legal lexicography to come to fruition, but we must also bear in mind that even if there are terms in abundance this does not guarantee their adoption by practitioners. One Malaysian judge (Faiza 1993: 105) has argued that provisions for the continued use of English in the interests of justice may have been necessary to compensate for gaps in the Malay legal lexicon but were not designed to excuse gaps in the vocabulary of individual lawyers. A Bangladeshi assistant judge (Ferdousi [personal communication] 2013) notes a preference among advocates for English terms even when Bangla equivalents are widely known. Quite apart from producing enough terminology, one of the toughest barriers for corpus planners to penetrate is the preference of professionals who live by their capacity to persuade for using words that have sufficient gravitas or precision (or, in some cases, ambiguity) to resonate in the minds of peers raised on the same discourses.

This leads us to the second strand of corpus planning: the generation of texts. While the thin quantity (Zubaidah 2002: 159) and poor distribution (Jayaram and Rajyashree 2000: 135) of translations are commonly cited as impediments to language reform, it should be noted that the first priority of corpus planners is to make available in the target language the legislation and rules most frequently cited in court. Hence a Malay version of the Penal Code was produced back in 1967 (*Straits Times* 1967) and the Road Traffic Act was among the 60 Malay translations completed in Malaysia by 1982 (Powell 2009: 163). Kiswahili texts are available for Tanzania's Primary Courts Civil and Criminal Procedure Rules and also for the Objects and Reasons sections appended to statutes (Rwezaura 1994: 112–113). The government of the Philippines has not commissioned any legislation in its national language, but one judge took it upon himself to translate the Civil, Penal and Family Codes and the Criminal Rules and Procedures (Gonzalez 1996: 230). As already mentioned, a number of jurisdictions, including Bangladesh, Hong Kong, Malaysia and Sri Lanka, publish new legislation in two or more languages. However, my discussions with legal practitioners in all of these lead me to believe there is still an overwhelming tendency to translate from English rather than draft directly in Bangla, Chinese, Malay or Sinhala (Powell 2012).

Translation, and drafting from scratch in new languages, present opportunities to reduce ambiguity and enhance transparency. While this chapter focuses on planning across languages, simplification and easification of legalese can certainly be thought of as falling within the parameters of legal language planning, and indeed some lawyers argue that putting laws into the vernacular is insufficient for greater transparency unless the register is made more accessible too (Patwary [personal communication] 2014). Plain language movements are not new. Tiersma (1999: 214) notes that 300 years ago a Charles XII called for documents to be in plain Swedish, and Sweden's justice ministry currently employs linguists to ensure compliance with a 1982 ordinance requiring clear and simple language. He also (Tiersma 1999: 217) feels emphasis upon plain English in United States law schools has led to more readable judgments. In Japan the recent introduction of lay judges has spurred efforts to make courtroom language more accessible (Okawara 2008).

While the desire to make documents and speech more comprehensible is laudable, plain language faces complex challenges. For one thing, corpus planners need to look beyond lexical to syntactical complexity, and when they do they may find conflicts between the needs of lay and legal readers. The tendency in English legislation to place qualifications as close as possible to what they qualify, for example, can make it cumbersome to read but prioritises legal certainty, and as Bhatia (2001:72) observes, avoidance of ambiguity overrides desire for accessibility. There is also the question of whether pursuing simplification is concordant with seeking legal equivalence in another language. As Mikkelson (2002: 2) points out in the context of legal interpreting, the goal is equality, not clarification. Fear of inaccuracy and inadvertent semantic shift is another issue facing plain language. Impatience with legalese can lead to errors when redrafting within the same language (Davies 2004: 96), and the risks are even greater across languages. In some cases deliberate semantic shift, rather than error, is suspected. There has long been debate in Malaysia over whether constitutional provisions for minor children's "parent or guardian" to decide their religion allows for unilateral conversion by one of them. It increased in intensity when the public became aware that "parent", initially translated in relevant Malay texts as *ibubapa* (widely read as 'parents', and assumed to uphold the interpretative principle that singular embraces plural), was later amended to *ibu atau bapa*, or 'either parent' (Lee & Blakkarly 2013).

In addition to codes and statutes, judgments and academic texts are important legal corpora that not only test out the meaning of new lexis but associate it with legal arguments and jurisprudence. From Bangladesh to the Philippines, however, judges and jurists continue to write overwhelmingly in English (Ferdousi [personal communication] 2013; Pasamba, in Powell 2012).

7 Acquisition planning

It is not enough to establish rules about and adapt languages for legal use unless measures are taken to ensure individual legal practitioners are proficient in the target legal medium. Yet far less effort has gone into acquisition planning than status or corpus reform. There is a wide assumption that the general proficiency achieved through general education can be drawn on when legal professionals attempt to practise law in a fledgling legal medium. Hong Kong has no requirement for Chinese in legal education (Hong Kong University PCLL 2012) despite the increasing importance of Cantonese in the lower courts and the bar's growing emphasis upon Mandarin skills (Yih 2009). Tonga may draft legislation bilingually but law is studied in English – and overseas (Lutui, p.c.2014). The Philippines has experimented with proceedings in Filipino yet there are no legal courses in it (Reyes 2009).

A number of jurisdictions do support bilingualism in legal education. In officially promoting Portuguese and Tetum as legal media while recognising the continued value of Indonesian in practice, Timor Leste runs law courses in Portuguese at its National University but allows candidate to take exams in Tetum or Indonesian at three other local institutions (Fernandes & Maceda [personal communication] 2010). Law graduates seeking to qualify as public prosecutors must complete a training course conducted in both Portuguese and Tetum (Figueiredo [personal communication] 2010). In Mauritius, which combines civil and common law through its French-British colonial legacy, the local LLB has obligatory courses in both French and English (Gunputh 2013: 62). South Africa, another mixed-law system, continues to support legal education in Afrikaans, even though it is unlikely law students could avoid English (Harms [personal communication] 2013). Canada has put considerable resources into bilingual legal education. The University of Ottawa has run parallel civil law and common law courses since 1957 and bilingual instruction began in 1977 (University of Ottawa 2012). Institut Joseph-Dubuc offers common law in French and civil law in English and McGill University holds summer schools in bilingual legal drafting (Blais 2009).

In Malaysia, candidates unable to certify Malay proficiency through school-leaving or other exam results are required to take a language test before they can be admitted to the bar (LPQB 2013). However, only two qualifying law departments (Universiti Malaya and Universiti Kebangsaan Malaysia) teach to any extent in the national language. In the former, students may opt to take exams in either language (Chew [personal communication] 2013), whereas in the latter at least one paper on any exam must be written in a different language from the others (Pey [personal communication] 2013). At all other domestic law schools instruction is in English. Lawyers may also be admitted upon passing the bar or solicitor's exams in England and Wales or Ireland or upon passing the Certificate of Legal Practice after studying in other Commonwealth law departments (LPQB 2013). The CLP may be sat in Malay or English but the great majority of candidates choose the latter (LPQB 2013).

Through much of South Asia it is possible to qualify as a lawyer in an indigenous language. The All Indian Bar Exam may be taken in eleven languages (Bar Council of India 2014). Language restrictions on exams in Pakistan have been dropped (Pakistan Bar Council 2014) and admission through Urdu is possible (Anis [personal communication] 2014). In Bangladesh, exams for subordinate court advocates and magistrates may be sat in either language, although those for the High Court are in English (Patwary [personal communication] 2015). From interviews at Dhaka International University (2014) I found a strong consensus among lawyers and law lecturers that a language-based class system had emerged in Bangladesh, with those qualifying in Bangla confined to less lucrative work. According to Ferdousi ([personal communication] 2013), the division is reinforced by higher bar fees for the higher courts, whose English-educated lawyers hardly bother with the lower courts. In Sri Lanka lawyers have been able to qualify in Sinhala, and in theory also in Tamil, although discussions at Sri Lanka Law College suggested they may be handicapped by a lack of courses and materials in these languages (Powell 2012), and there is evidence of linguistic social division there too. Since 2008 the College has been attempting to restore compulsory English (*The Island* 2008).

8 Degrees, patterns and effects of language planning

Status planning, corpus planning and acquisition planning have led to a number of different patterns of language contact, enabling language shift and influencing professional practice in legal domains. These range from the enforcement of monolingualism to support for multilingualism.

8.1 Regulation of relations among languages

Most legal systems function in a single language. Monolingualism may simply be assumed, especially where there are few doubts about which language has socioeconomic and political dominance, but sometimes it is established explicitly, as in the requirement for Danish under Denmark's Code of Civil Procedure or English under Botswana's Magistrates Courts Act – even though Setswana is often used in practice (Thekiso 2001). Imposing monolingualism is an instance of status planning just as much as accommodating multilingualism.

Where more than one language has official recognition there may be geographical separation, as in Switzerland's canton-based policy previously mentioned or Cameroon's Anglophone common law regions and Francophone civil law regions (Baaboh 2009). Separation according to court level is common and typically assigns indigenous languages to lower courts, sometimes alongside continued use of an elite exonormative language, while requiring the latter for higher courts. Hierarchical separation is particularly clear in Tonga, where English is absent from lower court proceedings (except for loanwords), but judges in the higher courts remind advocates that they will ignore any evidence *not* in English (personal observation 2013). In Sri Lanka, geographical and hierarchical separation are combined by installing Sinhala or Tamil for the subordinate courts according to region and English for the superior courts. The linguistic and legal rationales behind this kind of division are clear enough. Lower courts hear the majority of cases, many of them relatively straightforward and revolving around oral testimony that may be given in non-technical language. They are typically not courts of record and produce no jurisprudence. On the other hand the higher courts administer lengthier and more complex matters and make more use of written authorities and submissions, so conducting proceedings in languages new to the legal domain presents more of a challenge there. This tiered arrangement thus lowers corpus planning burdens. It may also serve political rationales by demonstrating to the public the legitimacy of postcolonial languages, since the majority of citizens who attend court, whether as defendants, witnesses, litigants or spectators, appear only at lower levels.

8.2 Effects of language planning on legal practice

The influence of language planning on legal practice becomes more complex and interesting when two or more languages are admitted in the same communicative events. This may happen where language policy is flexible enough to allow for bilingual proceedings (e.g. Malaysia), where bilingualism occurs despite official policy (e.g. in Botswana, or the U.S. small claims courts investigated by Angermeyer 2015), and where the language policy is silent (e.g. law offices and much private law). Legal bilingualism may be a burden for practitioners, but it also gives them opportunities for choosing the language they find most effective for the wide range of legal tasks they perform, from interviewing clients to writing and delivering submissions to researching precedents. Where planners have been disappointed by the progress of language shift they would do well to analyse bilingual legal practices to better understand task-, site- and interlocutor-based differences in legal communication and the reasons some languages are considered more suited than other to certain kinds of communication.

One aspect of language planning worthy of more extensive investigation is the effect it may have on recruitment into the legal profession. While conceding that Filipino was still ill-equipped for sophisticated legal argument, Gonzalez (1996: 231) saw the hold of English over law in the Philippines as effectively barring entry to those from rural areas and poorer backgrounds. The size and ethnic composition of Malaysia's bar has been transformed in the last twenty years (Majlis Peguam 2013), and although language policy in favour of Malay may only be part of the reason for this, it is not coincidental.

It is plausible that civil law adapts more readily than common law to new languages. French has almost disappeared from the legal systems of Indochina and Dutch from Indonesia. The lesser role of *stare decisis* in civil law may be significant. Codes are easier to translate than case law and may show considerable similarity across jurisdictions, as I observed in Dili when watching lawyers who had never studied Portuguese managing to work from authorised texts in it by making constant reference to unauthorised Indonesian equivalents (personal observation, 2010). On the other hand many civil law systems continue to operate in French or Portuguese, even in African polities where only a minority are fluent in them. It should also be remembered that civil law jurisdictions like Indonesia and Vietnam that successfully introduced national languages also experienced radical political and sociolegal transformation.

9 Conclusion: Language planning and access to justice

In his inaugural presidential address to the International Association of Forensic Linguists, Tim Grant (2015) attempted to unite diverse research on language and law under the overall aim of using language to improve the delivery of justice. I would argue that language planning serves and has considerable potential to further this aim. A great deal of work on language and law, from translation to authorship identification, is technical and apolitical, perhaps necessarily so. But improving the delivery of justice may also require a critical perspective that looks beyond the legal system to the political, social and economic relations in which it is situated. There may be good reasons for privileging certain languages and registers in legal communication, but these reasons should not be taken for granted, and the possibility of reforming language status, corpus or acquisition inevitably leads to deconstruction of the law's symbolic power. Moreover, constitutions, statutes, judgments and professional rules contribute crucially to public perceptions about linguistic authority, not only by laying down rules but by putting these rules into practice in the production of texts. Thinking about changing the medium of the law therefore entails examination of wider discourses, as well as individual texts.

Targeted at speech communities rather than individual legal participants, language planning doesn't remove the need for interpreting and translation, but it can reduce the incongruous practice of interpreters translating proceedings from elite legal languages that few understand and can improve transparency in the many jurisdictions where law is administered in a minority language. Whether justice has improved in Hong Kong or Malaysia with vernacular proceedings is difficult to answer since so many factors are involved. But vernacularisation can provide the groundwork for such improvement.

To avoid adding to language-borne injustice, planning should proceed cautiously, with periods of bilingualism bridging the older and newer legal media and registers. This places a heavy linguistic burden on legal practitioners but also affords them opportunities to choose the best linguistic tools for their trade. The role of bilingual lawyers is crucial, just as the role of lawyers as mediators between the law and their clients is crucial in monolingual jurisdictions, and so educational support should be prioritised. This has not been the case hitherto. While most Malaysian law schools do have some kind of course on legal Malay, they rarely go beyond teaching lists of lexis (UM Baseline Study 2014). This is pragmatically motivated inasmuch as it reflects the assumption that Malay will be used for less complex tasks, but it also reveals the weak intention of planners to make the national language a comprehensive medium of law. The dangers of creating language-based class division in legal professions must also be faced. Malaysia has not gone down this road as far as some South Asian jurisdictions, but evidence of linkage between language preference and career preference (UM Baseline Study 2014) shows that the danger is there.

By looking at bilingual law in practice we can gain insights into what legal communication entails. Suddenly replacing long-standing terms of art won't best serve the interests of justice, but neologisms can be improvements. (Legal Malay has at least five terms to cover the multiple legal meanings of 'charge'). Some legal communication has to be technical and elitist, but a lot of it need not be. There are understandable fears that bilingualism may increase the risk of ambiguity, but needing to explain law in two languages can also expose hidden or potential ambiguity, as in the translation of 'parent' as *ibubapa* mentioned above. Legal interpreting requires awareness of the various possible semantic and pragmatic meanings of legalese, but language planning adds to this awareness as it seeks lexicogrammatical equivalence on a long-term basis in multiple contexts.

References

Cases cited

Charlebois v City of St John [2005] [Canada SC]
Dato' Seri Anwar Ibrahim v Tun Dr Mahathir Mohamad [2010] 3CLJ 444 CA
Hernandez v. New York, 500 U.S. 352 (1991)
High Court of Uttarakhand vs State Information Commissioner [2010]
Ó Beoláin v. Fahy [2001] 2 I.R. 279
Police v Sikuea [1996] TOMC 1
R. v Tam Yuk-ha MA1385/1996
The State (Mac Fhearraigh) v. Mac Gamhna, 1983 T.É.T.S 29
Zainun bte Hj Dahan lwn *Rakyat Merchant Bankers Bhd & Satu Lagi* [1997] 4 CLJ

Personal communications

Anis, Muneeba (Pakistani legal educator and administrator) By email with the author, 26 August 2014.
Aung Htoo (Burma Law Council) Interviewed by the author in Bangkok and updated by email, October 2005 and November 2012.
Castillo, Kaline (Swiss journalist, bar candidate) Interviewed by the author in London, 8 January 2015.
Chew, Janet (Malaysian solicitor-advocate and lecturer) Interviewed by the author in Kuala Lumpur, 3 October 2013.
Ferdousi, Nahid (Bangladesh Open University) Interviewed by the author in Kuala Lumpur, 21 November 2013.
Fernandes, Bernardo and Macedo, Erika (Officers of Centro de Formação Juridico) Interviewed in Dili, 9 September 2010.
Figueiredo e Silva, Arlindo (Inspector to Supreme Council of Prosecutors) Interviewed in Dili, 9 October 2010.

Harms, Louis (former South African Supreme Court judge) Communication with the author by email, 27 May 2013.
Lutui, James (Tongan Attorney Chambers Office) Interviewed in Nuku'alofa, 10 March 2014.
Maosa, Thomas (Tanzanian barrister-at-law) (Communication with the author by email, 13 May 2013.
Myint Zan (Lecturer in law, Multimedia University) Interviewed in Melaka, 13 March 2013.
Ó Flatharta, Peadar (Dublin City University) Interviewed in Chiangmai and updated by email, December 2012 and May 2013)
Patwary, Shameem Haider (Barrister-at law, Dean, Dhaka International University) Interviewed in Dhaka, 11 April 2014.
Pey, Carol (Malaysian solicitor-advocate) Interviewed in Kuala Lumpur 11 November 2013.

Press reports

Hafiz Yatim. 2009. Anwar's suit struck out as document was in English. *Malaysiakini*, 12 September 2009 www.malaysiakini.com/news/119398 (accessed 12 November 2009).
Koshy, Shaila. 2013. Language makes the law. *The Star* (online edition), 15 September. http://www.thestar.com.my/News/Nation/2013/09/15/Education-Tun-Zaki-English-Medium-Schools.aspx (accessed 15 September 2013).
Lee Way Loon & Jarni Blakkarly. 2013. Subra blames translation error for conversion bill tiff. *Malaysiakini*, 2 July. http://www.malaysiakini.com/news/234529 (accessed 10 July 2013).
New Straits Times. 1981. Crash courses in court Bahasa. 14 October. p. 6.
Rashid Darham. 1990. Penggunaan bahasa Malaysia di semua mahkamah mulai hari ini [Use of Malay in all courts starts today] *Utusan Malaysia*, 1 June, p.13.
Reyes, Carmela. 2009. Bulacan uses Filipino in court trials. *Inquirer.net*, 20 August. http://article.wn.com/view/2009/08/20/Bulacan_uses_Filipino_in_court_trials/?section=TopStories&template=cheetah-photo-search%2Findex.txt (accessed 30 March 2013).
Siwach, Sukhbir and Hina Rohatki. 2012. 2.25) Use of Urdu In FIRs Baffles Courts, commoners. *Times of India* (Haryana Edition), 25 February. http://articles.timesofindia.indiatimes.com/2012-02-05/chandigarh/31026536_1_hasab-haryana-police-firs (accessed 18 December 2012).
The Island. 2008. Law College to switch to English medium: Chief Justice. 30 March, p.6.
The Singapore Free Press. 1960. Start Malay in the courts now, says Dr Zainal, 30 June, p.3.
The Straits Times. 1967. Language: I have chosen the peaceful way, 3 March, p.8.
The Straits Times. 1967. The Chief Justice rules on N-language, 20 August, p.2.
Tun Shin. 2013. The rule of law in Myanmar: perspectives and prospects. *New Light of Myanmar*. vol.X no.6, p.1. http://www.burmalibrary.org/docsMA2013/NLM2013-02-10.pdf (accessed 3 March 2013).
Utusan Malaysia. 1981. *Masa belum sesuai tetapkan guna bahasa Malaysia di Mahkamah* [Time not yet suitable to use Malay in courts.], 17 April, p.18.
Utusan Malaysia. 1983. *Tarikh penggunaan Bahasa Malaysia dalam mahkamah belum ditetapkan* [Date for use of Maly in courts not yet fixed], 24 March, p.6.
Utusan Malaysia. 1983. Penggunaan Bahasa Malaysia di mahkamah tak perlu dilaksana segera. [Use of Malay in court need not be implemented immediately.], 26 April, p.5.
Utusan Malaysia. 1984. *Permohonan jadi peguam tanpa ujian bahasa Malaysia ditolak* [Application to become lawyer without Malay test rejected], 2 June, p.3.
Utusan Malaysia. 1990. Bahasa Malaysia di mahkamah ditangguh [Postponement of Malay in court], 24 March, p.1.

Utusan Online. 1998. Nasib bahasa Melayu di mahkamah [The fate of Malay in court], 12 October. http://www.utusan.com.my/utusan/info.asp?y=1998&dt=1012&pub=utusan_malaysia&-sec=Rencana&pg=ot_02.htm#ixzz2fbq83aFV (accessed 30 April 2013).

Books, book chapters and articles

Abdullah Hassan. 1987. *30 tahun perancangan Bahasa Malaysia* [30 years of planning Malay). Kuala Lumpur: Dewan Bahasa dan Pustaka.

Abdullah Hassan. 1994. Problems of language assimilation in West Malaysia. In Abdullah Hassan (ed.), *Language planning in Southeast Asia*, 103–132. Kuala Lumpur: Dewan Bahasa dan Pustaka.

Ali Rahman and Mohammad Faravardin. 2009. Critical issues of language policy in multilingual educational contexts. *Buletinul* (Universitatii Petrol – Gaze din Ploiesti) LXI. 48– 57.

Altay, Ayfer. 2002. Difficulties encountered in the translation of legal texts: The case of Turkey. *The Translation Journal* 2002 6 (4). http://accurapid.com/journal/22legal.htm (accessed 10 September 2004).

Ammon, Ulrich, Norbert Dittmar, Klus J. Mattheier and Peter Trudgill (eds.). 2006. *Sociolinguistics/ Soziolinguistik – An international handbook of the science of language and society/Ein internationales Handbuch zur Wissenschaft von Sprache und Gesellschaft*. Vol. 3. Berlin: De Gruyter.

Angermeyer, Philip. 2015. Speak English or what? *Codeswitching and interpreter use in New York City courts*. New York: Oxford University Press.

Asmah Haji Omar. 1979. *Language planning for unity and efficiency: a study of the language status and corpus planning of Malaysia*. Singapore: RELC.

Asmah Haji Omar.2007. Malaysia and Brunei. In Andrew Simpson (ed.), *Language and national identity in Asia,* 337–359. Oxford: Oxford University Press.

Baaboh, Feh, Henry [Barrister with Henry, Samuelson &Co, Cameroon].2009. Cameroon Legal System. http://www.hg.org/attorney/henry-samuelson-and-co-/articles/35873 (accessed 18 June 2011).

Bangla Academy. 2014. Official website. http://www.banglaacademy.org.bd [Bangla pages translated by Dr Mahmud Hasan, Macquarie University.] accessed 30 January 2014).

Bar Council of India. 2014. Official portal. http://www.barcouncilofindia.org/ (accessed 20 February 2014).

Bastarache, Michel. 2012. *Les guaranties linguistiques: droits linguistiques humains ou instruments d'intégration social au Canada?* [Language guarantees: human rights or instruments of social integration in Canada?] Paper presented at *XIII AIDL-IALL International Conference*, Chiang Mai, December 2012.

Bhatia, Vijay. 1993. *Analysing genre. Language use in professional settings*. London/New York: Longman.

Bhatia, Vijay. 2011. Contested identities. Symposium on Interdiscursive colonization of arbitration practices: key perspectives. *AILA Conference*, Beijing, 25 August 2011.

Blais, François [Director Centre for Legal Translation and Documentation, University of Ottawa]. 2009. *Canada's jurilinguistic centres* (Language Portal of Canada, 2009.10.08). http://www.noslangues-ourlanguages.gc.ca/collaborateurs-contributors/articles/jurilinguistique- eng.html (accessed January 2013).

Bolton, Kingsley. 2008. English in Asia, Asian Englishes, and the issue of proficiency. *English Today* 24 (2). 3–12.

Bourdieu, Pierre. 1982. *Ce que parler veut dire. L'économie des échanges linguistiques* [What speech means. The economics of linguistic exchange]. Paris: Arthème Fayard.

Calvet, Louis-Jean. 1987. *La guerre des langues et les politiques linguistiques* [Language war and language politics]. Paris: Payot.
Calvet, Louis-Jean. 2002. *Le marché aux langues. Les effets linguistiques de la mondialisation* [The language market. Linguistic effects of globalisation]. Paris: Editions Plon.
Cheesman, Nick. 2011. How an authoritarian regime in Burma used special courts to defeat judicial independence. *Law and Society Review* 45(4). 801–830.
Cheung, Anne S.Y. 1997. Towards a bilingual legal system – the development of Chinese legal language. *Loyola of Los Angeles International and Comparative Law Review* 1997. 315–336.
Cleroux, Richard. 2011. The hill: Solution to bilingual judges falls short. *Law Times, 19 September* 2011. http://www.lawtimesnews.com/201109192514/commentary/the-hill-solution-to-bililngual-judges-issue-falls-short (accessed 20 January2013).
Cooper, Robert L. 1989. *Language planning and social change.* Cambridge: CUP.
Coperahewa, Sandagomi. 2011. The language situation in Sri Lanka. In Kaplan and Baldauf (eds.), *Language planning in the Asia Pacific: Hong Kong, Timor-Leste and Sri Lanka*, 160 –241. Abingdon: Routledge.
Corson, David. 1989. *Language planning across the curriculum.* Clevedon: Multilingual Matters.
Crown Law Tonga. 2013. Official portal of Tongan Justice Department. www.crownlaw.gov.to/ (accessed12 December 2013).
Davies, Eirian. 2004. Register distinctions and measures of complexity in the language of legal contracts. In J. Gibbons, V. Prakasam, K.V. Tirumalesh and H. Nagarajan (eds.), *Language in the law*, 82–100. Hyderabad: Longman Orient.
Davies, Rachel. 2012. *Hyrwyddo System Gyfreithiol Ddwyieithog yng Nghymru* [Facilitating a bilingual legal system in Wales]. University of Swansea, unpublished doctoral thesis. [English summary supplied by author.]
Dewan Bahasa dan Pustaka. 1986. *Istilah undang-undang* [Legal terminology]. Kuala Lumpur: Dewan Bahasa dan Pustaka.
Ethnologue. 2014. http://www.ethnologue.com/ (accessed October 2011).
Faiza Tamby Chik. 1993. Language and the law: the role of Malay and English in legal education and the practice of law. In Khaw Lake Tee (ed.), *Legal education in Malaysia Quo Vadis?* 103–107. Kuala Lumpur: University of Malaya.
Fuller, Janet. 1993. Hearing between the lines: style switching in a courtroom setting. *Pragmatics* 3.1. 29–43.
Gibbons, John. 1999. Language and the law. *Annual Review of Applied Linguistics 1999.* 156–173.
Gibbons, John. 2003. *Forensic linguistics.* Oxford: Blackwell.
Gill, Saran Kaur. 2005. Language policy in Malaysia: reversing direction. *Language Policy* (2005) 4. 241–260.
Gonzalez, Andrew. 1996. Incongruity between the language of law and the language of court proceedings: The Philippine experience. *Language & Communication* 16(3). 229–234.
Goodrich, P. 1984. Law and language: a historical and critical introduction. *Journal of Law and Society* 11(2).173–195.
Government of Hong Kong SAR Department of Justice. 2007. *The legal system in Hong Kong.* http://www.doj.gov.hk/eng/legal/ (accessed 28 September 2007).
Government of Sri Lanka. 2011. Official portal. http://www.priu.gov.lk/Cons/1978Constitution/Chapter_04_Amd.html (accessed 10 November 2011).
Grant, Tim. 2015. Keynote address delivered at the *12th Conference of the International Association of Forensic Linguists*, Guangzhou, July 9.
Gunputh, Rajendra Parsad. 2013. The professional and vocational training of lawyers according to the Anglo-Saxon model in a mixed legal system – the case of the Republic of Mauritius. In Izabela Kraśnicka & Magdalena Perkowska (eds.), *How to become a lawyer*, 57–74. Berne: Peter Lang.

Haarmann, Harald. 1990. Language planning in the light of a general theory of language: a methodological framework. *International Journal of Sociology of Language* 86 (1990). 103–126.

Harms, Louis [Former Deputy President, Supreme Court of South Africa]. 2012. Language and law in a multilingual society. *Potchefstroom Electronic Law Journal* 2012. 15. http://www.saflii.org/za/journals/PER/2012/15.html (accessed 20 December 2012).

Haugen, Einar. 1966. *Language planning and language conflict: the case of modern Norwegian.* Cambridge, MA: Harvard University Press.

Hill, Lloyd. 2010. Language and status: On the limits of language planning. *Stellenbosch Papers in Linguistics* 39. 41–58.

Hong Kong University PCLL. 2012. Website for Hong Kong University Postgraduate Certificate in Laws. http://www.ple.hku.hk/pcll/ (accessed 15 December 2012).

Hornberger, Nancy. 2006. Frameworks and models in language policy and planning. In Thomas Ricento (ed.), *An introduction to language policy. Theory and method, 24–41.* Malden, MA: Blackwell.

Jayaram, B.D. and K.S. Rajyashree. 2000 *State official language policy implementation.* Mysore: Central Institute of Indian Languages.

Jernudd, B.H. and J.Das Gupta. 1971. Towards a theory of language planning. In J.Rubin and B.H. Jernudd (eds.), *Can language be planned?* 195–215 Honolulu: University of Hawaii Press.

Kamarul Zaman Shaharudin, Rossilawaty Sheriff, Sa'odah Abdullah, Mohamed Hamizi Ghazali and Ismail Karmun (eds.). 2003. *Citra.* Kuala Lumpur: Dewan Bahasa dan Pustaka.

Kaplan Robert and Richard Baldauf. 1997. *Language planning from practice to theory.* Clevedon: Multilingual Matters.

Kärchner-Ober, Renate, Dipika Mukherjee and Maya Khemlani David. 2011. Conclusions: Multilinguality in the Malaysian context of nation-building and globalisation. In D. Mukherjee and M.K. David (eds.), *National language planning and language shift in Malaysian minority communities – speaking in many tongues,* 174–184. Amsterdam: Amsterdam University Press.

Kua Kia Soong. 2005. *The Malaysian civil rights movement.* Petaling Jaya, Selangor: SIRD.

Leibniz, Gottfried Wilhelm, Freiherr von. 1683/1917. *Ermahnung an die Deutschen. Von deutscher Sprachpflege.* [Admonition to the Germans: on German language cultivation]. Darmstadt: Wissenschaftliche Buchgesellschaft.

Leung, Janny. 2012. Judicial discourse in Cantonese courtrooms in postcolonial Hong Kong: the judge as godfather, scholar, educator and scolding parent. *The International Journal of Speech, Language and the Law* 19(2). 239–261.

Levesque, Gérard. 2012. L'exercise des droits linguistiques devant les tribunaux d'Alberta. Paper presented at *XIII AIDL-IALL International Conference*, Chiangmai, December 2012.

Lim Chap Sam and Norma Presmeg. 2011. Teaching mathematics in two languages: a teaching dilemma of Malaysian Chinese primary schools. *International Journal of Science and Mathematics Education* 9. 137–161.

Lo Bianco, Joseph. 2001. Viet Nam: Quoc Ngu, colonialism and language policy. In Nanette Gottlieb and Ping Chen (eds.), *Language planning and language policy: East Asian perspectives,* 159–206. Richmond, Surrey: Curzon Press.

Lo Bianco, Joseph. 2009. Critical Discourse Analysis (CDA) and Language Planning (LP): Constraints and applications of the critical in language planning. In Thao Lê, Quynh Lê and Megan Short (eds.), *Critical Discourse Analysis. An Interdisciplinary Perspective,* 101–118. New York : Nova Science.

Lo Bianco, Joseph. 2010. Language policy and planning. In Nancy H. Hornberger and Sandra Lee McKay (eds.), *Sociolinguistics and language education*, 143–173. Clevedon: Multilingual Matters.

LPQB. 2013. Portal of the Legal and Profession Qualifying Board, Malaysia. http://www.lpqb.org.my/ (accessed 1 September 2013).

Lundquist, Lita. 1995. Indefinite noun phrases in legal texts: Use, function and construction of mental spaces. *Journal of Pragmatics* 23(1). 7–29.
Majlis Peguam. 2013. *Bar Council Annual Report 2012/13*. http://www.malaysianbar.org.my/general_notices/bc_general_statistics_2013.html (accessed 30 November 2013).
Maley, Yon. 1994. The language of the law. In Gibbons (ed.), *Language and the law*, 11–50. London:Longman.
Maley, Yon, Christopher Candlin, John Crichton and Pieter Koster. 1994. *Orientations in lawyer-client interviews*. Working Papers No. 3, Centre for Language in Social Life, Department of Linguistics, Macquarie University.
Martin, Isabel Pefianco. 2012. Expanding the role of Philippine languages in the legal system. *Asian Perspectives in the Arts and Humanities* 2(1). 1–14.
Mead, Richard. 1988. *Malaysia's national language policy and the legal system*. New Haven: Yale.
Mellinkoff, David. 1963. *The language of the law*. Boston: Little, Brown & Co.
Mikkelson, Holly. 2000. *An introduction to court interpreting*. Manchester: St. Jerome.
Moeketsi, R.H. 1999. Re-defining the role of the South African court interpreter. *Newsletter of the National Association of Judiciary Interpreters and Translators* 8. 3–4. http://www.najit.org (accessed 20 April 2013).
Myint Zan. 2008. Legal education in Burma since the mid-1960s. *12 Journal of Burmese Studies*. 63–107.
Nekvapil, Jiří. 2006. From language planning to language management. *Sociolinguistica* 20. 92–104. http://uk-online.uni-koeln.de/remarks/d5134/rm2169329.pdf (accessed 4 April 2012).
Nencioni, Giovanni. 1986. L'Accademia della Crusca e la lingua italiana. In Paolo Ramat, Hans-Josef Niederehe and Konrad Koerner (eds.), *The history of linguistics in Italy*, 107–120. Amsterdam: Benjamins.
Ng Kwai Hang. 2009. *The common law in two voices. Language, law and the postcolonial dilemma in Hong Kong*. Stanford, CA: Stanford University Press.
Okawara Mami. 2008. *Shimin kara mita saibanin saiban* [市民から見た裁判員裁判 Lay judge trials as seen by citizens.] Tokyo: Meiseki Shoten.
Orts Llopis, María Ángeles. 2007. The untranslatability of law. Lexical differences in Spanish and American contract law. *European Journal of English Studies* 11(1). 17–28.
Pakistan Bar Council. 2014. http://pakistanbarcouncil.org/ (accessed 2014.6.20).
Perry, Amanda J. 200.) Is legal globalisation an impossible dream? National implementation of international standards. *CEPMLP Internet Journal* (Centre for Energy, Petroleum and Mineral Law Policy). http://www.dundee.ac.uk/cepmlp/journal/html/vol3/article3-4.html (accessed 2011.5.10).
Phillipson, Robert (ed.). 1992. *Rights to language: equity, power and education*. Mahwah, NJ: Erlbaum.
Powell, Richard. 2008a. *Motivations for language choice in Malaysian courtrooms and implications for language planning*. Kuala Lumpur: Universiti Malaya.
Powell, Richard. 2008b. Bilingual courtrooms: in the interests of justice? In John Gibbons and M.Teresa Turrell (eds.), *Dimensions of forensic linguistics*, 131–159. Amsterdam: John Benjamins.
Powell. 2009. The role of English in Southeast Asian legal systems. In Siebers and Hoffmann (eds.), *World Englishes: Problems – properties – prospects*, 155–177. Amsterdam: John Benjamins.
Powell, Richard. 2012. Legal vernacularisation and access to justice. Paper presented at the *Asian Regional Conference of the International Association of Forensic Linguists*, Kuala Lumpur, July 4–7.
Powell, Richard and Maya Khemlani David. 2011. Language alternation in Kenyan and Malaysian courts. In Anne Wagner and Cheng Le (eds.), *Exploring courtroom discourse: the language of power and control*, 227–250. London: Ashgate.

Rwezaura, Barthazara. 1994. Constraining factors to the adoption of Kiswahili as a language of the law in Tanzania. *Afrikanistische Arbeitspapiere: Schriftenreihe des Kölner Instituts für Afrikanistik* 37. 109–126.

Rubdy, Rani. 2008. Language planning ideologies, communicative practices and their consequences. In M. Martin-Jones, A.M. de Mejia and N.H. Hornberger (eds.), *Encyclopedia of language and education, 2nd edition, volume 3: Discourse and education,* 211–223. New York; Springer.

Šarćevič, Susan. 1997. *New approach to legal translation.* The Hague: Kluwer Law International.

Springer, George P. 1956. *Early Soviet theories in communication.* Cambridge, MA: MIT Press.

Thekiso, Elma. 2001. *A sociolinguistic analysis of communication processes in a bilingual court of law in Gaborone, Botswana.* University of Warwick unpublished PhD thesis.

Tiersma, Peter. 1999. *Legal language.* Chicago: University of Chicago Press.

Ting, Su-Hie. 2010. Impact of language planning on language choice in friendship and transaction domains in Sarawak, Malaysia. *Current Issues in Language Planning* 11(4). 397–412.

Tollefson, James. 2002. Introduction: critical issues in educational language policy. In James Tollefson (ed.), *Language policy in education, critical issues,* 3–16. Mahwah, NJ: Lawrence Erlbaum Associates.

UM Baseline Study. 2014. Baseline study on the communication skills of law students, Universiti Malaya, 11 June 2013 to 6 October 2014.

University of Ottawa. 2012. http://www.uottawa.ca/academic/info/regist/crs/0103/clEN/cl-eng3.htm (accessed 2012.12.1).

Wright, Sue. 2003. *Language policy and language planning: from nationalism to globalisation* Basingstoke: Palgrave Macmillan.

Yih, Dieter [former president of Law Society Hong Long]. 2009. *Becoming a lawyer in Hong Kong.* Presentation to Law Society of Hong Kong. Retrieved through personal communication with author, 2013.7.15.

Zaiton Ab. Rahman, Ramlah Muhamad. 1994. *Penterjemahan karya undang-undang* [Translating the law]. In Nik Safiah Karim and Faiza Tamby Chik (eds.), *Bahasa dan Undang-Undang,* 113–121. Kuala Lumpur: Dewan Bahasa dan Pustaka.

Zubaidah Ibrahim. 2002. *Court interpreting in Malaysia in relation to language planning and policy.* Universiti Malaya unpublished doctoral thesis.

Tommaso Agnoloni and Giulia Venturi
5 Semantic processing of legal texts

1 Introduction

Since 1977, when L. Thorne McCarty conceived and developed TAXMAN, the computer program "capable to performing a very rudimentary form of legal reasoning" (McCarty 1977), the main goal of applying Artificial Intelligence methods to the legal domain has been to teach computers how to reason with legal rules, how to perform legal interpretation by making explicit the content implicitly contained in legal documents, how to argue like a legal advocate, etc. The challenge "consists in finding a way to connect the computational models to tasks that attorneys, judges, and law students actually perform and texts they actually use" (Ashley and Grabmair 2015). Consequently, research and practice in the field of Artificial Intelligence and Law (AI&Law) address a broad range of topics dealing with the semantic content of legal documents: semantic and cross-language legal Information Retrieval, document classification, legal knowledge extraction, automated legal argumentation, construction of semantic resources and legal ontologies, explicit semantic annotation of textual content and representation as structured data *e.g.* Linked Data, etc. With the increasing availability of repositories of legal documents accessible as processable data, these tasks are getting more demanding: they require harvesting domain-specific knowledge on an unprecedented scale.

At the same time, it has always been well-known that "modeling what a lawyer does is more complex than modeling experts in technical/scientific domains" (Rissland 1985). On the one hand, as linguists claim, linguistic analysis of legal texts is more complex than the analysis of texts written in other domain-specific languages since legal language is not dramatically independent from every day speech (Mortara Garavelli 2001). It rather makes a specific use of lexical and syntactic peculiarities typical of ordinary language. Consequently, it can be seen both as an extension and a reduction of the possibilities offered by ordinary language. In addition, it is widely acknowledged that this sub-language is highly "convoluted and unnatural", to put in McCarty's words (McCarty 2009). On the other hand, making a computer able to perform legal reasoning entails that it would be able to "represent and reason about [...] situations using a great deal of commonsense knowledge as well as technical knowledge" (Rissland 1985).

In this context, it is of paramount importance the use of Natural Language Processing (NLP) techniques and tools that, when complemented with tools for knowledge management, enable computers to process the content (the semantics) of a large amount of documents by relying on the underlying linguistic structure. According to the literature, the use of NLP tools represents the starting point of different methodologies all devoted to automatically modeling domain-specific information starting from texts (Buitelaar, Cimiano and Magnini 2005). They play a crucial role in making it possible to overcome the traditional acquisition paradox: as knowledge is mostly conveyed in the text, content access requires understanding the linguistic structures representing content in text. In turn, content understanding presupposes that a considerable amount of domain knowledge is already in place. Starting from the assumption that all the relevant information is implicitly contained in the text and it is represented by its linguistic manifestations, a NLP-based approach allows bootstrapping domain-specific knowledge from texts through *knowledge-poor* language tools.

However, in past years little attention has been paid within the AI&Law community to how NLP can contribute to knowledge management tasks. Rather, researches in the field have been conducted mainly from a top-down perspective, uniquely stemming from domain-theoretical assumptions. The pivotal importance of NLP tools for accessing and managing the content of legal documents has long remained an *underground river* within the AI&Law community. Still in 2007, L. Thorne McCarty claimed that none of the research activities carried out so far "have attempted to tackle the natural language processing (NLP) problem head on, presumably because they assumed that full-scale NLP was just too difficult in a domain as complex as the law" (McCarty 2007).

Things have changed in the last few years when both the AI&Law and the computational linguistics communities started focusing on the automatic linguistic analysis of legal texts as starting point for further semantic processing tasks. Nowadays, NLP tools and techniques are mature enough to analyze these kinds of texts even though, as we will discuss later, some effort is still needed to adapt NLP tools to handle the specificity of legal documents. As Adam Wyner and Tom van Engers claim, "NL [Natural Language] isn't the problem! NL is the object of study" (Wyner and van Engers 2009). Accordingly, there has been a growing body of interest in using NLP techniques for a number of legal knowledge managements tasks, such as e.g. Argumentation Mining, i.e. the task of detecting, classifying and structuring legal arguments (e.g. support, against, conclusion) occurring in texts (Mochales Palau and Moens 2009; Kuhn 2010), Summarization of legal texts (Hachey and Grover 2006), Extraction of legal cases elements (e.g. names of parties or judges, roles of parties, meaning plaintiff or defendant) (Wyner 2010; Wyner and Peters 2010), Extraction of legal definitions (Walter 2009), Information Retrieval of legal cases (Maxwell, Oberlander and Lavrenko 2009), Extraction of textual amendment provisions (e.g. repeal, substitution) (Spinosa et al. 2009; Mazzei, Radicioni and Brighi 2009).

In 2010, the book *Semantic Processing of Legal Texts* (Francesconi et al. 2010b) made the point on the international interest in the field of NLP-based semantic processing of legal texts. Besides, a number of workshops has been organized on the topic. It is the case of the series of workshops on *Semantic Processing of Legal*

Texts (2008–2014)[1] and on *Natural Language Engineering of Legal Argumentation* (2008–2009),[2] of the workshop on *Applying Human Language Technology to the Law* (2011).[3] More recently the workshop on *Language and Semantic Technology for Legal Domain* (2015)[4] and the workshop on *Automated Detection, Extraction and Analysis of Semantic Information in Legal Texts* (2015)[5] were organized with the common aim to bring together an interdisciplinary group of scholars for a collaborative discussion about how matured NLP tools, machine learning and semantic technologies can be applied to the semantic processing of legal texts.

This contribution aims at providing an overview of the main approaches to the semantic processing of legal texts, combining views and perspectives of the computational linguistics and AI&Law communities. After introducing and discussing the main challenges encountered when accessing the content of corpora of legal documents (Section 2), in Section 3 the authors will present two main methods to semantic processing: a *top-down* approach relying on existing semantic resources and a *bottom-up* approach relying on Natural Language Processing and Information Extraction techniques. Different kind of resources (linguistic, lexical, conceptual) will be introduced and their differences, methodological premises, intended use and possible integration will be highlighted. Besides, the authors will show how NLP tools and techniques can be used to automatically extract the relevant knowledge contained in legal texts and to structure the extracted knowledge providing the starting point for a middle-out approach to the construction of domain-specific semantic resources (Section 4).

One of the main goal of this contribution is to discuss how the two research communities (the AI&Law and computational linguistics one) can benefit from the interaction of their approaches to semantic processing of legal texts: the legal artificial intelligence community can gain insight into the advantages offered by state-of-the-art linguistic technologies, and computational linguists can take advantage of the already existing legal resources (corpora as well as lexicons and ontologies) for training, adapting and evaluating state-of-the-art NLP technologies to the specificity of the legal domain.

---

1 https://sites.google.com/site/splet2014workshop/
2 http://wyner.info/nalea/index.php/jurix-2008-workshop-natural-language-engineering-of-legal-argumentation-nalela/
3 http://wyner.info/LanguageLogicLawSoftware/index.php/2011/01/29/icail-workshop-applying-human-language-technology-to-the-law/
4 http://eucases.eu/ranlp
5 http://www.lrdc.pitt.edu/ashley/icail2015nlp/

2 Semantic processing of legal texts: the main challenges

In this section the main challenges encountered when dealing with legal semantics and legal language will be discussed in relation with the construction and use of legal semantic resources, as well as with the process of automatic knowledge extraction from legal texts.

2.1 Law and language

Legal knowledge strictly depends on its linguistic expression: the law has to be communicated and social and legal rules are mainly transmitted through their oral and written expression. Moreover legal concepts change through time. Norms constitute the interpreted meaning of set of contexts, whose literal meaning is conditioned by the social dimension in which they are placed, whereby norms dynamically define and fix their object in relation to a continually evolving social context. Let us consider the creative power of the legislator in transforming terms of natural language in legal concepts: legislative definitions have a constitutive force, so we can assume that, for any new definition, a new concept is added in the legal system. As a consequence, legal concepts should be considered as a repository of meaning, whose content is dynamically modified by the influence of external factors. Changes in meaning of legal concepts occur within a diachronic process in relation to the cultural, political and social evolutions of the environment in which they are created. It is mainly through the work of the judiciary that the meaning of terms, like "public policy", "public morals", can be dynamically modified and registered. From a strictly semantic point of view, we cannot expect to find any direct 'referents' in reality, contrary to what happens for concepts in natural sciences, but, instead, examples of factual situations denoted by such kind of concepts.

If we move from a monolingual (and national) dimension to a multilingual (and transnational) dimension, a further element of complexity arises: legal terminologies used in both European and non-European legal systems express not only the legal concepts which operate in the different countries, but also reflect the deep differences existing between the various systems and the varying interpretations given by lawyers in each system. Given the structural domain specificity of legal language, we cannot talk about "translating the law" to ascertain correspondences between the legal terminology in various languages, since the translational correspondence of two terms satisfies neither the semantic correspondence of the concepts they denote, nor the requirements of the different legal systems.

In the European context, multilingualism affects the comprehensibility of legal documents from a dual point of view (Ajani 2007): on the one hand, the difficulty of establishing meaning correspondences (horizontal equivalences) between concepts that reflect different legal systems (and social/cultural contexts); on the other, the need to guarantee vertical consistency between the legal language of the national system and a transnational legal language, most importantly that of European Union law, where the need to produce conceptually equivalent legislative texts requires harmonised and inevitably generic terminological choices to be made. Several examples of the crucial difficulties in managing the multilingual panorama of European Community can be provided, showing how, in several social contexts, the terminological complexity reflects the problems of finding a methodology for bridging diversities and harmonising legal rules.

2.2 Adaptation of NLP tools to the legal domain

Similarly to other domains (see for example the case of the biomedical domain, McClosky and Charniak 2008), the use of NLP tools to analyze legal texts faces the issue of Domain Adaptation of tools originally developed to analyze newswire language. As firstly demonstrated by Gildea (2001), state-of-the-art tools suffer from a dramatic drop of accuracy when tested on domains outside of the data from which they were trained or developed on. One of the main challenges is concerned with the adaptation of syntactic dependency parsers to the analysis of domain-specific texts since syntactic parsing represents the starting point for a number of different text processing tasks, such as e.g. Information Extraction, Document Classification, Argumentation (Nivre 2006).

In spite of the fact that nowadays dependency parsing can be carried out with high levels of accuracy, the adaptation of syntactic parsers to new domains remains an open issue. In order to overcome this problem, the last few years have seen a growing interest in developing methods and techniques aiming at adapting current parsing systems to new domains (Nivre et al. 2007, Daumé et al. 2010). However, so far, very few attempts have been carried out to quantify the performance of dependency parsers on legal texts. Exceptions are represented by the *Domain Adaptation Track* (Dell'Orletta et al. 2013) organized at Evalita 2011, the evaluation campaign of NLP and Speech Tools for Italian,[6] and of the *First Shared Task on Dependency Parsing of Legal Texts* (Dell'Orletta et al. 2012) organized at the *Workshop on Semantic Processing of Legal Texts* (SPLeT).[7]

These two initiatives were both aimed at *i)* identifying specific challenges posed by the analysis of Italian and English legal texts, *ii)* obtaining a clearer idea of the performances of state-of-the-art dependency parsers when tested on this type of

---

[6] http://www.evalita.it/
[7] https://sites.google.com/site/splet2012workshop/home

Table 5.1: Dependency syntactic parsing performance before and after domain adaptation.

fig	Test	Performance	Performance after Domain Adaptation
Newspapers	Newspapers	82.09% LAS	–
Newspapers	Legal texts	75.85% LAS	80.83% LAS

texts, and *iii)* at developing and sharing multilingual domain specific resources. In those occasions, it resulted that dependency parsers have a drop of 6.24 percentage points when trained on newspaper texts and tested on legal documents. As shown in Table 5.1, where the results obtained by the best participant parsing system at Evalita 2011 *Domain Adaptation Track* (Attardi, Simi, and Zanelli 2013) are reported, parsing performances increase up to 5 percentage points when a domain adaptation strategy is devised.[8]

The drop of accuracy of parsing systems is motivated by the linguistic characteristics specific to the legal documents. Since state-of-the-art systems are statistical parsers based on machine learning algorithms, their performances tend to decrease when the training set (typically represented by newspaper articles) includes some main features hardly or never occurring in the analyzed texts belonging to a different domain. Starting for example from a raw text feature such as sentence length (calculated as the average of number of words per sentence), it resulted that the Italian and English legal texts collected for the *First Shared Task on Dependency Parsing of Legal Texts* contain longer sentences (i.e. with an average of 33.38 and 33.86 words per sentence respectively) with respect to the average sentence length of newspaper articles (23.61 and 24.49 words). Or, if we consider the morpho-syntactic level of analysis, the legal texts contain the highest percentage of prepositions (21.72% in the Italian texts and 18.27% in the English texts of the total amount of morpho-syntactic categories vs. 15.05% and 12.69% in the newspapers) and, only in the case of the Italian legal texts, an highest percentage of nouns (29.23% vs. 25.17% in the newspapers); on the contrary, they contain the lowest percentage of verbs (10% and 13.68% vs. 13.50% and 14.32% of the newspapers), pronouns (2.65% and 1.69% vs. 4.56% and 3% of the newspapers) and of full stops and commas (7.14% and 5.80% vs. 10.37% and 9.20%). While the different distribution of punctuation marks can suggest a sentence structure specific to the legal texts, the high occurrence of prepositions is strongly connected with their presence within long sequences of complements that modify a noun. It is well-known that this and other syntactic characteristics, such as for example, deep syntactic trees or long syntactic dependency links can negatively

---

8 The percentages reported in Table 1 refer to the Labeled Attachment Score (LAS), i.e. the percentage of tokens for which a system has predicted the correct syntactic head and dependency syntactic relation.

affect the transparency and understandability of legal texts. But, it is important to note here that these structural complexities also undermine the performance of the tools of automatic linguistic analysis.

Interestingly, the legal texts contain a higher percentage of newswire lexicon, i.e. about 80% in both languages. This reflects one of the main legal domain peculiarity: the fact that the legal language is not dramatically independent from every day speech but it rather stems from the specific use of common language words within this domain.

2.3 Discriminating between legal and world knowledge

As already noted, one of the main challenge in semantic processing of legal texts is that the legal content is tightly intertwined with common sense knowledge. This is mainly due to the fact that in the legal domain the meaning of a word is not intrinsically tied to the word itself but it rather stems from the specific use of the word within the legal sublanguage (Scarpelli 1976). In addition, it is well known that by its very nature, law deals with behavior in the world: it simultaneously *describes* the occurring events and *regulates* them. This is the reason why scholars committed to modeling legal domain knowledge have widely acknowledged with the challenge of designing legal knowledge organization systems where domain knowledge (i.e. *legal knowledge*) and knowledge of domains of interest to be regulated (referred to as *world knowledge*) are not intertwined. However, as pointed out by Breuker and Hoekstra (2004), the indiscriminate mixture of the two types of knowledge is a common attitude in constructing legal semantic resource such as for example legal ontologies. They point out that many legal ontologies collapse together "epistemological and ontological perspectives": domain independent concepts of law are mostly intertwined with common-sense notions which refer to social activities. Interestingly, they claim that "the domain ontologies developed in the various projects contained almost ninety-nine percent terms that belonged to the category *world knowledge*, i.e. the world the legal domain is about". On the contrary, a core ontology should exclusively include "typical legal concepts, like norm, responsibility, person (agent), action, etc.".

According to the state of the art in legal ontology design criteria (Casellas 2011), several levels can be established ranging from the more abstract *top or upper-level* ontologies, which include general concepts not domain-specific, and *core* ontologies, which provide top-level domain-specific (i.e. legal) concepts, to *domain-specific* ontologies, which organize world knowledge, providing a description of a specific domain of interest to be regulated. The architecture of the LRI-Core ontology (Hoekstra et al. 2009)[9] reported in Figure 5.1 provides an example of such a three-layer organization.

---

9 http://www.estrellaproject.org/lkif-core/

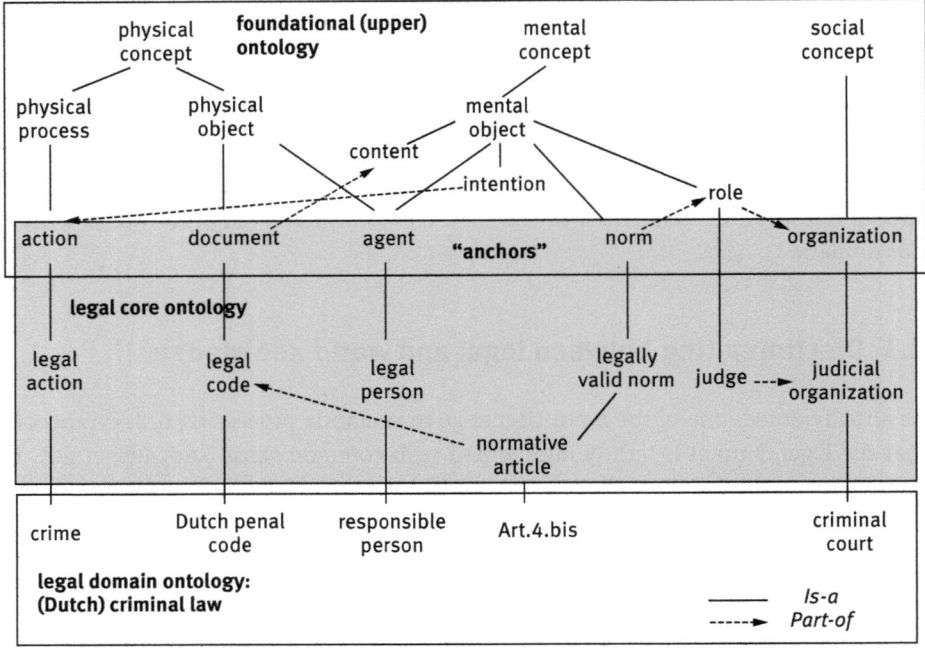

Figure 5.1: LRI-Core layers: foundational and legal core share *anchors* (high level concepts typical for law) (Breuker and Hoekstra 2004).

The most serious consequence is that "ontologies mixed with epistemological frameworks have a far more limited re-use and may pose more interoperability problems than clean ontologies" (Breuker and Hoekstra 2004).

2.4 Implicit and external knowledge: legal citations

A significant part of the knowledge conveyed by a legal document is only implicitly lexicalized in its text. Law is often expressed as a network of documents referring each other through legal citations. While an expert reader typically knows what the legal citation refers to and what is the meaning that it denotes, a layman as well as a machine has no chance to grasp the whole meaning of a text without reading or analyzing a number of referred texts.

Legal citations are therefore a special feature of a legal text that should be processed separately through specifically trained parsers able to identify and extract the significant components of a textual legal citation (issuing authority, date, number, etc.) and transform them into a formalized link that can be resolved to the referred text.

While drafting recommendation for well written legal citations exist, they are seldom followed by law makers, judges and legal practitioners, making the task of automatic legal reference extraction a challenging one requiring the coverage of a high variability of citation styles, abbreviations, relevant reference fields order and so on.

Reliable reference parsers able to identify legal citations (both to case law and legislation) in a text with high accuracy however exist. They typically rely on manually crafted rules based on regular expressions and grammars. For Italian legal texts *Linkoln*[10] and *Prudence* (Bacci, Francesconi, and Sagri 2013) are text analysis modules developed at ITTIG[11] able to identify legislative and judicial references from legal documents in plain text. The significant fields of the citation (issuing authority, type of cited document, date, number, subpartitions) are recognized, normalized, matched with admissible patterns and serialized in *urn:lex* and *ECLI* format which are respectively the standards *de facto* for legislative and jurisprudential sources identification.

Moreover legal citations are typically granular. They refer to a specific partition of a legal text which can be composed of hundreds of articles and paragraphs. In order to point the specific portion of text cited from a source, the formal structure of the referred document should also be caught. The way in which a legal text – typically legislation – is formally structured into chapters, articles and paragraphs is as well implicit knowledge which can be grasped by formally structuring the legal text with markup languages, typically XML. If legal texts are not natively available in structured format (which is the typical scenario) plain text can be preprocessed with structural parsers able to recognize legislative documents partitions and automatically markup texts in XML (typically legislative XML standards[12]). See for example *xmLegesMarker*,[13] a structural parser for Italian legislative texts able to identify their formal partitions: books, sections, chapters, articles, paragraphs, as well as titles and identifiers of the individual partitions. Though this kind of annotation carries little semantics in terms of the content of the norm, it provides a fine-grained structure of the text that ultimately allows to filter specific text portions for example to apply different weight to terminology extracted from different sections (*e.g.* from the titles

---

10 http://ittig.github.io/Linkoln/
11 Institute of Legal Information Theory and Techniques of the Italian National Research Council
12 Initiatives on adoption of XML standards for the representation of legislative document structures and metadata have been brought on both at national and international level in different countries in recent years. To cite the most successful, XML.gov in the U.S., Crown XML Schema in the U.K. provide the most rich and complete data- sets made available by governments in open XML. Other initiatives in European countries, like NIR (NormeInRete) standard in Italy or Metalex in the Netherlands have also lead to further development for a pan-African standard (AkomaNtoso) and to the international initiative of Metalex/CEN global interchange standard of legal sources.
13 www.xmleges.org

or from the body of partitions). Moreover the combination of legal references and structural markup of legal sources allows to establish a semantic link from the citing document, *e.g.* a judgment, and the knowledge and terminology carried by an external legal source. This depicts a scenario where typical legal information tasks and natural language processing approaches can be fruitfully combined to manage the peculiarities of legal texts.

3 Semantic processing of legal texts: two complementary approaches

In the literature on knowledge management, the process of accessing and structuring the content (the semantics) of a specific domain of knowledge is typically seen as an incremental process (Buitelaar, Cimiano and Magnini 2005). The various steps of knowledge organization can be arranged in a "layer cake" of increasingly complex subtasks, as illustrated in Figure 5.2. The process starts from the documents where the domain-specific knowledge is implicitly contained: it "implies the acquisition of linguistic knowledge about the terms that are used to refer to a specific concept in text and possible synonyms of these terms. An ontology further consists of a taxonomy backbone (is-a relation) and other, non-hierarchical relations. Finally, in order to derive also facts that are not explicitly encoded by the ontology but could be derived from it, also rules should be defined (and if possible acquired) that allow for such derivations."

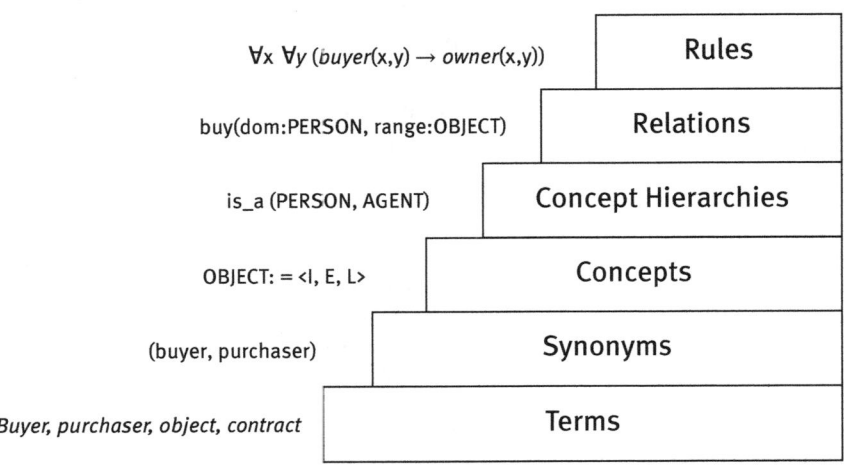

Figure 5.2: Ontology Learning Layer Cake (Buitelaar, Cimiano and Magnini 2005).

According to this view, we can model the semantics of legal domain assuming either a *top-down* or a *bottom-up* approach. In the former case, we exploit the domain-theoretical knowledge of domain experts to build taxonomies of concepts, rules, etc. (*top-down* approach). However, in this case the selected domain-specific concepts will not be anchored to any textual (linguistic) realizations thus posing problems of reusability of these concepts for accessing the content of new and large-scale legal document collections. Conversely, we can start from large collections of legal-relevant documents assuming that they contain the most relevant concepts (*bottom-up* approach). In this case, NLP tools and techniques can be fruitfully exploited to process the collected document collections and to automatically extract relevant knowledge that can be further organized (automatically or semi-automatically). In this way, the access and organization of the domain-specific knowledge will be constantly updated. However, we can run the risk of having a quite detailed representation of concepts and few general concepts unifying more specific ones. Or it might be also the case that the information automatically extracted from texts should be pruned by the pieces of information that are not relevant to the input document collection at hand.

A possible solution to overcome these pros and cons is represented by the so-called *middle-out strategy* which ensures both an anchoring of the conceptual model to domain-specific document collections and the coherence with general theories of the domain. Firstly, relevant terms of the domain are extracted from document collections and, secondly, these terms are linked to a semantic model of the domain defined independently from its linguistic manifestations. This approach has the virtue of counting with empirical evidence for the concepts proposed in the model[14] as well as with theoretical soundness, since the top-layers of the resulting conceptual model reveal the accepted theories of the domain. This approach to knowledge access and organization seems to be particularly appropriate for the legal domain since this domain of knowledge is "strictly dependent on its own textual nature" and accordingly "a methodology for knowledge extraction should take into account a combination of theoretical modeling and text analysis. Such a methodology expresses, in a coherent way, the links between the conceptual characterization, the lexical manifestations of its components and the universes of discourse that are their proper referents" (Francesconi et al. 2010a).

In what follows, *i)* we will provide an overview of the existing semantic resources for the legal domain and how they can be used assuming a bottom-up approach to domain-specific knowledge management and *ii)* we will introduce an example of how NLP tools and knowledge extraction techniques can be used to make explicit

---

14 By empirical evidence we refer here to the fact that concepts count with linguistic manifestations detected in domain relevant texts and can thus be expected to be part of the expert model of the domain.

and structure the semantic content implicitly contained in collections of legal texts. Finally, we will report an experiment where the two perspectives were fruitfully combined in a middle-out approach to the semantic processing of legal texts.

3.1 The top down approach: semantic resources for the legal domain

As previously discussed, conceptual access to a legal corpus or to a specific legal text is instrumental to support a variety of legal tasks. Structured semantic resources provide the conceptual layer between texts and services. Depending on their content, granularity and domain specificity, their level of formalization and ultimately the task they are intended to support, different kind of semantic resources can be distinguished: conceptual, lexical, formal. Moreover, in the framework of increasingly interconnected web resources provided by the Semantic Web paradigm, one of the goals is the integration of such different kind of resources in order to cover the whole gap, from lexical knowledge anchored to texts, to reasoning over formal statements. In the following, different kind of resources will be introduced and their differences, methodological premises, intended use and possible integration will be highlighted.

Legal thesauri

Traditional Knowledge Organization Systems (KOS), in the form of classification systems, controlled vocabularies, taxonomies, thesauri exist and have been used since a long time, particularly in libraries and then in digital libraries as a tool for the representation and indexing of information and documents.

Broadly speaking these are lists of terms (descriptors) possibly organized in hierarchies (BT *Broader Term*/ NT *Narrower Term* relations) and linked by generic RT (*Related Term*) relations. These kind of resources are therefore characterized by weak semantic constraints and do not address linguistic aspects of terminology. Their purpose is in fact typically oriented towards information retrieval and content tagging with document (or document partition) level granularity. Nonetheless, also thanks to their simplicity and low level of semantic commitment, they are of increasing importance and use in digital information management and applications. This is also due to the recent introduction of standards for their representation and exchange on the web. SKOS (Simple Knowledge Organization System)[15] is a W3C (World Wide Web Consortium) recommendation providing a format for the standard representation of KOS in interoperable, distributed, linkable and machine readable way.

---

15 http://www.w3.org/TR/skos-reference/

The fundamental difference between SKOS and other representation formats is that it is based on the principles of the Semantic Web. Differently from other existing standards, SKOS have been designed from the very beginning to allow the creation of modular KOSs that can be reused and referred over the web (interconnected controlled vocabularies). Semantic Web standards RDF and RDFS provide the infrastructure for the creation of a distributed network of data. Based on RDF, SKOS inherits its power in terms of flexibility and distribution. Since SKOS is represented in RDF, each concept has its unique identifier (its URI), that identifies it as a resource that can be univocally referred on the web and over which assertions can be stated. It may be used on its own, or in combination with formal knowledge representation languages such as the Web Ontology language (OWL). Using SKOS, concepts can be identified using URIs, labeled with lexical strings in one or more natural languages, assigned notations (lexical codes), documented with different types of notes, linked to other concepts and organized into informal hierarchies and association networks, aggregated into concept schemes, grouped into labeled and/or ordered collections, and mapped to concepts in other schemes.

In the legal domain, thesauri are widely used as a source of normalized descriptors to tag documents in legal databases, especially legislative databases. Eurovoc,[16] the multilingual thesaurus of the European Union, maintained and distributed by the Publications Office of the EU, covers all the subjects of European legislation. It is composed of more than six thousand descriptors, structured in 127 micro-thesauri and 21 domains. It provides a first level of management of multilinguality by providing the labeling of each abstract concept in the 26 official languages of the EU. This reflects the institutional role of the European Union to introduce harmonized legislation also by using aligned terminology among the different linguistic versions of an EU directive.

A more complex conceptual alignment issue arises when it comes to establish semantic equivalences among legal concepts described in national legal thesauri, equivalences which are not purely lexical but should reflect the correspondence of the "functional" meaning (its legal effect) of a legal concept in each national legislation. In such a case, as in the Legivoc initiative[17] whose aim is to create a network of national legal thesauri used to annotate national legislative corpora, alignment is not established at the lexical level with the translation of the concept labels, but by establishing semantic links using the SKOS properties of *exactMatch / broadMatch / narrowMatch / relatedMatch* among concepts of the different national thesauri.

---

16 http://eurovoc.europa.eu
17 http://www.legivoc.org

Legal lexicons

Computational lexicons are knowledge bases built to represent lexical meaning, providing explicit, basic knowledge background to machines to deal with natural language for text processing and analysis. The focus of this kind of semantic resource is on lexical knowledge.

While different kind of computational lexicons exist, differing for the type of content they represent (morpho-syntactic, terminological, semantic, mixed), we consider here semantic lexicons, among which Wordnet is one of the most popular and widespread resource (Fellbaum 2005).

Semantic lexicons like Wordnet are focused on the representation of the meaning of a word by distinguishing among its senses. Originally constructed for the English language, Wordnet partitions the lexicon in nouns, verbs, adjectives, adverbs which are in turn organized in sets of synonyms (synsets). Each synset denotes a lexical concept and then a specific sense. Synsets are linked through a variety of relations both linguistic and semantic, both hierarchical (specialization/generalization) and horizontal, forming a rich semantic network. Semantic lexicons are of course language dependent resources and the focus of the representation is both conceptual and terminological. They are typically characterized by concept density being their focus the representation of the general semantic knowledge of a substantial part of the lexicon of a language rather than of specific domains. Semantic lexicons like Wordnet also provide a basic level of semantic characterization of concepts in semantic domains, as well as a basic level of semantic relation among concepts (like the mentioned specialization/generalization namely hyponymy/hypernymy) with a very low level of axiomatization with respect to proper ontologies. Wordnet-like lexicons are therefore also often referred as lightweight ontologies.

Based on the original English Wordnet data model, many other Wordnets have been developed and distributed for other languages as a fundamental resource to support natural language processing tasks like Word Sense Disambiguation (WSD) and Semantic Role Labeling (SRL), as well as a support for tasks of information extraction, automatic classification and semantic tagging of documents by providing the anchoring between texts and more complex conceptual structures like formal ontologies.

Besides specialization to different languages, specializations of the resource to specific domains have been developed. In the legal domain JurWordNet (JWN) is a semantic legal lexicon constructed as a specialization of the Italian Wordnet (IWN) (Tiscornia and Sagri 2003). This kind of resource is able to complement the common language lexicon encoded in Wordnet with the specialized terminology used in the legal domain, as well as to take into account the different meaning that common-sense terms acquire when used in legal texts. Disambiguation of polysemies in specialized terminology lexicon should be considered extensively, as a distinction of the common meaning from the technical one. For instance, the Italian juridical term *canone,* means both the payment in money or in kind, against a contract; or, in the canonic right, a universal juridical norm. The Italian term *mora* is meant both as *unjustified lateness in discharging an obligation* and as *the amount of money due as fine against the delay*. Often, sense distinctions do not only concern the language, but also the differences in perceiving reality: for instance, to separate in a concept the role from the function, as for physical-substantial elements. The entry *President of the Republic* indicates the physical person, the constitutional body, and the holder of the state function. Or to distinguish between the normative content and the physical entity: the entry *contract* may be catalogued as a *privity*, as the physical entity of the paper, and as information content. In these cases the criteria followed to organize the concepts are based on assumptions external to the language. These are made explicit by adding a further level of conceptual specification to lexical concepts through their classification in classes of a (legal) ontology. This process also allows to set a mapping among terms of different languages. The approach is particularly effective in the legal domain, where the correspondence in not among terms, but among concepts, or often, juridical bodies.

LOIS (Peters, Sagri and Tiscornia 2007) is a multilingual legal Wordnet in five European languages (English, German, Portuguese, Czech, and Italian), where the monolingual lexicons are interconnected via an *Interlingual Index* to the English synsets; in this way semantic disambiguation and cross lingual retrieval can be coherently supported, even if the conceptual similarity on which the equivalence is based is left unexplained. However, when a consistent semantic interoperability is required, the best choice is to refer lexical knowledge to an external systems of concepts. In this case a solid ontology-based description of the domain would drive the process of multilingual alignment, thus providing the minimum core of common knowledge necessary to explain conceptual divergences and terminological misalignment.

Legal ontologies

The most well-known and complete definition of the term "ontology" in the computer science and information science field (Studer, Benjamins, and Fensel 1998) is that "an ontology is a formal, explicit specification of a shared conceptualization". From the definition one can argue that ontologies, in the computer science world, serve the purpose of representation of meaning among a community of interest (*shared*) in a processable format for machines (*explicit*) allowing further knowledge inference and consistency checking through logical statements (*formal*). Broadly speaking, ontologies, as semantic resources, provide language independent and richly axiomatised description of concepts. These might be very general and abstract concepts, or the specific concepts used in a certain domain. Several classifications of ontologies have been established based on the purpose, the generality (related to the level of detail of the conceptualisation), the level of formality (also related to the implementation language and the computational tractability) and the task they are intended to serve.

"The legal domain offers a perfect field for conceptual modelling and for ontology use in different types of intelligent applications and legal reasoning systems, not only for its complexity as a knowledge intensive area, but also for the high amount of data that it generates. Models of legal concepts, namely legal ontologies, play a crucial role in the cognition of legal contents, since they describe the main building blocks of legal knowledge" (Casellas 2011).

The typical distinction in terms of generality is between *foundational*, *core* and *domain* ontologies. Generic ontologies (often referred as "upper level" or "top level" or "foundational" ontology) define fundamental abstract and social concepts such as *state*, *event*, *process*, *action*, *component* etc. and *agent*, *role*, *task*, *social entity*, *organization* for what concerns the normative field. Often they provide a rich axiomatization of these concepts. Standard *de facto* among foundational ontologies are DOLCE[18] (Descriptive Ontology for Linguistic and Cognitive Engineering) and BFO[19] (Basic Formal Ontology). Core ontologies define concepts which are generic across a set of domains and are therefore situated between upper and domain ontologies, though the borderline is of course not so crisp. In the legal domain core ontologies are highly axiomatized and contain few concepts which are considered the least common denominator of all legal knowledge, including legal concepts like *norm*, *normative position*, *legal procedure*, *office*, *natural person*, *legal person*, *responsibility*, *legally defined institutions*. Some examples include Functional Ontology of Law (Valente and Breuker 1994), LRI-Core (Breuker and Hoekstra 2004), Core Legal Ontology (Gangemi et al. 2005), Applied Legal Epistemology (Mommers 2002), Ontology of Causality (Lehmann et al. 2004), LKIF-Core (Hoekstra et al. 2009). Domain ontologies express conceptualizations that are specific for a specific universe of discourse. The concepts in domain ontologies are often defined as specializations of concepts in the generic and core ontologies.

Legal ontologies are instrumental to a wide variety of tasks in legal information systems, for example:
- make conceptualizations explicit so that program can manage relations and distinctions among concept types;
- semantic integration and interoperability, *e.g.* for shared meaning in structured information exchange and reuse over the web;
- semantic indexing and search in Legal Information Retrieval by combining statistical techniques with *ontology*-based indexing;
- support multilingual search, translation and drafting by providing a conceptual abstraction level to the lexicon;

---

[18] http://www.loa.istc.cnr.it/old/DOLCE.html
[19] http://ifomis.uni-saarland.de/bfo/

- conformity checking *e.g.* to verify whether a social situation, modelled with formal concepts, is compliant with a legal regulation;
- reasoning with concepts (e.g., plug formal concepts into argument schema) in rule based engines;
- generate natural language arguments and explanations.

Legal ontologies may be constructed, as any other ontology, towards several purposes and they may have different levels of generality. Nevertheless some authors ascertain the fact that, different from the construction of ontologies in other domains, "law does not have its own ontological foundation" (Breuker and Hoekstra 2004), which leads to assume that ontology and epistemology are tangled in the conceptualization of legal core ontologies. From this point of view, law is a dynamic, normative field and its conceptualization would necessarily include those aspects, together with the representation of world knowledge or common sense knowledge.

Some critical points and lessons learnt on the design of legal ontologies have been raised during the last decade of increasing use of legal ontologies as a technique to represent legal knowledge (Ashley and Grabmair, 2015): there is still no agreement on what exactly should be specified in an legal ontology, nor on the level of detail an ontology should be specified at. At the core level their capacity to represent legal knowledge and its relation to the different existing legal theories is debated. At the domain level, ontologies should be designed for specific purposes and assessing their adequacy or suitability can only be done given the purpose for which they were created.

3.2 The bottom-up approach

In order to illustrate the bottom-up approach to semantic processing of legal texts we refer here to the methodology for knowledge extraction and management underlying T2K^2 (Dell'Orletta et al. 2014), a software platform developed by the ItaliaNLP Laboratory of the Institute of Computational Linguistics "Antonio Zampolli" of the CNR in Pisa.[20] T2K^2 relies on a battery of tools for Natural Language Processing, statistical text analysis and machine learning which are dynamically integrated to provide an accurate representation of the linguistic information and of the domain-specific content of English and Italian text corpora. It was tested and specialized for processing different typologies of legal documents, e.g. legislative texts (Lenci at al. 2009) and case law (Sagri et al. 2015), and document collections representative of different domains of knowledge, i.e. for extracting and organizing domain-specific knowledge implicitly contained in furniture product catalogues (Giovannetti et al. 2008) or in the

---

[20] http://www.italianlp.it/demo/t2k-text-to-knowledge/

analysis of technical documents such as patents and system requirements (Fantoni et al. 2013, Ferrari et al. 2014).

As detailed in Dell'Orletta and colleagues (2014), T2K^2 encompasses two main sets of modules, respectively devoted to carry out the linguistic pre-processing of the acquisition corpus and to extract and organize the domain knowledge contained in the linguistically annotated texts (see Figure 5.3). The underlying methodology starts from the basic assumption that the relevant domain-specific knowledge is contained in domain-specific document collections. Accordingly, by bootstrapping domain-specific knowledge from texts through *knowledge-poor* language tools, we can incrementally access the semantics of domain-specific document collections. This allows addressing both the need of an explicit representation of the textual content and the necessity of continuously customising this content with respect to specific application and/or user requirements.

Given a document collection in input, the collection is automatically enriched (i.e. annotated) with linguistic information at increasingly complex levels of analysis, represented by sentence splitting, tokenization, Part-Of-Speech tagging and syntactic dependency parsing. This phase of *Linguistic pre-processing* is performed by a battery of annotation tools developed by the ItaliaNLP Laboratory of the CNR of Pisa and the Department of Computer Science of the University of Pisa.[21] In particular, morpho-syntactic tagging is carried out by the POS tagger described in Dell'Orletta (2009) and dependency parsing by the DeSR syntactic parser (Attardi and Dell'Orletta, 2009) both representing state-of-the-art NLP tools for Italian and English. The document collection linguistically annotated represents the input for the following module of *Knowledge extraction*. This module is devoted to extract domain-specific entities denoting domain-specific concepts (i.e. terminology) as well as Named Entities specific to the domain under analysis.

According to the assumption that "terms are linguistic realizations of domain-specific concepts and are therefore central to further, more complex tasks" (Buitelaar, Cimiano, and Magnini 2005), terminology extraction is the first Knowledge Extraction step. In T2K^2 the layered approach to terminology extraction described in (Bonin et al. 2010a) is implemented. According to this approach, firstly, both candidate single terms, e.g. 'president', and multi-word terms, e.g. 'president of republic', are identified using linguistic filters (i.e. patterns of parts-of-speech such as for example sequence of noun+adjective, noun+preposition+noun, etc.) and state-of-the-art statistical measures (i.e. C-NC Value by Frantzi and Ananiadou, 1999). Secondly, a shortlist of well-formed and relevant candidate terms is re-ranked with respect to the associated contrastive score, reflecting their domain relevance which was computed on the basis of the comparative distribution of terms within the input document collections and a reference collection (referred to as *contrastive corpus*). In the final list, single and multi-word terms are ranked according to their decreasing contrastive score.

---

[21] http://www.italianlp.it/demo/linguistic-annotation-tool/

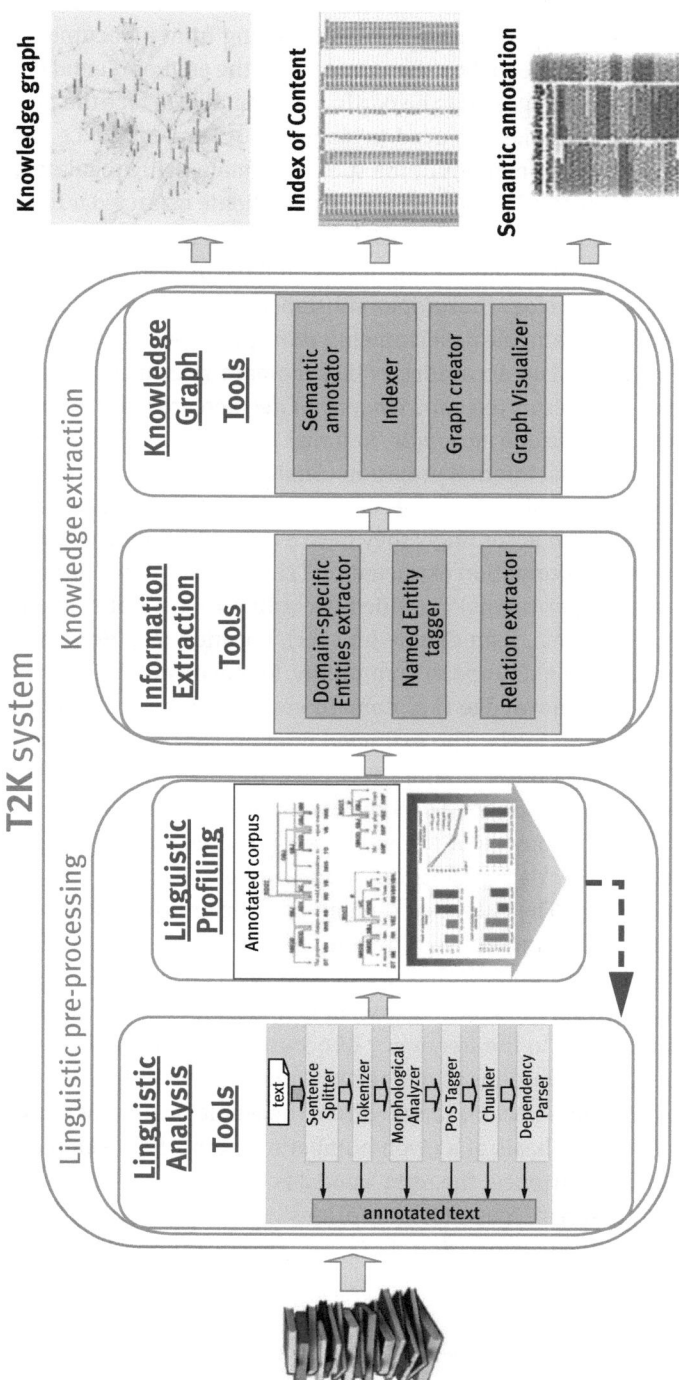

Figure 5.3: T2K² workflow.

As fully described in Bonin and colleagues (2010b) where the authors report the results of an extraction experiment carried out starting from a document collection constituted by Italian European directives concerning the environmental domain, this term extraction approach revealed to be particularly suitable to face the peculiar challenge posed by legal texts, i.e. the need to singling out legal terms, i.e. those which express *legal knowledge*, from terms of the specific domain being regulated, i.e. those which express *world knowledge*. In that case, the candidate extracted terms were contrasted against both a collection of texts testifying general language and of Italian European directives on consumer protection. In this final list of terms, the environmental terms (e.g. *sostanza pericolosa* 'hazardous substance', salute umana 'human health', *sviluppo sostenibile* 'sustainable development', *principio attivo* 'active ingredient') are in the top of the list ranked according to their domain relevance for the input collection, while the legal terms (e.g. *funzionamento del mercato interno* 'functioning of national market', *disposizione nazionale* 'national provision', *disposizione essenziale del diritto interno* 'essential internal provision of national law', *diritto nazionale* 'national law') are in the bottom since they are common to the environmental and consumer protection collections and accordingly they have a lower domain relevance score.

A further piece of information extracted by T2K^2 is a list *Named Entities*, i.e. a list of entities (mostly proper nouns) classified according to a set of semantic classes: Person (e.g. Barack Obama, Jean-Claude Juncker), Location (e.g. Romania, Republic Cyprus), Organization (e.g. European Community, Management Board).[22]

In T2K^2 extracted knowledge (i.e. domain-specific terms and Named Entities) is organized at different levels. The extracted domain-specific terms are organized into fragments of taxonomical chains, grouping terms which share the semantic head (e.g. 'free movement of goods', 'household goods', 'non-Community goods', etc. are classified as hyponyms of the more general term 'goods') or the modifiers defining their scope (e.g. 'data protection', 'data sources', 'data records' where 'data' is the shared modifier). The extracted domain-specific entities and named entities are also organized according to two different types of relations: co-occurrence and similarity relations. The former is the case of relations holding between entity mentions co-occurring within the same context. In this case, the relevance of the relation is weighted with respect to the frequency of occurrence or using the log-likelihood metric for binomial distributions as defined by Dunning (1993). To this end, different types of contexts can be selected, ranging from the whole document to the sentence or a span defined on the basis of a given number of tokens. For example, according to the frequency of occurrence, the term 'goods' is related (i.e. it occurs in the same contexts) with 'measures', 'customs authorities', 'customs territory', 'regulation', 'general rules', with the Organization 'EEC', etc. Or, according to the log-likelihood

---

[22] The reported examples refer to a knowledge extraction experiment carried out starting from a collection of Italian European directives on consumer protection.

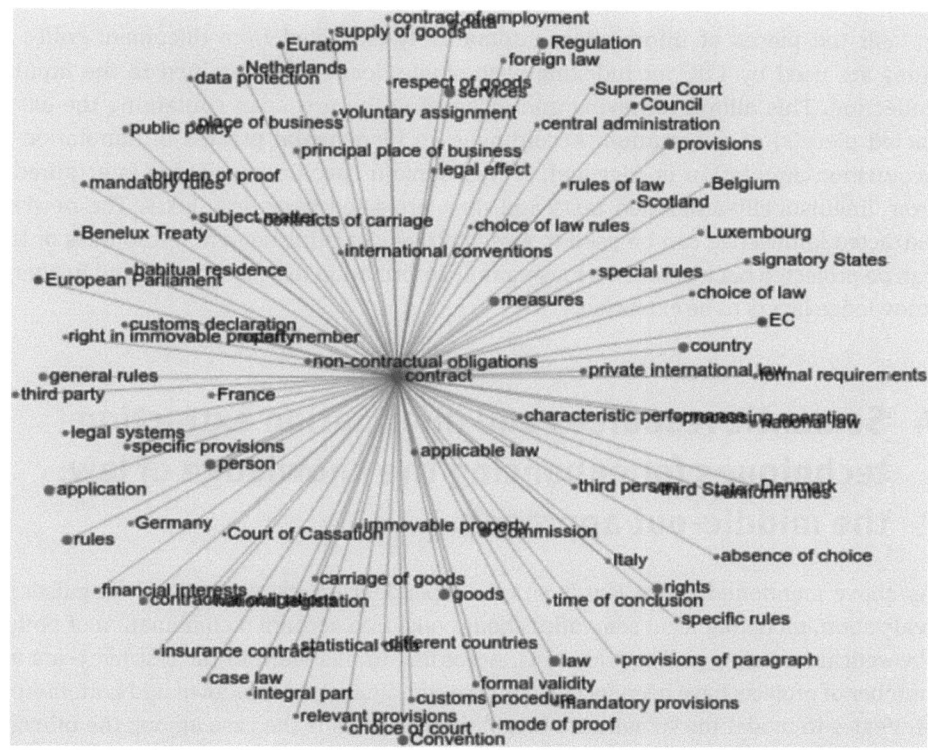

Figure 5.4: A screenshot of the knowledge graph extracted from the collection of Italian European directives on consumer protection.

metric, the term 'contract law' is in relation with 'country', 'formal validity', 'formal requirements', 'immovable property' or with the Organization 'Commission', etc.

The second type of relations, i.e. the similarity relations, are computed on the basis of the amount of contexts shared by the same entity mentions. This kind of relation is weighted on the basis of the cosine similarity between the entity context vectors. The components of each vector contain the association strength (computed in terms of log-likelihood) between the considered entity and its context entities. For example, the term 'data protection' share the same contexts of 'legal acts', 'principle of proportionality', 'legal instrument', 'conflict of laws', 'regulatory procedure', etc.

The extracted relations holding between domain-specific terms and Named Entities can be also visualized as a *knowledge graph* (see Figure 5.4) which can be surfed and used in a number of different graph mining analysis, such as e.g. extraction of all relations involving a given entity, or extraction of sub-graphs containing a given entity, or extraction of relations shared by two or more entities, or extraction of entities which share the same relations.

All the pieces of information automatically extracted from document collections are used by T2K^2 for indexing each single document contained in the input collection. This allows retrieving and visualizing the text span containing the extracted piece(s) of information. Accordingly, an incremental process of annotation-acquisition-annotation is triggered, where domain-specific knowledge is acquired from linguistically-annotated texts and then projected back onto texts. The newly extracted knowledge can be used to enrich already existing semantic resources or it can be projected back onto texts for semantic information to be annotated and further knowledge layers to be extracted.

4 Semantic resources and information extraction techniques for enhancing the knowledge of law: the middle-out approach

As above mentioned, since law is strictly dependent on its own textual (linguistic) realization, modeling legal semantics should take into account a combination of both theoretical modeling and text analysis. According to this view, in the last ten years a number of projects have been focusing on the combination of top-down and bottom-up strategies to model the semantics of legal domain. This is the case among the others of Walter & Pinkal (2009), Lame (2005), Lenci and colleagues (2009) who exploited Information Extraction techniques to derive domain-relevant terminology, concepts and relations from different typologies of legal texts as a primary step of the knowledge modeling process. A similar approach has been adopted in the construction for example of the LOIS Lexical ontology (Peters et al. 2007), the Ontology of Professional Judicial Knowledge (Casellas 2011), and the DALOS ontology (Agnoloni et al. 2009). Even if they differ with respect to the adopted methods and technologies, all these projects share a similar approach to modeling legal semantics. They all rely on a *middle-out* approach where domain-theoretical knowledge of domain experts and techniques of Information Extraction from collections of legal texts are jointly exploited. Namely, in the process of knowledge modeling, legal theory provides insights to construct semantic resources containing high-quality domain-specific information, and at the same time Information Extraction techniques based on Natural Language Processing tools guarantee the textual grounding of the terms, concepts and relations contained in the semantic resources.

The ontology built in the framework of the DALOS project (DrAfting Legislation with Ontology-based Support)[23] (Agnoloni et al. 2009) is a good example of how a domain-specific semantic resource can be conceived by adopting the *middle-out* approach. The project was designed to provide European law-makers with linguistic

---

23 www.dalosproject.eu (e-Participation 2006).

and knowledge management tools to be used in the legislative processes, in particular within the phase of legislative drafting. Relying on the same collection of legal texts written in four European languages (Italian, English, Dutch and Spanish), the underlying idea of the project is that the combination of multilingual terminology automatically acquired from texts and theoretical concepts defined a-priori by legal experts can enhance the accessibility and alignment of legislation at European level.

Accordingly, the DALOS architecture is organized in two layers. A first *lexical layer* containing multilingual lexicons automatically extracted using NLP tools and Information Extraction techniques from a collection of parallel corpora of EU legislation and case law written in four different languages, i.e. Italian, English, Dutch and Spanish.[24] This level is intended to describe the language-dependent expression of domain-specific concepts defined by legal experts. Extracted terms have been structured according to a WordNet-like data model (i.e. they have been automatically linked through linguistic relations such as synonymy, hypernymy, etc.), formally encoded[25] as instances of WordNet *Synsets* classes, identified by an URI and described by RDF object properties that model WordNet relations. Each *synset* is also linked to its textual referent, a text fragment encoded as an instance of the class *Partition* in the DALOS knowledge base.

The second layer is an *ontological layer* containing the conceptual modeling of the consumer protection domain at a language-independent level. Namely, it contains domain-relevant *concepts* defined a-priori by legal experts and linked to their corresponding monolingual *synsets* through the *hasLexicalization* relation. By providing an extensional characterization of the domain-relevant concepts, this layer represents a middle layer that allows mapping concepts with their linguistic realizations. It acts as a layer that aligns concepts at the European level, independently from the language and the legal order, where possible.

The resulting domain ontology formally describes the intentional meaning of core elements in the consumer law domain. The DALOS domain ontology is the result of an intellectual activity aimed at describing the domain of the consumer protection, selected as pilot case. It has been implemented as an extension of the Core Legal Ontology (CLO) (Gangemi, Sagri, and Tiscornia 2005) developed on top of DOLCE foundational ontology (Gangemi et al. 2002). Such an extension is addressed to cope with the entities of the selected domain and their legal specificities. In this knowledge architecture the role of a core legal ontology is to provide entities/concepts which belong to the general theory of law, bridging the gap between domain-specific concepts and the abstract categories of formal upper level or foundational ontologies such as, in our case, DOLCE.

---

[24] The consumer protection domain was selected as case study for the DALOS project. The whole document collection is composed by 16 EU Directives, 33 European Court of Justice Judgments and 9 Court of First Instance Judgments).
[25] RDF/OWL Representation of WordNet, http://www.w3.org/TR/wordnet-rdf/

The domain ontology is therefore populated by the conceptual entities which characterize the consumer protection domain. The first assumption is that all concepts that appear as definitions in the DALOS corpus are representative of the domain and, as a consequence, that several concepts used in the definitional contexts pertain to the ontology as well, representing the basic properties or, in other words, the 'intentional meaning' of the relevant concepts. Furthermore, the domain ontology contains generic situations having a legal relevance in the selected domain. Such domain-specific concepts are classified according to more general notions, imported from CLO, such as `Legal_role` and `Legal_situation`.

The ontological layer is meant to assign a domain-specific characterization to entities at a conceptual level, and consequently, to explain and validate terminological choices contained in the lexical layer. Furthermore, it enables to disambiguate concepts, setting their meaning in a specific domain and perspective. Figure 5.5 depicts the main part of the DALOS knowledge system, from ontology classes to lexical synsets.

The diagram depicted in Figure 5.5 makes clear how *Synset* resources in this knowledge model show both low level features deriving from their belonging to a lexicon in a specific language and invariant with respect to the domain, and high level features deriving from their association to a *Concept* object expressed as instance of the domain

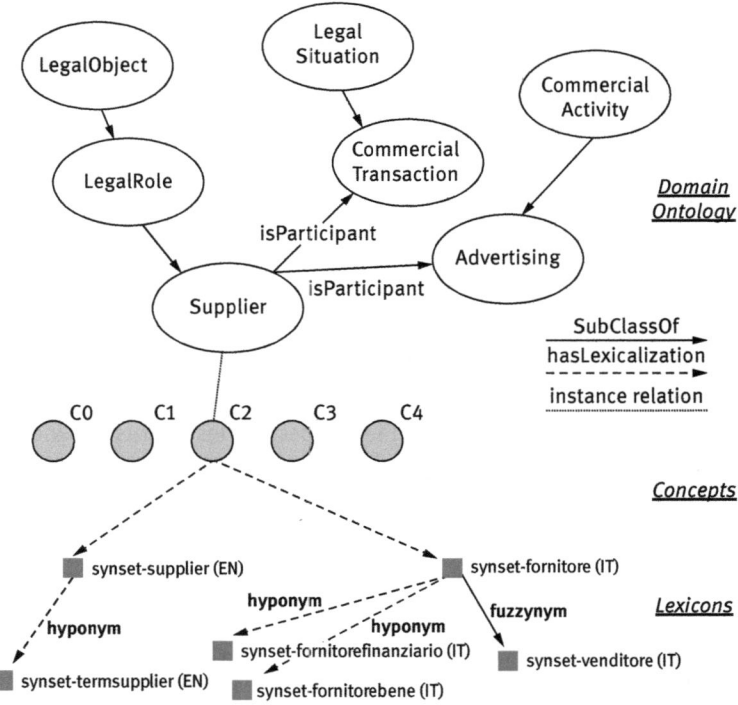

Figure 5.5: Extract of the DALOS Knowledge Base.

ontology. For example the concept object labelled as "C2" in the diagram is classified in the domain ontology as a "*Supplier*" and has two lexicalizations for two different languages. Thus, for each synset it is possible to list both its linguistic relations, typically WordNet relations, and its semantic relations with other synsets in the same or in a different lexicon. In fact, when applying the domain ontology, concepts assume new roles and particular properties that are valid only in the Consumer Protection semantic sphere.

5 Conclusion

Based on language and semantic technologies, research in knowledge acquisition and management made significant advancements in recent years towards its transformation into usable products (Ferrucci 2012). The achievement of a comparable goal in processing legal language still lags behind for a number of domain specific peculiarities and complexities outlined throughout this chapter. Yet, more and more domain specific resources, specialization of processing tools, reusable legal data and document corpora are being made available and the achievement of results of comparable precision and affordability of current general domain services can be expected within few years (Houlihan 2017).

Automated legal services based on legal data can have a significant impact on how users interact with the legal knowledge, being them legal professionals performing research on legal documents for justice or administrative tasks, or common citizens seeking a direct interaction with the system of rights, duties and procedures that regulate their relation with the State.

The use of language and semantic technologies, combined with traditional database search, is the mean to support tasks requiring improvement of legal information retrieval based on legal questions expressed in natural language, to assist legal professionals in their daily legal research duties by establishing nontrivial relations among documents based on their semantic content and legal context, to support language control in legal drafting for clarity, readability and unequivocal interpretation.

The theoretical framework and the technological and resource stack sketched throughout this chapter, highlight the levels of formal representation required and the need of different domain specializations of the processing tools and of the knowledge resources required to achieve such objective.

References

Agnoloni, Tommaso, Lorenzo Bacci, Enrico Francesconi, Wim Peters, Simonetta Montemagni & Giulia Venturi. 2009. A two-level knowledge approach to support multilingual legislative drafting. In Joost Breuker, Pompeu Casanovas, Michel C.A. Klein, Enrico Francesconi (eds.), *Law, ontologies and the semantic web: Channeling the legal information flood* (Frontiers in Artificial Intelligence and Applications, vol. 188), 177–198. Amsterdam: IOS Press.

Ajani, Gianmaria. 2007. Coherence of terminology and search functions. In *25 Years of European Law Online*, 129–136. Publications Office of the EC, Luxembourg.

Ananiadou, Sophia & John McNaught J. (eds.). 2006. *Text mining for biology and biomedicine*. London: Artech House.

Ashley, Kevin D. & Matthias Grabmair. 2015. *An introduction to artificial intelligence and law*. Tutorial at the 15th International Conference on Artificial Intelligence & Law ICAIL 2015, San Diego, June 8–12.

Attardi, Giuseppe & Felice Dell'Orletta. 2009. Reverse revision and linear tree combination for dependency parsing. In *Proceedings of NAACL-HLT 2009*, 61–64.

Attardi, Giuseppe, Maria Simi & Andrea Zanelli. 2013. Domain adaptation by active learning. In Magnini B., Cutugno F., Falcone M., Pianta E. (eds.), *Evaluation of natural language and speech tool for Italian* (LNCS-LNAI, vol. 7689), 77–85. Berlin/Heidelberg: Springer-Verlag.

Bacci, Lorenzo, Enrico Francesconi & Maria Teresa Sagri. 2013. A proposal for introducing the ECLI standard in the Italian judicial documentary system. In *Proceedings of the 26th International Conference on Legal Knowledge and Information Systems (JURIX 2013)*, 49–58. Amsterdam: IOS Press.

Bonin, Francesca, Felice Dell'Orletta, Giulia Venturi & Simonetta Montemagni. 2010a. A contrastive approach to multi-word term extraction from domain corpora. In *Proceedings of the 7th International Conference on Language Resources and Evaluation (LREC 2010)*, 3222–3229. La Valletta, Malta, 19–21 May.

Bonin, Francesca, Felice Dell'Orletta, Giulia Venturi, Simonetta Montemagni. 2010b. Singling out legal knowledge from world knowledge. An NLP-based approach. In *Proceedings of the 4th Workshop on Legal Ontologies and Artificial Intelligence Techniques (LOAIT 2010)*, 39–50. European University Institute, Fiesole, Florence, Italy, July 7.

Bosco, Cristina, Simonetta Montemagni, Alessandro Mazzei, Vincenzo Lombardo, Felice Dell'Orletta & Alessandro Lenci. 2009. *Evalita'09 parsing task: comparing dependency parsers and treebanks*. In *Proceedings of Evalita'09*.

Breuker, Joost & Rinke Hoekstra. 2004. Epistemology and ontology in core ontologies: FOLaw and LRI-Core, two core ontologies for law. In *Proceedings of the Workshop on Core Ontologies in Ontology Engineering (EKAW04)*, 15–27, Northamptonshire, UK.

Buitelaar, Paul, Philipp Cimiano & Bernardo Magnini. 2005. Ontology learning from text: an overview. In Paul Buitelaar et al. (eds.), *Ontology learning from text: methods, evaluation and applications* (Frontiers in Artificial Intelligence and Applications, volume 123), 3–12. Amsterdam: IOS Press.

Casellas, Nuria. 2011. *Legal ontology engineering: methodologies, modelling trends, and the ontology of professional judicial knowledge* (Law, Governance and Technology Series, vol. 3). Dordrecht: Springer.

Daumé, Hal, Tejaswini Deoskar, David McClosky, Barbara Plank & Jörg Tiedemann (eds.). 2010. *Proceedings of the workshop on Domain Adaptation for Natural Language Processing*, Uppsala, Sweden.

Dell'Orletta, Felice. 2009. Ensemble system for part-of-speech tagging. In *Proceedings of Evalita'09*.

Dell'Orletta, Felice, Simone Marchi, Simonetta Montemagni, Barbara Plank and Giulia Venturi. 2012. The SPLeT-2012 shared task on dependency parsing of legal texts. In *Proceedings of the Fourth Workshop on Semantic Processing of Legal Texts (SPLeT 2012)*, 42–51. Istanbul, 27 May.

Dell'Orletta, Felice, Simone Marchi, Simonetta Montemagni, Giulia Venturi, Tommaso Agnoloni & Enrico Francesconi. 2013. Domain adaptation for dependency parsing at Evalita 2011. In B. Magnini, F. Cutugno, M. Falcone, E. Pianta (eds.), *Evaluation of natural language and speech tool for Italian* (LNCS–LNAI, vol. 7689), 58–69. Berlin/Heidelberg: Springer-Verlag.

Dell'Orletta, Felice, Giulia Venturi, Andrea Cimino & Simonetta Montemagni. 2014. T2K^2: a system for automatically extracting and organizing knowledge from texts. In *Proceedings of 9th Edition* of *International Conference on Language Resources and Evaluation (LREC 2014)*, Reykjavik, Iceland, 26–31 May.

Dunning, Ted. 1993. Accurate methods for the statistics of surprise and coincidence. In *Computational Linguistics* 19(1). 61–74.

Fantoni, Gualtiero, Riccardo Apreda, Felice Dell'Orletta & Maurizio Monge. 2013. Automatic extraction of function-behaviour-state information from patents. *Advanced Engineering Informatics* 27 (3). 317–334.

Fellbaum, Christiane. 2005. WordNet and wordnets. In Brown, Keith et al. (eds.), *Encyclopedia of language and linguistics*, 2nd edn., 665–670. Oxford: Elsevier.

Ferrari, Alessio, Felice Dell'Orletta, Giorgio Oronzo Spagnolo & Stefania Gnesi. 2014. Measuring and improving the completeness of natural language requirements. In *Proceedings of the 20th International Working Conference on Requirements Engineering: Foundation for Software Quality (REFSQ 2014)*, 23–38.

Ferrucci, David A. 2012. Introduction to "This is Watson". *IBM Journal of Research and Development* 56(3.4).1.

Francesconi, Enrico, Simonetta Montemagni, Wim Peters & Daniela Tiscornia. 2010a. Integrating a bottom-up and top-down methodology for building semantic resources for the multilingual legal domain. In E. Francesconi, S. Montemagni, W. Peters, and D. Tiscornia (eds.), *Semantic processing of legal texts. Where the language of law meets the law of language* (Lecture Notes in Artificial Intelligence, volume 6036), 95–121. Berlin/Heidelberg: Springer-Verlag.

Francesconi, Enrico, Simonetta Montemagni, Wim Peters & Daniela Tiscornia. (eds.). 2010b. *Semantic processing of legal texts. Where the language of law meets the law of language* (Lecture Notes in Artificial Intelligence, volume 6036). Berlin/Heidelberg: Springer-Verlag.

Frantzi, Katerina & Sophia Ananiadou. 1999. The C-value / NC value domain independent method for multi-word term extraction. *Journal of Natural Language Processing* 6(3). 145–179.

Gangemi, Aldo, Maria Teresa Sagri & Daniela Tiscornia. 2005. A constructive framework for legal ontologies. In R. Benjamins, P. Casanovas, A. Gangemi, B. Selic (eds.), *Law and the semantic web* (LNCS, volume 3369), 97–124. Heidelberg: Springer.

Gangemi, Aldo, Nicola Guarino, Claudio Masolo, Alessandro Oltramari & Luc Schneider. 2002. Sweetening ontologies with dolce. In A. Gangemi, N. Guarino, C. Masolo, A. Oltramari, L. Schneider (eds.), *International Conference on Knowledge Engineering and Knowledge Management (EKAW 2002)*, (LNCS [LNAI], vol. 2473), 166–18. Heidelberg: Springer.

Gildea, Daniel. 2001. Corpus variation and parser performance. In *Proceedings of Empirical Methods in Natural Language Processing*, 167–202.

Giovannetti, Emiliano, Simone Marchi, Simonetta Montemagni & Roberto Bartolini. 2008. Ontology learning and semantic annotation: a necessary symbiosis. In *Proceedings of the 6th Edition of the International Conference on Language Resources and Evaluation, 28–30 May, Marrakech (LREC 2008)*, 2079–2085.

Hachey, Ben & Claire Grover. 2006. Extractive summarisation of legal texts. *Artificial Intelligence and Law* 14(4). 305–345.

Hoekstra, Rinke, Joost Breuker, Marcello Di Bello & Alexander Boer. 2009. LKIF Core: principled ontology development for the legal domain. In Joost Breuker, Pompeu Casanovas, Michel C.A. Klein, Enrico Francesconi (eds.), *Law, ontologies and the semantic web: channelling the legal information flood* (Frontiers in Artificial Intelligence and Applications, Volume 188), 75–94. Amsterdam: IOS Press.

Houlihan, David. 2017. *ROSS intelligence and artificial intelligence in legal research*. Bluehill Research Report Number A0280.

Kuhn, Florian. 2010. A description language for content zones of German court decisions. In *Proceedings of the Language Resources and Evaluation Conference (LREC2010), Workshop on Semantic Processing of Legal Texts (SPLeT 2010)*, 1–7, La Valletta, Malta.

Lame, Guiraude. 2005. Using NLP techniques to identify legal ontology components: concepts and relations. In Benjamins et al. (eds.) *Law and the semantic web. Legal ontologies, methodologies, legal information retrieval, and applications* (Lecture Notes in Computer Science, volume 3369), 169–184. Heidelberg: Springer.

Lehmann, Jos, Joost Breuke & Bob Brouwer. 2004. Causation in AI and Law. *Artificial Intelligence and Law* 12(4). 279–315.

Lenci, Alessandro, Simonetta Montemagni, Vito Pirrelli & Giulia Venturi. 2009. Ontology learning from Italian legal texts. In Joost Breuker, Pompeu Casanovas, Michel C.A. Klein, Enrico Francesconi (eds.), *Law, ontologies and the semantic web: channelling the legal information flood* (Frontiers in Artificial Intelligence and Applications, Volume 188), 75–94. Amsterdam: IOS Press.

Marinelli, Rita, Lisa Biagini, Remo Bindi, Sara Goggi, Monica Monachini, Paola Orsolini, Eugenio Picchi, Sergio Rossi, Nicoletta Calzolari & Antonio Zampolli. 2003. The Italian PAROLE corpus: an overview. In A. Zampolli et al. (eds.), *Computational linguistics in Pisa* (Special issue), XVI-XVII, Tomo I, 401–421. Pisa-Roma: IEPI.

Maxwell, Tamsin K., Jon Oberlander & Victor Lavrenko. 2009. Evaluation of semantic events for legal case retrieval. In *Proceedings of the Workshop on Exploiting Semantic Annotations in Information Retrieval (ESAIR 2009)*, 39–41, Barcelona, Spain.

Mazzei, Alessandro, Daniele P. Radicioni & Raffaella Brighi. 2009. NLP-based extraction of modificatory provisions semantics. In *Proceedings of the 12th International Conference on Artificial Intelligence and Law (ICAIL 2009)*, 50–57, Barcelona, Spain.

McCarty, Thorne L. 1977. Reflections on Taxman: An experiment in artificial intelligence and legal reasoning. *Harvard Law Review* 90. 837–893.

McCarty, Thorne L. 2007. Deep semantic interpretations of legal texts. In *Proceedings of the 11th international conference on Artificial intelligence and law (ICAIL2007)*, Stanford, California.

McCarty, Thorne L. 2009. Remarks on legal text processing: Parsing, semantics and information extraction. In *Proceedings of the Worskhop on Natural Language Engineering of Legal Argumentation (NaLEA2009)*, Barcelona, Spain.

McClosky, David & Eugene Charniak. 2008. Self-training for biomedical parsing. In *Proceedings of the Association for Computational Linguistics (ACL 2008)*, 101–104.

Mochales Palau, Raquel & Marie-Francine Moens. 2009. Argumentation mining: the detection, classification and structure of arguments in text. In *Proceedings of the 12th International Conference on Artificial Intelligence and Law (ICAIL 2009)*, 98–107, Barcelona, Spain.

Mortara Garavelli, Bice. 2001. *Le parole e la giustizia. Divagazioni grammaticali e retoriche su testi giuridici italiani* Torino: Einaudi.

Mommers, Laurens. 2002. *Applied legal epistemology. Building a knowledge-based ontology of the legal domain.* Leiden University Ph.D. thesis.

Nivre, Joakim. 2006. *Inductive dependency parsing.* Dordrecht: Springer.

Nivre, Joakim, Johan Hall, Sandra Kubler, Ryan McDonald, Jens Nilsson, Sebastian Riedel & Deniz Yuret. 2007. The CoNLL 2007 shared task on dependency parsing. In *Proceedings of the EMNLP-CoNLL 2007*, 915–932.

Peters, Wim, Maria Teresa Sagri & Daniela Tiscornia. 2007. The structuring of legal knowledge in LOIS. *Journal of Artificial Intelligence and Law* 15. 117–135.

Rissland, Edwina L. 1985. AI and legal reasoning. In *Proceedings of the International Joint Conference in Artificial Intelligence (IJCAI85)*, 1254–1260.

Sagri, Maria Teresa, Daniela Tiscornia, Simonetta Montemagni & Giulia Venturi. 2015. Neuroscienze e genetica comportamentale in un corpus di sentenze italiane alla luce dei risultati di elaborazioni linguistico-computazionali. In Nicola Lettieri and Sebastiano Faro (eds.) *Diritto, mente, cognizione*, 339–366.

Scarpelli, Uberto. 1976. La definizione nel diritto. In *Diritto e analisi del linguaggio*, 183–197. Milano: Edizioni di Comunità.
Smith, Barry, Michael Ashburner, Cornelius Rosse, Jonathan Bard, William Bug, Werner Ceusters, Louis J. Goldberg, Karen Eilbeck, Amelia Ireland, Christopher J. Mungall, Neocles Leontis, Philippe Rocca-Serra, Alan Ruttenberg, Susanna Assunta Sansone, Richard H. Scheuermann, Nigam Shah, Patricia L. Whetzel & Suzanna Lewis. 2007. The OBO Foundry: coordinated evolution of ontologies to support biomedical data integration. *Nature Biotechnology* 25. 1251–1255.
Spinosa, Pierluigi L., Gerardo Giardiello, Manola Cherubini, Simone Marchi, Giulia Venturi & Simonetta Montemagni. 2009. NLP-based metadata extraction for legal text consolidation. In *Proceedings of the 12th International Conference on Artificial Intelligence and Law (ICAIL 2009)*, 40–49, Barcelona, Spain.
Studer, Rudi, Richard V. Benjamins & Dieter Fensel. 1998. Knowledge engineering: Principles and methods. *Data Knowledge Engineering* 25(1–2). 161–197.
Thompson, Paul, John McNaught, Simonetta Montemagni, Nicoletta Calzolari, Riccardo del Gratta, Vivian Lee, Simone Marchi, Monica Monachini, Piotr Pezik, Valeria Quochi, CJ Rupp, Yutaka Sasaki, Giulia Venturi, Dietrich Rebholz-Schuhmann & Sophia Ananiadou. 2011. The BioLexicon: a large-scale terminological resource for biomedical text mining. *BMC Bioinformatics* 12(1). 397.
Tiscornia, Daniela & Maria Teresa Sagri. 2003. Metadata for content description in legal information. In *Proceedings of LegOnt Workshop on Legal Ontologies*, 2003.
Valente, André & Joost Breuker. 1994. A functional ontology of law. *Artificial Intelligence and Law* 7. 341–361.
Walter, Stephan. 2009. Definition extraction from court decisions using computational linguistic technology. In G. Grewendorf and M. Rathert (eds.), *Formal linguistics and law*, 183–224. Berlin: Mouton de Gruyter.
Walter, Stephan & Manfred Pinkal. 2009. Definitions in court decisions: automatic extraction and ontology acquisition. In J. Breuker, P. Casanovas, M.C.A. Klein, E. Francesconi (eds.), *Law, ontologies and the semantic web. Channeling the legal information flood* (Frontiers in Artificial Intelligence and Applications, volume 188), 95–113. Amsterdam: IOS Press.
Wyner, Adam & Tom van Engers. 2009. From argument in natural language to formalised argumentation: components, prospects and problems. In *Proceedings of the Workshop on Natural Language Engineering of Legal Argumentation (NaLEA2009)*, Barcelona, Spain.
Wyner, Adam. 2010. Towards annotating and extracting textual legal case elements. In *Proceedings of the IV Workshop on Legal Ontologies and Artificial Intelligence Techniques (LOAIT 2010)*, Fiesole, Italia, 9–18.
Wyner, Adam & Wim Peters. 2010. Lexical semantics and expert legal knowledge towards the identification of legal case factors. In *Proceedings of Legal Knowledge and Information Systems (JURIX) Conference*, 127–136. Liverpool, United Kingdom: IOS Press.

Part II: Forensic linguistics and court setting

Barbara Pasa and Lucia Morra
6 Implicit legal norms

1 Introduction

This chapter aims to provide further insight into implicit legal norms, building on previous studies on "cryptotypes" (Sacco 1980, 1989) on the one hand, and on "implicatures" (Grice 1975) on the other. In its background lies the idea that law is a socially valuable practice of regulation in a given time and place, a practice that reflects the variability of socio-legal conditions (Cotterrell 2015: 51): in such a practice, what counts in defining what is legal are particular social settings, namely the context. Endorsing this perspective allows seeing that different types of implicit legal norms serve the *prudentia* (carefulness) of jurists in different ways, their juristic experience in all its practical complexity, ethical ambiguity and contextual specificity. What should be understood in practice and in a particular time and place by the idea of law may be of special interest to judges and lawyers: as interpreters of the law, they are involved in a peculiar *inter-action* with the legislature and cannot ignore the fact that a legal text will imply more than it says. Legal communication, indeed, goes well beyond written texts or spoken words and extends to images, rituals, feelings and public performances as modes of human interpretation (Wagner and Sherwin 2014; Boehme-Neßler 2011). Furthermore, performance of an action, or of a duty, is normative in itself (Sacco 1995, 2015): hence, non-text law has a normative dimension (Sacco 1980; Kasirer 2003; Thompson 1993). In this perspective, the chapter analyses two cases of gender discrimination: the text of some Articles of the Italian Civil Code, Book I, on marriage and a well-known judgment of the Constitutional Court relying on the implicit assumption that *marriage* is essentially linked to a heterosexual paradigm as enshrined in the Italian Constitution; and the Californian Family Code that was amended in order to reject the implicit premise on which it relied, namely the idea of a *parent and child relationship* that can be instantiated by no more than two persons. From a methodological point of view, this analysis combines a functionalist approach, which emphasises law-as-rules, with a pure-hermeneutic-approach in which rules and concepts are merely the signifiers of a much deeper *mentalité* (cognitive structures that support and anchor positive law), so that it may be elsewhere than in legal texts that one may find the meaning of law. Such a combinatorial approach presupposes pluralising legal epistemology: it involves a shift from a single disciplinary focus on the law to a trans-disciplinary orientation.

2 Implicit dimension in law

Law contributes to the constitution of social facts by providing cognitive frames through which individuals apprehend social realities. At the same time, law is in itself an institutional fact, that is to say legal actors operate within an interpretative practice that the legal community created (Bell 1983). Law and society are aspects of a single reality. Thus, we are no longer tied to the conventional idea of law as an artefact of State power. Law is not only what law officials do and say they are doing, but it is also a reflection of social values, educational conditioning, ideology and economics (Twining 1997, 2005).

Such a premise means, among other things, that law is not only about the content of detailed legal rules and the structures and concepts used by doctrine and legal actors, but also about other implicit sources, foundational principles and values, assumptions underpinning them, and about the interaction of socio-economic and political values with the idea of law itself.[1] Discovering and engaging with legal rules, and more generally with the law as a whole, is an interpretative practice.

Interpretation is an "embedded and embodied practice by which interpreters recognise the contingency and plurality of law" (MacDonald 1986, 2000; McDonald and MacLean 2005: 725; Kleinhaus and MacDonald 1997; Sidnell 2003; Falk Moore 1978). Legal interpretative activity, in particular, is a relational and social practice that involves cognitive elements, some related to personal beliefs (MacDonald 1992: 61). Through an open-ended exploration of the multiple sites of normativity and of the multiple forms of legal communication we can understand law better. Roderick MacDonald called this approach *plurijuralism*. In the same vein, according to Rodolfo Sacco's theory of *legal formants* (Sacco 1980, 1991),[2] legal rules found in written constitutions, ordinary laws, court adjudications, and in non-text law in general (customs, for example) are composed, on the one hand, of formulated normative beliefs, and on the other, of unformulated assumptions. Close to these views, Brian Tamanaha coined a non-essentialist definition of law: "law is whatever people identify and treat through their social practice as law" (Tamanaha 2000: 296) and Ugo Mattei intended "law as a constantly negotiated process of making cultural connections (…) which captures the complex relationship among parts (individuals, duties, rights, powers) and the whole (law)" (Mattei and Capra 2015: 132). The interpretative practice by which interpreters recognize the plurality of law includes "both the process of devising and designing the law, and the process of decoding the law" (MacDonald and MacLean 2005: 757). To understand the phenomenon of law, we must then address the issue of multiple forms of communication within the legal sphere, forms which involve various social ordering situations (such as adjudication, legislation, and party autonomy), various actors (individuals, collective agents), and various modes of justification (such as legal rules, precedents, customary practices, authority,

---

[1] So the question is neither structural (what comprises law?), nor functional (what is law good for?), nor ontological (what is law?). The fundamental epistemological issue is that looking at the methods employed in legal reasoning brings to our attention a set of subjects distinct from traditional subjects in comparative research: not only rules, norms and functions, but also many different legal actors: legislators, judges, practitioners as lawyers or continental notaries, academics etc and individuals as final recipients too.

[2] His seminal work (Sacco 1980) is in Italian: *Introduzione al diritto comparato*.

and equity).³ Moreover, legal communication mediated through texts not produced by judges or legislators (such as stories, letters, posters, or websites) is just as important, if not more so, in contributing to constituting law – all these texts are interpretative sites in law. The same claim can be made about oral legal communication (i.e. trial practice, appellate pleading, public presentations to parliamentary committees or to corporate boards, client interviews, press conferences, and conversation with legal content).

The sense of the words in a legal message is bound up with and constitutive of the matrix of social relations through which they are generated and read (Grossi 2013: 27): all interpretation involves then practices that are inseparable from our embedded experience as social beings. Inquiring on these connections raises questions about the implicit normative dimension that permeates law, and induces a search of the implicit meanings hidden beneath the language that the law today is mainly expressed through. The research questions are whether it is possible to identify tacit rules that underlie and control social life in different legal communities and whether it is possible to understand how much they interfere with legal interpretation (Morra and Pasa 2015; Pasa 2015). It may be useful, if not necessary, to reveal patterns which are implicit but which have outward effects.

3 Cryptotypes and implicits in law: past and present

The *cryptotype* (a term imported from linguistics into law by Sacco) is the underlying pattern to be revealed, or made visible by logical or non-logical inferences from an explicit rule. A cryptotype amounts to a legal formant without an explicit linguistic formulation (Sacco 1991). The discovery of a cryptotype is facilitated when, as happens, a legal rule, a concept, or a principle implicit in one legal system is explicit in another legal system. Normally, jurists belonging to a given system find greater difficulty in freeing themselves from the cryptotypes of their system than in abandoning the rules of which they are fully aware. For some scholars, the subjection to cryptotypes constitutes the mentality of the jurist of a given country at a given time, and such differences in mentality are the greatest obstacle to mutual understanding between legal actors of different legal systems (Legrand 1999). We should thus try to unveil cryptotypes to foster better understanding of differences and similarities in a globalised world. Cryptotypes, however, are difficult to identify (Sacco 1991). Although a cryptotype can be intended as a part of the mentality, it does not coincide with it. Individuals often follow rules which they are not aware of, or which they would not be able to articulate

---

3 With some major differences: while, for instance, the judiciary shares a habitus which has its roots in the professional culture developed over generations, reflecting the legal knowledge of a certain place in a given time, the legislature has no reference community: the legislature has to translate contingent political, economic and social programs into textual propositions.

or explain. For instance, few would be able to formulate the language rule we follow when we say "three dark suits" and not "three suits dark" (Sacco 1991). Individuals often operate on the basis of a "sense of what would be morally wrong or right, or even illegal or legal", even in the absence of knowledge of the relevant rules or laws, and without being able to conceptualise what would be wrong about the relevant course of action. They can have "a feeling of entering forbidden territory without having a conception of the boundaries of that territory" (Schmitz 2013: 117).

Nonconceptual forms of intentionality and normativity, senses and feelings of what is familiar or unfamiliar, appropriate or inappropriate, right or wrong, have a social dimension and this means they may partially embody the identity of a group and its institutions, communal practices, and ways of living. They can express the shared background of a group because (and to the extent that) the background skills, tendencies, and habits that they display have been introduced and established in the joint interactions of the group.[4]

Implicit patterns played a fundamental role in the law of so-called "primitive societies[5]": where the law was unformulated, sources were implicit, acts were unspoken and the dichotomy between law and enforcement did not exist. The law was performed through acts accepted by others (Sacco 1995: 455): that was *mute law*.[6] Unacceptable acts immediately triggered reactions and measures taken for self-protection. Thus, performing acts and ceremonies, such as those for appropriation of land or for marriage, constituted the law: adherence to a rule was manifested by the spontaneous conduct of the members of the group. Although a major legal revolution took place when descendants of *Homo*

---

[4] The crucial point is that having a sense that something is right or wrong, legal or illegal, familiar or unfamiliar, is different from having the corresponding concepts or beliefs ("background assumptions" in the language of Searle), which are both unconscious and nonintentional, mental and physiological, more precisely neurophysiological: see Schmitz (2013). "Background assumptions" are those dispositions that become manifest in mental events and that are not themselves intentional states see Searle (1995: 133, 145). They produce behavior that is generally consonant with the rules, but they are entirely physiological.

[5] And still today within the so-called "Chthonic legal tradition": cf. Glenn (2010).

[6] Legal anthropology has traced back the origins of the basic structures of law far beyond the recent past covered by conventional legal history. The new historical perspective is *Macro-History*. The law of the fifth millennium B.C. was not the same as that in force 50,000 years before. The development of magical arts was a vital force of unprecedented vigor, able to produce radical innovations. Magic rituals made it possible to establish facts: ordeals were (and still are in the Chthonic tradition) the last in a long line of methods of proof with connections to the supernatural, to identify the person against whom the community had to proceed, and to find remedies to cure social noncompliance. Magic rituals were used to reinstate property owners, since magic spells were believed to be able to make objects deter misappropriations. Nobody has been able to establish the date of creation of magic, nor when it began to rule human beings' lives. We assume that it started to play a larger role as man transitioned from Inferior Paleolithic to Superior Paleolithic, but we do not know for certain. Nonetheless law existed even before magic, if we assume that law provides a means to prevent and solve conflicts throughout society. Wherever we find a society, we find law: cf. Sacco (2007).

Habilis began to use language, and a second disruptive revolution happened in the nineteenth century with the doctrine of the declaration of intent, unspoken acts and implicit sources continue to operate today. The law seems to have become a theoretical exercise, but social order and performance always have a practical dimension. Thus the recognition and study of such a practice and its (latent and pervasive) implicit normativity is an important area in current scholarship (Sacco 2015, 1980; Morra and Pasa 2015; Visconti 2010; Caterina 2012, 2009; Di Lucia 2009; Fiori 2009; Francavilla 2009; Graziadei 2009).

For example we occupy, we own, we abandon things,[7] or we follow certain uses and customary rules. We cannot deny that customary law is still a source of law in contemporary legal orders: a custom is grounded on instinctive behaviours infinitely stronger, in terms of persuasive power, than a group of legal scholars combined with a set of legal precedents. Since factual situations do not precede duties and rights, nor create them (e.g., while I am performing an act, I am observing a rule not yet in existence, but since the rule is not yet in existence, it cannot yet legitimate the conforming behavior, Sacco 1995), performance of an act, acquiescence, and respect for another's individuality are self-justifying. Only when cryptotypes are explicitly verbalised, are duties and rights clearly perceived as rules (and then we know we are exercising a right, or performing a duty) and passed on from one generation of jurists to another *as rules*. But how can cryptotypes be brought to the surface?

The tools of pragmatics offer a method.[8] When applied to key contemporary legal texts, such as statutes and judicial decisions, they bring to the surface not only implicit

---

7 As Sacco (1995) suggested, for example, jurists do not like to admit that the purpose of the law of property is possession; that the concept of ownership has been created to safeguard what individuals possess (by means of imposing exclusionary obligations on others); that those who claim ownership of property invoke the logical medium of possession; that the focal point of the law is ultimately possession, and not ownership.

8 Here we can only drop a hint to the discussed concept of "defeasibility" and to the related topic of "defeasible inferences" – pragmatic inferences within legal reasoning are typically defeasible "soft defeasibility thesis" (Alchourrón 2012). Cf. Ferrer Beltrán (2012); cf. also García Figueroa (2009); García-Yzaguirre (2012); recently Marmor (2016); Macagno, Walton and Tindale (2017).

If (Alchourrón 2012) we consider legal defeasibility as an "essential feature of law" (Sartor 2012), because every formal assiomatic system is incomplete and inconsistent, or in other words, undetermined and vague (Endicott 2001; 2014) then defeasible reasoning cannot be intended anymore as defective, or inadequate, but it must be considered as a "natural way in which an agent can cope with a complex and changing environment" (Sartor 2012: 116). Conversely, Guastini understands defeasibility as a consequence of the "act of interpretation" (Guastini 2012: 182). He describes a defeasible norm as a norm susceptible to implicit exceptions, which cannot be explicitly stated in advance; this in turn means that it is impossible to delimit circumstances that would represent genuine sufficient conditions for its use. For the author "literal interpretation is still interpretation" (Guastini 2012: 188), so there cannot be any neutral or value-free interpretation. He distinguishes then implicit norms in the strict sense, positive although unexpressed (because the interpreter can infer them from expressed rules), from implicit norms in a broad sense, the outcome of a creative activity in gap-filling by the interpreter: see (Guastini 2014, 2010).

beliefs, but specific cryptotypes: those habits, background skills, feelings and social practices and rules of conduct that people follow within groups, that ultimately guide the actions of the members of a community. When applied to legal texts, pragmatics tools unveil the connections between what lies outside the text and what is inside it: the tacit normative dimension is connected to the legal text through the halo of implicit meaning that intersects the "living law" where the legal text suggests, implies, or alludes. "The living law" Ehrlich wrote, is "the law which dominates life itself even though it has not been posited in legal propositions (…)" (Ehrlich 1913: 493), and the courts' concern about living law is becoming apparent.[9] The outside/inside perspectives being permeable,[10] the implicit halo of legal texts is in fact one of the major vehicles through which both social and personal beliefs and values contribute to legal interpretation, in shaping the meaning legal texts have in a given context of adjudication.

As for any text, also for legal texts (whether statutes, decrees or judicial decisions) elaborating this implicit halo proves necessary in interpretation, and calls for knowledge and values to be retrieved outside those expressed by both the literal surface of the text and the conceptual background shared by the legal community the text belongs to. Precisely, some regulative standards for argumentation elaborated by Marina Sbisà in the light of the Gricean theory (next §§), provide us with normative means (e.g. able to support the rational inferential path of a certain kind) for monitoring the text comprehension (what she calls "calculability of conversational implicature").

4 Unveiling implicit norms: the tools of pragmatics

As two examples will show (§§ 6.1 and 6.2), some implicit norms that silently rule the actions of a community may in fact be unveiled applying Paul Grice's theory of conversation (Grice 1975: 41–58) to legal texts.

---

9 Cf., for instance, the order no. 4701 of the *Tribunale dei minorenni di Bologna* (Bologna Juvenile Court), 10 November 2014, in which the court interpreted legal rules according to "the living law": it was a second parent adoption case, in which the mother of a child conceived by means of artificial insemination consented to the adoption of the daughter by her lesbian partner (they got married in the United States). Available at http://www.articolo29.it/wp-content/uploads/2014/11/14_11_10-Trib-minori-Bo-Ord-134-Cost.pdf (accessed 7 July 2017). The most relevant participant in the making of the Italian actual "living law" is the *Sezioni Unite della Corte di Cassazione* (the Supreme Court when it sits in Joined Chambers), as it has been recognized by the Constitutional Court in the decision of 11 February 2015, n. 11; confirmed by the *Cassazione* (Italian Supreme Court), 22 February 2016, n. 3376; and 13 May 2010, n. 18288. Cf. Salvaneschi (2016); Evangelista and Canzio (2005); Canzio (2008).
10 A different opinion is sustained by textualists: according to Justice Scalia: "legislation is a speech act and act of communication whereby the legislature by voting on a bill communicate a certain legal content, and that legal content is the content of the statutory law". Cf. Scalia and Garner (2012), and also Marmor (2014).

In Grice's perspective, speakers engaged in a verbal interaction may assume their exchange as ruled by expectations and restrictions for verbal production and interpretation that each party will respect and use to enrich the meaning of its utterances and to understand communicated content. On the background of these rules (or maxims),[11] the implicit meaning of the texts speakers produce may be rationally retrieved and analysed.

In order to understand how such a structure of mutual expectations is instantiated in the communicative exchange between the legislature and its recipients, differences between natural and legal communication have been analysed (Sinclair 1985; Miller 1990; Chiassoni 1999; Walton 2002; Marmor 2005, 2011, 2014; Neale 2007; Soames 2009, 2011, 2013; Poggi 2011; Morra 2011, 2015b; Carston 2013; Endicott 2014). In the first place, the time that elapses between the "utterance" of the legislature's proposition and its interpretations by recipients (courts, practitioners, public officials, academics, and citizens) provides legal language with a (descriptively challenging) trans-contextual character that suggests to consider the exchange between the legislature and the courts as a monologue formed by two principal independent agents, the legislature and the judicial authorities (Shaer 2013).[12] Some scholars have also pointed out that the legislature and the judiciary make a strategic, rather than cooperative, use of language (Marmor 2005, 2011, 2014).[13] Furthermore, the plurality of recipients makes it unclear who the parties to the conversation are; and, finally, the legislature's intention is not merely informative, but also normative: its communicative goal is to inform the audience of its normative intention so that citizens are provided with reasons for obeying the enacted laws.[14]

---

[11] The maxims in which Grice articulated his principle of cooperation are presumptions about utterances that listeners rely on and speakers use in communication. In cooperative exchanges of information, Grice argued, parties to conversation are guided by expectations of informativeness, truthfulness, relevance, and manner of the utterance they process. Grice treated "these rules not as arbitrary conventions, but as instances of more general rules governing rational, cooperative behavior". Cf. Davis (2014). Poggi (2011: 27) defines maxims as "formulations of customary hermeneutic, technical rules. According to von Wright's classification, technical rules (or directives) indicate a means to reach a certain goal, aiming not at directing the will of the receivers, but at indicating to them that their will is conditioned: in other words, that if they want to reach a certain goal, then they must maintain certain behavior".
[12] Amongst them, Ronald Dworkin, William Eskridge and Justice Antonin Scalia. Mark Greenberg advanced a radical position in Greenberg (2011). Marmor faced Greenberg's issues in Marmor (2014: 11–20).
[13] A thesis Marmor maintained in all his works. The view is endorsed with *distinguo* by Poggi (2011) and by Skoczeń (2015).
[14] Sometimes the legislature's inability to be (more) informative as regards specific behaviors or realities may be due to the unpredictability of the facts of specific cases that will be decided by the judges. But sometimes the legislature, although perfectly able to be maximally informative and to enact complex regulations in a specific domain, refrains from doing so, especially when detailed regulations could lead to controversial effects and it seems more reasonable to introduce vague concepts leaving the courts an amount of discretion and enabling them to decide on a case by case basis.

The set of these features makes the communicative exchange between the legislature and the judiciary very different from ordinary conversations, and yet it cannot be denied that also the parties to this peculiar kind of speech act linguistically do interact with a minimal common aim: the effectiveness of the legal order in which they operate, enacting laws and applying a plurality of sources. This means that a peculiar kind of co-operation holds even in their conversation,[15] although different from the principle that Grice exemplified for ordinary and collaborative conversation (Morra 2015b, 2016b; Morra and Pasa 2015).

A further *caveat* is necessary: analysing legal texts through a Gricean approach does not presuppose the endorsement of a particular theory of legal interpretation. It is a neutral practice that, *per se*, does not support any specific perspective on the relationship between the legislature and the courts (Morra 2016b). Detecting in a rational way the nuances of implicit meanings surrounding legal texts cannot (and should not) be considered as a method for solving interpretive problems that may arise in adjudication.[16] In fact, the Gricean approach considers the maxims of conversation in force in a communicative exchange as conducive to different and possibly conflicting *implicatures* when applied to the same portion of text; and in fact, rather than giving guidance for retrieving *the* implicit meaning of a text, Grice's theory aimed at providing tools for rationally motivating the meaning chosen from among a text's possible *implicata*. So, when applied to statutes, a Gricean approach cannot lead to univocal solutions when specific cases reveal the existence of an informative gap in a statute: it may only rationalise the interpretative options the text offers. Furthermore, when it is applied to judicial decisions, such an approach makes some implicit aspects of the architecture of legal reasoning detectable. It is precisely in this vein that some legal scholars have adopted it (Sinclair 1985; Miller 1990; Walton 2002).

5 Presuppositions and implicatures in legal texts

The normative variant of Gricean theory developed by Marina Sbisà (Sbisà 2007, 2015) appears particularly suited for analysing normative texts and their interpretations,

---

15 "In legislation, if cooperation breaks down, the rule of law breaks down. And the separation of powers between legislature and court depends on adherence by the courts to legal analogues of the conversational maxims." Cf. Endicott (2014: 8).
16 The form of Gricean approach here endorsed shares with textualism the idea that relevant communications are understood as they "would be grasped by a reasonable hearer aware of the legal and other background conditions of legislation" (Marmor 2014: 116–117); however it differs from a textualist approach in several crucial respects, first and foremost in its belief that, although implicatures depend also on the exact wording of the statute, many other factors beyond linguistic competence are relevant in deciding whether their inference is warranted in the particular context of interpretation (Morra 2015b; Morra and Pasa 2015; Moreso and Chilovi 2015).

and for extracting the implicit norms they are linked to. While the focus of Grice's theory was mainly on the speaker's communicative intention, in Sbisà's approach the emphasis is shifted onto the communicative intention of the text. Attributing a communicative agency [the capacity to act] to the text not only downscales the problem of the opacity of the communicative intention of the speaker (*speaker* referring in most contemporary Western legal orders to the legislature); it means that presuppositions and implicatures can be considered as additional information that interpreters must and may, respectively, retrieve in the text.

Presuppositions[17] are additional pieces of information suggested by lexical elements and syntactical constructions of a text: they are statements that are unexpressed but whose truth, nevertheless, must be assumed by interpreters when they accept as appropriate the utterance of the text. Holding a presupposition of a text as true is an interpretative restriction accepted by interpreters engaged in a communicative enterprise in which raising doubts about the status of the information given by the text would be inappropriate; in such circumstances, interpreters are likely to take into account the content of the presupposition without objection.

Implicatures, on the other hand, are pieces of information suggested by a text that enrich it without impacting on its truth value. While a conventional implicature is suggested by the use of a certain expression instead of another logically equivalent one, a conversational implicature can be inferred from the way in which a text is structured together with the assumption that it was produced in the specific context as a contribution fit for the purposes of the conversation in which the participants agreed to engage. When the inference is rationally motivated through argumentation, the piece of information vehicled by the implicature can plausibly be considered as part of what a text communicated when it was produced. In enacting a statute, members of the collective agency known as *the legislature* acknowledge that its formulation will express not only the implicatures they meant when they drafted it, but the implicatures the text will plausibly suggest in any context of interpretation (which they cannot know *a priori*); interpreters, for their

---

17 There is also a technical legal meaning of the term *presupposition*, which dates back to Windscheid and his writings (1892: 161, 201). The doctrine of tacit presupposition refers to contract law, with the aim of restricting the will of the contractual parties. The intention of a person is always related to a certain given set of facts; it has been formed on the basis of certain suppositions: if these suppositions are wrong, it is not always fair to hold that person to her words. On the other side, there is the community's interest in the certainty and predictability of the law. Thus, according to the doctrine of presupposition, the parties' expectations become an element of the contract as long as they formed a part of the contractual intention ("I want but I would not want if not" said Windscheid): in the case of non-fulfilment of the contract, these expectations are frustrated and the party has the *exceptio doli* to reclaim what she had given to the other party in order to perform the contractual obligation. Cf. Their (2011: 29). In our paper only *linguistic* presuppositions will be considered, namely presuppositions inferable from the text and its utterance.

part, accept the text as a container, a casing for their interpretations shaped by a multiplicity of varying contextual factors (Morra 2015b).

When used in textual analysis of statutes and judicial decisions, Sbisà's analytic tools prove useful for identifying characteristics, functions and uses of the implicit information that these texts convey (Morra 2011, 2015a, 2015b, 2016b; Morra and Pasa 2015; Sbisà 2015; Bairati 2015; Cassone 2015; Long 2015). Distinguishing what legal texts say, presuppose or suggest from what they do not communicate promotes awareness of the functions carried out by the different shades of implicit information surrounding them. Further, it makes it possible to justify the attribution of implicit meaning to these texts, linking the inference to a specific part of them; using argumentation and reasoning, interpreters may specify why they support one interpretative option instead of another one, making that attribution of meaning transparent and reasoned (Pasa 2015: 63). The tools of pragmatics applied to legal texts show how the implicit sense surrounding these texts modulates their applicability, and make transparent the reasoning that led the courts to attribute one implicit meaning instead of another possible one, according to rational criteria.

6 Implicit norms in gender issue: two examples

Connecting the *outside* to the *inside* dimension of law through a transparent and reasoned attribution of meanings proves particularly urgent when legal texts affect sensitive social issues. This is the case of *gender issues*.[18] As two examples will show, the awareness of what a cryptotype is in Sacco's terms, combined with the *normative* variant of Gricean theory developed by Sbisà for analysing legal texts, contributes to the emersion of traditional paradigms linked both to the social-symbolic organisation

---

18 By this expression, scholars of different disciplines usually refer to a plurality of questions. With regard to gender identity, many aspects are socially constructed, precisely how individuals perceive themselves as male or female or both or neither (one's internal sense of self). Gender expression is also socially constructed: one's outward presentation and behaviours are related to the set of roles and expectations assigned to males and females by the community. Finally gender roles do not imply any specific sexual orientation. Individuals whose gender identity does not match their assigned birth gender are called transgender. Being trans does not imply any specific sexual orientation, i.e. any attraction to people of a specific gender. When biological sex, gender identity and gender expression align, there is a level of congruence with the world around the individuals to the point that they feel part of the norm (they are also called gender-normative). The term *cisgender* usually refers to people whose sex assignment at birth corresponds to their gender identity and expression. The point here is that social privileges and their legitimization through law come from the assumption that the cisgender perspective is congruent and universal, not exceptional like the perspective of the transgender, agender, etc.

of sexuality and to our biological urge to reproduce and become parents, and makes the evolution of those paradigms detectable (Harding 2010; Pezzini 2012; Morra and Pasa 2015).

The first example concerns the *possibility for same-sex couples to get married* under Italian law after Constitutional Court judgment no. 138/2010 and after the enactment of Act no. 76/2016. The second example focuses on the question of what *parenthood* meant under the Family Code of California before and after an amendment enacted in 2014. In both examples, deliberately chosen to represent civil as well as common law systems, the questions raised by gender issues proved to be crucial in unveiling *cryptotypes* that covertly and/or unconsciously (*implicitly*) *drive* legal interpretative practice.

6.1 "Marriage" of same-sex couples and "two mothers" or "two fathers" in Italian law

The first example concerns the implicit norms relating to the heterosexuality of the couple in the text of the Italian Civil Code (hereinafter CC), Book I, on marriage (Morra 2011; Bairati 2015; Lorusso 2015).

Although most of the articles of the CC refer to those who want to marry, or those who have already married with gender-neutral expressions such as *spouse*, a few articles use the words *husband* and *wife* (Articles 107, 108, 143, 143bis, 143 ter 156 bis Italian CC). In particular, Article 107 CC, concerning the form of the marriage ceremony, considered as pivotal for interpretation, states that: "The registrar (*ufficiale dello stato civile*) declares the parties married only after each of them has declared their intention to take the other to be his/her wife/husband." The literal, or ordinary meaning of the words *husband* and *wife* is connected to the physical structure of reproductive organs used to assign sex at birth. Since nothing in the Civil Code indicates that *husband* and *wife* must be understood differently, that Y is a male is a condition for the effectiveness of the declaration of X, and vice versa: both statements are presuppositions underlying the text of Article 107 CC. The declaration of the registrar subsequent to both X's and Y's declarations presupposes those conditions (*X is a female* and *Y is a male*) have been satisfied, thus implying that the registrar can marry only individuals of the opposite sex.

The further question then arises as to whether the presupposition underlying Article 107 CC extends to all the other CC Articles on marriage that do not use the gender-specific words *husband* and *wife*. This seems logical, because if only couples consisting of a male and a female may make the declarations required by Article 107 CC, then, as a consequence, people of the same sex cannot marry. However, interpreters can apply this reasoning only after having activated an implicature with the purpose of preventing the incoherence and non-cohesion of the whole text on marriage contained in the CC. Since they can presume that Book I of the CC is a coherent text in which terms and their lexical analogues are used with a consistent meaning, in order to preserve this coherence and consistency they can assume that the specific meaning of *spouses* conveyed by the text of Article 107 CC [a heterosexual couple] modifies the gender-neutral meaning the term has in most Articles of Book I of the CC on marriage [a couple]. Namely, they activate a specific implicature I_1 (the presupposition peculiar to Article 107 CC that the couple must be composed of a *male* and *female* is *transferred to all the Articles* of the Book I of the CC), and this activation implies that marriage is open only to heterosexual couples. Implicature I_1 – which reflects the communicative intention with which the legislature enacted the rules on marriage in 1942 – had been activated by all recipients until same-sex couples challenged the *status quo* asking for admission to marriage. When these couples raised such a question before the Italian courts, judges could have retrieved another implicature in order to both preserved the coherence of the whole Civil Code's text on marriage and opened marriage to same-sex couples, namely implicature I_2 (the gender-neutral meaning of the terms *spouses* and *married couple* used in most Articles of the CC *broadens the specific meaning* the terms have in Articles 107 CC, 108, 143, 143bis, 143 ter and 156 bis). This inference is mainly grounded on the fact that, when the Italian legislature enacted the Civil Code containing the rules on marriage, same-sex couples were not included in the list of couples that cannot marry according to Article 87 CC – that is, those couples formed by individuals related by blood (ascendants and descendants in direct line), full or half siblings and persons connected by affinity in a direct line, or by adoption.

When required to evaluate whether the text of the Civil Code allows homosexual couples to marry, however, Italian courts always decided that it does not. They generally considered that, although the CC does not say explicitly that only couples formed by one male and one female can marry, it nevertheless gives sufficient indications to retrieve this piece of information and recognize it as an essential presupposition of the institution of marriage, a *core norm* extrapolated from Articles 107 CC, 108, 143, 143bis 143 ter and 156 bis that cannot be erased *via* interpretation. In conclusion, Italian trial courts held that the gender-neutral meaning of *spouse* and *married couple* could not have been extended to the whole Book I of the CC on marriage by substituting the terms *wife* and *husband* with gender-neutral words not related to biological sex (such as *spouse*) in the Articles with gender-specific terms.[19]

Dissatisfied with such a solution that did not recognise to same-sex couples rights and duties, some judges raised the question of constitutional validity of Articles 107, 108, 143, 143bis, 143 ter and 156bis CC that they had to apply to the case before them.[20]

---

19 As was proposed by some parts, and as was done, for example, in Spain in 2005: *Ley 13/2005, de 1 de julio, por la que se modifica el Código Civil en materia de derecho a contraer matrimonio, Boletín Oficial del Estado (BOE)*, no. 157, 2 July 2005, pp. 23632–23634.
20 On the peculiarities of the Italian Constitutional Court and its adjudication process, in English, see Barsotti et al. (2016).

When asked to consider the incompatibility of these Articles with the Constitution, the Constitutional Court, in its judgment no. 138/2010, declared the question of constitutional legitimacy manifestly unfounded and refused to rule upon the constitutionality of the challenged Articles, holding that its gap-filling activity would have redesigned the *core of those provisions*, a prerogative pertaining only to the legislature.[21] Although conservative,[22] the Court's interpretation unveiled a cryptotype – the exclusion of same-sex couples from marriage -, and thus made it available to legal discussion.

The attribution of this meaning to the legal text on marriage is, indeed, based on a cryptotype (Pasa 2015: 59) which requires a tacit compliance both with the "millennial tradition based on common sense", namely a natural order that considers marriage as the union between a male and a female – a tradition that the Italian Constitution recognises as the *foundation* of the rights of the family as a *natural*, spontaneous, *society* (Article 29 Const.[23]), and with the historical meaning the legislature had in mind when it produced both the text of the Constitution and of Book I of the CC on marriage in the '40s.[24] As a matter of fact, after the abovementioned judgment of the Constitutional Court which unveiled the cryptotype, the Italian Supreme Court (*Cassazione*), in its judgment no. 8097 of 21 April 2015, acknowledged that the heterosexual nature of marriage has legally lost its status of immutable paradigm (Pezzini, 2015b[25]) since it has proven to be a "standard which is subject to variation.[26]"

This contrastive dialogue between different judges (trial courts, the Constitutional Court and the Supreme Court) ultimately prompted the Italian legislature to introduce the "civil union", a specific legal protection for same-sex couples.

---

21 Cf. judgment no. 138/2010 and judgment no. 170/2014 of the Italian Constitutional Court available at http://www.cortecostituzionale.it/default.do (last access 10 September 2017).
22 The Constitutional Court recognized the heterosexuality of the couple as a fundamental, although only presupposed, condition of marriage at the time of the enactment of Book I of the CC on marriage.
23 "The Republic recognises the rights of the family as a natural society founded on marriage. Marriage is based on the moral and legal equality of the spouses within the limits laid down by law to guarantee the unity of the family".
24 A cryptotype which suggested to Italian Constitutional Fathers to draft an explicit patriarchal rule according to which: "The Republic protects mothers [*but not the fathers*!], children and the young by adopting necessary provisions". See Article 31(2) Italian Const.
25 As in an earlier decision dealing with the registration of a same-sex marriage celebrated abroad: *Cassazione* (Supreme Court) judgment no. 4182/2012, on which, among others, see Torino (2013).
26 Bernaroli struggled with gender dysphoria; in 2009, with the support of his wife, he travelled to Thailand, where he had sex reassignment surgery and became Alessandra. When Bernaroli officially changed name and gender, and she renewed her identity card, the Bologna Court annulled the marriage. The couple appealed the unwanted divorce and lost, but the Italian Supreme Court overturned the ruling, allowing them to stay married, until the legislature enacts a more appropriate legislation.

Act no. 76 of 20 May 2016[27] reflects how difficult it may turn out for positive law to meet the needs of a changing society. In fact, notwithstanding the Italian Supreme Court judgment no. 8097/2015, the legislature endorsed the traditional paradigm of marriage, as interpreted by the Constitutional Court, and it hermeneutically *locked* the marriage, reserving to same-sex couples a different institution, the civil union. Although the legislature projected duties and rights of marriage onto civil unions, providing that the rules which refer to marriage and contain the words "spouse", "spouses", or their equivalents, apply also to "each party of a civil union between same-sex persons" (Article 1, paragraph 20, Act no. 76/2016), it excluded the equivalence of meaning in two crucial issues, *filiation* and *adoption*, which traditionally characterize marriage as a relation between a male and a female.[28]

Once again, however, the shift towards a different paradigm is guided by the courts, which keep on[29] applying the special rules on adoption (Article 44, paragraph 1, letter d, Act no. 184/1983) that, as regards the so-called *second parent adoption*, protect "the best interest of the child". When doing so, the Courts are implicitly broadening the meaning terms like "parent", "mother", "father" and " son of / daughter of" traditionally had in the Italian legal system.

In 2014, for instance, the Juvenile Court of Rome[30] ruled on the second parent adoption admitting the full emotional and educational capacity of the adoptive mother in a same-sex couple, and the case reached the Italian Supreme Court, which in its judgment no. 12962 of the 22 June 2016 stated that: "the preferential treatment accorded to marriage should found a limit into the inviolable rights of the child,

---

27 Cf. the Italian Act 20 May 2016, no. 76: *Regolamentazione delle unioni civili tra persone dello stesso sesso e disciplina delle convivenze (Regulations of civil unions between persons of the same sex and discipline of cohabitation)* available at http://www.gazzettaufficiale.it/eli/id/2016/05/21/16G00082/sg (last access 18 September 2017). This statute is the outcome of several compromises between its promoters and the other parliamentarians, and it settled a legal institution for same-sex couples, the civil union (*unione civile*); it also recognised a (low) level of protection to the de facto cohabitation (*convivenza*).

28 "For the sole purpose of making the protection of rights effective and the duties deriving from a civil union between same-sex persons fulfilled, the provisions referring to marriage and the provisions containing the words 'spouse', 'spouses' or their equivalents, wherever they occur in statutes, legislative decrees, decrees and regulations, as well as in administrative acts and in collective labour agreements, shall apply also to each party of a civil union between same-sex persons. The aforementioned provision shall not apply to the Civil Code rules not explicitly mentioned in the present Act, as well as to the provisions of Act no. 1983/184. The foregoing shall be without prejudice of what is provided for and allowed by the current regulation on adoption".

29 Because, as we said in the previous ft., the final sentence of Article 1(20) states that "the foregoing shall be without prejudice of what is provided for and allowed by the current regulation on adoption".

30 *Tribunale dei Minorenni di Roma*, judgment no. 299 of 30.07.2014, confirmed by the Rome Court of Appeal (Juvenile Chamber), judgment of 23.12.2015, http://www.articolo29.it/wp-content/uploads/2015/12/SENTENZA-CORTE-APPELLO-ROMA-23-12-15.pdf (accessed 12 September 2016).

which cannot suffer harmful effects from a strict interpretation of the law.[31]" A few months later, the Turin Court of Appeal[32] protected the best interests of the child of two lesbians (married in Spain and then divorced), consenting the transcription of the Spanish child's birth certificate where the child is stated to have two mothers ("madre A" and "madre B" - in Spanish) at the City of Turin Civil Registry Office. This is a new possibility that, previously, the Italian courts had argued was "contrary to public order.[33]" The case reached the Italian Supreme Court, which in its judgment no. 19599 of the 30 September 2016[34] recognised the inclusion into the Italian legal system of a new instance of the legal concept of *madre* (mother) – a woman who both did not gave birth to her child *and* did not adopt it.[35] The City of Turin public officer who transcribed the Spanish birth's certificate, however, eschewed the reference to "mother A" and "mother B" as unnatural to be absorbed by the Italian legal system, and translated the reference to the parental relationship using the expression "figlio di A" (A's son) and "figlio di B" (B's son). But even if the Italian transcription of the Spanish birth's certificate does not mention the term "mother", it indirectly altered its meaning introducing in the legal ontology a new instance of the legal concept "son". Since the transcription of the Spanish birth certificate at the City of Turin Civil Registry Office, indeed, in Italy there is a child legally recognized as a son whose parents are both women, whereas up until now a child legally recognised as son/daughter of a woman could not be attributed a further legal parental relationship with another woman – as a matter of fact, this is a presupposition of Article 269(3) CC (proof of legal status of motherhood). The transcription of the Spanish birth certificate at the City of Turin Civil Registry Office then changed the meaning of the legal

---

31 *Cassazione civ., sez I*, judgment no. 12962 of 22.06.2016, http://www.neldiritto.it/public/pdf/12962_06_2016.pdf (accessed 12 September 2016).
32 Cf. *Corte d'Appello Torino, sez. famiglia*, decree of 29.10.2014, http://www.aiaf-avvocati.it/files/2015/01/Corte-appello-Torino-Decreto-ottobre-2014.pdf (accessed 21 September 2017).
33 *Corte d'Appello Torino, sez. famiglia*, cit. previous ft.
34 *Cassazione civ., Sez. I*, judgment n. 19599 of 30.09.2016, http://www.neldiritto.it/public/pdf/19599_10_2016.pdf (accessed 21 September 2017).
35 The implicit assumptions ruling parenthood in the EU, presupposing a gender-biased distribution of parental responsibilities and duties, were unveiled by the European Courts in sensitive cases involving surrogacy and adoption in same-sex couples: cf. the European Court of Justice, Case C-167/12 of 18 March 2014, *C. D. v S. T.* and in particular the Opinion of 23.09.2013 of the Advocate General Kokott, paragraph (46): "The objective of protection of maternity leave, which is enshrined as a fundamental right (...) demands the protection of the intended mother, irrespective of whether or not she breastfeeds the child." Comments by Moreno Pueyo (2015). Cf. also the European Court of Human Rights in *Paradiso and Campanelli v. Italy* (2015), Case 27 January 2015, referred to the Grand Chamber 01/06/2015, and confirmed by the Grand Chamber, 24 January 2017, according to which it is necessary that a child is not disadvantaged (in citizenship or identity, which are of paramount importance) because he was born to a surrogate mother. See also *Oliari and others v. Italy* (2015), Case 21 July 2015, and previously *X and Others v. Austria* (2013), Case 19 February 2013, §§ 107–110 and §§ 147-148-149.

concept of "son"; provided the interconnections this concept shares with those of mother and father, the transcription A's son and B's son necessarily entailed drawbacks also on the legal meaning of "mother" and "father". Further transcriptions of birth certificates of children of same-sex couples recently ruled by other Italian courts reinforced this bottom-up driving force which is changing the Italian legal paradigm of parenthood.[36]

Italian case law is thus moving toward a new parenthood paradigm, which provides for the possibility of a child to have two mothers, or two fathers (although, as before, not more than two parents).[37] This shift is generated by the court's intention of guaranteeing both the best interests of the child and the expectations of LGBTI people who desire to be parents, and it is not contrasted by the legislature, because Act no. 76/2016 does not mention the possibility for a party of a civil union between same-sex persons to create a legal and binding relationship with her/his partner's biological child, and so neither excludes it or allows it. Another implicit rule of the heterosexual paradigm of marriage, namely that children cannot have two mothers or two fathers, has been unveiled and objected.

6.2 "Parenthood" under the Family Code of California and polyamorous relationships and "plural marriage" in the U.S

The second example of a pragmatic reading of legal texts concerns the definition of "parenthood" provided by a provision of the California Family Code and its interpretations in some "hard cases" (Morra 2015a, 2016a). In the Seventies, in order to promote the best interests of a growing number of children born out of marriage, most western legal communities severed the concept of parenthood from the legal relationship between the parents of the child. Other tacit rules inferable from the paradigm traditionally ruling parenthood, such as the implicit definition of biologically determined (natural) parenthood as derived from the heterosexual paradigm of the couple, and the assumption that the terms *mother* and *father* identify unique parental roles, became explicit only when biotechnology made possible legal claims to which the traditional paradigm proved unable to provide a solution.

---

36 Trento Court of Appeal order (*Ordinanza della Corte d'Appello di Trento*) of 23.02.2017, available at http://www.dirittoegiustizia.it/allegati/PP_FAM_17tribTrento_s.pdf (accessed 16 March 2017).
37 On this point see Lucia Morra, Barbara Pasa, *Collective Agency, Intentionality and Communicative Intentions: The Case of the Legisla*ture, paper discussed at the Conference *Collective Agency and Speech Actions* at the University of Trieste in October 2016, see http://www2.units.it/ciml/eventi/?file=wks_agency.html (accessed 21 September 2017).

Before its amendment in January 2014, sec. 7601 of the California Family Code (FAM)[38] read as such:

> 'Parent and child relationship' as used in this part means the legal relationship existing between a child and the child's natural or adoptive parents incident to which the law confers or imposes rights, privileges, duties, and obligations. The term includes the mother and child relationship and the father and child relationship.

In the last sentence, the presupposition (P) activated by the definite article [the term includes *the* mother and child relationship and *the* father and child relationship] asserts the existence of *only one* (legal) mother-and-child relationship and the existence of *only one* (legal) father-and-child relationship: by logical consequence, then, a child can (legally) have only one mother and only one father. The logical consequences of the information provided by the presupposition differ according to two competing implicatures arising from ambiguity in the meaning of the verb *include*. Since *to include* means *to have (someone or something) as part of a group or total*, and also *to contain (someone or something) in a group or as a part of something* (Merriam-Webster Online), in that particular circumstance of interpretation the statement [The term includes the mother and child relationship and the father and child relationship] could be read as saying either I_1 ('parent and child relationship' includes *only* the mother-and-child relationship and the father-and-child relationship), or I_2 ('parent and child relationship' includes *among other (parental) relationships* the mother-and-child relationship and the father-and-child relationship).

In 1975, when sec. 7601 FAM was enacted, it was not that, overtly or not, the legislature wanted the statute to remain vague[39]; rather, the legislature did not even detect the possible ambiguity, because the context in which the statute was enacted impeded any implicature different from I_1. However, although in the Seventies socio-political circumstances did not suggest the activation of I_2, a few decades later the new political, social and legal context made it conceivable, desirable and possible, and thus the activation of I_1 was no longer automatic.

Differences between the informative content of the two implicatures can be appreciated by considering the different consequences of their merging with presupposition P, namely with the information that a child can have only one mother and only one father. Merged with I_1, P means that a child cannot have more than two legal

---

[38] Division 12. Parent and Child Relationship [7500–7961], Part 3. Uniform Parentage Act [7600–7730], Chapter 1. General Provisions [7600–7606].
[39] The vagueness given by different implicatures made available by a legal text can be considered as *overtly intended* when the legislature deliberately left open the interpretation due to the impossibility or inappropriateness of using an expression with a precise meaning, as happens in general clauses and with legal metaphorical terms still open to interpretation (amongst others, Endicott 2001; Morra and Bazzanella 2002); as *covertly intended* when precisely the ambiguity of the statute made possible the compromise through which the statute was approved (Marmor 2005; Morra 2010).

parents, a mother and/or a father; if we assign a literal or ordinary meaning to the terms *mother* and *father* (since they are not legally defined), it follows that if a woman or a man is already in a parental relationship with a child, someone of the same sex as the parent already legally recognized cannot be attributed a further parental relationship with the child. Conversely, merged with I_2, P means that a child may have more than two legally recognised parents: a mother, a father, and others, and that someone the child is biologically unrelated to can have a parental relationship with the child; that the unspecified potential parent cannot be recognized as a further mother or father of a child who already has a child-and-mother or child-and-father relationship; this does not exclude the possibility of someone of the same sex as the child's legally recognised mother/father having a parental relationship with the child.

Standard readings of sec. 7601 FAM, endorsing a heterosexual and patriarchal model of parenthood, remained undisputed until some "hard cases" were judged by the courts of the State of California. In one of them the courts had to decide whether it was possible to attribute a *natural parental relationship* to someone that met the criteria that in the FAM identified a presumed natural parent of a child, but could not be recognised either as the mother, since the child had already a (legally recognised) mother, or as the father, since this person was not a man. The question was decided in 2004 by the Court of Appeal of the Third District[40] that ruled that it was not possible, and then in 2005 by the Supreme Court of California[41] that reversed the decision of the Court of Appeal.

The facts of the case are as follows. Elisa and Emily lived together and decided to raise a family together. For this purpose, they both underwent artificial insemination and became pregnant by the same donor (Elisa gave birth to a girl, Emily to two twins). They parted two years after, and after some time Elisa stopped supporting Emily and the twins. The County (to which Emily had applied for financial help) sued Elisa. The trial court decided that she had to support the twins, but Elisa argued that under sec. 7601 FAM she could not be considered as a *natural parent* of the twins.

Questioned on the meaning of sec. 7601 of the California Family Code, the Court of Appeal adhered to the plausible original legislature's communicative intention, and stated that if a woman, or a man, already has a parental relationship with a child, someone of the same sex as the parent already legally recognised cannot be attributed a further parental relationship with the child. The Court argued that the precedents on which the trial court relied were inapposite for this case: they rather confirmed the heterosexual paradigm of parenthood since an individual biologically unrelated to a child was recognised as the child's natural parent only when she had the same sex as the lacking parent. Elisa, then, could not be considered a parent under sec. 7601 FAM. The Court acknowledged the unfairness of the consequences of its decision, but declared that a different judgment would have entailed an expansion "of the class of

---

40 *Elisa Maria B. v. Superior Court*, 118 Cal. App. 4th 966.
41 *Elisa B. v. Superior Court*, 37 Cal. 4th 108.

persons entitled to assert parental rights" reflecting a "public policy decision" that "should be left to the Legislature" due to the "complex practical, social and constitutional ramifications" it entailed.[42]

The Supreme Court of California reversed the decision, rejecting both the heterosexual and the pluralistic paradigm of parenthood incorporated respectively by I_1+ P and by I_2+ P, an ambiguous interpretive choice that revealed the difficulties that the *inter-action* between judiciary and legislature was facing at the time in tracking a swiftly changing society. The Court wrote that its choice avoided discrimination between adoptive and natural parents[43] and was coherent with its previous decisions ruling on the possibility for a child to have a same-sex parent *only* when the child did not have a second recognised legal parent. Furthermore, the decision guaranteed the best interests of the twins, because rejecting the presumption that Elisa was their parent would have deprived them of the support of a second parent; finally, Emily being out of work, it spared the County the heavy financial burden of supporting the twins, a weight implicitly communicated only in the statement of facts that mentions the serious health problems affecting one of the twins (information reported by the trial court, but not mentioned by the Court of Appeal).[44]

In 2011 the judgment of the Court of Appeal *In re M.C.*[45] rejected once again the heterosexual paradigm of the couple of parents, recognising two women as parents. It justified its decision, in fact, on the basis of the consequence of I_1 + P that a child cannot have more than two legal parents, a rule that the Californian Supreme Court had made explicit as an *obiter dictum* in the *Elisa* case. In *In re M.C.* more than two persons could have been considered as presumed natural parents of M.C. under sec. 7611 FAM (her biological mother, the woman this one had married shortly before her birth, her biological father, with whom she lived for some time after her birth), but the Court of Appeal held that sec. 7601 forbids such recognition. Recognising as natural parents of M.C. only her mother and her mother's spouse, the Court of Appeal regretted the consequences of its decision (since the M. C.'s biological mother was in jail and her spouse seriously ill, M.C. was taken into care by social services, and not by her willing biological father), but it held that recognising more than two parents would have proved disruptive for the text of sec. 7601 FAM. Further, the Court

---

42 *Maria B.* v. *Superior Court*, 118 Cal. App. 4th 966, at 10.
43 *Elisa B.* v. *Superior Court* 37 Cal. 4th 108, at 8. In 2003, the Californian Supreme Court had ruled on a second parent adoption in which the mother of a child conceived by means of artificial insemination consented to adoption of the child by the mother's lesbian partner: cf. *Sharon S.* v. *Superior Court*, 31 Cal.4th 417.
44 Providing factual support to reinforce its arguments, the Californian Supreme Court wrote: "Elisa gave birth to Chance in November, 1997, and Emily gave birth to Ry and Kaia prematurely in March, 1998. Ry had medical problems; he suffered from Down's Syndrome, and required heart surgery." *Elisa B.* v. *Superior Court* 37 Cal. 4th 108, at 2.
45 *In re M.C.*, 195 Cal. App.4th 197.

of Appeal requested that the legislature change the text in order to enable fair rulings in all extraordinary circumstances.

In 2014, the Californian legislature recognized the uptake of I_2 and its consequences as closer to its actual communicative intention, and amended sec. 7601 FAM in order to prevent any interpretative choice that could prohibit members of a homosexual couple from being both natural parents of the same child, including holdings that limited the possibility of attributing a parent and child relationship to both members of a homosexual couple in circumstances where this acknowledgement did not entail the recognition of more than two parents. The new text of sec. 7601 FAM gives now a definition of the legal concept of natural parent irrespective of biological links, and detaches its implicit (legal) meaning from the idea of couple, since it licenses the courts to recognise more than two parents for a child, although only one mother and only one father (the above-mentioned presupposition P is still maintained):

(a) 'Natural parent' as used in this code means a non-adoptive parent established under this part, whether biologically related to the child or not.
(b) 'Parent and child relationship' as used in this part means the legal relationship existing between a child and the child's natural or adoptive parents incident to which the law confers or imposes rights, privileges, duties, and obligations. The term includes the mother and child relationship and the father and child relationship.
(c) This part does not preclude a finding that a child has a parent and child relationship with more than two parents.
(d) For purposes of state law, administrative regulations, court rules, government policies, common law, and any other provision or source of law governing the rights, protections, benefits, responsibilities, obligations, and duties of parents, any reference to two parents shall be interpreted to apply to every parent of a child where that child has been found to have more than two parents under this part.

In its evolution towards a new legal paradigm that promises both to guarantee the best interests of the child, whatever the circumstances, and to meet claims for recognition advanced by LGBTI individuals who desire to be parents, the Californian legal system brought to the surface and finally rejected the implicit rule related to the number of possible parents, a rule lying at the core of the traditional heterosexual paradigm of marriage.

Another implicit norm part and parcel of the heterosexual paradigm of marriage, namely *marriages between same-sex persons are not allowed*, was eliminated throughout the United States by the decision of the Federal Supreme Court, in *Obergefell v. Hodges* of 26 June 2015[46] (previously, same-sex marriage had been legally recognised in about three-quarters of the States[47]). Interestingly enough, the decision legally

---

[46] The judgment is available at http://www.supremecourt.gov/opinions/14pdf/14-556_3204.pdf (accessed 21 July 2015).
[47] As of May 30, 2015, same-sex marriage existed in thirty-seven states (Alabama, Alaska, Arizona, California, Colorado, Connecticut, Delaware, Florida, Hawaii, Idaho, Illinois, Indiana, Iowa, Kansas,

unveiled a third implicit norm characterizing the hetero-marriage in western countries, namely the rule about the number of possible spouses. As about this implicit rule, scholars had already argued that an objective reading of the texts on marriage discloses the possibility of discussing the unconstitutionality of laws that implicitly limit civil marriage to couples (Den Otter 2015; Larcano 2006; Strassberg 2003)[48]: as for the case of gender biased/gender free expressions used in the legal texts on marriage, very few articles make it explicit that the number of spouses is limited to two individuals, and as in the case of the heterosexuality of the couple, different implicatures can be drawn to preserve coherence and cohesion of the legal texts.

As a matter of fact, in his dissenting opinion in *Obergefell v. Hodges* Justice Roberts argued[49]: "It is striking how much of the majority's reasoning would apply with equal force to the claim of a fundamental right to plural marriage. If "[t]here is dignity in the bond between two men or two women who seek to marry and in their autonomy to make such profound choices (...)" why would there be any less dignity in the bond between three people who, in exercising their autonomy, seek to make the profound choice to marry? If a same-sex couple has the constitutional right to marry because their children would otherwise "suffer the stigma of knowing their families are somehow lesser (...)" why wouldn't the same reasoning apply to a family of three or more persons raising children? If not having the opportunity to marry "serves to disrespect and subordinate" gay and lesbian couples, why wouldn't the same "imposition of this disability (...)" serve to disrespect and subordinate people who find fulfillment in polyamorous relationships?[50]"

As Nussbaum states, articulating and protecting spheres of personal liberty has been a crucial task of our tradition of constitutional law (Nussbaum 2010: xvi). Thus the claim of a fundamental right to a *plural marriage* could be the next step: at any rate, one may guess that in the next few years the question of whether the United

---

Maine, Maryland, Massachusetts, Minnesota, Montana, New Hampshire, New Mexico, Nevada, New Jersey, New York, North Carolina, Oklahoma, Oregon, Pennsylvania, Rhode Island, South Carolina, Utah, Vermont, Virginia, Washington, West Virginia, Wisconsin, and Wyoming and in the District of Columbia) Cf. *Marriage Center*, http://www.hrc.org/campaigns/marriage-center (accessed 1 July 2015). Quite differently from the Italian Constitution, the U.S. Constitution itself says nothing about marriage; therefore the States were entrusted with the whole matter of the domestic relations of husband and wife. The on-going debate about same-sex marriage is not only about gay and lesbian couples and their constitutional right; it is also about the legal definition of marriage and its extension to avoid the tendency to discriminate against different minorities.

48 Den Otter makes clear the relevant terminology, he discusses reasonable concerns about how women are treated in polygynous relationships, about child development and possible adverse consequences of judicial recognition of a constitutional right to "plural marriage".

49 576 U. S. ____ (2015) 21 Roberts, C. J., dissenting, available at http://www.supremecourt.gov/opinions/14pdf/14-556_3204.pdf (accessed 1 July 2016).

50 Justice Roberts quotes respectively Bennett (2009), Li (2014) and Den Otter (2015), estimating 500,000 polyamorous families in the United States.

States may continue to prevent even fully informed, consenting adults from marrying more than one person at the same time will be thoroughly analysed.[51]

7 Concluding remarks

The two examples illustrate how interpreters of legal texts may activate implicatures and their possible functions. More in general, they confirm that the law is not confined to the visible and usually written body of legal rules, although today professors and students still comfort themselves with the belief that texts *comprehensively* present the law in force. The retrieval of cryptotypes through the detection of presuppositions and implicatures and, more in general, the recognition of the tacit and implicit dimension of law, constitute one aspect of interpretative practice that cannot be explained in a straight and mere logical way, but nevertheless can be accounted for. Revealing the implicit information underlying legal provisions can help in tracing the way in which social and individual values contribute to the meaning given to legal texts in adjudication.

The two examples discussed in §6.1 and in §6.2 were both related to gender issues, but clearly the retrieval of cryptotypes through the tools of pragmatics may be a relevant exercise in all fields of law, to begin with migration law, criminal law, and labour law, where implicit beliefs and paradigms of action serving the socio-economic and political structure impinge on legal communities at large. This sort of exercise may well *not retrieve all* the shades of implicit meaning surrounding the norms, but it opens the retrieved cryptotypes to *rational inquiry,* which is possible only when statements become explicitly formulated.

From a comparative point of view, the application of such a methodology to gender issues highlights the circular relation between law and society: the existing body of legal doctrine and interpretive practices is a construct of relations of exclusion (such as those arising from history, gender, class and race) and, at the same time, legal institutions influence social structures and social knowledge. Moreover, the retrieval of the implicit dimension of law reveals the impact of cryptotypes into legal paradigms of *marriage* and *parenthood*, which are shifting differently at national level.

The emergence of cryptotypes silently shaping the traditional approaches to parenthood and marriage prompted in fact the research of new legal paradigms, with substantive differences in Western legal systems. As regards *parenthood*, as was seen, the Californian legislature settled that more than two parents can be legally recognised to a child, but the implicit rule that a child can have no more than one *mother* and

---

51 *Should Plural Marriage Be Legal?*, N.Y. TIMES: ROOM FOR DEBATE (Dec. 17, 2013), http://www.nytimes.com/roomfordebate/2013/12/17/should-plural-marriage-be-legal.

no more than one *father*, presupposing a gender-biased distribution of parental responsibilities and duties, still holds in court decisions; as opposed, while the Italian legislature still stands by the traditional paradigm of parenthood, the Italian judiciary is developing a new paradigm in which a child may have two mothers, or two fathers (but no more than two parents), in order to protect the best interests of the child and the desire of same-sex couples to become parents. As regards *marriage*, as was seen, while the Italian legislature missed the opportunity to recognize gender-neutral *marriage* through Act no. 76/2016, the Federal Supreme Court of US not only legally wiped out the heterosexual character of this institution, but it also disclosed the possibility of discussing a pluralistic paradigm of marriage – at least, a right to plural marriage is becoming apparent.

Interpretation is a practice by which interpreters can discover and project their identity, a practice by which they recognise both the contingency and plurality of law and the use (and *abuse*) of law as a mechanism of privilege and domination. Revealing the implicit dimensions of law may help to overcome social exclusion and subordination. What equality and justice are, and what the relationship between ideas of inequality and discrimination is (Butler 1990), are questions that cannot be avoided by all participants in interpretative practice.

Acknowledgments: This chapter is the product of collaborative research. Although it has been jointly discussed, Barbara Pasa contributed sections 2, 3, 6.1; Lucia Morra sections 4, 5, 6.2; while sections 1 and 7 were written jointly.

This essay is dedicated to the memory of Professor MacDonald, representative of the 'critical legal pluralism' movement. The paper has been discussed at the *Juris Diversitas* annual Conference on *The State and/of Comparative Law* (Limerick, June 2015).

References

Alchourrón, Carlos E. 2012. On law and logic. In Jordi Ferrer Beltrán & Giovanni Battista Ratti (eds.), *The logic of legal requirements: essays on defeasibility*, 39–52. Oxford: Oxford University Press.
Bairati, Lorenzo. 2015. La trascrizione del matrimonio omosessuale celebrato all'estero: argomentazioni e strategie interpretative tra implicito e non detto. In Lucia Morra & Barbara Pasa (eds.), *Questioni di genere nei testi normativi: crittotipi e impliciti*, 111–130. Torino: Giappichelli.
Barsotti, Vittoria, Paolo G. Carozza, Marta Cartabia & Andrea Simoncini. 2016. *Italian constitutional justice in global context*. Oxford, New York: Oxford University Press.
Bell, John. 1983. *Policy arguments in judicial decisions*. Oxford: Clarendon Press.
Bennett, Jessica. 2009. Polyamory: the next sexual revolution? *Newsweek*, July 28.
Boehme-Neßler, Volker. 2011. *Pictorial law. Modern law and the power of pictures*. Berlin, Heidelberg: Springer.
Butler, Judith. 1990. *Gender trouble: feminism and the subversion of identity*. New York: Routledge.

Canzio, Giovanni. 2008. Giurisprudenza di legittimità, precedenti e massime. *Questione Giustizia* (4). 51–61.
Capra, Fritjof & Ugo Mattei. 2015. *The ecology of law*. Oakland: Berrett-Koehler.
Carston, Robyn. 2013. Legal texts and canons of construction: a view from current pragmatic theory. In Michael Freeman & Fiona Smith (eds.), *Law and language. Current legal issues,* volume 15, 8–33. Oxford: Oxford University Press.
Cassone, Francesca. 2015. Procreazione e norme. Quali implicature? In Lucia Morra & Barbara Pasa (eds.), *Questioni di genere nei testi normativi: crittotipi e impliciti*, 131–147. Torino: Giappichelli.
Caterina, Raffaele (ed.). 2009. *La dimensione tacita del diritto*. Napoli: ESI.
Caterina, Raffaele. 2012. Il crittotipo, muto e inattuato. In Luisa Antoniolli, Gian Antonio Benacchio & Roberto Toniatti (eds.), *Le nuove frontiere della comparazione*, Atti I Convegno SIRD 5–7 maggio 2011, 85–97. Trento: Università Studi Trento.
Chiassoni, Pierluigi. 1999. Interpretive games: statutory construction through Gricean eyes. In Paolo Comanducci & Riccardo Guastini (eds.), *Analisi e diritto. Ricerche di giurisprudenza analitica*, 79–99. Torino: Giappichelli.
Cotterrell, Roger. 2014. Why jurisprudence is not legal philosophy. *Jurisprudence* 5(1). 41–55.
Davis, Wayne. 2014. *Implicature*. In Edward N. Zalta (ed.), *The Stanford encyclopedia of philosophy*. http://plato.stanford.edu/archives/fall2014/entries/implicature/.
Den Otter, Ronald C. 2015. Three may not be a crowd: the case for a constitutional right to plural marriage. *Emory Law Journal* 64(6). 1977–2046. http://law.emory.edu/elj/_documents/volumes/64/6/den-otter.pdf.
Di Lucia, Paolo. 2009. Il linguaggio dell'atto muto. In Raffaele Caterina (ed.), *La dimensione tacita del diritto*, 119–128. Napoli: ESI.
Ehrlich, Eugen. 1913. *Grundlegung der Sociologie des Rechts* [Fundamental principles of the sociology of law]. München: Duncker & Humblot.
Endicott, Timothy. 2001. Law is necessarily vague. *Legal Theory* 7(1). 377–383.
Endicott, Timothy. 2014. Interpretation and indeterminacy: Comments on Andrei Marmor's philosophy of law. *Jerusalem Review of Legal Studies* 10(1). 46–56.
Evangelista, Stefano & Giovanni Canzio. 2005. Corte di cassazione e diritto vivente. In *Foro italiano*, V, c. 82.
Falk Moore, Sally. 1978. *Law as process: an anthropological approach*. London: Routledge.
Ferrer Beltrán, Jordi & Giovanni Battista Ratti (eds.). 2012. *The logic of legal requirements: essays on defeasibility*. Oxford: Oxford University Press.
Fiori, Stefano. 2009. Regole, convenzioni tacite e diritto. Una possibile prospettiva della teoria economica. In Raffaele Caterina (ed.), *La dimensione tacita del diritto*, 85–96. Napoli: ESI.
Francavilla, Domenico. 2009. Diritto e conoscenza non linguistica. Osservazioni su origine, trasmissione e diffusione delle regole. In Raffaele Caterina (ed.), *La dimensione tacita del diritto*, 65–76. Napoli: ESI.
García Figueroa, Alfonso. 2009. Neoconstitucionalismo y derrotabilidad. http://studylib.es/doc/7467162/neoconstitucionalismo-y-derrotabilidad (accessed 22 September 2017).
García-Yzaguirre, José Víctor. 2012. La validez prima facie y el principio de derrotabilidad de las normas jurídicas. *Díkaion*. 459–487. http://www.redalyc.org/pdf/720/72028686007.pdf (accessed 22 September 2017).
Glenn, Patrick. 2010. *Legal traditions of the world: sustainable diversity in law*. Oxford: Oxford University Press.
Graziadei, Michele. 1999. Comparative law, legal history, and the holistic approach to legal cultures. *Zeitschrift Fur Europaisches Privatrecht* 1. 531–543.
Graziadei, Michele. 2009. La legge, la consuetudine, il diritto tacito, le circostanze. In Raffaele Caterina (ed.), *La dimensione tacita del diritto*, 49–64. Napoli: ESI.

Greenberg, Mark. 2011. Legislation as communication? Legal interpretation and the study of linguistic communication. In Andrei Marmor & Scott Soames (eds.), *Philosophical foundations of language in the law*, 217–256. Oxford: Oxford University Press.
Grice, Herbert-Paul. 1975. *Logic and conversation*. In Peter Cole & Jerry Morgan (eds.), *Syntax and semantics, vol. 3: Speech acts*, 41–58. New York: Academic Press.
Grossi, Paolo. 2013. *Prima lezione di diritto*. 19 edn. Roma/Bari: Laterza.
Guastini, Riccardo. 1993. *Le fonti del diritto e l'interpretazione*. Milano: Giuffrè.
Guastini, Riccardo. 2010. Introduzione alla teoria dell'interpretazione. In Visconti, Jaqueline (ed.), *Lingua e diritto. Livelli di analisi*, 61–74. Milano: ESEDRA.
Guastini, Riccardo. 2012. Defeasability, axiological gaps and interpretation. In Jordi Ferrer Beltrán & Giovanni Battista Ratti (eds.), *The logic of legal requirements: essays on defeasibility*. 182–192. Oxford: Oxford University Press.
Guastini, Riccardo. 2014. *La sintassi del diritto*. 2 edn. Torino: Giappichelli.
Harding, Rosie. 2010. *Regulating sexuality: legal consciousness in lesbian and gay lives*. London: Routledge.
Kasirer, Nicholas. 2003. Convoler en justes noces. In Pierre-Claude Lafond & Brigitte Lefebvre (eds.), *L'union civile: nouveaux modèles de conjugalité et de parentalité au 21e siècle*. 29–62. Cowansville: Éditions Yvon Blais.
Kleinhaus, Martha-Marie, Roderick A. MacDonald. 1997. What is critical legal pluralism? *Canadian Journal of Law and Society* 12(1). 25–46.
Larcano, Elizabeth. 2006. A "pink" herring: the prospect of polygamy following the legalization of same-sex marriage. *Connecticut Law Review* 38(1). 1065–1111.
Legrand, Pierre. 1999. *Fragments on law-as-culture*. Deventer: W.E.J. Tjeenk Willink.
Li, David K. 2014. Married lesbian 'throuple' expecting first child. *NY Post*, Apr. 23.
Long, Jöelle. 2015. Diritto italiano della famiglia e impliciti 'normativi'. In Lucia Morra & Barbara Pasa (eds.), *Questioni di genere nei testi normativi: crittotipi e impliciti*, 149–166. Torino: Giappichelli.
Lorusso, Annamaria. 2015. Percorsi semantici e pratiche interpretative: su alcuni usi degli artt. 2 e 29 della Costituzione. In Lucia Morra & Barbara Pasa (eds.), *Questioni di genere nei testi normativi: crittotipi e impliciti*, 167–180. Torino: Giappichelli.
Macagno, Fabrizio, Douglas Walton & Christopher Tindale. 2017. Analogical arguments: inferential structures and defeasibility conditions. *Argumentation* 31(2). 221–243.
MacDonald, Roderick. 1986. Vers la reconnaissance d'une normativité implicite et inférentielle. *Sociologie et Sociétés*, 18(1). 47–58.
MacDonald, Roderick. 1992. Academic questions. *Legal Education Rev*. 3(1). Article 3 http://epublications.bond.edu.au/ler/vol3/iss1/3 (accessed 22 September 2017).
MacDonald, Roderick. 2000. Regards sur les rapports juridiques informels entre langues et droit. *Revue de la common law en français* 3(1). 137–151.
MacDonald, Roderick. 2007. Unitary law re-form, pluralistic law re-substance: illuminating legal change. *Louisiana Law Review*. http://digitalcommons.law.lsu.edu/lalrev/vol67/iss4/7 (accessed 22 September 2017).
McDonald, Roderick & Jason MacLean. 2005. No toilets in park. *McGill Law Journal/Revue de droit de McGill* 50(1). 721–787.
McDonald, Roderick & Thomas McMorrow. 2007. Wedding: a critical legal pluralism to the laws of close personal adult relationships. *European Journal of Legal Studies* 1(1). 319–356. http://www.ejls.eu/1/15UK.pdf (accessed 22 September 2017).
MacDougall, Bruce. 2000. *Queer judgments: homosexuality, expression, and the courts in Canada*. Toronto: University of Toronto Press.
Marmor, Andrei. 2005. *Interpretation and legal theory*. 2nd ed. revised. Oxford and Portland: Hart Publishing.

Marmor, Andrei. 2011. Can the law imply more than it says? On some pragmatic aspects of strategic speech. In Andrei Marmor & Scott Soames (eds.), *Philosophical foundations of language in the law*, 83–97. Oxford: Oxford University Press.

Marmor, Andrei. 2014. *The language of law*. Oxford: Oxford University Press.

Marmor, Andrei. 2016. Defeasibility and pragmatic indeterminacy in law. In Alessandro Capone & Francesca Poggi (eds.) *Pragmatics and law. Philosophical perspectives*, 15–32. New York: Springer.

Miller, Geoffrey P. 1990. Pragmatics and the maxims of interpretation. *Wisconsin Law Review* 20(1). 1179–1227.

Moreno Pueyo, Manuel José. 2015. La prestación de maternidad en los casos de maternidad subrogada. Estado de la cuestión tras los pronunciamientos del TJUE de 18/03/14. *Revista española de Derecho del Trabajo*. 287–293.

Moreso, José J. & Samuele Chilovi. 2015. Interpretative arguments and the application of the law. https://www.academia.edu/12424691/Intepretive_Arguments_and_the_Application_of_the_Law (10 July, 2015). Forthcoming in Giorgio Bongiovanni, Gerald Postema, Antonio Rotolo, Giovanni Sartor, Douglas Walton & Chiara Valentini (eds.), *Handbook of legal reasoning and argumentation*. springer: Netherlands.

Morra, Lucia. 2011. Implicature conversazionali nei testi di legge. *Esercizi filosofici* 6(1). 214–231. http://www2.units.it/eserfilo/n6111.htm.

Morra, Lucia. 2015a. Genitorialità californiana. Analisi testuale della sec. 7601 del California Family Code. In Lucia Morra & Barbara Pasa (eds.), *Questioni di genere nei testi normativi: crittotipi e impliciti*, 181–200. Torino: Giappichelli.

Morra, Lucia. 2015b. Conversational implicatures in normative texts. In Alessandro Capone & Jacob L. Mey (eds.), *Interdisciplinary studies in pragmatics, culture and society*, 537–562. New York: Springer.

Morra, Lucia. 2016a. Implicit Information in judicial opinions. *Paradigmi* XXXIV (1). 81–98.

Morra, Lucia. 2016b. Widening the Gricean picture to strategic exchanges. In Alessandro Capone & Francesca Poggi (eds.), *Pragmatics and law. Philosophical perspectives*, 201–230. New York: Springer.

Morra, Lucia & Carla Bazzanella. 2002. Considerazioni sul "buon padre di famiglia". *Rivista critica del diritto privato* 20(1). 529–563.

Morra, Lucia & Barbara Pasa. 2015. Diritto tacito, diritto implicito e questioni di genere nei testi normativi. In Lucia Morra & Barbara Pasa (eds.). *Questioni di genere nei testi normativi: crittotipi e impliciti*, 1–11. Torino: Giappichelli.

Neale, Stephen. 2007. On location. In Michael O'Rourke & Corey Washington (eds.), *Situating semantics: essays in honor of John Perry*. 251–393. Cambridge: MIT Press.

Nussbaum, Martha. 2010. *From disgust to humanity. sexual orientation and constitutional law*. Oxford: Oxford University Press.

Pasa, Barbara. 2015. Dal crittotipo all'implicito: diritto tacito, muto, vissuto? In Lucia Morra & Barbara Pasa (eds.), *Questioni di genere nei testi normativi: crittotipi e impliciti*. 52–70. Torino: Giappichelli.

Pezzini, Barbara (ed.). 2012. *Genere e diritto. Come il genere costruisce il diritto e il diritto costruisce il genere*. Bergamo: Bergamo University Press.

Pezzini, Barbara. 2015. Oltre il "caso Bernaroli": tecniche decisorie, rapporti tra principi e regole del caso e vicende del paradigma eterosessuale del matrimonio. *GenIus* 1. 83–93.

Poggi, Francesca. 2011. Law and conversational implicatures. *International Journal for the Semiotics of Law* 24(1). 21–40.

Sacco, Rodolfo. 1980. *Introduzione al diritto comparato*. Torino: Giappichelli.

Sacco, Rodolfo. 1980. Comparazione giuridica e conoscenza del dato giuridico positivo. In Rodolfo Sacco (ed.), *L'apporto della comparazione alla scienza giuridica*, 204–247. Milano: Giuffrè.

Sacco, Rodolfo. 1989. Crittotipo. *Digesto disc priv., sez. civ.* IV, 39–40. Torino: Utet.
Sacco, Rodolfo. 1991. Legal formants: A dynamic approach to comparative law (Installment I and II). *American Journal of Comparative Law* 39(1–2). 1–34; 343–401.
Sacco, Rodolfo. 1993. Il diritto muto. *Riv. dir. civ.* Part I. 689–702.
Sacco, Rodolfo. 1995. Mute law. *American Journal of Comparative Law* 43(1). 455–467.
Sacco, Rodolfo. 2007. *Antropologia giuridica*. Bologna: Il Mulino.
Sacco, Rodolfo. 2015. *Il diritto muto*. Bologna: Il Mulino.
Salvaneschi, Laura. 2016. *Diritto giurisprudenziale e prevedibilità delle decisioni: ossimoro o binomio?*. http://milanosservatorio.it/wp-content/uploads/2016/04/salvaneschi-diritto-giurisprudenziale-e-prevedibilit%c3%a0-delle-decisioni-ossimoro-o-binomio.pdf (accessed 22 September 2017).
Samuel, Geoffrey. 2014. *An introduction to comparative law theory and method*. Portland: Hart Publishing.
Sartor, Giovanni. 2012. Defeasibility in legal reasoning. In Jordi Ferrer Beltrán & Giovanni Battista Ratti (eds.), *The logic of legal requirements: essays on defeasibility*. 108–136. Oxford: Oxford University Press.
Sbisà, Marina. 2007. *Detto non detto. Le forme della comunicazione implicita*. Roma/Bari: Laterza.
Sbisà, Marina. 2015. Normatività e comunicazione. In Lucia Morra & Barbara Pasa (eds.), *Questioni di genere nei testi normativi: crittotipi e impliciti*, 15–38. Torino: Giappichelli.
Scalia, Antonin & Brian Garner. 2012. *Reading law: the interpretation of legal text*. New York: West Group.
Schmitz, Michael. 2013. Social rules and the social background. In Michael Schmitz, Beatrice Kobow & Hans Bernhard Schmid (eds.), *The background of social reality. Selected contributions from the inaugural meeting of ENSO*. 107–125. Dordrecht: Springer.
Searle, John R. 1995. *The construction of social reality*. New York: The Free Press.
Shaer, Benjamin. 2013. Towards a cognitive science of legal interpretation. In Michael Freeman and Fiona Smith (eds.), *Law and language. Current legal issues,* volume 15, 259–291. Oxford: Oxford University Press.
Sidnell, Jack. 2003. An ethnographic consideration of rule-following. *Journal of the Royal Anthropological Institute* 9(1). 429–445.
Sinclair, Michael B. W. 1985. Law and language: the role of pragmatics in statutory interpretation. *University of Pittsburgh Law Review* 46(1). 373–420.
Skoczeń, Izabela. 2015. Implicatures within the legal context: a rule-based analysis of the possible content of conversational maxims in law. In Michał Araszkiewicz, Paweł Banaś, Tomasz Gizbert-Studnicki & Krzysztof Płeszka (eds.), *Problems of normativity, rules and rule-following*, 351–362. New York: Springer.
Soames, Scott. 2009. Interpreting legal texts: What is, and what is not, special about the law. In Scott Soames. (ed.), *Philosophical essays. 1: Natural language: What it means and how we use it,* 403–424. Princeton: Princeton University Press.
Soames, Scott. 2011. Toward a theory of legal interpretation. *NYU Law School Journal of Law and Liberty* 6(2). 231–259.
Soames, Scott. 2013. Deferentialism: A post-originalist theory of legal interpretation. *Fordham Law Review* 82(1). 101–122.
Strassberg, Maura I. 2003. The challenge of post-modern polygamy: considering polyamory. *Capital University Law Review* 31(3). 439–563.
Tamanha, Brian. 2000. A non-essentialist version of legal pluralism. *Journal of Law and Society* 27(2). 296–321.
Their, Andreas. 2011. Legal history. In Ewoud Hondius & Christoph Grigoleit (eds.), *Unexpected circumstances in European contract law*, 15–32. New York: Cambridge University Press.

Thompson, Edward P. 1993. *Customs in common: studies in traditional popular culture*. New York: The New Press.
Torino, Raffaele (ed.). 2013. *Le coppie dello stesso sesso: la prima volta in Cassazione*. Roma: RomaTrEPress.
Twining, William. 1997. *Law in context: enlarging a discipline*. Oxford: Oxford University Press.
Twining, William. 2005. Social science and diffusion of law. *Journal of Law and Society* 32(2). 203–240.
Visconti, Jacqueline (ed.). 2010. *Lingua e diritto. Livelli di analisi*. Milano: LED.
Wagner, Anne & Richard Sherwin (eds.). 2014. *Law, culture and visual studies*. Netherlands: Springer.
Walton, Douglas N. 2002. *Legal argumentation and evidence*. University Park, PA: Pennsylvania State University Press.
Windscheid, Bernhard. 1892. Die Voraussetzung. *Archiv für die civilistische Praxis* 78. 161.

Sabine Ehrhardt
7 Authorship attribution analysis

1 Introduction

Written language becomes the object of forensic analyses when it is used to commit a criminal offence and/or when it is relevant as a trace to an offender. For obvious reasons, offenders send their writings anonymously, and for similarly obvious reasons, law enforcement procedures are aimed at revoking this anonymity by disambiguating the authors of these texts. The linguistic discipline which focuses on the inference of author-specific characteristics from the characteristics of a text is commonly denoted as *authorship attribution* which is part of the multifaceted field of *forensic linguistics*. Forensic linguistics in its broader sense refers to all kinds of overlap of linguistics and law, e.g. how language is used and understood in various legal settings and how language is used in the context of criminal offences.[1] By this definition, a forensic linguist aims at determining the authenticity, meaning and intent of language events in the context of law and law enforcement.

The focus of the present paper is on forensic linguistics in its narrow sense, concentrating on the tasks of disambiguating authors and attributing authorship of anonymous texts. The term *forensic linguistics* is used in this narrow sense, i.e. to refer to linguistic analyses concerning authorship identification, attribution and profiling. The following sections are meant to provide a broad overview of the field and are therefore devoted to the objectives of forensic linguistic analyses (section 2: idiolect, scope, specific tasks), methods of analysis (section 3: qualitative, statistical and automatic approaches), and the objects of analysis (section 4: texts as offences and in the context of offences) especially taking into account the specific conditions that prevail in a forensic context.

2 Objectives of analyses

2.1 Idiolect and authorship

The basic assumption of forensic linguistics is the notion of idiolect. This means that language users show individual linguistic features which make them recognisable by their usage of language: "every language user has a unique linguistic style, or 'idiolect', and [...] features characteristic of that style will recur with a relatively stable

---

[1] For an overview of the interface of language and law, cf. for example Tiersma and Solan 2012; Gibbons 2011; Coulthard and Johnson 2007; Rathert 2006; Solan and Tiersma 2005.

frequency" (Coulthard, Grant and Kredens 2011: 536). This individuality in language use is caused by at least two factors: 1) Language acquisition is an individual process due to individual conditioning by culture, social class, educational background etc., and 2) language use is permanently influenced by each person's social, professional and cultural environment. Due to the influences on the biography of language users, they develop a repertoire of linguistic features as well as routines and preferences that characterise the linguistic competence of a person as individual (Fleischer 1996: 41; also cf. Dern 2009: 53–57).

Idiolect is primarily a theoretical concept. As a consequence, it is hard to determine what idiolect exactly is and where in each person's language use it manifests itself. Conversely, it is fairly easy to say what idiolect is not: It is not a clearly defined language profile which is consistently reproducible and immune to change. In fact, there are no universal linguistic features or feature sets which can always be used to discriminate between authors. This suggests that the concept of idiolect refers to the circumstance that an author's linguistic features are first and foremost characteristics of a group whose combination increases their scarcity value to such an extent that the entirety of an author's features appear to be individual. The lack of universally discriminating features is what makes the concept of idiolect rather difficult to handle and impossible to directly operationalise.

Forensic linguistics as a forensic science is aimed at inferring from a text an author's idiolect. This aim seems to presuppose that each text is written by a single author – a presupposition that is problematic. Before conducting an examination and of course during the process of an examination, the linguistic expert needs to be aware of indications that more than one person was involved in the making of a text. There are different forms and functions of authorship to a text (Grant 2008: 217–218). Talking about authors in the common sense of the word we are referring to what has been described as "executive author", i.e. "the compiler of the verbal text up to the point where it is judged suitable for publication in one or another form" (Love 2002: 43). Love continues by pointing out that "executive authorship can be either solo or collaborative" (Love 2002: 43). The implications for authorship attribution analysis are obvious in that the collaborating authors should be treated separately, which is at best a difficult matter to handle; often it is an impossible task. In addition to indications of collaborative authorship,[2] there may also be traces of "precursory authorship" which means that the current text reflects influences of earlier texts. Transferred to forensic linguistic case work, an example of precursory authorship is the adherence of radical left-wing authors to writing conventions of the left-wing terrorist scene like the RAF, "Rote Armee Fraktion"

---

2 Collaborative authorship is sometimes also denoted as *multiple authorship* (cf. Kniffka 2007: 151, Dern 2009: 61, Fobbe 2011: 41–44).

(*Red Army Faction*).³ In times when responsibility claims were not published on specialised internet platforms, these conventions were only known to members of the radical scene. By adhering to particular conventions an author – usually by intention – conveyed the information that the responsibility claim is authentic.

A further kind of authorship that is relevant for forensic linguistics is "revisionary authorship". In Love's terminology, this denotes influences on a text due to editing and revising processes which are best described with reference to chronology because they occur subsequent to the phase of executive authorship (Love 2002: 47). Published texts like papers in radical scene magazines, but also (pseudonymous) letters to the editor might have undergone more or less extensive editing and revising.

Consideration of the different forms of authorship is an essential preparatory step in the examination of forensic material.⁴ Essentially, it needs to be performed as a result of the difficult situation that forensic linguistics is aimed at describing or attributing a particular author of a text despite the fact that texts are not necessarily written by single authors.

2.2 Scope of authorship analyses

Forensic linguistics can be applied in a variety of situations. For authorship attribution, a distinction can be made based on the stage of criminal proceedings at which the forensic analysis is needed. It may be requested to either support preliminary proceedings and the investigatory phase or to evaluate linguistic evidence for court proceedings.⁵ The difference between these two settings does not necessarily show itself in the methodology to be applied but rather in the specific tasks and questions to be answered by the forensic scientist, the way results are presented in reports and in limitations concerning the admissibility.

For investigations, linguistic findings do not have evidential value but serve to enable investigators to evaluate traces and to base investigatory decisions upon these findings, e.g. by deciding which leads to follow first or by reducing the set of suspects. The means to reach these aims may be authorship attribution analyses just as they are also commissioned by courts (or for court proceedings) like text comparisons; but there are further tasks that are usually not relevant for court proceedings like

---

3 The RAF was a German terrorist group which was founded in 1970 and which declared its dissolving in 1998. The group kidnapped and murdered more than 30 police officers, judges, prosecutors, politicians, bankers etc. Characteristic for their writings, the main body of the text was in small letters, followed by a set of slogans in capital letters, and concluded by their logo in connection with the name of the RAF commando unit "Kommando [+ *name*]".
4 See section 3 for a detailed description of the entire process of critically inspecting the objects of analysis as the preliminary to a forensic examination.
5 A further field for application is intelligence gathering which is similar to investigations (possibly less constrained by regulations ensuring the suitability for further use in legal proceedings).

the analysis of larger amounts of data with respect to topic and vocabulary as well as the analysis of texts for a sociolinguistic profile of an anonymous author. Reports for these activities are rather descriptive and explanatory than evaluative.[6] With the separation of investigation and the forensic analysis of traces (which is common in many judicial systems), forensic practitioners are not necessarily in command of enough information from investigations to be fully aware of the significance of their results, especially concerning the question which aspect of their analysis is indeed crucial to investigators. Therefore, the discussion of linguistic features in great detail, especially those findings that are ambiguous in their interpretation serves the overall purpose because, to the linguist, it may not be known where the links to other fields of the investigation are. Of course, these instances of ambiguity as well as the robustness of findings must be clearly stated nevertheless.

For court proceedings, the objective of a linguistic analysis is more constrained. The main task is the evaluation of linguistic evidence for the judge or the jury (depending on who is the trier of fact in the relevant judicial system). In some countries, the courts have raised the question of the admissibility of linguistic evidence and established standards to secure basic scientific principles in the application of forensic sciences. The impact of the Daubert criteria on forensic linguistics in the U.S. and in other countries have been extensively discussed since the *Daubert v. Merrell Dow Pharmaceuticals* ruling in 1993 (e.g. cf. Tiersma and Solan 2002, Coulthard 2013). In countries having an inquisitorial judicial system, the admissibility of forensic evidence seems to be less of an issue due to the nature of these judicial systems with a pre-eminent judge vested with complete authority to "assess, appreciate and evaluate the weight of evidence brought to him within the context of the case" (Margot 1998: 71). Obviously, there are also regulating mechanisms to the pre-eminence of the judge as presented by the code of criminal procedure and the risk of appeal.

Apart from the admissibility of forensic evidence, an equally important discussion centres on how to evaluate forensic findings and subsequently on evaluative reporting. Empirical forensic sciences like handwriting analysis, speaker recognition and forensic linguistics alike used to make probabilistic statements about whether an unknown trace originates from a known source in the interpretation of their findings (Dern 2009: 75–78), which means that an expert offers an opinion on the probability of a hypothesis given the evidence, i.e. posterior probability. But this expression of evidential value is considered as "logically incorrect conclusions" (Broeders 1999: 228) and is strongly debated since at least the end of the 1990s (e.g. Robertson and Vignaux 1995). In 2015, a guideline was published by ENFSI, the European Network of Forensic Science Institutes, recommending the application of the Bayes theorem within a

---

[6] In ENFSI (2015: 24–27), a distinction is made between four different types of reporting (intelligence, investigative, technical, and evaluative), though the differences do not seem to be relevant and applicable in all forensic sciences.

likelihood-ratio-based approach[7] to the evaluation of forensic findings stating that the forensic evaluation of evidence should be based on exhaustive and mutually exclusive hypotheses formulated in pairs, and the assignment of a likelihood ratio (LR) addressing each of the competing propositions: "The likelihood ratio measures the strength of support the findings provide to discriminate between propositions of interest." (ENFSI 2015: 6). The main difference between the two approaches of evaluating evidence is that the first approach addresses the probability of a hypothesis given the evidence (i.e. posterior probability) whereas the LR-based approach addresses the evidence given the hypotheses (i.e. LR).[8] Beside logic, an advantage of the LR-based approach is the possibility to combine the LRs of independent variables by multiplying them.[9] However, difficulties arise for forensic sciences which lack population-level data necessary for the calculation of LRs. The suggestion to estimate LRs instead of calculating them is still under debate as it might cause further issues, e.g. differing estimations by different experts and a misleading impression of objectivity and robustness which does not in fact exist.

Again, the phase of criminal proceedings that a linguistic analysis is meant to serve (investigation vs. court proceedings) is not necessarily influencing the choice of methodology of the forensic analysis because investigative support and evaluation of evidence are equally dependent on sound scientific procedures. But the difference is most reflected in the reporting of forensic linguistic findings and the tasks that are relevant.

2.3 Authorship attribution tasks

There are several objectives that forensic linguistic analyses can have. This section focuses on forensic tasks involving the analysis of anonymous texts with the aim to disambiguate an author of a text or to attribute a text to an author, i.e. authorship profiling, comparative analyses, and the use of corpora of forensically relevant texts.[10]

---

7 The author is indebted to a colleague for the remark that the above mentioned approach is often called *Bayesian approach* disregarding that also a probabilistic statement can be Bayesian in fact.
8 Cf. Jessen (this volume, chapter 9 [4.2]) for the Bayes theorem in the odds form. Concerning the interface of forensic sciences and the courts, there is the conflicting situation that, on the one hand, the judge is ultimately interested in posterior odd statements and that, on the other hand, these statements presuppose prior odds that the forensic scientist is not supposed to know.
9 Though this is possible in theory, a potential problem for this procedure is that the hypotheses have to be truly the same. It would be up to the judge to decide on the sameness of hypotheses as presented in expert reports of different forensic sciences.
10 There are further tasks with the aim to determine the authenticity of texts and to make statements about the author of a text, e.g. involving text samples, statements or just expressions which are wrongly attributed to an author as it may happen in protocols of police interviews. For an overview cf. Coulthard and Johnson (2007) among others.

2.3.1 Authorship profiling

The task of disambiguating the author of an anonymous text is straightforwardly faced by analysing the language of that text and inferring from the analysed linguistic characteristics to the author. This procedure is a profiling task and essentially non-comparative in nature. Due to the lack of comparison material, it is occasionally referred to as "single text problem" (Grant 2008: 222; Coulthard, Grant and Kredens 2011: 536–537) including cases in which the "single text" may in fact be a set of text samples known to be of common origin and, thus, pooled in order to be analysed collectively.

The objective of authorship profiling tasks is the categorisation of an author with respect to social influences and biographical aspects, the evaluation of author intentions and aims pursued with the text as well as the assessment under which circumstances a text was produced (cf. Dern 2009: 64).[11] It is important to note that authorship profiling tasks are not aimed at the psychology or personality of authors but at the influences that prevailed during these authors' language acquisition phase, that still prevail in their current language use, and that, thus, allow categorisations according to social and biographical aspects. Referring to authorship profiling tasks by terms like "sociolinguistic profiling" (Coulthard, Grant and Kredens 2011: 538), "describ[ing] an author *qua* author" (Olsson 2004: 98) and "Text Analysis" (Dern 2009: 64–66; Ehrhardt 2013: 68) emphasises the purely linguistic nature of this analysis and the indispensable dissociation from other (forensic) sciences und procedures.

Authorship profiling requires the extensive examination of the questioned text in terms of collecting and systematising the essential linguistic characteristics of this text as the basis of interpretation (cf. section 3 for a possible method of analysis). In general, the interpretation of linguistic features aims at the aspects presented in Table 7.1.

There are further aspects which might be in the focus of linguistic analyses, e.g. an author's sex, the seriousness of threats as well as deception detection, but as far as is known, these topics are hard to approach with linguistic methodology alone.

Of course, it is crucial to take into account the possibility that authors intentionally disguise their linguistic behaviour by manipulating their language use (cf. section 4). Manipulations can be detected quite well as authors usually do not have the kind of in-depth linguistic knowledge required for a complete shift of authorship status. Despite the realistic possibility to detect manipulations they might be effective nevertheless because they successfully prevent the interpretation of authentic linguistic features. In short, the success of manipulations as an author's strategy to cover up linguistic traces is largely independent of the success of detecting manipulations.

---

11 An assessment of how a text was produced may be a valuable information for investigations per se but this assessment is also part of the evaluation of linguistic findings, e.g. in the explanation of the origin of particular linguistic characteristics like spelling errors that are typing errors actually (cf. section 3.1).

Table 7.1: Relevant aspects in authorship profiling tasks.

Language classification	Assessment of language usage as native or non-native: If the author is writing in a foreign language there might be the possibility to point out which language the author's mother tongue actually is, although, the statement about a group of closely related languages (e.g. Slavic, Romance, Germanic languages) seems to be more practicable.[1]
Regional variety	Markers of dialect and accent: By this, an assessment of the author's origin and current place of residence is aimed at – although with the reservation that dialect and accents are language features that are less easily accessible in writing than they are in samples of spoken language.
Age	Approximation to age ranges: Linguistic markers of these ranges may be the use of obsolete spellings, expressions and grammatical forms, the use of teenage slang, just emerging tokens and inflection forms as well as experience in text composition in different communicative situations.
Linguistic competence, Education, Social background	These three aspects are closely related: Linguistic competence is assessed by analysing texts with respect to an author's skills in writing and text composition. As these skills (among others) are standard skills of higher education, the level of education is deduced from the linguistic competence displayed in a text sample. On the basis of the assumption that level of education and social class are likely to be correlated, the social class of authors is derived from their linguistic competence and the presumed level of education. Indications of these aspects may be provided by text structure, thematic development, vocabulary and layout.[2] The precision of assessments regarding education and social class can vary greatly, and, depending on the text sample in question, it may not be possible at all to draw conclusions.
Profession, Special interests	An author's professional knowledge and special interests are assessed on the basis of technical terminology and particular expressions which are not part of standard or commonly known vocabulary and thus presumed to be acquired while carrying out an occupation as well as in vocational training. However, this assessment is getting increasingly difficult as specialised knowledge has become more easily available, e.g. due to information platforms at the internet.[3] For this reason, it is part of the task to differentiate between genuine use of technical language and seeming specialised knowledge. Clues to an authentic use of technical terminology are formulations which do not contain just proper nouns as technical terms but also other parts of speech, especially verbs, and of course the correct use of technical terminology. Texts may also show that an author assumes something as known/unknown which is in fact not (to laymen). In addition to technical terminology, a text sample also needs to be assessed with respect to how skilled in writing and text composition an author is since this information may hint at a professional orientation involving the professional use of (written) language.

(continued)

Table 7.1: (continued)

Attitude	The analysis of an author's choice of expression may provide indications to attitudes, beliefs and views. For example, the German adjective "ungläubig" [infidel] is nowadays more or less exclusively used by people with an Islamic background (either to distance themselves from non-Muslims or from other Islamic orientations).[4] Similarly, using the noun phrase "kapitalistische Verwertungslogik" [capitalist logic of exploitation] in line of an argument hints at the rather left-wing political view of an author, and deictic expressions like *here* define an author's perception of his/her personal space possibly interpretable in terms of a region and/or identifcation with a particular group.

Notes:
[1] Assessing the presumed mother tongue of an author is often a delicate matter due to the variety of languages that might be relevant and the natural limits of an analyst's expertise. The discussion of the assessment with experts of the language(s) in question is an appropriate measure to improve the strength of the result.
[2] Layout is just partly linked to linguistic theory. Including layout in linguistic analyses serves the purpose of assessing an author's adherence to text models (e.g. text components in formal writing) and – if possible – skills of word processing. The analysis of text layout is not meant to describe and interpret an author's choice of typeface, font, printer or pen.
[3] Additionally, Braun observes a tendency of the standard language to become more and more scientific because of a general popularisation of sciences (Braun 1998: 41).
[4] The remark above only refers to the meaning of "ungläubig" in the narrow, religion-related sense of the word. The adjective is also frequently used in different contexts, e.g. "ungläubig den Kopf schütteln" [shaking the head in disbelief].

In general, the procedure of interpreting the occurrence or the quality of linguistic characteristics with respect to influences on language acquisition and language use implies the risk of overrating and misinterpreting. Coulthard, Grant and Kredens are correct in their reasoning that it is the reversal of scientific method that provokes these risks: "Normal scientific method moves from observation of a large number of examples to a generalization. Profiling involves taking a single example and, by matching it to a well-founded generalization, drawing a conclusion about that instance." (2011: 538). The risks of misinterpretation and overrating can be minimised by basing assessments on approved reference material and, more importantly, statistical evaluations of linguistic features. Reservations against author profiles are justified if assessments seem to be exclusively based on intuition and (personal) experience of the profiler.

2.3.2 Text comparison

In contrast to the task of authorship profiling, text comparisons require at least two text samples for analysis. Prior to the actual comparison task, the hypotheses that the analysis addresses need to be outlined including a clarification about the constellation of the text samples. A multitude of constellations are possible but they can be interpreted in terms of the three setup options *1:1*, *1:N* and *N:N*. The clarification of the comparison setup is less straightforward than it seems as this process is usually based on information which is already interpreted with respect to authorship by the party commissioning the request for comparison. This information might be misleading conditioning information and should be checked for plausibility[12] before conducting a text comparison to avoid the risk of a design error of the comparison task as well as to avoid the risk of incorrectly pooling text samples in order to analyse them collectively.

The basic comparison setup (*1:1* or pairwise) involves just two text samples. Comparisons in which there is just one text of questioned authorship are also termed *authorship verification* (cf. Potha and Stamatatos 2014: 313–314). Koppel, Schler and Argamon (2013) refer to authorship verification tasks as the "fundamental problem of authorship attribution", and they point out that this setup is at the core of other setups as well: "Plainly, if we can solve this problem, we can solve the standard attribution problems [...] as well as many other authorship attribution problems." (Koppel, Schler and Argamon 2013: 326).

A pairwise text comparison can be further specified with respect to whether a text of questioned authorship is to be compared to a text of known authorship or of questioned authorship as well. The first constellation (questioned vs. known material) is the more typical one because it includes standard forensic comparison of anonymous texts with text samples of suspects. The latter constellation (questioned vs. questioned material) serves the purpose of establishing the basis to combine the investigations of so far unsolved but possibly related cases.

The *1:N* setup is a task of increased difficulty and the *N:N* setup even more so. Both can be interpreted (or operationalised) as a series of pairwise comparisons. In computational linguistics and biometrical approaches, *N* is specified either as a closed set of candidates (set includes author of questioned material) or as an open set (set may or may not include author of questioned material). The effect of this distinction is that the linguistic features of candidate authors need to be weighted differently (due to different prior odds) in the course of the comparison. In forensic linguistics, a text comparison is mostly an open-set attribution task, i.e. the question to be answered is *Was the questioned text written by one of the candidate authors and if so who?*. Comparisons of the kind *Who of the candidate authors has written the questioned text?* which would be a closed-set attribution task are commissioned much less commonly. A closed-set comparison requires a completed pre-selection of possible authors; but conditioning circumstances and results of investigations are seldom that precise.[13]

---

12 Such a plausibility check would be part of the critical inspection of texts as described below (section 3.1).
13 Potha and Stamatatos do not perceive this scenario as unrealistic because "in many forensic applications the investigators are able to filter out most of the persons in a case and produce a

Consequently, the most common situation is that some persons are suspected to have written an anonymous text without excluding that another person (outside the circle of suspects) could have written the questioned material.

What has just been called the "underlying questions" of a text comparison refers to the hypotheses or propositions that need to be formulated before the analysis. The definition of these preliminaries is the essential step because they define the conceptual framework in which the analysis is conducted. This step is of course closely related to the discussion of how to evaluate linguistic findings, i.e. the results of a text comparison, which was briefly addressed at the end of the last paragraph (cf. section 2.2). There are several approaches under discussion and in use, e.g. the assignment of likelihood-ratios (cf. ENFSI 2015), the use of a scale of verbal probability statements (cf. Dern 2009: 75–78), and the use of categorical statements complemented by an expression about the strength of certainty (cf. Coulthard 2010: 480–484). The application of these approaches is partly dependent on the methods used to extract linguistic features (cf. section 3) but not solely.[14]

Disregarding the ongoing discussion which approach is suited best to serve both the demands of science and judicial proceedings, the actual procedure for a comparative linguistic analysis is basically the same. First of all, each of the involved text samples is analysed separately and independently by extracting the linguistic features that will be the basis for the evaluation. The extraction implies the collection and the systematisation of linguistic data. Both the data collection itself as well as the features it contains can be relevant for the comparison. The linguistic data is then further analysed with respect to similarities, differences and its typicality for a population of relevant language users. Eventually, the results of that process are evaluated, i.e. conclusions are drawn addressing the hypotheses that have been formulated in the preliminaries to the text comparison.

2.3.3 Corpora of forensically relevant texts

Similar to the establishment of identification services for DNA, handwriting and firearms, texts of criminal cases can be used to build up a corpus or database for identification purposes. Of course, the realisation depends on the possibility to obtain relevant texts in quantities large enough to allow for general insights in particular

---

closed-set of suspects" (Potha and Stamatatos 2014: 313). There may be differences internationally in how much information an expert is in command of to treat justifiably a comparison request as closed-set attribution task. Under the condition that the information about a set of candidate authors being closed is reliable, this task presents the less complicated challenge.

14 Experts applying automated and quantitative approaches tend to make use of the likelihood-ratio-based approach whereas experts using qualitative approaches seemingly prefer other frameworks (cf. section 3).

types of criminal activity (and maybe concentrating on a certain geographical region). For example, the German Bundeskriminalamt (BKA) hosts and develops the so-called *Corpus of Incriminating Texts* by collecting and processing all the anonymous texts that are analysed there.[15] The forensic linguistics department started this work in 1990 and is now in command of a database which serves as an identification service for several types of texts like blackmail letters and extremist/terrorist responsibility claims. Each anonymous text that is submitted for forensic linguistic examination is subjected to a corpus search, i.e. salient features concerning choice of expression, topic, deviations from standards of writing and text composition etc. are used as search items in this procedure. In addition to the identification of texts that are presumably written by the same author as the latest anonymous writing, the focus of interest is on linking offences, e.g., by uncovering similarities in the modus operandi.

Instances in which a text-based identification service was successful involve the detection of links between cases of the same offence type and of different offence types. Concerning the same-offence linking, it is known that the rate of repeat offenders (and repeat writers of anonymous texts) is substantial in fields of criminal activity like extortion, assault and slander. As a result to implementing the text-based identification service, the forensic linguistics department of the BKA was able to detect a connection between two extortion cases which were committed to the detriment of a municipal utility company and a large chemical enterprise. What was unusual about this case is the time interval of 20 years between the two offences. The extortion committed earlier could not be solved back then whereas, in the current extortion, the offender was arrested during the handover of money. With the linking of the two cases via a linguistic database search, the offender could be held responsible for both offences.

Of course, police records are also effectively used to link cases, especially within a field of criminal activity. The task gets harder when it comes to types of offences which appear to be very unlikely to have been committed by one and the same person. There was such an instance in 2011 when a German intelligence service captured e-mails announcing an Islamist terrorist attack. The author of those e-mails offered further information in return for financial favours. The database search resulted in a match regarding a series of extortion letters against a local drugstore chain which unmasked the author of the e-mails as ordinary extortionist who was then quickly discovered and prosecuted.

These two examples show that a text-based identification service is a powerful tool regardless of the type of offence.[16] The possibility to link cases of seemingly unrelated fields of criminal activity presumably presents the biggest advantage to classical

---

15 Other examples of forensic text corpora are the compilation of suicide notes as described in Shapero (2011) as well as the corpus of threatening texts called Communicated Threat Assessment Database (Simons and Tunkel 2014: 199).
16 For further fields in which corpora are used in forensic linguistics cf. Coulthard (1994) and Kredens and Coulthard (2012).

police records. However, this kind of work depends on the constant incorporation of anonymous texts into the database which is hard to achieve without the help of law enforcement agencies.

3 Methods of analysis

With the basic assumption, the scope and the tasks of authorship attribution analyses being outlined we now turn to the questions of how forensic examinations are conducted and which methods are being used. Basically, forensic examinations consist of three parts: the critical inspection of the objects of analysis, the diagnosis of findings and the evaluation of findings.

3.1 Critical inspection of the objects of analysis

Before conducting a forensic analysis, the text samples under examination should be evaluated with respect to their suitability for the analysis at hand. Text characteristics that have potentially an effect on conducting linguistic examinations include the aspects presented in Table 7.2.

Table 7.2: Aspects for critical inspections of examination material.

Quantity of the material	Texts may be too short or too long for the method of analysis that is intended to be used. There may also be an unfavourable difference in length between text samples submitted for comparative analyses.
Quality of the material	Texts may be only partially legible due to incomplete transmissions of data or damages by fire, explosions, water etc. Apart from that, texts may not have been submitted as original copy but as duplicates with modifications unintentionally caused during the process of duplication, e.g. corrupted or missing parts due to data conversion or copying.
Date of origin	Due to the fact that linguistic behaviour may change in the course of time, texts submitted for comparative analyses may show differences which are a result of the time interval of their respective origin and which do not necessarily indicate different authors.
Mode of text production	Differences or similarities between texts may be caused by their modes of production rather than author-specific characteristics. This might be especially relevant in comparative examinations of handwritten and electronically generated texts as the writing process has an influence on the occurrence of particular linguistic features, e.g. typing errors, and those features that are caused by the default or typing settings in electronic communication devices, e.g. automatic word completion.

Table 7.2: (continued)

Type of text	Analogously to mode of text production, it is important to distinguish between features caused by the chosen type of text and those which display linguistic preferences of an author. The disparity between these categories becomes more intelligible in comparisons of text samples of the same type which means that a match situation should always be attempted in a comparative task.[1]
Attribution of authorship by commissioning party	Parties commissioning a request for authorship analysis may deliver texts which are assumed to be of common origin. Since pooling[2] text samples can be of advantage for the analysis, this assumption must be checked for its plausibility. The procedure may include a test for homogeneity of prominent linguistic, textual and extra-textual features.[3] An analysis which has been conducted under false presuppositions is rendered unsuited for investigation and presentation in court likewise. Cases are known in which the false presuppositions became obvious during the presentation in court and, thus, severely compromised the expert's current and subsequent work.
Indications of collaborative authorship	As outlined in section 2.1, texts may not have been written by a single author. If there are indications of collaborative authorship or editing/revising processes, it needs to be made clear in which ways the analysis is influenced or limited.

Notes:
[1] In more detail than above, Dern (2009: 62–63) lists as potentially limiting factors for an analysis text length, quality of duplicate, date of origin and type of text.
[2] Pooling is the act of combining separate text samples into one set under the assumption that all the segments in the set belong to the same author.
[3] For instance, extra-textual features like handwriting may reveal deviations to such an extent that pooling is not justified. This has recently happened in Germany where the judge of court proceedings in a large terrorist case commissioned a text comparison of an anonymous pamphlet with handwritten texts of the defendant. These comparison texts were forms of the defendant's prison which are used there to request permissions (like the participation in sports classes) and which have to be filled in by hand and personally signed by the applicants. Despite the correct attribution to the defendant (which became clear due to a particular requested permission and the corresponding identification number), the request – including the signature – was written in an apparently different hand than the other texts. Consequently, this text had to be excluded from the analysis.

From a linguistic point of view, the conditions of forensic examinations are usually not what is considered to be optimal. A critical inspection of the items submitted for examination serves the purpose of making clear under which conditions an examination is conducted as well as which results can and, equally important, cannot be expected. As the outcome of a critical inspection takes its influence in the analysis and especially in the evaluation of findings, the process of a forensic examination becomes more transparent and understandable when its conditions are presented beforehand and separately from the other parts of the examination.

3.2 Diagnosis of findings

The methods that are used to analyse texts within the scope of forensic examinations are not entirely agreed upon by forensic practitioners. On the contrary, there is a great variety of approaches. A basic dividing line is usually drawn between qualitative and quantitative approaches, although, the term *quantitative approach* seems to be too limited in scope for its intended coverage. What is subsumed under this heading is better being described as statistical and automated methods of analysis.

For authorship analysis, each of these approaches has its advantages. Qualitative approaches make use of multitude of independent features and, thus, reach a remarkable depth of description and analysis. Statistical and automated approaches usually incorporate population-level data and they are tested for reliability and validity– both being perceived as increasing the strength of evidence. Conversely, each of these approaches has its weaknesses. For qualitative approaches, the lacking possibility to test their reliability and validity might not be in line with demands of judicial systems concerning the admissibility of forensic evidence. Furthermore, large amounts of data cannot be fully analysed with time and effort balanced. Statistical and automated approaches are limited in the number of features that can be used for an analysis. The challenge for methodological development probably lies in the smart combination of the approaches as to make the most of each's advantages for the ultimate aim to increase the strength of evidence in authorship analysis.

3.2.1 Qualitative approaches

Qualitative approaches are characterised by a generally non-standardised collection of data grounded in those parts of linguistic theory that explain the processes of language production, language use and potential influences on both. The subsequent evaluation of data is based on interpretation and judgement. Despite their grounding in scientific theory, qualitative methods (and their results) are occasionally suspected to be subjective and/or arbitrary as their reliability and validity is generally not tested. To respond to this suspicion, qualitative methods and the interpretation of findings are often complemented by empirical, e.g. corpus-based, studies and statistical analyses of linguistic characteristics; although only selected characteristics are accessible with these approaches.

The full range of approaches to analyse anonymous texts cannot be addressed here. Major theoretical treatments of forensic linguistics and their application to case work are presented in several books and papers by McMenamin (2002), Coulthard (2004), Shuy (2006) and Kniffka (2007), to name only few influential works.

As an example to demonstrate how qualitative linguistic methods can be applied in forensic examinations, a method will be outlined that is in use in German law enforcement for several years.[17] The method comprises the combined qualitative analysis of numerous linguistic features. The features of a text are described with regard to their relation to linguistic and communicative norms. Linguistic and communicative norms differ with respect to their binding force. The underlying assumption is that language is both a system governed by rules and a system providing alternatives and equivalents which can be chosen from according to appropriateness. Error analysis[18] is applied to detect and classify systematic violations of norms (errors) as well as non-systematic violations (mistakes). The procedure comprises several steps by which errors and mistakes are identified, described, explained with respect to their origin as well as evaluated in relation to unmarked and accepted occurrences. The errors and mistakes of a text are classified with regard to the level of language (e.g. punctuation, grammar, vocabulary), type (e.g. omission, addition, substitution) and specific category (e.g. capitalisation, word division, case inflection) resulting in a typology of systematic and non-systematic violations of norms for that particular text.

In addition to the analysis of errors and mistakes, the stylistic features of a text are analysed. This analysis is conducted on all levels of language including text structure and layout, as each might show salient features by which an author's style of writing and text composition can be described. While the criterion for evaluating errors is the dichotomy *correct* vs. *incorrect*, stylistic features are evaluated according to their quality and appropriateness in the specific context. The analysis of an author's style is approached from two perspectives: From the perspective of text production (author's perspective), language offers a repertoire of alternatives to choose from. From the perspective of text reception (reader's perspective), these stylistic choices are evaluated according to their quality and compliance with expectations that the text provokes, e.g. by its layout, forms of address, subject etc. It is important to consider both perspectives; without an evaluation of possible alternatives, the description of stylistic features that are actually used in a text falls short of its full informational value – even more so as there is always a gap between the level of describing an author's individual style and the perception of style markers (cf. Grant and Baker 2001). Therefore, the analysis of stylistic features presents a difficult task due to the issue of describing individual perceptions of style (Fobbe 2011: 108). This procedure also implies the identification of salient features and the scaling of their salience. Studies on the frequency and distribution of features with the help of reference corpora provide the complementation of qualitative stylistic analyses.

The approach of combining error analysis and stylistic analysis results in an extensive data collection which describes each text and its author in a very detailed manner. Apart from that, it offers an additional level for evaluation as, beside the

---

17 For a more detailed description cf. Baldauf 1999, Dern 2009: 67–70, Fobbe 2011: 104–155.
18 Error analysis has been developed in the context of language learning. It is concerned with understanding (successful and erroneous) language production and its implications on language teaching (Corder 1967, James 1998).

features themselves, the collection of features can be evaluated with respect to typicality and plausibility of composition. Especially in the context of linguistic manipulations, the check of the data collection for plausibility has proven to be valuable. Linguistic manipulations as a means of disguise can often be detected because manipulators lack the linguistic understanding to take into account all levels of language that are affected by their chosen strategy, e.g. pretending to be a non-native writer. Instead, they are manipulating only those levels of language that they are aware of like spelling and morphology which results in constellations of errors and mistakes that deviate from the language use of genuine non-natives (cf. Dern 2008).

The method just presented has produced good results in law enforcement over a long period of time.[19] Nevertheless, it provides some challenges. The first challenge is a result of the purely qualitative nature which is in contrast to contemporaneous developments and demands for validity testing. The second challenge results from the dependence on the amount of material which has to be large enough to be reasonably expressive for linguistic analyses, but which must not be too large for the method to be applicable at all.[20] This means that it is sensible to also invest in statistical and automated approaches for at least two reasons – to face the demand for testing and to enlarge one's portfolio of methods for authorship analysis.

3.2.2 Statistical and automated approaches

Due to the extensive digitisation which comprises nearly all areas of life and work, it seems to be a modern trend to invest in the development and application of statistical and automated approaches. This assumption turns out to be wrong considering that the first attempts of "nontraditional authorship attribution studies"[21] date back to the 1960s, more concrete to the analysis of *The Federalist* papers (Mosteller and Wallace 1964). According to Stamatatos 2009, the statistical research of that time and until the 1990s was dominated by "attempts to define features for quantifying writing style" (Stamatatos 2009: 538), also known as *stylometry*,[22] which was intended as a

---

[19] Expert reports produced with this method are constantly checked against results from investigations and the outcome of court proceedings. Furthermore, the method has been standardised and accredited according to ISO 17020 in order to prevent misapplication and ensure reliability as far as it is possible for qualitative methods.
[20] Although linguistic analyses generally benefit from large amounts of material, it is not per se an advantage to use all the material that is available. Beside the need to select suitable texts for analysis (cf. section 3.1), it may be necessary to restrict an examination to texts which are likely to add information about an author's writing style with time and effort balanced.
[21] The term *nontraditional authorship attribution* is used in contrast to qualitative, human-expert-based approaches (Stamatatos 2009: 538).
[22] For a survey of the history of stylometry cf. Holmes (1994).

computer-assisted way of working on authorship questions. Fully automated approaches do not seem to have been in the focus for most of the time until now.

Statistical methods work in different degrees of complexity. Descriptive statistics can be applied with a relatively simple test design, for example by analysing a selected feature which is then evaluated with respect to rareness[23] and – in comparative analyses – by testing differences for significance (e.g. with the help of a t-test). Among the features used for these statistic evaluations are usually figures which serve as measurement of lexical richness like type-token ratio, lexical density and the number of hapax legomena (i.e. words that appear only once in a text), but also figures which quantify the various components of texts, e.g. distribution and frequency of punctuation marks, average word length, average number of syllables per word, average sentence length etc. Juola describes these approaches as a "summary statistic" which is extracted because of the underlying idea that "different authors will vary, noticeably and consistently, along this statistic" (2008: 9). But analogous to traditional authorship studies, selected linguistic features do not universally function as discriminators between authors. Therefore, the approaches relying on single features or small feature sets did not prove to be successful over a variety of different types of texts. Results improve when features of different types (character-based, lexical, syntactical, and semantic features) are combined.

As with qualitative approaches, the variety of methods developed to use or approximate automated procedures for authorship attribution cannot be addressed here. Juola (2008) and Stamatatos (2009) provide excellent overviews. While early studies in this line of research focused on literary texts, interest today has switched to electronically generated and digitally transmitted types of text (e.g. Grant 2013; Sousa Silva et al. 2011 among others) – not least because text messages and instant messages are available in large amounts.

Two studies which combine an automated procedure with a likelihood-ratio-based approach of evaluation have been presented by Ishihara (2014 and 2017). On the basis of a non-forensic SMS corpus, Ishihara tested the performance of a text comparison system. For this purpose, he created four datasets with messages by 24, 34, 43 and 85 authors. Each dataset contained two text groups of each author compiled by chronologically sorting the text messages up to a length of 200, 1000, 2000, and 3000 words. As method for data extraction, Ishihara uses the N-gram language model in which a text is modelled as a series of N-grams[24] and their associated probabilities (as a result of their frequencies). The data were then used to calculate a score for each comparison of two texts. The score formula, as presented in Doddington (2001: 2522), puts the degree of similarity between two message groups in relation (*log ratio*) to the typicality of one of the two message groups against a cross-validated background model which was built on the basis of all text groups in the test except those two just

---

23 This refers to the concept of typicality (compared to a defined population) as outlined in section 3.3.
24 An N-gram is a sequence of language items with N defining the length of the sequence; e.g., word bigrams and trigrams are sequences of two or three words, respectively.

compared.[25] By way of logistic regression, the calculated scores are calibrated in order to convert them to likelihood ratios (LRs). The performance of the system is finally evaluated with the value log-likelihood-ratio cost (C_{llr}) as a gradient metric to assess the overall performance of a system.[26] The magnitude of LRs and scores as well as the discriminatory power of the system are discussed with the help of Tippett plots.[27] In his 2017 study, Ishihara again tests the performance of a text comparison system, this time using a forensic corpus of chatlog messages used to prosecute paedophiles (Ishihara 2017: 71). As method of data extraction, he chose several word-based and character-based stylometric features like Yule's I, type-token ratio and unusual-word ratio (Ishihara 2017: 73). The system performance was evaluated by calculating the equal error rate (EER) and the log-likelihood-ratio cost (C_{llr}).

The results of both studies suggest that automatic text comparison systems are suited to discriminate between same-author and different-author messages if the amount of text material is large enough (Ishihara 2014: 38–43; Ishihara 2017: 67). For the different data sets in the 2014 study, the results improve with the sample size and it becomes obvious that the performance of such systems and consequently the evaluation of findings depends on the availability of relevant population-level data for modelling backgrounds (Ishihara 2014: 43–44, Ishihara 2017: 92).

That sample size is the key issue in automated approaches has also been shown in two studies conducted with authentic forensic material from the BKA corpus of incriminating texts. The study design resembled that of Ishihara (2014 and 2017). The first test served as a pilot study with only a small database which led to somewhat distorted background models and problems in converting the scores to LRs (Ehrhardt 2015). In the main test, the data base consisted of 84 authors and 144 different parameter combinations of N-gram-based data with each parameter combination presenting an independent text comparison system. For the result of a particular comparison of two texts from the data base, the score was transformed into a likelihood ratio. The subsequent comparative evaluation of the systems has shown that an approach like this is altogether promising (EER: 13%, C_{llr}: 0.4381985 for the best performing parameter combination [Ehrhardt 2017]). But still, limitations in sample size, especially of data for the background set, had a clear effect in the study.

Researchers of related fields of application have also struggled with problems of population size. For forensic voice comparison systems, the influence of the background population size has been analysed. Equal error rates can become unstable below a population size of 20 speakers; but they start to get stable with 30 speakers

---

[25] For further explanations of how the scores are calculated cf. Doddington 2001 and the verbalisation in Ishihara (2014: 35–37).
[26] With reference to Morrison (2011: 93) and Brümmer and du Preez (2006), Ishihara (2014: 37–38) explains the advantage of C_{llr} as scalar value for performance assessment.
[27] Jessen (this volume, chapter 9 [4.5]) gives a short explanation of how Tippett plots are read, and he provides references for further reading on method validation.

and even more so with 60 speakers (Kinoshita and Ishihara 2014: 217).Thus, the major obstacle for this line of research is the lack of appropriate corpora. It would appear that this obstacle can be remedied for some cases considering that modern communicative devices are based on electronically generated texts which easily mount up to several megabytes in size.

3.3 Evaluation of findings

For the evaluation of findings, it is important to be aware of three relevant dichotomies: 1) *consistency* and *distinctiveness*, 2) *intra-author variation* and *inter-author variation*, 3) *similarity* and *typicality*. These concepts' relevance results from the demand in authorship analysis to assess linguistic characteristics with respect to their discriminative power and their evidential value. Consistency refers to the assumption that an author's linguistic characteristics are sufficiently consistent to recur with a frequency that makes this author recognisable by his/her characteristics. Furthermore, it is a basic assumption of authorship analysis that the consistent characteristics of an author are sufficiently distinctive to discriminate that author from most other authors.[28] Comparative linguistic analyses rest upon these assumptions. However, problems arise due to two circumstances: Neither is consistency a stable criterion to describe an author's characteristics nor is distinctiveness a stable criterion to discriminate authors on the basis of their characteristics. Instead, both consistency and distinctiveness show variations. For authorship analysis, it is relevant to know with how much variation characteristics occur – both for a single author and between different authors. The variation within an author's characteristics is called intra-author variation, the variation of characteristics between different authors inter-author variation. The optimal situation for comparative analyses is low intra-author variation and high inter-author variation, because in that case an author would show features which are very different from those of other authors. The worst situation for comparative analyses is just the other way round, i.e. high intra-author variation and low inter-author variation which means that authors vary with respect to their characteristics so much that there might be a substantial overlap with characteristics of other authors.[29] In the course of comparative analyses, linguistic characteristics are assessed regarding their intra-author and inter-author variation with the ultimate aim to determine the degree of distinctiveness between two authors and to put this into relation to their respective consistency. Characteristics which show high intra-author and

---

28 Cf. Grant (2010) for the discussion that the assumptions of consistency and distinctiveness render the notion of idiolect as theoretical grounding of authorship analysis superfluous.
29 For an illustration of the four possible constellations in the quality of intra-/inter-individual variation the reader is referred to Jessen (this volume, chapter 9 [2.1]). He also discusses the relevance of similarity and typicality in the context of forensic voice comparisons.

low inter-author variation are less suited to discriminate between authors, i.e. their discriminating power is limited, and vice versa.

Distinctiveness describes the distance of an author's characteristics to another author's characteristics. The opposite concept, i.e. similarity, describes the closeness of characteristics between two authors. The determination of the degree of distinctiveness or similarity between two authors as a result of a comparative analysis is incomplete as there is no indication made about how likely it is that this very degree of similarity (distinctiveness likewise) can occur with respect to other authors as well. This additional, but necessary information is provided by an assessment of typicality which is a frequency measure in relation to the relevant population and which expresses the evidential value of the characteristics that are analysed. The statement that characteristics of two authors resemble each other to a high degree carries more evidential value if the characteristics are proven to occur only rarely in the population of all relevant authors. Vice versa, characteristics with a high degree of similarity but which are quite common in frequency for a population do not have much evidential value for the comparison of two authors' texts. The combined concepts of similarity and typicality are also reflected in the calculation of scores and, eventually, likelihood ratios as it was described above. As it was shown there, the score formula contains a similarity part, i.e. the comparison of text A to the model of text B, and a typicality part, i.e. the comparison of text A to the background model which was created on the basis of all texts (or on a predefined background set) in the test and which represents the relevant population.

The evaluation of findings is the crucial issue when it refers to the task of expressing the results of a comparative analysis for use within the scope of legal proceedings. The ultimate aim of a comparative task for the expert is to take a position to at least two mutually exclusive hypotheses. It is generally agreed upon that the analysis of linguistic characteristics does not provide sufficient grounding for categorical statements regarding those hypotheses (Dern 2009: 75). However, Broeders (1999: 237–238) suspects that conclusion frameworks like the use of verbal probability scales allow just that – categorical statements which are just hedged by statements of subjective conviction. Furthermore, it has been recognised that the basis for the use of verbal probability scales is often logically flawed in the sense that it addresses posterior probabilities, i.e. probability of one hypothesis concerning identity or non-identity given the evidence which consists of the results of the linguistic analysis, instead of addressing the probability of the evidence given the (at least two and mutually exclusive) hypotheses. In contrast, the likelihood-ratio-based approach has been promoted as logically correct way for the evaluation of evidence (cf. ENFSI 2015). The presentation of results differs accordingly: Common verbal probability scales include statements like *It is highly probable that the texts just compared are written by the same author.* (cf. Dern 2009: 76) whereas the result within the LR-based framework is expressed as *The forensic findings provide moderately strong support for the proposition that suspect A has written the text rather than for the proposition that an unknown person has written the text.* (cf. ENFSI 2015: 17). However, the application of the LR-based approach presents a dilemma for qualitative forensic linguistics as it lacks the population-level data that is the basis for the calculation of likelihood ratios. In this context, Coulthard refers to the problem of getting this data and he comes to the conclusion that "forensic linguists do not have access to population statistics" (Coulthard 2010: 483). This is certainly true for the qualitative analysis of many linguistic characteristics, though surely not for the entirety. Advocates of automated approaches in forensic linguistics seem to be better positioned as these methods are already designed to work with data of a relevant population which means that these methods take into account only those features that are apt for an application based on probabilities and statistics. But so far, automated approaches do not have a depth of description as qualitative approaches have and, therefore, automated approaches have not been brought to such a level of maturity that they can substitute qualitative methods. Proponents of the LR-based approach seem to disregard qualitative approaches to a large extent. To the best of the author's knowledge, qualitative linguistic analyses that make use of the conceptual framework of the LR-based approach have not been presented yet in the relevant literature. This suggests that recognition has not yet been won about the point that the analysis of data and the formulation of conclusions can follow different approaches.

The decision on a framework of evaluating findings may be influenced by the methods that are used to extract the relevant linguistic data (as it was already remarked). The necessity of a reliable and correct representation of conclusions should not be affected though. Independently of the methods involved, conclusions always require the consideration of basic principles and concepts for the evaluation of findings. Additionally, the context in which the conclusions are presented has to be taken into account. Ultimately, a trier of fact is confronted with the task to decide on the answer to a binary question. Experts and their evaluation of forensic findings are meant to assist in this process which implies that first and foremost forensic experts are obliged to make exactly clear how their conclusions are to be understood.

4 Objects of analyses

Forensic linguistics has been well described as a linguistic and as a forensic field of research and application (cf. references in section 1). This does not hold true for the objects of forensic linguistic analyses. Publications concentrate on few selected types of texts, with extortion letters (Artmann 1996; Brinker 2002; Busch 2006; Dern 2009: 141–191; Seifert 2010; Fobbe 2011: 72–100 among others),[30] suicide notes (Leenaars 1988; Ammon 1994; Olsson 2004: 159–164; Sanger and McCarthy Veach 2008; Shapero

---

30 Extortion letters seem to have been particularly well researched in German forensic linguistics.

2011, among others) and, more recently, text or micro-blogging messages (Sousa-Silva 2011; Grant 2013; Ishihara 2014, among others) being at the centre of those efforts. The knowledge of text patterns, models and types is essential for forensic linguistics as well as the differentiation between linguistic features that are influenced by text type and those that are idiosyncratic.

As follows, a description will be presented of the AnoText corpus of the German Bundeskriminalamt (BKA) containing text samples that have been objects of forensic examinations in law enforcement within a period of ten years.[31] As a total, the AnoText corpus includes 1,707 writings (903,918 tokens) which date from 2003 to 2012. The writings of the corpus will be described as to how they relate to criminal offences, what type of text they are, and how anonymity has been accomplished by the author of a text. The AnoText corpus represents a repository of forensic texts and, thus, conveys the diversity of these texts. Before describing the particularities of each type of text, the similarities will be pointed out.

There are three features that the writings in AnoText have in common. Firstly, they are *texts* in the sense that they have been produced in the "graphic code" (Koch and Oesterreicher 1985: 17). The corpus does not contain protocols of audio material resulting from monitoring of telecommunications as these protocols are hard to assess with respect to the linguistic influence that other persons beside the speaker have had upon them.[32] Of course, the differences between spoken and written language still have to be taken into account when analysing the texts.

The second common feature of the AnoText writings refers to the *context* they are taken from. Each of the writings has been the object of criminal investigation and/or prosecution. The way they gained that status may differ, though. As traces, these texts have a causal connection with a criminal offence; and this causal connection might be given by the fact that a text is either found at the location of the victim of an offence, is found at the crime scene, is written by an offender, contains information of an offence, shows an ideological connection to an offence, or presents the means of committing an offence. Despite the common denominator of the forensic context, this listing already shows that there is virtually no restriction to the form that a forensically relevant text may take.

The third shared feature of the texts is the *anonymity* of their authors. To obtain anonymity writers have different possibilities at their disposal (cf. Fobbe 2011: 52), although the majority of them simply abstain from signing and including optional

---

[31] For a more detailed discussion cf. Ehrhardt (2017).
[32] Producing a written record of spoken language generally implies a change to the object, e.g. by (intentionally or unintentionally) correcting ungrammatical sequences, by deleting pauses/laughter/coughs/hesitators, by interpreting acoustically ambiguous sequences, by removing instances of simultaneous speech or by adapting utterance parts to make them easier comprehensible. In short, the written records are usually not produced as a genuine transcription, which would be an exact duplicate.

information like a return address.[33] Because anonymity is a marked feature of text types like letters and e-mails, authors repeatedly comment on why they want to stay anonymous by writing about their fear of prosecution and the danger of getting detected by persons somehow involved in the offence in question. A special case of anonymization is linguistic disguise which refers to the intentional manipulation of linguistic features with the aim to either dissimulate or simulate. Dissimulations are arbitrary manipulations of – to non-linguists – easily accessible linguistic features with the aim of covering up a potentially revealing idiosyncrasy. In comparison, simulations are strategies of linguistic manipulations to simulate characteristics of other authors to divert suspicion from the actual author (Ehrhardt 2007; also cf. Dern 2008, Bredthauer 2013). In a broader sense, simulation also comprises the use of pseudonyms and code words which are a widespread phenomenon in extortion letters. In cases of fraud, some authors deliberately choose to write under the name of somebody else (without further linguistic manipulations). All in all, the feature of ancnymity is disputable for about 20 writings of the AnoText corpus as they have names and return addresses included. However, the authenticity of these names and addresses are called into doubt by the investigators and/or the actual owners.

Despite the properties the texts of the corpus have in common, the corpus is in fact characterised by heterogeneity. In order to develop a typology of text types, it is important to highlight the features that differentiate and classify the corpus. The main differentiation between texts can be made on the basis of their relation to the criminal offence. Two types can be distinguished, namely those writings which present the offence themselves and those writings which appear in the context of criminal offences.

4.1 Texts as offences

The first category ("text as offence") makes up about 60 % of the corpus (i.e. 1,034 texts), but is limited only to a few types of text, namely to extortion letters, threatening messages and defamation letters in which language is used to commit the offence itself because the usage of particular speech acts or the particular combination of speech acts constitutes the elements of the offence.[34] This way, the texts are

---

33 This is not tantamount to omitting an address at all. For many authors, text models seem to have such a strong binding force that they cannot leave out information that is typically included. In their need to adhere to conventional models of writing, authors substitute authentic information by fake names, addresses etc.
34 Tiersma and Solan deal with the phenomenon of "language crimes" (2012: 340) by discussing the offences *solicitation, conspiracy, bribery, threatening* and *perjury*. The text samples they describe or give as examples differ in some aspects from the writings that are contained in the *AnoText* corpus which seems to be less diverse with respect to types of texts in the category "text as offence".

classified according to their communicative function (TO EXTORT [= TO THREAT + TO DEMAND], TO THREAT, TO INSULT). Furthermore, these texts can be classified according to the type of text that is usually chosen by the authors of these writings. For incriminating texts, generally accepted and conventionalised types or models of texts do not exist. Still, each competent language user can both recognise and produce an extortion letter (threatening and defamation letters likewise). If authors do not have a model which fits their communicative intention and which they can adhere to, they choose from the existing repertoire of text types of everyday language and adapt them to their needs. Therefore, the most widely chosen text type for the category "text as offence" is the letter – either in a formal, business-like form or in a colloquial form depending on the author's attitude towards the addressee among other factors. In the course of the technical developments that the means of written communication have undergone, the letter became less relevant in the last decades. This development is also reflected in the text types of the AnoText corpus. Until a couple of years ago, the preferred communication medium for blackmailers has been the letter, it then changed to e-mails, and has now changed to the multiple communication possibilities provided by the internet, e.g. contact or request forms of websites. The choice of medium is to a large extent dependent on what the author thinks is best to serve his/her need of anonymisation.

A further possible aspect to differentiate between the category "text as offence" is the addressee and the "sphere of action"[35]. Concerning extortion letters, most of the texts belong to the official sphere because they are addressed to firms. This is not very surprising as the probability of getting large amounts of money appears to be higher when extorting a successful company than a single person, especially if in that case it might be easiest to carry out an impersonal extortion which seemingly presents less risks of detection. With respect to threatening letters, it is interesting that only 53 writings (3.1 % of the total) are addressed to private individuals, whereas 211 (12.4 %) are directed against people who are either well-known or generally perceived as influential (politicians, judges, police officers, priests etc.). Concerning defamation letters, there is a specific type of text in which the addressee represents a whole group of people which are defamed because of their religion or nationality. These writings usually have a right-extremist background. In German criminal law, this offence is subsumed under the section 130: "Volksverhetzung" [incitement to hatred] and it is treated differently than libel and slander due to the historical experience that German nationalism leading to World War II was spurred by the legal toleration of defamation and propaganda against minori-

---

35 According to Brinker (2001: 139ff.), communication can be differentiated with respect to the sphere of action: *private communication* refers to communication among persons privately known to each other, *official communication* refers to communication among business partners etc. and differs from private communication in the degree of obligation it lays on the communicants, *public communication* refers to communication via media like articles, TV, radio and corresponding internet presence.

ties. German post-war legislation sought to prevent further nationalist movements, especially anti-Semitic offences, by revising the corresponding section (cf. Reichel 2001: 144ff.).

In summary, the majority of the writings of AnoText belongs to the category referred to as "text as offence". They show a close relation to the offence in question as the author is committing the offence by means of speech acts.

4.2 Texts in the context of criminal offences

The second category, namely "texts in the context of offences", makes up about 40 % of the AnoText corpus (i.e. 673 writings). The relatively unspecific designation already hints at the fact that this group of samples features various forms of relations to an offence. This relation is comparatively close in cases where the author is the actual offender and takes responsibility of the offence with his text. The corpus contains 216 written responsibility claims. Naturally, their main communicative function is the avowal of having committed an offence but these writings usually comprise more than that. Authors do not just state what they have done but also elaborate on their motivation. This explanation or justification of the deed can be seen as a supplementary communicative function of responsibility claims. Furthermore, this group of texts can be differentiated with respect to the necessity of the avowal which goes along with the sort of offence. Confessions can be described as rather private, even intimate writings of a lone operator who voluntarily gives insights into what has driven him/her to commit the offence. In contrast, responsibility claims that accompany extremist and terrorist offences are written in the name of a group of people. The individual author stays in the background for the benefit of the group. Responsibility claims constitute an inherent element of a radical left-/right-wing offence. Because they appear in temporal proximity to the offence it is obvious that they are included in the plot of the offence right from the start. The absence of a responsibility claim after an extremist/terrorist attack is highly likely to be commented on by the media (Lübbe 2002: 128). The authors' motivation for writing such claims is twofold – they intend to present their political or ideological position, and by pointing to the social context, they try to justify the offence. By that means, the offence is no longer considered an ordinary criminal act but a deed intended to reach an important goal such as the improvement of social conditions. Because of this pretension of the authors Lübbe has termed responsibility claims as „Trivialitätsdementis" [denials of triviality] (2002: 129). In contrast to confessions, responsibility claims are addressed to the public. The combination of both radical offence and responsibility claim can be described as a communicative strategy in which the offence is meant to focus the public's attention on the conditions explained in the accompanying responsibility claim (cf. Unterholzner 2012: 32–34). Formally, responsibility claims consist of the actual avowal (which is usually placed at the very beginning of the text and which is rather short) and various components that serve a secondary communicative function such as a portrayal of the radical group responsible for the offence, justification of the offence connected with an evaluation of selected aspects of society and politics, slogans, calls for action, announcements of further actions as well as comments on media reporting and visibility.

Texts that are similar to responsibility claims in form and content are position papers of radical left-/right-wing groups. These texts comprise 8.9 % of the corpus (i.e. 152 texts). In comparison to responsibility claims, their relation to an offence is less close as position papers are just expositions of ideological beliefs. From the investigator's point of view, position papers are associated with radical offences although they might be free of any hints to actual offences. The content of those papers is similar to responsibility claims: portrayal of the radical group, evaluation of selected aspects of society and politics, slogans, calls for action, and announcements of further actions. But in contrast to responsibility claims, position papers may also be devoted to discussing more general aspects like fundamental social and political issues and the line of action to enforce political aims. In Germany, there was a public debate provoked by the positions papers of the *militante gruppe* [militant group] that lead the discussion about whether or not serious crimes are appropriate means to enforce political aims.

The last clearly distinguishable group of "texts in the context of offences" comprises texts in which anonymous writers provide leads for investigators. These tip-off writings make up about 10 % (i.e. 173 texts) of the AnoText corpus. Tip-offs provide information concerning offences that the author believes not to have been solved yet. With his text, the author presents himself towards the addressee who usually is a law enforcement authority as being a witness, an accessory to the crime or a helper for the police. Most of the texts provide leads to persons supposedly involved in a crime. Some authors also try to elaborate on offenders' motivation. Similar to confessions, tip-offs may not be authentic. The need for recognition on the part of the author may be writing motive. Also, they may have been written in an attempt to defame somebody. Whether or not a tip-off writing is authentic cannot usually be gathered from the writing itself but from the background of the case which, however, might not be available at the time a tip-off is received. That is the reason why tip-off writings are perceived as forensically relevant.

The remaining writings of the AnoText corpus cannot sensibly be integrated into a typology of forensically relevant types of texts. With a quantity of 133 texts (i.e. 8 %), these samples present a considerable group. This is a result of the fact that there is no correlation between text type and its appearance in the context of a criminal offence. In principal, each type of text can show a connection to an offence. Therefore, the group of miscellaneous texts includes samples of a great variety of text types – be it love letters, complaints, applications, letters from official authorities, petitions, instructions, poems and fiction to name only a few.

To sum up, the writings that have been objects of forensic examinations present a decidedly heterogeneous group of texts. The majority of them can be described in a typology of types of texts because they are used as a result of communicative demands which exist in relation to committing an offence, or, to put it the other way round, there are types of offences which are likely to be accompanied by writings. Due to their relation to offences, these writings show describable characteristics in language use, topic, and structure; although they might be modelled upon conventional text types. The remaining part of the corpus consists of texts which do not have a relation to offences per se. Their only common feature is that of disputed authorship.

Further criteria to classify forensically relevant texts cannot universally be applied to all of the mentioned types of text. Depending on the writing or a group of writings, it might be instructive to analyse the medium that was used to transmit a text, the manner to anonymise a text, the intention of the author as directly or indirectly displayed in a text as well as aspects of quantity and text structure against the background of other representatives of the same type.

5 Conclusion

Authorship attribution as a forensic science is ambivalent in its status. On the one hand, forensic linguistics is a discipline with a long scientific tradition and an active research community. Its application in a forensic context is regularly requested, and there are numerous examples of how linguistics has served criminal prosecution when "classical" forensic sciences could not be applied. On the other hand, it does not belong to the core disciplines of forensic sciences. Neither is forensic linguistics inherent part of most forensic science laboratories throughout the world, nor has it accepted standards of methods and training, nor is it represented in organisations concerned with the development of forensic sciences like ENFSI and OSAC, to name only two organisations. What are the reasons for this limited acceptance despite a strong demand of its services?

It can be noticed that the application of linguistics in the forensic context differs substantially – both on national and international level. This is partly due to differences in judicial systems and judicial decisions concerning the admittance of linguistic evidence in court. But partly differences arise from the working conditions. Taking Germany as an example, its situation is characterised by heterogeneity and fragmentation.[36] The majority of forensic linguistics experts are working in the academia. To the best of the author's knowledge, experts with this university background apply their science to case work just as a side-line job. In contrast, full-time practitioners

---

[36] For a more detailed account of German forensic linguistics cf. Ehrhardt (2013: 64–65, 71–73).

are small in number. Some of them work in law enforcement since Germany is one of few countries to have forensic linguistics expertise included into the scope of services offered by the Forensic Science Institute of the BKA.[37] A very small number of German experts of forensic linguistics is employed in consulting firms. As far as is known, there are just a handful of private enterprises in this line of business and, at least for one of these, the focus rather seems to be on handwriting analysis with forensic linguistics only to complement it. The fragmented nature of German forensic linguistics is enforced by the lack of a national board of practising experts. Thus, the development of methods, working standards and ethics is impeded and cannot be retrieved by those who request forensic linguistic expertise.

In relation to the admissibility of linguistic evidence to court, it has been pointed out that forensic linguistics might suffer from a reputation of lacking "scientificness" because proof of its scientific quality by way of error rates and validity testing is hard to come by, at least for some methodological approaches. Nevertheless, risks of inferior expert's work can be minimised by measures which serve the purpose of quality assurance and transparency. The management of quality includes both standardisations as a means to assure consistency and the concept of best practice as a means to improve the overall performance. In addition, issues like experts' competence, integrity and compliance with scientific practice can be addressed by codes of ethics.[38] Quality assurance can be pursued to differing extents. Forensic science laboratories are usually accredited, which means that they operate a quality management system according to norms like those of the International Organisation for Standardization (ISO). But as most practitioners are not employed in larger institutes, experts of forensic linguistics must strive for alternative measures like peer review and combining different methods to back up results.[39] The development of standards and best practice manuals would confront some of the reservations held against authorship attribution analysis more effectively.

---

[37] Lately, the Landeskriminalamt Berlin has also included two kinds of linguistic analyses into its scope of services.
[38] For instance, the *International Association of Forensic Linguists* has published a code of ethics which comprises a set of values and recommendations for appropriate practice (IAFL Code of Practice). Depending on an organisation's policy, codes of ethics may have the same binding force as other quality-assuring regulations. On its website, the IAFL does not proclaim enforcement capacity for its code of practice due to the association's nature as professional organisation with a strong academic focus (www.iafl.org/resources; accessed 25 October 2017).
[39] A survey among German forensic linguists has shown that experts apply a great diversity of quality-assuring measures. Due to the fragmented nature of linguistics as a forensic science, a consistent approach of handling these issues did not yet emerge – in spite of a recognised demand (Ehrhardt 2013: 72–73).

References

Ammon, Georg. 1994. Zum Aussagewert von "Abschiedsbriefen". *Archiv für Kriminologie* 193. 163–172

Artmann, Peter. 1996. *Tätertexte: Eine linguistische Analyse der Textsorten Erpresserbrief und Drohbrief*. München.

Baldauf, Christa. 1999. Zur Signifikanz sprachlicher Merkmale im Rahmen des Autorschaftsnachweises: Ansätze und Desiderate der forensischen Linguistik. *Archiv für Kriminologie* 204(3/4). 93–105.

Braun, Peter. 1998. *Tendenzen in der deutschen Gegenwartssprache*. Stuttgart: Kohlhammer.

Bredthauer, Stefanie. 2013. *Verstellung in inkriminierten Schreiben – Eine linguistische Analyse verstellten Sprachverhaltens in Erpresserschreiben und anderen inkriminierten Texten*. Köln: Wissenschaftsverlag.

Brinker, Klaus. 2001. *Linguistische Textanalyse: Eine Einführung in Grundbegriffe und Methoden*. Berlin: Erich-Schmidt-Verlag.

Brinker, Klaus. 2002. Textsortenbeschreibung auf handlungstheoretischer Grundlage (am Beispiel des Erpresserbriefs). In Kirsten Adamzik (ed.), *Texte – Diskurse – Interaktionsrollen: Analysen zur Kommunikation im öffentlichen Raum*, 41–59. Tübingen: Stauffenburg-Verlag.

Broeders, A.P.A. 1999. Some observations on the use of probability scales in forensic identification. *Forensic Linguistics: The International Journal of Speech, Language and the Law* 6(2). 228–241.

Brümmer, Nico & Johan du Preez. 2006. Application-independent evaluation of speaker detection. *Computer, Speech and Language* 20(2–3). 230–275.

Busch, Albert. 2006. Textsorte Erpresserschreiben. In Sigurd Wichter & Albert Busch (ed.), *Wissenstransfer – Erfolgskontrolle und Rückmeldung aus der Praxis*, 51–66. Frankfurt: Peter Lang.

Corder, Stephen Pit. 1967. The significance of learner's errors. *International Review of Applied Linguistics* 5(4). 161–170.

Coulthard, Malcolm. 1994. On the use of corpora in the analysis of forensic texts. *Forensic Linguistics: The International Journal of Speech, Language and the Law* 1(1). 27–43.

Coulthard, Malcolm. 2004. Author identification, idiolect, and linguistic uniqueness. *Applied Linguistics* 25(4). 431–447.

Coulthard, Malcolm & Alison Johnson. 2007. *An introduction to forensic linguistics – Language in evidence*. London: Routledge.

Coulthard, Malcolm. 2010. Experts and opinions – In my opinion. In Malcolm Coulthard & Alison Johnson (eds.), *The Routledge handbook of forensic linguistics*, 473–486. London: Routledge.

Coulthard, Malcolm. 2013. On admissible linguistic evidence. *Journal of Law and Policy* XXI(2). 441–466.

Coulthard, Malcolm, Tim Grant & Krzysztof Kredens. 2011. Forensic linguistics. In Ruth Wodak, Barbara Johnstone & Paul Kerswill (eds.), *The SAGE handbook of sociolinguistics*, 259–544. Los Angeles etc.: Sage.

Dern, Christa. 2008. Wenn nix zahle dann geht dir schlecht: Ein Experiment zu sprachlichen Verstellungsstrategien in Erpresserbriefen. *Zeitschrift für germanistische Linguistik* 36(2). 240–265.

Dern, Christa. 2009. *Autorenerkennung: Theorie und Praxis der linguistischen Tatschreiben analyse*. Stuttgart: Boorberg.

Doddington, George. 2001. Speaker recognition based on idiolectal differences between speakers. In *Proceedings of the European conference of speech communication technology (Eurospeech '01)*, 2521–2524. Aalborg: Aalborg University.

Ehrhardt, Sabine. 2007. Disguise in incriminating texts – theoretical possibilities and authentic cases. Paper presented at the 8th Biennial Conference on Forensic Linguistics / Language and Law, University of Washington, Seattle, 12–15 July 2007.

Ehrhardt, Sabine. 2013. Forensic linguistics accredited: Four years of experiences with ISO 17020 in authorship analysis. In Rui Sousa-Silva, Rita Faria, Núria Gavaldá & Belinda Maia (eds.), *Bridging the Gap(s) between Language and the Law – Proceedings of the 3rd European Conference of the International Association of Forensic Linguistics*, 64–75. Porto: Faculdade de Letras da Universidade do Porto. http://ler.letras.up.pt/site/default.aspx?qry=id03id1477&sum=sim (accessed 25 October 2017).

Ehrhardt, Sabine. 2015. Handling 'big data': From qualitative methods to automated processes in forensic linguistics. Paper presented at the 7th European Academy of Forensic Science Conference, Prague, 6–11 September 2015.

Ehrhardt, Sabine. 2016. Texte als Straftat und im Straftatkontext. In Ekkehard Felder & Friedemann Vogel (eds.), *Handbuch Sprache und Recht – Handbuchreihe Sprachwissen Nr. 12*. Berlin: Walter de Gruyter.

Ehrhardt, Sabine. 2017. Automatic forensic text comparison: A discussion about linkage to linguistic theory and evaluation of evidence. Paper presented at the 13th Biennial IAFL Conference, Proto, 10–14 July 2017.

ENFSI. 2015. *Guideline for evaluative reporting in forensic science*. http://enfsi.eu/wp-content/uploads/2016/09/m1_guideline.pdf (accessed 25 October 2017).

Fleischer, Wolfgang, Georg Michel & Günter Starke. 1996. *Stilistik der deutschen Gegenwartssprache*. Frankfurt, Berlin: Peter Lang.

Fobbe, Eilika. 2011. *Forensische Linguistik: Eine Einführung*. Tübingen: Narr.

Gibbons, John. 2011. Towards a framework of communication evidence. *International Journal of Speech, Language and the Law* 18(2). 233–260.

Grant, Tim. 2008. Approaching questions in forensic authorship analysis. In John Gibbons & M. Teresa Turell (eds.), *Dimensions of forensic linguistics*, 215–229. Amsterdam & Philadelphia: John Benjamins.

Grant, Tim. 2010. Txt 4n6: Idiolect free authorship analysis. In Malcolm Coulthard & Alison Johnson (eds.), *The Routledge handbook of forensic linguistics*, 508–522. London: Routledge.

Grant, Tim. 2013. TXT4N6: Method, consistency, and distinctiveness in the analysis of SMS text messages. *Journal of Law and Policy* 21(2). 467–494.

Grant, Tim & Kevin Baker. 2001. Identifying reliable, valid markers of authorship: a response to Chaski. *Forensic Linguistics* 8(1). 66–79.

Holmes, David I. 1994. Authorship attribution. *Computers and the Humanities* 28(2). 87–106.

IAFL Code of Practice. http://www.iafl.org/jscripts/tiny_mce/plugins/imagemanager/files/IAFL_Code_of_Practice_1.pdf (accessed 25 October 2017)

Ishihara, Shunichi. 2014. A likelihood ratio-based evaluation of strength of authorship attribution evidence in SMS messages using N-grams. *International Journal of Speech, Language and the Law* 21(1). 23–49.

Ishihara, Shunichi. 2017. Strength of forensic text comparison evidence from stylometric features: a multivariate likelihood ratio-based analysis. *International Journal of Speech, Language and the Law* 24(1). 67–98.

James, Carl. 1998. *Errors in language learning and use: Exploring error analysis*. London: Longman.

Juola, Patrick. 2008. *Authorship attribution*. Boston & Delft: Now.

Kinoshita, Yuko & Shunichi Ishihara. 2014. Background population: How does it affect LR-based forensic voice comparison?, *International Journal of Speech, Language and the Law* 21(2). 191–224.

Kniffka, Hannes. 2007. *Working in language and law – A German perspective*. Basingstoke & New York: Palgrave Macmillan.

Koch, Peter & Wulf Oesterreicher. 1985. Sprache der Nähe – Sprache der Distanz. Mündlichkeit und Schriftlichkeit im Spannungsfeld von Sprachtheorie und Sprachgeschichte. *Romanistisches Jahrbuch* 36. 15–43.

Koppel, Moshe, Jonathan Schler & Shlomo Argamon. 2013. Authorship attribution: What's easy and what's hard?. *Journal of Law and Policy* 21(2). 217–332.

Kredens, Krzysztof & Malcolm Coulthard. 2012. Corpus linguistics in authorship identification. In Peter Tiersma & Lawrence Solan (eds.), *The Oxford handbook of language and the law*, 504–516. Oxford: Oxford University Press.

Leenaars, Antoon A. 1988. *Suicide notes*. New York: Human Science Press.

Love, Harold. 2002. *Attributing authorship – An introduction*. Cambridge: Cambridge University Press.

Lübbe, Hermann. 2002. Bekennerschreiben und freundlichere Konsensdementis. *Zeitung für Literaturwissenschaft und Linguistik* 126. 128–143.

Margot, Pierre. 1998. The role of the forensic scientist in an inquisitorial system of justice. *Science & Justice* 38(2). 71–73.

McMenamin, Gerald R. 2002. *Forensic linguistics: Advances in forensic stylistics*. Boca Raton & London: CRC Press.

Morrison, Geoffrey S. 2011. Measuring the validity and reliability of forensic likelihood-ratio systems. *Science & Justice* 51(3). 91–98.

Mosteller, Frederick and David L. Wallace. 1964. *Inference and disputed authorship: The Federalist*. Reading, MA: Addison-Wesley.

Olsson, John. 2004. *Forensic linguistics: An introduction to language, crime and the law*. London & New York: Continuum.

Potha, Nektaria & Efstathios Stamatatos. 2014. A profile-based method for authorship verification. In Aristidis Likas, Konstantinos Blekas & Dimitris Kalles (eds.), *Artificial intelligence: Methods and applications – SETN 2014 Proceedings*, 313–326. Heidelberg: Springer.

Rathert, Monika. 2006. *Sprache und Recht*. Heidelberg: Winter.

Reichel, Peter. 2001. *Vergangenheitsbewältigung in Deutschland: Die Auseinandersetzung mit der NS-Diktatur in Politik und Justiz*. München: C. H. Beck.

Robertson, Bernhard & G. A. Vignaux. 1995. *Interpreting evidence: Evaluative forensic science in the courtroom*. Chichester, New York: Wiley & Sons.

Sanger, Sandra & Patricia McCarthy Veach. 2008. The interpersonal nature of suicide: A qualitative investigation of suicide notes. *Archives of Suicide Research* 12(4). 352–365.

Seifert, Jan. 2010. Verstellungs- und Imitationsstrategien in Erpresserschreiben – Empirische Studien zu einem Desiderat der forensisch-linguistischen Textanalyse. *Zeitschrift für angewandte Linguistik* 52. 3–27.

Shapero, Jess. 2011. *The language of suicide notes*. Birmingham: University of Birmingham PhD thesis. http://etheses.bham.ac.uk/1525/1/Shapero11PhD.pdf (accessed 25 October 2017).

Shuy, Roger W. 2006. *Linguistics in the courtroom: A practical guide*. Oxford: Oxford University Press.

Simons, André & Ronald Tunkel. 2014. The assessment of anonymous threatening communications. In J. Reid Meloy & Jens Hoffmann (eds.), *International handbook of threat assessment*, 195–213. Oxford: Oxford University Press.

Solan, Lawrence M. & Peter M. Tiersma. 2005. *Speaking of crime: The language of criminal justice*. Chicago: The University of Chicago Press.

Sousa-Silva, Rui, Gustavo Laboreiro, Luís Sarmento, Tim Grant, Eugénio Oliveira & Belinda Maia. 2011. 'twazn me!!;(' Automatic authorship analysis of micro-blogging messages. In Rafael Muñoz, André Montoyo & Elisabeth Métais (eds.), *Natural language processing and information systems*, 161–168. Berlin, Heidelberg: Springer.

Stamatatos, Efstathios. 2009. A survey of modern authorship attribution methods. *American Society for Information, Science and Technology* 60(3). 538–556.

Tiersma, Peter & Lawrence M. Solan. 2002. The linguist on the witness stand: Forensic linguistics in American courts. *Language* 78(2). 221–239.

Tiersma Peter & Lawrence Solan. 2012. The language of crime. In Peter Tiersma & Lawrence Solan (eds.), *The Oxford handbook of language and the law*, 340–353. Oxford: Oxford University Press.
Tiersma Peter & Lawrence Solan (eds.). 2012. *The Oxford handbook of language and the law*. Oxford: Oxford University Press.
Unterholzner, Bernhard. 2012. *Bekennerschreiben: Kommunikation als Ereignis*. Saarbrücken: Akademikerverlag.

Georgina Heydon
8 Topic management in police-suspect interviewing

1 Introduction

Over the last three decades, a significant shift has occurred in the field of police interviewing mainly led by the police authorities in England and Wales who have sought to address deficiencies in interviewing practice by developing training programs based on empirical research findings (Baldwin 1993; Bull & Milne 2004; Clarke & Milne 2001; Moston, Stephenson & Williamson 1992; Pearse & Gudjonsson 1996). Although this might seem unremarkable for scholars accustomed to working with client agencies in education, medicine, marketing and a range of other fields, the move towards research-based training for police interviewers in the UK, Australia, New Zealand and now many other parts of the world demonstrates a recognition that interviewing is teachable skill – something that was not widely accepted by police prior to the mid-1980s. Until the introduction of tape recorders into police interview rooms following the UK Police and Criminal Evidence Act in 1984, police interviewing was regarded as either a natural talent, or a skill best acquired on the job, through an ad hoc apprentice-like model (Griffiths and Milne 2005: 167). However, with the sudden availability of masses of recorded interviews to police management, British psychologists were engaged to undertake large-scale surveys of interview data and identify improvements that could be addressed by research-based training materials (Baldwin 1993; Pearse & Gudjonsson 1996). Although the international research supporting interviewing has been dominated over the past two decades by the discipline of psychology, recently a number of studies focusing on the language of police interviewing have demonstrated the valuable contributions to be made by forensic linguists (Cotterill 2001; Edwards 2006; Haworth 2013; Heydon 2005; Johnson 2008; Rock 2007).

The basis for the evidence-based police interviewing model developed initially in the UK, and now more widely applied, is the Cognitive Interview (Geiselman, Fisher, MacKinnon & Holland 1986). The information gathering and questioning phases of this model commonly utilise structured conversation to facilitate an "account" from an interviewee. This "Account phase" (see note (1) below) consists of selected topics or subjects addressed chronologically or thematically and generally introduced by the interviewer after an initial "free" disclosure by the interviewee.

This structure is based on proven psychological principles associated with concepts such as memory, rapport and questioning. While originally intended for interviewing eyewitnesses (Clarke and Milne 2001), the cognitive interview model also known as the PEACE model[1] has proven equally effective as the basis for police interviews with suspects. An established model for cognitive interviews with suspects is the Conversation Management model (Shepherd 2007) where the Account phase with structured questioning is supplemented with evidentiary questions and challenges to the suspect's account. Further developments of the model have included sophisticated techniques for uncovering deception, such as the Strategic Use of Evidence (Vrij, Granhag, Mann & Leal 2011). All of these models of interviewing are broadly termed "investigative interviewing", emphasizing the focus on information gathering rather than the elicitation of a confession.

Investigative interviewing models dominate training programs in the UK, Australia and New Zealand, and are being developed and tested for police forces around the world, from Mozambique to Indonesia. However, another prominent model of interviewing, the Reid Method (Senese & John E. Reid and Associates. 2005), is used mainly in North America and has also generated significant research interest especially in behavioural psychology. There are a number of critical features that separate the Reid Method from the investigative interviewing approach, the most obvious of which is the emphasis on obtaining a confession and the focus on credibility assessment, or lie detection. In general, the Reid Method advocates a coercive approach through its "nine step interrogation" technique and includes practices that would render the evidence inadmissible in some jurisdictions (e.g. Australia), such as the use of deception to persuade a suspect to confess. The use of the Reid Method is not without controversy (Snook, Eastwood, Stinson, Tedeschini & House 2010), but its critics are in a weakened position empirically because complete police interviews are not recorded electronically in most jurisdictions where the method is used.[2] It is notable that it was the introduction of recorded police interviews following the Police and Criminal Evidence Act in the UK that led to significant changes to police interviewing practices there.

Nonetheless, it is still relevant to our discussion to encompass the interviewing practices of North American police officers since many of the underlying techniques and requirements are the same. For example, building rapport and eliciting high quality, detailed narratives are both identified in the Reid Method as important goals for an interviewer. While there might not be the same concerns about voluntariness and the admissibility of evidence produced by the suspect or witness, the reliability of the information is still vital to a successful investigation. With this in mind, we

---

[1] The PEACE model is named for a mnemonic referring to the five main phases of the investigative interview: Planning & Preparation; Engage and Explain; Account; Closing; Evaluation. It has been the standard model of witness interviewing in England and Wales since it was first introduced in 1992. (See Central Planning and Training Unit 1992.)
[2] Usually a recording device is used to capture just the confession following what might be several hours, or even days, of interviewing and interrogation.

will now turn to the central concern of this chapter, which is the development and management of topics in police interviews.

2 Topics in police interviews

As the basic cognitive interview model has developed, police and academic researchers have begun to recognize that subject or topic coverage within an interview is a complex process (see most recently Walsh & Bull 2015). Topics might include items that constitute direct evidence, such as things that an interviewee heard, saw or did in the immediate vicinity of an incident. However, topics covered in an interview might also include information that an interviewee holds, but which is not direct evidence, for example knowledge of friends or associates of a murder victim, or where witnesses sought for an investigation may be found. Notably, the product of an interview will almost always comprise both evidence that might become part of the courtroom trial (Heffer, Rock & Conley 2013), and other information or intelligence that will be used to further the investigation. Therefore, the planning and structuring of an interview is now a complex task where the issue of chronology must be combined with a division of evidence/intelligence.

Given the complexity of the interview structure, and the inclusion of two distinct types of subject matter – direct evidence and indirect information or intelligence – it is incumbent upon police investigators to find some way to navigate the various subjects that might be covered in an interview. This is not simply a matter of working through a list of items relevant to the offence: some subjects might be introduced during the Account that are not on the police agenda at all, but which cannot be dismissed as irrelevant without further investigation. Some subjects might be known to the investigator but assume greater relevance and priority in light of other disclosures made by the interviewee. In short, the interview is dynamic, and a good interviewer must be responsive and adaptable to topic shifts, whenever they occur.

This chapter aims to unpack the structure of interviews from a linguistic perspective and demonstrate that choosing the right strategy when changing the topic in a conversation can:
a) have a dramatic impact on the rapport between interactants;
b) affect the capacity of interviewees to volunteer reliable information; and
c) affect the admissibility of evidence.

Rapport has been repeatedly identified as a critical factor in the success of an interview (Collins, Lincoln & Frank 2002; Griffiths & Milne 2006; Vallano & Compo 2011). Part of being a competent interviewer means being able to build and sustain an appropriate level of rapport over the course of an interview. To some extent, this will be contingent upon the character and mood of the interviewee, as well as the personality of the interviewer. However, the appropriate management of topics is a simple way of improving rapport or at the very least, reducing the dominance of the interviewer at the interactional level.

Voluntary confessions are fundamental to a fair trial and a technique that can optimize opportunities for interviewees to freely offer new information, whether evidential or not, is surely worth including in interviewing training. This chapter will demonstrate how the appropriate management of topics can be critical in offering interviewees an opportunity to make a voluntary statement, as well as ensuring that the interview as a whole is less likely to be challenged in court on the grounds of undue pressure being applied to the interviewee. Admissability of interview evidence is a key concern for prosecutors, and is affected by police behaviour and practices in the interview room. Although admissibility has become less of a concern with the introduction of electronic recordings in many jurisdictions, inappropriate interviewing methods and a lack of voluntariness of a suspect's statement continue to result in costly delays in the justice process and undermine procedural fairness and public trust (Dixon 2006; Williams 2000)

In order to describe the structure of an interview, we must first take a nuanced and empirically-based approach to the analysis of conversation as a social activity. Conversation Analysis (CA), an ethnomethodological approach to the analysis of talk between two or more participants, is particularly concerned with the way in which speakers take turns at talk and how different types of utterance are used to achieve social and communicative goals (Levinson 1983; Sacks, Schegloff & Jefferson 1974). In addition to turn-taking, CA provides a set of tools for analyzing the initiation, maintenance and shift of topics in the turn-by-turn construction of a conversation. It is therefore well-suited to this study of managing subjects in a police interview, especially in light of the implications of the "chain rule" (Frankel 1990), described below.

The following section first describes the general rules of turn-taking before examining the special rules of turn-taking in an interview. This provides the basis for an analysis of topic management, and in particular the strategies that are available to speakers when they want to change or pursue a topic. We can then return to consider the impact of topic management strategies on rapport, voluntariness and admissibility. In the course of this chapter, readers will be introduced to some of the basic terminology of conversation analysis. This can be used to produce a simple schematic for training interviewers in effective and strategic topic management.

3 Conversation Analysis

Conversation Analysis (CA) is a method of analyzing talk that describes the rules that speakers apply to regulate interactions, such as being able to determine who will speak next (Sacks et al 1974). This may seem trivial, yet even the briefest of conversations between two or more people is a highly rule-governed social activity requiring split-second timing and the almost instantaneous interpretation of a raft of social cues and structures, just to know when to speak and what to say. Analysts working within the CA tradition are able to specify the cues that speakers use to achieve such remarkable levels of cooperation and this research has identified the means by which speakers are able to moderate the timing of speaker change to avoid interruption and (unintended) simultaneous talk. The work of Sacks et al (1974) demonstrates that in multi-party talk, there are rules that govern the passing of the floor amongst the participants and in any interaction there are rules about what kind of turn can follow a previous turn. Clearly, these rules are not inviolate; however, as a set of norms they are powerful and, when broken, require redress to maintain social cohesion – consider the work that is done by participants to manage interruption or simultaneous talk so that social harmony is maintained. We will not discuss the actual rules of turn-taking here, as it is not directly relevant to this analysis, but it is important to note that these rules exist and produce powerful constraints on participants in a conversation.

When Conversation Analysis began to establish the rules of casual conversation, the importance of relevance had already been identified as part of a Cooperative Principle (Grice 1975) that governs interactions between speakers. Using the CA approach to spoken data, Harvey Sacks and his colleagues demonstrated that this is also embedded in conversational structure, and indeed part of being a successful interactant is being able to offer a relevant response, and being able to identify the relevance of another's contribution, through inference if the relevance is not immediately obvious (Sacks 1987). Thus, when one party to a conversation makes an initial contribution (an "initiation" turn), it requires a second contribution (a "response" turn) from another party in order to function properly as part of a successful interaction. And the content and function of this response turn is limited by the initiation: it must be appropriately relevant to the content of the initiation, and it must match the function of the initiation. In other words, each part of this two-part exchange can only make sense if the other part is executed properly by the conversational partner. A question – *what is the time?* – has no function in a conversation if it is not followed by a relevant response – *I don't know, three-thirty, time for lunch* – or a response that might be made relevant through further clarification – *I'm holding a coffee* (inference: *I can't turn my wrist to see my watch and tell you the time*). If there is no response, or no inference can be made that the next turn is an answer to the question, then the question is no longer functioning as a request for information about the time. It may, in some very highly specific set of circumstances, function in some other way, such as an admonition for time-wasting or a philosophical observation, but this would require a lot of inferential work on the part of the interactants, unless that function was somehow more explicitly conveyed. Part of this requirement for relevance is the selection of the appropriate type of turn. A question requires an answer turn in response; an invitation requires an acceptance turn or a declining turn; an accusation requires an admitting turn, or a denial turn; a greeting requires another greeting turn (Bilmes 1988).

Finally, and perhaps most obviously, the order of the two types of turn is also critical to their successful functioning in a conversation. Except in certain television quiz shows,[3] responses must always follow initiations in order to function properly. Thus, initiations are characterized as turns that require a relevant and appropriate type of response in the next turn, and in this way, CA finds that the initiation and the response are two parts of a pair of turns that must occur in a specific order and in close proximity in the conversation. For this reason, such turns are called "adjacency pairs" and they are the building blocks of conversation (Schegloff & Sacks 1973). In order to understand the importance of these observations, particularly to social harmony, consider the slight that is suffered when one party offers a greeting that is not followed by a reciprocal greeting turn. Questions must be completed with relevant answers, invitations insist upon acceptance or refusal and accusations require a confession or a denial. It is true that other responses are possible to any of these types of initial turns, but this deviation would be noticed by participants and require some explanation – *I'll let you know about the party when I've checked my diary.*

These general rules of relevance across pairs of turns continue to apply in an interview, and must therefore be observed in order to build social harmony and rapport (cf Heydon 2011). We will return to this aspect of interviewing later, where we will show how police interviewers can use this knowledge to avoid unnecessary and harmful damage to their rapport building efforts as they interact with suspects and witnesses. However, we will first discuss an important difference between interviews and other conversations, which is the rules about who speaks next. In an interview, unlike ordinary conversation, a special rule of turn taking called the chain rule (Frankel 1990) keeps returning the "floor" to the interviewer.

In his analysis of doctor-patient communication, Frankel (1990) identified the special turn-taking rules of an interview in an institutional setting. Sacks et al (1974) had already established that the rules of turn-taking in ordinary conversation allow parties to select the next speaker (including themselves in self-selection) so that potentially any party can take a turn at initiating a new adjacency pair. The important difference between ordinary conversation and an institutional interview is that in the latter, only the professional party has automatic access to initiations. Quite simply, and just as the *I'm asking the questions here* cliché makes clear, the interviewer is in charge of initiations while the interviewee is confined to responding to these questions (Greatbatch, 1988). That is what makes it an interview. Even when the interviewee does produce an initiation turn, such as a clarification, the floor and the right to produce initiations, returns to the interviewer immediately after that adjacency pair is completed. Thus the following sequence from an interview is typical of this pattern:

---

3 In the US quiz show *Jeopardy*, the answer to a question is provided and the contestant supplies the relevant question. However, this is not actually a new turn taking rule per se, as it is in fact an agreed inversion of the accepted norm whereby the quiz master is actually understood to be asking something like: 'If the answer to a question were given as X, what is the question that would have preceded that answer?'

Excerpt 1 From police interview with a suspect recorded in Victoria, Australia showing insert sequence and application of the chain rule

Line	Speaker ID	Turn function	Turn
403.	pio1:	*Police question (Q1)*	so you didn't bother saying anything to them
404.			that the glass was broken or
405.	IN1:	*Suspect question (Q2)*	to who
406.	pio1:	*Police answer (A2)*	to Betty ... in at the store
407.	IN1:	*Suspect answer (A1)*	no. that happened af-
408.			when I walked out
409.			when I wal-
410.	pio1:	*Police Question (Q3)*	yeah but you didn't stop to think you'd go back in
411.			and tell them that you've broken their front door
412.	IN1:	*Suspect Answer (A3)*	[nup]
413.	pio1:	*(continues Q3)*	or anything
414.	IN1:	*(continues A3)*	nup.
415.			she knew it was broken
416.			you could hear it going
417.			I heard it ... going.
418	pio1:	*Police Question (Q4)*	what was your reason for assaulting Ian.
419.	IN1:	*Suspect Answer (A4)*	over that phone call
420.			cause that's ... the only place that it would have came from...

This pattern of Question 1, Question 2, Answer to 2, Answer to 1 is called an insert sequence (Levinson 1983: 304–305). It does not, as demonstrated in this example, change the default turn-taking rule that allocates initiations to the interviewer and responses to the interviewee. The subsequent turns show that the question initiation turns continue to be allocated to the police interviewer (Q3 and Q4). In this way, the participants create a "chain" of question-answer pairs with a strict regulation of turn type distribution (Frankel 1990; Heydon 2005). This chain rule has extremely important implications for topic management, which we will discuss below.

4 Topic management in interviews

We established above that there are specific rules of turn-taking that apply to interviews, and that an important feature of interviews is the default allocation of initiations to the interviewer and responses to the interviewee. This gives interviews their characteristic question-answer structure, but it also has important implications for the management of topics by participants. The management of topics in interviews is the main focus of this section.

Topics are introduced by participants to a conversation as a way of contributing new information, or eliciting new information from other speakers. In ordinary conversation, any participant has the potential to introduce a new topic to the conversation, and any other participant can choose to maintain that topic during their turn at talk, or change the topic to a new one. The easiest way to introduce a new topic into a conversation is to use an initiating turn that contains that topic: *Did you hear about Bill's new car?* The next speaker is then obligated, according to the maxims of cooperation (Grice 1975) to provide a response that is relevant to the topic of that initiation: *Sure – everyone's talking about it.* Initiations are by far the turn of choice for new topics. To introduce a new topic in a response turn requires a different strategy (Jefferson 1984). First the speaker must respond to the preceding initiation, and only then can they move towards their new topic: *Sure, everyone's talking about it. But you know I don't think a new car is the key to happiness – since I started yoga, I think it's all about the mind-body balance.* This kind of gradual shift is used by speakers to demonstrate adherence to Grice's maxim of relation, and to maintain a cooperative stance with the first speaker, but still manage to change the topic. Nonetheless, the flexibility of ordinary conversation allows for the next turn to be used by the first speaker to return to his/her topic: *Well, you can have your yoga – I reckon a new Porsche would make me pretty happy right now. I hear it handles like a dream.*

But interviews do not have this level of flexibility, at least not in their default state. When all the initiations are allocated to the police interviewer by the 'chain rule' (see above), this simultaneously grants the interviewer access to topic changes at almost every turn. At the end of every initiation-response sequence, the application of the chain rule means that the floor by default returns to the interviewer. In this way, the interviewer is provided with another opportunity to start a new topic, with no structural obligation to maintain the relevance of the previous turn, because it was a response. This is not at all like ordinary conversation – in fact if such a pattern were to emerge during a casual conversation, it is likely that the responding party would protest: *I feel like I'm being interrogated here!*

This raises an important point about topic management and interviewing: the chain rule of interviewing results in topic initiations being unequally distributed in favour of the interviewer. In fact, having only access to response turns, the interviewee is very limited in their capacity to introduce a new topic. Following the discussion above, we can identify two distinct strategies for changing the topic in an interview (or any interaction): the first is a *disjunctive topic shift* and occurs in **initiations** when the interviewer introduces a new topic without any reference to, or acknowledgement of, the topic of the previous interviewee turn. The second type of topic shift is a *stepwise topic transition* which can be employed by interviewees in **response** turns, just as our hypothetical speaker above moved from the topic of Bill's new car, to the benefits of yoga.

Analysis of police interview data in Heydon 2005 finds that police officers have a tendency to rely on disjunctive topic shifts as in lines 210 and 212 in the following example:

Excerpt 2 From police interview with a suspect recorded in Victoria, Australia showing stepwise and disjunctive topic shifts

Line	Speaker ID	Turn function	Turn
199.	pio7	Police topic initiation	right and um when you purchased that did you ah
200.			believe it to be a certain substance
201.	SPT7	Suspect topically relevant response	yeah yeah //oh-*
202.	pio7	Police topic initiation	what* did you believe it to be
203.	SPT7	Suspect topically relevant response	well marijuana
204.		Suspect topically relevant response	it was compressed in a little block n=
205.	pio7	Police Minimal response	=all right=
206.	SPT7	Suspect stepwise topic transition	=I thought I'd get a whole lot more than what I got but
207.	pio7	Police Minimal response	all right
208.	SPT7	Suspect stepwise topic transition	cause I was hoping to have some for Christmas
209.			to tell the truth but hh
210.	pio7	Police discourse marker	now
211.	SPT7	Suspect stepwise topic transition	it's all gone
212.	pio7	Police disjunctive topic initiation	police in searching your premises
213.			searched the underneath of your house
214.			are you aware of that
215.	SPT7		yeah

In fact, disjunctive topic shifts account for the majority of all topic changes in the interactions that comprise the Account phase of the interviews with adult suspects used for this study. Stepwise topic transitions rarely occur in police interviewer turns, but are frequently found in interviewee turns, which is consistent with the chain rule allocating all the response turns to interviewees. The excerpt above also gives several examples of the suspect using stepwise topic transitions to achieve topic change in the interview, in lines 206, 208 and 211.

The distribution of topic management tools in this way has important implications for the three key aspects of police interviewing referred to in the Introduction above: rapport building; reliability of intelligence obtained in the interview; and the admissibility of interview evidence. Each of these will be discussed further below.

5 Discussion

5.1 Rapport building

Disjunctive topic shifts are found by Heydon (2005) to provide a means by which police interviewers can maintain control of the interview content and exclude topics that have been introduced by the suspect through stepwise topic transitions. This level of control over the interview content is found to be unnecessary, especially in light of the structural features of an interview that automatically pass topic control to the interviewer with initiation turn types (Heydon 2005: 174–179). On the contrary, the current PEACE model of interviewing training encourages the interviewer to pass control to the interviewee (Milne & Bull 1999), although as illustrated above, this is very difficult to achieve because of the chain rule of interviews.

As we found earlier, an arrangement where one party continually asks questions and controls the topic shifts is very dissimilar to ordinary conversation, and this feature of interviews naturally creates a considerable barrier to putting the interviewee at ease. Building rapport in an interview has been shown to be critical to eliciting reliable and detailed accounts (Collins et al. 2002; Griffiths & Milne 2006; Vallano & Compo 2011; Walsh & Bull 2015), so a turn-taking structure that emphasizes the distance between the participants requires some attention.

The use of disjunctive topic shifts in particular is problematic for interviewers who are attempting to build rapport. Interviewers are instructed to be "active listeners" during the Account phase (indeed, at any time that the interviewee is taking a turn at talk), yet there is little in the investigative interviewing literature to suggest what this might entail. There is some mention of the use of receipt markers or feedback to encourage further contributions – *uh huh, go on, and then what happened?* – and some discussion of behavioural strategies, such as nodding and taking up a synchronous body position, but little about what to do when an interviewee turn ends, as it inevitably must (see for instance Milne & Bull 1999; Stacey & Page 2012). Royce (2005: 10) provides a set of active listening instructions for crisis negotiators, drawn from an earlier FBI source, and the verbal and non-verbal acts that are described are consistent with the approaches described more broadly in the UK-based training material as rapport building. However, this specific active listening skills development does not seem quite as far advanced in the investigative interviewing literature as in the crisis negotiation field.

An understanding of topic change strategies can fill this gap, because taking a new turn and changing topic is essentially the only option left to the interviewer when the interviewee no longer responds to the abovementioned invitations to continue his or her turn. In this situation, our earlier analysis indicates that interviewers tend to rely on disjunctive topic shifts. However, this does not offer the interviewee any acknowledgement of his or her prior turn, and indeed dismisses the value of that turn (Heydon 2005). This may be intentional, as a means to control the allowable contributions by the interviewee, or it may be simply due to carelessness, stress or ignorance of the damage that disjunctive topic shifts might cause to the rapport building process.

The avoidance of disjuncture in topics is taken for granted when we converse with a friend, or conduct a business conversation with colleague or even a stranger. The topic of a participant's prior turn is typically acknowledged before a new topic is initiated, and often a speaker will attempt to make a link between the old topic and their new topic with a stepwise topic transition. This observation offers interviewers two straightforward strategies to manage the change in topics that will eventually occur in any interview:
- acknowledge the content of the interviewee's prior turn; and
- link the upcoming new topic with the interviewee's prior topic.

The first strategy may involve some feedback or a token of acknowledgement, such as *thanks for providing so much detail* or *yes, you mentioned earlier that you were in a hurry to leave.* Importantly the language must remain neutral and the interviewer must avoid offering an evaluation of the interviewee's topic.

The second strategy involves more effort, and may be combined with the first. In this instance, the interviewer needs to create a series of stepwise topic transitions to move from the interviewee's topics to the new interviewer topic. This is especially useful when the interviewee wants to backtrack to an earlier interviewee topic: *thanks for providing so much detail about the car. You mentioned earlier that when the car arrived you were not in such a good position to see it – can you tell me how you came to get a better view of the car later?*

5.2 Reliability of intelligence

The use of topic initiations that are interviewee-centered can make an important contribution to maximizing the reliability of information provided by the suspect or witness. As we have seen, the default conversational structure of an interview is one where the interviewer has consistent access to initiations such as questions, which are the most powerful topic management tools. In this way, the normal rules of an interview mean that the interviewer controls the choice of topic. This may be relevant at times during the interview and the strategic introduction of specific subjects may be crucial to a successful interview (Shepherd 2007). However, at the start of the Account phase, when the interviewee is invited to give a free narrative, the first priority must be to ensure that the interviewee has exhausted their own subject matter before the interviewer begins to strategically introduce new topics (Milne & Bull 1999). This avoids contamination of the interviewee's story with police intelligence or priorities, since every police topic change imposes a police agenda on the interviewee's narrative.

In addition, while the interviewee is producing a narrative based on their memories of an event, the accuracy and reliability of their story can be threatened if their cognitive load is increased by a sudden change of topic requiring retrieval of a memory from a different area of the brain (Fisher & Geiselman 1992; Milne & Bull 1999). The emphasis on allowing the interviewee to produce a free narrative without interruption from the interviewer is central to the principles of investigative interviewing because of its value in protecting the integrity of the interviewee's story and minimizing disruption of the memory retrieval process.

In terms of topic management, this means that the topic choice must, as far as possible, rest with the suspect or witness in the interview during the free narrative phase, and the probing questions that follow. The police-led topic changes must wait until the interviewer is confident that there are no further topics that the interviewee will introduce spontaneously. This can be quite difficult to establish, especially since interviewees are commonly reluctant to initiate a topic shift, or introduce new material that is not requested. This can apply even when the interviewee is asked repeatedly if they wish to add anything further to the interview, and when they do actually have important new information to contribute, as in the following extract from Heydon (2005):

Excerpt 3 From police interview with a suspect recorded in Victoria, Australia showing reluctance of suspect to introduce new topics, even when explicitly requested by the police interviewer.

Line	Speaker ID	Turn function	Turn
290.	Pio2:	Police Topic	(2.0) so there was (0.6) absolutely no reason
291.			(.) why you should have treated 'er in that manner
292.	SPT2:	Suspect response	(1.0) nup
293.		(long silence)	(12.6) ((soft intermittent paper shuffling sounds during silence))
294.	pio2:	Police request for new information	was there anything else that (.) a:h you wish to add to (0.2) what's happened
295.	SPT2:	Suspect silence, then denial then new topic initiation	(2.8) no:oh jus (2.0) if you wanna (h)know what (h)happened y'know

296.	(.) we- (0.8) we went back to Littlevillage
297.	(2.0) I didn't have my ke:ys hh
298.	(0.4) um (0.4) to get in (0.8) to the (.) hotel
299.	so (0.6) we went back to u:m (0.6) her place in Satellite River
300.	(2.6) talked until (1.8) five 'clock in the morning

As is clear from the example above, the onus falls on the interviewer to permit ample time during the free narrative phase so that interviewees can respond with longer turns that might include stepwise topic transitions. SPT2 here pauses twice for between two and three seconds in line 295 when negotiating a topic shift in order to pick up the thread of his narrative that had earlier been disrupted by a police agenda topic (establishing whether there was a reason for the offence – see line 290). SPT2 also downgrades his own topic initiation – *jus (2.0) if you wanna (h)know what (h)happened y'know* – which emphasizes his reluctance to take the floor even when explicitly invited to do so.

Permitting the interviewee time to develop their own topics is an important step in handing over control of the interview to the witness or suspect, at least in the elicitation of a free narrative that marks the beginning of the Account phase. In so doing, interviewers reduce the chance that their own questioning, and topic management, might contaminate the interviewee's evidence, because the control of the topics is then largely managed by the interviewee. It also allows interviewees to introduce new material that has not been covered by the interviewer, and might have been otherwise missed, as nearly occurred in the example above.

It is a simple fact that interviewees will struggle to provide information that is not requested unless they have access to resources that allow them to change the topic as they see fit. The stepwise topic transition therefore plays an important role in ensuring that the reliability of evidence is not compromised through omission.

In England and Wales, there is an important corollary to this discussion, and this relates to the caution. Suspects in these jurisdictions are required to "mention when questioned something that you later rely on in court" or risk an adverse inference being drawn by the Court from their failure to disclose such evidence during the interview. However, a suspect may claim that they were not questioned about a specific event or detail that they later rely on for their defence, and so it is incumbent upon investigating officers to ask as many questions as are necessary to cover any of these likely defences. Nonetheless, just as in other jurisdictions that do not have such a caution, the interviewer-led questioning should be conducted *after* the suspect has exhausted their own topics in relation to the investigation.

5.3 Admissibility of evidence

The extent to which a confession was made voluntarily by a suspect is often tested in court, and an important consideration will be the role of the interviewer in eliciting the confession. As we have seen, topic management provides an important opportunity to differentiate between an interviewer-led interview, and an interview where suspects or witnesses are able to volunteer information. By relying on disjunctive topic shifts in turn initiations, police interviewers run the risk of excluding topics introduced by the interviewee, and dominating the choice of subjects in the interview.

During the elicitation of a confession, a turn structure that favours the interviewee's contributions has obvious advantages. If interviewees are able to execute stepwise topic transitions to introduce new information, and these turn shifts are permitted or even encouraged by the interviewer, it will be easier to show later that any admissions made during the interview were made voluntarily. There will be fewer instances of police assertions being used to elicit an agreement from the suspect, which is a weak form of confession and one that might well be challenged in court by the defence counsel. The statements that make up a confession must be produced by the suspect in his or her own words without any pressure or coercive force from the police interviewer, and the only topic management structure that permits this is one where suspects are able to move in and out of topics as required in order to produce their own admissions. Clearly, if the interview is structured so that topics are managed and changed predominantly by the police interviewer, there is a risk that any admissions will appear to have been suggested or led by the interviewer.

Even at the investigative level, admissions or observations provided by witnesses and suspects alike are more reliable and more easily attributable to the interviewee later if they have been produced in a topic that they themselves have introduced. Where the topics in an interview are entirely managed and introduced by the interviewer, and interviewees are led through the narrative created by the police interviewer, it will be easier for witnesses or suspects to distance themselves from these statements later on the basis that they did not frame the topics or choose the words used to describe the object, person or event.

The management of topics by the participants in an interview can be assessed in post-interview evaluations as a way of identifying weaknesses in the evidence that might arise if the key admissions were made in police-led topics. Thus the analysis of topic management can make an important contribution to both brief preparation and training. This is discussed in more detail below.

6 Implications for practice

The discussion above has demonstrated the importance of topic management to three critical aspects of police investigative interviewing: rapport building, reliability of the interviewee's account and admissibility of the evidence. Conversation Analysis provides tools that reveal the impact of turn-taking structures on topic management, and demonstrates that interviewees are in a weak position when it comes to changing the topic, compared with the interviewer. While police training materials currently emphasise the need for interviewers to pass control to the interviewee for the free narrative and subsequent probing phases, and to avoid introducing police topics before the interviewee has completely exhausted their own topics, there is little in the literature or interviewing guidelines to suggest how this might be achieved in practice.

This chapter suggests that police might benefit from some instruction in turn-taking structures, and the nature of topic management. The two types of turn transition identified in the CA literature – disjunctive and stepwise – are easily understood when illustrated with examples and provide a framework for officers to manage topics more effectively. The current literature tends to focus on turn-taking phenomena that are more visible to non-specialists, like interruptions, silences or minimal responses, but this is confusing because in fact these turn types are not consistently productive or unproductive. A turn that appears to be an interruption might in fact be evidence of scaffolding that builds a close affinity between speakers; silences that in one context might allow time for an interviewee to gather their thoughts and recall extra details, might in another context be felt by the interviewee as pressure to say anything to fill the gap, no matter how accurate or reliable the information; minimal responses can operate to encourage the interviewee to keep talking but can also indicate that the police interviewer agrees with the interviewee, which is usually entirely inappropriate.

Keeping the training focus on topic management and the different types of topic shift avoids these confusing categories of turn types, and allows police interviewers and trainers to identify successful interviewing strategies more consistently. An evaluation tool like the Griffiths Question Map (Griffiths & Milne 2006) maps the questions asked by an interviewer according to several broad categories (open, closed, yes/no, leading etc) and then draws conclusions about the efficacy of the interview and the skills of the interviewer according to the pattern of questioning. However, while this has value in assessing the quality of the questioning, the GQM does not reveal anything about the quality of the information produced by the interviewee. At the very least, an evaluation tool that categorized topic initiations could distinguish between police topics and interviewee topics, and in conjunction with the GQM, such an analysis could plot when those initiations occurred in relation to the question types being used by the interviewer. This topic management-based evaluation would capture the extent to which an interviewee had been able to volunteer new information in the course of the interview, and how that particular interviewee responded to specific question types, rather than the GQM outcome, which is only able to assess the interviewer behaviour, and not the interviewee responses.

7 Concluding remarks

This chapter has identified several aspects of topic management that are closely linked to evidence-based investigative interviewing. The importance of applying linguistic analysis to police interviewing within the accepted models (i.e. Cognitive Interviewing and PEACE) is key to the acceptance of new training techniques by police practitioners. A great deal of research already exists demonstrating the efficacy of these models and police agencies are unlikely to be interested in new techniques that are not consistent with existing practice. This is especially true in the United Kingdom, but also in New Zealand, Norway, and increasingly in Australia and Canada and even the United States of America where the Reid Method has dominated practice for several decades. This chapter is intended to demonstrate in part how linguistic analytic tools can indeed enhance and extend these existing models of investigative interviewing training and practice, and in addition, to demonstrate specifically how topic management is a crucially relevant phenomenon that can be used to improve rapport building, as well as the reliability and admissibility of evidence in criminal cases. It seems likely that similar analyses of topic management can also be applied to other legal questioning settings, including mediations, restorative justice conferencing, tribunals, and review boards.

References

Baldwin, John. 1993. Police interview techniques: establishing truth or proof? *The British Journal of Criminology* 33(3). 325–352.

Bilmes, Jack. 1988. The concept of preference in conversation analysis. *Language in Society* 17. 161–181.

Bull, Ray & Becky Milne. 2004. Attempts to improve the police interviewing of suspects. In G. D. Lassiter (ed.), *Interrogations, confessions, and entrapment*, 181–196. New York: Kluwer Academic.

Clarke, C. & R. Milne. 2001. National evaluation of the PEACE investigative interviewing course. *Police Research Award Scheme*. London: Home Office.

Collins, Roger, Robyn Lincoln, & Mark G. Frank. 2002. The effect of rapport in forensic interviewing. *Psychiatry, Psychology and Law* 9(1). 69–78. doi: 10.1375/pplt.2002.9.1.69

Cotterill, Janet. 2001. Domestic discord, rocky relationships: semantic prosodies in representations of marital violence in the O. J. Simpson trial. *Discourse and Society* 12(3). 291–312.

Dixon, David. 2006. A window into the interviewing process? The audio-visual recording of police interrogation in New South Wales, Australia. *Policing and Society: An International Journal of Research and Policy* 16(4). 323–348. doi: 10.1080/10439460600968123

Edwards, Derek. 2006. Facts, norms and dispositions: Practical uses of the modal would in police interrogations. *Discourse Studies* 8(4). 475–501.

Frankel, Richard. 1990. Talking in interviews: a dispreference for patient-initiated questions in physician-patient encounters. In G. Psathas (ed.), *Interaction competence*, 231–262. Washington DC: University Press of America.

Geiselman, R.E., R.P. Fisher, D.P. MacKinnon & H.L. Holland. 1986. Enhancement of eyewitness memory with the cognitive interview. *American Journal of Psychology* 99. 385–401.

Greatbatch, David. 1988. A turn-taking system for British news interviews. *Language in Society* 17. 401–430.

Grice, H.P. 1975. Logic and conversation. In P. Cole & J. L. Morgan (eds.), *Speech acts (Syntax and Semantics Volume III)*, 41–58. New York: Academic Press.

Griffiths, A. & R. Milne. 2006. Will it all end in tiers? Police interviews with suspects in Britain. In T. Williamson (ed.), *Investigative interviewing : rights, research and regulation*, 167–189. Cullompton, UK; Portland, Or.: Willan.

Haworth, K. 2013. Audience design in the police interview: The interactional and judicial consequences of audience orientation. *Language in Society* 42(1). 45–69. doi: 10.1017/S0047404512000899

Heffer, Chris, Frances Rock & John M.Conley. 2013. *Legal-lay communication : textual travels in the law*. Oxford; New York: Oxford University Press.

Heydon, Georgina. 2005. *The language of police interviewing : a critical analysis*. New York: Palgrave Macmillan.

Jefferson, Gail. 1984. On stepwise transition from talk about a trouble to inappropriately next-positioned matters. In J. M. Atkinson & J. Heritage (eds.), *Structures of social action: studies in conversation analysis*, 191–222. Cambridge: Cambridge University Press.

Johnson, A. J. 2008. Changing stories – Achieving a change of state in suspect and witness knowledge through evaluation in police interviews with suspects and witnesses. *Functions of Language* 15(1). 84–114. doi: 10.1075/fol.15.1.06joh

Levinson, Stephen C. 1983. *Pragmatics*. Cambridge: Cambridge University Press.

Milne, Rebecca & Ray Bull. 1999. *Investigative interviewing : psychology and practice*. Chichester ; New York: Wiley.

Moston, Stephen, Geoffrey M. Stephenson & Thomas Williamson. 1992. The effects of case characteristics on suspect behaviour during police questioning. *The British Journal of Criminology* 32. 23–40.

Pearse, John & Gisli H. Gudjonsson. 1996. Police interviewing techniques at two South London police stations. *Psychology, Crime & Law* 3. 63–74.

Rock, Frances. 2007. *Communicating rights: the language of arrest and detention*. Houndmills: Palgrave Macmillan.

Sacks, Harvey. 1987. On the preferences for agreement and contiguity in sequences in conversation. In G. Button & J. Lee (eds.), *Talk and social organisation*, 54–69. Clevedon, Philadelphia: Multilingual Matters.

Sacks, Harvey, Emanuel Schegloff & Gail Jefferson. 1974. A simplest systematics for the organisation of turn-taking for conversation. *Language* 50(4). 696–735.

Schegloff, Emanuel & Harvey Sacks. 1973. Opening up closings. *Semiotica* 8(4). 289–327.

Senese, Louis C. & John E. Reid and Associates. 2005. *Anatomy of interrogation themes : the Reid technique of interviewing and interrogation* (1st edn.). Chicago: John E. Reid and Associates.

Shepherd, Eric. 2007. *Investigative interviewing : the conversation management approach*. Oxford; New York: Oxford University Press.

Snook, B., J. Eastwood, M. Stinson, J. Tedeschini & J. C. House. 2010. Reforming investigative interviewing in Canada. *Canadian Journal of Criminology and Criminal Justice* 52(2). 215–229.

Stacey, Harriet & Alison Page. 2012. *Investigative interviewing: a guide for workplace investigators*. Canberra City: WISE Workplace.

Vallano, J. P. & N. S. Compo. 2011. A comfortable witness is a good witness: rapport-building and susceptibility to misinformation in an investigative mock-crime interview. *Applied Cognitive Psychology* 25(6). 960–970. doi: 10.1002/acp.1789

Vrij, A., P. A. Granhag, S. Mann & S. Leal. 2011. Outsmarting the liars: Toward a cognitive lie detection approach. *Current Directions in Psychological Science* 20(1). 28–32. doi: 10.1177/0963721410391245

Walsh, D. & R. Bull. 2015. Interviewing suspects: examining the association between skills, questioning, evidence disclosure, and interview outcomes. *Psychology Crime & Law,* , 21(7). 661–680. doi: 10.1080/1068316x.2015.1028544

Williams, J. W. 2000. Interrogating justice: A critical analysis of the police interrogation and its role in the criminal justice process. *Canadian Journal of Criminology-Revue Canadienne De Criminologie* 42(2). 209–240.

Michael Jessen
9 Forensic voice comparison

1 Introduction

The task of Forensic Voice Comparison (henceforth FVC) is to compare one or several recordings of a questioned speaker with one or several recordings of a suspect.[1] Its goal is to help the court or other mandating authorities (i.e. parties requesting a FVC) decide whether the suspect said the questioned speech. The role of the FVC expert in this process – after in-depth analysis of the different voice patterns involved – is to report strength of evidence, i.e. whether the analysed evidence supports the same-speaker hypothesis (questioned speaker and suspect are identical) or the different-speaker hypothesis (they are not identical) and how strong this support is.

Even under favourable conditions FVC is difficult. Speakers differ in many ways, but from what we know today there is no unique pattern that distinguishes one speaker from everyone else without any overlap. When voice comparison occurs under real-world forensic conditions the difficulty is increased due to various technical limitations and behavioural influences. For example, recordings submitted for FVC analysis can be relatively short (e.g. just 5 to 20 seconds net duration, i.e. with pauses or the voices of other speakers removed), there can be environmental noise, signal distortions, lossy compression, or strong reverberation. Forensically relevant speech will also most commonly be telephone-based, which means that some frequencies are filtered out. On the behavioural side, speech might be spoken loudly, under stress, under the influence of alcohol, with a common cold, or even with a deliberate voice disguise. Despite these difficulties (but also depending on the particular case), FVC is possible and can provide useful information for the parties requesting a FVC.

This chapter will address the principles of FVC (section 2). It will subsequently characterize two methodological approaches in FVC analysis – the auditory-acoustic approach (section 3) and the automatic and semiautomatic approach (section 4). The conclusion addresses how the different approaches can be used together (section 5).

The approaches to FVC shown in this chapter cover those that are used frequently in the international practice of this field, which was surveyed in Gold and French (2011) and Morrison et al. (2016). The automatic and the semiautomatic approach are organised into one larger category here (based on the common use of likelihood ratios), but they can also be seen as separate approaches.

---

[1] Alternative terms for "questioned speaker" are "unknown (speaker)", "offender", or "perpetrator". Alternative terms for "forensic voice comparison" are "forensic speaker comparison", "forensic speaker identification", or "forensic speaker recognition".

2 Fundamental tasks and concepts of Forensic Voice Comparison (FVC)

2.1 Speaker-discriminatory power and intra- vs. inter-individual variation

In a FVC case, a wide variety of characteristics of the voice patterns of the questioned speaker and the suspect is compared.[2] The range of speaker characteristics (also referred to as "speaker-discriminatory features" or simply "features" in this chapter) and the methods behind them will be presented more systematically in section 3 and 4. A fundamental question to ask in FVC is: what is the speaker-discriminatory power of a speaker characteristic, i.e. how speaker-specific is it? Obviously, the more speaker-discriminatory a characteristic is, the more useful it will be for FVC in general, i.e. not only for a specific FVC case, but for FVC as a field in general. The concepts most relevant to this question are intra-individual variation and inter-individual variation.

The voice is not constant within the individual; even the same utterance spoken twice will generate a different physical output. This situation is called *intra-individual variation*. Intra-individual variation can be purely linguistically determined, for example variations of a vowel due to the segmental context in which it occurs and the level of prosodic prominence with which it is spoken. Intra-individual variation can also be increased due to mismatched conditions, i.e. striking technical, speech-stylistic or other behavioural differences between the questioned-speaker recording and suspect recording. For example, the questioned material might be from a video recording of an outdoor scene, whereas the suspect recording might be from an intercepted telephone conversation. This difference will probably have an influence both on the technical conditions and on the speech style used. Other behavioural mismatch factors include speaking with or without a cold, intense stress, alcohol or drug influence, and, perhaps most extremely, voice disguise.

The term *inter-individual variation* refers to the fact that different individuals differ in their speaker characteristics. Without inter-individual variation FVC would not be possible.

The relation between these two types of variation and the notion of speaker-discriminatory power is as follows: the less intra-individual variation a speaker characteristic has and the more inter-individual variation it has, the higher its speaker-discriminatory power (Nolan 1983). Figure 9.1 presents an abstract representation of this

---

[2] In FVC, the term "voice" is used in a broad sense that includes the entire ensemble of features capable of distinguishing speakers, not only characteristics of the voice source and its supralaryngeal filtering, but also many habitual patterns, such as speech tempo and speech rhythm, as well as patterns of language varieties (dialects etc.).

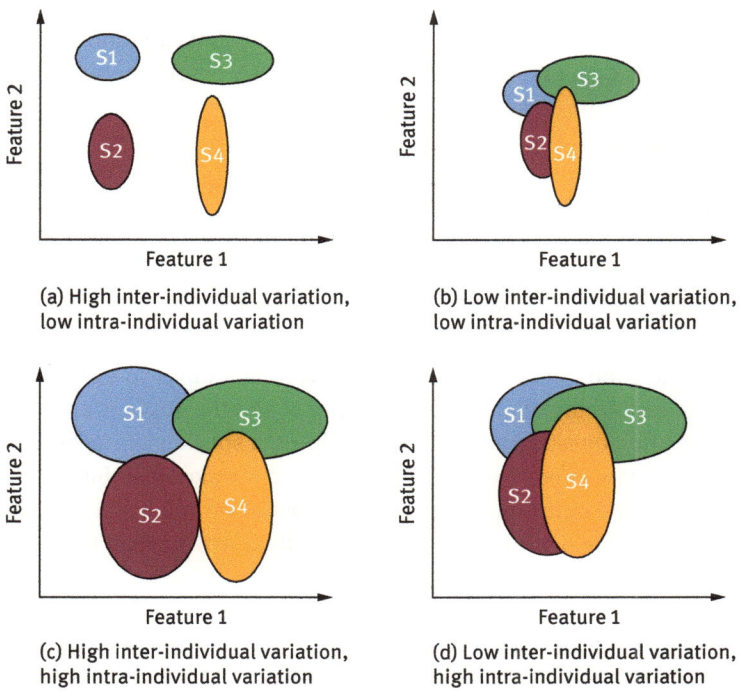

Figure 9.1: Abstract representation of different combinations of intra-individual and inter-individual variation. The notation "S" stands for speaker.

interplay between intra-individual and inter-individual variation. Four speakers (S1 to S4) are represented in a two-dimensional space involving two different speaker characteristics (called "features" in the figure). These could for example be average fundamental frequency plotted against articulation rate, each with different scaling of the axes.[3]

Plot (a) of the figure represents the ideal situation: intra-individual variation, represented by ellipses, is relatively small and inter-individual variation, represented by the distance between ellipses, relatively large. As a consequence, the areas in two-dimensional space occupied by the different speakers do not overlap; each speaker is separated from every other in this space. In plot (b), intra-individual variation is still small but inter-individual variation is small too and as a consequence the spaces occupied by the speakers begin to overlap. In plot (c), inter-individual variation is as large as in (a), but now intra-individual variation is large too, so there is overlap

---

[3] Using a two-dimensional feature representation in Figure 9.1 is particularly favourable for illustrating the essence of the argument. Any other number of features, and hence dimensions, would be possible too. Section 2.3 will address the point that the dimensions should preferably be maximally uncorrelated.

similar to (b). Plot (d) represents the worst situation: intra-individual variation is large and inter-individual variation small. The consequence is massive overlap between the speaker spaces (cf. Rose 2002: 10–18 for related ways of visualising speaker spaces).

2.2 Similarity and typicality

As mentioned in section 2.1, a fundamental question to ask in FVC is: what is the speaker-discriminatory power of a specific speaker characteristic? A second fundamental question to ask is: what is the evidential value of a specific speaker characteristic when it is used to compare questioned and suspect recordings in a concrete FVC case? These two questions are related but not identical and the answers are only partially connected. The first question addresses the value of a speaker characteristic in general: For example, how good is articulation rate as a speaker-discriminatory feature in general? The second question addresses the information value of a speaker characteristic in a specific case. For example: how valuable is articulation rate as a speaker-discriminatory feature in this particular FVC at hand?

In order to understand this second type of question and the principles behind it, it is important to introduce the concepts of similarity and typicality. Before that step is taken, the following terminological detail needs to be addressed. Speaker characteristics have different *instantiations* or *values*. For example, if mean fundamental frequency is the speaker characteristic, there can be a whole range of different values with which this speaker characteristic can be instantiated. A male speaker with a high-pitched voice, for example, might have a mean fundamental frequency value of 160 Hz and a male with a more common voice pitch might have a value of 120 Hz; 160 Hz and 120 Hz are different instantiations of the speaker characteristic called average fundamental frequency. Whereas in this example of a speaker characteristic there is a gradual scale of possible instantiations, there can also be speaker characteristics with a binary distinction between the presence and the absence of that characteristic. For example, some speakers may make use of falsetto voice or may use a stereotypical expression such as *you know*, whereas others do not. Another option is categorical steps on a scale, a point to be addressed in section 3.3. The concepts of similarity and typicality apply to gradual, binary, and stepwise speaker characteristics though in slightly different ways; the situation that will be illustrated below in Figure 9.2 is one involving gradual instantiations.

Similarity is the closeness of the instantiation of a specific speaker characteristic in the speech of the questioned speaker to the speech of the suspect. For example, the mean fundamental frequency might be 115 Hz for the questioned speaker and 120 Hz for the suspect. This is quite close, and therefore these instantiations have high similarity. The greater the similarity, the stronger the evidence for identity between questioned speaker and suspect. The smaller the similarity, the stronger the evidence that they are non-identical.

Typicality is the degree to which the particular instantiation of a speaker characteristic in the questioned speaker is common or uncommon relative to the frequency

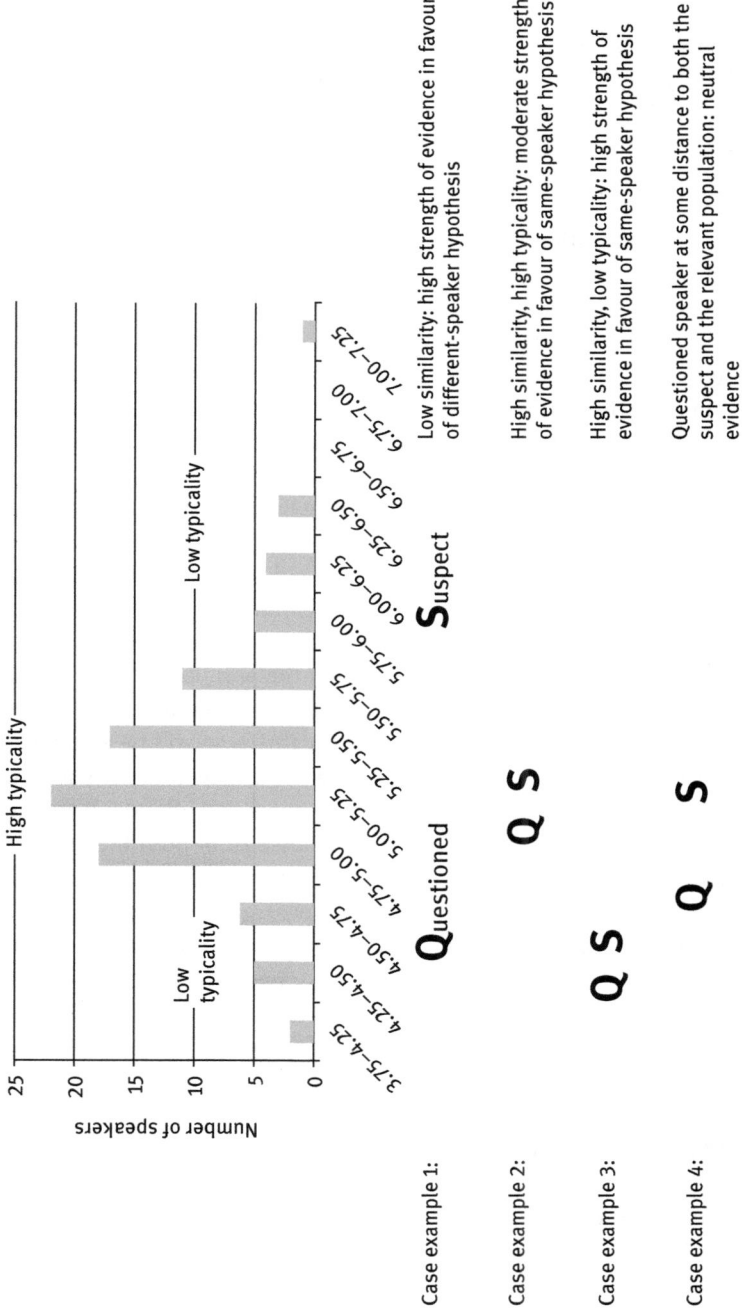

Figure 9.2: Histogram of articulation rate in a population of 100 male adult speakers of German. Articulation rate ranges expressed in syllables per second on x-axis, number of speakers (out of 100) on y-axis. Four hypothetical cases are illustrated.

of different instantiations in the relevant population. The relevant population can be defined in various ways but often it is defined as a set of adult speakers with the same sex and the same language as the one found in the questioned speaker. High typicality means that the instantiation of the speaker characteristic is quite common in the relevant population, and low typicality means that it is quite uncommon. For example, a mean fundamental frequency value of 120 Hz has high typicality among German male speakers and a value of 160 Hz has low typicality, i.e. the latter is an unusually high value (Künzel 1987; Jessen, Köster and Gfroerer 2005). The lower the typicality of a feature manifestation in a case, the stronger the evidence for identity between questioned speaker and suspect (see also Rose 2002 for explanations and illustrations of similarity and typicality throughout his book).

Figure 9.2 illustrates the principles explained in this subsection. The speaker characteristic illustrated is articulation rate. Figure 9.2 shows a histogram of different articulation rate values (expressed in syllables per second) in a population of 100 male adult speakers of German (from Jessen 2007). For illustration purposes, four hypothetical cases are shown underneath the histogram.

In case 1, the similarity between the articulation rate instantiation of the questioned speaker and the one of the suspect is very low. One would be far more likely to get a situation like this if the suspect and questioned speaker were different than if they were the same. In case 2, similarity between the articulation rate instantiation of the questioned speaker and that of the suspect is high. However, the articulation rate instantiation of the questioned speaker is also typical of the population. One would be only slightly more likely to get this situation if the suspect and offender were the same person than if they were different individuals (why this is so will be explained in section 4.2). In case 3, similarity is as high as in case 2, but now typicality is low. One would be far more likely to get this situation if the suspect and offender were the same. In case 4, the questioned speaker is at some distance from both the suspect and from the centre of the population. In a case like that the evidence is neutral (non liquet), i.e. one would be just as likely to get this if the suspect and questioned speaker were the same as if they were different. Other situations in which an analysis might result in a non liquet conclusion occur when the quality or quantity of the material is very poor or when different features point into very different directions, i.e. when the strength of evidence from some important features is contradictory.

2.3 Multidimensionality and (in)dependence of speaker features

Rose (2002: 14) says that "voices are multidimensional objects". In order to distinguish one speaker from another there is no single dimension, i.e. no single speaker-characterizing feature that would be sufficient for that purpose. An illustration of a single dimension has been given in Figure 9.2 (articulation rate) and an abstract representation of two dimensions has been given in Figure 9.1, but in reality there are many more dimensions on which speakers can be distinguished. The task of a FVC is to address as many dimensions, i.e. is to describe as many speaker characteristics, as possible. Since there are obvious practical limits to that task, it is reasonable to select speaker characteristics for the analysis procedure that are as independent from another as possible. In statistical terms, probabilities involving independent features can be multiplied – a principle that is used efficiently in DNA analysis. This principle is important when speaker information is treated in fully quantitative terms (of the type to be addressed in section 4). But the principle of preferring maximally independent speaker characteristics is a good guideline also when the analysis is more qualitative (see section 3). To give some examples of independence, long-term formant frequencies, fundamental frequency, and articulation rate are essentially uncorrelated with another (Moos 2010; Gold 2014). Likewise, Hughes et al. (2017) report that features from the domain of laryngeal auditory voice quality are essentially independent of long-term formants and automatic speaker recognition.

Degree of correlation can be investigated empirically, as in the cited studies, or judged based on theory. For example, there is no reason in phonetic/linguistic theory why average fundamental frequency should correlate with the kind of greeting expressions that a speaker uses. Lack of correlation can also be "created" with signal processing methods such as cepstral coefficients, discussed in section 4.3.

For speaker characteristics that have been proven to carry particularly important speaker-discriminatory information it might also make sense to describe related characteristics even when they are to some level correlated. For example, the cepstral coefficients used in automatic speaker recognition (section 4.3) are to some extent correlated with formant frequencies because both are correlates of vocal tract anatomy and physiology. Vocal tract acoustics have shown to be strongly speaker-discriminatory. As discussed in Rose (2002, 2003) and Jessen (2008), analysis of cepstral coefficients and formant frequencies has mutual advantages and disadvantages and it makes sense to look at both of them in a FVC. Rose (2003) mentions among the most important advantages of cepstral coefficients and formant frequencies, respectively, that the former are on average more speaker-discriminative and that the latter are more interpretable because they are based on well-researched relations between articulation, acoustics, and perception within phonetic theory.

3 Methodological approaches I: The auditory-acoustic approach

3.1 Introduction and history

Since the 1980s there has been broad consensus that FVC should use both auditory-based and acoustic-based methods in phonetics (and linguistics) (Nolan 1983; Künzel 1987; Baldwin and French 1990; Hollien 1990). This broad (though not unanimous) consensus is still maintained up to the present (Gold and French 2011). Examples of auditory-phonetic speaker characteristics are auditory voice quality and dialect patterns. Examples of acoustic-phonetic speaker characteristics are mean fundamental frequency and formant frequencies. Some speaker characteristics have both auditory and acoustic components, e.g. articulation rate (syllables are identified auditorily; the combined duration of a sequence of syllables is measured acoustically).

The approach of combining auditory and acoustic aspects of phonetics (as well as aspects of linguistic analysis that occur on other levels than phonetics and phonology) is addressed with different terms in the literature, but all with largely equivalent meaning. These include: "(combined) auditory-acoustic" (Nolan 1997), "auditory-instrumental" (Gfroerer 2003), "linguistic-acoustic" (Foulkes and French 2012), "auditory phonetic + acoustic phonetic" (Gold and French 2011), and "auditory-acoustic-phonetic by forensic practitioners (qualitative opinion)" (Morrison et al. 2016).

The view that both auditory and acoustic properties should be taken into account when performing a FVC is in part a reaction to earlier approaches in which only acoustic or only auditory aspects had been taken into account. A well-known example of the former is the voice print approach, launched in the USA in the early 1960s. The voice print approach has been criticised on many accounts, not just on being limited to acoustic characteristics (this limitation has in fact been relaxed in later revisions of the original approach). Critical reviews of the voice print approach are given by Nolan (1983), Hollien (1990), and Rose (2002). Purely auditory analysis has been performed from the 1960s until the 1980s by some British phoneticians who essentially regarded the analysis behind FVCs as a kind of very detailed dialect analysis – attempting to proceed to the point where dialects become idiolects. However, Nolan (1990) showed a case example in which purely auditory analysis led to a conclusion that, based on external evidence, would most probably have been a false identification. By including acoustic analysis such a conclusion was challenged because consistent acoustic differences in formant structure occurred between the questioned and suspect recordings that had no other known explanation than the non-identity of the speakers. Further arguments against a purely auditory approach are presented in Nolan (1994).

Contrary to these one-sided approaches, the main idea behind the auditory-acoustic approach is to describe the speaker characteristics of the speakers to be compared from as many linguistic and phonetic perspectives as practically possible. This diversity of perspectives is one of the strongest assets of the auditory-acoustic approach.

3.2 Range of speaker characteristics

Although it is not possible here to provide a full list of linguistic and phonetic speaker characteristics used within the auditory-acoustic approach, Table 9.1 provides examples of speaker characteristics frequently used by practitioners in the

Table 9.1: Speaker characteristics frequently used in the auditory-acoustic approach.

Speaker-discriminatory features	Remarks
Average fundamental frequency (f0)	Measure of the central tendency of the f0 distribution in a recording. Most commonly used is mean f0 (Künzel 1987; Jessen, Köster, and Gfroerer 2005), but also mode and median of f0 are used as parameters (Hudson et al. 2007). Average f0 (as a cover term for all three measures, but most commonly the mean) has an anatomical foundation: the longer the vocal folds (= vocal cords), the lower the average f0, everything else being equal. This is why, on average, women have higher-pitched voices than men (Simpson 2009), but there are also inter-individual differences within the sexes. However, average f0 is also subject to sources of intra-individual variation. One particularly strong factor is vocal loudness: if an individual speaks louder than in his/her neutral setting, f0 will rise (Jessen, Köster, and Gfroerer 2005, incl. further references). An overview of various other factors is presented by Braun (1995). In addition to or instead of average f0 some practitioners use base-level f0, which is the lowest f0 value or range of values that a speaker produces. Some methods of capturing the lowest end of the f0 distribution are presented by Kraayeveld (1997) and Lindh and Eriksson (2007).
Variability of fundamental frequency	Variability index of the f0 distribution in a recording. Commonly used parameters are the standard deviation and the Varco (coefficient of variation, i.e. standard deviation divided by the mean). It has been pointed out that f0 standard deviation is positively correlated with f0 mean and should be normalised with parameters such as Varco (Künzel 1987; Kraayeveld 1997). If f0 standard deviation is expressed in terms of Varco, the correlation disappears almost entirely (Jessen, Köster, and Gfroerer 2005). In the interest of keeping correlation between different speaker features as low as possible, f0 varco is more informative than f0 standard deviation.
Formant frequencies (F1, F2, F3)	Formant frequencies can be measured locally, i.e. separated according to vowel category (Rose 2002, 2010; Rose and Winter 2010; Morrison, Zhang, and Rose 2011), or globally in the form of Long Term Formant Distributions (Nolan and Grigoras 2005; Becker, Jessen, and Grigoras 2008; Moos 2008, 2010; Gold 2014). In addition to these static measures, it is possible to measure the temporal dynamics of formants that are found in diphthongs or other vocalic sequences (McDougall 2004, 2006; Morrison 2009, 2011) and these trajectory features have been shown to produce stronger evidence than point measurements, even for monophthongs (Rose 2015). Static formant frequencies have an anatomical foundation: among other factors, the longer the vocal tract, the lower the formant frequencies (Reetz and Jongman 2009 for the principles; Simpson 2009 for female-male differences). F2 and F3 are quite stable against most technical and behavioural factors, but F1 is more affected, e.g. raised in loud as opposed to neutral speech (Jessen, Köster, and Gfroerer 2005 for further literature); raised in telephone speech (Byrne and Foulkes 2004; Lawrence, Nolan, and McDougall 2008). F4 is usually very close to the upper limit of the telephone passband and cannot be measured reliably in telephone speech.

(continued)

Table 9.1: (continued)

Speaker-discriminatory features	Remarks
Auditory voice quality	Different laryngeal voice qualities (e.g. creaky voice, breathy voice, harsh voice) or supralaryngeal voice qualities (e.g. nasal voice, pharyngealised voice, lip-rounded voice), or voice qualities with both laryngeal and supralaryngeal aspects (tense vs. lax voice). Most of these auditory voice qualities (which are also referred to as "settings", especially with the supralaryngeal voice qualities) have been described by John Laver (Laver 1980; see also Mackenzie Beck 2005). For further discussion of auditory voice quality in forensic phonetics see Köster and Köster (2004) and Nolan (2005). A current research project at University of York provides further exploration of Laver-style auditory voice quality and its correlation with acoustic parameters (French et al. 2015; Hughes et al. 2017).
Speech tempo	One frequently used speech tempo parameter is Articulation Rate (AR). AR is measured in terms of syllables per seconds in passages with fluent speech production (pauses and other non-fluencies are excluded in the measure). Syllables can be defined canonically, i.e. in terms of the number of syllables according to standard pronunciation (documented in pronouncing dictionaries), or phonetically, i.e. in terms of the number of syllables that were actually spoken (for literature on AR in forensic phonetics, see Künzel 1997; Jessen 2007; Cao and Wang 2011; Gold 2014; Amino and Osanai 2015).
Filled pauses	Filled pauses (= fillers) are the expressions that are commonly written as *uh* or *uhm* in English (Corley and Stewart 2008). Speakers can differ, among other things, in terms of how often they use these filled pauses (per constant time unit, e.g. per minute) and in how the filled pauses are manifested acoustically (de Leeuw 2007; Jessen 2012; Braun and Rosin 2015; Hughes, Wood, and Foulkes 2016).
"Idiolect"	– Combination of different language varieties (regional, social, foreign-language accented) or specific combination of different features within a language variety. A special case of the latter occurs if different speakers differ in the *degree* of a variety (e.g. strong Russian accent vs. weak Russian accent). – Linguistic-phonetic / phonological details that are independent of a language variety. Examples include VOT (Allen, Miller, and DeSteno 2003) and stop epenthesis (Yoo and Blankenship 2003).[1] Moosmüller (1997) for further examples. Sound change is a source of idiosyncrasies (de Jong, McDougall, and Nolan 2007; Stuart-Smith and Timmins 2010), which belongs in this or the preceding category. – Forensic-linguistic features, including idiosyncratic aspects of morphology, syntax and the lexicon; stereotypical expressions such as greetings and "empty" (semantically non-referential) expressions; discourse patterns. (Jessen 2012 for this typology of idiolectal features)
Some further speaker-discriminatory features	– Breathing (acoustic patterns, type, location, frequency) (Kienast and Glitza 2003) – Non-fluencies (beyond filled pauses), e.g. silent pauses, syllable lengthening, stutter-type behaviour, speech errors, sentence interruptions, and corrections (McDougall, Duckworth, and Hudson 2015)

Table 9.1: (continued)

Speaker-discriminatory features	Remarks
	– Specific intonation characteristics (beyond f0 average, variability, and base-level) (Nolan 2002; Leemann et al. 2014; Rose 2013b; see also Kinoshita, Ishihara, and Rose 2009; Kinoshita and Ishihara 2014) – Non-speech vocalisations (e.g. laughing, throat clearing, clicking) (Hirson 1995; Gold 2014) – Articulatory precision ("slurred" vs. precise speaking). Articulatory precision is related to coarticulation (more coarticulation in less precise speech) (Nolan 1983) – Speech rhythm (e.g. syllable-timed speaking in a stress-timed language) (Leemann, Kolly, and Dellwo 2014) – Speech pathology features (e.g. lisp, stutter) (Nolan 1997)

Note:
1 VOT (Voice Onset Time, i.e. the time between the release of a stop and the onset of voicing in the following vowel) and stop epenthesis (i.e. inserted stops in words such as *ten^{t}se*) are subject not only to individual variation, but also to dialectal variation or differences between languages (Braun 1996 and Fourakis and Port 1986 for examples of dialectal variation).

field of forensic phonetics and acoustics. Some of the more recent overviews of the auditory-acoustic approach, including some speaker characteristics not mentioned here, are given by Nolan (1997), Hollien (2002), Gfroerer (2003, 2014), Künzel (2004), French and Harrison (2006), Jessen (2008, 2010, 2012), Watt (2010), Eriksson (2012), Foulkes and French (2012), and French and Stevens (2013).

3.3 Application of the approach in casework

A concrete FVC that is based upon the auditory-acoustic approach takes into account the principles summarized in section 2. Its central task is to deal with similarity and typicality. For each of the speaker characteristics analysed in a case (see Table 9.1 for examples), the forensic expert makes an assessment of the degree of similarity between questioned speaker and suspect and s/he also determines how typical the particular instantiation of a speaker characteristic found in the questioned speaker is relative to the relevant population of speakers. The way of making similarity judgments differs depending on whether the speaker characteristic is auditory or acoustic and depending on how many instantiations (binary, gradual, or with discrete steps) a speaker characteristic has. If the instantiation is binary, for example the presence vs. absence of a lisp (speech impediment, also known by the term sigmatism), there are just two possible outcomes: either similarity is high (both questioned speaker and suspect show a lisp; or both of them do not have it, which would be much less informative) or it is low (only one of them shows a lisp). With auditory features a scale with discrete steps may be used. For example, harsh or breathy voice quality may be judged on a scale from zero to two (Nawka and Anders 1996). In that case there are several similarity values. In this example, similarity is maximal if the questioned speaker and suspect have the same degree of harsh or breathy voice quality and it is minimal if they lie at opposite ends of the scale. If acoustic measurements are used, the instantiations are gradual (unless the expert prefers to discretise the measurements by dividing the gradual scale into regions). One way of dealing with gradual acoustic measurements that is frequently used in the auditory-acoustic approach is to plot the measurements in a graph and to assess the degree of similarity based on the plot (for examples see Nolan and Grigoras 2005; Jessen 2010; Foulkes and French 2012). If the measurements of the questioned speaker fall within the range of values measured in the suspect this would constitute a case of high similarity. (Often in casework there is more speech material coming from the suspect than from the questioned speaker.)

The second task is to assess typicality. Again, it matters whether the speaker characteristic is auditory or acoustic and how many instantiations a speaker characteristic exhibits. In the case of the binarity example given above, presence of a lisp can be considered of very low typicality since most speakers do not have a lisp; absence of a lisp, on the other hand, has high typicality. In the voice quality example, harsh voice judged with a degree of two on the scale of Nawka and Anders (1996) is uncommon since this is a level usually associated with pathological voices and hence has low typicality, whereas harsh voice with level zero has higher typicality, since most speakers do not have a harsh voice quality. When using acoustic measurements, typicality is usually defined on a gradual scale. For example, as mentioned in section 2.2, 120 Hz is a fundamental frequency instantiation with high typicality among German male speakers and 160 Hz is an instantiation with low typicality in this population. Ideally, the assessment of typicality of a feature instantiation is based upon a scientific study of the frequency of different instantiations in the relevant population. Unfortunately, studies of that sort are relatively rare. There exist a few such studies of average fundamental frequency (e.g. Künzel 1987; Jessen, Köster and Gfroerer 2005 on German; Hudson et al. 2007; Gold 2014 on English; Lindh 2006 on Swedish), on articulation rate (e.g. Jessen 2007 on German; Cao and Wang 2011 on Chinese; Gold 2014 on English) and on long-term formants (e.g. Moos 2008, 2010 on German; Gold 2014 on English). But for most other speaker characteristics (and most languages) no such population studies exist. This holds true in particular for auditory features. For example, there is no known study on the different degrees of harsh voice quality in a population (cf. French et al. 2015 and Hughes et al. 2017 for new developments in that domain). If no population study exists on a given speaker characteristic, typicality can still be assessed if the forensic expert has relevant experience from her/his work or even simply as a phonetically/linguistically trained observer of speech behaviour encountered in everyday life. Here it is the auditory features that have the advantage over acoustic ones. For example, when encountering a strong degree of harshness in a case, the expert can probe her/his perceptual memory of past casework or of voices encountered in everyday life or in the media and can make a reasonable estimate of how typically the degree of harshness in the forensic case is found in the population. The accuracy of such experience-based typicality judgments is necessarily limited and they carry a substantial amount of subjectivity.

Based on the similarity judgment and the typicality judgment for a given speaker characteristic, strength of evidence of that characteristic is estimated according to the principles illustrated in Figure 9.2. This procedure is carried out for all speaker characteristics analysed in the case. As mentioned above, these characteristics should usually be as independent from each other as possible. Finally, in a FVC case, the strength of evidence is judged for the combination of all the speaker characteristics analysed in the case and a final conclusion is reached.

4 Methodological approaches II: The automatic and semiautomatic approach and the likelihood ratio

4.1 Introduction and history

While the auditory-acoustic approach to FVC has been used since the 1980s, two other strands of methodology relevant to FVC have been developed since the late 1990s. One strand is the combination of forensic-phonetic analysis with the Bayesian approach to forensic inference. This connection was made first by Phil Rose and is explained in his book Rose (2002) (see also Rose 2003). The Bayesian approach and the notion of the likelihood ratio, to be explained shortly, have been introduced to the forensic sciences as an effective and logically coherent way of interpreting and modelling forensic evidence (Robertson and Vignaux 1995) and it is a very active approach in the forensic sciences today. The approach that emerges from this combination of Bayesian inference and phonetically based FVC will be called *Forensic Semiautomatic Speaker Recognition* (FSASR) in this chapter. As will be explained further in section 4.4, the prefix "semi" in FSASR accounts for the fact that phonetic analysis requires manual activity by the phonetician and therefore the procedure is not fully automatic; what is automatic are methods of statistic modelling and machine learning, to be discussed shortly.

The second of these strands is automatic speaker recognition. Automatic speaker recognition is a field of speech technology that addresses tasks such as speaker verification and speaker identification in applications such as access control to sensitive areas or sensitive information. With a few exceptions, automatic speaker recognition was of no interest for forensics until the later 1990s. The reason for this was that forensic material was too difficult to meet the requirements of these systems. Whereas many automatic speaker recognition systems are based on text-identity (e.g. same passphrases spoken during training and when requesting access), FVC frequently requires text-independence. Moreover, most FVCs involve telephone-transmitted data, which is another characteristic many automatic speaker recognition systems did not have to cope with at the time. There are further limitations of the quality, quantity and speech style in forensic material that automatic speaker recognition systems were not prepared for. Technological and conceptual improvements have addressed these challenges, one important landmark study being the dissertation of Reynolds (1992) in which the method of Gaussian Mixture Modelling (GMM) was introduced to speaker recognition. A recent overview of automatic speaker recognition is provided by Hansen and Hasan (2015).

Although over time automatic speaker recognition had achieved the flexibility to deal with a variety of forensically realistic situations, only some proponents or developers of automatic speaker recognition were interested in its forensic application. Among those who are, most accept the Bayesian approach and the use of likelihood ratios. One of the earliest accounts of combining automatic speaker recognition with Bayesian methods in forensics was the dissertation by Meuwly (2001). At least by 2007 the need for making this connection became the dominant view (Gonzalez-Rodriguez et al. 2007; Ramos 2007). This Bayesian-based approach to automatic speaker recognition will be referred to as *Forensic Automatic Speaker Recognition* (FASR) in this chapter. The terms FSASR and FASR are also used and explained in a recent guideline document on these topics (Drygajlo et al. 2015).

In the INTERPOL survey documented by Morrison et al. (2016), the semiautomatic approach is referred to as "acoustic-phonetic by forensic practitioners (statistical model)" or simply as "acoustic phonetic statistical". The automatic approach is subdivided into "human-supervised automatic approaches by forensic practitioners" and "fully automatic approaches by non-forensic practitioners". According to the description in the survey, the former category involves "phoneticians or signal-processing engineers who carefully select and prepare recordings which are then analysed using signal-processing algorithms including the use of statistical models to calculate the strength of the evidence". It is this category of human-supervised automatic approaches by forensic practitioners that is intended when the automatic approach (FASR) is covered in section 4.3.[4]

---

[4] A term related to "human-supervised automatic approaches by forensic practitioners" that is found in the literature is called "human-assisted automatic speaker recognition", abbreviated as HASR. HASR has a narrow and a broad reading. In the narrow reading, the human factor involves aspects of auditory-based data preparation, such as the removal of portions from unrelated speakers or the removal of pauses or signal distortions, and that reading corresponds to the description of the human-supervised automatic approaches by forensic practitioners cited here. In the broad reading of HASR, the human factor is also seen as a second source of evidence beside the automatic analysis, for example by estimating speaker identity or non-identity from listening to the recordings holistically or even by combining FASR with the auditory-acoustic approach or FSASR (Gold and French 2011; Schwartz et al. 2011). It is the narrow reading of HASR that is addressed here when discussing FASR.

4.2 Bayesian approach and the likelihood ratio

Central to the Bayesian approach is Bayes' theorem. One way of formulating Bayes' theorem is called the odds form. Adapted to the purposes of FVC, it can be expressed as shown in Figure 9.3 (cf. Rose 2002: 63 and Morrison 2010: 23 for analogous expressions and explanations of the formula).

In this formula, $H_{\text{same speaker}}$ stands for the hypothesis that the questioned speaker is identical to the suspect, and $H_{\text{different speaker}}$ stands for the hypothesis that the questioned speaker is someone else other than the suspect in the relevant population. The term "E" stands for forensic speech evidence, which in the case of FVC is the result of the analysis of the different speaker characteristics (or one speaker characteristic at a time). "p" stands for probability and "|" stands for "under the condition of" or simply "given".

The *posterior odds* are the probability that the questioned speaker and the suspect are the same given the speech evidence, divided by the probability that the questioned speaker is someone else given the same speech evidence. The posterior odds are calculated by multiplying the likelihood ratio with the prior odds.

The *prior odds* are the probability that the questioned speaker and the suspect are the same divided by the probability that the questioned speaker is someone else before the speech evidence is adduced. In a forensic case this is information that the forensic expert usually has no access to. Whether or not questioned speaker and suspect are identical before even looking at any speech evidence (or other evidence from the forensic sciences) is information that has to do with general circumstances of the case, for example about how many individuals had access to a given telephone handset at a given location and moment in time or about how many individuals had a motive to commit a specific crime.[5]

The *likelihood ratio* (henceforth LR) is the probability of the speech evidence given that the questioned speaker and the suspect are the same, divided by the probability of the same speech evidence given that the questioned speaker is someone other than the suspect. Within the Bayesian approach to forensics it is the task of the

$$\underbrace{\frac{p(H_{\text{same speaker}}|E)}{p(H_{\text{different speaker}}|E)}}_{\text{Posterior Odds}} = \underbrace{\frac{p(E|H_{\text{same speaker}})}{p(E|H_{\text{different speaker}})}}_{\text{Likelihood Ratio}} \times \underbrace{\frac{p(H_{\text{same speaker}})}{p(H_{\text{different speaker}})}}_{\text{Prior Odds}}$$

Figure 9.3: The odds form of Bayes' theorem applied to FVC.

---

[5] In other contexts the prior odds are also referred to as the "base rate". Calculating or estimating probabilities without taking into account the base rate is a frequently encountered cognitive error. An explanation of base rate neglect and other cognitive errors is given by Kahneman (2011).

forensic expert to provide the LR, which is a measure of the strength of the evidence, as explained below. The task of providing the prior odds and of calculating the posterior odds from the prior odds and the LR (not just the LR from speech evidence but from other forensic evidence as well) is the duty of the court.

The LR has the interesting characteristic of providing a very straightforward way of quantifying the strength of evidence in a given FVC. As was explained in section 2.2, the greater the similarity between questioned speaker and suspect, the stronger the evidence that the two are identical, and the smaller the similarity the stronger the evidence that they are non-identical. In the Bayesian approach this similarity aspect is expressed in the numerator of the LR. It was also explained in that section that the lower the typicality, the stronger the evidence in favour of identity and vice versa. In the LR this typicality aspect corresponds to its denominator (see Rose 2002 for the connection between the LR and similarity/typicality). Since the LR is a ratio, the value of that ratio is increased by either increasing its numerator (i.e. increasing similarity) or by decreasing its denominator (i.e. decreasing typicality). This way, strength of evidence, i.e. the degree of support in favour of or against identity between questioned speaker and suspect, can be straightforwardly quantified. The LR also captures the direction of the evidence, i.e. whether it supports identity or non-identity: If the LR is larger than 1 there is more evidence in favour of identity than against it, and if the LR is smaller than 1 there is more evidence against identity than in favour of it. Often the LR is expressed as logarithm. In that case the value at which the direction of the evidence changes is at zero (this will be shown in Figure 9.9).

Before making specific comments about methods used in FASR and FSASR in the following subsections, the principles behind LR calculation can be shown in the following two figures adopted from Morrison (2010).

Figure 9.4 represents a case in which similarity is high and typicality is low. The x-axis presents a scale of gradual (i.e. continuous) values of an acoustic-phonetic parameter – in this case fundamental frequency in Hz, but it could be any other gradual parameter. The y-axis shows probability density. The vertical line (green in colour), when extended down to the x-axis, represents a measurement result for the questioned speaker (here: about 150 Hz). The slim Gaussian distribution to the right (blue in colour) represents the distribution of all acoustic values measured in the suspect modelled normally. The broader Gaussian distribution to the left (red in colour) represents the distribution of acoustic values measured in a relevant population (e.g. adult male speakers of English or German), again modelled normally. In this example similarity is (maximally) high because the vertical line from the questioned speaker lies right in the middle of the distribution of the suspect. At the same time typicality is low because the value of the questioned speaker lies at the margin of the distribution of the population. The LR is calculated by taking the y-axis probability density values at two locations in the graph. The first location is where the vertical line intersects the suspect distribution (here the probability density value is

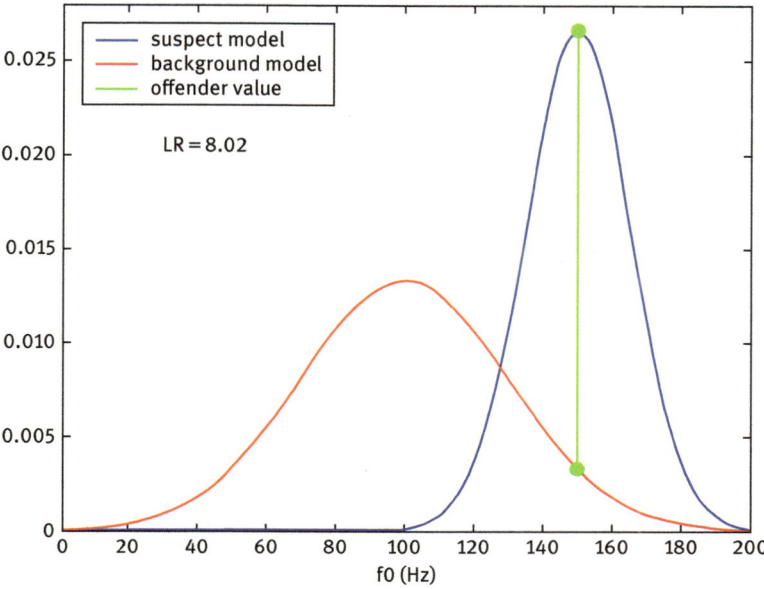

Figure 9.4: Schematic illustration of LR-calculation in a case with high similarity and low typicality (from Morrison 2010; copyright Geoffrey Stewart Morrison 2010, used with permission).

about 0.027) and the second location is where the vertical line intersects the population distribution (here the probability density value is about 0.0035). The former value constitutes the numerator of the LR and the latter the denominator. After dividing the two values a result of about 8 is obtained. This is the LR-value in this example. Expressed verbally, the value means that one would be eight times more likely to observe the questioned acoustic value if it had come from the suspect rather than some other randomly chosen individual from the relevant population. The case example shown here is the same in principle as "case example 3" illustrated in Figure 9.2 in preparation for the discussion of the auditory-acoustic approach. In both examples the illustrated configuration is of high similarity and low typicality. The difference is that within the auditory-acoustic approach strength of evidence can merely be estimated, whereas here with the LR method strength of evidence can be fully quantified.

Figure 9.5 shows a case with high similarity – as in Figure 9.4 – but also with high typicality. It corresponds to "case example 2" illustrated in Figure 9.2. In this example the LR is lower because the denominator of the LR is higher than in the low-typicality situation shown in Figure 9.4. Interestingly the LR is not unity (one) despite the fact that the value of the questioned speaker is located in the middle of not just the suspect distribution but also the population distribution. The reason that in this situation the LR is higher than one is because in this example (and usually in general) the

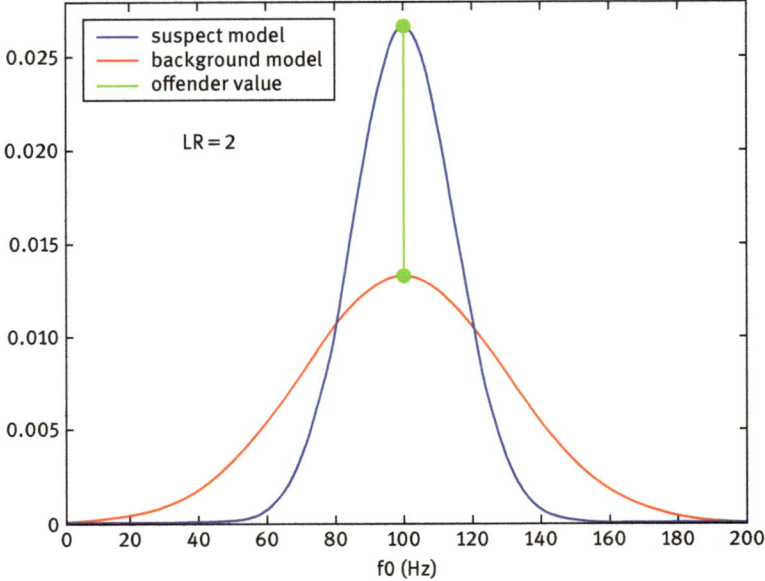

Figure 9.5: Schematic illustration of LR-calculation in a case with high similarity and high typicality (from Morrison 2010; copyright Geoffrey Stewart Morrison 2010, used with permission).

distribution of values in the population is broader than the distribution of values in the suspect. In other words, inter-individual variation is larger than intra-individual variation – as it should be if a feature is useful for distinguishing between different speakers (see section 2.1).[6]

---

[6] More technically, the key facts to understand LR>1 in Figure 9.5 are: (1) A probability distribution has to have an area under the curve of 1; both of the Gaussians in Figure 9.5 (as well as Figure 9.4) occupy that same area. (2) The probability density of a normal distribution is partly a function of its dispersion (the parameter is the standard deviation). Consequently, the greater the dispersion, the lower the maximum value of the probability density function that can be achieved given the same area under the curve. Some situations in which the configuration in Figure 9.5 becomes relevant are shown by Rose (2017). In his case examples it was possible to quantify the numerator of the LR but not the denominator, since no background population was available. He argues that if similarity between questioned speaker and suspect is high, there will be some evidence in the direction of identity, even though the particular strength of evidence is not known. He points out that this is possible under the plausible assumption that inter-individual variation for well-investigated FSASR features (such as formants) will be broader than intra-individual variation, as illustrated in Figure 9.5. He also demonstrates that strong *dis*similarity between questioned and suspect material argues against identity, no matter how the characteristics of the background population (see "case example 1" in Figure 9.2). He points out that any missing typicality information is something that should be mentioned to the court.

If in Figure 9.5 the vertical line occurred at the left intersection of the distributions (at about 80 Hz) or the right one (at about 120 Hz) the LR would be 1 and evidence would be neutral; this corresponds to "case example 4" in Figure 9.2. Expressed verbally, one would be just as likely to get such a value under the same-speaker hypothesis as under the different-speaker hypothesis (cf. Figure 9.3). In other words, it does not tell us anything more than we already know from the existing evidence: it does not make us change our previous beliefs.

So far it was illustrated how the LR is calculated. To conclude this subsection, three examples will be given of how a LR is combined with prior odds in order to arrive at the posterior odds, as shown in Figure 9.3. In these examples the LR is kept constant and the prior odds are varied. Let us assume that the LR of the speech evidence is 8, which can also be expressed at 8/1. Let us now assume that there are 5 people including the suspect who could have said the incriminating speech. In that case, the prior odds are 1/4, and multiplied with the LR of 8/1 we arrive at the posterior odds 8/4. These posterior odds can be converted into a probability (number between 0 and 1) by calculating 8/(8+4), which is 0.67 (Robertson & Vignaux 1995: 15). Expressed as percentage, this is a 67% probability the incriminating speech was produced by the suspect. In the second example, the LR is 8/1 again, but this time there are 100 people including the suspect who could have said the incriminating speech. The prior odds are 1/99 and the posterior odds 8/99. The posterior probability expressed as percentage is 8/(8+99) = 8%. In the final example, there is only one other speaker who could have said the incriminating speech. The prior odds are 1/1 and with LR 8/1 the posterior odds are 8/1. The posterior probability expressed is 8/(8+1) = 89%. In casework, the LRs achieved by individual features or combinations of features are often higher and the posterior odds then will be correspondingly higher as well (or lower with LR values <1).

4.3 Forensic automatic speaker recognition

Forensic Automatic Speaker Recognition (FASR) is based on acoustic features, but these acoustic features usually differ from the ones familiar in acoustic phonetics, such as fundamental frequency or formant frequencies, which were summarized in Table 9.1. One type of acoustic feature that is most frequently used in FASR is called *cepstral coefficients*. There are several versions of cepstral coefficients, including MFCC (Mel Frequency Cepstral Coefficients) and LPCC (Linear Prediction Cepstral Coefficients). MFCCs are found most frequently in automatic speaker recognition (as well as in applications such as speech recognition or language recognition) and they are explained in introductory texts to automatic speaker recognition such as Rosenberg, Bimbot, and Parthasarathy (2008). LPCCs have also been used in both research and casework, including by the phonetician Phil Rose. Rose (2013a) provides a very accessible step-by-step introduction to cepstral analysis using LPCCs.

A forensic-phonetic study using both MFCCs and LPCCs has been presented by Hughes (2014). Cepstral coefficients are "short-term spectral features" as termed by Kinnunen and Li (2010). These short-term spectral features are intended to (primarily) capture the acoustic characteristics of the vocal tract. Capturing the speaker-discriminatory aspects of the vocal tract is also the intention behind formant analysis, mentioned in Table 9.1. But the information captured by these two methods is not the same. On the one hand, cepstral analysis provides more information about the spectrum than formants; for example, it provides information not only about spectral peaks, but also spectral valleys, and not only about vowels (the primary domain of formants) but also consonants. On the other hand, formant analysis is more robust against noise, whereas noise components in the spectrum will be included in the cepstral coefficients, though there are methods which attempt to disregard noise components (see Rose 2013a for illustration).

The technical idea behind cepstral analysis is that the shape of the speech spectrum is characterized by a relatively small number of coefficients that are uncorrelated or almost uncorrelated. Speech spectra are extracted by sliding a window of about 20 to 30 milliseconds duration through an entire recording of a speaker (without pauses) at a rate of about 100 times per second. For each window, a number of cepstral coefficients (13 or a similar value) is calculated. Moreover, the same number of so-called delta coefficients can be calculated. Delta coefficients capture the changes between adjacent cepstral coefficients and they are a way of capturing speech dynamics. (Otherwise the temporal order of the coefficients is not processed, which is a difference to automatic speech recognition, were temporal structure is crucial.) The entire process of spectral extraction and the calculation of cepstral coefficients proceeds automatically.

The outcome of this procedure is a series of feature vectors with a dimensionality corresponding to the number of coefficients. For example, for a 20-second long recording, there is a series of two thousand 26-dimensional feature vectors (if the extraction rate is at 100 per second and 13 MFCCs with deltas are included). This is a complex data set that needs to be modelled statistically in order to capture the essential characteristics of the speaker. The most commonly used way of calculating a speaker model is called Gaussian Mixture Modelling. A *Gaussian Mixture Model (GMM)* is the additive output of several (about 32 or more) Gaussians (Hansen & Hasan 2015: 86 for details). A simple example of GMMs is given in Figure 9.6.

The right-hand GMM in Figure 9.6 (i.e. the tall, pointy peak marked with a bold line, blue in colour) represents a model of a suspect and consists of four different (thin-lined) Gaussians in one-dimensional space. The left-hand GMM (i.e. the bold-lined structure with a saddle, red in colour) represents the background model, to be explained shortly. The figure illustrates not cepstral coefficients but fundamental frequency (f0; see Table 9.1). Fundamental frequency is one-dimensional and a small number of Gaussians can be enough to capture the shape of the f0-distribution of a speaker. As we saw, typical cepstral representations are 26-dimensional and a

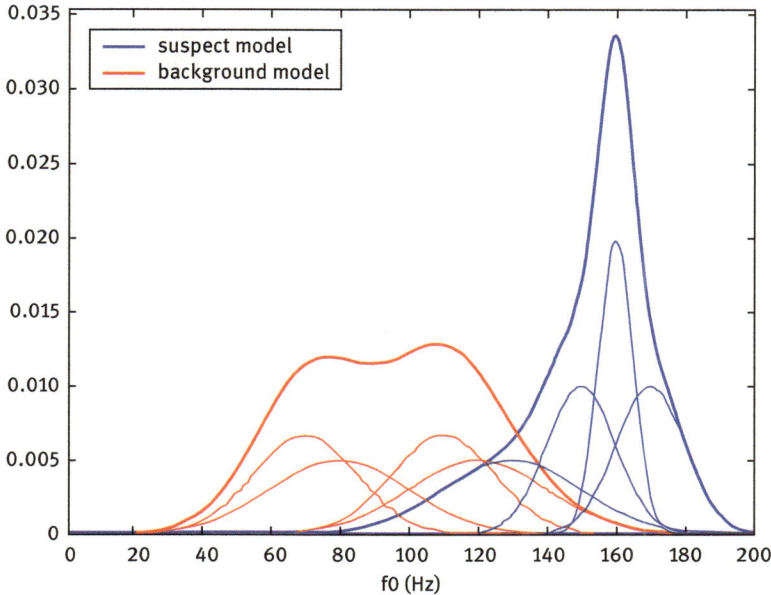

Figure 9.6: Schematic illustration of Gaussian Mixture Models for suspect data and the background model. As in Figures 9.4 and 9.5, the x-axis represents an acoustic feature (here: fundamental frequency) and the y-axis probability density (from Morrison 2010; copyright Geoffrey Stewart Morrison 2010, used with permission).

possible number of Gaussians is 32; needless to say, this is far more than can be illustrated visually. The figure also demonstrates that Gaussian Mixture Modelling and cepstral analysis do not necessarily go hand in hand; there can be GMMs of classical acoustic-phonetic features (as illustrated here with f0 or as in Becker, Jessen, and Grigoras 2008 using long-term formants) and there are other ways of modelling cepstral information than with GMMs (for example with so-called support vector machines; Hansen and Hasan 2015). Using GMMs for acoustic-phonetic features is a typical semiautomatic application, to be addressed in section 4.4.

Forensic Automatic Speaker Recognition (FASR) is compatible with the Bayesian approach and the calculation of likelihood ratios (LR) that was explained in section 4.2. There are different ways of arriving at LRs. One of the simplest ones, called the Direct Method by Alexander (2005), is explained here as follows. After extracting cepstral coefficients for both the questioned speaker and the suspect, the suspect data are modelled with a GMM. Another GMM will be calculated for a relevant population, i.e. a set of speakers that are unrelated to a case but that have similar overall characteristics – such as sex and language – as the compared speakers and who speak in a similar speech style under similar conditions. Another term for this population of unrelated speakers (and their models) is Universal Background Model (UBM) or simply background model. This stage of the analysis is again illustrated in Figure 9.6. It shows on the right-hand side the GMM of the suspect and to the left-hand side the GMM of the relevant population (again, for simplification the illustrated feature is f0, not cepstral coefficients).[7]

The next step of the analysis is to determine where the extracted cepstral coefficients-based feature vectors of the questioned speaker occur relative to the GMM of the suspect. In the simplified model in Figure 9.6, the result from the questioned speaker is one value on the x-axis. In reality, since there are many feature vectors per questioned recording, averaging is applied. Furthermore, the comparison between questioned recording and suspect model takes place in something like 26-dimensional space, not the one-dimensional space illustrated here. In Figure 9.7, a hypothetical result from the questioned speaker is included as a vertical line (green in colour). This result is also referred to as the Evidence. Comparison between the questioned-speaker result and the model of the suspect shows that the evidence value of the questioned speaker intersects

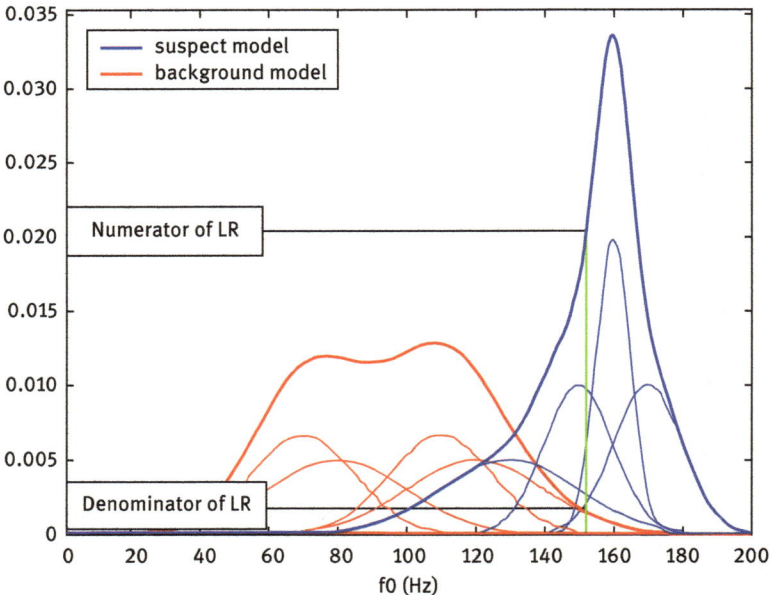

Figure 9.7: Same illustration as in Figure 9.6, now supplied with Evidence (i.e. acoustic value(s) for the questioned speaker) and with horizontal lines indicating the probabilities at the points where the evidence intersects suspect model (right) and background model (left). Expanded from Morrison 2010; copyright Geoffrey Stewart Morrison 2010, used with permission.

---

[7] In the approach of Reynolds, Quatieri, and Dunn (2000), the UBM has a size of about 512 Gaussians or more. The suspect GMM is not calculated independently from the UBM but derived from it by an adaptation procedure in which the GMM representing the UBM is modified according to the characteristics of the suspect data.

the suspect model at a probability density value of 0.020. This probability density value constitutes the numerator of the LR. Subsequently, the questioned-speaker result is compared with the background model and the intersection between the questioned-speaker value and the background model occurs at a probability density value of about 0.002. This value constitutes the denominator of the LR. The LR in this illustration would be 10.

This procedure of arriving at LRs in Figure 9.7 is entirely analogous to the illustrations in Figures 9.4 and 9.5 and it corresponds to the LR concept in the formula in Figure 9.3. The LR that is shown more abstractly in Figure 9.3 looks like in Figure 9.8 when applied to FASR.

The method shown so far summarizes core procedures of FASR (see also Becker 2012; Drygajlo 2011 for overview). There are several more extensions to this procedure and several more issues to address, a few of which will be mentioned here briefly.

One of the important topics is *calibration*. As characterized in section 4.2, the LR value at which the evidence is maximally uncertain is at LR=1 (or log LR=0). With a value of one, the evidence provides as much/little support of speaker identity as it does of speaker non-identity. A FASR system in which this point of maximal uncertainty is at or near the value of LR=1 (or a log LR value of zero) when a method validation is carried out (section 4.5) is called a calibrated system. The FASR method of LR calculation shown above (Direct Method) often does not provide a fully calibrated outcome. In an uncalibrated system the point of maximal uncertainty takes a value that clearly deviates from LR=1. Although it is possible to some extent to arrive at meaningful results without a calibrated system, calibration is a desired property of a system. LR values that are not calibrated are called LR scores or simply scores. Several methods have been proposed in the literature to convert scores into calibrated LRs. One of them is called the scoring method (Alexander 2005; Gonzalez-Rodriguez et al. 2006; Drygajlo 2011; a brief illustration of the scoring method is also shown in Jessen 2008), another is called logistic regression calibration (Brümmer et al. 2007; Morrison 2013 and Rose 2013a for tutorials and demonstrations). Another recent proposal is presented by Solewicz, Jessen, and van der Vloed (2017).

Another issue is the handling of *mismatch problems*. As mentioned in section 2.1, mismatch means that the behavioural or technical conditions in the questioned recording differ from the ones in the suspect recording. Several proposals have been made to address the mismatch problem in FASR, some of them apply to the level where MFCCs (or other features) are extracted, some apply to the level of GMM modelling and some apply to the scoring level, i.e. scores can be readjusted according to conditions (Kinnunen and Li 2010 and Enzinger 2015 for general overview; Alexander 2005 for score-level compensation; Enzinger, Morrison, and Ochoa 2016 for earlier-level compensations). Mismatch compensation has aspects of calibration (especially

$$LR = \frac{p(CC_{questioned}|GMM_{suspect})}{p(CC_{questioned}|UBM)}$$

Figure 9.8: Likelihood ratio concept used with the Direct Method of Forensic Automatic Speaker Recognition (CC = Cepstral Coefficients, other abbreviations explained in text).

score-level compensation), but it is also intended to increase speaker-discriminatory performance compared to uncompensated comparisons.

A recent approach to FASR is called the *i-vector approach* (Dehak et al. 2011). In the i-vector approach GMMs are calculated not only for the suspect but also the questioned speaker (GMMs are adapted as described in the preceding footnote). The essential information from the GMMs (the means in particular) is represented as high-dimensional vectors called supervectors. The dimensionality of these supervectors is reduced into largely independent fixed-length vectors by a specific compression process; the results are the i-vectors. In subsequent steps, the most discriminative speaker information is emphasised (along with providing further dimensionality reduction) using LDA (Linear Discriminant Analysis), and scores are calculated with methods such as PLDA (Probabilistic Linear Discriminant Analysis). Later steps of the analysis, such as calibration, proceed in essentially the same manner as in earlier FASR approaches.

4.4 Forensic Semiautomatic Speaker Recognition

As shown in section 4.3, FASR consists roughly of three stages: feature extraction, speaker modelling (with GMM or by other means), and the calculation of a score or likelihood ratio that captures the strength of evidence of a particular voice comparison numerically. The division into these three essential stages applies not only to FASR, but also to Forensic Semiautomatic Speaker Recognition (FSASR). The content of the second and third stage is very much the same in FASR and FSASR. The main difference lies in the feature extraction stage. The features used in FASR are extracted automatically and they usually derive from the domain of speech technology (automatic speech recognition, speaker recognition etc.), which is the case for cepstral coefficients such as MFCCs. The features used in FSASR, on the other hand, are extracted (or supervised) manually and they usually derive from acoustic phonetics. Since acoustic phonetics is a source of information for the auditory-acoustic approach as well (section 3), there is overlap between FSASR and the auditory-acoustic approach, which is addressed towards the end of this subsection.[8]

The features used in FSASR include vowel formant centre frequencies (Gonzalez-Rodriguez et al. 2007; Rose and Winter 2010; Morrison, Zhang, and Rose 2011), formant dynamics in diphthongs modelled by curve fitting methods (Morrison 2009, 2011), long-term formants (Becker, Jessen, and Grigoras 2008; Gold 2014; Jessen, Alexander, and Forth 2014), and f0-distribution parameters such as mean, variance,

---

[8] The term semiautomatic speaker recognition has also been used in the past for methods of FVC that quantify speaker differences but not necessarily within the Bayesian framework and with the calculation of LRs (Meuwly 2001 for overview).

skewness, and kurtosis (Kinoshita, Ishihara, and Rose 2009; Kinoshita and Ishihara 2014). These features normally require the input of a phonetician. For example, although formant tracking or pitch tracking methods automate the extraction of formants and fundamental frequency, there can be tracking errors that have to be corrected manually. Moreover, selecting, identifying and segmenting the vowels, diphthongs or other linguistic units that are subject to a FSASR method is usually performed manually. It is this manual contribution by the phonetician that is meant by the prefix "semi" in FSASR.

In order to arrive at a clear distinction between FSASR and FASR, the presence/absence of manual input is more reliable as a criterion than the distinction between different feature types. The reason is that there can be cross-overs between the combinations shown so far. One example are segmental cepstra (Rose, Osanai, and Kinoshita 2003; Rose 2013a). The features used in segmental cepstra are cepstral coefficients just like in FASR. But unlike in FASR, cepstral analysis is limited to certain sounds (consonants or vowels) and these have to be selected manually (unless they are automatically identified and segmented with speech recognition methods). Segmental cepstra are classified here as a FSASR method because of their manual involvement; if classification were based on the feature type, it would have to be classified as a FASR method. Another type of cross-over occurs with methods in which features typically used in FSASR are extracted fully automatically, i.e. without any manual involvement or supervision (e.g. in Gonzalez-Rodriguez 2011 on automatic extraction and modelling of formant dynamics or in Alexander et al. 2016 on automatic long-term formant analysis). These methods are classified here as FASR because feature extraction is automatic, although based on features typical of FSASR.

Whereas FASR and FSASR differ at the feature extraction stage, the speaker modelling and the calculation of an LR are the same in principle, but there can be differences in complexity. The features used in FSASR usually have fewer dimensions than the cepstral coefficients used in FASR. As shown, MFCCs used in FASR might have 26 dimensions (13 coefficients plus deltas) or more. Acoustic-phonetic features usually have fewer dimensions. For example, fundamental frequency normally is a one-dimensional feature and if delta features are included a two-dimensional one (but see Kinoshita, Ishihara, and Rose 2009 and Kinoshita and Ishihara 2014 for more dimensions). If three formants are measured the resulting feature vectors are three-dimensional and with changes included six-dimensional. There are also examples of acoustic-phonetic features with more dimensions, but rarely exceeding ten. The range of sounds covered by the features is also usually more extensive in FASR than in FSASR. With MFCC, all sounds are covered, whereas, for example, formants are only measured in vowels (or only in some types of vowels) and fundamental frequency is only defined in voiced sounds. Because of these differences in complexity, speaker modelling (and in part LR calculation) can be simpler in FSASR than in FASR. This affects the number of dimensions that need to be modelled and the number of Gaussians necessary in GMM analysis. For example, Becker, Jessen, and Grigoras (2008) and

Jessen, Alexander, and Forth (2014) show that three to eight Gaussians (not 32 or more as in FASR) are sufficient to capture the speaker information in long-term formants.

A method for modelling speakers and calculating LRs other than the GMM-based one shown in section 4.3 is called MVKD (Multivariate Kernel Density). Whereas the GMM-based approach (also called GMM-UBM approach) originally stems from the field of automatic speaker recognition, MVKD is a method that was developed within the forensic sciences in general (Aitken and Lucy 2004; see also Rose 2002 for predecessors of this method and Morrison 2011 for a study in which both methods are compared on the same data set and in which the two methods are explained in detail). The models used in MVKD are simpler than in the GMM-UBM approach and the number of dimensions that can be captured meaningfully is limited to about ten. But when applied to the features used in FSASR, they both perform well (some studies cited in the second paragraph of this subsection used GMM-UBM, others used MVKD). No matter which of these methods for speaker modelling and the calculation of LRs is used, the execution of the method proceeds automatically with suitable computer software as soon as all the speaker data and necessary background data are provided, hence the component "automatic" in the name "semiautomatic".

When the semiautomatic approach is compared with the auditory-acoustic approach addressed in section 3, both similarities and differences can be noted. What the auditory-acoustic approach has in common with FSASR is that in both approaches speaker-discriminatory features from the domain of acoustic phonetics are used. There are no principled reasons why FSASR cannot also be applied to auditory characteristics or even to linguistic features outside phonetics and phonology. This would require that the ability to calculate LRs be extended to more features than acoustic-phonetic ones. Although there are no LR-based methods for auditory analysis that are as established as the ones for acoustic analysis (covering acoustics both within FSASR and FASR), some options have been shown in the literature (Kinoshita 2001 [also discussed in Rose 2002: 304–306]; Elliot 2002; Schwartz et al. 2011; Aitken and Gold 2013; French et al. 2015).

In the manner proposed in this chapter, the difference between FSASR and the auditory-acoustic approach is defined to lie in the way in which similarity and typicality are expressed. In the auditory-acoustic approach they are expressed in qualitative terms, but in FSASR they are quantified in terms of a likelihood ratio. This distinction is also made in Drygajlo et al. (2015), as well as in Morrison et al. (2016) with slightly different terminology. The rigorous quantification used in FSASR makes certain requirements on the data provided. Importantly, there have to be case-relevant data for a background model and the FSASR method needs to be validated, which requires a test data set with more than one recording per speaker (see section 4.5) of at least about 20 speakers. This currently can/has not been provided for many speaker characteristics used in the auditory-acoustic approach. As a consequence, the set of speaker characteristics (features) used in FSASR is generally smaller than the one used in the auditory-acoustic approach. However, as shown by Rose (2013b), when a population is collected that is dedicated to the properties of the case (e.g. by including words and expressions found in both the questioned and suspect recordings), all the ingredients for full LR-quantification of a variety of features in FSASR are there (see also Enzinger, Morrison, and Ochoa 2016 for dedicated population-building in FASR).

In some descriptions of the auditory-acoustic approach cited in section 3 it is left open as an option that statistical analysis leading to LRs may be applied if possible. This would mean that FSASR is part of the auditory-acoustic approach. It is proposed here instead that FSASR should be granted a standing of its own rather than being limited in status to an optional procedure within the auditory-acoustic approach. This is not intended to mean that the use of FSASR is obligatory in FVC, but it is intended to mean that the scientific complexity and forensic relevance of calculating LRs based on auditory-acoustic data is duly acknowledged.

4.5 Method validation

For any analysis method or set of methods used in FVC it is desirable to know what the recognition rate is, or, more technically speaking, how well it is possible to separate pairs of recordings that originate from the same speaker from pairs of recordings that originate from different speakers. This is possible to some extent both for the auditory-acoustic approach and for FASR/FSASR, but it works particularly well for the latter approach. The main reason for this is that due to the automatic components involved in both FASR and FSASR it is possible to automatically calculate the results of many comparisons. For example, in a dataset of 40 recordings in which 20 speakers are involved and where there are two recordings per speaker, there are 400 comparisons (20 times 20), of which 20 are same-speaker comparisons and 380 are different-speaker comparisons. To perform 400 comparisons is entirely unrealistic for the auditory-acoustic approach but is very realistic for FASR and FSASR. (For FASR it can be a matter of minutes or less, for FSASR it requires a dataset with manually corrected input, but as soon as this is available, computation takes about the same time as in FASR.) To perform such a set of comparisons (or even larger sets) is called method validation, which means that the performance of a system (a method or set of methods used in FASR/FSASR) is tested in order to show how well it works.[9]

There is a variety of different ways to document the speaker-discriminatory performance of a system. These performance indicators can either be single values or graphical displays, from which a variety of important information can be read. An example of a very useful display is the Tippett plot (named after a statistician

---

9 Another way of validating FVC than the one shown in this section is to limit the number of comparisons to a smaller set of about ten to fifteen or less. With that restriction, analyses from all approaches are realistic (Cambier-Langeveld 2007 and Schwartz et al. 2011 for examples).

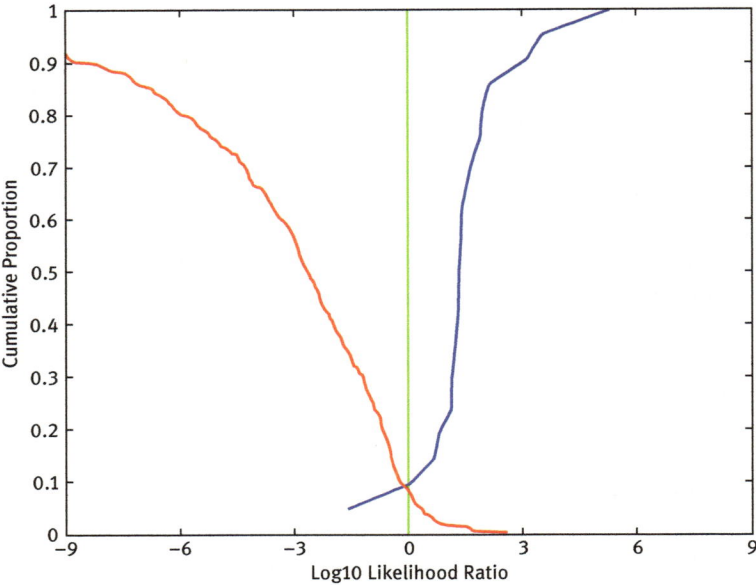

Figure 9.9: Example of a Tippett plot. X-axis: log10 likelihood ratio; Y-axis: Cumulative proportion.

with that name). Such a Tippett plot is shown in Figure 9.9, based on the analysis of long-term formants with the GMM-UBM method on a subset of the corpus Pool 2010 (Jessen, Köster, and Gfroerer 2005).

The Tippett plot reads as follows: the curve (cumulative proportions) rising towards the right (blue in colour) displays the log LRs of all the same-speaker comparisons and the curve falling towards the right (red in colour) displays the log LRs of all the different-speaker comparisons. As expected, the log LRs for the same-speaker comparisons are higher on average than those of the different-speaker comparisons. But there is overlap. The intersection of these curves is the point of maximal uncertainty. Since this point has a value of (or very near to) log LR=0, this is a well calibrated system (cf. the paragraph on calibration in section 4.3). Calibration had been performed with cross validation calibration.[10] The Tippett plot is useful for, among others, two reasons. Firstly, it simply gives a clear descriptive presentation of all the log LRs obtained in a data set. For example, one can see that the lowest log LR value of all same-speaker comparisons in the data set is at about –1.5 and the highest is at about 5.

---

10 Morrison (2011) for details on the cross validation calibration method. Thanks to Ewald Enzinger for performing this method and for creating the Tippett plot shown in Figure 9.9. Jessen, Alexander, and Forth (2014) for the GMM-UBM method used to generate the scores before calibration.

Secondly, the value on the y-axis on which the two curves intersect is meaningful: it is called the Equal Error Rate (EER). The EER is a type of single-value performance indicator; the lower the value, the better the speaker discrimination performance. In this case the EER is slightly below 0.1 (i.e. 10%). This means that if the intersection between the two curves, which due to good calibration is at log LR=0, is taken as the decision threshold (see the vertical line, green in colour), there is an about 10% chance to make a false identification error (i.e. all the different-speaker values with log LR>0) and likewise there is an about a 10% chance to make a false rejection error (i.e. all the same-speaker values with log LR<0).

Overviews of Tippett plots and EER, as well as on several other performance values and displays, are given, among others, by van Leeuwen and Brümmer (2007), Morrison (2010), Drygajlo (2011), Ramos et al. (2013), and Haraksim (2014). Further information on method validation, but also on FASR and FSASR in general, is presented in Drygajlo et al. (2015). An example of a method validation based on forensic casework is provided by Solewicz et al. (2012). Van der Vloed, Bouten, and van Leeuwen (2014) describe another forensically based corpus and validation results from it.

A Tippett plot can also provide a more quantitative view of the relations between intra- and inter-individual variation that were illustrated qualitatively in Figure 9.1. The log LR scale of the Tippett plot is not only informative about the direction of the evidence (log LR>0 supporting identity, if calibrated, and vice versa for non-identity) and its strength, but it can also be seen as a quantification of acoustic similarity: the lower the value, the lower the similarity. If inter-individual variation is high, as shown in Figure 9.1 (a) and (c), the acoustic similarity between recordings in different-speaker comparisons is low. In the Tippett plot this means that the different-speaker distribution (red in colour) is located at the relatively lower (i.e. left) end of the x-axis-scale. If inter-individual variation is low, as shown in Figure 9.1 (b) and (d), the different-speaker distribution has higher values and is located further to the right on the scale. If intra-individual variation is low, as in Figure 9.1 (a) and (b), the acoustic similarity between recordings in same-speaker comparisons is high and the same-speaker distribution (blue in colour) occurs far to the right of the Tippett plot. If however intra-individual variation is high, as Figure 9.1 (c) and (d), the acoustic similarity when speakers are compared with themselves is lower and the same-speaker distribution lies somewhat more to the left of the scale. From these relationships it can be understood why the pattern shown in Figure 9.1 (a) is the optimal one. When inter-individual variation is high and intra-individual variation is low, the different-speaker distribution occurs far to the left of the Tippett plot and the same-speaker distribution far to the right. In that situation overlap between the two distributions is very small (or even absent in very clean data) and the EER is very low, hence speaker recognition performance is high. In the less favourable combinations of intra-individual and inter-individual variation shown in Figure 9.1 (b) to (d), overlap is stronger and the EER will be higher; it will be highest for the situation shown in Figure 9.1 (d).

5 Conclusion

In this contribution an introduction has been given to the principles of FVC. Two approaches have been shown within which forensic voice comparison (FVC) analyses can be carried out. These are, firstly, the auditory-acoustic approach and, secondly, the automatic and semiautomatic approach. Both of these approaches have mutual advantages and disadvantages.

The strong asset of the auditory-acoustic approach is that it includes a wide range of speaker characteristics. This has the advantage of adding robustness to the conclusion since the question of identity vs. non-identity is examined from the perspective of multiple, maximally independent speaker-discriminatory features. The weak side of this approach is that the assessments of similarity and typicality are qualitative and (with some features) quite strongly dependent on subjective judgment and experience.

Conversely, the automatic and semiautomatic approach (FASR and FSASR) has the advantage of allowing for full quantification of similarity and typicality and the resulting likelihood ratio and it is much less reliant on subjective judgment. Its disadvantage is that presently the range of speaker characteristics used in FASR and FSASR is limited to acoustic features, and within that domain, the main emphasis lies on vocal tract acoustics.

If both of the approaches are used in a FVC case the analysis can benefit from the advantages of both of them, and the reliability and robustness of the conclusion is likely to increase. Since the analysis results of FASR and FSASR methods are numerical, but the analysis results of the auditory-acoustic approach are qualitative, it will not be possible to combine both into a final numerical conclusion and the final conclusion will therefore have to be qualitative, i.e. expressed verbally. If, instead, full quantification in the form of an LR is intended, a reasonable diversity of speaker characteristics should be analysed, at least some of them more theory-driven (informed by phonetic/linguistic theory) than the cepstral coefficients used in FASR alone (cf. González-Rodríguez et al. 2014). An example of such a fully numerical approach is given by Rose (2013b).

At the end of all the analyses performed within a FVC case, it is necessary to arrive at a conclusion relevant to the speaker identity/non-identity question that the court (or any other mandating authority) is interested in. This conclusion is not only a condensation of all the analytical results in the case, it is also a form of communication interface between forensic scientists and their scientific methods on the one hand, and the goals and mindsets of the legal experts (judge, prosecution and defence lawyers) involved in preparing the judicial decision-making process on the other hand. Having in mind this interface function of the conclusion, the conclusion framework, i.e. the way in which conclusions are presented in general (i.e. for all cases), is something that should be negotiated in a way that both the forensic scientists and the legal experts (plus the jury, depending on the legal system) can understand and are satisfied with. This is not at all an easy task and it is not surprising that the ways in which conclusions are expressed differ widely between different countries and even within countries. (This holds for forensic science in general, not just for FVC.) The topic of conclusion frameworks is complicated and requires a separate treatment. What this chapter has concentrated on instead is to explain the forensic science behind forensic voice comparison. Some Information on conclusion frameworks and their use internationally is provided by Gold and French (2011) and Morrison et al. (2016). No matter which conclusion framework is adopted, it remains the central task for the FVC expert to give the court an indication as to whether the results of the analysis support the same-speaker hypothesis or the different-speaker hypothesis and how strong the evidence in support of either hypotheses is.

Acknowledgements: The author is particularly grateful to Phil Rose and Dom Watt for detailed comments throughout the chapter. Many thanks are also expressed to Finnian Kelly for providing valuable input on questions concerning automatic speaker recognition. Comments from my BKA colleagues in the early stages of this chapter are gratefully acknowledged as well.

References

Aitken, C.G.G. & D. Lucy. 2004. Evaluation of trace evidence in the form of multivariate data. *Applied Statistics* 53. 109–122.

Aitken, Colin & Erica Gold. 2013. Evidence evaluation for discrete data. *Forensic Science International* 230. 147–155.

Alexander, Anil. 2005. *Forensic automatic speaker recognition using Bayesian interpretation and statistical compensation for mismatched conditions*. Lausanne: EPFL dissertation.

Alexander, Anil, Oscar Forth, Alankar Aryal Atreya & Finnian Kelly. 2016. VOCALISE: A forensic automatic speaker recognition system supporting spectral, phonetic, and user-provided features. *Proceedings of ODYSSEY 2016* (Bilbao).

Allen, J. Sean, Joanne L. Miller & David DeSteno. 2003. Individual talker differences in voice-onset-time. *Journal of the Acoustical Society of America* 113. 544–552.

Amino, Kanae & Takashi Osanai. 2015. Cross-language differences in articulation rate and its transfer into Japanese as a second language. *Forensic Science International* 249. 116–122.

Baldwin, John & Peter French. 1990. *Forensic phonetics*. London: Pinter.

Becker, Timo. 2012. *Automatischer forensischer Stimmenvergleich*. Norderstedt: Books on Demand.

Becker, Timo, Michael Jessen & Catalin Grigoras. 2008. Forensic speaker verification using formant features and Gaussian mixture models. *Proceedings of INTERSPEECH 2008* (Brisbane), 1505–1508.

Braun, Angelika. 1995. Fundamental frequency – How speaker-specific is it. In Angelika Braun & Jens-Peter Köster (eds.), *Studies in forensic phonetics*, 9–23. Trier: Wissenschaftlicher Verlag Trier.

Braun, Angelika. 1996. Zur regionalen Distribution von VOT im Deutschen. In Angelika Braun (ed.), *Untersuchungen zu Stimme und Sprache / Papers on speech and voice*, 19–32. Stuttgart: Steiner.

Braun, Angelika & Annabelle Rosin. 2015. On the speaker-specificity of hesitation markers. *Proceedings of the 18th International Congress of Phonetic Sciences* (Glasgow).

Brümmer, Niko, Lukáš Burget, Jan Černocký, Ondřej Glembek, František Grézl, Martin Karafiát, David van Leeuwen, Pavel Matějka, Petr Schwarz & Albert Strasheim. 2007. Fusion of heterogeneous speaker recognition systems in the STBU submission for the NIST speaker recognition evaluation 2006. *IEEE Transactions on Audio, Speech, and Language Processing* 15. 2072–2084.

Byrne, Catherine & Paul Foulkes. 2004. The 'mobile phone effect' on vowel formants. *The International Journal of Speech, Language and the Law* 11. 83–102.

Cambier-Langeveld, Tina. 2007. Current methods in forensic speaker identification: Results of a collaborative exercise. *The International Journal of Speech, Language and the Law* 14. 223–243.

Cao, Honglin & Yingli Wang. 2011. A forensic aspect of articulation rate variation in Chinese. *Proceedings of the 17th International Congress of Phonetic Sciences* (Hong Kong), 396–399.

Corley, Martin & Oliver W. Stewart. 2008. Hesitation disfluencies in spontaneous speech: The meaning of um. *Language and Linguistics Compass* 2. 589–602.

De Jong, Gea, Kirsty McDougall & Francis Nolan. 2007. Sound change and speaker identity: An acoustic study. In Christian Müller (ed.), *Speaker classification II: Selected projects*, 130–141. Berlin: Springer.

De Leeuw, Ester. 2007. Hesitation markers in English, German, and Dutch. *Journal of Germanic Linguistics* 19. 85–114.

Dehak, Najim, Patrick Kenny, Réda Dehak, Pierre Dumouchel & Pierre Ouellet. 2011. Front-end factor analysis for speaker verification. *IEEE Transactions on Audio, Speech, and Language Processing* 19. 788–798.

Drygajlo, Andrzej. 2011. Voice: Biometric Analysis and Interpretation of. *Wiley Encyclopedia of Forensic Science*. Published Online: 15 Dec 2011, DOI: 10.1002/9780470061589.fsa1034.

Drygajlo, Andrzej, Michael Jessen, Stefan Gfroerer, Isolde Wagner, Jos Vermeulen & Tuija Niemi. 2015. *Methodological guidelines for best practice in forensic semiautomatic and automatic speaker recognition*. Frankfurt: Verlag für Polizeiwissenschaft. [also accessible at http://enfsi.eu/wp-content/uploads/2016/09/guidelines_fasr_and_fsasr_0.pdf].

Elliot, Jennifer, R. 2002. *OKAY, what are the odds? Strength of auditory evidence in forensic speech analysis using Bayes' likelihood ratios*. Canberra: Australian National University MA thesis.

Enzinger, Ewald. 2015. *Implementation of forensic voice comparison within the new paradigm for the evaluation of forensic evidence*. Sydney: University of New South Wales dissertation.

Enzinger, Ewald, Geoffrey Stewart Morrison & Felipe Ochoa. 2016. A demonstration of the application of the new paradigm for the evaluation of forensic evidence under conditions reflecting those of a real forensic-voice-comparison case. *Science and Justice* 56. 42–57.

Eriksson, Anders. 2012. Aural/acoustic vs. automatic methods in forensic phonetic case work. In Amy Neustein & Hemant A. Patil (eds.), *Forensic speaker recognition. Law enforcement and counter-terrorism*, 41–69. Berlin: Springer.

Foulkes, Paul & Peter French. 2012. Forensic speaker comparison: A linguistic-acoustic perspective. In Lawrence M. Solan & Peter M. Tiersma (eds.), *Oxford handbook of language and law*, 557–572. Oxford: Oxford University Press.

Fourakis, Marios and Robert Port. 1986. Stop epenthesis in English. *Journal of Phonetics* 14. 197–221.

French, Peter & Philip Harrison. 2006. Investigative and evidential applications of forensic speech science. In Anthony Heaton-Armstrong, Eric Shepherd, Gisli Gudjonsson & Davis Wolchover (eds.), *Witness testimony, psychological, investigative and evidential perspectives*, 247–262. Oxford: Oxford University Press.

French, Peter & Louisa Stevens. 2013. Forensic Speech Science. In Mark Jones & Rachel Anne-Knight (eds.), *The Bloomsbury companion to phonetics*, 183–197. London: Continuum.

French, Peter, Paul Foulkes, Philip Harrison, Vincent Hughes, Eugenia San Segundo & Louisa Stevens. 2015. The vocal tract as a biometric: output measures, interrelationships, and efficacy. *Proceedings of the 18th International Congress of Phonetic Sciences* (Glasgow).

Gfroerer, Stefan. 2003. Auditory-instrumental forensic speaker recognition. *Proceedings of EUROSPEECH 2003* (Geneva), 705–708.

Gfroerer, Stefan. 2014. Sprechererkennung und Tonträgerauswertung. In Gunter Widmaier (ed.), *Münchener Anwaltshandbuch Strafverteidigung* (second, revised edition), 2682–2707. München: Beck.

Gold, Erica. 2014. *Calculating likelihood ratios for forensic speaker comparisons using phonetic and linguistic parameters*. York: University of York dissertation.

Gold, Erica & Peter French. 2011. International practices in forensic speaker comparison. *The International Journal of Speech, Language and the Law* 18. 293–307.

Gonzalez-Rodriguez, Joaquin. 2011. Speaker recognition using temporal contours in linguistic units: the case of formant and formant-bandwidth trajectories. *Proceedings of INTERSPEECH 2011* (Florence), 133–136.

Gonzalez-Rodriguez, Joaquin, Andrzej Drygajlo, Daniel Ramos-Castro, Marta Garcia-Gomar & Javier Ortega-Garcia. 2006. Robust estimation, interpretation and assessment of likelihood ratios in forensic speaker recognition. *Computer Speech & Language* 20. 331–355.

Gonzalez-Rodriguez, Joaquin, Phil Rose, Daniel Ramos, Doroteo T. Toledano & Javier Ortega-Garc a. 2007. Emulating DNA: Rigorous quantification of evidential weight in transparent and testable forensic speaker recognition. *IEEE Transactions on Audio, Speech, and Language Processing* 15. 2104–2115.

González-Rodríguez, Joaquín, Juana Gil, Rubén Pérez & Javier Franco-Pedroso. 2014. What are we missing with i-vectors? A perceptual analysis of i-vector-based falsely accepted trials. *Proceedings of ODYSSEY 2014* (Joensuu), 33–40.

Hansen, John H.L. & Taufiq Hasan. 2015. Speaker recognition by machines and humans – A tutorial review. *IEEE Signal Processing Magazine*, Nov. 2015. 74–99.

Haraksim, Rudolf. 2014. *Validation of likelihood ratio methods used in forensic evidence evaluation: Application in forensic fingerprints*. Enschede: University of Twente dissertation.

Hirson, Allen. 1995. Human laughter – A forensic phonetic perspective. In Angelika Braun & Jens-Peter Köster (eds.), *Studies in forensic phonetics*, 77–86. Trier: Wissenschaftlicher Verlag.

Hollien, Harry. 1990. *The acoustics of crime. The new science of forensic phonetics*. New York: Plenum Press.

Hollien, Harry. 2002. *Forensic voice identification*. San Diego: Academic Press.

Hudson, Tobi, Gea de Jong, Kirsty McDougall, Philip Harrison & Francis Nolan. 2007. F0 statistics for 100 young male speakers of Standard Southern British English. *Proceedings of the 16th International Congress of Phonetic Sciences* (Saarbrücken), 1809–1812.

Hughes, Vincent S. 2014. *The definition of the relevant population and the collection of data for likelihood ratio-based forensic voice comparison*. York: University of York dissertation.

Hughes, Vincent, Sophie Wood & Paul Foulkes. 2016. Strength of forensic voice comparison evidence from the acoustics of filled pauses. *The International Journal of Speech, Language and the Law* 23. 99–132.

Hughes, Vincent, Philip Harrison, Paul Foulkes, Peter French, Colleen Kavanagh & Eugenia San Segundo. 2017. Mapping across feature spaces in forensic voice comparison: the contribution of auditory-based voice quality to (semi-)automatic system testing. *Proceedings of INTERSPEECH 2017* (Stockholm), 3892–3896.

Jessen, Michael. 2007. Forensic reference data on articulation rate in German. *Science and Justice* 47. 50–67.

Jessen, Michael. 2008. Forensic phonetics. *Language and Linguistics Compass* 2. 671–711.

Jessen, Michael. 2010. The forensic phonetician: Forensic speaker identification by experts. In Malcolm Coulthard & Alison Johnson (eds.), *The Routledge handbook of forensic linguistics*, 378–394. London: Routledge.

Jessen, Michael. 2012. *Phonetische und linguistische Prinzipien des forensischen Stimmenvergleichs*. München: LINCOM.

Jessen, Michael, Olaf Köster & Stefan Gfroerer. 2005. Influence of vocal effort on average and variability of fundamental frequency. *The International Journal of Speech, Language and the Law* 12. 174–213.

Jessen, Michael, Anil Alexander & Oscar Forth. 2014. Forensic voice comparisons in German with phonetic and automatic features using VOCALISE software. *Proceedings of the Audio Engineering Society 54th International Conference* (London), 28–35.

Kahneman, Daniel. 2011. *Thinking, fast and slow*. London etc.: Penguin (published in Penguin Books 2012).

Kienast, Miriam & Florian Glitza. 2003. Respiratory sounds as an idiosyncratic feature in speaker recognition. *Proceedings of the 15th International Congress of Phonetic Sciences* (Barcelona), 1607–1610.

Kinnunen, Tomi & Haizhou Li. 2010. An overview of text-independent speaker recognition: From features to supervectors. *Speech Communication* 52. 12–40.

Kinoshita, Yuko. 2001. *Testing realistic forensic speaker identification in Japanese: A likelihood ratio based approach using formants*. Canberra: Australian National University dissertation.

Kinoshita, Yuko, Shunichi Ishihara & Philip Rose. 2009. Exploring the discriminatory potential of F0 distribution parameters in traditional forensic speaker recognition. *The International Journal of Speech, Language and the Law* 16. 91–111.

Kinoshita, Yuko & Shunichi Ishihara. 2014. Background population: how does it affect LR-based forensic voice comparison? *The International Journal of Speech, Language and the Law* 21. 191–224.

Köster, Olaf & Jens-Peter Köster. 2004. The auditory-perceptual evaluation of voice quality in forensic speaker recognition. *The Phonetician* 89. 9–37.

Kraayeveld, Johannes. 1997. *Idiosyncrasy in prosody: Speaker and speaker group identification in Dutch using melodic and temporal information*. Nijmegen: Catholic University of Nijmegen dissertation.

Künzel, Hermann J. 1987. *Sprechererkennung: Grundzüge forensischer Sprachverarbeitung*. Heidelberg: Kriminalistik Verlag.

Künzel, Hermann J. 1997. Some general phonetic and forensic aspects of speaking tempo. *Forensic Linguistics* 4. 48–83.

Künzel, Hermann J. 2004. Tasks in forensic speech and audio analysis: a tutorial. *The Phonetician* 90. 9–22.

Laver, John. 1980. *The phonetic description of voice quality*. Cambridge: Cambridge University Press.

Lawrence, Sophie, Francis Nolan & Kirsty McDougall. 2008. Acoustic and perceptual effects of telephone transmission on vowel quality. *The International Journal of Speech, Language and the Law* 15. 161–192.

Leemann, Adrian, Marie-José Kolly & Volker Dellwo. 2014. Speaker-individuality in suprasegmental temporal features: Implications for forensic voice comparison. *Forensic Science International* 238. 59–67.

Leemann, Adrian, Volker Dellwo, Hansjörg Mixdorff, Maria O'Reilly & Marie-José Kolly. 2014. Speaker-individuality in Fujisaki model f0 features: Implications for forensic voice comparison. *The International Journal of Speech, Language and the Law* 21. 343–370.

Lindh, Jonas. 2006. Preliminary descriptive f0-statistics for young male speakers. *Lund University, Dept. of Linguistics and Phonetics Working Papers* 52. 89–92.

Lindh, Jonas & Anders Eriksson. 2007. Robustness of long time measures of fundamental frequency. *Proceedings of INTERSPEECH 2007* (Antwerpen), 2025–2028.

Mackenzie Beck, Janet. 2005. Perceptual analysis of voice quality: The place of vocal profile analysis. In William J. Hardcastle & Janet Mackenzie Beck (eds.), *A figure of speech. A festschrift for John Laver*, 285–322. Mahwah: Lawrence Erlbaum Associates.

McDougall, Kirsty. 2004. Speaker-specific formant dynamics: An experiment on Australian English /aI/. *The International Journal of Speech, Language and the Law* 11. 103–130.

McDougall, Kirsty. 2006. Dynamic features of speech and the characterization of speakers: towards a new approach using formant frequencies. *The International Journal of Speech, Language and the Law* 13. 89–126.

McDougall, Kirsty, Martin Duckworth & Toby Hudson. 2015. Individual and group variation in disfluency features: a cross accent investigation. *Proceedings of the 18th International Congress of Phonetic Sciences* (Glasgow).

Meuwly, Didier. 2001. *Reconnaissance automatique de locuteurs en sciences forensiques: l'apport d'une approche automatique*. Lausanne: EPFL dissertation.

Moos, Anja. 2008. *Forensische Sprechererkennung mit der Messmethode LTF (long-term formant distribution)*. Saarbrücken: Universität des Saarlandes MA thesis.

Moos, Anja. 2010. Long-Term Formant Distribution as a measure of speaker characteristics in read and spontaneous speech. *The Phonetician* 101/102. 7–24.

Moosmüller, Sylvia. 1997. Phonological variation in speaker identification. *Forensic Linguistics* 4. 29–47.

Morrison, Geoffrey Stewart. 2009. Likelihood-ratio forensic voice comparison using parametric representations of the formant trajectories of diphthongs. *Journal of the Acoustical Society of America* 125. 2387–2397.

Morrison, Geoffrey Stewart. 2010. *Forensic voice comparison*. In I. Freckelton & H. Selby (eds.), Expert evidence (Chapter 99). Sydney: Thomson Reuters.

Morrison, Geoffrey Stewart. 2011. A comparison of procedures for the calculation of forensic likelihood ratios from acoustic-phonetic data: Multivariate kernel density (MVKD) versus Gaussian mixture model – universal background model (GMM-UBM). *Speech Communication* 53. 242–256.

Morrison, Geoffrey Stewart. 2013. Tutorial on logistic-regression calibration and fusion: converting a score to a likelihood ratio. *Australian Journal of Forensic Sciences* 45. 173–197.

Morrison, Geoffrey Stewart, Cuiling Zhang & Philip Rose. 2011. An empirical estimate of the precision of likelihood ratios from a forensic-voice-comparison system. *Forensic Science International* 208. 59–65.

Morrison, Geoffrey Stewart, Farhan Hyder Sahito, Gaëlle Jardine, Djordje Djokic, Sophie Clavet, Sabine Berghs & Caroline Goemans Dorny. 2016. INTERPOL survey of the use of speaker identification by law enforcement agencies. *Forensic Science International* 263. 92–100.

Nawka, Tadeus & Lutz Christian Anders. 1996. *Die auditive Bewertung heiserer Stimmen nach dem RBH-System. Doppel-Audio CD mit Stimmbeispielen*. Stuttgart: Thieme.

Nolan, Francis. 1983. *The phonetic bases of speaker recognition*. Cambridge: Cambridge University Press.

Nolan, Francis. 1990. The limitations of auditory-phonetic speaker identification. In Hannes Knifka (ed.), *Texte zur Theorie und Praxis forensischer Linguistik*, 457–479. Tübingen: Niemeyer.

Nolan, Francis. 1994. Auditory and acoustic analysis in speaker recognition. In John Gibbon (ed.), *Language and the law*, 326–345. London: Longman.

Nolan, Francis. 1997. Speaker recognition and forensic phonetics. In William J. Hardcastle & John Laver (eds.), *The handbook of phonetic sciences*, 744–767. Oxford: Blackwell.

Nolan, Francis. 2002. Intonation in speaker identification: an experiment on pitch alignment features. *Forensic Linguistics* 9. 1–21.

Nolan, Francis. 2005. Forensic speaker identification and the phonetic description of voice quality. In William J. Hardcastle & Janet Mackenzie Beck (eds.), *A figure of speech. A festschrift for John Laver*, 385–411. Mahwah: Lawrence Erlbaum Associates.

Nolan, Francis & Catalin Grigoras. 2005. A case for formant analysis in forensic speaker identification. *The International Journal of Speech, Language and the Law* 12. 143–173.

Ramos-Castro, Daniel. 2007. *Forensic evaluation of the evidence using automatic speaker recognition systems*. Madrid: Universidad Autónoma de Madrid dissertation.

Ramos, Daniel, Joaquin Gonzalez-Rodriguez, Grzegorz Zadora & Colin Aitken. 2013. Information-theoretical assessment of the performance of likelihood ratio models. *Journal of Forensic Sciences* 58. 1503–1518.

Reetz, Henning & Allard Jongman. 2009. *Phonetics. Transcription, production, acoustics, and perception*. Chichester: Wiley-Blackwell.

Reynolds, Douglas A. 1992. *A Gaussian Mixture Modeling approach to text-independent speaker identification*. Atlanta: Georgia Institute of Technology dissertation.

Reynolds, Douglas A., Thomas F. Quatieri & Robert B. Dunn. 2000. Speaker verification using adapted Gaussian mixture models. *Digital Signal Processing* 10. 19–41.

Robertson, Bernard & G A Vignaux. 1995. *Interpreting evidence. Evaluating forensic science in the courtroom*. Chichester etc.: Wiley

Rose, Philip. 2002. *Forensic speaker identification*. London: Taylor and Francis.

Rose, Philip. 2003. *The technical comparison of forensic voice samples*. In I. Freckelton & H. Selby (eds.), Expert evidence (Chapter 99). Sydney: Thomson Lawbook Company.

Rose, Phil. 2010. The effect of correlation on strength of evidence estimates in forensic voice comparison: uni- and multivariate likelihood ratio-based discrimination with Australian English vowel acoustics. *International Journal of Biometrics* 2. 316–329.

Rose, Phil. 2011. Forensic voice comparison with secular shibboleths – a hybrid fused GMM-multivariate likelihood-ratio-based approach using alveolo-palatal fricative cepstral spectra. *Proceedings of the 2011 International Conference on Acoustics, Speech and Signal Processing (ICASSP)* (Prague). 5900–5903.

Rose, Phil. 2013a. More is better: likelihood ratio-based forensic voice comparison with vocalic segmental cepstra frontends. *The International Journal of Speech, Language and the Law* 20. 77–116.

Rose, Phil. 2013b. Where the science ends and the law begins: likelihood ratio-based forensic voice comparison in a $150 million telephone fraud. *The International Journal of Speech, Language and the Law* 20. 277–324.

Rose, Phil. 2015. Forensic voice comparison with monophthongal formant trajectories – A likelihood-ratio-based discrimination of "schwa" vowel acoustics in a close social group of young Australian females. *Proceedings of the 2015 International Conference on Acoustics, Speech and Signal Processing (ICASSP)* (Brisbane). 4819–4823.

Rose, Phil. 2017. Likelihood ratio-based forensic voice comparison with higher level features: research and reality. *Computer Speech & Language* 45. 475–502.

Rose, Phil, Takashi Osanai & Yuko Kinoshita. 2003. Strength of forensic speaker identification evidence: multispeaker formant- and cepstrum-based segmental discrimination with a Bayesian likelihood ratio as threshold. *The International Journal of Speech, Language and the Law* 10. 179–202.

Rose, Phil & Elaine Winter. 2010. Traditional forensic voice comparison with female formants: Gaussian mixture model and multivariate likelihood ratio analysis. *Proceedings of the 13th Australasian International Conference on Speech Science and Technology* (Melbourne), 42–45.

Rosenberg, A.E., F. Bimbot & S. Parthasarathy. 2008. Overview of speaker recognition. In Jacob Benesty, M. Mohan Sondhi, Yiteng Huang (ed.), *Springer handbook of speech processing*, 725–741. Berlin: Springer.

Schwartz, Reva, Joseph P. Campbell, Wade Shen, Douglas E. Sturim, William M. Campbell, Fred S. Richardson, Robert B. Dunn & Robert Granville. 2011. USSS-MITLL 2010 Human Assisted Speaker Recognition. *Proceedings of the 2011 International Conference on Acoustics, Speech and Signal Processing (ICASSP)* (Prague), 5904–5907.

Simpson, Adrian P. 2009. Phonetic differences between male and female speech. *Language and Linguistics Compass* 3. 621–640.

Solewicz, Yosef A., Timo Becker, Gaëlle Jardine & Stefan Gfroerer. 2012. Comparison of speaker recognition systems on a real forensic benchmark. *Proceedings of ODYSSEY 2012* (Singapore), 86–91.

Solewicz, Yosef A., Michael Jessen & David van der Vloed. 2017. Null-Hypothesis LLR: A proposal for forensic automatic speaker recognition. *Proceedings of INTERSPEECH 2017* (Stockholm), 2849–2853.

Stuart-Smith, Jane & Claire Timmins. 2010. The role of the individual in language variation and change. In Carmen Llamas & Dominic Watt (eds.), *Language and identities*, 39–54. Edinburgh: Edinburgh University Press.

Van der Vloed, David, Jos Bouten & David A. van Leeuwen. 2014. NFI-FRITS: A forensic speaker recognition database and some first experiments. *Proceedings of ODYSSEY 2014* (Joensuu), 6–13.

Van Leeuwen, David A. & Niko Brümmer. 2007. An introduction to application-independent evaluation of speaker recognition systems. In Christian Müller (ed.), *Speaker classification I: Fundamentals, features, and methods*, 330–353. Berlin: Springer.

Watt, Dominic. 2010. The identification of the individual through speech. In Carmen Llamas & Dominic Watt (eds.), *Language and identities*, 76–85. Edinburgh: Edinburgh University Press.

Yoo, Isaiah WonHo & Barbara Blankenship. 2003. Duration of epenthetic [t] in polysyllabic American English words. *Journal of the International Phonetic Association* 33. 153–164.

Chris Heffer
10 Narrative practices and voice in court

1 Introduction

Understanding forensic narrative helps us to understand better both the nature of the legal process and the nature of narrative. Since legal cases fundamentally concern disputed stories of wrongdoing, narrative remains highly significant to the legal process in general and the trial context in particular. However, the institutional and evidential complexity of a trial, along with its anti-narrative legal constraints, challenge our literary- and conversation-based conceptions of narrative. For example, while narrative texts found in legal contexts can tell us something about the language of narrative, they tell us relatively little about legal communication in context. It is fruitful, then, to consider forensic narrativity in terms of practices rather than text (Bamberg 2011). Furthermore, these narrative practices are embedded within a rhetorical legal process and are thus intertwined with the demands of evidence, the constrictions of legal regulation, and the circumstances of adversarial conflict. To understand the narrativity of the trial, then, we need to consider not just the textual product (narrative text, however that is defined) but also such discursive practices as emplotment, story negotiation, character navigation and narration (Heffer 2012), which lead to the construction of the forensic narrative. When we combine this analysis with an analysis of voice (Heffer 2013a) we can go some way towards a discussion of narrative inequality in the trial.

The chapter begins with the paradox that narrative is central to the trial and yet apparently peripheral to trial discourse. I then consider various approaches to solving this paradox and conclude by showing how narrative is embedded in forensic rhetorical practice. Next I introduce the two models of narrative navigation and voice projection and show how they are relevant to an analysis of narrative inequality and loss of voice at trial. The remainder of the chapter applies these models to a particular case, considering first inequalities of emplotment and story negotiation, then inequalities of narration, and finally inequalities of character navigation.

2 The centrality of narrative in court

Legal cases fundamentally concern stories of wrongdoing and courts evaluate those stories to establish whether or not a remedy is required. Forensic stories, stories designed to convince a legal decision-maker, are predicated on evidence but that evidence is never complete or unequivocal: if it were, there would be no need for a trial. The forensic value of stories is that they enable complex bodies of evidence to be reduced to simple cognitive templates that can be more easily fitted to offence categories. Stories are thus natural vehicles for presenting the patchwork of available, admissible, agreed and disputed "facts" with which lawyers work in court. They "provide the most obvious link between everyday analytical and communicational skills and the requirements of formal adjudication procedures" (Bennett & Feldman 1981: 10).

The centrality of narrative in the forensic arena was clearly manifest in Athenian courts of the fourth century BCE. Without the intricate institutional structures of present-day Western trial systems, litigants simply stood up before the *dikastai* (the lay judges) and tried to persuade them of their case (Carawan 2007). In their carefully constructed forensic orations, the aim was to come across as natural and spontaneous, and narrative is our most effective vehicle for achieving this aim. It is not that these narratives were unconstrained: as today, they had to be carefully constructed to serve the rhetorical goal of persuading the fact-finders of the defendant's guilt or otherwise (Heffer 2013b). Furthermore, while Attic orations might have revolved around a central forensic narrative, they also included much specific argumentation, including legal argumentation. As today, the primary speech genre of "forensic discourse" (I use the term in the Aristotelian sense of rhetorical discourse about the justice of past actions) was argument not storytelling. Nevertheless, narrative was used as the primary *means* of argumentation and so was manifestly central in Athenian forensic oration.

The centrality of narrative cannot be taken for granted, on the other hand, in contemporary Western trial systems. With the development of detailed substantive and procedural law, complex institutional structures of law enforcement, increasing demands for evidential grounding of decisions and intricate due process procedures, trial discourse has become highly fragmented. This discursive fragmentation has been confirmed through fine-grained linguistic and discourse analytic studies of the investigation and trial in both adversarial systems (e.g. Stygall 1994; Harris 2001; Cotterill 2003; Heffer 2005) and inquisitorial ones (e.g. Komter 1998; Heydon 2005; Hannken-Illjes 2011), thus demonstrating that the legal process is, in many respects, "anything but a narrative" (Stygall 1994: 118). Cases are framed by abstract legal charges that severely circumscribe the tellable domain. Parties can and do challenge the admissibility of evidence both before and during trial, further restricting narrative scope. Rules of evidence set strict constraints on how evidence, and thus narrative, may be presented in court, so that some mainstays of literary and conversational narration (evaluation, hearsay, opinion and speculation) are either prohibited or closely controlled (Conley & O'Barr 1990). Witnesses are examined in a question-answer format and rarely have a chance to narrate for more than a few words at a time (Heffer 2005). Many witnesses provide scientific or other technical explanations and opinions that bear very little relation to narrative discourse. And witnesses' accounts are constantly open to challenge: through opposing counsel's objections, cross-examination and legal submissions to the judge. Narrative discourse may appear more overtly in the lawyers' opening and closing speeches (Cotterill 2003; Harris 2005) but these speeches are not considered as "evidence" on which the fact-finders should base their verdicts. The legally circumscribed, narrationally constrained, structurally fragmented and verificatory nature of trial discourse, then, militates against viewing it in narrative terms.

At the same time, though, the evidence from psychology and both legal and lay accounts suggests quite strongly that participants orient to the trial as narrative either solely or in combination with a legal orientation. For example, jurors appear to process and assess trial evidence not as discrete items to be weighed up individually but as coherent and plausible stories (Pennington & Hastie 1986). Judges also appear to make decisions by comparing the forensic story with culturally-shared stock narratives (Wagenaar, van Koppen & Crombag 1993). Advocacy manuals written by legal professionals very often discuss the trial lawyer's task in terms of presenting their "story" to the jury (Stone 1984) and lawyers wonder what was the "hole in the story that hung him" when they lose a case (Engel 2000: 55). Lay witnesses also tend to want to tell their story in court (Conley & O'Barr 1990).

There is an essential paradox, then, in the centrality of narrative in court: legal cases fundamentally concern (and are oriented to by participants as) stories of wrongdoing, yet pre-trial and trial genres are rarely narrative in structure or discourse. This chapter will suggest a solution to that paradox between perception and performance by focussing on the *discursive practices* involved in narrative construction and maintenance – practices that permeate the pre-trial and trial processes – rather than on the specific *textual product* of narrative discourse. This reflects a gradual but general move in the humanities and social sciences from text to practice (Bourdieu 1990; Scollon 2001) and a more specific recent turn towards practice in narrative inquiry (De Fina & Georgakopoulou 2008). I shall also link this work on narrative practice with practices of voice projection outlined in my Voice Projection Framework (Heffer 2013a).

3 From narrative text to narrative practice

Forensic narrative can be considered from a number of perspectives ranging from textual analysis to sociocultural practice. These perspectives are to some extent complementary. For example, although I shall be advocating a broad practice approach to narrativity in the trial, it is also important to maintain a rigorous linguistic approach to the identification of narrative discourse.

3.1 Narrative as event and evaluation

A good place to start an investigation of narrativity in the trial is Labov and Waletzky's (1967) analysis of the structure of oral narrative since there are significant similarities between their Personal Experience Narratives and trial narratives. Labov and Waletzky isolated two core functions in oral narrative: the referential and the evaluative. The referential function was to recapitulate experience in an ordered sequence of clauses that matched the temporal order of the original experience. The evaluative function of narrative, on the other hand, was to show the listener that it was worth telling the tale, that the story had a point.

The referential function was conveyed primarily through temporally ordered independent "narrative" clauses, often linguistically cued through the past simple or preterite tense:

> He *attacked* me and the friend *came* in and she *stopped* it

These clauses were said to be "bound", since changing the order would result in a changed story:

> She *stopped* it and the friend *came* in and he *attacked* me

The definition of a "minimal narrative" as "any sequence of clauses which contains at least one temporal juncture" (1967: 28) is useful as it enables us to distinguish quite rigorously between narrative and non-narrative discourse in the trial. It enables us to identify quite brief witness turns as examples of narrative discourse: "He ran up and punched me". Often in witness examination the lawyer will provide the temporal juncture through an explicit temporal sequence adverbial such as *then*, thus creating a minimal narrative across two witness turns:

> A. He ran towards me.
> Q. What did he do <u>then</u>?
> A. He punched me.

And it enables us to recognise narrative responses to questions that are not designed to elicit narrative, as in "narrative expansions" in answers to yes-no questions (Galatolo & Drew 2006). Furthermore, examinations of "narrative" witnesses tend to take them chronologically through their story (Heffer 2005) and, while this appears to be less the case in US trials (Stygall 1994; Cotterill 2003), English and Welsh legal professionals try as far as possible to sequence witnesses in the order of the events in dispute (Heffer 2005). Most importantly, though, Labov and Waletzky's definition enables us to distinguish witness turns that are evidently not narrative in nature, as in the case of most expert witness turns. A rigorous linguistic definition of minimal narrative helps us to avoid the poststructuralist pitfall of defining narrative text as "any minimal linguistic (written or verbal) act" (McQuillan 2000: 7), a definition that can only lead us into a semiotic cul-de-sac where "narrative" is synonymous with "speech act" and we are unable to distinguish the scientific explanation of a ballistics expert from the story of a lay eyewitness. What the scientific expert and the lay eyewitness are doing with words in court is quite different and it seems important to be able to establish that difference through discourse. As identified by linguists such as Stygall (1994), Harris (2005) and Heffer (2005), the comparative lack of narrative discourse in a social practice founded on assessing competing stories is a central issue that needs to be addressed in accounts of the trial rather than something that can be glossed over by defining the issue out of existence.

At the same time, a *minimal* narrative for definitional purposes is by no means a *felicitous* one: a temporally ordered sequence of clauses does not make a *good* narrative. What makes a narrative a *personal experience narrative* rather than a neutral *account* is the evaluative function. For Labov and Waletzky, the evaluative function was conveyed both through "free clauses" they called Evaluation, which suspended the narrative action to comment on it in some way (e.g. "I was frightened"), and through evaluation devices internal to the narrative clauses themselves. Internal evaluation is a wave-like phenomenon, "a condition that holds true during the entire narrative" (Labov 1997: 401). As in Personal Experience Narrative, evaluation in Forensic Narrative permeates the telling and can be found both within narrative clauses, in such forms as intensifiers (increasing salience), comparators (indicating what might have happened but didn't) and explicatives (explicitly motivating the action), and in free clauses that explicitly or implicitly comment on the action.

3.2 Narrative as Discourse Structure

Labov and Waletzky (1967) observed that well-formed personal experience narratives tended to have a number of constituent elements. Labov (1972) noted that these elements tended to respond to some basic questions an audience might have about one's narrative:

> Abstract – What is this about?
> Orientation – Who, when and where?
> Complicating Action – What happened?
> Evaluation – So what?
> Resolution – What happened in the end?
> Coda – Why's this relevant now?

Labov was certainly *not* suggesting that the absence of any one of these structural elements (apart from minimal complicating action) precludes the presence of narrative. Furthermore, the elements are still identified through rigorous clause-based microstructural analysis and it is unhelpful to extend the functional labels to units such as the trial itself that are clearly not narrative in their discursive structure. Adopting a serious textual/discourse approach to narrative means focussing only on those stretches of trial discourse which *do* display narrative structure, whether in the form of a minimal two-clause narrative, a common Orientation–Complicating Action–Evaluation structure or (quite rare in court) a "fully-formed" narrative. Harris, for example, has shown that some US opening speeches and some witness turns conform to a modified version of Labov's personal experience narrative. Heffer (2005) has also identified Labovian structure in English opening statements.

When applied to trial narrative, this perspective helps us to note both similarities and distinctions between personal experience and forensic narratives. For example, both Harris (2001, 2005) and Heffer (2005) have noted that opening statements, some long witness turns and the examinations-in-chief of key witnesses can be seen to conform to a Labovian structure but that forensic narratives are heavily weighted towards Orientation, and the Evaluation, which Harris calls the "Point", is always related to the legal charges. At the same time, focussing on narrative-as-discourse-structure can give the impression, as Stygall and Harris claim, that the trial is simply not narrative in nature. Perhaps the narrativity of the trial is a common myth disseminated by fictional courtroom dramas and debunked by scientific discourse analysis. Certainly, the overall structure of the adversarial jury trial – opposing opening statements, recursive witness examination with the internal dialectic of direct and cross-examination, opposing closing arguments – resembles much more a debate than a narrative (Heffer 2005). Civil Law trials, founded as they are on the written "case file" rather than oral testimony (Komter 2002), are even less narrative-like in structure.

However, this is the etic perspective of the external linguistic observer and the normative perspective of the legal regulator. The emic perspective of both lay and legal participants, as we have seen, is that narrative is central to the enterprise. Furthermore, one should not fall into the corpus linguistic trap of confusing *frequency* with *salience*. Those who have sat through an entire trial will know that not all elements in a trial are equally salient: some witnesses are more important than others; some parts of a witness examination are more crucial than others; cross-examination tends to be more intense than examination-in-chief, and so on. It is quite possible that, although statistically narration makes up a smaller percentage of the trial than one might expect, those moments of narration are significantly more *salient* than the non-narrative discursive moments. The problem is that, as with most interesting questions, salience is very difficult to measure in the field.

3.3 Narrative as cognitive schema

The question of salience is particularly relevant to a third narrative perspective: narrative as a cognitive schema. What is crucial in this view (e.g. Bennett & Feldman 1981, Pennington & Hastie 1986) is the overall story content perceived and constructed by the fact-finding listener, while the actual discourse dynamics of the trial are considered relatively unimportant. This perspective links with the traditional narratological distinction between the cognitive "story" and linguistic "discourse" (Chatman 1978). The trial evaluates the prosecution/claimant's story of a crime or civil wrong but much of that evaluation will not be in the form of narrative discourse. The decision-makers (jury, judge, magistrate) may well assess the evidence in narrative terms but this could all be a post-evidential cognitive construction. Discourse analysts have re-introduced trial text (and legal agency) to this account to the extent that they see the parties as presenting some form of skeleton narrative text in their opening speeches which is then "fleshed out" by successive witnesses in direct examination during the evidential phase (Snedaker 1991; Cotterill 2003; Heffer 2005). However, narrative practice itself is still considered to be restricted primarily to the lawyers' construction and co-construction of narratives in their opening and closing speeches and in direct examination of witnesses.

This cognitive narrative perspective is crucial to an overall account of narrative practices in the trial, but it is inadequate in that it fails to show links between the discursive construction of stories by the lawyers/witnesses and the cognitive constructions of stories by the decision-makers. A better link can be achieved by going beyond the story semantics (the story that is being constructed in the trial) to consider the "narrative pragmatics" of testimony, or the way the jury will match the testimonial behaviour of witnesses to "narrative typifications" of how witnesses testify and what one can infer from that testimonial practice (Jackson 1988). The semiotic practices involved in establishing and undermining the credibility of witnesses as narrators can then be seen as an essential part of a lawyer's overall narrative practice, and much of this occurs in cross-examination, which is generally considered to be anti-narrative in nature.

3.4 Narrative as a cultural-cognitive mode of discourse

Another perspective that goes beyond narrative discourse but tries to maintain the connection with unfolding discourse is to see narrative as a pervasive cultural-cognitive mode of discourse operating throughout the trial, but one whose manifestation is severely weakened by co-existing anti-narrative forces. Chief among the anti-narrative forces are the types of legal constraints outlined earlier. However, trial lawyers try to negotiate those legal constraints in a way that will work to their narrative advantage. Both Harris (2005) and Heffer (2005) have worked with Bruner's distinction between narrative and paradigmatic modes of reasoning (Bruner 1986, 1996). Heffer (2005) argued that legal professionals engaged in a hybrid "legal-lay discourse" that arose from a constant tension between these modes. A better term might have been "logico-narrative discourse" since "legal-lay discourse" has been understandably confused with "legal-lay communication" (Heffer, Rock & Conley 2013; Tracy & Delgadillo 2013). This approach shows the importance of *narrativity* (having the qualities of narrative) to the trial and it indicates how narrativity can come into play even in judges' legal instructions to juries. It also stresses the ongoing and dynamic tensions found in trial discourse, which I now link to broader tensions between rhetoric and rights (Heffer *forth.*). However, this perspective does not sufficiently explain how a party's narrative is constructed and then sustained through the trial; in other words, what narrative *practices* are involved in conveying the trial story to the jury.

4 The embedding of narrative in forensic rhetorical practice

A practice has been described as an action with a history (Bourdieu 1977: 78). A discursive action becomes a *practice* when it is repeated over time in a similar institutional context and becomes normalized as the "thing to say" in that context. It is now quite common to consider narrative in terms of its functional embedding within a given sociocultural practice (De Fina & Georgakopoulou 2012). Given the emphasis in narrative inquiry on conversational narrative, the narrative practice perspective has emphasised the notion of "small stories" (Bamberg & Georgakopoulou 2008) and how salient aspects of narrativity emerge in small snippets of talk-in-interaction outside canonical self-sufficient narrative texts. Here we need to consider the much bigger unit of the trial and see how narrative is embedded in the rhetorical practice of the trial process. I shall first discuss the embedding of narrative in institutional practice and then specifically its embedding in forensic rhetorical practice.

4.1 Institutional practice

Forensic narrative shares features with other institutional narratives. There has been much focus in research on institutional discourse (Freed 2015) on the social and discursive asymmetries between speakers in institutional contexts. In court, legal professionals are likely to be socially more powerful than witnesses not only due to their powerful professional status as lawyers or barristers but also because of their elite socioeconomic and educational background: in the mid 2000s, 67% of barristers in England and Wales came from professional/managerial classes and 32% did their degree at Oxford or Cambridge in comparison to 1% of all university goers (Zimdars & Souboorah 2009: 24). As with other institutional representatives, trial lawyers also hold much greater discursive power: they have both greater control over the ongoing discourse (they ask the questions, witnesses answer) and a much greater understanding of the discursive rules of the game. As in other institutional contexts, the lay narratives of witnesses are elicited through a question-answer format that will bring out the institutionally-required information, or "facts", as efficiently as possible. And the narrative that is co-constructed is one that will fit the institutional and rhetorical requirements of the examining lawyer, with the result that the story the lay witness brings to court often gets institutionally "mangled" (Linde 2003: 520), frequently resulting in dissatisfaction with the process.

Often in the literature on institutional narrative this "mangling" has been seen as a distortion of "natural" conversational forms of narration. Yet there is nothing "natural" or "spontaneous" about any form of narration: "a storyteller is not free to narrate just anything, in just anyway at any place or time to any audience" (Langellier & Peterson 2004: 19). As children are gradually socialized into narrative ("narrative socialization"), and narrative skills are implicitly and explicitly taught both at home and at school, "they learn what can be, or could be, told as a story, and how it may or may not be told to particular audiences" (Linde 2015: 1). Furthermore, narrative skills are unequally distributed and few become highly proficient narrators (and when they are, the skill tends to be recognized both socially and professionally). In a rather similar way, in law school, students learn how to legally frame the narratives underlying cases (Mertz 2007). As they develop their legal framing skills, they work with their professors to co-construct coherent and cohesive legally-framed narratives (Mertz 2007: 154). The issue, then, is not that conversational narration is free while institutional narration is highly regulated but that lay participants have not been socialized into the institutional rules of the game. Indeed, those who have frequent contact with an institution, such as expert witnesses in court, can develop a quite sophisticated understanding of its discursive rules.

4.2 Forensic rhetorical practice

The fact that narrative in court is embedded in the specific rhetorical situation (Bitzer 1968) of a legally-regulated trial in which competing parties try to persuade decision-makers of the guilt or otherwise of the defendant further shapes the process and form of the narrative (Heffer 2013b). Firstly, forensic narrative is highly evidential in contrast to conversational narrative. Hearsay is not permitted and any unsubstantiated claims will be challenged by the opposing party. Secondly, forensic narrative is subject to legal constraints, both in terms of what can be talked about (it must be relevant to the charges) and how it can be talked about (the rules of evidence). Thirdly, and certainly within adversarial systems, lawyers are engaged in an overall rhetorical practice of persuading the legal decision-maker (judge, jury, magistrate) of the guilt or otherwise of the defendant. As in all rhetorical situations, the persuasive goal is paramount. While research has often focused on the way legal constraints shape trial discourse, the persuasive goal is arguably far more important in terms of narrative practices. Thus, the lawyer will control the witness not so much to ensure that the rules of evidence are followed as to ensure that the story develops in the most rhetorically efficacious fashion. Furthermore, each genre within the trial comes with its own narrative forms, rules and expectations. Opening and closing speeches by the prosecution and defence lawyers may contain narratives about the disputed incident but opening statements are not meant to be evaluative (though they frequently are) while closing arguments are openly evaluative.

If it is accepted that the primary function of forensic discourse in court is to persuade fact-finders to convict or acquit the defendant, then the *principals* (Goffman 1959) in criminal cases (the State and the Defendant) authorize trial lawyers to act (including speak) on their behalf and to use their legal and communicational expertise to bring about the desired goal of conviction or acquittal. In this rhetorical context, witness testimony is evidence that is adduced by lawyers in constructing their forensic narrative of the case. If witnesses, who mostly do not know the lawyer's master narrative, had equal narrative rights, the result would be a very inadequate form of forensic rhetoric that would make the decision-maker's task more difficult.

The model of narrative navigation outlined in the next section expressly works within an understanding of the overall forensic rhetorical situation.

5 Narrative navigation and voice projection

In the remainder of this chapter, I shall endeavor to show how two models of trial communication I have developed over the past few years can complement each other and contribute to our understanding of forensic narrative practice.

5.1 Narrative navigation

The Narrative Navigation model (Heffer 2012) is an attempt to account for an institutional storyteller's practices in conveying a coherent and persuasive story to an intended audience in narrationally-constrained complex rhetorical contexts. In the rhetorical situation of the trial, forensic narrators (trial lawyers) steer their stories of the crime or civil wrong through the complex trial process. As in Attic oration, narrative is seen as the primary vehicle through which trial lawyers convey their theory of the case to the jury and/or judge. But given the extreme discursive fragmentation of contemporary pre-trial and trial processes, narrative navigation, like physical navigation, involves both plotting a route and maintaining that route in the changeable conditions of ongoing trial discourse. Narrative navigation in the trial involves four key elements: emplotment, story negotiation, character navigation and narration.

Emplotment involves plotting the forensic story to fit both *institutional parameters* (especially the charges on the indictment) and the audience's *folk psychological narrative scripts*. Thus, in England and Wales, a story of murder must include plot elements that will demonstrate the legal requirement of "intending to kill or seriously harm" the victim, but a "good" forensic plot will also include elements that indicate a motive, as required by folk psychological scripts. The forensic story, often called the "master narrative" (Bamberg 2004), is first plotted by the legal teams before the trial and then presented in the Opening Statement (Snedaker 1991) in jury trials. This provides the skeleton plot that is fleshed out in witness examination and returned to in the Closing Argument. Narrative inequalities arise when the forensic plot available to one party more closely matches folk psychological scripts than that of the other party, as we shall see in the case of "road rage" discussed below.

Story negotiation involves negotiating with other trial participants the permissible scope of the narrative presented in court and the salience of putative narrative elements. We are never "free to narrate anything" but whereas the line between "sanctioned and non-sanctioned narratives" (Barton 2000) is often implicit in most non-institutional contexts, in court it is made very explicit in negotiations about admissibility. Negotiations can take various forms: in private between lawyers or between lawyers and the judge; in open court but out of the hearing of the jury; and in open court and in the hearing of the jury. This is the most controversial element of the model because while plot has traditionally been seen to underlie narrative and character navigation occurs frequently within narration, story negotiation almost never involves narration or narrative discourse. However, forensic narratives are heavily circumscribed by these negotiations and when the judge admits or fails to admit a key narrative element, this, as we shall see, can lead to a narrative inequality that might radically affect the rhetorical effectiveness of the lawyer's master narrative.

Character navigation involves ascribing and managing the identities of the key participants. Character may be ascribed in opening statements and "built up" during examination-in-chief, but then that construction needs to be sustained through the aggressive deconstructive process of cross-examination, and it is there that much of the character navigation work takes place, and as much through the lawyer's questions as the witness's answers. To that extent, character navigation is not simply an aspect of emplotment or narration. It is also fundamental to a forensic case both because decision-makers tend to see negative dispositions as motivating criminal actions and because the plausibility of the story is dependent on the credibility of the witnesses. The notion of character navigation is adapted from Bamberg's (2011) concept of "identity navigation". According to Bamberg, speakers navigate their identities between points on three continua: high/low agency; sameness/difference; and constancy/change. In court, though, it is the *lawyers'* positioning of the witness rather than the witness's positioning of themselves that is of central importance to the emerging forensic narrative. The prosecution will attempt to ascribe *high agency* to the defendant as this indicates criminal responsibility while the defence might attempt to show that he or she is a *low agency* victim of circumstances. The prosecution will attempt to show that the behaviour of the defendant diverged from the legal *norm* of the "reasonable person" while the defence will claim that his behaviour was societally *normal*. Finally, prosecutors will tend to focus on showing *constancy* of "bad character" since a sudden *change* of temperament can be used to mitigate incriminating actions, such as turning murder into manslaughter.

Finally, there is **narration** itself. Narration is defined by the existence of narrative discourse in any form from a narrative expansion in a witness's answer to a full-blown Labovian narrative embedded in an opening statement. It should be noted that none of the trial genres are *narrative* genres as such. Where narration exists, it is *embedded* within the genre. *Direct narration* is where the lawyer narrates directly to judge and jury in her opening and closing speeches and it is where emplotment, narration and character navigation come together. There is also a form of quasi-direct *antagonistic narration* in cross-examination in which the cross-examiner puts her version of events to the witness (and thus the jury) while totally ignoring the witness's responses:

Q. He got out of the car and came towards you with nothing in his hands.
A. No, he didn't.
Q. And you struck out at him again.
A. I did not.
Q. He put his hands up to defend himself.
A. No, he didn't.
Q. You had lost your temper with him.
A. No.

(Cross-examination of Sheila Bush)

Mediated narration, or witness-mediated narration, is where the lawyer narrates *through* the witness in examination-in-chief. The witness, to the trial lawyer, is effectively like an internal narrator to a novelist, except that the lawyer has to work much harder to keep control over her narrators. The lawyer, through focused questioning, will navigate the witness very carefully through her (that is, the lawyer's) storyline, making sure both that all case-significant details come out (referential function) and that these are evaluated by the witness (evaluative function), but also avoiding such forensic traps as hearsay, omission and testimony that is detrimental to the lawyer's case. The advantage for the forensic rhetorical agent, or 'rhetor', of witness-mediated narration is that the witness, who has first-hand experience of the storyworld, provides authenticity and plausibility to the story and will hopefully *engage* the jury in the narrative.

Table 10.1 below roughly summarises the manifestation of narrativity in an English jury trial. "Matters of law" in column 1 is the name given to legal discussions that occur out of hearing of the jury (who are sent out of court) and might occur at any point in the trial. While they are the principal site of story negotiation, such negotiations also take place during pre-trial speech events not included here. The other indications of "navigation focus" in column 2 are very rough. Narration is not indicated as a focus of the defence closing speech (the defence do not have an opening speech in England) because the defence task is to instill doubt in the jury by challenging the prosecution story and their portrait of the defendant. Nevertheless, the defence will often still provide a narrative of what happened in the trial.

An analysis of narrative navigation can reveal *narrative inequalities*, particularly between prosecution and defence. For example, certain plots (though factually true) will not play with jurors; the judge might favour one party or the other in negotiations over the

Table 10.1: Narrativity in an English jury trial.

Trial Genre	Navigation focus	Embedded narrative	Narrators	Type of narration
Prosecution opening statement	Emplotment, narration, character navigation	Crime story	Prosecutor	Direct
Prosecution examination-in-chief	Narration, character navigation	Complainant/ eyewitness/ police story	Prosecutor + witness	Mediated
Defence examination-in-chief	Narration, character navigation	Defendant/ eyewitness story	Defence lawyer + defendant/ witness	Mediated
Cross-examination	Character navigation	Case putting	Cross-examiner	Antagonistic
Prosecution closing speech	Narration, character navigation	Trial story/crime story	Prosecutor	Direct
Defence closing speech	Emplotment, character navigation	Trial story	Defence lawyer	Direct
Matters of law	Story negotiation	—	—	—

admission of narrative elements; some identities are easier to manage than others; and narration in witness examination is at the mercy of the witness's narrative competence.

The Narrative Navigation model accounts for the agentive practices of powerful institutional narrators arguing their case in court. Witnesses and defendants in that account are *characters* manipulated by trial lawyers in navigating their stories through the trial. The witnesses' *own* stories are considered immaterial. There is nothing inherently *unjust* about this from a forensic perspective: the lawyers are trying to put their best case to the decision-makers to ensure that, from their perspective, *justice* is done (which is not to say that there are not some unscrupulous lawyers who will take a purely strategic approach irrespective of their sense of where justice lies). If witnesses were allowed to tell their own stories freely, the case would lose focus and decision-makers lose concentration and focus, which might have a negative impact on the justice of the final decision. However, in such institutional narrative dynamics, witnesses clearly lose voice. The Voice Projection Framework (Heffer 2013a, 2018) tries to account for this loss of voice.

5.2 Voice projection

The Voice Projection Framework (Figure 10.1) involves three key elements: perspective, responsive understanding and projection. *Perspective* covers the ways of being

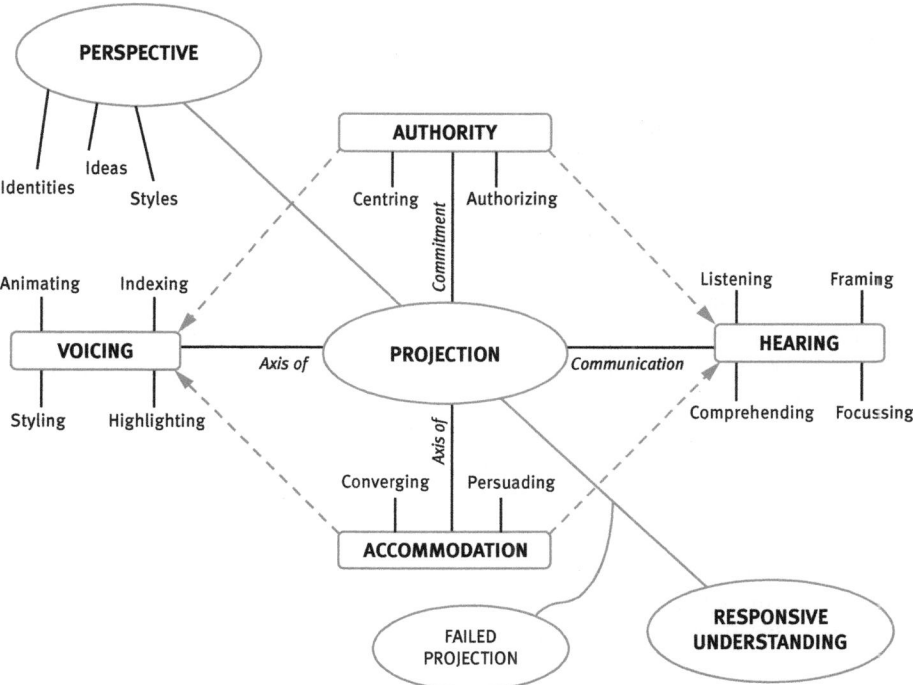

Figure 10.1: The Voice Projection framework.

(Identity), ways of thinking (Ideas) and ways of speaking (Styles) that the speaker projects to an audience when they are "given voice". The defendant, for example, may wish to project to the audience that they are a decent person with polite manners who has been unjustly accused. *Responsive understanding* (after Bakhtin 1986) is when the audience understand what we are "getting at" to the point where they are able to actively respond – either positively or negatively – to what we have said. Responsive understanding is not persuasion: the audience may not agree or they may turn our request down but they will leave us feeling that we have "been heard". Witnesses will often feel that they have not been responsively understood by the decision-makers partly because it is ultimately not their perspective that is being conveyed to the jury or judge but that of the lawyer. *Projection* is the way voice carries to an audience, whether intentionally or unintentionally, and so is at the heart of the Framework. When a voice fails to project, we can say that the speaker "loses voice".

Projection combines communicational elements (voicing and hearing) with power elements (authority and accommodation). *Voicing*, or giving semiotic expression to one's perspective, involves *animating*, or physically conveying voice through sound, sign and other forms of semiosis, and *styling*, or the selecting and arranging of words, sentences, paragraphs and so on. A witness narrator may lose voice because they are prevented from saying (animating) what they "need" to say or because they say it in a strong accent that cannot be understood by the court. They may also lose voice because they speak in a powerless style (Conley & O'Barr 1990) that devalues in the hearer's mind what they have to say or in an overly technical style (e.g. expert witnesses) that will not be comprehended by the jury or judge. Voicing also involves guiding audience interpretation by pointing to particular ways of reading what is said (*indexing*) and stressing the salience of certain elements (*highlighting*). These are particularly vital elements in the rhetorical context of the trial and the forensic narrator will control indexing and highlighting through focused questioning in a way that will best support her case. However, this means that the personal stories that lay people bring to court will recede into the background and might give a sense of loss of voice. On the other hand, an "unreliable" witness can do damage to the forensic narrator's attempt to guide interpretation.

While speakers can anticipate and guide interpretation, hearers are by no means passive recipients and they will willingly or unwittingly impose their own interpretations on what they hear. Accordingly, successful voice projection is dependent on processes of hearing matching processes of voicing but outside the control of the speaker. *Hearing* involves both physical *listening* (or reading) and mental *comprehending*. The legal or lay narrator's voice will fail to project if the audience is not paying attention (the cognitive demands of concentrating on 6 hours a day of evidence are considerable) or if a juror has impaired hearing or difficulty reading, or if the discourse is too complex or the hearer insufficiently intelligent to understand. Hearing also involves crucial interpretative practices – schematic *framing* and selective *focusing* – that are guided, but certainly not determined, by the speaker's indexing and highlighting. The same speech act or event can be framed in very different ways by different individuals and communities, and with different values. In one fraud case I observed, a self-representing litigant indexed as "normal" a level of corrupt behaviour that the jurors visibly found shocking. Focussing makes salient certain aspects of the voicing and backgrounds others. While this can be guided by highlighting, if we are already predisposed towards a certain interpretation, it can become difficult not to cherry pick our salient elements. This is illustrated very well in Roger Shuy's analysis of the discourse of undercover agents in entrapment cases, in which the agents are so focused on listening for incriminating statements that they fail to hear clearly stated exculpatory ones (Shuy 2017). One key aspect of a forensic narrator's expertise is achieving a closer match between indexing and framing, highlighting and focusing.

Working alongside the communicative axis of voicing and hearing is an axis of commitment to authority or accommodation. *Authority* constrains opportunities for narrative voicing and hearing by imposing discursive and other norms through the practices of *centring* (Silverstein 1998; Blommaert 2005), the institutional imposition of normative standards, and *authorizing* (Bourdieu 1991), or the conferring of authority and legitimacy on speakers and discourse. Forensic narrators are constrained by the rules of evidence enforced by the legal institution but are also authorized to control narration during witness examination. Witnesses may sense a loss of voice from not being able to introduce hearsay or by being constantly interrupted in their narration. *Accommodation,* or the extent to which the speaker adapts their speech to the audience, involves practices of *converging,* or adapting to the communicative norms of the speaker, and *persuading,* or being rhetorically efficacious. Trial lawyers, determined to win their case, are generally very good at accommodating to the jury but they will often *diverge* from witnesses, particularly in cross-examination, when it is in their strategic interests to do so. For example, cross-examiners will often use complex syntax with child witnesses so as to deliberately confuse them. It is very difficult for narrative witnesses to accommodate to the Court, on the other hand, as they are likely to know neither the legal framework nor the lawyer's master narrative.

6 Narrative inequality and loss of voice at trial

One important application of the models outlined above is that they can help us analyse narrative inequality and loss of voice at trial. According to Hymes, narrative inequality is concerned with "rights to use narrative, with whose narratives are admitted to have a cognitive function" (Hymes 1996: 109), or a probative function in the forensic context. For example, Blommaert (2001), Eades (2008) and Ehrlich (2013) have shown how the narratives of certain lay participants in the legal process (asylum seekers, Aboriginals, rape victims) are read as little more than "noise" (Blommaert 2001) by the legal system. My interpretation of narrative inequality, though, is much broader and more practical and concerns the unequal distribution of narrative resources in a given context that affect the narrator's ability to convey their narrative effectively. Clearly, as has been pointed out many times in the literature, there is narrative inequality between lawyer and witness deriving from the unequal distribution of telling rights. However, as indicated above, it is not actually clear that witnesses should have a *right* to equality of narrative practice with lawyers in court. In a sense, the narrative inequality between lawyer and witness is institutionally legitimated by the forensic rhetorical situation. The most consequential form of narrative inequality in the trial, then, is not between lawyer and witness but between prosecution and defence. Accordingly, narrative inequality in the trial is best investigated not through interactional asymmetries but through the narrative practices of the trial lawyers. We might also distinguish between *structural inequalities,* which derive from the sociolegal and psychological system of norms and rules, and *strategic inequalities,* which restrict the lawyer's scope of action in a given case, though it is not always easy to distinguish between the two. At the same time, the witness's *loss of voice* is very important for two reasons. Firstly, it is an issue in itself where such loss can lead to a sense of disempowerment or even humiliation, particularly in the intimidating environment of cross-examination (Henderson, Heffer & Kebbell 2015).

Secondly, where witnesses lose voice, this can have a negative impact on the forensic rhetor's case itself. Consequently, loss of voice needs to be integrated into an analysis of narrative inequality.

I shall now explore this thesis in a brief analysis of a case I have analysed previously as a "typical Crown Court trial" (Heffer 2005) and as an illustration of narrative navigation (Heffer 2012).[1] In the anonymized case of *R v Speak*, two young women were riding along a narrow country lane when the defendant came up behind them in a jeep. The prosecution, represented by Mr Rider, claim that Speak, tooting his horn and swearing abuse at the women, forced the first woman up the bank, "rammed" into the back legs of the second horse, and then, after stopping, rushed at the second rider, Sheila Bush, with a steering-wheel clamp and hit her on the leg. The defence, represented by Mr Spurs, claimed that Speak passed the first horse by driving up onto the verge and then Bush lashed out at him with her whip and, when he stopped to ask why he had done this, she continued to hit and abuse him. The trial was held over two days and involved three charges: (1) dangerous driving; (2) possession of an offensive weapon; and (3) common assault. I shall attempt to show both the narrative inequalities between prosecution and defence and the loss of voice suffered by the defence witnesses.

7 Plotting and negotiating the forensic story

We should start by noting that the defence generally suffer structural narrative inequality in emplotment because of the folk psychological rule that "The prosecutor rarely brings innocent people to trial" (Wagenaar, van Koppen & Crombag 1993: 43). The law tries to counteract this inequality through the presumption of innocence and a high standard of proof but it is not easy for some jurors (or judges) to override a presumption of guilt. The defence are at a further strategic disadvantage in this case, though, because the defendant and the events can be so easily made to fit with lay narrative scripts of road rage that are likely to have been held by the provincial jurors. The prosecutor is easily able to match his narrative *indexing* with the jury's likely *framing* of events. A narrative requires a stable storyworld that is disrupted by some form of disequilibrium (Herman 2009: 9). Mr Rider emphasises that the normal state is one shared by the provincial jurors with whom he aligns (the defendant, on the other hand, has come up from the city). In his closing speech, when outlining the "proper way" of overtaking horses, he uses inclusive "we" ("in our county", "We all") to align with the jury, and the subsequent impersonal "one" and "you" appear to fall within the pronominally inclusive range:

---

[1] I have mostly used different examples from those in Heffer 2012.

> I am sure it is the sort of thing which often happens in our county. We all, no doubt, have had the experience of driving along, coming across riders, and one knows that if there is nothing coming towards you, you get well on to the other side of the road, drive very slowly past, and you only accelerate when you are well past. That is the proper way of dealing with overtaking horses.
> (Defence closing argument)

The "trouble" (Bruner 2004), which is legally in the form of three separate charges (dangerous driving, possession of a weapon and assault), is *indexed* as the one lay category of "road rage" and Mr Rider *highlights* in his closing speech that the "one incident" "divided up into three charges" is clearly one of "road rage". With this central theme, he then ensures during the trial through *focussed* questioning that most of the behaviours commonly associated with road rage (James & Nahl 2000) are *highlighted* in the testimony: aggressive driving, close tailgating, sounding the horn excessively, hitting other "vehicles" (in this case a horse), shouting verbal abuse ("Get out of the fucking way"), making threats ("I'll give you what for"), exiting the car to start a confrontation, using or threatening to use an offensive weapon (a steering-wheel clamp), assaulting other road users. The road rage is further aggravated, according to the prosecution, by the vulnerability of the victims. Mr Rider *highlights* this aspect in his closing speech through stylistic parallelism, the vocative "members of the Jury", and the contrast between "injury" and "a few yards":

> They were on horses who are easily frightened. They could have bolted. They could have thrown them. They could have sustained injury. Their beloved horses could have been seriously injured. All for the sake, members of the Jury, of a few yards.
> (Prosecution closing speech)

In theory, though, the prosecution and defence plots could have been symmetrical stories of road rage. When Mr Rider puts the prosecution case to the defendant in cross-examination, Speak rashly suggests (at turns 241 and 243) that it was the young women who were raging:[3]

238 Q. Do you get wound up while you are driving a car if incidents occur?
239 A. I'm not aware of being unusually wound up about anything.
240 Q. You see, because I do put to you that this was a particularly grave example of what has sadly become known as road rage.
241 A. Yes, exactly.
242 Q. Was it not?
243 A. Not on my part.
(Cross-examination of Defendant. My emphasis)

Mr Spurs, though, recognizes that this would stretch folk psychological narrative scripts too far: "road rage" prototypically evokes testosterone-filled aggressive males protected within the metal cage of a car, not the behaviour of an unprotected female rider trotting along a country road. There would be too great a mismatch between the narrator's *indexing* of an interpretation and the audience's likely predispositional *framing* of the event. He opts, then, for the safer story of middle class arrogance and irritation at an impatient working class driver. The problem is that this fits less well with the audience of provincial (and probably middle class) jurors.

Defence and prosecution, then, are not on equal terms with respect to choice of plots available to them both because of structural inequalities created by folk psychological norms (presumption of guilt) and strategic inequalities resulting from the easy fit of the prosecution plot to lay narrative scripts of road rage likely to be held by the audience of provincial jurors. This makes the job of matching *indexing* and *framing* much easier for Mr Rider than Mr Spurs.

Prosecution and defence do have equal structural rights to challenge the scope of the opposing party's narrative (what can be told by whom) by questioning the admission of evidence. However, decisions on admissibility are in the hands of the judge and there has been a tendency towards "liberal – if not lax – standards of admissibility" in English courts (Roberts & Zuckerman 2004: 528). In ordinary cases in which the defendant is not wealthy, then, this gives strategic advantage to the prosecution, who have the power and resources to enlist forensic, medical and other experts. The defence in this case try to exclude in particular two "expert" opinions that lend weight to the claims that the defendant's driving was dangerous and that he assaulted Bush. While it is received wisdom that opinions are only admitted in court if they are given by an expert on matters that are beyond the knowledge and understanding of the jury, in fact "the courts do *not* insist on any 'common knowledge' or 'abnormality' criterion" (Roberts and Zuckerman 2004: 311) but on a "probative helpfulness" criterion, which leaves considerable scope for strategic judicial decisions. However, the judge in this case (a barrister acting as a part-time "recorder") appears to accept opinions that depend not only on "ubiquitous" rather than "specialist" expertise (Collins & Evans 2007) but also that do not "help" the jury more generally. Firstly, with regard to the statement of a police expert on the Highway Code (an official government booklet giving guidance to road users), defence counsel, Mr Spurs, points out to the judge in negotiation out of hearing of the jury:

> MR SPURS: ... The last thing, "Horses are unpredictable animals." It is a matter of common sense. It is not a matter which perhaps the jury requires expert evidence on. ...
>
> THE RECORDER: I would have thought the unpredictable nature of horses has some relevance to the issue of whether driving close to them and making a lot of noise in the vicinity is going to be a potential cause of danger.
>
> MR SPURS: That may be. I am not going to really object to that. It is a matter of common sense.

Mr Spurs' stated lack of objection to the point needs to be seen in the light of the normal give-and-take of negotiation. In the quite lengthy negotiation from which this passage is extracted, he does not "push" the point and "settles" for inclusion of an opinion, which in this rural area is simply "common sense", because he has a more serious objection to make. Namely, he objects to inclusion of Dr Clark's opinion that bruises on Bush's leg were "entirely consistent with her account" of being hit with a steering-wheel clamp (Heffer 2012: 280–81). He points out that:

There is no evidence to say that this doctor is in any way an expert as to injuries or their causation. What one normally finds, if it is an important point, a forensic pathologist who is experienced in wounds or damage or whatever is the sort of person who gives that evidence. ... There is nothing in the statement to show the expertise on the part of the doctor. That witness is a general practitioner.
(Defence submission to judge)

The judge, though, replies:

THE RECORDER: That may be the case. I would not imagine for a moment the jury are going to have any difficulty in making up their own mind whether the bruise in the photographs is consistent with what is alleged to have happened.

MR SPURS: Yes.

THE RECORDER: It is a bit of a fuss about nothing.

Ironically, the judge both allows the opinion, thus recognizing the doctor's expert status, and implies that it will not be probatively helpful for the jury, thus suggesting it should not be admitted. Yet this is not "a bit of a fuss about nothing" because an *authorised* statement from an *authoritative* figure is likely to *confirm* for the jury what they might already think, thus putting it beyond reasonable doubt. Furthermore, if the judge had ruled against the expert opinion, a vital inferential link in the prosecution story would have been severed since the doctor's opinion provides the only corroborating evidence beyond the potentially complicit complainants for both the possession and assault charges.

Prosecution and defence, then, have unequal power in determining narrative scope in this case both because of a general laxity in admitting evidence (which can work in the defence's favour in other cases) and because the judge seems happy to stretch the scope of the forensic narrative to include elements of expertise that are, on his own admission, not probatively helpful for the jury.

8 Practices of forensic narration

There is also serious inequality in the narrational power of prosecution and defence. Structurally, while lawyer and witness have unequal telling rights, prosecution and defence theoretically have the same telling rights: they both examine and cross-examine witnesses under the same legal constraints. Strategically, though, prosecution and defence often have very unequal narrational resources at their disposal, in terms of both number and narrative impact of witnesses. Here, the prosecution are able to make use of two fairly skilful and committed witness narrators (the riders), plus the experienced officer in charge of the case and two "expert" witnesses. The defence, on the other hand, have the defendant, who is a "powerless" narrator by any measure, and a young eyewitness (Peters) who is such a reluctant witness that he has to be summoned and picked up by a process server. Conley and O'Barr (1990), amongst others, have provided empirical evidence of how certain interactional behaviour can enhance or diminish credibility. For example, "powerless" narrators (ones who use features such as hedges, filled pauses and honorifics) are considered less credible by mock jurors than "powerful" ones who do not use those features, and witnesses who testify in a "narrative" style are considered more credible than those who testify in a "fragmented" style. Here, the prosecution witnesses Bush and Walters are typical "powerful" speakers while the defendant Speak and the defence's one reluctant eyewitness (Peters) are clearly powerless ones. While credibility is generally seen as a matter of persuasion rather than voice, there is clearly a threshold of credibility required before a speaker can reach first base in terms of responsive understanding: I will not respond to what you are "getting at" if I do not believe you are telling the truth.

The lead prosecution witness, Sheila Bush, shows both a powerful style and accommodation to forensic narrative requirements in her examination-in-chief:

23 Q. ... whilst you were riding along the road, both you and Miss Walters on your horses, what happened around about noon?
24 A. We heard a car approaching from behind on this road. Because it was a very narrow road, we decided to trot up to get to the corner shown in photograph No.1 to let the vehicle get past. He was impatient. He came up behind us. He started honking his horn and shouting abuse at us.

In this simple example of co-tellership, we find the three central elements of narrative discourse identified by Labov: Orientation summed up in the barrister's question; Complicating Action conveyed through a causally-connected series of events relating to the crime – (we) *heard ... decided*, (he) *came up ... started* (honking); and a set of evaluative clauses (legal Point) and clausal elements (evaluation) which together allocate blame to the defendant: *it was a very narrow road ... he was impatient ... honking his horn and shouting abuse.* Not only is her voice likely to have projected successfully to the jury, but in doing so it is putting the case effectively for the prosecution.

The defendant, Reginald Speak, on the other hand, shows a distinctly powerless style in examination-in-chief, as can be seen from his very first answer:

1 Q. ... The police officer suggested when you showed him some injuries on your hands that you contact a doctor.
2 A. I did attempt to. It was Saturday evening. The surgery is a very little practice in Stalham. On the Monday I went down there to make an appointment and I was told the earliest appointment I could get was a Wednesday afternoon. Wednesday tea-time, frankly, four days had gone by and it was really hardly worth turning up ---- There was hardly anything left ---- There were just weals and cuts. It wasn't sort of ---- They had just about healed up frankly

(Examination-in-chief of Speak)

However, there is a far more significant problem in terms of the defendant's voice. The prosecution have a significant structural advantage in narration since they control the investigation process. Given that the tape of the police interrogation of the defendant was played to the court during the examination of the officer in charge of the case (as part of the *prosecution* case), this account produced under duress becomes the defendant's definitive "narrative" which defence counsel feels he cannot "repeat" during examination-in-chief of the defendant. He begins his examination as follows (immediately preceding the above extract):

> 3 Q.   Mr. Speak, I am going to ask you some questions about the events of 12 April of this year. The Jury have just heard your narrative, and your answers, to the police officer later on that evening. I am not going to repeat all that. I am just going to ask you a couple of things to clarify one or two points.

He ends his very brief examination (720 words in total) *highlighting* the need not to repeat:

> 19 Q.   You gave your explanation on the tape. I am not going to cover all of that again. It would be repetitious.

The result is very different, and far less engaging, than the fully-formed narrative co-constructed by prosecutor and lead witness Bush at the opening of the trial (see Heffer 2005). In not allowing the defendant to tell his story in the "friendly" co-narrational context of examination-in-chief, a potentially more positive *animation* and *styling* of his story is effectively suppressed. Mr Spurs would almost inevitably have helped scaffold a more persuasive story as Mr Rider does with the more competent Bush. *Recontextualizing* a story in a more positive environment is not at all the same thing as simply *repeating* it. However, this distinction between repeating and recontextualizing, which is well established in linguistic anthropology (Bauman & Briggs 1990) and fundamental in legal contexts (Heffer, Rock & Conley 2013), is not common knowledge and Mr Spurs is probably right in presuming that neither the judge nor jury would tolerate what they might perceive as a simple *repetition* of evidence. This is not a question of suppressing the defendant's voice, as often occurs in US trials, to avoid self-incrimination during cross-examination. Given that juries in England and Wales are allowed to infer probative significance from a defendant's silence, defendants will invariably testify and Speak, following his brief examination-in-chief, faced a gruelling cross-examination of 132 turns and 4600 words.

There is significant narrative inequality also between the corroborating witnesses. Whereas Walters, the prosecution's witness, has a distinctly narrative style of testimony (she produces the longest witness turns in the trial), Peters, the defence eyewitness, has a distinctly fragmented style. Under cross-examination, he also comes across as extremely unreliable:

> 132 Q.   So, Mr. Speak contacted you a week or so after this incident.
> 133 A.   I cannot guarantee that it was a week. It could've been a day. It could've been a month.
> 134 Q.   Forgive me, Mr. Peters. You are not terribly sort of precise about these things.
> 135 A.   Because I'm not precise within myself.
> 136 Q.   I am sorry?

> 137 A. I am not precise in what happened within myself because I can't ---- It was ten months ago – maybe more. I'm not too sure. April.
> 138 Q. That is ten months ago, was it?
> 139 A. I think so. (Pause) No, it's not. It's five/six months. Even still, I ----
>
> (Cross-examination of Peters)

In short, there is extreme narrative inequality between the prosecution and defence internal narrators. But that is not all. The prosecution also have access to material resources that can bolster the rhetorical effectiveness of the verbal narration. Exploiting the potential of multimodal narration as an engagement device, Bush's account is accompanied by photos of the road, two of which include a police car "to show the width of the road". The police car in the photo, though, fills the entire width of the road despite the defendant's claims that he drove up onto the verge. This lends a visual sense of confinement to the horse riders' lexical refrains that the defendant *"squeezed past"* and *"forced"* them into the hedge (my emphasis):

> 60 A. He came up very close behind Ginger's horse and *forced* her to go up the bank.
> 61 Q. Can we see the bank she was *forced* to go up?
> 62 A. Probably No.4 again, just before the hedge.
> 63 Q. Is it on the left or the right as we look at the photograph?
> 64 A. She'd be on the right-hand side as we look at it.
> 65 Q. Where the high bushes are?
> 66 A. Yes.
> 67 Q. Ginger was *forced* by him up that bank?
> 68 A. Yes.
>
> (Examination-in-chief of Sheila Bush)

This visual sleight of hand transforms the mere geographical *place* into an evaluatively significant *space* (De Certeau 1988: 118) in the crime story. The combination of visual confinement and the repetition of words like "squeezing" and "forcing" also *indexes* the local cultural *frame*, shared with other rural people and made salient in the closing speech, of how one *practices* a country lane when one comes across horses. The trick is picked up by Mr Spurs in his cross-examination of the officer in charge of the case, which begins with a sarcastic "nicely positioned":

> 1 Q. Just a couple of things. As far as the photographs are concerned, it shows a picture of a police car nicely positioned in the middle of the road. When you interviewed him, and prior to these photographs being taken, Mr. Speak had explained that when he went past the horses, he had been up on the verge. Did you take any photographs showing the position of the vehicle on the verge?
> 2 A. No, I did not.
> 3 Q. Would that not have been useful to show us what sort of gaps there were to get past?
>
> (Cross-examination of PC Glory)

However, PC Glory is the last witness in the prosecution case, long after the examination of the principal narrator, Bush, above. The prosecution, then, exploit both structural and strategic inequalities of narration to give them a distinct advantage in the narrative performance at trial.

9 Character navigation and cross-examination

Finally, the prosecution have both structural and strategic advantages with respect to character navigation. Structurally, they present all their evidence first. This allows them to build up characters in examination-in-chief and then simply try to maintain these under cross-examination. It also means that when they cross-examine the defendant, they have already built up their own picture of him. And, as we have seen, the defendant's own narrative is embedded in the examination of the officer in charge of the case. Mr Rider, the prosecutor, effectively encapsulates the already-presented prosecution case in the opening of his cross-examination of Mr Speak:

> 1 Q. You are a man with a short fuse, are you not, Mr. Speak?
> 2 A. I am not – not at all.
> 3 Q. You are a man who just could not be bothered to wait a few seconds until the horses got to the corner fifty yards ahead, could you?
> 4 A. I had no reason to ---- I wasn't in a hurry at all.

The availability of the "short fuse" metaphor gives a strategic advantage because it allows the prosecution to focus not on a specific *change* in behaviour ("losing it") but on the underlying *constancy* of character that "causes" it. The focus here is not on the defendant's presumed impatience at a given point in the narrative but on his inherently bad character ("You are a man with ..."; "You are a man who ..."). The "short fuse" provides the motivation for the sudden explosion of "road rage" that narratively explains the defendant's criminal actions. At the same time, the prosecution are careful to make sure that Speak retains *high agency* ("just could not be bothered") rather than being seen as the *low agency* victim of a condition such as Intermittent Explosive Disorder (IED) (Galovski 2006).

The defence, on the other hand, are forced into a corner with respect to character. Since it is implausible in terms of lay narrative scripts to claim that the horse riders exploded in road rage, they focus on a momentary *change* of mood, losing one's temper, as Mr Spurs puts to Bush in cross-examination:

> 21 Q. No, so, why did you hit out at him with your whip?
> 22 A. Because it is a reflex action. As he hit my horse, she spun round. I hit out as a reflex action to protect her.
> 23 Q. By the time he is coming past, he is no longer attacking her. It is not reflex action.
> 24 A. No.
> 25 Q. You had lost your temper ....
>
> (Cross-examination of Sheila Bush)

She has supposedly lost her temper with an "oik", which is British slang for an ignorant, ill-educated, lower-class person:

> 373 Q. You expected him to wait. You thought to yourself, "He can wait till we get to the corner and then get past." You did not like the fact that he managed to get past. Here he was, this oik coming back and saying, "What's going on? What are you hitting me for?"

However, if the jury accept the road rage script, they are likely to excuse the strongly provoked outburst from the complainant.

A potentially more effective defence strategy, then, as summed up in Mr Spurs' closing speech, is to contrast the *constant* bad character conveyed by the prosecution – a "man who has such a short fuse that he is not even going to wait a second or two behind a car; a man who is so foul-mouthed that every other word is an F word; a man who clearly is arrogant; who is aggressive; who cannot control his temper" – with their own face-to-face experience of the defendant in court: "Is that the sort of person he struck you as when he gave his evidence?" However, Speak comes across as artificially polite in his testimonial style and so gives the impression of a momentary *change* of character on occasion of the trial hiding a more *constant* impoliteness. His use of honorifics is extremely rare and distinctly powerless in the English courtroom:

8 Q. They were not stationary then, were they?
9 A. No, sir.
10 Q. You were a short distance away from the corner.
11 A. That's true, yes, sir.
12 Q. So, all you had to do was be patient and drive behind the two horses as they continued walking to the corner, was it not?
13 A. That's true, sir, yes.

(Cross-examination of Speak)

While it is well established in the literature (e.g. Conley and O'Barr 1990) that working-class witnesses with limited education tend to hypercorrect to the formality of the courtroom situation and that therefore nothing can be construed probatively about their awkward style, most jurors will not know this. In trying to gain voice, Speak is probably losing it.

Once again, then, we find unequal access to narrative in the relative power of prosecution and defence to ascribe and maintain character in both the crime story and the trial story. It is difficult, in short, for the defence to escape the discursive "othering" (Said 1978) of the working-class urban defendant by the middle class provincial jurors.

10 Conclusion

In this chapter I hope to have shown both the centrality of narrative practices to the trial process and how the frameworks of Narrative Navigation and Voice Projection can inform our understanding of narrative inequality and loss of voice in the trial. Focussing on the practices of Narrative Navigation (emplotment, story negotiation and character navigation, as well as narration) can give a sense of the "bigger" picture of narrativity in the trial and where forensic inequalities really lie. Focussing on the practices of Voice Projection, which make salient hearing as well as voicing, authority as well as accommodation, can reveal not only how witnesses lose voice beyond the discursive asymmetry of witness examination but also how severe loss of voice in a witness can damage the forensic rhetor's case, and thus impact on justice. I originally believed *R v Speak* to be what lawyers call an "easy" case. Viewing the case through the lenses of narrative navigation and voice projection, though, has made me realize that though the case may remain "easy" in the sense of securing a guilty verdict, that ease is uncomfortably linked to the structural and strategic narrative inequalities faced by the defence. An *easy* case is not necessarily a *just* case.

Inevitably, there are limitations to this analysis. The frameworks are both relatively new and relatively untested and I would expect to make considerable modifications in the light of forthcoming critique and further attempts at application. I intend over time to strengthen the links between the elements and sub-elements of the frameworks and nitty-gritty linguistic realisations of those elements. However, one could never produce more than a set of available linguistic resources that *might* be used in realizing a given function. Both frameworks have been based on analyses of Anglo-American jury trials. In theory, there is no reason why either framework should not work in analyzing trial discourse in civil cases or in inquisitorial systems. The anti-narrative forces may be greater in the latter, but we are still dealing with stories of wrongdoing, while the practices of voice projection should apply to any context. However, it remains to be seen what would happen in practice.

Finally, limitations of space have not permitted me to discuss how these frameworks might lead to reform of legal-institutional practice. Perhaps the general point is the need to maintain strong due process procedures to counteract the prosecution's structural narrative advantages. The fact that defendants have only a qualified right to silence in England and Wales means that suspects will talk in police interviews and then tapes of these interviews will be played to the jury by the prosecution. But if a defendant is going to be cross-examined in court, they should have the right to a full and friendly examination-in-chief that will bring out their story in the best possible light rather than depending on the story elicited in the hostile environment of police interrogation. Otherwise, they lose their voice, the defence lose the voice of their key witness and the result is a serious narrative inequality in the trial process.

References

Bakhtin, Mikhail. 1986. *Speech genres and other late essays*. Austin: University of Texas Press.
Bamberg, Michael. 2004. Considering counter narratives. In M. Bamberg & M. Andrews (eds.), *Considering counter narratives: narrating, resisting, making sense*, 351–371. Amsterdam: John Benjamins.
Bamberg, Michael. 2011. Narrative practice and identity navigation. In J.A. Holstein & J.F. Gubrium (eds.), *Varieties of narrative analysis*, 99–124. London: Sage.

Bamberg, Michael & Alexandra Georgakopoulou. 2008. Small stories as a new perspective in narrative and identity analysis. *Text & Talk – An Interdisciplinary Journal of Language, Discourse & Communication Studies* 28(3). 377–396.
Barton, Ellen. 2000. Sanctioned and non-sanctioned narratives in institutional discourse. *Narrative Inquiry* 10(2). 341–375.
Bauman, Richard & Charles L. Briggs. 1990. Poetics and performance as critical perspectives on language and social life. *Annual Review of Anthropology* 19. 59–88.
Bennett, W. Lance & Martha S. Feldman. 1981. *Reconstructing reality in the courtroom*. London: Tavistock.
Bitzer, Lloyd. 1968. The rhetorical situation. *Philosophy and Rhetoric* 1. 1–14.
Blommaert, Jan. 2001. Investigating narrative inequality: African asylum seekers' stories in Belgium. *Discourse and Society* 12(4). 413–449.
Blommaert, Jan. 2005. *Discourse*. Cambridge: Cambridge University Press.
Bourdieu, Pierre. 1977. *Outline of a theory of practice*. Trans. by Richard Nice. Cambridge: Cambridge University Press.
Bourdieu, Pierre. 1990. *The logic of practice*. Trans. by Richard Nice. Cambridge: Polity.
Bourdieu, Pierre. 1991. *Language and symbolic power*. Trans. by Gino Raymond & Matthew Adamson. Cambridge: Polity Press.
Bruner, Jerome. 1986. *Actual minds, possible worlds*. Cambridge, MA: Harvard University Press.
Bruner, Jerome. 1996. Frames for thinking: Ways of making meaning. In D.R. Olson & N. Torrance (eds.), *Modes of thought: explorations in culture and cognition*, 93–105. Cambridge: Cambridge University Press.
Bruner, Jerome. 2004. Life as narrative. *Social Research* 71(3). 691–710.
Carawan, Edwin. 2007. *Oxford readings in the attic orators*. Oxford: Oxford University Press.
Chatman, Seymour. 1978. *Story and discourse*. London: Cornell University Press.
Collins, Harry M. & Robert Evans. 2007. *Rethinking expertise*. Chicago: University of Chicago Press.
Conley, John M. & William M. O'Barr. 1990. *Rules versus relationships: The ethnography of legal discourse* (Language and Legal Discourse). Chicago: University of Chicago Press.
Cotterill, Janet. 2003. *Language and power in court: a linguistic analysis of the O.J. Simpson Trial*. Basingstoke: Palgrave.
De Certeau, Michel. 1988. *The practice of everyday life*. Berkeley, CA: University of California Press.
De Fina, Anna & Alexandra Georgakopoulou. 2008. Narrative analysis in the shift from texts to practices. *Text & Talk* 28(3). 275–281.
De Fina, Anna & Alexandra Georgakopoulou. 2012. *Analyzing narrative: discourse and sociolinguistic perspectives*. Cambridge: Cambridge University Press.
Eades, Diana. 2008. *Courtroom talk and neocolonial control*. New York: Mouton de Gruyter.
Ehrlich, Susan. 2013. Post-penetration rape and the decontextualization of witness testimony. In Chris Heffer, Frances Rock & John M. Conley (eds.), *Legal-lay communication: textual travels in the law*, 189–205. New York: Oxford University Press.
Engel, Susan. 2000. *Context is everything: the nature of memory*. New York: W.H. Freeman and Company.
Freed, Alice F. 2015. Institutional discourse. *The International Encyclopedia of Language and Social Interaction*. 1–18.
Galatolo, Renata & Paul Drew. 2006. Narrative expansions as defensive practices in courtroom testimony. *Text & Talk* 26(6). 661–698.
Galovski, Tara E. 2006. *Road rage: assessment and treatment of the angry, aggressive driver*, 1st edn. Washington, DC: American Psychological Association.
Goffman, Erving. 1959. *The presentation of self in everyday life*. London: Penguin.
Hannken-Illjes, Kati. 2011. Narratives as resources in criminal case work. *Narrative Inquiry* 21(1). 175–188.

Harris, Sandra. 2001. Fragmented narratives and multiple tellers: Witness and defendant accounts in trials. *Discourse Studies* 3(1). 53–74.

Harris, Sandra. 2005. Telling stories and giving evidence: The hybridisation of narrative and non-narrative modes of discourse in a sexual assault trial. In Joanna Thornborrow & Jennifer Coates (eds.), *The sociolinguistics of narrative*, 215–237. Amsterdam: John Benjamins.

Heffer, Chris. 2005. *The language of jury trial: a corpus-aided analysis of legal-lay discourse*. Basingstoke: Palgrave Macmillan.

Heffer, Chris. 2012. Narrative navigation: Narrative practices in forensic discourse. *Narrative Inquiry* 22(2). 267–286.

Heffer, Chris. 2013a. Projecting voice: Towards an agentive understanding of a critical capacity. Cardiff Papers in Language and Literature. Cardiff. Reprint Edition.

Heffer, Chris. 2013b. Revelation and rhetoric: A critical model of forensic discourse. *International Journal for the Semiotics of Law* 26(2). 459–485.

Heffer, Chris. 2018. When voices fail to carry: Voice Projection and the case of the 'dumb' jury. In A. Durant & J. Leung (eds.), *Language, power and law: the invisible exercise of power through language*, 207–235. Cambridge: Cambridge University Press.

Heffer, Chris. forth. *Rhetoric and rights: a theory of forensic discourse*. New York: Oxford University Press.

Heffer, Chris, Frances Rock & John M. Conley (eds.). 2013. *Legal-lay communication: textual travels in the law*. New York: Oxford University Press.

Henderson, Emily, Chris Heffer & Mark Kebbell. 2015. Cross-examination and discourse. In T. Grant, G. Oxburgh, T. Myklebust & B. Milne (eds.), *Communication in forensic contexts: integrated approaches from psychology, linguistics and law enforcement*, 181–208. Hoboken, NJ: Wiley & Sons.

Herman, David. 2009. *Basic elements of narrative*. Malden, MA: Wiley-Blackwell.

Heydon, Georgina. 2005. *The language of police interviewing: a critical analysis*. Basingstoke: Palgrave Macmillan.

Hymes, Dell. 1996. *Ethnography, linguistics, narrative inequality: toward an understanding of voice*. London: Taylor and Francis.

Jackson, Bernard S. 1988. *Law, fact and narrative coherence*. Liverpool: Deborah Charles Publications.

James, Leon & Diane Nahl. 2000. *Road rage and aggressive driving: steering clear of highway warfare*. Amherst, NY: Prometheus Books.

Komter, Martha. 1998. *Dilemmas in the courtroom: a study of trials of violent crime in the netherlands*. Mahwah, NJ: Lawrence Erlbaum Associates.

Komter, Martha. 2002. The suspect's own words: The treatment of written statements in Dutch courtrooms. *Forensic Linguistics: The International Journal of Speech, Language and the Law* 9(2). 168–192.

Labov, William. 1972. *Language in the inner city*. Philadelphia: University of Pennsylvania Press.

Labov, William. 1997. Some further steps in narrative analysis. *Journal of Narrative and Life History* 7(1–4). 395–415.

Labov, William & J. Waletzky. 1967. Narrative analysis: Oral versions of personal experience. In J. Helms (ed.), *Essays on the verbal and visual arts: Proceedings of the 1996 Annual Spring Meeting of the American Ethnological Society*, 12–44. Seattle: University of Washington Press.

Langellier, Kristin M. & Eric E. Peterson. 2004. *Storytelling in daily life: performing narrative*. Philadelphia: Temple University Press.

Linde, Charlotte. 2003. Narrative in institutions. In Deborah Schiffrin, Deborah Tannen & Heidi E. Hamilton (eds.), *The handbook of discourse analysis*, 518–535. Oxford: Blackwell.

Linde, Charlotte 2015. Memory in narrative. *The International Encyclopedia of Language and Social Interaction*. Wiley, 1–9.

McQuillan, Martin (ed.) 2000. *The narrative reader*. London: Routledge.
Mertz, Elizabeth. 2007. *The language of law school: learning to 'think like a lawyer'*. Oxford: Oxford University Press.
Pennington, Nancy & Reid Hastie. 1986. Evidence evaluation in complex decision making. *Journal of Personality and Social Psychology* 51(2). 242–258.
Roberts, Paul & Adrian Zuckerman. 2004. *Criminal evidence*. Oxford: Oxford University Press.
Said, Edward W. 1978. *Orientalism*. Harmondsworth: Penguin.
Scollon, Ron. 2001. *Mediated discourse: the nexus of practice*. London: Routledge.
Shuy, Roger. 2017. *The deceptive ambiguity of institutionally powerful police, prosecutors and undercover agents*. New York: Oxford University Press.
Silverstein, Michael. 1998. Contemporary transformations of local linguistic communities. *Annual Review of Anthropology* 27. 401–426.
Snedaker, Kathryn. 1991. Storytelling in opening statements: Framing the argumentation of the trial. In David Papke (ed.), *Narrative and the legal discourse*, 132–157. Liverpool: Deborah Charles.
Stone, Marcus. 1984. *Proof of facts in criminal trials*. Edinburgh: W. Green & Son.
Stygall, Gail. 1994. *Trial language: differential discourse processing and discourse formations*. Amsterdam: John Benjamins.
Tracy, Karen & Erica L. Delgadillo. 2013. Troubling the legal-lay distinction: Litigant briefs, oral argument, and a public hearing about same-sex marriage. In Chris Heffer, Frances Rock & John M. Conley (eds.), *Legal-lay communication: textual travels in the law*, 226–244. New York: Oxford University Press.
Wagenaar, Willem A., Peter J. van Koppen & Hans F.M. Crombag. 1993. *Anchored narratives: the psychology of criminal evidence*. Hemel Hempstead: Harvester Wheatsheaf.
Zimdars, Anna & Jennifer Souboorah. 2009. *Some observations on meritocracy and the law: the profile of pupil barristers at the Bar of England and Wales 2004–2008*. London: Bar Council.

Part III: **Legal language outside of court**

Alan Durant and Jennifer Davis
11 Linguistic analysis in trade mark law: current approaches and new challenges

1 Introduction

Trade mark law is prominent among areas considered of special interest to scholars concerned with language in the legal sphere. In introductions to forensic linguistics, the field is regularly listed along with document authorship, speaker identification, product warnings, the meaning of defamatory statements, and other topics (Coulthard and Johnson 2007; Gibbons and Turell 2008).

There are two main reasons for this level of interest. The first reason is that, traditionally and almost certainly still, most trade marks consist of verbal signs (or "figurative" marks comprised of words in a given stylisation, or "get-up").[1] So the question of which verbal signs are registrable as trade marks, and whether use of such signs by third parties will infringe the proprietary rights of trade mark owners, invites analysis and discussion. The second reason concerns a different level of language use: namely, the terminology through which trade mark law governs the verbal signs which function as marks. That terminology amounts to a legal metalanguage of specialised semiotic/legal terms which operate in tandem with other legal terminology. Basic terms include "sign" itself or "figurative" as used above, as well as "distinctive", "descriptive" and "generic". Each term in this cluster is used in ways that overlap with but are not the same as how the same term is used in linguistics or in general discussion of language. Along with other technical terms describing effects that signs may produce, including "dilution", "blurring" and "tarnishment", as well as nonce terms favoured as professional shorthand by counsel and judges (such as "side by side use" or "double identity"), such words create the apparatus through which trade marks are conceptualised and classified.

An important field of commercial language behaviour is in this way legally regulated by means of a conceptual framework which differs significantly from any corresponding terminology or approach in linguistics or related fields. It is unsurprising, therefore, that the language of trade marks should not only interest lawyers but also linguists, including professional linguists who in some jurisdictions are engaged as expert witnesses in trade mark disputes.

This chapter describes the interaction that has taken place between law and linguistics on the subject of trade marks. We begin with a summary of the main

---

[1] Barton Beebe and Jeanne Fromer, in a recent (2018) article we discuss below, estimate that by the end of 2016 there were over 2 million active trade mark registrations on the (US) Patent and Trademark Office's register, of which more than 95% included text and more than 75% consisted only of text (Beebe and Fromer 2018:956-7) As far as we are aware, no equivalent data are available for UK marks.

legal measures governing verbal signs used as marks, taking European Union trade mark law as our main reference but introducing US law where appropriate. We then describe how courts address language-related questions in particular, and ask how compatible the understanding of communication relied on in trade mark law is with accounts developed in linguistics. Highlighting both commonality and contrast, we examine the contribution made to trade mark law by linguists in two major traditions: an applied linguistic tradition of expert evidence, illustrated below principally by the work of US linguist Roger Shuy; and an interdisciplinary tradition of efforts to understand trade marks in semiotic terms, illustrated by an influential article by US legal scholar Barton Beebe (Beebe 2004). We then consider some "intermediate" studies between linguistics and trade mark law: studies which use linguistic scholarship to support arguments for changes in the law. In these sections, our illustrations are concerned with the work of US scholars who have paid most attention to linguistic issues in trade mark law. We go on, however, to explore how far similar insights might illuminate approaches taken by the European courts and the challenges they face. We conclude by asking how linguistic contributions to trade mark law might develop through further collaboration between lawyers and linguists.

2 Trade marks: the legal context

Before exploring areas of overlap between trade mark law and linguistics, we should introduce the main sources of trade mark law itself, as well as key economic and social assumptions that have determined its scope.

The degree of protection afforded to registered trade marks is determined by a combination of national, regional and international legislation. The Paris Convention[2] ensures among other things that foreign nationals have a right to register their marks on the same terms in any Convention country as any national of that country. The TRIPS agreement (1994),[3] which derives from the WTO (World Trade Organisation), sets out minimum standards for national or regional protection of trade marks. In the European Union (EU), a process of harmonisation of trade mark law has taken place between Member States; so final interpretation of trade mark law in this jurisdiction falls to the European Court of Justice (now known as the CJEU, formerly the ECJ). In the United States, trade mark law is governed by a combination of the federal Lanham Act[4] and laws passed by individual states, although (as with EU trade mark law) such protection must be consistent with TRIPS and the Paris Convention.

---

[2] The Paris Convention for the Protection of Industrial Property, 1883 (as amended September 28, 1979). The Convention has 176 signatories.
[3] The Agreement on Trade Related Aspects of Intellectual Property Rights, 1994.
[4] The Lanham (Trademark) Act (Pub.L. 79-489, 60 Stat. 427, enacted July 5 1946, codifed at 15 U.S.C. 1051 et seq. (15 U.S.C. ch. 22))

International conventions set rules and minimum standards for registered trade mark protection. But protection is almost exclusively national in scope. A UK or German registration will protect a registered mark only within the borders of the UK or Germany; a US trade mark registered under federal law will only protect that mark within the US. There are nevertheless some exceptions to this principle. These include the European Union Trade Mark (EUTM), whose protection extends across the European Union as a whole,[5] and signs protected under the Madrid Protocol,[6] whose protection covers signatory countries.

In most jurisdictions, it is also possible for businesses to claim protection for marks which have not been registered. In the UK and to some extent in the US, the law of passing off will prevent misleading use by a third party of an unregistered trade mark which has become distinctive of a particular business. In passing off cases, however, what the law seeks to protect is not the trade mark as such, nor primarily the interest of consumers, but the goodwill of the business which might be harmed by third-party use, for example through loss of sales or damage to reputation. The labelling by a leading supermarket of a chocolate bar which was not made in Switzerland as SWISS CHALET (together with a picture of a Swiss chalet)[7] was for instance held to be a misrepresentation which would damage the goodwill of Swiss chocolate producers. Although consumers who attribute desirable qualities to "Swiss chocolate" would be the direct victims of such a misrepresentation, it was not their interests that were at the centre of the action but those of Swiss producers. In addition to passing off measures, unfair competition laws in many jurisdictions (including continental Europe and the United States) can protect unregistered trade marks from unauthorised use by third parties. The main aim of this area of law is to protect the public at large, as much as the first user of the mark. Finally, consumer protection laws designed to prevent conduct harmful to consumers may protect unregistered marks if those marks are used deceptively.

The relevance of this general context is that, in contrast with the protection of unregistered marks, what the registered trade mark regime is designed to protect is not the business goodwill which the trade mark represents but the trade mark itself.

---

5 Decisions on the registration of an EUTM (formerly a CTM) are taken by the EUIPO (formerly the OHIM) in Alicante. A decision may be appealed to the Opposition Division, the Board of Appeal, and then to the General Court, before finally to the CJEU. The EUTM is regulated by Regulation (EU) No. 2015/2424 of the European Parliament and of the Council of 16 December 2016.
6 Protocol Relating to the Madrid Agreement Concerning the International Registration of Marks (as amended on November 12, 2007). On English and European trade mark law, see Aplin and Davis (2017); and Waelde, Brown, Kheria & Cornwell (2016).
7 *Chocosuisse Union des Fabricants Suisses de Chocolat v Cadbury Ltd* [1998] ETMR 205. Throughout the chapter we present signs used as marks (whether registered or not) in uppercase. This is not a fully satisfactory convention, in that some marks are distinguished in part by whether any, some or all their letters are in uppercase or lowercase (e.g., "AquaPerfect"); also, many verbal marks are registered in a "figurative" form, being distinctive partly on the basis of their font, colour and other aspects of design.

This major difference makes linguistic investigation of such marks far more pertinent. Unlike unregistered trade marks, which can generally only be transferred between businesses along with attendant goodwill, registered marks can be licensed or sold without the underlying business.[8] When that happens, although the registered trade mark is understood as a badge of origin it may in fact communicate very little about the origin of goods or services on which it is placed. The mark might, for example, represent the business of the retailer of such goods, as with a supermarket's own brand products. Or it may have been acquired by a company which bears no direct responsibility for producing the goods that carry the mark. An example of this second possibility is the multinational drinks corporation Diageo, whose trade marks include JOHNNY WALKER for Scotch whisky, GUINNESS for stout, and VEUVE CLIQUOT for champagne. In terms of production, a single developing-world factory may manufacture clothing that will carry a number of different, in some cases world-renowned trade marks.

Protection of trade marks by means of registration is of primary benefit to a proprietor. But the justifications most commonly given for trade mark protection go beyond that narrow interest. Protection of a registered trade mark functioning as a badge of origin is claimed both to reduce consumer search costs and to ensure the quality of goods. These effects follow because such costs will be reduced if the proprietor maintains a good and consistent quality over time. Registration, it follows, encourages producers to expend on quality; and consumers will be willing to pay a premium price for trade-marked goods because they gain the benefit of known quality (Landes and Posner 1987). These advantages would be lost if the trade mark ceases to act as a badge of origin.

Sometimes a trade mark is recognised as carrying additional messages apart from indicating the origins of the goods. For instance, it may serve as a vehicle for other attractive qualities which attach to those goods or services. In such circumstances it is proprietors' interests which are paramount in granting protection. In an early EU trade mark case, *Arsenal Football Club v Reed*, it was suggested by the Advocate General that a distinctive mark might indicate not just quality but also reputation, as well as the renown of the producer or even "a way of seeing life".[9] In order for such effects to be conveyed by a trade mark, the proprietor may have had to make a considerable investment in building particular ways of perceiving or understanding the mark, an investment that may also be deemed worthy of protection against those who would seek to free ride on it.

Increasingly EU trade mark law has been interpreted as designed to protect such additional meanings, which go beyond the earlier role of a mark as purely an indication of origin. Such additional meanings contribute to what are referred to as "brand values";

---

8 Many registered trade marks acquire wider meanings beyond being perceived solely as a badge of origin. Arguably, these meanings attach as much to the underlying business as to the mark, and are sometimes referred to as "brand values". To this extent, they share something in common with the idea of goodwill.

9 *Arsenal Football Club plc v Reed* (Case C-206/01 [2002] ECR I-10273 at AG 46.

and some of the complexity surrounding verbal trade marks, both from a linguistic and a legal perspective, arises from those extra meanings. The CJEU has acknowledged such meanings in a number of decisions. For example, in *Sigla SA v OHIM* the General Court identified other "messages" that a mark might convey as: "...luxury, lifestyle, exclusivity, adventure, youth"; and the Court went on to acknowledge that such messages can exist independently of goods or services to which they attach.[10] Recently, the CJEU has gone further, suggesting that as well as acting as a badge of origin trade marks may serve further functions including communication, investment and advertising. Perhaps of most interest to linguists is what has been called the "communication function". As yet, however, the CJEU has not elucidated precisely what "communication function" means, beyond a mark's ability to reflect the quality of goods on which it is placed or to act as an advertising tool. Nevertheless, recent judicial focus on the sign's various meanings beyond that of an indicator of origin, and on its multiple functions, accentuates the potential importance and relevance of approaches seeking to understand such phenomena, such as approaches based on linguistics and semiotics.

3 Trade mark law: provisions which raise questions about language

What legal measures within this general framework are most relevant in understanding language use in this area of law? The answer lies in a number of important details.

The EU Trade Marks Directive (TMD)[11] defines a registerable sign as "any sign capable of being represented graphically which is capable of distinguishing the services of one undertaking from those of other undertakings". A trade mark may consist of a word or combination of words, but it may alternatively consist of a shape, colour, sound or even a smell (or some combination of any or all of these), as long as it can be represented graphically in a manner which is "clear, precise, self-contained, easily accessible, intelligible, durable and objective", and capable of acting as a badge of origin.[12] The new Trade Mark Directive has dropped the necessity for graphic representation, in part to accommodate more easily non-verbal or visual signs, such as for example smell marks.

---

10 *Sigla SA v Office for Harmonisation in the Internal Market* (Trade Marks and Designs) (OHIM) (EU.T.2007:93).
11 First Council Directive 89/104/EEC, 21 December 1988, to approximate the laws of the Member States relating to trade marks, codified as Directive 2008/95/EC. The codified version contains an annexe (Annex II) which tabulates correspondence between the 1989 and 2008 directives. There is now a new Trade Mark Directive: Directive (EU) 2015/2436 of the European Parliament and of the Council to approximate the laws of Member States relating to trade marks (Recast).
12 *Siekmann v Deutsches Patent-und Markenamt* (Case C-273/00) [2002] ECR I-11737.

The distinctiveness of a sign, including its capacity to act as a badge of origin in relation to the goods and services against which it is registered (as classified according to the 1957 Nice Classification, which divides products and services into categories),[13] is judged, like so much else in trade mark law, through the eyes of the "average consumer", who is deemed to be "reasonably well informed, reasonably observant and circumspect". It is assumed that such a consumer will be the average consumer for the goods or services for which registration is sought, and further assumed that the consumer will consider the mark as a whole and not break it down into constituent parts. For example, it was held that the sign SAT.2 for satellite dishes might be distinctive even though SAT on its own might not.[14] A distinctive mark might in principle be as short as one letter (e.g., the Greek character "alpha", for beer),[15] or as long as a slogan such as I CAN'T BELIEVE IT'S NOT BUTTER! for margarine.[16]

In principle, signs in different media are treated equivalently. A verbal mark may be initially distinctive either because it is an invented word, such as KODAK, or because it consists of a word or combination of words which bear no relation to the goods or services against which those words are used; a common example of this given by the UK courts is NORTH POLE for bananas. Some marks may also be distinctive if they are merely suggestive of the goods or services against which they are registered: for instance, AIRBUS for a passenger airplane. Conversely, a sign will not be registered if it is judged to lack distinctiveness, or if it is held to be descriptive, or if it is common to the relevant trade. An example of a non-distinctive mark might be a common name such as NICHOLS for retail services, or a slogan such as TAKE A BREAK for chocolate bars. A descriptive mark might be a geographic name, or even a neologism such as DOUBLEMINT for gum, created out of two descriptive words.[17]

Signs which may for any of those reasons initially lack a capability to act as a badge of origin may nevertheless acquire distinctiveness as what is called a "secondary meaning" over time and through use on the market. Once again, the measure of acquired distinctiveness will be whether the mark in question is perceived as a badge of origin by the average consumer for the relevant goods and services. Conversely, a registered trade mark may be declared invalid if it is shown to have lacked distinctiveness at the time of registration. Or it can be revoked if it has become deceptive or generic over the period since registration. Most famously, both aspirin and the trilby hat lost trade mark protection by becoming generic.

---

13 The Nice Agreement concerning the International Classification of Goods and Services for the Purposes of the Registration of Marks (1957), administered by WIPO (the World Intellectual Property Organization).
14 *SAT.1 Satellitenfersehen GmbH v OHIM* (Case C329/02) P [2004 ECHR I-8317.
15 *BORCO-Marken-Import Matthiesen* (Case C 265/09) [2011] E.C.R. I-8265.
16 Registered as a UK trade mark by Unilever in 1990 for margarine and other spreads.
17 *OHIM v Wm Wrigley Jr Company* (Case C-191/01) P [2003] ECR I-12447.

The principle that an initially non-distinctive trade mark may be registered on proof of distinctiveness acquired through use betrays the neo-classical economic underpinnings of the TMD. It also impacts on what had traditionally, in some jurisdictions, been a protected public domain or "commons" of non-proprietary words and other signs. Prior to the TMD, in many jurisdictions including the UK and Germany trade marks would not be registered even if they were distinctive, if they were also marks that other traders might wish to use. Thus, HAVE A BREAK for chocolate bars was denied registration in 1983 because at that time the court held that, in a period when an increasing number of people "snacked", the phrase HAVE A BREAK would be valuable to other traders. But HAVE A BREAK was successfully registered in 2007, following implementation of the TMD and after lengthy litigation, on the basis that it had acquired distinctiveness through use (Davis and Durant 2015). Obviously some words may be descriptive or non-distinctive in one context but not in another, depending on the type of goods against which they are registered. An example would be use of CARIBBEAN for bananas and for skiing equipment: based on the reasoning above we can assume CARIBBEAN would not be registered without evidence of acquired distinctiveness for bananas but would be seen as inherently distinctive in relation to skiing equipment.

Another reason a sign will not be registrable (a so-called "relative ground", one of the TMD's "further grounds for refusal or invalidity concerning conflicts with earlier rights"), is if it conflicts with an earlier registered mark. There are several grounds for such conflict; some require proof of consumer confusion and some do not. The grounds are important because, with a few exceptions, they also constitute the basis for infringement actions. An identical sign used on identical goods (so-called "double identity") will be barred from registration or, if used on the market, may be found to have infringed an earlier mark even without proof of consumer confusion. In such circumstances it is difficult to suppose that the average consumer would not be confused as to the origin of the goods or services at issue.[18] In contrast with identical signs, similar signs used on similar goods (or identical signs used on similar goods, or similar signs used on identical goods) will only be refused registration, or found to infringe, if the average consumer is likely to be confused. Whether a likelihood of confusion exists depends on a host of factors including: visual, aural (phonetic), and/or conceptual similarity between the two signs; the degree of distinctiveness of the registered mark; how much attention will be paid to both the mark and the sign at issue by the average consumer (which will depend on the nature of the goods and how they are sold); and the degree of similarity between those goods. "Similarity", in

---

18 This situation has been complicated by recent CJEU decisions which have held that infringement depends on the use of the later sign affecting one or more functions of the registered trade mark including but not limited to its origin function. See for example, *L'Oreal SA v Bellure NV* [2009] (Case C-487/07) ECR I-5185.

such circumstances, is in part linguistic but as can be seen not exclusively a linguistic property of the signs at issue.

To take an example, in the case of *Picasso*[19] the proprietors of the PICASSO trade mark as used on automobiles objected to registration of PICARO, also for cars. The CJEU decided that, while PICASSO was a distinctive mark on account of the fame of the painter, it was not a distinctive mark for cars. In *BSH Bosch v OHIM*,[20] other factors were taken into account. In that case, the applicant sought to register the word AQUA-PERFECT as a EUTM for kitchen goods including washing machines. Its application was opposed by Bosch, which had the registered mark WATERPERFECT for many of the same goods, also including washing machines. In deciding whether the marks were similar enough to cause confusion, the EU General Court examined the following considerations: the level of attention exercised by consumers (high in relation to washing machines; not high in relation to daily kitchen goods); the degree of visual similarity, as the words were of similar length; the presence of phonetic similarity, in that the words had the same number of syllables, a common element "perfect" and first syllables of similar length and sound; and that there was conceptual similarity, as the marks had the same "semantic content" (the average EU consumer would know that *aqua*[21] was Latin for water and even non-English speakers would understand the meanings of *water* and *perfect*). In light of these similarities, and despite the fact that the earlier mark had only a weak distinctive character, being somewhat descriptive, the court held there was a likelihood of confusion.

Further forms of analysis may be introduced where registered marks convey messages that extend beyond their role as an indicator of origin. It is a commonplace, for example, that the meaning of a trade mark nurtured on one category of goods can transfer to others. The VIRGIN mark, which began life applied to sound recordings, has been registered for financial services, air travel and beverages, among other things. Virgin describes its mark as connoting "service quality", "fun", and "value for money", as well as "competence" and "rule breaking", all of which are connotations which relate substantially or wholly to commercial use of VIRGIN rather than to the word *virgin* as found in other contexts.[22] That a trade mark can embody such additional meanings is recognised by the TMD and also in the US, notably by the Trade Mark Dilution Revision Act (2006). Under the TMD a registered trade mark with a reputation (a category defined by the mark's degree of public recognition, taking into consideration factors including its market share, the intensity as well as geographical extent and duration of its use, and the scale of investment made by the undertaking in

---

19 *Ruiz Picasso v OHIM* (Case C-361/04 PO [2006] ECR I-643.
20 *BSH Bosch und Siemens Hausgerate GmbH v OHIM* (T-123/14) EU:T:2015:52; GC.
21 We follow the convention here of representing citation forms for words in italics and representations of meaning in quotation marks.
22 http://www.integratedbrands.org/brands/virgin/@@details. Compare the claimed associations with the dictionary meanings and symbolic associations conventionally associated with virgin.

promoting it) is protected against any attempt by a third party to register the same or a similar sign, or to make unauthorised use of the registered mark, if such use would take unfair advantage of or be detrimental to the distinctiveness or reputation of the registered mark. This is so even if the third-party sign is used in relation to dissimilar goods or services, and even if the average consumer would not be confused. In such cases the average consumer is taken to make a "link" between the registered mark and the sign, in that use of the later sign will "call to mind" the earlier registered mark.[23]

The overall purpose of these relatively recent prohibitions is to protect a registered mark not against confusion as to origin but against three other, potentially damaging consequences of commercial use by a third party if the consumer makes the relevant link. Each is legally defined but difficult to apply. First, trade marks with a reputation are protected against "dilution" of their distinctive character (sometimes referred to as "blurring"). For example, use of the sign BOTUMAX for pharmaceuticals was held to dilute the distinctiveness of the mark BOTOX for similar goods.[24] Second, marks with a reputation are protected against damage to that repute, as a result of use of the same or a similar mark on less desirable goods or services. This is known as "tarnishment", and an early example recognised by the Benelux court was the effect on the repute of the mark CLAERYN for gin by the use of the sign KLAREIN for toilet cleaner.[25] Thirdly, a proprietor might suffer damage as a result of another trader "free riding" on the repute of its registered mark. Notice that in this third category there is no damage to the mark as such: simply by attaching the registered mark to its own goods, a third party may be held to have appropriated attractive qualities from that mark without rewarding the proprietor who nurtured them. Thus, in *L'Oreal v Bellure*[26] the defendant used the names of L'Oreal's expensive perfumes to describe their own cheaper smell-alike scents. In this case, the defendant was found to be free riding on L'Oreal's carefully nurtured, exclusive reputation.

4 Contributions by linguists

The brief introduction we have given to the context and key provisions of trade mark law allows us now to address the question of how linguistic expertise has been brought to bear on this highly detailed legal framework. Linguists, we suggest, have engaged in dialogue with trade mark law and lawyers in two main ways. They have given expert evidence in trade mark cases; and they have sought to develop a more general semiotic understanding of how trade marks function. We introduce each

---

[23] *Intel Corp Inc v CPM UK Ltd* (Case C-252/07) [2008] WLR (D) 371 at 42/.
[24] *Farmeco AE Dermokallyntika v OHIM* [2010] ECLI:EU:T:458 (General Court).
[25] *Colgate Palmolive v Lucas Bols* (Claeryn/Klarein) [1976] IIC 420.
[26] *L'Oreal SA v Bellure NV* [2009] (Case C-487/07) ECR I-5185.

approach in turn; then we discuss some examples of work in which a more interdisciplinary approach to issues in trade mark law has been attempted.

4.1 Expert evidence in trade mark disputes

It is difficult to know exactly how widespread linguistic evidence is in trade mark cases. This is partly a result of differing admissibility considerations between jurisdictions, and partly because most cases settle before reaching court. Any expert evidence or advice that has been given will not form part of the public record if a settlement arrived at in advance of court proceedings is subject to a confidentiality agreement. What is clear, despite this, is that expert linguistic evidence is far more likely to be either adduced or admitted in US cases than in the UK or EU (or in most other jurisdictions).

This difference between jurisdictions is not new. US courts have always been more willing to admit empirical evidence of any description in trade mark cases than UK courts. In English law, in early cases a judge would frequently decide whether there had been an infringement (or make some other adjudication) based on his own assessment and without benefit of evidence. An interesting example of an early collision between that approach and the possibility of linguistic expertise can be found in the late nineteenth-century case *Harden Star Hand Grenade Fire Extinguisher Company's Trade Mark*,[27] in which the question for the court was whether the trade mark HAND GRENADE FIRE EXTINGUISHER was descriptive. The plaintiffs submitted an affidavit from a "philologist" (Mr. Henry Morley LL.D, Professor of English Literature at University College London) stating that the mark's four words were not "words of common use in the English language" and qualified as a "fancy" phrase. To counter this assertion, the applicant produced an affidavit by a Mr Silvanus Thompson, formerly Professor of Experimental Physics at University College Bristol, to the effect that the four words "formed an admirable description of the article, and that there was nothing fancy about them, and that they were purely descriptive" (134). According to the judge, Chitty J, this was the first time expert evidence had been adduced "to explain the English language". But he rejected that evidence, saying it was a matter of common sense and, by implication, a matter within the competence of the judge to decide. "This is not a question", he opined, "and I say this emphatically – for a grammarian or a philologist. It is a question of the ordinary fair meaning of the terms to any ordinary Englishman" (134).

The role of empirical evidence in trade mark cases has continued to be contentious, despite many examples of professional advice being given as well as occasional courtroom testimony. A relatively rare example of linguistic evidence in a UK trade

---

[27] RPC (1886) 3(9), 132-7.

mark case is the UK linguist Chris Heffer's testimony in *Bambino Mio v Cazitex*,[28] both at first instance and on appeal. While Heffer's evidence appears to have been sympathetically received, little was said in the report of one hearing, and nothing at all in the other, as to its legal significance. Such a tendency for linguistic evidence to be included in law reporting either only minimally or not at all may nevertheless be not so much a comment on its significance or otherwise as a reflection of the fact that trials follow multiple lines of legal reasoning; evidence given by expert witnesses may be subordinate to other steps of potentially greater legal importance.

Given a reluctance on the part of most English and European judges to admit linguistic evidence in trade mark cases, it is scarcely surprising that the most prominent linguistic experts in trade mark law have been Americans, in particular the US academics Roger Shuy and Ronald Butters (in an interview in 2010 the latter commented that trade mark cases amounted to about three quarters of his forensic linguistic consultancy work).[29] In our brief discussion below, first we exemplify the approach typically taken, illustrating our account from the work of Roger Shuy (whose *Linguistic Battles in Trademark Disputes* (2003) remains the most widely cited study in the field). Then we compare that general approach with three European cases which have decided the same kinds of question without the benefit of expert evidence.

Shuy's book discusses ten cases, reporting the author's involvement in trade mark litigation over approximately two decades. Of the ten cases, seven were reported in US law reports; and five, Shuy points out, involved an opposing linguistic expert. The core features of Shuy's approach emerge clearly in one case turning on whether use of the phrase HEALTH SELECTIONS, as the name of a new food product, infringed the trade mark HEALTHY CHOICE.[30] Shuy's analysis (2002:69–80) examines similarities and differences determining how far the two marks sound the same (phonetics), look the same (morphology, their word structure), and/or have similar meaning (semantics, explored through relative synonymy).

In assessing the sound structure of the disputed marks, Shuy draws attention to evidence given in an earlier trade mark case by another US linguist, Jerrold Sadock, involving the marks LITTLE DOLLIE and LITTLE DEBBIE for cupcakes. In that earlier case, Sadock had used a form of phonological analysis called distinctive feature analysis to demonstrate that the sounds of the two marks were only 13% different. Distinctive features are aspects of sounds that indicate the minimal contrasts between sounds systematically used in a language (Chomsky and Halle 1968). Structural analysis of such features (in effect, a grid of the components of consonants and vowels in the two marks) had allowed Sadock to provide a quantitative assessment of how far

---

28 *Bambino Mio v Cazitex* [2009] EWCA Civ 922
29 "Interview with Seemaab Naseem". Aston University: Centre for Forensic Linguistics.
30 *ConAgra Inc v Acme Commercial Corp*, US District Court for the District of Nebraska, Civil Action No 8: CV 91-119.

the two phrases resembled each other; and Sadock produced a detailed chart in court indicating the existence or absence of each specified feature. Following Sadock's example, Shuy reports that he produced an equivalent analysis and found the quantitative outcome similarly compelling. But he comments that, although the lawyers he was working with were impressed, they doubted whether such detailed presentation would be effective in court. So Shuy produced a simpler analysis, summarising the degree of difference in a manner likely to be more accessible to general, "ordinary" language users.

Among linguistic specialisms, it is worth noting that phonetic/phonological evidence is usually considered the most decisive in court. This is because the sound structure of language is scarcely accessible to untrained language users, while what language means (with exceptions in areas such as dialect, jargon, and words loaned from other languages) is often considered to fall within the normal competence of a language user, and certainly of a judge.

Meaning questions were nevertheless central in another case in which Shuy was called: *McDonald's Corporation v Quality Inns International*.[31] In that case, in which McDonald's alleged infringement by the hotel chain Quality Inns following the latter's decision to create a new brand, McSleep Inns, Shuy examined what he calls "the meaning of a patronymic prefix": effectively, what *Mc* means when used to create new compounds such as *McNugget, McFlurry,* and *Mcjob*.

As in virtually all litigation, the legal issues in *McDonald's* were wide-ranging. Shuy's linguistic contribution drew on collected corpora of language use, and combined dictionaries with a database of newspaper, magazine and media use as well as with use of *Mc* collected from relevant commercial sectors. His analysis prompted him to group together attested instances of the prefix into seven major types: proper names, alliterative patterns based on proper names, acronyms, McDonald's product names, Macintosh-related computer products, parodies of a fast food product or service, and other uses conveying more general meanings of "basic, convenient, inexpensive and standardised". Shuy acknowledged that it is not possible for a linguist to say exactly how consumers understand "Mc", stressing that he did not set out to answer that question. A linguist, Shuy emphasises, is concerned with language patterns which show what a word *can* mean, and therefore how consumers might be expected to understand it based on established conventions of use. Shuy contrasts this kind of evidence with survey evidence – commonly used in trade mark cases, in the US and sometimes in Europe – which reports what actual consumers have said about what they thought (for example whether they were confused, or whether sign X called sign Y to mind).

McDonald's prevailed in Shuy's case, and the court's reception of his evidence, as he recalled it later, reveals attitudes towards semantic analysis which differ from those shown towards phonetic evidence. Courtroom questioning mostly concerned

---

31 US District Court for the District of Maryland, Civil Action No. PN-87-2606.

method, especially how different senses associated with a word-form are divided up and grouped together, and so with how many meanings there are (a complicated and not fully scientific construct either in semantics or lexicography). Questioning related to those issues prompted further probing of how far divergent inferences as regards the meaning of "Mc" might be warranted by alternative linguistic approaches.

Two brief illustrations cannot of course do justice to Shuy's evidence; and the linguistic issues described here do not represent the only kinds of question explored in linguistic evidence either by Shuy or other linguists. Other issues have included the boundary between descriptive and imaginative or associative signs; the meaning of words transferred across languages (as in Heffer's UK evidence on an English-speaking consumer's likely understanding of the word *bambino*); and the significance of generic senses reported in dictionaries. Butters (2007) has also written on trade mark dilution, and in doing so summarised how, in his view, linguistic expertise can be useful in three main ways: by "providing evidence for the determination of one dimension of fame"; by "providing evidence with respect to the validity of the mark where genericness issues are raised by the defendants"; and by "determining the likelihood of blurring and tarnishment with respect to the phonological, morphological, and semantic characteristics of the mark" (Butters 2007:518). Butters describes these three concerns as still "rather conservative goals", suggesting that linguists could potentially also shed light on the nature of tarnishment by applying expertise sometimes brought to bear on alleged defamatory statements or by adapting how linguists assess whether trade marks violate federal trade mark law forbidding "immoral, deceptive, or scandalous matter; or matter which may disparage" (2007:518). These areas suggest a substantial forensic linguistic agenda for the future. Because linguistic consultancy in trade mark cases is often not written up, however, it remains unclear how much use has been made since the article was published of linguistic evidence of each of these kinds, or how far the wider aim Butters intimates – that of "shedding light on the nature of" tarnishment or other aspects of trade mark law (2007:518–9) – has been achieved.

4.2 European parallels and differences

US courts, we have said, tend to be more willing to admit linguistic evidence than European courts. Yet broadly equivalent issues arise in European cases, and are dealt with without assistance from linguists. A brief comparison with how European courts have addressed such issues may therefore help to focus the question whether, and if so how far, UK and European courts are disadvantaged by lack of expert linguistic evidence. We consider this issue by referring briefly to three cases; each appears initially to be primarily a matter of two verbal signs with disputed similarity in their form.

1. The 1999 case *Lloyd Schuhfabrik Meyer v Klijsen Handel* concerned whether the degree of similarity between the signs LLOYD and LOINT'S, for shoes, would lead to consumer confusion.[32] The CJEU held that it would, and that aural similarity between the two was sufficient to cause confusion even in the absence of visual or conceptual similarity. The Court's judgment was arrived at without expert assistance. An impressionistic judicial assessment was made of the view of the average consumer, with attention directed not only to similarity between the signs themselves but also to similarity between the types of product in question and the methods used in marketing them. Although the court's assessment did not draw on expert evidence, it still took account of sound patterns including: the same number of syllables; similarity of features between the two marks' final consonant clusters (with the possessive apostrophe "s" in "Loint's" disguising the base form *Loint* which is closer to LLOYD); and greater saliency attributed to similarity occurring at the beginning of the two marks rather than at the end. No doubt these similarities could have been described more precisely by linguists. But expert evidence on such linguistic characteristics could only have been introduced (if either side had applied to submit it) at the cost of greater procedural complexity and expense – both of these also being important considerations for the courts to assess in case management.
2. The 2014 case *Volvo v OHIM* involved more complicated linguistic argument.[33] The case concerned the disputed signs VOLVO and LOVOL for cars, and the General Court confirmed earlier decisions made in proceedings by the Opposition Division and the Board of Appeal, which had held that LOVOL was neither conceptually, visually nor aurally similar to VOLVO.[34] The Board of Appeal had presented its linguistic reasoning in detail. The complainant, Volvo, submitted that both signs contain five letters and both consist of combinations of the letters "v", "o" and "l". The capital letters "V" and "L", it contended, were both angular characters, so their geometric structure was also similar. Volvo further submitted that the marks had the same vowel sequence ("o" followed by "o") as well as a parallel A-B-A pattern in their consonants: one has v-l-v; the other l-v-l. At syllable level, Volvo stated that both marks are characterised by "vol" and "vo" "and/or their inversion". On pronunciation, it argued that (i) the syllables "vol", "vo" and "lov" have striking similarities; (ii) both signs repeat the vowel "o", which dominates the way each sign is pronounced; and (iii) both signs contain "the soft consonants 'l' and 'v'", which, when pronounced, "do not create any strong sounds". As regards conceptual comparison, Volvo expressed the view that it is

---

[32] *Lloyd Schuhfabrik Meyer & Co GmbH v Klijsen Handel BV* (Case C-342/97) [1999] ECR I-3819.
[33] *Volvo Trademark Holding AB v Office for Harmonisation in the Internal Market (Trade Marks and Designs) (OHIM)* (Case T-524/11) [2015] ETMR 10.
[34] All three of these courts, in turn, hear appeals from the EU IPO. Appeals from the General Court go to the CJEU.

impossible to compare the signs in question, since neither has a meaning in any EU language. It submitted nevertheless that consumers coming across LOVOL would be intrigued by a new mark for cars and would ask themselves whether that new mark had any connection with an old and highly reputed trade mark for cars; on that basis they would be led to associate LOVOL with VOLVO.

The Board of Appeal rejected those arguments. It acknowledged that the signs at issue shared four out of five letters but observed that those letters did not appear in the same order. On aural comparison, the Court found that the mere fact that the marks had the same number of syllables was of no importance. Rather, given the difference between the vowel sounds in both syllables of the respective signs (since the same letter "o" is pronounced differently on each of the four occasions it occurs), the marks were aurally dissimilar. Moreover, the signs differed in their initial letters ("v" and "l"), as well as in their first syllable ("vol" and "lo"). On this point the court noted that – according to case law, rather than citing linguistics – consumers normally attach more importance to the beginnings of words. Nor could Volvo base any valid argument on supposed similarity between the capital letters "L" and "V". On this point the court reasoned that, rather than looking for similarity, the average consumer instinctively contrasts letters of the Roman alphabet. Drawing on case law again rather than linguistics, the Board found it unlikely that the average consumer would divide the marks into their respective syllables so as to create an anagram and on that basis associate LOVOL with VOLVO.

Patterning by means of sound reversal or inversion was given particular attention. On Volvo's argument that the first syllable of LOVOL is a reversal of "vol", the Court noted that Volvo had not provided any example of an EU language according to whose rules the trade mark LOVOL breaks down into the syllables "lov" and "ol". On the contrary it stated that, according to the rules of many if not most EU languages, LOVOL analyses into the syllables "lo" and "vol". Volvo could therefore not validly argue that both marks are composed only of the syllables "vol", "vo" and "lov". Even assuming that the first syllable of LOVOL could be "lov", Volvo had not provided any evidence to substantiate its assertion that the average consumer would divide a short meaningless word into syllables and then read the first syllable backwards.

As can be seen, the Board's reasoning in this case (confirmed by the General Court) is attentive to detail and by no means linguistically naive, despite no expert linguists being called. At various points technical linguistic contrasts are invoked, for example how the letters "l" and "v" are articulated differently: "'l' is an alveolar consonant, whereas 'v' is a labiodental consonant". Sometimes linguistic concepts and terminology do falter, as for instance in this description of the VOLVO sign: "the juxtaposition of the consonants 'l' and 'v' means that the space between those sounds is slightly compressed, whereas, in the word LOVOL, the vowels and consonants are alternated, with the result that pronunciation of that word is more flowing. Consequently, the signs at issue have a different rhythm of pronunciation" (at paragraph 44). While legal and linguistic commentary relate awkwardly at some points, however, in general they appear complementary even where concerned with sound patterns which, we have noted above, tend to be the aspect of language most in need of specialist expertise.

3. Our third case, the 2015 case *Maier v ASOS*, also ostensibly turns on sound and visual similarity: between the marks ASSOS and ASOS applied to clothing.[35] At first instance, it was submitted that the public did not consistently distinguish between pronunciation of the two signs by using a long vowel (as in *stay*) for ASOS and a short vowel (as in *cat*) for ASSOS. During proceedings, Asos also accepted that ASOS was commonly misspelt as ASSOS, including in consumer search requests typed into Internet browsers. The judge, Rose J, held that there was both visual and aural similarity between the signs. She also accepted that the mark ASSOS was inherently distinctive, and that, although it did have a meaning in Greek ("best"), it did not have any descriptive meaning when used in connection with clothing.

What is striking in the official transcript of the Court of Appeal hearing, however (where the Court confirmed the lower court's judgment), is that only 4 out of 259 paragraphs (including Sales, LJ's dissent) are concerned with visual, aural and conceptual similarity between the two signs. The other 255 paragraphs deal with other issues between the parties, including the relation between the goods being marketed (general versus specialist cycling clothing), styles of marketing online, and respective market segments (upper versus popular), as well as the availability and merits of available defences.

Do these cases permit any more general comparison as regards the value of linguistic evidence regarding trade marks? While in each case similarity between verbal marks will understandably appear to linguists to be primarily a matter of the formal characteristics of the respective signs, for the courts – following a principle also embedded in a great deal of linguistic thinking, the requirement to analyse language use in context – similarity must be assessed in the context of the parties' business practices. It is not surprising therefore that in many cases the most important legal issues may be more concerned with provisions governing use of marks in particular kinds of commercial undertaking, or in their marketing contexts, than with their linguistic form. Potentially, expert linguistic evidence could have been submitted in any of the three cases we have discussed, if one of the parties had applied to do so and if the judge ruled such evidence admissible. But the legal value of such evidence would have depended on a variety of factors, including many concerned with language use in a given context rather than language form.

---

35 *Roger Maier, Assos of Switzerland SA v ASOS plc, ASOS. com Ltd* [2015] EWCA Civ 220.

4.3 Semiotic analysis of trade mark law

Expert linguistic evidence in trade mark disputes is not, we suggested above, the only context in which trade mark law has been of interest to linguists. We now illustrate another major approach, less concerned with judgments made by one particular court than with questions about how courts in general decide (and should decide) trade mark disputes. To illustrate this direction, we discuss the most influential exemplar of that approach: an influential article by US law academic Barton Beebe, "The Semiotic Analysis of Trademark Law" (Beebe 2004).

Beebe seeks to understand trade mark law as a whole, including the procedural and policy issues it raises, by bringing broad linguistic concepts to bear. His overall argument is that economic approaches to trade mark analysis (e.g., emphasising the efficiency-enhancing function of trade marks by reducing search costs and encouraging investment) have not succeeded in explaining satisfactorily either the crucial concept of trade mark "distinctiveness" or more recent notions such as trade mark "dilution". One of his aims, accordingly, was to develop a richer account of such concepts, by viewing trade mark law through the lens of semiotics. Beebe urges that the concept of distinctiveness should be reconceptualised as two (distinct) types: "source distinctiveness", denoting a trade mark's source-indicating capability; and "differential distinctiveness", a trade mark's degree of separation in terms of sound, form and meaning from other marks around it (this kind of distinctiveness he bases on the capability of formal contrasts to convey conceptual or evocative effects, and is not related to the badge of origin function).

The ambition of Beebe's arguments emerges most clearly from his historical account of trade mark law's development. But the consequences he claims are current. Beebe proposes that, in different circumstances, courts should assess different axes of a sign's functional potential: whether or not it possesses "source" distinctiveness, when evaluating its eligibility for protection against infringement; and how far a sign has "differential" distinctiveness, when what is in question is the scope of its protection against infringement. The theoretical basis for this proposal lies in early twentieth-century descriptions of how signs signify; indeed Beebe suggests that trade mark law has developed an almost parallel understanding of signs to that present in semiotic thinking.

Two established accounts of how signs function are juxtaposed in Beebe's article with judicial opinions in US cases and with theoretical scholarship on trade marks, including work by Schechter and Posner. The first, semiotic account is that developed by Ferdinand de Saussure; the other comes from the work of logician and polymath C. S. Peirce.

In a discipline-defining but now infrequently read series of lectures transcribed and edited after his death, Saussure (1983 [1916]) suggested that signs consist of two elements or aspects: a signifier (or formal material: for a trade mark, what is commonly considered the whole "sign" but what in Saussure designates more narrowly the verbal form or sound); and a signified (an idea or concept conveyed by association with that signifier). For Saussure, the two aspects were inseparable, like (in his famous image) the recto and verso of a sheet of paper. Communication, he argued, is made possible not by either aspect on its own but by the relations that signs consisting of these two aspects enter into. Saussure identifies two kinds of relation, hence Beebe's proposed two kinds of distinctiveness: a relation of "signification", in which a sign means something in the world (Saussure's example is that a five-franc coin can be exchanged for a loaf of bread); and a relation of "value", through which the sign takes its place in a system of contrasts with other signs around it (the five-franc coin is equivalent to five one-franc coins). Communication ulitises both kinds of relation. The sign's potential to refer to things in the world had of course been acknowledged for centuries; Saussure's innovation was to draw attention to how far meaning is produced by – and how much it depends on – the system or network of structural relations which creates the contrasts between signs. This aspect of Saussure's thinking (his other main achievement was to shift the emphasis of linguistics away from philological enquiry towards systemic, "synchronic" analysis) has been important, though also often challenged, in a great deal of subsequent thinking about meaning and more generally about the relation between language, thought and reality.

The second account of signs Beebe draws on comes from the work of C. S. Peirce. Peirce's model is sometimes called triadic, or triangular, because, as well as having a tangible symbol (signifier) and cognition produced in the mind (signified), Peirce also insisted on the importance of a third element: the thing referred to (the referent). Peirce's resulting model consists of a physical sign that creates a concept, with these two aspects in combination pointing to an extra-linguistic referent. Modern linguistics, it should be noted, is no longer so preoccupied with these fundamental characteristics of sign functioning, and typically describes the relations entered into by verbal signs in different terms, such as sense relations, denotation and connotation, and reference. But the nature of the sign has continued to play an important role in semiotics generally, as well as in literary and cultural theory.

Beebe's central insight in the article was to show how semiotic terminology can be used to describe many features of trade mark law, mapping legal developments onto how signs work in general. To simplify somewhat, he divides the history of trade mark signification into three phases: a "classic triadic structural relation of the trade mark"; a more recent "dyadic structural relation of the trade mark"; and an emergent phase of the "floating signifier and hypermark". The main difference between the three phases, Beebe suggests, concerns how the three elements of a semiotic sign, as described above, function in relation to one another.

In Beebe's "classic, triadic structural relation", the qualification of a word or symbol to function as a trade mark required three elements:
1. A tangible symbol or device (a signifier)
2. Use of that symbol as a mark by a manufacturer or seller of goods or services (those goods being the signifier's referent – though note here the complication of Saussure's relative lack of engagement with reference, as well as the difficulty in

trade mark law in distinguishing consistently between goods and the commercial undertaking as the sign's referent)
3. Performance of the function of identifying and distinguishing the goods from goods made or sold by others (in Beebe's conceptualisation, a signified combining the goods with their associated goodwill based on quality, reliability, etc.)

In describing this "classic" structure, Beebe draws attention to difficulties in such an account, including the risk of merging together product, producer, and goodwill in a reduced concept of a sign's "meaning". But a deeper instability in the three-way relation, he suggests, runs through the more recent development of trade mark law.

In Beebe's view, the "classic" three-part structure now coexists with a newer, "dyadic" structure in which the mark's function relates more to what is signified (goodwill, positive affect, resonance or evocation) than to any referent. Accompanying this second phase or structure, Beebe contends, is a new level of commodification of semiotic sign value, creating an "industrial production of social distinction" (2004:624) The kinds of social distinction in question are contrasts between associations (i.e., aspects of the signified) rather than qualities of a referent, the commercial source. If there is a material referent in this newer commercial structure, that referent is no longer a matter of producers or products but "the consumer himself". He/she is "the commodity-form about which the trade mark is designed to convey information" (2004:659).

Such weakening of the role of the referent in the nexus of producer and product was, Beebe maintains, already under scrutiny in Schechter's writing in the 1920s, in a commercial movement away from the "strict source" requirement associated with mediaeval guilds (when marking products could be a liability as much as an asset) towards an "anonymous source theory" reflecting modern modes of industrial production (Schechter, 1926–7). The outcome of such changes, Beebe argues, is that courts have now become willing to protect promotional extensions of trade marks far beyond their traditional source-denotative function. (2004:660).

Beebe's third phase, that of the "floating signifier and the hypermark", is more speculative. He notes that trade mark regimes continue to change in tandem with wider shifts in commerce and culture, and have become a system of marketing communication and consumer information in which a tangible mark (the signifier) may now only imply a signified that is "so indefinite or contested as to constitute an 'empty category'" (2004:667). Not only is there no identifiable referent, but the signifier is empty of connoted meanings of a kind that might underpin social distinction by appealing differently to different consumers. Beebe comments that in this phase, "There is only distinctiveness from, not of" (2004:669). Trade marks operate to achieve such "differential distinctiveness", or contrast with surrounding signs (Saussure's "value"), without any reference to a source (Saussure's "signification"); and consumers interpret trade mark signifiers in this altered marketplace as if the signs are designations of source without questioning whether they are, or giving any particular meaning to what "source" designation indicates.

Beebe extrapolates from this theoretical-historical analysis a series of arguments why courts should move towards decisions based on his two types of distinctiveness. He submits, for example, that dilution is concerned with differential distinctiveness rather than source distinctiveness: it occurs because, by being similar, two signifiers lessen each other's degree of contrast even where there is no issue of confusion. He also discusses the relation between trade mark tarnishment and dilution. In recent developments, Beebe contends, the trade mark signifier creates the goodwill it communicates, generally by means of what, echoing Schechter, he describes as "vast expenditures in advertising... which the courts concede should be protected to the same extent as plant and machinery" (2004:685). Extended protection granted to creating rather than reflecting goodwill, Beebe argues, is part of a contemporary trade mark landscape riven by contradictions.

4.4 The challenge of greater interdisciplinarity

We turn now to two directions in recent publications which attempt closer integration between trade mark law and linguistic analysis than either applied linguistic evidence or semiotic overview. The approaches we describe have in common that, in more concrete ways than Beebe's general semiotic account, they bring linguistic evidence and argument to bear in advancing critiques of particular trade mark law doctrines and in order to advocate legal changes. Together, the articles we describe might in this way be thought an "intermediate" direction for research.[36]

In a recent article, "Are we running out of trademarks? An empirical study of trademark depletion and congestion" (Beebe and Fromer 2018), Beebe and co-author Jeanne C. Fromer (2018) argue that two related phenomena, trade mark "depletion" and trade mark "congestion", threaten the ability of trade mark regimes to fulfil the policy objectives of promoting efficient and fair competition and minimising consumer search costs. Their article presents evidence of increased trade mark scarcity, and points to the likelihood in future of a shortage of suitable verbal signs for prospective trade mark proprietors to register and use.

To understand their research, it is necessary first to consider what trade mark depletion and congestion are. The term "trade mark depletion" refers to the using up, in relevant commercial fields, of available signs.[37] Trade mark law has typically presumed an inexhaustible supply of unclaimed, potential verbal trade mark signs that are likely to be as competitively effective as those already claimed. The authors submit that this is a testable empirical assumption and that it is incorrect. The supply of competitively effective marks, they argue, is exhaustible and has already reached

---

36 Possible such directions were influentially outlined and encouraged in Dinwoodie (2008).
37 The concept of trade mark "depletion" is first outlined in the US Supreme Court decision in *Qualitex Co. v. Jacobson Products Co.* 514 U.S. 159 (1995).

a severe level of scarcity, with the consequence that the overall ecology of the trade mark system is at risk.

The availability of potential trade mark signs is complicated, the authors assert, by the likelihood that some signs are more suitable for trade mark purposes than others. Marketers, for instance, urge that verbal marks should be short; and common words are also considered desirable by comparison with neologisms because their everyday use can impart feelings including familiarity and authenticity. Signs with such characteristics have also shown themselves to be easy to pronounce and recall, and are valued especially where a word's connotations reinforce a brand's message. Marketing experts also advise against descriptive words or phrases, because such signs will not be granted legal protection on registration as inherently distinctive. Would-be trade mark proprietors nevertheless often choose evocative signs in order to convey information about characteristics of the product, even at the risk of losing distinctiveness, in the belief that the leverage of recognition and recall may compensate for the need for additional investment in advertising to cultivate acquired distinctiveness. Such considerations reflect a general point: that, given limits to human cognition and communication, some signs enjoy a competitive advantage as trade marks over others.

"Trade mark congestion" describes a related process. Even if a mark is already registered, this fact does not preclude other undertakings from registering the same or a similar mark in connection with different goods or services. Many marks, Beebe and Fromer point out, have multiple registrants in different classes. By 2015, for example, there were according to their data over 100 active single-word US registrations for ACE across the Nice classes, owned by nearly 100 different registrants (Beebe and Fromer 2018:1012–3). Even where such "parallel use" of the same mark does not confuse consumers as to commercial source, it may diminish a given mark's distinctiveness by creating a potentially diluting or blurring effect.

In these circumstances new trade mark applicants are increasingly obliged to resort to less competitively effective marks. With almost every naturally occurring one-syllable word already claimed, commercial undertakings select longer signs or portmanteau (combined or blended) words, or strategically drop vowels or change spellings in existing words, or devise neologisms. The authors argue that such complexity and potential obscurity can lead to increased consumer search costs and contribute to an erosion of the public, linguistic domain.

To test their sense that serious problems surround the availability of verbal signs, Beebe and Fromer assess evidence that conflicts with the intuitive consensus about an unlimited supply of verbal signs. They examine all trade mark applications filed at the US Patent and Trademark Office from 1982 until 2015; they analyse registrations for the most frequently used words and surnames in American English by consulting COCA (the Corpus of Contemporary American English) and US Census data on the most frequently occurring names. They also scrutinise an original dataset of phonetic representations of word marks, in order to estimate scope for further user-friendly neologisms. Finally, because of the contemporary significance of Internet domain names, they assess registration data for domain names at the .com top-level.

The extensive empirical data they collected consistently show increased use of, scarcity in, and pressure on signs available for registration as marks. Applications and publication rates have varied by year but risen steeply overall, albeit with an increased rate of refusals because of impermissible similarity with already registered signs. Looking forward, the authors report on the availability of one-syllable neologisms, examining all combinations compatible with English sound patterns. In some Nice classes they report that half of all one-syllable possibilities have been claimed. Extending their analysis to likelihood of confusing similarity, the authors claim results are even starker. Since a word mark registration in a given class depletes not only the word it matches but also all similar words in the same class whose use would confuse consumers as to source, the authors argue that a full assessment of depletion should include not only identity but also non-identical similarity between claimed marks and the supply of possible new signs. Calculating relative distance between strings of letters by using a tool to count the number of operations (such as insertion, deletion, or transposition) required to transform one into another, the authors report that nearly all new signs based on frequent words would be confusingly similar with an active trade mark registration. Even as regards possible one-syllable neologisms, the authors show that over half of the most frequent syllables in American English have been claimed as one-syllable marks; and in their examination of top-level .com domain name registrations, the authors found almost complete saturation.

Beebe and Fromer conclude their article by turning to policy initiatives that might mitigate the effects of depletion and congestion they claim to have demonstrated. Among initiatives they discuss is variable pricing for registration in different fields, depending on level of congestion, in order to internalise costs that such registration imposes on competitors. Citing evidence that, among audited registrations over a two-year pilot period roughly half could not be verified as being in use as claimed, they also urge increased maintenance and renewal fees for trade marks, as well as a general tightening of enforcement procedures.

The other direction in recent scholarship we wish to draw attention to we can illustrate by reference to two related articles by US trade mark scholar Jake Linford.[38] Like Beebe and Fromer, Linford argues in favour of changes in trade mark law. His arguments, however, are not based, like theirs, on "big data" but on theoretical work on language change. Linford discusses how far analysis of "semantic shifts" (i.e., linguistic processes of meaning change) can illuminate the relationship between signs claimed as trade marks and goods to which they are attached. Linford's focus in each of the two articles we describe is an established category of verbal signs as

---

38 Linford, Jake. 2015a. A linguistic justification for protecting "generic" trademarks; Linford, Jake. 2015b. The false dichotomy between suggestive and descriptive trademarks.

understood in trade mark law: in one article, so-called "generic" marks, in the other "suggestive" (sometimes known as "imaginative" or "associative") marks. These two categories form part of what in US trade mark law is called the "Abercrombie scale" (or "spectrum"): an arrangement of different types of sign and their relation to goods promulgated in the case of *Abercrombie & Fitch Co. v. Hunting World, Inc.*[39] (The US categories broadly correspond to distinctions we described above in relation to UK and European law.)

The Abercrombie scale lists five categories of trade mark signs (or potential signs), which we illustrate here in relation to words or phrases: "fanciful" (made-up words, such as XEROX); "arbitrary" (words with no discernible connection between sign and the class of goods to which it is applied: our example for UK signs was NORTH POLE for bananas; Linford uses the standard but more problematic US example APPLE for computers)[40]; "suggestive" (signs where the goods are evoked imaginatively by the sign: Linford exemplifies this class by GLEEM and SKINVISIBLE, for toothpaste and cosmetics; an active mental leap is needed to connect sign with goods); "descriptive" (signs which identify characteristics or qualities of the goods; Linford's main example is SEALTIGHT, for fasteners); and "generic" (signs which name a category of goods within which the sign is proposed – inevitably unsuccessfully – as a source indicator for one particular supplier: Linford discusses the made-up examples COMPUTER for computers and HELICOPTER for helicopters, as well as, he argues more problematically, HOG initially for big and then specifically for Harley Davidson motorcycles).

The Abercrombie categories characterise types of relationship between sign and class of goods. They are not formal categories like phoneme or verb, or names for general tropes like metaphor or synecdoche. Although several of the relations do depend on figurative tropes which extend or transfer meaning (e.g. metaphor and metonymy), the categories also depend crucially, as we stressed above, on situations of commercial use for any given sign. What makes the categories a "scale" is that they represent an ordering of relations, such that, when a prospective mark is assessed, a judgment as to which category it is in has major legal and commercial consequences: the top three categories "fanciful", "arbitrary" and "suggestive" are all considered inherently distinctive, and so registrable on application; "descriptive" signs can only be registered on demonstration of acquired distinctiveness ("secondary meaning"), assessed by an analysis of commercial context; "generic"

---

39 *Abercrombie & Fitch Co. v. Hunting World, Inc.*, 537 F.2d 4, 9-11 (2nd Cir. 1976).
40 Seeking to register APPLE for computers is generally considered to create a homonym (two identical forms with no connection in meaning, and so an arbitrary relation between the two meanings: fruit and computer). Alternatively, however, the sign might in context be argued to convey metaphorical meanings, and polysemous extension: a computer might be viewed as "natural" like an apple, or a new beginning like "A is for Apple", or, especially if visualised with a bite taken out of it, the sign might symbolise digital entry into (Biblical) knowledge acquired from the tree of life.

signs, at the bottom, cannot be registered at all (even if acquired secondary meaning were shown).

In each of the two articles we consider, Linford links his discussion of a particular sign type to a doctrinal issue. In one of the articles (Linford 2015a), he urges an extension of possible protection, proposing a change to the US doctrine of "trademark incapacity" or "de facto secondary meaning" ("de facto" in this context means something like "legally insignificant"); the result would be that marks considered "generic" could be – as they now cannot be – granted protection as distinctive source indicators, if satisfactory proof were submitted of acquired distinctiveness. In the other article (Linford 2015b), Linford proposes a reduction in available protection, by withdrawing treatment of "suggestive" marks as inherently distinctive and instead requiring proof of secondary meaning in such instances, as for "descriptive" marks.

To understand Linford's arguments, it is necessary to consider further the relationship between the Abercrombie scale and semantic change. A trade mark is created, Linford suggests, when a "source identifying" meaning is added to an existing word (or phrase), or when a word is invented to identify the commercial origin of a product. Where the sign in question is already in use in the language, then its existing meaning or meanings are extended and it becomes polysemous; where a neologism is created, then its source-indicating meaning is its first and only meaning.

What is important for Linford is that distinctions made in the Abercrombie scale appear mostly to align with mechanisms of "semantic shift"; and in areas where there appear to be discrepancies between the two he urges that trade mark treatment of signs should be reconfigured so that it better reflects wider, demonstrated principles of language change. "Generic" signs, he points out in the article on this category of signs, have in many instances in the history of languages undergone semantic narrowing (to a prototypical or particular instance); so there should be no obstacle in registering formerly generic signs as trade marks where the narrowing change of meaning can be demonstrated to a satisfactory standard. "Suggestive" signs in the Abercrombie scale, he argues in the article on a "false dichotomy" between "suggestive" and "descriptive signs", are in processing terms more similar to "descriptive" signs than they are to "arbitrary" signs; both, he suggests, are typically polysemous (either by metaphorical or metonymic transfer); and signs with these properties have been shown in experimental studies to enjoy processing advantages that result in easier recognition and recall by comparison with (homonymic) signs, where there is no link between a sign's earlier meaning and its new meaning. Extrapolating from experimental modelling of language change mechanisms to trade mark use, Linford concludes that allowing registration of suggestive signs because they are assumed to be inherently distinctive confers an unjustified advantage on them, as well as an anti-competitive commercial advantage on the undertaking which owns them.

This account of Linford's arguments inevitably simplifies greatly the author's engagement with semantic theory and trademark doctrine.[41] But it does illustrate the speculative character of the two articles, and may be useful in highlighting difficulties to be faced by anyone seeking to progress such lines of research in the future. Four areas of difficulty are worth noting. First, although the Abercrombie categories are often described as forming a "scale", suggesting step-changes at relevant borderlines (albeit with inevitable fuzzy borderline disputes), they are also, as Linford notes, alternatively viewed as a "spectrum": this alternative description foregrounds how far signs within a given category range in semantic space between adjacent categories and may differ considerably from each other as well as from signs in other categories. Secondly, pairings of signs and categories of goods are generally not made in trade mark law entirely in the abstract; both for registration and infringement purposes they are modulated, for the sign by its particular design, juxtaposition and use and for the goods by particulars of commercial context. Third, transfer of ideas from principles of semantic change to trade mark doctrine is a bold step, both theoretically (from descriptive linguistic reconstruction, through psycholinguistic experiments, to normative application to processes of naming) and practically (from naturally occurring language change to commercial naming and regulation). Fourthly, the metalanguage currently shared by trade mark law and linguistics may not be adequate to support the necessary linkages of argument between fields. The idea of "meaning", to take one key example, is difficult to apply consistently unless distinctions are made at least between denotation, connotation, and reference, and unless it is also shown how such distinctions are to work in relation to naming. Further, if an analogy is to be made between "efficiency" of language change mechanisms (or of "communication" more generally) and efficiency in consumer search costs, then more nuanced terminology and attention to contexts of use is likely to be needed. So too with the attractive-sounding "regular" semantic change, which like many terms already in use in trade mark metalanguage is linguistically both polysemous and vague, and could mean "consistent and rule-governed", "periodic", or even just "usual and ordinary".[42]

---

41 In the course of the two articles, Linford brings together late nineteenth-century philological accounts of semantic change (including Bréal's celebrated classification of mechanisms such as sense widening, narrowing, amelioration and pejoration), with later developments in semantics ranging from Ullmann through to cognitive semantic accounts such as Blank's (1999) typology of motivations for lexical semantic change, Klepousniotou's (2002) comparison between the processing of homonymy and polysemy, Croft and Cruse's (2004) analysis of construal processes, and the 'invited inference' theory of regularity in semantic change developed in Traugott and Dasher (2005). For detailed discussion of such semantic approaches, see Geeraerts (2010).
42 At the very beginning of their study, Traugott and Dasher (2005) point out that not all areas of the lexicon show the same degree of regularity in semantic change. Most irregularity, they note, occurs in fields where words ("primarily in the nominal domain") are exposed to "reference and therefore to changing life-styles and ideologies". Such words are scarcely subject to regular models of language change because they are "particularly susceptible to extralinguistic factors such as change in the nature or the social construction of the referent." (Traugott and Dasher 2005: 3-4).

5 What role for linguistics in trade mark law?

The various directions in established and newer linguistic approaches to trade marks that we have outlined differ not only in aims and method, but also in strategy: in how they seek to engage with and inform trade mark law's procedures and institutions. The "expert evidence" approach is essentially a kind of applied linguistics. It offers expertise in particular cases and stays within that expertise by remaining detached from legal procedures and reasoning. In contrast, "semiotic" and more fully interdisciplinary approaches urge dialogue between linguistics and trade mark jurisprudence but remain problematic, we suggest, in connecting generalisations with specific legal issues under debate. While all the approaches offer insights into how trade mark signs work, none in its present form offers a fully satisfactory way forward as regards longer term collaboration between lawyers and linguists.

Turning from analysis and critique towards our own suggestions for fresh lines of enquiry, we now consider whether there might be more fruitful ways to address the sorts of questions and problems in trade mark law we have described. One way of framing the issues we see as important is to acknowledge that both legal and linguistic analysis of trade mark signs occurs in three related conceptual areas (areas we differentiate from stages in legal proceedings such as registrability assessment and infringement litigation). In each, the approaches taken by the respective disciplines parallel each other but never fully coincide. To this extent, engagement between the two disciplines is arguably still as much a non-encounter as an encounter.

The three conceptual areas, or domains of enquiry, we have in mind are: (i) analysis of formal features and meanings of particular signs used as marks; (ii) generalisation or idealisation of sign interpreters' /consumers' perceptions and behaviour; and (iii) appeals to empirical evidence. We consider each separately, and inevitably very briefly.

5.1 Analysis of signs used as marks

It would be impossible for trade mark registrars and courts to avoid borrowing words and categories from general and more technical linguistic usage to identify and compare the verbal phenomena they are examining (e.g. consonants, vowels, and syllables; or parts of speech and basic grammatical relations). Familiar metalinguistic categories of this kind may be considered "ordinary words of English" rather than legal terms of art and are often used, at least as viewed from a linguistic perspective, imprecisely or even incorrectly by the courts. Such categories are defined more exactly in linguistics than in law, and are subject to theoretical investigation as parts of the language system. For the courts' descriptive purposes, however, special expertise in using such terms seems unnecessary in most cases (e.g. it is possible to know sufficiently that the four sounds made by the one letter "o" in the two signs VOLVO and LOVOL differ from one another without phonemic categorisation). Labelling the properties of signs more precisely might help clarify discussion, but it brings significant disadvantages of cost and complexity; so there seems good sense in a legal presumption that assessing the relative similarity or difference between the features of marks encountered in a supermarket or car showroom should be kept as simple as possible (particularly because commercial setting may have an impact on how the respective signs are perceived).

There are two other kinds of terminology, however, that invite greater interdisciplinary interest. Less familiar, more interpretive concepts are sometimes used in trade mark analysis including "neologism", "loan-word", "figurative", "connotation", and "parallelism". The characteristics, use and consequences of such categories seem less clear. These are no longer ordinary words of English in any ordinary (rather than legal) sense, and appear to have become legal terms of art, though only in the sense of being terms only decipherable by lawyers and not subject to other scrutiny rather than because they have clear definitions or standards of use. Beyond such categories there are also complex legal constructs such as "visual, aural and conceptual similarity", a compound which includes estimation of degree and processes of combination and balancing in creating a more impressionistic global assessment.

Faced with such an array of terms and associated concepts, some linguists have urged that trade mark lawyers and linguists should work together to define terms, so that relevant terminology is translatable between the two fields. This, it might be argued, could lead to increased procedural clarity and legal certainty. As many of the examples above suggest, however, many language-related terms in trade mark law are not purely metalinguistic; they combine linguistic meaning with other characteristics: e.g. a specific contextual relation (a connection between sign and class of goods); a wider contextual relation (use of a sign within specialised marketing practices of a given field of commerce); and a normative implication (the legal consequence for a sign of falling inside or outside a given linguistic-legal category, such as being "distinctive"). Legal application of such concepts requires combined linguistic and commercial assessment, within a precisely specified legal framework. Linguistic research into such terms and concepts, both in general and as applied in particular cases, needs accordingly to be an interdisciplinary form of investigation.

5.2 How consumers perceive and construe signs

A similarly complicated interface is to be found between linguistic and legal thinking in our second area. To appreciate the significance of this area, it is necessary first to say more about the average consumer, who in European trade mark law is assumed to be reasonably well-informed, reasonably observant and circumspect (and whose US cousin has been attributed similar characteristics: "the ordinary purchaser in the exercise of ordinary care and caution in such matters").[43] Assigning interpretive authority to a generalised consumer in this way inevitably involves idealisation: an act of abstraction towards selected characteristics based on potentially quite different alternative processes, including generalisation from the behaviour of observed consumers; normative assessment derived from a general theory or value system, related in this case to consumption; and creation of a legal construct for reasons of procedural efficiency.

Viewed from the perspective of how the idealisation is made the average consumer in trade mark law hovers between different conceptions. The average consumer is average for the classes of goods to which the sign in question relates rather than general across all marketing situations, and pays greater or less attention to different kinds of purchase. Recently, the CJEU has also identified a second average consumer: the average internet user, who is assumed to have the same characteristics as the original but with more or less actual knowledge of how websites function.[44] Both online and in the real world, the average consumer is presumed to be a rational market actor: a utility-maximizing individual able to process information in order to make the most advantageous choice (Davis 2005).

Trade mark signs are viewed as one element of the information available to the average consumer in making rational choices. When that average consumer is deciding how verbal signs look or sound, however, or what they mean or what other signs they link to or call to mind, these characteristics are inevitably supplemented with other, tacit linguistic and psychological assumptions that do not take the form of standards (such as "reasonably well-informed" or "circumspect") but are specific capabilities or behaviours, including noticing, inferring, comparing, and linking. Those linguistic and psychological capabilities contribute to being "circumspect" or "reasonably well-informed", but cannot be derived from any normative category. In assessing how the average consumer might react in specific circumstances without recourse to evidence, frequently legal authorities simply put themselves in the place of the average consumer. They did so for example when a EUTM registration was sought for SOLVO for computer programs and was opposed by the proprietor of VOLVO for automobiles. The General Court assumed that the average consumer of SOLVO software would be a "professional" who would "scrupulously" examine the software and possibly even meet the provider's employees. On that basis, the average consumer would be unlikely to be confused.[45] Alternatively however, it might be argued that an understanding of the capabilities or behaviours that the relevant average consumer brings to bear can only be derived either from actual evidence in specific cases, or from what is understood through idealisations made in other fields about how people behave, for example how they see and interpret signs, or compare and recall them. It is therefore an interesting

---

43 *McLean v Fleming* 96 U.S. 245, 24 L. E.
44 *Google France Sarl v Louis Vuitton Mallettier* (Case C-236/08-238/08) [2010] E.C.R. I-2417 at 99.
45 *Grebenshikove v OHIM* (T-394/10) [2014] ETMR 22 at 35-36.

research problem how behaviours and capabilities involved in trade mark law relate to equivalent idealisations made about communicative behaviour in linguistics.

Linguistics does of course have its own forms of idealisation about language users. But such idealisations are devised in relation to the field's own research goals, rather than concerned with the characteristics or kind of behaviour attributed to the average consumer. There may as a result be little to be gained by referring to present linguistic idealisations in trying to understand how verbal signs used as trade marks are perceived and understood. This point can be illustrated by reference to the most well-known linguistic idealisation, Chomsky's concept of linguistic competence in generative grammar; in that context, idealisation refers to a native speaker's knowledge of language as a system of rules such that he or she can produce and understand an indefinite number of sentences, many never formulated or heard before, and can recognise grammatical mistakes and ambiguities (Chomsky 1965). Linguistic competence understood in this way relates ultimately to a research claim about linguistic innateness, and differs fundamentally from the kind of behavioural generalisation involved in the idea of the average consumer. It is true that a less obviously dissimilar idealisation was put forward in sociolinguistics soon after Chomsky, in Hymes's notion of communicative competence (Hymes 1966), an idealisation based not only on grammaticality as in Chomsky but modelling the ideal speaker/hearer's knowledge that permits production and comprehension of utterances appropriate to the setting or context in which they occur (i.e., a concept of competence that incorporates social determinants such as the relationship between speaker and hearer and the time and place of speaking). What seems clear, however, is that neither form of linguistic idealisation aligns easily with the very different abstraction involved in the legal concept of the average consumer. While incompatibility between legal and linguistic generalisations may have little practical consequence in law – where judges will almost certainly continue, in most instances, to decide what the average consumer's view would be based on impression or their own example – it raises new and interesting interdisciplinary possibilities as regards how far linguistics or psychology might contribute to understanding "average consumer" assessments.

5.3 Appeal to empirical evidence

Both trade mark law and linguistics place a high value on evidence, but not necessarily evidence of the same things, or for the same purpose, or discovered by the same methods. In European law, the CJEU has made it clear that empirical evidence such as the extent of use of a mark and consumer opinion polls may be deployed in helping to decide whether or not a mark is distinctive in the eyes of the average consumer. But there is a difference in this respect between the treatment of distinctiveness and of confusion. In UK cases concerned with confusion, the courts have generally treated the average consumer as a "hypothetical legal construct", about whose views the court can "make up its own mind" without the necessity of "counting heads". In *Hearst Holding v AVELA*, Birss, J gave a pithy description of the relationship between the average consumer and the test for confusion. He noted that the parties to the case were agreed that the average consumer "is a legal construct and that the test is to be applied objectively by the court from the point of view of that constructed person. The word "average" denotes that the person is typical. The term "average" does not denote some form of numerical mean, mode or median."[46] Less frequently, the courts will accept that likelihood of confusion is a matter of individuals whose views might be measured by empirical evidence, including opinion polls (Davis 2015). But generally they take the view that empirical evidence of confusion is expensive to gather and rarely probative.[47]

In this context, it is worth asking what kinds of linguistic evidence would demonstrate best how far the courts' decisions could be assisted by linguistic expertise, either in addition to or instead of the kinds of survey evidence more readily admitted at present. Such evidence could potentially take a number of different forms (leaving aside evidence from introspection, i.e. searching one's intuitions for examples and counterexamples in relation to a particular linguistic claim). Linguistic evidence might consist of any one or a combination of the following:

1. Acoustic, experimental phonetic, and theoretically derived phonological evidence (as regards how words are pronounced, including the pronunciation of trade mark neologisms; or regarding the relative saliency of first and subsequent syllables in words).
2. Corpus linguistic searches for tokens of a given word or phrase, to establish frequency-of-use, common collocations, or comparison with use of the same or other signs. Such investigation could potentially help to show, as Heffer tried to, whether the word *bambino* is used in English often enough and in suitable circumstances to make it recognisable as meaning "baby or young child"; or how often and where the English word "baby" is followed by "dry", as a way of exploring whether the phrase "Baby Dry", somewhat controversially registered as a mark, occurs in descriptive contexts in addition to use as a suggestive brand name for nappies.[48]
3. Psychological or psycholinguistic research into the perception of signs, including: what they evoke; how easily they are recalled and what triggers such recall; how similar a sign is perceived to be in relation to other signs; the relative likelihood of association between different signs; and how multiple meanings ascribed simultaneously to signs co-exist and relate to each other (a topic increasingly relevant in the context of additional functions attributed to trade mark signs, and perhaps especially complex in relation to slogans (Davis and Durant 2011).

---

46 *Hearst Holding Ltd v AVELA Inc* [2014] EWHC 439 (Ch).
47 *Interflora v Marks & Spencer* [2014] EWCA Civ1403.
48 *Proctor & Gamble Co v OHIM* (C383/99 P) [2001] ECR I-6251.

6 Conclusion

The possible new lines of enquiry we are drawing attention to in this chapter in some instances resemble current forms of forensic linguistic evidence, and might be submitted in that form in jurisdictions which permit such evidence. But whether linguistic research would assist a court in a given case should not in our view be the only test of whether such research is worth doing. A more general significance is also possible: contribution to a legal and academic culture of trade mark discussion that may not impact on particular cases but contributes to the development of the area of law as a whole.

Alongside the necessary interdisciplinarity of such research, another characteristic seems indispensable: engagement with the procedural exigencies of trade mark law. For example, the first two of the three domains we proposed above as suitable for further linguistic enquiry will always be present in trade mark cases. There will always be formal analysis of signs by legal authorities applying statute and case law (e.g., both as regards absolute and relative grounds of registration, and in infringement cases); and there will always be an assessment of the view of the average consumer, situated in the relevant commercial context. What will not always be present is empirical evidence, the area perhaps most favoured among linguists. Often, indeed, such evidence is found by the courts to be unhelpful even where submitted. Even if the courts were more enthusiastic than they now appear to be, however, there would still be a difficulty. If such evidence were required in all cases in support of the view to be taken of the average consumer, or even in most, judicial systems dealing with trade mark cases would grind to a halt, or at least become prohibitively expensive for most claimants.

In the EU, where there are 24 official languages, the burden of acquiring expert evidence in trade mark cases is almost certainly exacerbated. Frequently, in cases involving either registration of a word or phrase as a EUTM or in a subsequent dispute, the legal authorities may need to take account of its meaning in more than one language. Perhaps unsurprisingly, the courts have generally concluded that such disputes may be resolved by recourse to the average consumer without a need for expert translation. An example is *Intra-Presse v Golden Balls Ltd*,[49] which ultimately came before the CJEU. In *Intra-Presse* it was necessary for the courts to assess the similarity between two signs *Golden Balls* and *Ballon D'Or*. Intra-Presse, a French company, had a EUTM registration for BALLON D'OR. Golden Balls Ltd sought registration for GOLDEN BALLS for a wide variety of goods identical and similar to those for which *BALLON D'OR* had already been registered. The case reached the General Court, which found for the applicant in those proceedings, Golden Balls Ltd, and the decision was endorsed by the CJEU. The General Court held, *inter alia*, that the average consumer, including the average Francophone consumer who would generally have a weak understanding of English,

---

[49] *Intra-Presse SAS v OHIM, Golden Balls Ltd* [2015] ETMR 6.

would not see the marks as meaning the same thing. Furthermore, the clear difference between the linguistic origins of the two marks would make any immediate discovery of a shared hidden meaning for the signs more difficult, both for Francophone and Anglophone consumers with an average level of attention. Finally, the General Court held that, in any event, it was improbable that the result arrived at through an analysis of the translation would spontaneously enter the head of the average consumer concerned, contemplating a simple purchase of everyday consumer goods. The decision was reached without taking into account any empirical evidence at all about, for example, the level of understanding of either Francophone or Anglophone consumers. Nor did the General Board require advice from an expert translator.

The approach of the EU courts in the "Golden Balls" case emphasises once again that, despite the frequently high financial stakes which result from corporate investment in branding, there is an eminently practical reason for adopting a notion such as the average consumer and limiting the kind and scale of evidence submitted, much as in the past judges were willing to rely on their own "common sense". Practical and procedural considerations should accordingly be incorporated into future interdisciplinary thinking, alongside recognition that trade mark lawyers have a strong motivation to explore the complex language issues raised in trade mark law and are likely to be as highly adept in doing so as linguists.

References

Aplin, Tanya & Jennifer Davis. 2017. *Intellectual property law: text, cases, and materials*, 3rd edn. Oxford: Oxford University Press.

Beebe, Barton. 2004. The semiotic analysis of trademark law. 51 UCLA Law Review. 621–624.

Beebe, Barton and Jeanne C. Fromer. 2018. Are we running out of trademarks? An empirical study of trademark depletion and congestion. *Harvard Law Review* 131. 945–1045.

Bently, Lionel, Jennifer Davis & Jane Ginsberg (eds.). 2008. *Trade marks and brands*. Cambridge: Cambridge University Press.

Blank, Andreas. 1999. Why do new meanings occur? A cognitive typology of the motivations for lexical semantic change. *Historical Semantics and Cognition* 61.

Butters, Ronald. 2007. A linguistic look at trademark dilution. *Santa Clara High Technology Law Journal* 24(3). 507.

Butters, Ronald. 2008. Trademarks and other proprietary terms. In John Gibbons & Mary Teresa Turell (eds.), *Dimensions of forensic linguistics*, 231–248. Amsterdam: John Benjamins.

Butters, Ronald. 2010. Interview with Seemaab Naseem. Aston University: Centre for Forensic Linguistics.

Chomsky, Noam. 1965. *Aspects of the theory of syntax*. Cambridge, MA: MIT Press.

Chomsky, Noam & Morris Halle. 1968. *The sound pattern of English*. Cambridge, MA: MIT Press.

Croft, William & Cruse, D. Alan. 2004. *Cognitive linguistics*. Cambridge: Cambridge University Press.

Coulthard, Malcolm & Alison Johnson. 2007. *An introduction to forensic linguistics: language in evidence*. London: Routledge.

Davis, Jennifer. 2005. Locating the average consumer: his judicial origins, intellectual influences and current role in European trade mark law. *Intellectual Property Quarterly* 183. 189–196.

Davis, Jennifer. 2015. Revisiting the average consumer: an uncertain presence in European trade mark law. *Intellectual Property Quarterly* 15. 21–24.

Davis, Jennifer & Alan Durant. 2015. "Have a Break" and the changing demands of trade mark registration. *Queen Mary Journal of Intellectual Property* 5(2). 132–156.

Davis, Jennifer & Alan Durant. 2011. To protect or not to protect? The eligibility of commercially-used short verbal texts for copyright and trade mark protection. *Intellectual Property Quarterly* 4. 345–370.

Dinwoodie, Graeme. 2008. What can linguistics do for trademark law. In Lionel Bently, Jennifer Davis & Jane Ginsberg (eds.), *Trade marks and brands,* 140–157. Cambridge: Cambridge University Press.

Durant, Alan. 2008. How can I tell the trade mark on a piece of gingerbread from all the other marks on it? Naming and meaning in verbal trade mark signs. In Lionel Bently, Jennifer Davis & Jane Ginsberg (eds.), *Trade marks and brands,* 107–140. Cambridge: Cambridge University Press.

Geeraerts, Dirk. 2010. *Theories of lexical semantics*. Oxford. Oxford University Press.

Gibbons, John & Mary Teresa Turell (eds.). 2008. *Dimensions of forensic linguistics*. Amsterdam: John Benjamins.

Hymes, Dell. 1966. Two types of linguistic relativity. In W. Bright (ed.), *Sociolinguistics,* 114–158. The Hague: Mouton.

Klepousniotou, Ekaterini. 2002. The processing of lexical ambiguity: homonymy and polysemy in the mental lexicon. *Brain and Language* 81. 205.

Landes, William & Richard Posner. 1987. Trademark law: an economic perspective. *Journal of Law and Economics* 30 (2). 265–309.

Linford, Jake. 2015a. A linguistic justification for protecting "generic" trademarks. *Yale Journal of Law and Technology* 17. 110–170.

Linford, Jake. 2015b. The false dichotomy between suggestive and descriptive trademarks. *Ohio State Law Journal* 76(6). 1367–1421.

Saussure, Ferdinand de. 1983 [1916]. *A course in general linguistics*. Edited by Roy Harris. Oxford: Blackwell.

Schechter, Frank. 1926–7. The rational basis for trade mark protection. *Harvard Law Review* 40. 813–833.

Shuy, Roger. 2003. *Linguistic battles in trademark disputes*. Basingstoke: Palgrave Macmillan.

Traugott, Elizabeth C. and Richard Dasher. 2005. *Regularity in semantic change*. Cambridge: Cambridge University Press.

Waelde, Charlotte, Abbe Brown, Smita Kheria & Jane Cornwell. 2016. *Contemporary intellectual property: law and policy*. 4th edn. Oxford: Oxford University Press.

Cases referred to

Abercrombie & Fitch Co. v. Hunting World, Inc., 537 F.2d 4, 9–11 (2nd Cir. 1976).
Arsenal Football Club plc v Reed (Case C-206/01 [2002] ECR I-10273.
Bambino Mio v Cazitex [2009] EWCA Civ 922.
BORCO-Marken-Import Matthiesen (Case C 265/09) [2011] E.C.R. I-8265.
BSH Bosch und Siemens Hausgerate GmbH v OHIM (T-123/14) EU:T:2015:52; GC.
Chocosuisse Union des Fabricants Suisses de Chocolat v Cadbury Ltd [1998] ETMR 205.
Colgate Palmolive v Lucas Bols (Claeryn/Klarein) [1976] IIC 420.
ConAgra Inc v. Acme Commercial Corp, US District Court for the District of Nebraska, Civil Action No 8: CV 91–119.
Farmeco AE Dermokallyntika v OHIM [2010] ECLI:EU:T:458 (General Court).
Google France Sarl v Louis Vuitton Mallettier (Case C-236/08-238/08) [2010] E.C.R. I-2417.

Grebenshikove v OHIM (T-394/10) [2014] ETMR 22 at 35–36.
Hearst Holding Ltd v AVELA Inc [2014] EWHC 439 (Ch).
Intel Corp Inc v CPM UK Ltd (Case C-252/07) [2008] WLR (D) 371.
Interflora v Marks & Spencer [2014] EWCA Civ1403.
In the Matter of the Harden Star Hand Grenade Fire Extinguisher Company's Trade Mark. RPC (1886) 3(9), 132–7.
Intra-Presse SAS v OHIM, Golden Balls Ltd [2015] ETMR 6.
Lloyd Schuhfabrik Meyer & Co GmbH v Klijsen Handel BV (Case C-342/97) [1999] ECR I-3819.
L'Oreal SA v Bellure NV [2009] (Case C-487/07) ECR I-5185.
McDonald's Corporation v. Quality Inns International, US District Court for the District of Maryland, Civil Action No. PN-87-2606.
OHIM v Wm Wrigley Jr Company (Case C-191/01) P [2003] ECR I-12447.
McLean v. Fleming 96 U.S. 245, 24 L. E.
Proctor & Gamble Co v OHIM (C383/99 P) [2001] ECR I-6251.
Qualitex Co. v. Jacobson Products Co. 514 U.S. 159 (1995).
SAT.1 Satellitenfersehen GmbH v OHIM (Case C329/02) P [2004 ECHR I-8317.
Roger Maier, Assos of Switzerland SA v ASOS plc, ASOS. com Ltd [2015] EWCA Civ 220.
Ruiz Picasso v OHIM (Case C-361/o4 P0 [2006] ECR I-643.
Siekmann v Deutsches Patent-und Markenamt (Case C-273/00) [2002] ECR I-11737.
SIGLA SA v Office for Harmonisation in the Internal Market (Trade Marks and Designs) (OHIM) (EU.T.2007:93).
US District Court for the District of Maryland, Civil Action No. PN-87-2606.
Volvo Trademark Holding AB v Office for Harmonisation in the Internal Market (Trade Marks and Designs) (OHIM) (Case T-524/11) [2015] ETMR 10.

Roger W. Shuy
12 Defamation, language and linguistics

1 Introduction

Linguistics can play an important role in virtually every area of life, including law. One such intersection is the area of defamation because persons who accuse another of defamation usually base their claims on the words and expressions that constitute their accusations. This chapter describes how linguists can provided assistance in defamation cases by calling on their tools of speech acts, grammatical referencing, discourse structure, verbal framing, malicious language, and the meaning conveyed by the texts in evidence.

2 Definitions of defamation

Defamation laws can be complex and sometimes difficult for even lawyers to understand. In United States courts, charges of defamation require Plaintiffs to demonstrate a defamatory effect. The *Restatement (Second) of Torts § 558 (1976)* defines an utterance as defamatory "if it tends to harm the reputation of another as to lower him in the estimation of the community or to deter third persons from dealing with him."

Black's Law Dictionary defines defamation as: "An intentional false communication, either published or publicly spoken, that injures annother's reputation or good name." Some legal jurisdictions including Scotland, use the terms *libel, slander,* and *defamation* synonymously, while in other parts of the world including the United States, *libel* is used for written defamation and *slander* for spoken defamation. The majority of defamation cases are brought against newspapers, magazines, radio and television stations, and various forms of electronic media. Plaintiffs in the United States are required to prove that defendants knew that their communication was false and that it was published with malice and reckless abandon. This contrasts with British defamation law in which defendants have to prove that the accusations against them are false. In the old days insults led to bloody duels, but by now apparently humanity has advanced beyond that stage, now substituting monetary awards for the former vindication brought by physical injury or death. Mere insults do not qualify as defamation in American law, although other jurisdictions such as Germany include insults as one type of defamation.

2.1 The development of defamation law

For many years the U.S. Supreme Court declined to protect the media from lawsuits, relying on the guaranteed freedom of the press found in the First Amendment of the

Bill of Rights. However, in 1994 in the case of *New York Times Co. v. Sullivan* (376 U.S. 254 1964) the Supreme Court revolutionized defamation law by ruling that public figures could not prevail against the media unless reporters used "actual malice." The Court defined actual malice as "information that was false" or was published "with reckless disregard of whether it was false or not." Therefore, if malice or ill-will could be proved and if the published information could be shown to be false, charges of defamation had a good chance to succeed.

2.2 The role of understanding legal terminology

Legal scholars and practitioners alike struggle in their efforts to determine the meaning of various vague but commonly used law terms, especially adverbs such as *intentionally, willfully, recklessly, maliciously, knowingly, voluntarily*, and phrases such as *reasonable doubt, heat of passion, malice aforethought, preponderance of the evidence* and *willful premeditation* (Shuy 2014: 31–43). They are not alone in this, however, for even lexicographers find these abstract expressions hard to pin down.

Intentionality is one of the most difficult terms to define in any context (Searle 1983), for in a perfect world to know intentions would require probing into the minds of speakers and writers, but at the present time we have nothing like DNA evidence to guide us. Defamation cases are no exception. It can be difficult to prove that defendants knew that their alleged defamatory statements were false, that their act was intentional, that their message contained malice, that it was conveyed recklessly, and that it qualifies for what the statutes call being "published." But these abstract expressions are prevalent in the law and courtroom, largely because there are no other suitable terms to replace them. The linguist's task is to find clues in the language within the evidence that can help support what these terms can mean.

3 Linguistics and defamation

The following presents some of the ways linguistic analysis can be useful in defamation cases. It includes speech acts, discourse structure and framing, grammatical referencing, malicious language, and conveyed meaning.

3.1 The role of speech acts in defamation

It was a highly respected law professor who had also trained as a linguist who suggested two important additions to the conventional definition of defamation: (1) that it is a linguistic act and (2) that it constitutes the illocutionary speech act of accusing (Tiersma 1987: 304). Although at that time little had been written about the speech act of accusing, Tiersma's suggestion fits nicely into the legal arena's notion of defamation. To directly perform the ordinary act of accusing someone of something, the speaker must convey that an offensive act had occurred in the past, identify who performed and was responsible for that offensive act and note that the act was undesirable. It is possible that law had not thought of defamation as an accusation because the speech act of accusing is not usually accomplished performatively ("I accuse you of doing X").

Tiersma then describes an accusation as: "...an utterance with the force of an accusation is an attribution of responsibility to someone for a blameworthy act or state of affairs...that lays responsibility for an act that violates community norms at the feet of the accused," adding, "an accusation is meant to evoke certain consequences, such as lowering the wrongdoer's reputation or imposing punishment" (306). His observation contrasts with the law's conventional focus on the perceived effect on the receiver of the defamatory message and places the emphasis on the language used by the sender of that message. The receiver may feel defamed, but proof of the source of this feeling can be found in the way language is used by the person who originated the purported defamation. As obvious as this might seem, it was a relatively new idea in defamation cases, which had previously relied mostly on the receiver's perception of alleged defamation.

Two aspects of slander and libel do not fall within the province of linguistic analysis: determining the truth or falsity of the statements in the message and the type and extent of injury claimed by the plaintiffs. The specific language used by the sender of the message, however, is a fruitful area for linguistic analysis.

Since defamation is a linguistic act, both slander and libel cases offer considerable opportunities for linguistic analysis. Pragmatics, including implicatures and speech acts (Austin 1962; Searle 1969; Fernandez and Cairns 2010) can prove useful for identifying and distinguishing among assertive, directive, commissive, expressive, and declarative expressions in defamation disputes. Because defamation law protects opinions, what counts as a felicitous speech act of giving an opinion can have considerable value to litigators and identifying indirect speech acts can be equally important. Tiersma (1987) points out that the law of defamation conventionally has focused on the effect of the purported defamatory utterance on the alleged victims rather than on the illocutionary force of the author's speech act of accusing. Since defamation cases begin with the plaintiff notifying the defendant about the perceived harm along with a request for an apology, the felicity of the speech acts of both the plaintiff's requesting and the defendant's speech acts of apologizing are also important aspects of the linguistic analysis.

3.2 The role of grammar in defamation

It is often the case that analysis of the pronouns and deixis in defamation case evidence can help explain otherwise unclear or ambiguous grammatical relationships.

Unless pronouns like "we," "it" and "they" have clearly identified references, their meaning is unclear. The same is true for deictic references such as "that," "these," and "those" as well as articles such as "the" and "a." When the language evidence is unclear about these references, claims about their meanings can be challenged. Major problems in defamation cases can arise out of the potential ambiguity of grammatical expressions.

3.3 The role of discourse structure in defamation

As mentioned above, defamation cases can rely heavily on the assumption of intentionality, which is a very difficult matter to identify and prove. What the participants intended is something that nobody is able to determine with scientific certainty. Nevertheless, the language that people use provides some useful clues about their intentions. Often the focus of litigants centers on the smaller language units of sentences or phrases, which in criminal cases are called "smoking gun" expressions. On some occasions, the alleged smoking guns found in purported defamatory statements can be neutralized by discovering the ways they occur within larger discourse units (Shuy 2011, 2013, 2014).

There are no clearer clues to the intentions of speakers than their agendas revealed by the topics they choose to bring up and recycle. Topic introductions are the clearest evidence available about what people have on their minds and their intended contributions to a discourse. This does not necessarily defuse other portions of the evidence that may point to defamation, but it can situate those portions in the discourse context by showing that the overall intention of the speakers as revealed by their agenda was something other than purposely defaming their targets.

3.4 The role of discourse framing in defamation

Discourse framing (Goffman 1974; Tannen 1993) is still another area of language structure that can contribute to the analysis of defamation cases. Discourse is comprised of units of information that in written text consist of paragraphs or other identifiably marked units, while in spoken communication the most relevant units are topics. Both written and spoken discourse include framing of some sort, usually by way of an introduction that tells the receiver what to expect the message to be about and a conclusion reprising the result. In some defamation cases, the discourse framing can play a role that the actual text does not clearly convey. Such framing can take different realizations.

Radio news programs, for example, can begin with suggestions or hints of defamatory information that frame the remaining content of the program which includes only benign, non-defamatory information. When defamatory suggestions introduce following statements that convey no defamatory accusations, the result can create an effect on receivers that is the same as if the follow-up information was actually defamatory. This same effect can be produced by beginning television shows with photographs or other images that suggest something bad about the person being discussed and even though the following actual text tiptoes around making any verbal defamatory statements, the defamatory effect remains.

3.5 The role of malicious language in defamation

Malicious language certainly seems like a bad thing, but there is not always complete agreement about what it is. In his *Dictionary of Modern Legal Usage,* Garner (1995: 545) says that in the legal context malice is synonymous with "intentional" and "reckless" but not the way most people understand it as "wicked" or "evil." Intentionally used reckless language that conveys malice usually takes the form of sarcasm (mocking or contemptuous statements), exaggeration (distortion of a seemingly normal event), rhetorical questions (providing the answer in the question), and the use of pejorative terms (such as referring to a politician's trips as "junkets"). Although jurors in defamation cases are often instructed to consider whether the language evidence is malicious or, more commonly, if it had malicious intent, it is not easy for the plaintiff to prove that the defendant's language was malicious. If the language in question is spoken (slander), the heightened emotion of speakers may reveal their malicious anger that exposes itself in name-calling or sarcasm. In defamation cases comprised of written language (libel), punctuation sometimes is the key, such as when exclamation marks are used frequently, especially multiple exclamation marks. This can give the appearance that the writer is angrily shouting with malicious intent.

Therefore, when linguists are consulted in defamation cases, they can know that the law considers defamatory statements as intentional, false and harm the receiver's reputations by using malicious language. The potential handarm caused by malicious language is only part of what linguistic analysis of the evidence can point out.

3.6 The role of conveyed meaning in defamation

Conveyed meaning is often accomplished by innuendo and malicious language that creates inferences that can be made from fact-like statements. Language can be explicit or it can provide room for receivers to infer other meanings. Explicit accusations are inherently negative, but when they are made less explicitly, they leave considerable wiggle room for different interpretations or inferences. Contextualizing indirect speech acts can help analysts understand that the conveyed meanings can be very different from that which they otherwise appear to be.

One form of conveyed meaning is innuendo in which the utterance constitutes some form of unwanted ascription toward the target of the comment (Fraser 2001: 206). This conveyed and implied meaning encourages a statement to be considered defamatory as long as the reader or listener knows the relevant facts upon which that innuendo is based. Bach and Harnish (1979: 101) observe that the key to innuendo is its intentionality and deniability. Fraser (2001: 215) points out that innuendo addresses only the audience of the larger community, differentiating it from insinuation, which is directed to a target or specific audience. Addressing the larger community relates directly to the requirement that defamation widely harms the reputation of a target. Interestingly, the stain caused by innuendo can remain even when the accusation that it entails is later proven false. On the whole, however, innuendo is not the strongest evidence of defamation, as the court observed in *Strada v. Connecticut Newspapers, Inc.*, (477, A.2d at 1012), concluding that public officials may not base a charge of actual malice on claimed innuendo.

4 The problem of the ordinary reader

If linguistic analysis is not used in defamation cases, decisions have to be made in some other way. Durant (1996) observes that defamatory meaning is often decided by the "ordinary reader" test, which is not a test in the usual sense of that term, but instead is a subjective assessment made by triers of the facts. The question of what constitutes this ordinary reader rears its head in many civil and criminal law cases, including defamation cases. Tiersma (1987) points out that one of the problems of relying on the impressions of the ordinary reader is that doing so ignores or overlooks the actual language evidence that causes that ordinary reader to assume a particular meaning and feel the way they do. When defamation is defined primarily by its effect on the plaintiff, this subjective feeling is obvious from the start of a trial and may easily influence triers of the fact to rely heavily on it instead of understanding the defendant's language evidence, which is a far better indicator for determining whether or not such defamation exists.

5 Defamation cases illustrating the use linguistic analysis

Defamation lawsuits come in many types and shapes. The plaintiffs can be corporations, unions, medical practitioners, or individuals and groups that claim to have been defamed. The following examples of defamation cases are organized by the above-mentioned linguistic tools that have been found useful to the attorneys who litigated those cases. For further details about how linguistic analysis helped resolve these defamation cases, see Shuy (2010), where the cases described here receive greater elaboration.

5.1 Speech act analysis a lawsuit brought by a company against its union

In 1994 the union contract expired at Grinnell Fire Protection Systems Company, America's largest manufacturer, installer, and provider of maintenance for automatic fire protection systems. The company tried to negotiate a new contract with its union but was not successful, after which the union members went on strike. As is often the case, the company hired replacement workers to do the jobs of the striking union employees. Believing that these replacement workers were unskilled in the tasks required of them, the union hired a public relations firm to produce letters, handbills, direct-mail pieces, and a paid commercial announcement that was widely aired on radio stations in an effort to expose what it believed to be unfair treatment by the company. This material was sent all over the country declaring:

> Grinnell's skilled fire protection workers have walked off sites in your area leaving systems designated to save your life in the hands of workers with little or no experience. The question for you is does that sprinkler above your head even work?

This announcement added that Grinnell was increasing its profits by making a "calculated and cold-blooded decision" to destroy the workers' existing health care system and that the company was now using replacement workers whose work could endanger the safety of employees in companies where Grinnell systems were now in place. One handbill said, "It takes only one bad installation of a sprinkler system to spell the difference between life and death." Another said, "What happens when the company hired to prevent fires causes them?" A direct mail piece sent to contractors said, "If Grinnell is still charging you the same as when it had skilled union sprinkler fitters and you're expecting the same degree of workmanship, YOU'VE BEEN HAD."

Grinnell's response was to file a defamation lawsuit against the union, claiming that it had published false and malicious defamatory statements about the company.

It is beyond the scope of linguistic analysis to evaluate the truth or falsity of the union's claims that the replacement workers were unskilled and that their work was substandard. However, the union's speech act of accusing the company that the current situation endangered workers' lives in the places where replacement workers had installed new systems was subject to speech act analysis to determine whether this accusation was presented as a fact or as an opinion. This analysis was important, because virtually all expressions of opinion are protected by the First Amendment to the United States Constitution. The union claimed that their statements represented their opinions and did not claim to be facts.

Factual statements relate to things that have actual existence, things that are done, that have objective reality, and can be verified. If they have already happened, they are represented by verbs in the past tense. If they are states of being, they are usually represented by verbs in the present tense. All of the union's statements were couched in the past tense and were verifiable facts, such as "they substituted strikebreakers," "they gave wage cuts of 20%," "they refused to negotiate," and "they used unskilled workers."

In contrast, opinions represent the senders' judgments, views, or appraisals that they form in their minds. They evidence a belief stronger than an impression but less strong than positive knowledge. Opinions usually concern the present or future time. The union claimed that the following statements in their letters to occupants and owners of building with Grinnell's sprinkler systems were opinions:

> Grinnell hopes to increase profits
> You'll be affected
> Grinnell trades health for profits
> You may lose your life
> The job may be more dangerous
> A bad installation can lead to death
> The company may cause fires
> This may put you in danger
> This will change the face of the industry
> [not using Grinnell] could save your life
> [using Grinnell] can give you a false sense of security

All of the items on this list fit the conventional definition of opinions by expressing a present or future state even though none are accompanied by the usual signals that mark them as opinions such as "in our opinion," "it seems," "we think," or "it would appear to us." Even the statements containing the conditionals "may" and "could," were not outwardly couched as opinions that would say something like "we think that you may lose your life."

How then could Plaintiff Grinnell charge the union with defamation? One answer came with the identification and use of indirect speech acts, which occur when the locution and illocution of a speech act are not in syntactic alignment. At trial, the union's claim that its messages were opinions rather than purported facts failed because these alleged opinions were shown to be indirect speech acts in which speakers say what they mean, but they also mean something more than they say. Searle (1979: 60–61) says that speakers convey meaning that is more than they say by using indirect speech acts to hearers "by way of relying on their mutually shared background information, both linguistic and nonlinguistic, together with their powers of rationality and inference." Indirect speech acts produce an effect similar to that of irony, metaphor, hints, and insinuation. They say what they mean but they convey something else at the same time. Psychologists use the construct of schemas in essentially the same way (Bartlett 1932).

5.2 Speech act analysis in the lawsuit brought by a widow against her insurance company

A second example of the use of speech act analysis in a defamation case is one brought by the widow of Frank Doramus, who held a life insurance police with Jackson National Life Insurance Company. Doramus currently had a policy for $500,000 that designated his wife as beneficiary. In 1988 he tried to add an additional $300,000 to that policy. His application form required him to take a new physical exam, and the result of this exam showed that he was HIV positive. The insurance company then notified Doremas that his request for additional coverage was denied, but claimed that because of the confidential nature of health information, the company could not inform him about why his application was rejected. The law specified that the applicant can request this information, but when the company complies with this request, the information must be sent only to the applicant's health provider and not to the applicant.

Doramus did not make his request until March 1991 and his health provider received it in April. Doramus then died in June. His widow received the face value of the $500,000 policy, but during the following year she filed a lawsuit against the insurance company, claiming that its failure to notify her husband that he had HIV had significantly reduced her husband's life expectancy and had exposed her to potential harm. The U.S. District Court entered a summary judgment in favor of the insurance company in 1995, ruling that the company was not required to disclose the reason for denying Mr. Doramus's application. This decision was later upheld in the Fifth District Court.

Mrs. Doramus then sought the help of her congressman, who wrote to the insurance company on her behalf. The company wrote back to the congressman and his professional staff, saying that Mrs. Doramus was "absurdly litigious," adding that Mr. and Mrs. Doramus "had been involved in at least 32 court proceedings."

The media then got hold of the story. When the insurance company heard that *Dateline NBC* was planning a national story about this, its senior vice president sent two documents to the network, one called "Doramus Case Chronology," and the other called a "White Paper." These documents were intended, as its writer admitted, "to get *Dateline's* proposed story turned." The two documents indicated that Mr. and Mrs. Doramus had a sordid past, engaged in a disreputable life style of illegal drugs and extramarital sex, and had exposed themselves to AIDS long before the insurance company was involved. The company said it was being defrauded by the Doramuses because they knew that Mr. Doramus was dying of AIDS at the time when he tried to purchase the additional coverage. Mrs. Doramus's attorney claimed that the insurance company was now misleading *Dateline NBC*. The company also had made these same accusations to the congressman who had tried to help Mrs. Doramus during her meeting with him in the presence of his staff at his Washington DC office. The company's claims easily met the requirement that the alleged defamation was "published."

The story did not end there. In 1997 the Maryland House of Delegates Committee on Economic Matters was planning to sponsor a bill that would require insurance companies to disclose the results of adverse medical test results directly to the applicants who were denied coverage. Jackson National then sent a letter to various members of the state's legislative committee, claiming that Mrs. Doramus was a "liar" who was engaged in "dishonest and disreputable conduct." The company also sent similar letters to media outlets and insurance commissions in California, Texas, and other states. These documents further revealed that the company threatened to expose these accusations if Mrs. Doramus were to cooperate with *Dateline's* planned program.

By then there could be no question about whether the insurance company's efforts were intentional, whether they injured Mrs. Doramus's reputation, and whether they were published. The remaining battleground about whether or not the information was false was outside the expertise of a linguist and was the responsibility of the lawyers to prove.

It is clear enough that the company's published information injured the reputation of Mrs. Doramus. Jackson National's various publications were replete with accusations that Mrs. Doramus had made false statements, and that the company's letter to her was intended to silence her. They published these accusations and accompanied them with supporting information. The insurance company's lawyers countered that the letters were merely giving Mrs. Doramus advice, not accusing her of anything. But the speech act of advising is very different from the speech act of accusing. When advising someone, one takes the listener's perspective, as in "If I were you, I would not continue in this." Instead, the letter told her, "This must stop," clearly a directive supporting the accusation rather than mere advice. Receivers of advice have control over what they will do with that advice, in contrast with the letter's threat to expose what they believed they knew about Mrs. Doramus if she cooperated with *Dateline's* planned program. By definition, receivers of threats are obligated to take the consequences if they don't comply. Advising and threatening are not the proper basis for a defamation case, but accusations are relevant, as speech act analysis demonstrates. Conditions for the speech act of accusing must (1) represent a current event or state of affairs in which the speaker has the authority and ability to make the accusation; (2) the speaker must have evidence for the truth of the accusation; (3) the speaker must believe the accusation to be true, accurate, and not in the hearer's best interest; (4) the accusation is not obvious to the hearer; and (5) it is not necessary for the hearer to take evasive action because the event is now past and not repairable.

At a subsequent hearing in which this analysis was presented, the Court concluded that in the context of the ongoing dispute, the insurance company's letter to Mrs. Doramus was a sufficient accusation for her to bring a defamation suit against Jackson National.

5.3 Discourse framing in the case of a celebrity against a TV network

In 1980 NBC's *Nightly News* produced at program called "Wayne Newton and the Law" that was followed a few months later by two other programs with the same name and on the same topic. The famous singer had announced that he intended to purchase assets in a Las Vegas hotel. The gaming commission rules that obtain for such purchases require applicants to be investigated and interviewed in order to determine whether or not they have any connection with organized crime. When Newton appeared before the gaming commission, he admitted that he had met a man named Gino Penosi when he was a seventeen year-old singing at the Copacabana in New York. Penosi was in that audience and offered Newton a hundred dollars if he would sing Penosi's favorite song. Newton sang it but refused to take Penosi's money. Subsequently Penosi brought his mob friends with him to hear Newton sing several more times, each time offering him money with Newton refusing it. Penosi had been making bets with his friends that Newton would turn down his offers of money. After one such concert, Penosi invited Newton and his mother to his home for dinner. They accepted, and Newton testified that this was the extent of their relationship.

Newton explained all of this to the gaming commission and thought no more of it. As he was leaving the hearing, NBC reporter Brian Ross followed Newton to his car awaiting him outside to ask more questions about his relationship with Penosi. Ross somehow learned that Newton recently had made several phone calls to Penosi. Ross asked about this and whether Newton knew other mafia figures. Newton replied that he did not. Celebrities are used to such ambush interviews by the media and Newton ended it as quickly as possible.

The first program of the NBC series was aired shortly after this, describing Newton as "under investigation" for his involvement in the purchase of the hotel. This was accurate, but the word, "investigation," can convey a more sinister meaning than it meant to the gaming commission. The news anchor, John Chancellor, introduced the program with two large, equal-sized photos on the screen, one of Gino Penosi and the other of Newton, framed next to each other as though they were equals in the information to follow. This clear association of Newton with the mob was framed visually before a single word was said in the program.

The following verbal discourse framing was equally damaging to Newton. Topic analysis of the first program indicated that there were six topics introduced by Ross:

1. A video clip of the FBI stakeout of Penosi's home was shown with voiceover pointing out that Penosi was a New York hoodlum and believed to be the Gamino family's point man in West Coast narcotics and show business.
2. A verbal description of Penosi's Grand Jury investigation, noting that Penosi is the key figure in the investigation of the hotel that Newton was planning to purchase. In the background Newton can be heard singing the lyrics to one of his songs, "I think I'm going out of my mind."
3. A verbal description saying that Newton makes a million dollars a week and is buying the hotel for $85 million even though he has run into financial difficulties, adding that the grand jury is investigating the role of Penosi in "the Newton deal."
4. Ross saying that Newton asked Penosi for help with a problem. Penosi took the problem to the Gambino family who took care of it and made Penosi Newton's "hidden partner in the proposed hotel purchase." Ross reported that Newton denied this but said he knows Penosi as a fan and friend but does not know about any connections with the Gambino family.
5. Ross then said, "the authorities say Newton is not telling the whole story" and is expected to be the first witness in the grand jury investigation of Penosi, adding that Newton "was angry when we asked him questions." It then showed clips of the ambush interview at the point when Newton said, "I really don't care what you want."
6. Ross reported his parking lot interview with Newton about Penosi, in which Newton told Ross he doesn't know Penosi. Ross added, "the feds say that eleven calls were made between Newton and Penosi and that this is part of the FBI investigation of the East Coast mob's involvement in narcotics and racketeering in the entertainment world."

The topic framing is clear. Topics 1, 2, and 6 framed the discourse at the beginning and end with the criminal Penosi. Even though the program was called "Wayne Newton and the Law," the topics about the singer placed him in the middle of topics framed by Penosi and the mob. This framing encouraged a direct criminal association of the two men. The two follow-up programs in the series had virtually identical discourse and visual framing.

Although linguistic analysis cannot deal with the factual evidence of cases, Newton's attorney was able to show that the program was wrong in many of its alleged facts. It was true, however, that Newton had recently telephoned Penosi to request his help with a personal problem that had nothing to do with the purchase of the hotel. Newton recently had received threats to his four year-old daughter's life. Since Newton felt that the police had not been helpful, he remembered his old acquaintance, Penosi, and called him to see if he could help. After Newton requested this help, the threats stopped, but whether or not this was due to Penosi's involvement was never resolved. The discourse framing analysis, however, was instrumental in helping with Newton's charges of defamation by NBC. The defendant clearly harmed

Newton's reputation, intentionally accused him of a connection with the mob, and published the information very broadly.

5.4 Discourse framing by a radio news program

Discourse framing also was central in a defamation case brought by a Minnesota woman against the local television station and the county sheriff. In 1993 Dennis Stokes was murdered while he was sleeping in bed. As is common in such cases, the sheriff suspected the victim's spouse, Terri Stokes, who appeared to have the motive and opportunity. But after five months, the police still couldn't find enough evidence to indict her. At that point a local television station was interested in the case and invited the sheriff to report the progress of his investigation.

The program began with a discourse frame that set the table for listeners to understand that a previous local murder in which a wife killed her husband is the same as the current program about the wife of Dennis Stokes:

> Male reporter: During the last few weeks you've probably seen or read about the latest in the so-called I-35 murder.
>
> Female reporter: A widow and her one-time boy friend have been indicted for murdering her husband. Well, tonight's Dimension examines another case where the victim's widow is coming under close scrutiny.

Even though Terri Stokes was a suspect, the police had not been able to find enough evidence to indict her. The program's discourse framing encouraged listeners to believe that Terri Stokes was a killer just like the wife in the recent I-35 murder case. It made for a juicy news program but it also contributed a defamation lawsuit against the television station.

5.5 Grammatical referencing in a defamation case against a radio station

During one interview by the media in the case in which Terri Stokes was accused of murdering her husband, the sheriff reported that "the only suspect" was Terri Stokes. A disagreement arose when the radio station did not agree that the sheriff had spoken the word, "she," when he said:

> Sheriff: Somebody walked directly to the house, up the stairway, into the bedroom and, it appears, shot him while he was sleeping. [She] pulled the trigger. This was a personal thing. I think it was a well planned out, methodical execution.
>
> Reporter: By his wife?
>
> Sheriff: She's the one and only suspect.

> Reporter: Do you have any doubts about the direction you are going?
>
> Sheriff: No...when you start focusing on her, she tries to get away from the question. You close in on her, she runs.

Careful listening to the tape of the program made it clear that the sheriff did indeed say "she pulled the trigger." A defamation case could have been filed based on this exchange alone, except that the station denied that the sheriff said "she" here, which grammatically related "the only suspect was his wife" with "[she] pulled the trigger." But this important pronoun reference was not the only language evidence in which the sheriff claimed that Terri Stokes committed the murder. In addition to the dispute over whether the sheriff said "she," the defense claimed that up to this point the sheriff was using the speech act of giving an opinion rather than the speech act of stating a fact. But there was agreement on both sides that he clearly said that Terri Stokes was the "only suspect."

This became important when few months later, the nationally syndicated radio news show, *American Journal*, aired its own story about the murder and again an interview with the sheriff was the centerpiece. In it the sheriff said this:

> Voice over: Police believe the family man's killer was someone very close to him.
>
> Reporter: Now police say they have only one suspect.
>
> Sheriff: The suspect walked directly into that house, up the stairs, into the bedroom, and shot Dennis Stokes right between the eyes while he was sleeping.

The crucial matter was that the sheriff previously had said that Terri Stokes was the "only" suspect. Now he said "*the* suspect" using the article that refers to something previously identified, as opposed to *a* suspect, which has an unidentified referent. His "only suspect," Mrs. Stokes, was now promoted to *the* suspect who committed the murder. This grammatical reference was a clear accusation that conveyed the meaning that Terri Stokes, not some unspecified person, was the murderer. Since Mrs. Stokes was never indicted, this accusation, along with the previous use of the disputed "she," was the basis of the defamation case brought against both the sheriff and the radio station.

5.6 Grammatical referencing in a defamation case against a speaker at a national conference

Grammatical referencing also played a role in the defamation case brought against Horst Rechelbacher, the founder and owner of the popular Aveda hair products and distribution company. After he sold his company to Estee Lauder, the magazine, *Beauty Mfg*, interviewed Rechelbacher and quoted him directly as saying:

> And this is something I always wanted to do but wasn't as successful because I didn't have the muscle Lauder has – to clean up the distribution. Some of our distributors weren't interested

in promoting our philosophy, system of sales, and mission. Some were really polluting certain markets, ignoring the terms of contracts with them. They were selling to anybody and everybody, particularly to phantom salons.

Rechelbacher went on to cite Northern California as an example of the "polluted market" that had been cleaned up by Lauder. Even though all of Rechelbacher's place references contained plural nouns, one of the distributors in the audience believed that these references were directed to him alone and brought a defamation suit against Rechelbacher that was dismissed on several grounds, including this grammatical referencing.

5.7 Conveyed meaning in the defamation case against the television network

In the defamation case brought by Wayne Newton, the program's words, "investigation," "deal," "not telling the whole story," and Newton's decontextualized quote to the reporter, "I don't care what you want," conveyed more information than the program actually said, thereby encouraging listeners to the infer that something bad was involved.

5.8 Conveyed meaning in the defamation case against the radio station

During the follow up programs in the Terri Stokes defamation case, the radio station reported that she had "made plans" and "left town," suggesting that she had done so in order to avoid being indicted and conveying meaning to listeners that suggested her guilt. Also in that case, the media's adverbs such as *supposedly* and *secretly,* cast suspicion and doubt on her actions. When the reporters said that their calls to her "went unanswered," this conveyed to listeners that this "only suspect" was hiding something even though there could be perfectly benign reasons why she chose to not respond to persistent ambush interviews by pesky journalists.

5.9 Malicious language in a dispute between professional organizations

One example of a dispute over malicious language occurred in a 1982 defamation case brought by Georgia otolaryngologists against the Georgia Society of Plastic Surgeons after the latter published an article in the *Journal of the Medical Association of Georgia* called, "Things Are Never What They Seem: Skim Milk Masquerades as Cream" (vol. 71, 103–105). The Georgia otolaryngologists, known for a medical practice involving the ear, nose, and throat, were accused of invading the specialty of plastic surgeons when they began performing surgery on the neck and head, an area that the plastic surgeons believed to be encroachment their own anatomical territory.

The article contained a great deal of name-calling that the otolaryngologists considered defamatory including "cosmetic surgeons without portfolio" and "this maverick group." The plastic surgeons also used sarcasm as they objected to the name and practice of the otolaryngologist's professional organization, saying, "my, my, the potential for word combinations is positively underwhelming," "Georgia plastic surgeons were amused to see [this development]," and [they] do not wish to encumber themselves with years of training." Also objectionable were several rhetorical questions that presuppose their own answer, as in, "Is this how competent plastic surgeons are trained?" and "can just anyone in the fraternity do cosmetic surgery?" And of course the plastic surgeons' reference to the practice of otolaryngology as "skim milk" was high on the list of the complaints. Sometimes even punctuation can be sarcastically malicious, especially when quotation marks are used to set off expressions, as in this article's use of "would-be physicians."

5.10 Malicious language in the company's defamation case agaist its union

In the Grinnell defamation case discussed above, the union's inflammatory expressions such as "Grinnell made a cold-blooded decision," "you've been had," "attempt to destroy the health-care system," and "suffer loss of property and even life" aroused enough emotion and anger to suggest that these expressions were malicious.

5.11 Malicious language in the defamation case against the speaker at a conference

A similar charge was made in the defamation case against Horst Rechelbacher in which the plaintiff also claimed that Rechelbacher used malicious language in a speech that he gave before 5,000 Aveda distributors and employees. Unfortunately for the plaintiff's lawyers, they couldn't come up with anything convincing. The speech was videotaped, offering more visual information that could have revealed such anger and spite than could an audiotape or written language.

Often what is *not* said means as much as what *is* said. Rechelbacher calmly said he was "embarrassed" about the distributors who didn't follow Aveda's philosophy, but he did not use exaggerated terms such as "disgusted," "mortified," or "sickened." His voice and language were calm and unemotional with no loudness, high pitch, speeded speech, or other signs of heightened negative emotion. He used no imperatives even when he talked about the distribution problems in Northern California and made no menacing gestures. The plaintiff's lawyers made much of the Rechelbacher's semi- closed fist as he spoke of "other distributors." But research in gestures shows that a fist or semi-closed fist is used to communicate many ideas such as promoting or emphasizing a point being made, presenting new ideas, and simply the impression of holding objects. At any rate, closer examination of the videotape showed that he was not making a true fist. His thumb was beside his index finger rather than across it and as he spoke his hand was moving left to right in a gesture that commonly signals a contrast of one thing with another. This, coupled with the grammatical referencing noted earlier, gave no indication that Rechelbacher was using malicious language to defame the distributor who sued him.

6 Conclusions

The linguistic features most useful in analyzing the evidence in defamation cases are: the speech acts used; the grammatical references, the discourse structure; the language framing revealed by means of topic analysis of texts or visual displays; the use of malicious language; and the use of conveyed meanings. Description of these language features described here were used successfully by retaining attorneys.

In other defamation cases that I've worked on, the results of my analysis have not been helpful to the retaining attorneys. When I searched for these language features and didn't find convincing evidence of their presence, my only alternative was to report this to the retaining lawyers, at which point not surprisingly my relationship to the case ended. I did not consider this a failure on my part, however, because these analyses at least alerted the attorneys to the problems they had to face. Most of the time they were grateful for this; other times not so much.

References

Austin, John. L. 1962. *How to do things with words*. Cambridge MA: Harvard University Press.
Bach, Kenneth and Robert Harnish. 1979. *Linguistic communication and speech acts*. Cambridge: Cambridge U Press.
Bartlett, Frederic. 1932. *Remembering: a study of experimental and social psychology*. Cambridge: Cambridge U Press.
Black's Law Dictionary. 1999. St. Paul MN: Thompson West.
Durant, Alan. 1966. Allusions and other 'innuendo' meanings in libel actions: the value of semantic and pragmatic evidence. *Forensic Linguistics* 3(2). 195–210.
Fraser, Bruce. 2001. An account of innuendo. In Robert Harnish (ed.), *Perspectives on semantics, pragmatics and discourse: a festschrift for Ferenc Kiefer*. Amsterdam: John Benjamins.

Fernandez, Eva M. and Helen S. Cairns. 2010. *Fundamentals of psycholinguistics*. Hoboken NJ: John Wiley and Sons.
Garner, Bryan. 1995. *Dictionary of modern legal usage*. New York: Oxford University Press.
Goffman, Erving. 1974. *Frame analysis*. New York: Harper.
Searle, John. 1969. *Speech acts: an essay in the philosophy of language*. Cambridge: Cambridge University Press.
Searle, John. 1979. *Expression and meaning*. Cambridge: Cambridge University Press.
Searle, John. 1983. *Intentionality: an essay in the philosophy of mind*. Cambridge: Cambridge University Press.
Shuy, Roger W. 2010. *The language of defamation cases*. New York: Oxford University Press.
Shuy, Roger W. 2011. *The language of perjury cases*. New York: Oxford University Press.
Shuy, Roger W. 2013. *The language of bribery cases*. New York: Oxford University Press.
Shuy, Roger W. 2014. *The language of murder cases*. New York: Oxford University Press.
Tannen, Deborah. 1993. What's in a frame? Surface evidence for underlying expectations. In Deborah Tannen (ed.), *Framing in discourse*, 14–54. New York: Oxford University Press.
Tiersma, Peter. 1987. The language of defamation. *Texas Law Review* 66. 303–350.

Peter Robson
13 Future directions in law and popular culture: a British perspective

1 Introduction: law and popular culture and its spread

Law and popular culture has truly come of age. The books, collections of essays and individual essays that have been published over the past 20 years constitute a clear and growing area of academic endeavour on film (see References) and to a lesser extent television (ibid). Most recently scholars have reached out to emphasise the links with other related fields (see Wagner and Sherwin 2014; Ogletree and Sarat 2015; Sharp and Leiboff 2016; Picart, Jacobsen and Greek 2016). There have been, however, limited links with the related field of law and literature and few individual scholars work in both areas. There is a wealth of both material as well as a range of different approaches. Some of these show the way in which the use of popular culture can supplement legal study and involve truly imaginative approaches to areas of scholarship (Robson 2005). As with much intellectual endeavour there is scholarship which uses specialist language which demands a high degree of sophistication from the audience. There is also always the issue of methodology. In essence, why readers should find writers' comments and analysis convincing is not always made entirely clear.

Studies in the field of law and popular culture are paradoxical. They are, on the one hand, highly international. We watch, it seems, the same films and see the same television series whether we are in North America, Europe or Australia. Developments, however, are significantly local affairs. Our legal systems are markedly different, whether it be approaches – common law to Codes – or personnel – elected judges to professional civil servants. Our educational practices are quite distinctive. The role of the media in the shaping of perceptions of law and justice are determined by very different histories (Asimow et al. 2005).

The impact and resonance, then, of much of what we are looking at and discussing, is different. This may well explain the rather different directions in which work is developing.

This comment on the future of law and popular culture suggests reasons as to why some of these developments have taken place. The perspective recognises the particularity of different cultural backgrounds. The account from Australian scholars of the emergence of cultural legal studies is specific to the Antipodes (Sharp and Leiboff 2016). The German perspective on law and film, too, demonstrates quite specific elements, (Machura 2016) as do those accounts from American scholars (Sarat 2009). Whilst recognising these differences, there are, however, many areas of congruence which this essay seeks to address. It also indicates some of the problems that the developments are likely to produce. The common problems resolve themselves into related matters of methodology, the use of language and issues of focus. A possible way forward with an unambiguous focus, clear methodology and simple language is provided to counter the notion that the critical elements in this essay amount to no more than negative carping with no alternative programme suggested. It examines areas of justice on television which are both specific to Britain but which, it is suggested, illustrate much broader themes of relevance with this jurisdiction and which are based on a close reading of material in its historical and material context.

2 Legal scholarship in context

In order to appreciate how cultural legal studies might develop it is worth going back to the problematic nature of legal studies themselves. Most disciplines have debates about methodology. Legal education has an even more fundamental underlying conflict since it is involved in training for the legal profession and legal practice as opposed to a discrete intellectual inquiry. There has always been a split on what one is aiming to achieve with the process. This is, admittedly, less of an issue for those from cognate disciplines. The majority of the scholarship, however, which we are involved in here comes from within the world of law and legal studies.

The approach one takes to uncovering the nature of law and how it operates depends crucially on the questions one wants answered. These in turn depend on who is making the inquiries and in what circumstances. The questions which a bright young student of law is likely to ask about the operation of justice are perhaps likely to be centred more on how justice is achieved than the immediate concerns of a lawyer representing poor or disadvantaged clients. These are more likely to be more concerned with rather more mundane matters such as "will my client be able to stay in their current accommodation". He or she will be aware that the big questions of the fairness of the system may have to wait for another day, irrespective of how important they may actually be in determining, for instance, that minority ethnic applicants never achieve success before particular judges. The broader social context, too, is highly important. The significance of what the common law or statutory position of anyone seeking legal assistance is hugely affected by whether or not the justice system is perceived to be fair and open to all. It may be, however, that not having money denies people access to proper advice and representation. It may also be that being a certain sex, ethnicity or sexuality is known or thought to affect one chances before the law, either in terms of the way the rules are applied or enforced. So, taking this into account, it should be clear that which particular approach is adopted, does not take place in some kind of vacuum in which people opt to become "doctrinal" lawyers or "socio-legal" lawyers. It is more a question of teasing out what approach best serves one's immediate purpose. The overarching concern of many has been to uncover how it is that the legal system which promises so much in terms of the equal treatment of the laws, so consistently operates in the interests of the few against the interests of the many and why this is either not known about or allowed to happen without greater social conflict. It is to answer questions like this that scholars have asked not just questions about the impact of particular sets of rules but more importantly what contribution is made to this situation by the way law is represented in books, films and on television. This is the most recent kind of approach found in Law Schools. It links, however, with issues which have fascinated scholars since the dawn of modern legal education and beyond.

3 Modern legal scholarship

It is a paradox that the apparently newest approach to examining and understanding law has, in fact been with us since the emergence of formal legal education. In Britain this did not emerge until the nineteenth century. Law faculties have been in existence for many centuries before this but with a limited role in the preparation of legal profession. This was done by the professions (Abel-Smith and Stevens 1967).

Legal education as distinct from in-house professional training for lawyers by the profession has only been with us in the United Kingdom since the 1870s (Robson 1979, 2012). Until the reform of legal education the then limited number of Universities had Faculties of Law and Professors who wrote on a range of practical and philosophical issues. What they did not have, however, was students. They did not offer degrees. There were some desultory courses offered to trainee lawyers but the reports to the Committee of Legal Education in 1865 from the great institutions of learning in the middle of the nineteenth century paint a sorry picture. When universities started to take undergraduates and offer courses in law from the 1870s there were two approaches. One was to offer a degree in the style we are familiar with today from the United States – the postgraduate first degree. This focused on the details of the operation of the legal system and was geared towards teaching professional practical subjects to those graduates who had commenced working in the legal profession. These young men – and they were, by order of the courts (Jex-Blake v Senatus of Edinburgh University 1873 11 M 784), all men – had received their education at University already with a degree, usually in some Arts subject so were in some sense "educated". The degree could focus on those areas of practice which were central to the working life of the lawyer. Teaching on these part-time degrees, for instance, was undertaken at the beginning of the day, at lunchtime and at teatime to enable these new graduates to combine their study with full-time work as trainee lawyers. The second approach which many lawyers opted for was the in-house training route. Here would-be lawyers completed a period of service in legal firms as articled clerks or apprentices while taking examinations set by the local legal professional societies. It was in this context of focused professional training that legal education as a distinct degree for school leavers commenced on a broad scale.

Debates about what should be in the legal syllabus, which were later encountered during the expansion of higher education in the 1960s, and the dominance of the full time degree addressed the crucial issue of balance (Robson 1979). On the one hand there was the focus on professional training and the day-to-day practical concerns of the profession to have useful well-trained staff joining them from University. On the other hand it was recognised that there was a need for would-be lawyers to reflect on the nature of law and its relationship with justice. This featured heavily in all the debates on the nature and function of the law degree. There was consensus that there was more to a University law degree than merely providing training for the profession. Education required more and this was recognised in the inclusion of compulsory subjects like Jurisprudence and somewhat bizarrely, Forensic Medicine. These would allow the formation of fully rounded lawyers for the future, capable of disputation and contemplation above the narrow details of the common law and emerging statutory codes and the dangerous view that the law is the law. The aim was to produce the kind of lawyer whom the distinguished lawyer and internationally recognised novelist, Sir Walter Scott talked of when he distinguished between the lawyer as "a mechanic, a mere working mason" and one with some knowledge of history or literature who might call himself "an architect" (Guy Mannering 1815).

The point about law and popular culture is that it takes us into a realm of enterprise which socio-legal scholars have, as yet, ventured only in a very limited way. It completes the circle of enquiry about how law and justice really operate. It looks not just at the actions and practices of the justice system, but at what factors help to drive the success or failure of laws and legal systems. By taking seriously the culture of law in the form in which the system is presented to the public it can help give a richer picture than previously available. It is not, however, ever likely to be the dominant approach to law but it provides rich possibilities to complement other scholars' work. The difference is not so much in the different methodologies adopted, however, but rather the kinds of questions which are posed. It has emerged in a variety of different forms.

4 Law and literature

One of the by-products of the nineteenth century debates was the notion that popular culture could provide an insight into the legal process. As long ago as 1913 John Marshall Gest's *The Lawyer in Literature* was the first of a stream of writing about law which showed the link to literature. Building on Wigmore's 1908 list of legal novels, this early collection of the more literary thinking from within the legal community was very much in the spirit of establishing the lawyer as a fully rounded scholar and was followed by other such collections. We find this approach most recently in the 1998 selection *The Literature of the Law* with its selection of extracts from some of the more literary passages from judgments of common law judges on topics as diverse as law and the downtrodden, law in wartime, the law and justice and judicial infirmities (Harris 1998).

As Michael Freeman points out, this link to literature was the recognition of something that has fascinated writers and scholars for hundreds of years (Freeman 2005: 1). Freeman noted that law's engagement with popular culture goes back to the mists of time. Within the Old Testament there are jurisprudential issues aplenty and these expand greatly in Ancient Greece. The themes and issues which Freeman adverts to have, in fact, formed the very stuff of this first way of linking law and popular culture. With their roots in Gest's collection there has been scholarship on the interface between law and literature for the past century. In addition to essays appearing in mainstream legal journals, there has been the *Journal of Law and Literature* since 1969 – originally this appeared as the *Cardozo Studies in Law and Literature* and was published under that title until 1996 – and the Columbia *Journal of Law and the Arts*. Their pages catalogue a vast store of scholarship which examines the literature and law relationship in two principal ways. The less practiced approach is to study the literary forms which judges and lawyers employ in their work. Most people do not read traditional legal texts and the interest remains strictly within the legal community. There is, in addition, a focus on how law is represented within literature. What this involves is looking to what examining works of literature can bring to the understanding of law both within the legal community and outside it. This is of particular importance in the process of legal education. The editors of one collection of essays on law and literature, for instance, suggested that drawing on the insights of literature allows key legal issues to be brought to life in ways which orthodox legal materials cannot rival (Morison and Bell 1996: 1).

This is the principal focus of much of law and literature's scholarship. The 1999 volume of the prestigious Current Legal Issues series from the University of London was devoted to Law and Literature and spans over 750 pages. There are some 32 essays with coverage of playwrights such as Shakespeare and Ibsen and such novelists as Scott, Thomas Hardy, Edgar Allen Poe and Angela Carter. Not only are legal themes mined within literary sources but there is also some attention paid to the literary elements within traditional legal sources such as trials. The contents, however, indicate that the interests of many scholars are with quite specific areas such as the Guernsey Witchcraft Trials of 1617 and the captivity of native North American children. The later collection under the broader heading of Law and Popular Culture appeared in 2005 and continues this splatter gun approach. The vast storehouse of literature is raided by scholars to provide a launch pad for developing arguments on such issues as children's literature, Gothic novels, JG Ballard's work and jurisprudence. Within the specialist Journals, putting aside the permanent fascination with Shakespeare, there is no unifying theme or themes but only a restless search by scholars for new ways to illustrate their current pre-occupations whether it be Bertolt Brecht, Arthur Miller's *The Crucible*, Herman Melville's *Bartleby, the Scrivener* or Laurence Stern's *Tristram Shandy*.

It is evident, then, that the area flourishes today. In addition to the literature and journals noted, there are courses on law and literature available in many Law Schools and the programme of the Association for the Study of Law, Culture and Humanities provides a focus for those working in this area. The work of law and literature scholars sits alongside that of writers on the products of the twentieth century, the cinema and TV. It is, however, quite distinct. It maintains the approach which first animated people to link law and literature. It is worth doing because, like scholarship on Shakespeare, the Romantic Poets or French Realists, it can tell us something profound about human nature and human motivation. As Lincoln Faller put it:

> [l]iterary texts are ... able to escape or smooth over strongly felt contradictions in belief and practice that other kinds of texts have difficulty dealing with. This can make them powerful instruments for 'solving' social and political problems ... or alternatively escaping the insufficiency in the face of such problems of other, supposedly more reality-orientated forms of discourse (Faller 1993: xv [cited in Morison and Bell: 1]).

This, then is the promise and potential insight provided by law and literature. It allows us at its best to contemplate such "contemporary" issues as consent, power and rape by looking at the relationship between Alex and Tess in *Tess of the D'Urbervilles* afresh (Freeman and Lewis 1999: 167) or the broader theme of violence against women (Graycar 1996). The work of Alice Walker in *The Color Purple* similarly provides an element of distance from people's own preconceptions and perspectives to allow debate to be framed in a way with which people are likely to be less threatened. By looking through the eyes of characters, the issues are no less real but less personalised. An overview of the scholarship shows two things. It demonstrates that there is a wealth of material and issues with which to engage. It also highlights two of the reasons why this is an area which has been seen as marginal. The texts are not always accessible. There is in some of most feted writing a curious style which mixes standard academic discussions of footnoted propositions with soaring high flown literary imaginings. Reading the works of such writers as Goodrich (1996) and Aristodemou (2000), for instance, is often akin to reading a novel. Some critics within academe find these works hugely inspiring and liberating. To others they are largely impenetrable. They are certainly a challenge to any student commencing their study of law. Lawyers have to get used to being perplexed but it does not aid an approach when insights are hard to glean because of the method of expression. It is a problem which cannot be shirked that literary criticism is an area where pellucid exposition is not always in the ascendant. The language is frequently at best murky. The writings examined by scholars tend not to engage with any contemporary writing. Thus we find Posner looking at Homer, Shakespeare, Dickens, Dostoevsky and Kafka. Greek myths feature heavily in the scholarship of law and literature and a strong intellectual pedigree is essential.

Engagement with more recent work is rare (Meyer 2001; Robson 1996 and 2014a). The expansion of the legal novels from the early 1990s with the work of Grisham, Turow, Bernhardt and a whole host of others has been largely ignored in favour of "classics".

So here we have a niche area with a recognised body of scholarship and adherents who still face the suspicion that what they are doing is merely a diversion or amusement for the high-minded. The problem for those seen as offering no more than playful comments on law in great literary works is to connect this enterprise to the rest of the syllabus of the average law student. As a "sideline" for academics it may be guaranteed to preserve, and perhaps enhance, status but is not a viable career path and threatens to be always on the margins. The potential to become more engaged with the issues of the day, however, is there. Discussions on the thin lines between anarchy, law and order and a police state can often be highlighted effectively through fictional characters and analysing their actions as well as themes like the impact of feminism (Freeman and Lewis 1999: 191, 219 ; Thornton 2002). There is, though, no sign of any kind of work to link the interpretation of these books and plays with how the public perceive them and what impact they might make. This potential for engagement outside the narrow group of fellow scholars into civil society is a major feature behind developments since 1996 in relation to the visual media. As we shall see, however, here the temptation of academics to engage in arcane debates remains. It is in this area that the more recent excursions into the visual media offer both parallels and, potentially, an alternative.

5 Law and film

The emergence of an interest in law and film as a major focus in publishing terms has occurred in the twenty years since 1996 with some 18 books, 10 edited collections and 8 special journal issues in the area (These appear in the References and in Robson and Silbey's [2012] Introduction). It seems clear that this is an area with considerable potential. As indicated at the start of this essay, however, there are problems which need to be explored. The rise in film and law has a clear foundation stone. It is the assertion and perception that film influences how we see law and justice. This has been the fundamental notion that has inspired writers to explore a range of films. Looking at popular culture also stems from and complements concerns within traditional Sociology of Law and Socio-Legal studies with the social construction of law and its socio-political nature. What has emerged has been a raft of work with both practical and intellectual concerns.

The concern of the earlier scholarship was to draw attention to how law was mis-portrayed in film as well as to use the visual media simply to capture the attention and interest of law students. The use of film as an illustrative teaching/pedagogic tool continues to be a worthwhile focus for lecturers and students alike. Much scholarship has been on individual films (see for example Puaux 2002; Nieto and Fernandez 2004; and Strickland, Foster and Banks 2006). It has been complemented by rather more ambitious attempts to use film's content to illustrate changes in the way social issues are treated and who wields power in society (Greenfield, Osborn and Robson 2001, 2010). Film portrayals and the issues covered and not covered have been used to chart the rise of women lawyers, for instance and the changes in the ways oppressed minorities have been treated. From *I am the Law* (1939) through *Adam's Rib* (1949) and *Jagged Edge* (1987) to *Legally Blonde* (2000) we can see the changes in the visibility and role of women in the law. The fate of ethnic minorities and the LGBT community under the law has received rather less coverage (Moran 1998). Mainstream film material has, until recently (*Brokeback Mountain* 2005; *I Love You Phillip Morris* 2009); *Behind the Candelabra* 2013), been rather scarcer. Again this material whether, utilised in individual doctrinal law classes, theory courses like Jurisprudence or Sociology of Law or in bespoke Law and Film courses meets the need for a modern version of the rounded lawyer. There are, however, two developments, which link law and popular culture with socio-legal studies and professional concerns and which seem likely to provide much of the reason to believe that this visual media focus of modern law and popular culture can break out of the ghetto of academic marginalisation which has bedevilled law and literature.

Firstly there is the application to legal practice of the techniques of storytelling and rhetorical persuasion which can be observed in cinema. In much of Western legal culture the adversarial nature of the legal process involves the techniques of persuasion as much as technical legal knowledge. The ways in which both juries and lawyers understand the process of legal decision-making suggests that legal material is increasingly presented in cinematic terms. It is not just that juries expect the cases to resemble what they have seen on screen. Lawyers and judges themselves derive their role models within practice from fictional presentations of law (Meyer 2001). This interpenetration of reality and popular culture means that the scope of law and popular culture has moved beyond testing the fictional against the "real". The "real" is constructed by lawyers who tactically mould their arguments to fit into their audience's popular cultural expectations (Sherwin 2000). This is done both in technological terms and in narrative terms. Juries are assisted by a range of audio-visual aids. In complex trials the issues are presented in the narrative forms with which the jury is familiar, that of the fictional film or TV trial. This development has important implications for the next generation of lawyers as well as for those with an interest from a theoretical angle on the representation of the law and its actors within popular culture and is important for the Law School of the 21st century.

The second link which has made limited headway but which promises for the future is the attempt to link the ruminations of scholars on the likely impact of the media on people's behaviour with concrete empirical evidence. Rather than simply assume that the media have an impact on behaviour and that is why governments have always tried to censor what the people can see, there are now studies which seek to illustrate exactly how this occurs. This was done in 1973 by Vincenzo Tomeo in *Il Giudice Sullo Schermo* but no English translation has yet been published although I have this in hand. Jessica Silbey has pointed out that there has been a split of emphasis between "law" and "film" somewhat akin to the "law in literature/law as literature" split noted above. This "law-in-film" part looks at how debates within law are conducted within film. How does law order our world in film? Within this broad field of "Law-in-film", Silbey has noted that this scholarship looks at how film shapes our expectations of law and justice in the world at large. Her suggestion "film, *no less than law*, (my emphasis) changes our perceptions of reality" is one thing which is the bedrock of interest in law and popular culture (Silbey 2007: 567). Other writers, from Macaulay (1987) to Sherwin (2000) to Denvir (2004) have made similar suggestions. It has been driven by the exposure of people in the twentieth century to film and then television. Steven Stark estimated that by the time a child in America in the 1980s had reached secondary school age they had been exposed to some 10,000 hours of television on crime and that this shaped their outlook on law and order issues (Stark 1987). Assessing it, however, he suggested was a far from easy task.

The position remains remarkably similar over 30 years later (Robson and Schulz 2016: *passim*). In the twenty-first century there have been a number of attempts to address it. For example, one team of international scholars conducted a study across six disparate jurisdictions on the ways in which law students derive their notions about justice and its relation to law. This revealed that the media including films and TV, did indeed play a major role in the formation of ideas about justice and the legal system (Asimow et al. 2005). By contrast, Kimberlianne Podlas (2009, 2012) as well as Salzmann and Dunwoody (2005) have examined the impact of television and found its impact to be rather less than had been assumed. Further attempts to assess the impact of the media on audiences have been chronicled by Machura (2011), as well as later related work by Machura, Love and Dwight (2014). Although these are all limited studies they do indicate the beginnings of a potentially valuable link between law and popular culture and socio-legal approaches to legal phenomena.

The rather less well-trodden path of some scholars in the field is to suggest that '"film-as-law" is a study of filmic practices that are as pervasive and effective as legal ones in the ways in which they influence and inspire social order' (Silbey 2007: 557, fn 29). This film studies focus has been noted and there have been various attempts made to utilise the insights from this other discipline. Dominated though as the field is by those with a legal rather than film studies background, this has not proved a fertile area. It does, however threaten to shift the area into a kind of self-indulgent emphasis with the nuances of film theory at the expense of engaging those coming from a legal angle. James Elkins has explained that it is precisely because there is an emphasis on the legal that makes film and the law in its more legal-centric form so appealing to scholars and students within Law Schools (per Elkins 2004: 824). Work linking into film studies has emerged (Picart, Jacobsen and Greek 2016) as well as much needed empirical research (Robson and Schulz 2016; Podlas 2009).

6 Law and TV

Whilst scholarship on law and film has flourished, there has been relatively little published on the small-screen lawyer and legal processes. Even in light of the major developments in Spain, where cultural images of law have been examined in extensive detail in a multi-volume series from the Valencia publishers Tirant Lo Blanch under the head of "*cine y derecho*," (Robson 2009: 117) that work has neglected the broader "*cultura popular y derecho*" and television representations scarcely feature at all in the 47 volumes produced by June 2017 (www.tirant.com (last consulted 12 June 2017)) reveals only The West Wing Law Política Como Promesa (October 2016). The same holds true for French and Italian scholarship. In Germany, by contrast, there has been extensive debate and scholarship in this area (Machura 2012).

The dearth of scholarship devoted to television as opposed to cinema in the law and popular culture field is ironic. Television reaches the vast majority of the population. It is more democratic in its processes and distribution mechanism than is film. It provides news, dramas, documentaries and comedies seven days a week, twenty-four hours a day. Cinema, the pre-eminent source of mass entertainment since the early 1920s, is on the decline. Visiting the cinema is now a luxury and is reserved for a relatively small population of Western audiences. The rise of television as the dominant source of entertainment and information, in light of the world's growing focus on the rule of law and international relations, demands consideration in the law and culture scholarship. Robust studies of law and television will complement law school courses on law and literature, law and film, and law and popular culture more broadly.

Most television scholarship about law focuses on the police and not on legal processes or lawyering (Rafter 2006; Lenz 2003). This is likely because the adjudication phase of law, with lawyers and courts, does not feature in the vast majority of police or prison television dramas. The separateness of the trial process from detention and imprisonment is a consistent feature of a considerable body of programmes in Britain and the United States. The split between the apprehension and the adjudicatory phases is stark with the former dominating television coverage across the world. In a study of 14 countries in 2014 around 95% of the law and justice programming on television was on the police and the question of crime detection (Robson and Schulz 2016).

This is an issue which is being addressed and there is new scholarship developing both analysing the nature of the television product as well as its reception and the production process (Robson and Silbey 2012). The allure of the rather more glamorous and seemingly prestigious world of cinema remains, however. One needs to add to this the mundane reality that television series occupy more hours than individual films as well as the older series being unavailable for study. For reasons unconnected with any intrinsic importance as a cultural object there is likely to be a continuation of the existing hierarchy of prestige. Law and literature will continue to enjoy prestige with its links back to the Greeks, Shakespeare and Dickens. The prospects for work between those principally concerned with law and film and the burgeoning field of law and television remain unclear. Existing links need to be strengthened, though, if the full potential for law and popular culture is to be realised by looking at the impact. These possibilities seem more promising, though, than linking the literary and visual worlds. Whether or not this will encompass an examination of the economic structures which determine the content of the culture which we are exposed to is even more problematic but it is a feature which continues to be unfashionable although it is something which the 2016 transnational study addresses (Robson and Schulz 2016).

7 Problems in law and popular culture

There are a number of particular problems within the field of law and popular culture. These centre around the methodology and language adopted within much of the work in the field. There is then the imbalance of resources devoted to television as compared to film. In this section I make a number of suggestions in the spirit of one keen to see this field of interest expand and grow in influence rather than develop into an exotic irrelevant sideline incomprehensible to all but a few specialists.

7.1 Methodology

How one decides what the subject matter is and how enquiry should be carried out was an issue largely overlooked in the early scholarship. Here were arresting new resources – the visual media – to highlight a range of questions in relation the practice of law. Exactly what one did with this new text was determined by one's traditional method of analysing texts for their "meaning". This was the link between traditional doctrinal "black letter" scholarship and socio-legal approaches. The implications of an interpretation for a single client expanded to look at the class, gender and race impacts. Hence scholars started to use cases and legislation to illustrate the ways in which groups and individuals had exercised authority and power in society. From concrete and specific conflicts over such issues as slavery, inadequate housing or working conditions or the role of power in the family, the waxing and waning of power and influence could be demonstrated. Law, even the common law, was shown then as not simply a set of rigid rules with an impenetrable origin but a battleground of social struggle. Film and TV were no different. They were simply different texts which had both clear meaning on the surface as well as other rather more oblique significance and potential meanings. Thus we had *The Man Who Shot Liberty Valance* seen as a metaphor for two different concepts of the nature of law (Denvir 1996: 24). One way of law emerging is organically through the will of the people, whilst the other is to be handed "down" from some authoritative source. A slightly different spin was put on the film Thelma and Louise. Spelman and Minow discussed the crucial theme which crops up in both legal discourse as well as more broadly, namely, the role of confidence in the legal system (Denvir 1996: 270).

Much of this early work was relatively modest in its goals. It often traced how the legal *zeitgeist* had altered and illustrated this with films (Greenfield 2005; Strickland, Foster and Banks 2006). The problem, though is the way in which the cinematic evidence is used as a key to the *zeitgeist*. How does a trend become significant? How many films should we be looking at? What period of time might we observe? What about the issue of changes in different generations' perceptions of earlier films? I have sought to address these issues in discussing vigilante films. Here the time frame for the relevant films was determined by the impact of censorship banning the cinematic glorification of revenge until the 1970s (Robson 2016a; 2016b).

There are other concerns where we move beyond the imprecise, but hugely attractive boundaries of *zeitgeist*. Mark Tushnet examines the film Class Action in terms, not of its significance as an illustration of class politics or professional ethics but as a site for psychoanalytic discussion (in Denvir 1996: 54 ff). He sees the film as a struggle between father and daughter. Austin Sarat, for his part, looks at a range of issues in *The Sweet Hereafter*. He reads the film for its potential to illustrate psychoanalytic perspectives drawn from Lacan (Sarat 2000). What is interesting in both these examples is that they each use the highly contentious perspective of Lacan in relation to the law of the father.

Although the early calls to action on popular culture from Macaulay and Friedman both referred to television, as well as film, most of the work which took up the challenge to examine popular visual culture engaged with film. The role of the first scholars was to provide a stimulating supplement to legal education. The legal education enterprise has traditionally been dominated by professional concerns. What film was used for was to highlight and emphasise. With the new availability of accessible video recordings in the 1990s this work was made considerably easier. An early issue was of the absence of any kind of clear theoretical perspective informing the analysis (Black 1999). The work looking at different kinds of films had a tendency to be highly descriptive. This stemmed from the nature of the task which scholars were addressing with film. As has been explained in greater detail elsewhere this was a subsidiary role (Osborn 2001). The doctrinal or social science analysis was primary. The film texts were examples of these ideas in action. More recently the films themselves seem to have become the focus. This shift into a cultural or film studies framework alters the nature of the scholarly enterprise. It may produce more rigorous "film" scholarship but does it advance our understanding of such issues as gender, ethnic or class interaction and oppression?

Another stream of activity in law and film centred on the storytelling features of law and film (Silbey 2001). There is admittedly, a parallel between the way in which trial lawyers seek to construct a narrative and the way in which some cinema is narrative in its form. This common feature of storytelling, though, neither exhausts what is involved in the operation of the justice system nor what occurs in film. Much of day-to-day legal practice is involved in negotiating between parties as to how future relations will be conducted. There will be discussions about how past conduct has not met stipulated criteria. When allied to the complex enterprise of drafting documents to encompass these scenarios and prevent against undesired outcomes it is hard to see why this set of practices should be portrayed as storytelling. The narrative convention in film may be dominant but much "art house" and even mainstream cinema takes a very different approach.

The question, though, for us is not so much whether or not the characterisation of law as storytelling is inadequate but, rather whether the range of studies Silbey indentifies as "law-in-film" can be usefully contained within a single framework. I would suggest that different methodologies are at work. Different interests and foci exist. Just as legal scholarship ranges from the doctrinal black letter through socio-legal to philosophical analysis, so too law and film has its distinct constituents. The problem lies in failing to recognise that the distinct approaches come with different sets of criteria of relevance. When scholars shift between different approaches without acknowledging this change, they run the risk of their work being misinterpreted or critiqued for failing to do something which it was not trying to do. Descriptive work or taxonomic surveys often cover extensive amounts of material without appearing to engage explicitly with theory. Theoretical insights, in turn, are sometimes premised on very limited evidence. These limitations need to be addressed in the pursuit of richer scholarship. Whether that is turned, as I would wish to see it, towards demystification of the politics of popular culture, is another issue.

7.2 Language

Although this might be seen as the least significant complaint the question does need to be raised by scholars. As part of the enterprise of specialisation and perhaps for the less worthy goal of academic kudos, there is a tendency towards increasing written obscurity tending towards obfuscation. Journals expand in both size and numbers and the contents are aimed at specialist audiences. The same occurred with Marxist analysis in the 1970s. Those lacking the background in a discipline need not start to read. People who may have thought they were interested in law and literature or critical studies have only to open the Journals catering to these areas to find a bewildering array of language and styles unfamiliar to the standard educated reader. The solution, as always is to purchase a dictionary. Academics cannot be expected to dumb down. They might, however, pause to wonder what their interventions are achieving. Read by few and understood by even fewer, there seems little point in engaging in law and popular culture if the students, members of the profession and the public are excluded effectively from the discourse.

My own goals have always been clear and simple. I see the point of examining law and popular culture as part of a mission to explore how the phenomenon of law affects people in their daily lives, both the positive as well as the adverse impact. I do this in the substantive law classes I teach, working in the tradition developed from realism and now found in critical legal perspectives. Here, in my own case, the classes examine how the protections for those in poverty or who are homeless or subject to discrimination operate using social science data beyond the skeleton of the formal rules and regulations. In countries where inequality abounds and oppression on the basic of class, sexuality, disability, gender and ethnicity are rampant, how is law actually able to challenge those practices? Insofar as the protections offered may be totemic do these imperfect legal solutions buttress the positions of those with lawful authority? Specifically, in relation to popular culture, what is their role in suggesting to us that we are genuinely protected by fine phrases like "reasonable" or "just and equitable" and that worthy concepts like "the rule of Law" are not hollow mockeries like the rights under Stalins' 1936 Constitution? (Getty 1991). Is the legal world of the movies and television a site for the vindication of ordinary people's struggles in a way which is far removed from the perpetuation of daily injustice? The aim is not to develop new frontiers in film studies but to illuminate and enrich the study of law and justice using popular culture as an accessible tool to this end. In broad terms it is instructive to assess whether or not the version of law and justice which is encountered is reflexive and supportive of the *status quo* or contains within it a critique of the institutions and their working and are refractive (Black 1999). These are issues which I have considered in the context of the early films of John Grisham's novels (Robson 2001)–currently under revisal but with the same broad conclusion) and in the justice films of Sidney Lumet (Robson 2006) and which strike me as allowing a useful starting point to assess the political significance of popular culture and its changes over time. It is what my colleagues Steve Greenfield and Guy Osborn have sought to do in our collaborative work (Greenfield 2001, Osborn and Robson 2010).

7.3 Shifting the focus

The tendency in law and popular culture studies in the past, often has been relatively modest in the coverage of films or television material. Scholars have by and large examined individual films and analysed what these had to say to us in relation to issues of law and justice. The majority of the writing in the special collections and Journal pieces have followed this line. Thus, for instance, from Denvir's 1996 *Reel Justice* and the San Francisco University Picturing Justice symposium through to the Baltimore Law Review Special Collection on Law and Film in 2007 we find writers taking on board individual films like *Adam's Rib* (Kamir 2000; see also Sanderson and Somerlad 2006), *The Accused* (Silbey 2009) and *North Country* (Korzec 2007). The general expectation, as we see in an issue of the International Journal of Law in

Context and the treatment of *Robocop* (Robertson 2008), is to focus on a single film. The problem, of course, is that the conclusions one can draw from a single film are limited. The reading of films changes over time. Alternatively writers have selected a theme and illustrated this with a selection of films. How film has dealt with a particular issue such as capital punishment (Harding 2005), corporate misconduct (Robertson 2005) or the ethnic minority experience has been explored (Robson 2002).

Selecting big themes and applying a longitudinal approach is, however, best suited for books and generally less appropriate for the essay format. I am, however, impressed with the approaches of Richard Sherwin and Marianna Valverde. Sherwin adopts an approach which involves looking at both the text and the broad context of the period being examined (Sherwin 1996). He has sought to draw rather more elaborate conclusions from limited material without, in my view, stretching our credibility. In his examination of the making and re-making of the film *Cape Fear*, Sherwin draws conclusions about the nature of shifts in American society and the role of lawyers between the late 1950s and the early 1990s. His comments appear perceptive and well-grounded at the general level, although one might cavil that there could be greater social science data on levels of respect for lawyers and changing societal roles of lawyers. Valverde points to the value of locating specific cultural products within their cultural context. She draws our attention to the value of format analysis (Valverde 2006) as a way of differentiating between cultural products to see better how representation is structured and presented. By combining these two approaches I hope to take these cultural phenomena and provide a richer picture than by focusing solely on the different content. I do this looking at products separated in time by 40 years which have the potential to illustrate a changed perception of justice. The objects of my focus are two television series and the goal is to see whether this adds to our understanding of superficially different representations of key actors in the justice system, judges.

I argued some years ago on a number of occasions that television should be looked at in rather greater depth (Robson 2007a, 2007b) and that to continue with a focus on film cuts down on what we can usefully say in terms of the impact of popular culture on society. The films provide a version of how law operates. The television shows, too, indicate the issues confronting society when systems of justice operate. Here we can see the bigoted jury in *To Kill a Mockingbird* (1962), ignoring the evidence, to convict Tom Robinson and the dangers of vigilante justice in *The Star Chamber* (1983). We can see the trade-off made by prosecutors to secure a conviction in *The Accused* (1988). We learn how backstreet abortion blighted the lives of women and their families prior to the legalisation of abortion in *Vera Drake* (2004). I fully appreciate, and am to a significant degree seduced, by the attractions of the glamour of film but do wonder whether we should not be devoting at least equal time to television. The undernoted is a modest contribution to what I would argue is the only way to develop if we are genuinely interested in the impact of popular culture, as opposed to simply film, in relation to law and justice. Elsewhere I have adopted a similar approach to two television legal series with female protagonists to indicate how the portrayal of feminism and social issues have altered between the early 1970s and the second decade of the twenty-first century (Robson 2014b).

8 Assessing the local – from *Mr Justice Duncannon* to *Judge John Deed*

Whilst not wishing to be parochial it also seems to me that it is worthwhile examining TV lawyers in the first place at least in their specific jurisdictional context. It is, I think, vital that the different ways in which such things as how prosecution authorities are constituted, the distinct paths to a judicial career or appointment and how lawyers are paid be recognised in any attempt to survey and assess the representation of the justice system on television. In addition, it is of importance that the structure of the television medium at the specific time and place be noted since this has an impact on the types of programmes made and not made. It may turn out in the end that the links between the versions of TV lawyers encountered in different jurisdictions are overwhelming and that looking at Germany tells us exactly what we gain from looking at the United States or Britain. Similarly the way programmes are produced and financed in different countries may turn out to be much the same. To this end we commissioned essays from a range of 14 different countries on the specifics of television programming on law and justice in 2014 (Robson and Schulz 2016). As we suspected that this was not so. The important thing was to gain a clearer picture from noting the specifics of programmes. Where power lies in making decisions about whether issues are to be pursued in the courts and what kinds of programming receives approval adds to our understanding. At the broader level, this is what we did in the transnational survey in 2014. By way of a further step in this direction the rest of this essay looks in detail at the British legal system as portrayed on television in two series which had a similar focus. One is drawn from 1963 and the other from 2005. Both portray the justice system from the point of view of a High Court judge. It seems to me that this gives us an opportunity to see how law, justice and television itself have altered in the period between the showing of *Mr Justice Duncannon* and the arrival *Judge John Deed*.

What is particularly interesting is that in the examination we can see a conscious attempt to create a character and situation which differs from the reflexive *status quo* supportive scenario that is encountered in much of popular culture's portrayal of justice. In this examination we move from the world and worldview of the British judge and fiction writer of the 1950s and 1960s Henry Cecil to that of contemporary author, Gordon F Newman. We shift from an era of deference to judicial pronouncements to a sustained critique of those interpreting and applying the law. Judges are in the early period ethereal figures almost beyond our ken and absent from the public eye. They do not appear in public discourse. They are amateurs drawn from the practicing Bar and appointed by the senior judge, the Lord Chancellor in an arcane manner meeting unspecified criteria. In the twenty-first century the role and visibility of judges has not altered. The principal change is that they apply for their posts and their appointment is done through the Judicial Appointments Board. The change in the composition of the Bench from being a collection of white, privately educated middle class men has not been dramatic in the years between 1963 and the turn of the century.

The legal disputes we encounter in the world of Henry Cecil appear to be cosy. The characters are daft eccentrics. People are well-meaning, if ineffectual. There are scamps and rogues. This is a world of decent folk occasionally overstepping the mark and of genuine misunderstandings. The world of Gordon Newman, as exemplified in his *Law and Order* series (BBC TV DVD (2006) 1978) and other work is gritty and sleazy. There are really nasty characters. Villains employ shotguns not charm and witty one-liners. Lawyers are happy to provide perjured evidence. Police more than ready to lie and subvert the justice system – to "fit up" any villain who is "due" unless of course enough money can be provided by way of a "bung" (bribe). What one might expect is that the world of *Mr Justice Duncannon* has been supplanted by a much harder edge picture of judicial work addressing the issues of a politicised legal apparatus in the twenty-first century *Judge John Deed*.

8.1 The context of TV

The black and white two channel world of 1963 is the one occupied by Andrew Cruickshank's *Mr Justice Duncannon* and his fellow judges. One channel is funded by a licence fee payable for all TVs, the other relies on commercial advertising for its income. The BBC where Duncannon appeared made programmes in-house. By the time *Judge John Deed* appears on the scene he is competing with five terrestrial channels and a multitude of cable and satellite offerings (Robson and Schulz 2016). He also appears on the public funded channel. External commissioning now takes place within a changed framework of small competitive companies seeking to provide their product to one of many specialised outlets. When *Mr Justice Duncannon* appeared the level of cinema attendance was still buoyant. By the time Judge John Deed appeared cinema and TV's modes of delivery had altered to accommodate DVDs, home cinema and streaming through the internet. These sit alongside the traditional carefully scheduled TV programming and multiplex cinema releases. Which delivery format will determine the market product in the future is far from clear to observers and those within the industry.

One factor which needs to be noted too is the curious paradox of the relative importance of individual television programmes back in the early 1960s and their different status in the new millennium. They are far more plentiful and available from a vast range of sources. The products of the 1960s, though far fewer in number were treated cavalierly. Technological developments mean that it is far easier to produce the programmes as well as to store. We have a situation where something as interesting and path-breaking as *Mr Justice Duncannon* exists only on the pages of the Frank Muir archive at Sussex University. The tapes are listed in no archive and must be presumed wiped. Thankfully the whole world can obtain access to Martin Shaw's *Judge John Deed* in the comfort of their own homes, any time with the DVD version.

8.2 Lawyer portrayals in the 1960s

What is, perhaps, initially surprising about the Duncannon portrayal is that it addresses complex issues of justice at a time when either the humorous or sensational side was typically encountered. The lawyer-centred series that were found in 1962 were four in number on British television. On the one hand were two British products and on the other two US imports (*Perry Mason*, 1957–66); *The Defenders*, 1961–65). We could watch either *Boyd QC* solving crimes and appearing in his wig in court. His popularity was reflected in a prime time slot at 8 p.m. on weekday evenings. It ran over 78 episodes for some eight years between 1956 and 1964. He appeared for both defence and prosecution and did not always win his cases. Again the tapes are wiped although 3 episodes are available online. Alternatively for one short period in 1962 there was a comedy offering from the BBC, *Brothers in Law*. This was based on the light hearted writings of county court judge, Henry Leon. He published 24 books between 1951 and 1977 along with three collections of short stories and seven non-fiction works on legal themes.[1]

The success of *Brothers in Law* both as a book, on the radio and as a 1957 film saw it transfer to television in April 1962. It ran for 13 half hour episodes until 10 July that year. Typical story lines stress Roger Thursby's incompetence in making a plea in mitigation (*Brothers in Law* Episode 1, broadcast 6th April 1962) and in seeking damages for an industrial injury (*Brothers in Law* Episode 2, broadcast 13th April 1962). What we are seeing is how a young and inexperienced youth finds his feet at the Bar. He triumphs by accident and whilst it stops short of farce it exploits the situations for laughter rather than to make a pointed critique of the nature of

---

1 Novels – The Painswick Line (1951); No Bail for the Judge (1952); Ways and Means (1952); Natural Causes (1953); According to the Evidence (1954); Brothers in Law (1955); Friends at Court (1956); Much in Evidence (1957); Sober as a Judge (1958); Settled Out of Court (1959); Alibi for a Judge (1960); Daughters in Law (1961); Unlawful Occasions (1962); Independent Witness (1963); Fathers in Law (1965); The Asking Price (1966); A Woman Named Anne (1967); No Fear or Favour (1968); Tell You What I'll Do (1969); The Buttercup Spell (1971); The Wanted Man (1972); Truth With Her Boots On (1974); Cross Purposes (1976); Hunt the Slipper (1977). **Short story collections** – Full Circle (1948); Portrait of a Judge (1964); Brief Tales from the Bench (1968) – all published by Michael Joseph, London.

the British justice system or its then amateurish method of legal education. The programmes were shown on a Friday evening at 8:50 p.m. at what has become known as "primetime". The actor taking the part of a judge in the final episode, "Counsel for the Prosecution", had just commenced playing Dr Cameron in the adaptation of AJ Cronin's medical stories *Country Doctor* and *The Little Black Bag*. These were shown as *Dr Finlay's Casebook* and ran for 9 years. In his first break from filming this medical series Andrew Cruickshank took the opportunity to reprise his role as Mr Justice Duncannon for a six-episode series between January and February 1963.

The style is though rather more serious than that encountered in *Brothers in Law*. The writers were the same. The basic plots were provided by the same county court judge and writer, Henry Leon, using his nom-de-plume Henry Cecil. Comedy tyros, Frank Muir and Dennis Norden were charged with the task once again of collaborating to render the scripts appropriate for transmission. Dialogue was not Cecil's strong point. There is an optimism, though, about the outlook. The glass of whisky connoisseur *Mr Justice Duncannon* is very much half full.

What is interesting is that in this brief excursion into the life and thoughts of a judge, the writers took the opportunity to address serious themes and weighty issues. The style and approach to some extent calls to mind what we find with John Mortimer's *Rumpole*. The Old Bailey hack seems to be in danger of being remembered as a light comic figure memorable for his spouting of poetry at inappropriate moments, quaffing poor quality claret and being browbeaten by his harridan wife, Hilda (Bergman 2009) . This image of Horace Rumpole and his self-presentation as a bit of buffoon, however, ignore two things. In the first place, a significant proportion of the storylines in the programmes in which we see Rumpole over the years do feature serious issues. These range from rape ("Rumpole and The Honourable Member" (1978) and sexual harassment ("Rumpole and the Quacks" (November 25th 1991) through police corruption ("Rumpole and the Learned Friend" (May 1st 1978); "Rumpole and the Miscarriage of Justice" (November 5th 1992) and racially motivated crimes ("Rumpole and the Fascist Beast" (June 19th 1979) to murder ("Rumpole and Golden Thread" (October 18th 1983); "Rumpole and the Sporting Life" (November 8th 1983; "Rumpole and the Right to Silence" (November 11th 1991) and manslaughter ("Rumpole and the Summer of Discontent", November 4th 1991). Although Mortimer has a fondness for the "scallywag" Timpson family of south London rogues they actually feature in issues which are themselves of significance, like the manufacturing of evidence and defective identity parades. In addition, it is worth pointing out that this is not just my reading of the Rumpole stories. The intention of the author, John Mortimer, which I am sure he achieved, was to introduce a decent left-leaning liberal politics to his audience. The trick was to do this through the mouth of an apparent pillar of the Established order, the barrister, Horace Rumpole. Mortimer opined about Rumpole's that "he does say a good many of the things I think and if I said them they might sound rather leftish and off-putting, but when given voice by Rumpole they become crusty, conservative and much more appealing" (*Rumpole of the Bailey* (2003) Interview with Sir John Mortimer (DVD, Acorn Media).

In *Mr Justice Duncannon* the judge also wrestles with issues of some substance. In the first episode, "Burden of Proof" (MJD (1) transmitted Friday 18th January 1963), for instance he examines what we actually mean by the standard of criminal proof, "beyond a reasonable doubt". His original attempt to turn this standard into common language that one needs to "feel sure" runs into difficulties when the judge tries to explain what this in turn means (MJD (4)transmitted Friday 1st February 1963 – shown out of sequence). He is aided and abetted on his quest by fellow judges and by an encounter with a traffic warden. The tone is light but the issue is quite a serious one. The script produces wry smiles rather than belly laughs. In his next outing, "Brief to Counsel" (MJD (2) transmitted Friday 25th January 1963) the question of judicial bullying and abuse of their position in relation to counsel is explored through the device of having an old flame suggest to Duncannon that he has a reputation as being rude and crusty with young counsel. He duly bends over backwards to be fair only to discover that the young counsel is in fact the son of his lady friend. The same kind of exposure of judicial humanity is seen in "The Whole Truth" where Mr Justice Duncannon struggles to deal with the issue of truth telling. A religious witness is unwilling to swear an unqualified oath since he points out that only God can know what the truth and that a mere mortal can merely "do his best to tell the truth". The subsequent jailing of the witness and the public outcry on behalf of the wronged would-be truth teller foreshadow the whole debate about the relationship between community values and those of the remote figures on the Bench – an issue covered in his fiction like many of Cecil's TV and radio storyline – "Friends at Court" (1956). In "Trial and Error" (MJD (5) transmitted Friday 8th February 1963 – shown out of sequence), the issue of judicial bullying of counsel is again raised along with the question of the appropriateness of imprisonment as opposed to imposing a fine on someone who is well-off and would not notice the impact of a fine. We then see how judges have different personalities and distinct ways of seeing the law and interpreting evidence in "A Case of Whisky" (MJD (3) transmitted Friday 15th February 1963 – shown out of sequence). Again the approach is quite cerebral but like the previous encounters we see our protagonist's judicial omniscience being exposed at the end of the episode. Finally, in the last numbered script, "Orders Not to Pay" (MJD (6) transmitted Friday 22nd February 1963 – shown out of sequence) we encounter Mr Justice Duncannon being hoist by his own petard again when required to admit that the rule which he had stated as the law in his edition of a textbook on recovery of debts was "ill-considered and superficial".

Here, then we have a picture of a judge who is human. Whilst being by no means a modernist he does not have self-conceit. What the series showed, though, was the extent to which the judge is at the mercy of others in terms of setting an agenda. It also indicated the dramatic possibilities as well as limitations of the judicial format for ensuring discussion of interesting and conflicting ideas. Some in the Duncannon series were thrashed out in court with the sparring of counsel and the judiciary

("Brief to Counsel", 25 January 1963; "Orders Not to Pay", 22nd February 1963). Others involve judges in discussion in court ("A Case of Whisky", 15th February, 1963) or providing informal soundings and advice to Mr Justice Duncannon ("The Whole Truth", 1st February, 1963). Contacts with members of the public were also used to provide a forum for debate ("Trial and Error", 8th February 1963) discussion with wife of counsel over abuse of power by powerful people ; "Burden of Proof" (loc cit) discussion with traffic warden over witness credibility). Mr Justice Duncannon played a man who had not married and no family was ever alluded to so that the possibility of chewing over the issues confronting him in his work had no domestic forum. It seems clear, though, from the flow of legal stories and simplicity of the settings mean that further series could have been managed. In the Cecil books we read of the development in the character of Roger Thursby from raw and inexperienced barrister in 1955 (*Brothers in Law* (1955) to Queen's Counsel in 1956 (*Friends in Court* (1956) and finally on to the bench in 1958 (*Sober as a Judge* (1958). The first stage provided us with 13 TV episodes and some 39 radio programmes. Andrew Cruickshank, the embodiment of Mr Justice Duncannon, however, returned to take up his medical duties as Dr Cameron in the long-running and hugely successful TV series *Dr Finlay's Casebook* (1962–1971; 8 series and 178 episodes) ministering to douce rural Tannochbrae and, perhaps, more importantly, the industrial urban Knoxhill. Cecil also had an interest in reflecting on the legal system and in its operation in his non-fiction works *(Brief to Counsel* (1958 and 1972); *Not Such an Ass* (1961); *The English Judge* (1970) and to an extent in his autobiography *Just Within the Law* (1975: Chapters 14–17). Like his fiction, he has greater affection for the system of justice than *animus* against it defects. Cecil continued to produce a stream of stories up until his death in 1977. Given slightly different circumstances, particularly the unavailability of the principal actor, then, the brief experiment with *Mr Justice Duncannon* could have had a longer life and the concept of the judicially centred TV drama might have become less of a rarity.

8.3 Developments in the 20th century

Why it took another 40 years before a judge took centre stage needs to be placed in some kind of context. The early programmes mentioned above have been followed by a huge number of different kinds of portrayals of both the justice system and law in general. Both police procedurals and court centred programming has been an ever present on our screens. Much of this has been home produced providing versions of the British systems. Here is a template in which high drama can be played out with a clear resolution and myriad different plot lines. At its most basic the thrice weekly series *Crown Court* lasted for some 12 years and 735 episodes. The ever-present themes of the loss of liberty, damage to feelings and reputation and tales of cruelty and heartbreak that pass through the courts on a daily basis mean that there is an apparently endless fund of fresh narratives. The trick has been over the past 50 years how to package these in different ways for new audiences. Although the 1970s saw a female protagonist in *Justice* (1972, 4 – 26 episodes) and an ethnic minority lead in *Black Silk* (1985, 8 episodes) only a handful of British offerings have been as long-running as the series *Sutherland's Law* (1973, 76 – 46 episodes), where the inquisitorial role of the Scottish Procurator Fiscal was embellished to provide us with a detective series dressed up as a lawyer show. The success of *L.A. Law* in returning us to the lawyer's office in the 1980s has led most subsequent efforts at legal drama series to replicate the ensemble style. Even the series which focused on an individual like *Rumpole* and *Kavanagh QC* have used the "case/home/office" structural divisional device to allow for a range of different relationships and perspectives to be covered. In these series we have the three distinct compartments of the legal case and its progress in court. This is set in the context of developments and tensions within the workplace environment. To these features are added the vicissitudes of family life in a variety of ways.

8.4 The new millennium

The era since 2000 has been particularly fruitful not simply in the number of British TV lawyers on show but their diversity. There is a sense in which writers and producers have confidence in the "legal drama" format. We have seen a parade of different groups of lawyers seeking to capture the public imagination – and viewing figures. These have principally been based around a recognised TV face – *Close and True* (2000) with multi-series TV star Robson Green and long-established television actor James Bolam; *In Defence* (2000) with soap star Phil Mitchell (Ross Kemp); *Fish* (2000) with *Dr Who* star Paul McGann; *Trust* (2002) again with Robson Green; *The Brief* (2004) with comedy star Alan Davies; *Outlaws* (2005) with *Quadrophenia* actor Phil Daniels; *New Street Law* (2007–2009) with screen star John Hannah and comedian John Thompson; *Kingdom* (2008–2009) with popular TV polymath Stephen Fry and *Silk* (2011–2014) with one of Britain's leading TV and stage actors, Maxine Peake. They also included ensemble pieces of relative unknowns – *Wing and a Prayer* (1997), *Mortimer's Law* (1998) *North Square* (2000) (Robson (2007b: 82–84) and *Coroner* (2015). They were all conventional in their focus on a legal practice and the work of its members pursuing justice in a range of different court settings. None was successful in securing a long run and becoming the new *Rumpole* or *Kavanagh Q.C.* The reasons ranged from poor reviews to lack of the availability of actors with fresh projects to low audience figures.

The "office" or "barristers' chambers" mould, though has been well and truly broken with the setting of such entertainment in a judge's chambers in *Judge John Deed*. The series was created, written and produced by Gordon F Newman. Known for his coruscating exposé of the corruption of the world of justice in his 1978 series, *Law and Order*, Newman sees the glass as already smashed and ready to use on someone. Eschewing the conventional, Newman chose to use the unlikely setting of the High

Court some 40 years since *Mr Justice Duncannon* had been the focus for a legal series. Whilst there is a sense with *Mr Justice Duncannon* that he is merely reacting to what life throws up in his court, *Judge John Deed* has an agenda. Despite the patent fact that the judiciary have no role in the allocation of what issues are brought before the courts, we get the feeling that Deed is in control. He is fishing in the streams of litigation for cases that will give him the opportunity to ensure that injustice is rooted out. From his unprivileged working class Northern background he knows that all is not as it seems in the world of law.

Unseen and powerful forces are seeking to influence the smooth running of his courts. These may take the form of the Government with an interest in ensuring that some individual receives special treatment ("Rough Justice:, 26th November 2001) – MI5 informer whose sentence for domestic abuse is to be nominal) or of the private construction industry seeking to minimise their responsibility for breaches of health and safety regulations which have led to the death of a young casual worker on one of their sites ("Duty of Care", 3rd December 2001) – corporate manslaughter charges reinstated at the behest of Deed). The military and diplomatic world are also secretive and loath to open up to the scrutiny of the justice system ("Silent Killer", 27th January 2006); "War Crimes", 9th January 2007); "Evidence of Harm", 26th January 2007). The set-up of the *Judge John Deed* series, is however, utterly unlike that of his 1960s predecessor. Not only does Deed have a family but he has a split and dysfunctional family. He is related by marriage to a senior member of the judiciary as well as having both his daughter and his sometime mistress working as barristers and often appearing before him. He also comes into frequent contact with his ex-wife whose father is an influential senior judge. The opportunities for ethical conflicts are extensive although these are glossed over as the "Establishment" seek to discipline and control Deed. The mysterious Lord Chancellor's Department attempts to restrict and limit what Deed can do. Deed uses his own informal network of contacts to protect and further his own interests – which are, of course, noble. Deed is not venal. He is promiscuous and sexually irresponsible but he retains within him the heroic commitment to his vision of justice. In one early instance, a man, who is so overwhelmed by grief at his daughter's death that he seeks revenge on the perpetrator, will not defend himself. Deed manages to manoeuvre the unwilling defendant to make a pre-sentence statement that allows the jury to change its mind and find him not guilty ("Exacting Justice", 9th January 2001). The rationale for Deed's action is a simple gut instinct that this man does not deserve a life sentence for reacting just as Deed would have done had his own daughter been run over by a dangerously driven car.

Within his world Deed has powerful allies in the lower court officials. His P.A., Rita "Coop" Cooper, is happy to accept the pejorative term used for these vital cogs in the machinery of justice, by one of the judges. To him they are POLEs – persons of low esteem. They are able to protect Deed from the oversight that the Lord Chancellor's Department (LCD) would wish to exercise over Deed's professional and personal life. This conflict is given a personal edge through the device of having Deed conduct a brazen affair with the wife of one of the senior civil servants in the LCD. Deed, then is the classic rogue figure with whom TV viewers are familiar from popular culture. He is brilliant but not one to be cowed by the rules. From cinema we are familiar with Harry Callahan (*Dirty Harry* (1971); *Magnum Force* (1973); *The Enforcer* (1976); *The Dead Pool* (1988) and Martin Riggs (*Lethal Weapon* (1987); *Lethal Weapon 2* (1989); *Lethal Weapon 3* (1992); *Lethal Weapon 4* (1998). In television we know our detectives will be dismissive of doing the paperwork and will be happy to cut corners in pursuit of instinctive policing. The line is long in Britain from Endeavour Morse (Inspector Morse; Endeavour) and Andy Dalziel (Dalziel and Pascoe) to Jack Frost (Frost) and Jim Taggart (Taggart). The trope is so well recognised that it is hard to think of a "justice" series where the hero is not at odds with the authorities and their restrictions. What Newman has done is to transfer this characteristic to a place where following strict procedures would seem to be a quintessential feature of the role. He has shown us that law can be flexible in the right hands and that even apparently rigid, hierarchical institutions like the law are capable of a degree of flexibility. This is done in a series where contemporary controversies are also raised including race ("Hard Grating", 6th January 2006) and a wide range of medico/legal issues ("Hidden Agenda", 17th December 2001; "Nobody's Fool", 12th December 2002; "Everyone's Child", 19th December 2002; "Health Hazard", 27th November 2003); "Separation of Power", 10th February 2005; "Lost Youth",2nd January 2006; "Silent Killer", 27th January 2006; "Heart of Darkness", 10th February 2006), as well as the dangers of reality TV ("Popular Appeal", 17th February, 2005).

9 Assessing the television judges and their eras

It is the contrast between the two judicial portrayals that appears at first glance to provide a clear snapshot of two very different eras. Examining the individual lawyer programmes between 1962 and 2005 we can see a shift with some themes and issues remaining constant and others changing quite markedly. Sexism and racism are an ever-present. The abuse of power by police and lawyers recurs. Looking though at the world of *Mr Justice Duncannon*, on the one hand, and his successor, *Judge John Deed*, on the other, the difference might seem to have been truly seismic. The change, though, is in superficial style more than in substance. It is possible to read Cecil as fluffy and insubstantial and Newman as gritty and realistic (Robson (2014a)). One is just light entertainment and the other providing a powerful social critique. *Mr Justice Duncannon* might seem to be the great uncle of Stephen Fry's 21st century creation, market town solicitor Peter Kingdom (*Kingdom* – 1st series – 2007; 2nd series – 2008 ; 3rd series – June 2009. Critically panned but with strong audience figures of 6 million + leading to re-commissioning). This world of comfortable minor problems with eccentric British characters in which problems vanish when common sense prevails is classically supportive of the established order. In fact, the similarities are rather more extensive and the tradition of thoughtful reflection which Mr Justice Duncannon brings to social and legal questions is encountered in the subsequent work. What has really altered is the context of a much more fully realised personal life. Beneath the quizzical gaze of *Mr Justice Duncannon* quite profound questions are raised to which there are no simple pat solutions. Cecil's achievement was to dress these debates in the flummery of the British courtroom scene. Perhaps, like his successor as the leading British author on legal topics John Mortimer, he was able, thereby, to achieve a more palatable style of debate.

The problem, though, of course for both Cecil and Mortimer is that what people tend to remember is the style not the substance. What remains, like Lewis Carroll's cat is the grin. Paradoxically a related problem occurs with our reading of Judge John Deed. What we remember are his lurid sexual encounters. The profoundly serious issues in the cases pale by comparison with his unjudicial private life and his personalised jousting with the Establishment.

The question of context also needs to be factored into any assessment of these two distinct cultural products. It is not so much that the nature of society and social issues have not actually changed so much as how the two writers provide their vision of their society. At the time when Henry Cecil was writing his unthreatening accounts of the travails of untrained amateur ingénu, Roger Thursby and his like, the police were fabricating evidence; judges like Lord Goddard were giving highly prejudicial charges to juries in capital murder cases – provided word for word from the court transcript in *Let Him Have It* (1989); razor gangs in Glasgow were causing mayhem; Teddy Boys were swaggering through the streets – although the Teddy Boy phenomenon can be seen as a "moral panic" produced by the press headlines there was involvement of some of their number in the race riots of 1958 and racial tensions and attacks in Nottingham and Notting Hill were taking place. The contemporary British films of the time painted different portraits of Henry Cecil's Britain. A steady stream of post-War British films showed a society riven by lack of opportunity, poverty, alienation and conflict. The conflicts are sometimes profoundly political as in the IRA drama *Odd Man Out* (1946). The focus may be on lives which are drab and only tangentially connected with law – *It Always Rains on Sunday* (1947) or there may be a central focus on organised crime and gangsters – *Brighton Rock* (1947) or youth and gang culture - *The Blue Lamp* (1949). Here, however, is a Britain unrecognisable from watching sanitised versions of the justice system like *Eight O'Clock Walk* (1953), *Witness for the Prosecution* (1957) or *Brothers in Law* (1957). The point is not really which of these versions is more accurate but that they represent two facets. One is a focus on a particular segment of society. The other is the level of optimism of the writing.

Social realism and escapist drama are two very different kinds of film but the contrast between early sixties films like *The Boys* (1961) and *The Fast Lady* (1963) is instructive. Both involve at some point the courts and we see two very different Britains. *The Boys,* taking its cue from Ted Willis' essays on British social relations,

No Trees in the Street (1958) and *Flame in the Streets* (1961) paints a bleak picture of a narrow and introspective British society. The Willis films ask questions about social inequality and prejudice in the same way as showing a restless dangerous almost *film noir* version of Britain. Allied to the rejection of an unyielding class system seen in *Room at the Top* (1958) and *Saturday Night and Sunday Morning* (1960) we have a perspective which stresses the urban backdrop to crime and order problems (Hutchings 2001). *The Fast Lady*, on the other hand, is in the tradition of *Doctor in the House* (1953), *Genevieve* (1953) and *The Constant Husband* (1955) and finds us in a country of mild eccentricity where people rub along tolerably well. To highlight this point, we can look at two of Sir Cliff Richard's films to see the contrast. In one we have the depressing alienated youth culture portrayed in *Serious Charge* (1959) and in the other its upbeat equivalent in *The Young Ones* (1961) – see also *What a Crazy World* (1961) for a cheerful rendering of poverty – and racial stereotypes played out for comic effect. Same settings and characters but with a positive mood change. Writers and commentators like Gerald Gardiner (Gardiner and Martin 1963), Ludovic Kennedy (1964), and David Yallop (1967), in contrast to Cecil's non-fiction, adopted a distinctly more pessimistic approach stressing that the legal system, in particular, might have fine visually uplifting traditions but that these were leading to serious miscarriages of justice. In the world of *Mr Justice Duncannon* we have a baffled kind of optimism that we will muddle through. *Judge John Deed* knows that the forces of self-interest will not be easily thwarted and that the prospects for social stability hang by a thread. The world where there is a filmic reflection on British social life hardly figures in the time of John Deed. It has been replaced by fantasy cinema. This ranges from the hobbits of Tolkien in the Lord of the Rings trilogy, the spoof spy Johnny English and the James Bond franchise. It is left to niche "arthouse" directors Ken Loach (*My Name is Joe* (1998); *Bread and Roses* (2000); *Sweet Sixteen* (2002); *Ae Fond Kiss* (2004)) and Mike Leigh (*Secrets and Lies* (1995); *All or Nothing* (2002); *Vera Drake* (2004)) to shine a light on contemporary poverty, racism and alienation. The televisual world of reality TV, soap operas and medical series are where we go for ethical conflicts. The judge wrestles with his dilemmas on his own. His world is not different from that of his predecessor. Dangers and moral panics abounded in the early 1960s with multiple murderers Peter Manuel, Myra Hyndley and Harry Roberts in our lives. They have, however, been glossed over and largely forgotten in a rosier recollection of the world inspired by catchy pop songs, Mini Coopers and England winning the World Cup – all packaged together along with witty gangsters in *The Italian Job* (1969).

10 Concluding remarks

When in the mid-1980s calls went out for scholars to look beyond the actual operation of the legal system to see how this world was presented in the media this opened a new and exciting chapter in socio-legal scholarship. Those very first examples mixed comments about film and television in equal measure. Much ink has since been spilt in this area. The dangers I alluded to at the beginning of this essay are beginning to be confronted. It seems to me that a great opportunity is being lost to investigate how representations affect those who learn from them if the future does not assess the whole field, including television. Simply offering readings of films at one moment in time does not adequately address these concerns. Moreover, this work with an altered focus also would do well to go beyond the contested meanings of these works and look at the impact on opinion, ideally at different times and on different groups. Obtaining the resources to conduct extensive empirical research is another question. The majority, however, of the more recent work still focuses on the big screen. It would be a sad day if the attractions of a tangential connection with the glamorous world of film and of providing a reading of individual films were to continue to skew the efforts and scholarship of writers to the detriment of a rich plural picture of how law and popular culture interact.

References

Abel-Smith, Brian and Robert Stevens. 1967. *Lawyers and the courts*. London: Heinneman.
Aristodemou, Mària. 2000. *Law and literature*. Oxford: Oxford University Press.
Asian Law Journal. 1998. Race, law and film. *Asian Law Journal* 1.
Asimow, Michael (ed.). 2009. *Lawyers in your living room: law on television*. Washington: ABA.
Asimow, Michael, Kathryn Brown, and David Papke (eds.). 2014. *Law and popular culture: international perspectives*. Cambridge: Cambridge Scholars Press.
Asimow M., S. Greenfield, J. Guillermo, S. Machura, G. Osborn, P. Robson, C. Sharp and R. Sockloskie. 2005. Perceptions of lawyers: a transnational study of student views on the image of law and lawyers. *International Journal of the Legal Profession* 12. 407.
Asimow, Michael and Shannon Mader. 2004. Law and popular culture New York: Lang.
A symposium on film and the law. 1997. *Oklahoma City University Law Review* 22(1).
Bergman, Paul. 2009. Rumpole and the bowl of comfort food. In Michael Asimow (ed.), *Lawyers in your living room: law on television*. Washington: ABA.
Bergman, Paul and Michael Asimow. 1996. *Reel justice – the courtroom goes to the movies*. Kansas City, MO: Andrews McMeel.
Black, David. 1999. *Law in film: resonance and representation*. Urbana and Chicago: University of Illinois Press.
Chase, Anthony. 2002. *Movies on trial: the legal system on the silver screen*. New York: The New Press.
Denvir, John (ed). 1996. *Legal reelism: movies as legal texts*. Urbana and Chicago: University of Illinois Press.
Denvir, John. 2004. The slotting function: how movies influence political decisions. *Vermont Law Review* 28. 799.
Elkins, James. 2004. Reading/teaching lawyer films. *Vermont Law Review* 28. 797.
Faller, Lincoln. 1993. *Crime and Defoe: a new kind of writing*. Cambridge: Cambridge University Press.
Freeman, Michael and Andrew Lewis (eds.). 1995. *Law and literature*. Oxford: Oxford University Press.
Freeman, Michael (ed.). 2005. *Law and popular culture*. Oxford: Oxford University Press.

Gardiner, Gerald and Andrew Martin (eds.) 1963. *Legal reform now*. London: Gollancz.

Gest, John. 1913 [1999]. *The lawyer in literature*. London: Sweet & Maxwell.

Getty J Arch. 1991. State and society under Stalin: constitutions and elections in the 1930s. *Slavic Review* 50(1). 19.

Goodrich, Peter. 1996. *Law in the courts of love: literature and other minor jurisprudences*. London: Routledge.

Graycar, Regina. 1996. Telling tales: Legal stories about violence against women. *Australian Feminist Law Journal* 7(1). 79–93.

Greenfield, Steve and Guy Osborn. 2005. The double meaning of law: does it matter if film lawyers are unethical. In M. Freeman (ed.), *Law and popular culture*, 638. Oxford: Oxford University Press.

Greenfield Steve and Guy Osborn (eds.). 2006. *Readings in law and popular culture*. Abingdon: Routledge.

Greenfield, Steve, Guy Osborn and Peter Robson. 2007. Genre, iconography and British legal film. *Baltimore Law Review Law and Cinema Special Issue* 36. 371.

Greenfield, Steve, Guy Osborn and Peter Robson. 2001. *Film and the law*. London: Cavendish.

Greenfield, Steve, Guy Osborn and Peter Robson. 2010. *Film and the law: the cinema of justice*. Oxford: Hart.

Guéry, Christian. 2007. *Justices à l'écran*. Paris : Institut des Hautes Etudes sur la Justice.

Gunn, David (ed.). 1993. *The lawyer and popular culture: proceedings of a conference*. Littleton: Fred B Rothman.

Harding, Roberta. 2005. Reel violence: popular culture and concerns about capital punishment in contemporary American society. In Michael Freeman (ed.), *Law and popular culture*, 358. Oxford: Oxford University Press.

Harris, Thomas. 1987. *Courtroom's finest hour in American cinema*. Metuchen, NJ & London: The Scarecrow Press.

Harris, Brian (ed.). 1998. *The literature of the law*. London: Blackstone Press.

Hutchings, Peter. 2001. Beyond the new wave: realism in British cinema 1959–63. In R.P. Murphy (ed.), *The British cinema book*. London: BFI.

Jarvis, Robert and Paul Joseph. 1998. *Prime time law: fictional television as legal narrative*. Durham, NC: Carolina Academic Press.

Kamir, Orit. 2000. X-raying Adam's Rib: multiple readings of a (feminist?) law-film. *Studies in Law, Politics and Society* 22. 103.

Kamir, Orit. 2006. *Framed: women in law and film*. Durham, NC: Duke University Press.

Kennedy, Ludovic. 1964. *Ten Rillington Place*. London: Gollancz.

Kornstein, Daniel. 1994. *Kill all the lawyers? Shakespeare's legal appeal*. Princeton, NJ: Princeton University Press.

Korzec, Rebecca. 2007. Viewing *North Country*: sexual harassment goes to the movies. *Baltimore Law Review Law and Cinema Special Issue* 36. 303.

Law and cinema [Special Edition]. 2007. *Baltimore Law Review* 36.

Law and film [Special Issue]. 2001. *Journal of Law and Society* 29.

Law and popular culture [Special Issue]. 1998. *Legal Studies Forum* 22(3).

Law in film/film in law [Special Issue]. 2004. *Vermont Law Review* 28. 797.

Lenz, Timothy. 2003. *Changing images of law in film and television crime stories*. New York: Peter Lang.

Levi, Ross. 2005. *The celluloid courtroom: a history of legal cinema*. Westport CT: Praeger.

Linera, Miguel Angel Presno and Benjamin Rivaya (eds.). 2006. *Una introducción cinematográfica al derecho* [A cinematic introduction to law].

Lucia, Cynthia. 2005. *Framing female lawyers: women on trial in film*. Austin: University of Texas Press.

Macaulay, Stewart. 1987. Images of law in everyday life: the lessons of school, entertainment and spectator sports. *Law and Society Rev*iew 21. 185.

Machura, Stefan. 2011. Media influence on the perception of the legal system. In K. Papendorf, S. Machura and K. Andenæs (eds.), *Understanding law in society*. Zurich and Berlin: Lit Verlag.

Machura, Stefan, 2012. The German sociology of law: a case of path dependency. *International Journal of Law in Context* 8. 506–523.

Machura, Stefan, Thomas Love and Adam Dwight. 2014. Law students' trust in the courts and the police. *International Journal of Law, Crime and Justice* 42. 287–305.

Machura, Stefan. 2016. Law and cinema movement. In Caroline Picart, Michael Jacobsen and Cecil Greek, (eds.), *Framing law and crime: an interdisciplinary anthology*. Madison & Teaneck, NJ: Farleigh Dickinson University Press.

Machura, Stefan and Peter Robson (eds.). 2001. *Law and film*. Oxford: Blackwell.

Masson, Antoine and Kevin O'Connor (eds.). 2007. *Representations of justice*. Bruxelles: Peter Lang.

Meyer, Phil. 2001. Why a jury trial is more like a movie than a novel. *Journal of Law and Society* 28(1). 133.

Moran, Leslie. 1998. 'Heroes and Brothers in Love: The male homosexual as lawyer in popular culture'. *Studies in Law Politics and Society* 18.

Moran, Leslie, Elena Loizidou, Ian Christie and Emma Sandon (eds.). 2004. *Law's moving image*. London: Glasshouse Press.

Morison, John and Christine Bell (eds.). 1996. *Tall stories? Reading law and literature*. Dartmouth: Aldershot.

Nieto, Francisco Soto and Francisco J Fernández. 2004. *Imágenes y Justicia: el derecho a través del cine [Images and Justice; law through cinema]*. Madrid: La Ley.

Ogletree, Charles and Sarat Austin. 2015. *Punishment in popular culture*. New York: New York University Press.

Osborn, Guy. 2001. Borders and boundaries: locating the law in film. In Stefan Machura and Peter Robson (eds.), *Law and film*. Oxford: Blackwell.

Picart, Caroline, Michael Jacobsen and Cecil Greek, (eds.). 2016. *Framing law and crime: an interdisciplinary anthology*. Madison & Teaneck, NJ: Farleigh Dickinson University Press.

Podlas, Kimberlianne. 2009. Impact of television on cross-examination and juror 'truth' 14. *Widener Law Review* 483.

Podlas, Kimberlianne. 2012. Testing television: studying and understanding the impact of television's depictions of law and justice. In P. Robson and J. Silbey (eds.), *Law and justice on the small screen*. Oxford and Portland, OR: Hart Publishing.

Posner, Richard. 1988. *Law and literature*. Cambridge, MA: Harvard University Press.

Puaux, Francoise (ed.). 2002. La justice à l'écran. *CinémaAction* 105. Conde-sur-Noireau: Corlet-Telerama.

Rafter, Nicole. 2006 (2000). *Shots in the mirror*. Oxford: Oxford University Press.

Rapping, Elayne. 2003. *Law and justice as seen on tv*. New York New York University Press.

Robertson, Michael. 2005. Seeing blind spots: corporate misconduct in film and law. In M. Freeman (ed.), *Law and popular culture*, 385. Oxford: Oxford University Press.

Robertson, Michael. 2008. Property and privatisation in *RoboCop*. *International Journal of Law in Context* 4(3). 117

Robson, Peter. 1979. *Housing and the judiciary*. Glasgow: University of Strathclyde.

Robson, Peter. 1996. Images of law in the fiction of John Grisham. In J. Morison and C. Bell (eds.), *Tall stories? Reading law and literature*. Dartmouth: Aldershot.

Robson, Peter. 2001. Adapting the modern law novel: filming John Grisham. In *Law and film* (eds) Stefan Machura and Peter Robson (eds.), *Law and film*. Oxford: Blackwell.

Robson, Peter. 2002. Fade to grey: portraying the ethnic minority experience in British film. *International Journal of the Sociology of Law* 3. 235.
Robson, Peter. 2005. Law and film studies; autonomy and theory. In M. Freeman (ed.), *Law and popular culture*. Oxford: Oxford University Press.
Robson, Peter. 2006. The justice films of Sidney Lumet. In Steve Greenfield and Guy Osborn (eds.), *Readings in law and popular culture*. London and New York: Routledge.
Robson, Peter. 2007a. Lawyers and the legal system on TV: the British experience. *International Journal of Law in Context* 2(4), 333–362.
Robson, Peter. 2007b. Developments in law and popular culture: the case of the tv lawyer. In Antoine Masson and Kevin O'Connor (eds.), *Representations of justice*, 75–93. Bruxelles: Peter Lang.
Robson, Peter. 2009. Law, Hollywood and the European experience. *Studies in Law, Politics and Society: Symposium on Film*, 117.
Robson, Peter. 2012. Law and Popular Culture (in An Introduction to the Study of Law ed Simon Halliday). Edinburgh, W Green.
Robson, Peter. 2014a. The law through the eye of courtroom comedy: the light legal procedural in context. In Michael Asimow, Kathryn Brown and David Papke (eds.), *Law and popular culture: international perspectives*. Cambridge: Cambridge Scholars Press.
Robson, Peter. 2014b. Women lawyers on tv – the British experience. *Nordic Journal of Law and Social Research* 5. 101–116.
Robson, Peter. 2016a. Beyond the courtroom: vigilantism, revenge and rape-revenge films in the cinema of justice. In Caroline Picart, Michael Jacobsen and Cecil Greek (eds.), *Framing law and crime: an interdisciplinary anthology*. Madison & Teaneck, NJ: Farleigh Dickinson University Press.
Robson, Peter. 2016b. Vengeance in popular culture. Oxford Research Encyclopedia Criminology and Criminal Justice. www.criminology.oxfordre.com (accessed 12 June 2017).
Robson, Peter and Jennifer Schulz (eds.). 2016. *A transnational study of law and justice on tv*. Oxford: Hart.
Robson, Peter and Jessica Silbey (eds.). 2012. *Law and justice on the small screen*. Oxford: Hart.
Salzmann, V. and P. Dunwoody. 2005. Do portrayals of lawyers influence how people think about the legal profession. *Southern Methodist University Law Review* 58. 411.
Sanderson, Peter and Hilary Somerlad. 2006. Gender, power and law in screwball comedy: re-viewing *Talk of the Town* and *Adam's Rib*. In Steve Greenfield and Guy Osborn (eds.), Readings in law and popular culture. Abingdon: Routledge.
Sarat, Austin. 2000. Imagining the law of the father: loss, dread and mourning in *The Sweet Hereafter*. *Law and Society Review* 34. 5.
Sarat, Austin, Anderson, Matthew and Frank, Catherine O, 2009. Cambridge: Cambridge University Press.
Sarat, Austin, Lawrence Douglas and Martha Umphrey (eds.). 2005. *Law on the screen*. Stanford: Stanford University Press.
Sharp, Cassandra and Marett Leiboff (eds.). 2016. *Cultural legal studies: law's popular cultures and the metamorphosis of law*. Abingdon and New York: Routledge.
Sherwin, Richard. 1996 *Cape Fear*: Law's inversion and cathartic justice. *University of San Francisco Law Review* 30. 1023.
Sherwin, Richard. 2000. *When law goes pop: the vanishing line between law and popular culture*. Chicago: University of Chicago Press.
Silbey, Jessica. 2001. Patterns of courtroom justice. In Stefan Machura, and Peter Robson (eds.), *Law and film*. Oxford: Blackwell.
Silbey, Jessica. 2007. Truth tales and trial films. *Loyola of Los Angeles Law Review* 40. 551–557.
Silbey, Jessica. 2009. A witness to justice. In Austin Sarat (ed.), *Studies in law politics and society*, (Studies in Law, Politics and Society, Volume 46), 61–91. Emerald.

Stark, Steven. 1987. Perry Mason meets Sonny Crockett: the history of lawyers and the police as television heroes. *University of Miami Law Review* 42. 229.

Strickland, Rennard, Teree Foster and Taunya Banks (eds.). 2006. Screening justice: the cinema of law. Buffalo, NY: William S. Hein & Co.

Symposium on law and film. 1991. *Legal Studies Forum* 15. 199.

Symposium: picturing justice: images of law and lawyers in the visual media. 1996. *University of San Francisco Law Review* 30. 891.

Thornton, Margaret (ed.). 2002. *Romancing the tomes*. London: Routledge.

Tomeo, Vincenzo. 1973. *Il giudice sullo schermo*. Bari: Laterza.

Valverde, Mariana. 2006. *Law and order: images, meanings and myths*. London: Routledge.

Villez, Barbara. 2005. Séries télé: visions de la justice. Paris: Presses Universitaires de France.

Villez, Barbara. 2010. Television and the legal system. London: Routledge.

Wagner, Anne and Richard Sherwin. 2014. *Law, culture and visual studies*. Dordrecht: Springer.

Ward, Ian. 1995. Law and literature. Cambridge: Cambridge University Press.

Ward, Ian. 1999. Shakespeare and the Legal Imagination. London: Butterworths.

Yallop, David. 1967. *To encourage the others*. London: Gollancz.

Part IV: **International legal settings**

Silvia Ferreri
14 Multilingual interpretation of European Union law

1 Introduction: the multilingual option

A long-standing decision from 1958 still affects the present situation of languages within the European Union. At the time, when the languages used in the six original member States of the European Common Market were very few when compared with today's 24 languages, it seemed quite logical to provide in EEC Regulation 1/1958 that: "Article 1. The official languages and the working languages of the institutions of the Community shall be Dutch, French, German and Italian."

Under this rule, workloads could be managed reasonably well, considering that minor (in terms of number of native speakers) languages such as the Luxembourg language (*Lëtzebuergesch*), or Belgium's Flemish spoken, were not granted the title of "official languages."[1]

The commitment to multilingualism is also repeated in art. 20, 2 (d) of the 2007 Treaty on the Functioning of the EU, according to which "Citizens of the Union shall enjoy (...) (d) the right to petition the European Parliament, to apply to the European Ombudsman, and to address the institutions and advisory bodies of the Union in any of the Treaty languages and to obtain a reply in the same language."

Problems related to the management of several versions of European documents have obviously become much more serious with the joining of several new countries, especially those belonging to Central and Eastern Europe. This is the reason why so much discussion is taking place on the "language policy after the enlargement"[2] (Pozzo and Jacometti 2006).

---

[1] Some regional languages, such as Basque, Catalan, Galician, Scottish Gaelic and Welsh have a "co-official" status in the sense that the documents are translated into these languages, on the basis of specific agreements with the Member States where these languages are used and with the economic support of those States. The Ministers of Foreign Affairs reached the agreement in 2005. http://euobserver.com/news/19323.
[2] Pozzo, Barbara & Jacometti, Valentina (eds.). 2006. Le politiche linguistiche delle istituzioni comunitarie dopo l'allargamento. Milan: Giuffré.
Schübel-Pfister, Isabel. 2005. Enjeux et perspectives du multilinguisme dans l'Union européenne: après l'élargissement, la "babelisation". Revue du Marché Commun et de L'union Européenne. 332.
Some interesting data in Marí, Isidor & Strubell, Miquel (Open University of Catalunya). The linguistic regime of the European Union: Prospects in the face of enlargement.

A specific consideration deserves attention. A rather critical remark made by Advocate general Jacobs points out that [3]:

It is a fiction to say that the legislature has considered all the language versions. What of legislation adopted by the Six? Each accession increases the number of texts that were not originally authentic in all the current languages.

It would, however, be contrary to the accession treaties to suggest that only those language versions existing at the time the legislation was adopted are authentic.

We should therefore consider that some texts have become authentic *ex post*, after the Member State using a different language has actually joined the Union. As a result, from the beginning of our reflections on the subject, we must contend with issues relating to compromise. For instance, there is an element of fiction in saying that the Irish version of a 1967 regulation is authentic, since Ireland only joined the "European club" in 1973.

The European Court of Justice has dealt with equality issues between all the languages. In the Skoma case (C-161/06) at point 37, it ruled that regarding legislation that existed prior to a State's accession: "an act adopted by a Community institution, such as the regulation at issue in the main proceedings, cannot be enforced against natural and legal persons in a Member State before they have the opportunity to make themselves acquainted with it by its proper publication in the *Official Journal of the European Union*".[4]

This is a consequence of the need for legal certainty, ruling that legislative acts enacted before the accession of a State to the Community (now Union) must be translated into the language of all member States to be made binding on the citizens. Publication on the *Official Journal* is part of the process of making the law accessible to citizens.

2 Advantages and disadvantages

On the positive side of the arrangement reached in 1958, two arguments attract our attention.

Firstly, everyone agrees that cultural diversity is an important asset, and that different languages reflect differences in culture. Linguistic issues are highly sensitive and are part of the identity of many ethnic groups in Europe. Often, demands for independence are linked to the existence of a particular language in a specific area

---

[3] Jacobs, Francis. 2003. How to interpret legislation which is equally authentic in twenty languages. Lecture at European Commission, seminars on quality of legislation, Legal Revisers Group, Brussels. October 20. http://ec.europa.eu/dgs/legal_service/seminars/agjacobs_summary.pdf.
[4] European Court of Justice. C-161/06. Skoma-Lux sro v Celní ředitelství Olomouc. https://eur-lex.europa.eu/legal-content/EN/TXT/?uri=CELEX%3A62006CJ0161.

that sets part of the population apart from the rest of the country (the obvious reference is to Catalonia, the Basque country, the Flemish region in Belgium, Scotland and so on).

Secondly, when legislation is expressed in more than one language, it may well be that the intent of the legislator is better explained by comparing the various versions of the same text. Where the intent may result fuzzy in one language, another version may be more explicit.

On the negative side, of course, the main complaint concerns the complex mechanisms necessary to maintain 24 parallel versions of all documents[5] (Solan 2008), the uncertainty connected with the fact that the various versions may be divided into majority and minority groups (or into even more fragmented groups) and the observation that in fact, apart from official declarations of equality, English has largely taken over, at least as working language at the institutional level.

A study performed some years ago by the Commission observed for the first time that more documents had been drafted in English than French (55% and 42% respectively). Just a few years later in 2009 a survey of Commission staff found that over 90% regarded English as their main drafting language. The 2009 survey found, however, that only a small minority of those writing in English are native speakers, just 13%. Rather alarmingly 54% of drafters "rarely or never have their documents checked by a native speaker.[6]"

Obviously the discrepancies between what is done in practice during the political negotiations (English as *lingua franca*) and the multilingual final version of the agreed documents reflect real needs. Providing simultaneous translation for all meetings of all working groups is simply not feasible, and the use of "bridge languages" (*langues-pivot*) helps at least in the safeguarding of the principle of multilingualism.

There actually is an area in European Union law where the French language still competes with English: the case law (*jurisprudence*) of the European Court of Justice. Under the rules of procedure of the European Court of Justice[7], the language used during the trial (procedural language) depends on the requests of the parties to

---

[5] Solan, Lawrence M. 2008. The Interpretation of Multilingual Statutes by the ECJ. Brooklyn J. International Law 34 (9). 276. According to Solan managing many linguistic versions results in "a daunting task for a court that must resolve disputes over a statute's applicability (...) The opportunity for inconsistencies among the various language versions is so profound that it would not be surprising if the entire system collapsed under its own weight." The author is more optimistic, as shown in the following pages.
[6] Report on the survey in the Directorate General for Translation publication Languages and Translation, Issue 1. 4.
http://ec.europa.eu/dgs/translation/publications/magazines/languagestranslation/documents/issue_01_en.pdf.
[7] https://eur-lex.europa.eu/legal-content/EN/TXT/?uri=LEGISSUM:ai0049.

the case[8]. However, according to the internal arrangement of the court, discussions between the judges take place in French, in order to establish one shared language that may directly be used without the mediation of translators[9] (Gallo, in Pozzo and Jacometti 2006). The internal agreement has been made to allow for a common means of communication, so that judges can address each other on a shared basis. When Eastern European countries joined the EU, some debate took place on the possibility of moving towards English as a substitute common language, but the existing practice finally won majority consent. This choice influences the organization of the linguistic services: French translators are generally under greater pressure, leading to a larger number of civil servants appointed[10] (Oddone in Pozzo and Jacometti 2006).

In the parallel institution of the Council of Europe, the Strasbourg European Court of Human Rights, judges may discuss in either English or French as both these languages are official languages of the Council of Europe.[11] That said, a certain trend toward English as working language may be detected in the Council.

---

8 Art. 37, 1: "In direct actions, the language of a case shall be chosen by the applicant (…) 3. In preliminary ruling proceedings, the language of the case shall be the language of the referring court or tribunal."

9 Gallo, G. 2006. Organizzazione e caratteristiche dell'attività di traduzione nell'ambito della Corte di Giustizia delle Comunità Europee. In Pozzo, Barbara & Jacometti, Valentina (eds.). *Le politiche linguistiche delle istituzioni comunitarie dopo l'allargamento*. Milan: Giuffré. 251.

Oddone, Beatrice. 2006. La traduzione giuridica alla Corte di Giustizia delle Comunità Europee. Problemi e tecniche. In Pozzo, Barbara & Jacometti, Valentina (eds.). *Le politiche linguistiche delle istituzioni comunitarie dopo l'allargamento*. Milan: Giuffré. 277; Brady, Hugo. 2014. Twelve Things Everyone Should Know About the European Court of justice. *The thinks in French*. Center for European Reform. 35.

https://www.cer.eu/publications/archive/report/2014/twelve-things-everyone-should-know-about-european-court-justice.

Edward, David expresses the opinion of one of the past judges at the European Court of Justice, in Edward, David. 1995. How the Court of Justice works. *European Law Review*. 539–546. Recently also: Stotz, Rüdiger (Director General, Directorate Library, Research and Documentation, Court of Justice of the European Union). 2014. *The interpretation of legal texts by the Court of Justice of the European Union*. Second European Symposium on Improving the Comprehensibility of Legal Provisions, Federal Ministry of Justice and Consumer Protection, Berlin. November 11.

10 Oddone, B. 2006. La traduzione giuridica alla Corte di Giustizia delle Comunità Europee. Problemi e tecniche. In Pozzo, Barbara & Jacometti, Valentina (eds.). *Le politiche linguistiche delle istituzioni comunitarie dopo l'allargamento*. Milan: Giuffré. 277.

11 Translation into the 38 other languages (for 47 member States) takes place at a later stage: not every document is translated ("The selection of the most important cases is made by the Bureau following a proposal by the Jurisconsult").

https://www.echr.coe.int/Pages/home.aspx?p=caselaw&c.

http://www.echr.coe.int/Pages/home.aspx?p=caselaw/HUDOC/translations&c=.

Linguists belonging to countries that have recently joined the EU have observed that the past influence of French on the *acquis communautaire* is noticeable. This is especially true in the comparison of the style of documents before and after the joining of common law countries, which has affected the structure and terminology of European Union law[12] (Šarčević 2001 and Bajčić in Gotti and William 2010).

In the past, several proposals have been put forward with the aim of simplifying the linguistic arrangement. One radical project was designed by the so-called *Druon Manifest*, which proposed the use of the French language as the most apt to express legal notions in Europe.[13] An alternative option, proposed by the Scandinavian countries, was for each speaker in a public debate in the European institutions to use his/her own native language, but to be required to listen to replies, discussions, questions in English, to diversify the active and passive use of English (generally better managed in the passive situation, rather than in expressing complex notions with an appropriate terminology).[14] A rather extreme proposal suggested that a limited number of official languages could be selected for discussions, as long as everyone agrees to express himself/herself in a language different from his/her native one. Finally, we should mention that the conclusions of the Barcelona European Council meeting in 2002 suggested that all citizens should learn not only a second international language to communicate in business, but also a third independently chosen language, to help preserve languages less required for efficiency reasons, but still practiced within the EU.[15] As it was argued in 2008 "the European Union should advocate the idea of personal adoptive language. The idea is that every European should be encouraged to freely choose a distinctive language, different from his or

---

[12] Šarčević, Susan. 2001. *Legal translation: preparation for accession to the European Union*. Reijeka: Faculty of law, University of Reijeka.
Bajčić, Marina. Challenges of Translating EU Terminology. In Gotti, Maurizio & William, Cristopher. 2010. *Legal Discourse across Languages and Culture*. Bern: Peter Lang AG.
[13] Manifeste pour le français, langue juridique de l'Europe, 2004, available at the website of the *francophonie*.
https://www.francophonie-avenir.com/Archives/Index_MD_Manifeste-Druon_pour_que_le_francais_soit_la_langue_juridique_de_l%27Europe.htm.
[14] The Swedish Language Council (a semi-official body) has actually envisaged the possibility of the preservation of Swedish as an active tool of expression, but that the passive role may be carried out in English – translation would be ensured only from Swedish and not into Swedish – (*Draft Action Programme for the Promotion of the Swedish Language*, published with an English translation by the Swedish Language Council in 1998).
http://www.sprakochfolkminnen.se/om-oss/kontakt/sprakradet/om-sprakradet/in-english.html.
[15] Presidency conclusions of the Council of the European Union.
http://www.consilium.europa.eu/uedocs/cms_data/docs/pressdata/en/ec/71025.pdf.
Also, in the same direction, Conclusions on language competences to enhance mobility, Brussels 2011.
http://www.consilium.europa.eu/uedocs/cms_data/docs/pressdata/en/educ/126373.pdf.

her language of identity, and also different from his or her language of international communication.[16]"

A great loss stemming from the increased use of English as a working language lies in the lost opportunity for the clarification of concepts that are connected to the co-drafting of documents in more than one language. Research conducted on behalf of the EU Commission on 'Document quality in public administrations and international organisations' has evidenced that several multilingual States consider the parallel drafting of documents in more than one language very helpful in the clarification of policy, to avoid use of expressions that belong only to one of the cultures involved, and so on. In Canada for instance when French versions of Canadian laws were mere literal translations of the English version, the results were rather 'stilted in terms of style, so that jurists who had to interpret the text were forced to refer to the source language. Such a translation technique was perceived as being in contradiction with the principle of language equality. Therefore, the method used to draw up laws in French and English had to evolve to avoid literal translation and to ensure that, as regards private law, it can be understood in the legal context of both civil and common law[17] (Wellington 2001).

The adoption of co-drafting has given rise to perceived changes in federal legislation:

> (...) the historical rigidities of bilingual drafting have been relaxed to a degree. It is no longer necessary for the French version to track the sentence structure and wording of the English version. (...) On the English side, common law drafting has evolved toward a higher level of generality and abstraction, which has brought it more in line with civilist style.[18]

Unfortunately the research has also demonstrated that several international institutions have renounced the previous practice of negotiating legal texts in several languages in parallel, due to economic concerns that have suggested that the co-drafting process be dropped, at least at the level of working groups.[19]

---

16 The policy of encouraging the learning of two foreign languages rather than one was recommended in the Maalouf Report. 2008. *A rewarding challenge, How the Multiplicity of Languages could Strengthen Europe*.
The group of intellectuals for Intercultural Dialogue set up at the initiative of the European Commission included 9 distinguished scholars of different disciplines. As an incidental remark, the report also notes "as regards the language of international communication, we are well aware that most people would today opt for English."
17 Wellington, Louise M. 2001. *Bijuralism in Canada: Harmonization Methodology and Terminology*. Canada, Department of Justice.
18 Cabinet Directive on Law-Making of the Government of Canada of 1999. See Government of Canada Privy Council Office. 2001. *Guide to making Federal Acts and Regulations* (2nd edn.). Part II, Making Acts.
19 For instance within the United Nations, the UNOV (United Nations Office Vienna) respondents to the research questionnaire have emphasized that because of budgetary tightening, greater rigor is

3 Consequences of having all linguistic versions as authentic

The most obvious consequence of the deliberate choice to avoid the selection of a privileged language is that no one can safely refer to one single version of a normative text: the minimum precaution that must be taken is that of comparing a number of linguistic versions[20] (Tiersma and Solan 2012).
a) Fundamental legislation (primary law).
   The problem does not concern only secondary legislation, but also the fundamental documents that have established the EU itself.
   As an example we may recall that on the issue of how to raise a reference for a preliminary ruling (art. 177 of the 1957 Treaty, now art. 267 of the Treaty on the functioning of the EU) a certain discrepancy exists between the literal English and German versions of the same provision. The German text (Abstract 3) seems to imply that the issue must be argued by one of the parties to the case and that the judge of last instance must forward the question to the European Court of Justice.[21]

---

applied in deciding whether a document should be edited and/or translated; for example following the proliferation of working groups for various commissions, it was decided that working group documents would not be edited or translated: Document quality control in public administrations and international organisations, Brussels, 2013. 231.
https://publications.europa.eu/en/search-results?p_p_state=normal&p_p_lifecycle=1&p_p_id=portal2012searchExecutor_WAR_portal2012portlet_INSTANCE_q8EzsBteHybf&resultsPerPage=10&facet.collection=EUPub&language=it&SEARCH_TYPE=SIMPLE&queryText=document+quality+control&.
20 On the difficulty involved in this exercise: Tiersma, Peter & Solan, Lawrence (eds). 2012. *The Oxford Handbook of language and law*. Oxford: Oxford University Press.
21 Art. 267, 3: "Wird eine derartige Frage in einem schwebenden Verfahren bei einem einzelstaatlichen Gericht gestellt, dessen Entscheidungen selbst nicht mehr mit Rechtsmitteln des innerstaatlichen Rechts angefochten werden können, so ist dieses Gericht zur Anrufung des Gerichtshofs verpflichtet." The sentence causing some doubt is the first ("wird eine … Frage … bei einem einzelstaatlichen Gericht gestellt").
The English version: "Where any such *question is raised* in a case pending before a court or tribunal of a Member State against whose decisions there is no judicial remedy under national law, that court or tribunal shall bring the matter before the Court" [emphasis mine].
In French: "Lorsqu'une telle *question est soulevée* dans une affaire pendante devant une juridiction nationale dont les décisions ne sont pas susceptibles d'un recours juridictionnel de droit interne, cette juridiction est tenue de saisir la Cour" [emphasis mine].
The German version would have been closer to the other languages if it had been structured in the following manner: "Stellt sich eine Frage" (Stotz, Rüdiger. 2014. *The interpretation of legal texts by the Court of Justice of the European Union*, at the *Second European Symposium on Improving the Comprehensibility of Legal Provisions*. Federal Ministry of Justice and Consumer Protection, Berlin. November 11).

The correct interpretation given by the European Court of Justice has clarified that the mere fact that a party contends that the dispute gives rise to a question concerning the interpretation of Community law does not mean that the court or tribunal concerned is compelled to consider that a question has been raised within the meaning of Article 177. On the other hand, a national court or tribunal may, in an appropriate case, refer a matter to the Court of Justice of its own motion.[22]

b) Secondary legislation.

Regarding secondary legislation, on the issue of comparing the various linguistic versions, the European Court of Justice has repeatedly stated the following principle:

> when a single decision is addressed to all the member states the necessity for uniform application and accordingly for uniform interpretation makes it impossible to consider one version of the text in isolation but requires that it be interpreted on the basis of both the real intention of its author and the aim he seeks to achieve, and in the light in particular of the versions in all four languages.[23]

And since the Cilfit case (1982), it is a settled principle that "community legislation is drafted in several languages and that the different language versions are all equally authentic. An interpretation of a provision of community law thus involves a comparison of the different language versions.[24]"

More recently the European Court of Justice reiterated this approach[25] by stating: "(38) It is settled case-law that the wording used in one language version of a provision of European Union law cannot serve as the sole basis for the interpretation of that provision, or be made to override the other language versions in that regard. Such an approach would be incompatible with the requirement for uniform application of European Union law."

---

[22] European Court of Justice. Case 283/81. Srl Cilfit and Lanificio di Gavardo SpA v Ministry of Health. Point 9.
http://eur-lex.europa.eu/legal-content/EN/TXT/PDF/?uri=CELEX:61981CJ0283&from=EN.
[23] European Court of Justice. Case 29/69. Erich Stauder v. City of Ulm.
http://eur-lex.europa.eu/legal-content/EN/TXT/HTML/?uri=CELEX:61969CJ0029&from=EN.
References by the court are to European Court of Justice. Case C-372/88. Cricket St Thomas. Paragraphs 18–19; European Court of Justice. Case C-149/97. Institute of the Motor Industry. Paragraph 16; European Court of Justice. Case C-239/07. Sabatauskas and Others. Paragraphs 38–39.
[24] European Court of Justice. Case 283/81. Srl Cilfit and Lanificio di Gavardo SpA v Ministry of Health. Point 9.
http://eur-lex.europa.eu/legal-content/EN/TXT/PDF/?uri=CELEX:61981CJ0283&from=EN.
[25] European Court of Justice. Case C-451/08. Helmut Müller GmbH v Bundesanstalt für Immobilienaufgaben.
http://curia.europa.eu/juris/liste.jsf?language=en&num=C-451/08.

In the case concerned, in a request for a preliminary ruling[26] (on Directive 2004/18, a directive on public procurement for building activities for public bodies), interpreters found that in defining the concept of "public works contracts": "(36) While the majority of the language versions use the term 'work' for both the second and the third variants, the German version uses two different terms, that is to say, *Bauwerk* ('work') for the second variant and *Bauleistung* ('building activity') for the third."

The conclusion was that "the provisions of Directive 2004/18 do not apply to a situation in which one public authority sells land to an undertaking, even though another public authority intends to award a works contract in respect of that land but has not yet formally decided to award that contract."

Linguists interested in legal issues have often scrutinized European Court of Justice case law to elaborate on the process by which a common core of meaning is identified by European judges[27] (Solan 2007).

c) Independent meaning.

Beyond the necessary comparison of various linguistic versions, the European Court of Justice has also clearly stated that expressions used in European legislation have an independent meaning from that assigned to the similar sounding phrases in the Member States. This means that even if some expressions recall domestic experiences, interpreters should be wary in assuming that there actually is any identity between national and supranational legal terms.[28] Readers are

---

26 The Court (paragraph 37) also found that "the German version of Article 1(2) (b) is the only one which provides that the activity referred to in the third variant must be realised not only 'by whatever means' but also 'by third parties' (*durch Dritte*)." The full title of the legislative text is: Directive 2004/18/EC of the European Parliament and of the Council of 31 March 2004 on the coordination of procedures for the award of public works contracts, public supply contracts and public service contracts. *Official Journal* (L134). 114.

27 Solan, Lawrence. 2007. Statutory Interpretation in the EU: The Augustinian Approach. *Brooklyn Law School Research Papers* (78).
http:/ssrn.com/abstract=998167 (accessed March 3, 2015).
European Court of Justice. Case C-228/87. Pretura Unificata di Torino v. X. At page 21, the notion of "emergency" is identified by comparing several language versions of a regulation on water contamination. The author also recalls another case where the German version deviated from all other languages: European Court of Justice. Case C-64/95. Lubella v. Hauptzollamt Cottbus (bitter cherries – *Suesskirschen* – rather than sweet one).
Šarčević, Susan (ed.). 2013. *Language and Culture in EU Law: Multidisciplinary Perspectives*. London: Ashgate.

28 European Court of Justice. Case C-283/81. Cilfit. Paragraph 19:
"Even where the different language versions are entirely in accord with one another, ... community law uses terminology which is peculiar to it. Furthermore , it must be emphasized that legal concepts do not necessarily have the same meaning in community law and in the law of the various member states."
And paragraph 20:

often confronted with the notion of a *sui generis* expression in European Court of Justice case law.[29] The judges regularly point out that European terms may not easily fit in the domestic web of legal concepts.

d) Extrinsic means of interpretation.

In front of such a complex situation, the words themselves may be insufficient, even if expressed in several languages.

Here too we may consider some of Advocate General Jacobs' observations:

> it has sometimes been suggested that the judgment in Cilfit seems to impose an exacting requirement to national courts in calling on the national courts to compare all the language versions. But in fact the principle that all language versions are equally authentic means that no single version is authentic. Linguistic discrepancies can rarely be resolved just by comparison of different versions. National courts would be better advised to apply the ECJ's approach to interpretation and to seek an effective and appropriate solution having regard to the context and the purpose.[30]

In technical legal terms this consideration emphasizes the need for a purposive interpretation (also defined "teleological"): as no single text is "authentic", the reader must consider the intention of legislator in the drafting of a text[31] (Gambaro

---

"Every provision of community law must be placed in its context and interpreted in the light of the provisions of community law as a whole, regard being had to the objectives thereof and to its state of evolution at the date on which the provision in question is to be applied."

29 Opinion of the Advocate General Kokott. In European Court of Justice. Case C-583/11. Inuit Tapiriit Kanatami and Others v European Parliament and Council of the European Union. Point 31–32:

"(31) It cannot be denied that in some language versions of the Treaties there is a certain degree of similarity between the term 'regulation' within the meaning of the second paragraph of article 288 TFEU and the expression 'regulatory act' (...) However, to equate the expressions 'regulation' and 'regulatory act' on the selective basis of a few language versions of the FEU Treaty would disregard the fact that the European Treaties are now equally authentic in 23 different languages (Article 55 (1) TEU and Article 358 TFEU). In many EU official languages there is certainly no etymological link between the terms 'regulation' and 'regulatory act'. (32) It must therefore be assumed that the expression 'regulatory act' is a *sui generis* term of EU law, in whose interpretation regard must be had to the objective of the Treaty provision in question, the context in which it is used, and its drafting history." https://eur-lex.europa.eu/legal-content/EN/TXT/?uri=CELEX%3A62011CJ0583.

30 Opinion of the Advocate General Jacobs in the above-mentioned conference and in European Court of Justice. Case C-292/00. Davidoff & Cie SA v Gofkid Ltd. Point 34.

"Where a legislative provision is clear, it is in principle unnecessary and undesirable to look behind the terms adopted. That having been said, however, in the present case the drafting history of the Directive – which is closely linked to that of the Regulation – tends to support a literal interpretation." http://curia.europa.eu/juris/document/document.jsf?text=&docid=47256&pageIndex=0&doclang=EN&mode=lst&dir=&occ=first&part=1&cid=56345.

31 Gambaro, Antonio. 2007. Interpretation of Multilingual Legislative Texts. *Electronic Journal of Comparative Law* (December 2007).

http://www.ejcl.org/113/abs113-4.html.

2006). To this end, the history of the provision (e.g. pre-existing rules that have been amended) and the preparatory works – as it will be clarified further in a following paragraph – may be relevant.

Several years ago, Antonio Gambaro observed that the literal comparison of texts is often insufficient and that in these circumstances more than in others, the interpreter is induced to search for the intention of the legislator which does not have much in common with intention in a psychological sense. It is more a matter of attributing to the rules a sense which is in conformity with the purpose assigned to them.

In effect, in Community case law, the teleological criterion prevails even if it is used in an unrefined way compared to the masterful teachings of Aharon Barak (Barak 2005). Evidence of this can be found in the Océano case (case C. 240/98).

This well-known case[32] concerned the application of Directive 93/13 EEC and its article (6, 1) stating that unfair clauses in contracts that have been agreed upon with consumers "shall not be binding on the consumer". The expression, flexible in its meaning, needed judicial clarification.

Consideration of the purpose of a specific rule is also relevant with regards to the principles governing EU activity in particular in accordance with the *effet utile* notion (or *effectivité*/'effectiveness' principle)[33] that emphasizes the effort to give full effect to European interventions.[34]

This purposive approach has also been justified on the basis of a fundamental international treaty: the 1969 Vienna convention on the law of treaties, specifically Article 33. According to this provision, if a comparison of different language versions of a text reveals differences, the interpretation that best reconciles the text and the purpose should be adopted.[35]

---

[32] European Court of Justice. Case C-240/98. Océano Grupo Editorial SA v. Roció Murciano. http://curia.europa.eu/juris/liste.jsf?num=C-240/98.
The problem concerned uncertainty of the power of a court to establish its own motion (*ex officio*) that an unfair clause would be unenforceable.
[33] European Court of Justice. Case C-429/07. Inspecteur van de Belastingdienst v X BV. Point 36–39. http://curia.europa.eu/juris/liste.jsf?language=en&num=C-429/07.
[34] European Court of Justice. Case C-119/05. Ministero dell'Industria, del Commercio e dell'Artigianato v Lucchini. Point 61. It mentioned the "settled case-law that a national court which is called upon, within the exercise of its jurisdiction, to apply provisions of Community law is under a duty to give full effect to those provisions, if necessary refusing of its own motion to apply any conflicting provision of national legislation."
http://curia.europa.eu/juris/document/document.jsf?text=&docid=62742&pageIndex=0&doclang=EN&mode=lst&dir=&occ=first&part=1&cid=112127.
[35] According to Advocate General Jacobs, this approach "may be compared with, but is not the same as, other bodies confronted with multilingual texts such as the European Court of Human Rights and the World Trade Organisation."

Many recent European Court of Justice decisions, which make reference to a long list of precedents, can be found where an interpretation giving effect to the purpose of the European legislator is favoured.[36]

4 Common law jurisdictions: a cautious attitude

A certain suspicion has sometimes surrounded this teleological approach to interpretation, especially in common law countries where, traditionally, any reading of legislation that deviates from the literal meaning of the exact words used by the legislator is very cautiously used[37] (Zweigert and Kötz 1998 and Mann 1983).

It would be difficult to express the opposition between the two traditions better than in Lord Denning's words, in a decision delivered by the English Court of Appeal,[38] while comparing the English and the continental approach to legal interpretation:

> the draftsmen of our statutes have striven to express themselves with the utmost exactness. They have tried to foresee all possible circumstances that may arise and to provide for them.
>
> They have sacrificed style and simplicity. They have foregone brevity. They have become long and involved. In consequence, the Judges have followed suit. They interpret a statute as applying only to the circumstances covered by the very words. They give them a literal interpretation. If the words of the statute do not cover a new situation – which was not foreseen – the Judges hold

---

Jacobs, Francis. 2003. How to interpret legislation which is equally authentic in twenty languages. Lecture at European Commission, seminars on quality of legislation, Legal Revisers Group, Brussels. 20 October.
http://ec.europa.eu/dgs/legal_service/seminars/agjacobs_summary.pdf.
36 European Court of Justice. Case C-487/12. Vueling Airlines SA v Instituto Galego de Consumo de la Xunta de Galicia. Point 31:
"Where there is divergence between the various language versions of a European Union legal text, the provision in question must be interpreted by reference to the purpose and general scheme of the rules of which it forms part (see, in particular, judgments in European Court of Justice. Case C-30/77. Bouchereau. Paragraph 14; European Court of Justice. Case C-482/98. Italy v Commission. Paragraph 49; and European Court of Justice. Case C-52/10. Eleftheri tileorasi and Giannikos. Paragraph 24)."
37 Zweigert, Konrad & Kötz, Hein. 1998. *An Introduction to Comparative Law* (3rd edn). Oxford: Clarendon Press. 265; Twining, William & Miers, David. 1999. *How to do Things with Rules* (4th edn). London: Butterworths; Mann, Francis A. 1983. Uniform Statutes in English Law. *Law Quarterly Review* 99 (3). 376–406.
38 England and Wales Court of Appeal. Civil Case 14/1974. H.P. Bulmer v. J Bollinger SA. Paragraph 10. http://www.bailii.org/cgi-bin/markup.cgi?doc=/ew/cases/EWCA/Civ/1974/14.html&query=Bulmer+and+v+and+Bollinger+and+%281974%29&method=boolean.

that they have no power to fill the gap. To do so would be a "naked usurpation of the legislative power" (see *Magor and St. Mellons R.D.C. v. Newport Borough Council* [1952] Appeal Case 189).

The gap must remain open until Parliament finds time to fill it.

How different is this Treaty. It lays down general principles. It expresses its aims and purposes. All in sentences of moderate length and commendable style. But it lacks precision. It uses words and phrases without defining what they mean. An English lawyer would look for an interpretation clause, but he would look in vain. There is none. All the way through the Treaty there are gaps and lacunae. These have to be filled in by the Judges, or by Regulations or Directives. It is the European way.

Seeing these differences, what are the English Courts to do when they are faced with a problem of interpretation? They must follow the European pattern. No longer must they examine the words in meticulous detail. No longer must they argue about the precise grammatical sense. They must look to the purpose or intent. To quote the words of the European Court in the *Da Costa* case (1963) 2 *Common Market Law Review* at page 237, "they must deduce from the wording and the spirit of the Treaty the meaning of the Community rules." They must not confine themselves to the English text. They must consider, if need be, all the authentic texts, of which there are now eight, see Sociale Verzekeringsbank (1968) 7 *Common Market Law Review* 151."

Common lawyers' preference for a literal reading may be influenced by the generally prompt reaction of the United Kingdom legislator when shortcomings and loopholes in the legislation are pointed out by the courts.

In a study, published by Patrick S. Atiyah and Robert S. Summers several years ago[39] (Atiyah and Summers 1989), this aspect of the United Kingdom legal system was emphasised to explain the difference of attitude between United States and English courts. In the United States of America, courts have often used a purposive approach and have made early recourse to preparatory works of legislation to argue an interpretation issue, while the English tradition has been rather reluctant to adopt a similar approach. It is only more recently (1992) that the courts have admitted the use of preparatory works in judgments.[40] The authors of this study attributed the difference of approach to the different processes of legislation and especially to the readiness of the legislator in the United Kingdom to pass an amendment of an act when a gap or an ambiguity is discovered much more readily than in the United States of America (both at State and federal levels).

A similar observation is expressed by Advocate General Jacobs, reasoning that the reason why it is more necessary for the to take a purposive approach considering

---

39 Atiyah, Patrick S. & Summers, Robert S. 1987. Form and Substance in Anglo-American law. Oxford: Clarendon Press.
40 United Kingdom House of Lords. Appeal Case 593/1992. Pepper (inspector of taxes) v. Hart. http://www.bailii.org/uk/cases/UKHL/1992/3.html.

the difficulty of amending the Treaty-or of amending legislation in the case of Council acts. The European Court of Justice cannot take the approach of many English courts which determine the meaning of a provision, acknowledge that that meaning may have unfortunate consequences, but state that it is up to the legislator to alter the text if it does not like those consequences.[41]

5 Some criticisms

On a general level, we must observe that there is indeed an element of optimism in the expectation that in the reading EU texts, judges and lawyers will go beyond the reading of a couple of versions of the same document: any further enquiries will be prevented by the simple fact that most do not know more than a couple of foreign languages[42] (Derlen 2007).

Observers more closely involved with the functioning of EU institutions have also expressed some scepticism.

The effort to find a precise solution to interpretation issues may conflict with the deliberate choice of some legislation to maintain a certain level of vagueness, as has sometimes been noticed by judges of the European Court of Justice. An enlightening conference held by former European Court of Justice judge Konrad Schiemann on the issue of *The advantages of obscurity: the drafting of EU legislation and judgments*[43] illustrated the need for some flexibility in European sources and the strategies followed by the European Court of Justice to avoid taking position on issues that are not ripe for decision and are extremely controversial (one such example can be found in the missing definition of "embryo").[44]

---

41 Jacobs, Francis. 2003. How to interpret legislation which is equally authentic in twenty languages. Lecture at European Commission, seminars on quality of legislation, Legal Revisers Group, Brussels. October 20.
42 Derlén, Mattias. 2007. A Castle in the Air – Practical Problems of the Multilingual Interpretation of European Community Law. *Umeå Studies in Law* (16). 678.
43 Sir Schiemann, Konrad. 2013. The advantages of obscurity: the drafting of EU legislation and judgments. Seminar at the Institute of Advanced Legal Studies, International Association of Legislation, London. October 7.
https://ial-online.org/recording-the-advantages-of-obscurity-the-drafting-of-eu-legislation-and-judgments/.
44 Many situations go beyond the explicit regulation of EU law: in European Court of Justice. Case C-506/06. Mayr v. Bäkerei und Conditorei Gerhard Floeckner. the Court of Justice had to decide whether *in vitro* fertilization of *ova* (before transfer into the uterus) may be considered "pregnancy" in order to decide whether an employee qualified for protection from dismissal on grounds of equal treatment for women and men.
http://curia.europa.eu/juris/liste.jsf?language=it&num=C-506/06.

It is however worthwhile underlining that the European Court of Justice seems to conduct a rather thorough examination of the various linguistic versions, as exemplified in cases where the judges compare several texts, such as comparing the Dutch version of an article in a directive with 9 other versions.[45]

6 Where to look for the purpose of legislation?

The European Court of Justice has often indicated that the introductory part of EU legislative acts is relevant in defining the aims of the provisions approved by the European legislator.

In the area of air passengers' rights, the Sturgeon[46] case seems archetypal.[47]

There, the court (paragraph 41) stated:

> as the Court has made clear in its case-law, it is necessary, in interpreting a provision of Community law, to consider not only its wording, but also the context in which it occurs and the objectives pursued by the rules of which it is part (see, *inter alia*, Case C-156/98 *Germany v Commission* [2000] ECR I-6857, paragraph 50, and Case C-306/05 *SGAE* [2006] ECR I-11519, paragraph 34).
>
> (42) In that regard, the *operative part* of a Community act is indissociably *linked to the statement of reasons* for it, so that, when it has to be interpreted, account must be taken of the reasons which led to its adoption (Case C-298/00 P *Italy v Commission* [2004] ECR I-4087, paragraph 97 and the case-law cited) [emphasis mine].

In the specific investigation on the issue whether delayed passengers could ask for the same compensation paid to passengers who have had their flight cancelled, the Court said:

> (49) In view of the objective of Regulation No 261/2004, which is to strengthen protection for air passengers by redressing damage suffered by them during air travel, situations covered by the regulation must be compared (...).

---

45 European Court of Justice. Case C-445/09. IMC Securities BV v Stichting Autoriteit Financiële Markten. Point 26.
http://curia.europa.eu/juris/document/document.jsf?text=&docid=107264&pageIndex=0&doclang=EN&mode=lst&dir=&occ=first&part=1&cid=84038#Footnote*.
46 European Court of Justice. Joined Cases C-402/07 & C-432/07. Sturgeon and Others. http://curia.europa.eu/juris/liste.jsf?language=en&num=C-402/07.
47 The conclusion reached in Sturgeon have been further extended in the following European Court of Justice. Joined Cases C-581/10 & C-629/10. Nelson and Others v Deutsche Lufthansa AG & TUI Travel and Others v Civil Aviation Authority.
http://curia.europa.eu/juris/document/document.jsf?text=&docid=128861&pageIndex=0&doclang=EN&mode=lst&dir=&occ=first&part=1&cid=253017.

(50) In this instance, the situation of passengers whose flights are delayed should be compared with that of passengers whose flights are cancelled.

(51) In that connection, Regulation No 261/2004 seeks to redress damage in an immediate and standardised manner and to do so by various forms of intervention which are the subject of rules relating to denied boarding, cancellation and long flight delay (see, to that effect, IATA and ELFAA, paragraph 43).

(52) Regulation No 261/2004 has, in those measures, the objective of repairing, *inter alia*, damage consisting, for the passengers concerned, in a loss of time which, given that it is irreversible, can be redressed only by compensation.

(53) In that regard, it must be stated that that damage is suffered both by passengers whose flights are cancelled and by passengers whose flights are delayed if, prior to reaching their destinations, the latter's journey time is longer than the time which had originally been scheduled by the air carrier.

The conclusion reached by the Court (including delays beyond cancellation of flights as reasons for damages) has caused strong reactions, as a previously unaddressed situation has been brought within the scope of the Regulation on the strength of an argument referring to the introductory part of the legislative text. The United Kingdom commentators have been rather upset by this approach, as evidenced in the titles of some articles published right after the delivery of the judgment.[48]

In an extra-judicatory comment, Judge Malenovský (who acted as rapporteur in the IATA and ELFAA 2006 case) has explicitly referred to the recital introducing the policy of the legislation and affirming the need for an increased protection of air passengers.[49] Starting with this consideration, the court in the Sturgeon case concluded that a difference between passengers who have had a flight cancelled and those who may have suffered a long delay, but have reached the destination under the original number of the flight would be unjustified, violating the principle of equality.[50]

---

[48] In the UK, comments by Lord Mance have been especially critical (referring to a "bold interpretative approach": United Kingdom Supreme Court. Case 59/12. X v. Mid Sussex Citizens Advice Bureau. Paragraph 44). In France, Le Bot, F. 2013. La protection des passagers aériens dans l'Union Européenne. *Revue trimestrielle droit européen* (49). 753–771: comments in academic literature speaking of "constructive reading" and "*contra legem* interpretation."

[49] Malenovský, Jiří. 2014. EU Passenger Rights. Conference EU Law in the Member States. Air Passenger Rights, 10 Years on, at Collège d'Europe. Bruges. September 26–27.
https://www.coleurope.eu/events/conference-eu-law-member-states-air-passenger-rights-10-years.

[50] Point 38–39 of the Sturgeon case:
"(38) as the Polish Government notes in its written observations, the distinction the Regulation introduces between cancellation and delay may lead to passengers who find themselves in objectively similar situations being treated differently.
(39) That unavoidably raises the (fundamental) question as to whether the Regulation violates the principle of equal treatment."

Strikingly enough, the Court has set aside arguments presented on the preparatory works of the Regulation where the issue of delayed flights had been raised but not included in the final version of the regulation.[51]

The Advocate General Sharpston in her conclusions in the Sturgeon case, observes[52]:

In the explanatory memorandum to its original proposal for a regulation,[53] the Commission noted, at point 20, that "[c]ancellation by an operator (...) represents a refusal to supply the service for which it has contracted, except in exceptional circumstances beyond its responsibility, such as political instability, severe weather conditions, inadequate security and unexpected safety failures (...)." At point 23, it stated:

> although passengers suffer similar inconvenience and frustration from delays as from denied boarding or cancellation, there is a difference in that an operator is responsible for denied boarding and cancellation (unless for reasons beyond its responsibility) but not always for delays. Other common causes are air traffic management systems and limits to airport capacity. As stated in its communication on the protection of air passengers, the Commission considers that in present circumstances operators should not be obliged to compensate delayed passengers.

In the Advocate General comments (paragraph 32) "It is not all that easy to discern the logic behind the distinction that the Commission was there drawing."

What is striking in this case is that a certain hypothesis had been considered by the Commission and deliberately disregarded. There was a conscious decision not to include the protection of passengers experiencing long delays.

Yet the Court, in its judgment on this case, has finally given more weight to the issue of equality than to coherence with the *preparatory works* of the regulation. One would be tempted to say that the court has actually made policy choices rather than interpretation.

---

[51] An extensive discussion on the preparatory works of the regulation took place in the first of a series of cases involving this rather controversial piece of legislation. In European Court of Justice. Case C-344/04. IATA and ELFAA. Paragraphs 49–59. the discussion considered the process by which the initial text was amended (especially art. 5 was re-drafted by the Conciliation Committee provided for in article 251 EC).
http://curia.europa.eu/juris/document/document.jsf?text=&docid=57285&pageIndex=0&doclang=EN&mode=lst&dir=&occ=first&part=1&cid=593132.
[52] Opinion of Advocate General Sharpston. European Court of Justice. Joined Cases C-402/07 & C-432/07. Sturgeon v Condor Flugdienst GmbH and others. Pararagraph 31.
http://curia.europa.eu/juris/document/document.jsf?text=&docid=76092&pageIndex=0&doclang=EN&mode=req&dir=&occ=first&part=1&cid=597895.
[53] Proposal for a regulation of the European Parliament and of the Council establishing common rules on compensation and assistance for air passengers in the event of denied boarding and cancellation or long delays of flights. Commission of the European Communities. 2001. Explanatory memorandum to the original Commission proposal (COM [2001]) 784 final). Brussels.

We should also consider that preparatory works are occasionally not very helpful: tracing the reasons for changes in terminology is often frustrating.

For instance, the process of selecting the most appropriate words to indicate the defence that the air company may use in the opposition to compensation demands, by invoking extreme conditions (article 5), is rather puzzling.

In the process of approval of regulation 261/2004 a change in terminology occurred: "Initially, reference was made to 'Act of God' which was then substituted by 'exceptional circumstances' "[54] (Carnimeo 2013).

When reading the Proposal for a regulation[55] one is struck by the Commission's observation (at point 20), that "[c]ancellation by an operator (...) represents a refusal to supply the service for which it has contracted, except in exceptional circumstances beyond its responsibility, such as political instability, severe weather conditions, inadequate security and unexpected safety failures" [emphasis mine].

This definition did not last until the final version of the regulation.

Advocate General Sharpston in her conclusions on the Sturgeon case says: "in the text of Article 5 of the Regulation as adopted, (...) the 'exceptional circumstances' referred to by the Commission are re-christened 'extraordinary circumstances'."[56]

The frequent changes of expression have not been very helpful in clarifying which events are included in this clause of "force majeure"[57] and long discussions are ongoing even after an intervention by National Enforcement Bodies of the various states that have agreed on a Draft list of extraordinary circumstances during a meeting held on 12 April 2013.[58]

In general terms, we should consider that the use of legislative preparatory works has increased in later years. This is due to the fact that in the early period of uniform legislation not all materials were accessible[59] and the Court of Justice inclined to

---

54 Carnimeo, Nicolò. 2013. Passengers Protection: Development and Analysis. *Aviation Space Journal* 12 (1). 2–10.

55 Commission of the European Communities. 2001. Explanatory memorandum to the original Commission proposal (COM [2001]) 784 final). Brussels.

56 In a previous opinion (Opinion of the Advocate General Shrapston. In European Court of Justice. Case C-396/06. Kramme. Paragraph 50), Advocate General Shrapston had already explained that: "The *travaux préparatoires* also support a literal interpretation. In the course of them, 'force majeure' was altered to 'extraordinary circumstances'. According to the Council's statement in the *Common Position*, that change was made in the interest of legal clarity."
http://curia.europa.eu/juris/document/document.jsf?text=&docid=63514&pageIndex=0&doclang=EN&mode=lst&dir=&occ=first&part=1&cid=599820#, Footnote25.

57 Traditionally international texts on transport law have used the notion of "force majeure" to limit the liability of the carrier: e.g. Lemarié, Alexis. 2012. *La force majeure en droit du contrat de transport maritime*. Sarrebruck : Editions universitaires européennes.

58 http://ec.europa.eu/transport/themes/passengers/air/doc/neb-extraordinary-circumstances-list.pdf

59 Some considerations in the Opinion of the Advocate General Kokott. In European Court of Justice. Case C-583/11. Inuit Tapiriit Kanatami and Others v European Parliament and Council of the European

exclude references to documents that were not reflected in the final version of an official act.⁶⁰ Lately, the policy has somewhat relaxed, as shown in several recent cases.⁶¹

As a limit to investigations on the policy implemented by EU legislative texts we have to consider that sometimes it is hard to delve into the introductory comments ("recitals") that precede the actual binding articles, as they may be extensive. Occasionally they are much more numerous than the specific provisions. Such is the case of e.g. directive 2013/48/EU on the right of access to a lawyer in criminal proceedings⁶²: 59 recitals for only 18 articles; and EU Directive 95/46/EC – The Data Protection Directive: 72 recitals and 34 articles.⁶³ The more controversial the issue, the more the number of recitals seems to increase: compromise is often reached by inserting an issue in the introduction, rather than in the body of the regulating text.⁶⁴

Union. Point 32: "Drafting history (...) has not played a role thus far in the interpretation of primary law, because the *travaux préparatoires* for the founding Treaties were largely not available. However, the practice of using conventions to prepare Treaty amendments, like the practice of publishing the mandates of intergovernmental conferences, has led to a fundamental change in this area. The greater transparency in the preparations for Treaty amendments opens up new possibilities for interpreting the Treaties which should be utilised as supplementary means of interpretation if, as in the present case, the meaning of a provision is still unclear having regard to its wording, the regulatory context and the objectives pursued."
http://curia.europa.eu/juris/document/document.jsf?text=&docid=132541&pageIndex=0&doclang=EN&mode=lst&dir=&occ=first&part=1&cid=116521
60 European Court of Justice. Case C-292/89. The Queen and The Immigration Appeal Tribunal, ex parte Gustaff Desiderius Antonissen.
http://curia.europa.eu/juris/showPdf.jsf?text=&docid=96732&pageIndex=0&doclang=EN&mode=lst&dir=&occ=first&part=1&cid=114059.
"(17) The national court referred to the declaration recorded In the Council minutes at the time of the adoption of the aforesaid Regulation No 1612/68 (...) on the abolition of restrictions on movement and residence within the Community for workers of Member States and their families."
"(18) However, such a declaration cannot be used for the purpose of interpreting a provision of secondary legislation where, as in this case, no reference is made to the content of the declaration in the wording of the provision in question."
61 European Court of Justice. Case C-58/08. Vodafone Ltd et al. V Secretary of State for Business, Enterprise and Regulatory Reform. Point 45, 55 and 58 of the judgment quoting "the explanatory memorandum to the proposal for a regulation and point 2.4 of the impact assessment."
http://curia.europa.eu/juris/document/document.jsf?text=&docid=79665&pageIndex=0&doclang=EN&mode=lst&dir=&occ=first&part=1&cid=115728.
62 Directive 2013/48 EU of the European Parliament and of the Council of 22 October 2013 on the right of access to a lawyer in criminal proceedings (...) and in European arrest warrant and on the right to have a third party informed upon deprivation of liberty and to communicate with third persons and with consular authorities while deprived of liberty.
http://eur-lex.europa.eu/LexUriServ/LexUriServ.do?uri=OJ:L:2013:294:0001:0012:EN:PDF.
63 Directive 1995/46 EC of the European Parliament and the Council – The data protection Directive.
http://www.dataprotection.ie/viewdoc.asp?DocID=91&m=
64 Jeckel, Sebastian (Head of Division, Permanent Representation of the Federal Republic of Germany to the European Union). An overview of the EU legislative process: Heinkelmann, Bärbel

7 Two equally criticized approaches

As mentioned above, European drafters try to avoid giving the impression that legal notions used in Brussels actually belong to the legal tradition of one of the member States: this is both because it may cause suspicion in some of the other member States, and also because not all the implications of a domestic concept may suit the structure and competences of European institutions. Often legal concepts are closely connected with judicial or administrative procedures and remedies to enforce some of the consequent rights. It would be a great risk to assume that a notion borrowed from one of the States' experiences also carries the same web of mechanisms deemed necessary to implement it at the State level. As it is well known, the competence of the EU in procedural matters is still limited.

Therefore some expressions such as "estoppel", *effet utile*, "proportionality" that may stem from English common law,[65] French administrative law or the German constitutional tradition are recognized in European terminology, yet interpreters should isolate these terms from their roots, abandon any expectation rooted in their national education and connect them with the EU context.

The problem with this approach is that it is rather demanding on the audience.

It is not clear how far interpreters can really monitor distinct ways of reading legal terminology and avoid (even inadvertent) expectations of certain consequences as a result of a familiar notion.

It is also unclear what exact meaning the transplanted term should take, at least when the European Court of Justice has not had an opportunity to clarify it (a process that may take some time, as a real case must arise and be brought to the Court's attention).

Unfortunately lawyers pose similar arguments also when the European legislator creates a neologism. In this case as well, one may expect questions revolving around the exact meaning of a term and complaints on the "fuzzy" nature of EU legislation.

EU Regulation 261/2004 on air passengers' rights provides a recent example of the difficulty of striking the right balance between traditional expressions that may

---

(Officer, Commission GD JUST). 2014. Scope and limits of comprehensibility in the drafting process, The European Commission as an Example. Second European Symposium on Improving the Comprehensibility of Legal Provisions, Berlin. November 11.

65 As is well known, Judge Pierre Pescatore drew a comparison (which was later very successful) between the attitude adopted by the European Court in the famous *Ratti* case (C 148/78) and the prohibition of acting in a contradictory way:

"the Court brings for the first time into its ruling an element which may be linked to the English concept of 'estoppel', if I may use so loosely an expression which has, as I am told, a more technical meaning in English law." (Pescatore, Pierre. 1983. The doctrine of "direct effect": an Infant Disease of Community Law. *European Law Review* (8). 155–169).

cause unwanted assumptions about the implications of the words and alternative or new meanings. As mentioned above, the airways company is exempted from some of its obligations to assist passengers if the flight is delayed or cancelled due to "extraordinary circumstances" (article 5, n. 3). The expression is in itself flexible, as the regulation presents examples and does not specify a full list of cases that may fall within the range of this provision[66] and has been criticized for deviating from the traditional and familiar notion of "force majeure".[67]

Notwithstanding these uncertainties of meaning, the choice of a "neutral language" is often a deliberate choice in the drafting of international texts, to avoid clauses that would automatically result in an assumption by the reader stemming from his or her background.

Many examples of attempts to harmonise the rules of certain sectors that are especially affected by international transactions are available in uniform law texts. In the UNIDROIT *Principles of international commercial contracts*, the obvious examples are "agreed payment for non-performance" (instead of "penalty clause" or "liquidated damages clause"), and "hardship" (instead of "excessive benefit" or other expressions).[68]

8 Problems of translation or problems of clarity?

Negotiations of legislative texts are always complex procedures where compromises must be accepted. At the international level this difficulty is increased because negotiators have limited comprehension of each other's legal background.

---

[66] European Court of Justice. Case C-12/11. McDonagh v. Ryanair ("not exhaustively defined in the Regulation, even though Recitals 14 and 15 of its preamble provide several examples, including notably air traffic management decisions and meteorological conditions incompatible with the operation of the flight concerned").
[67] In Carnimeo, Nicolò. 2013. Passengers Protection: Development and Analysis. *Aviation Space Journal* 12 (1). 2–10. "it would be desirable to insert a definitive list of exceptional circumstances in the Regulation, possibly accompanied by the provision of traditional exemptions, such as Act of God and force majeure or at least have the Commission publish guide-lines on the interpretation of exceptional circumstances, in order to ensure uniform application."
The European Consumers' Centre Network. 2005. Air Passenger Rights: Consumer Complaints 2005, A Summary & Analysis of Consumer Complaints reported to the European Consumer Centre Network. Paragraph 5.3. 23: "The use of 'exceptional circumstances' on the evidence sent to ECCs indicates that there is a lack of clarity about what it covers."
[68] International Institute for the Unification of Private Law. 2010. Art. 1.6 (2) UNIDROIT Principles 2010. Rome. http://www.unilex.info/dynasite.cfm?dssid=2377&dsmid=14311.

An unforgettable piece of ironic representation of a conference drafting an international uniform law was written by Gyula Eörsi and bears the title: *Unifying the Law (A Play in One Act, with a Song)*.[69]

This masterpiece of satirical writing on legal issues reflects all the possible misunderstandings, strategic manoeuvres and linguistic devices utilised to hide disagreement and reach an apparent consent. The expression "a dog shall bark" during the fictional discussions described by Eörsi is carried through all shades of meanings to reach a final workable, very wide and undetermined meaning.

Beyond the literary dimension, an interesting historical testimony is offered by one of the delegates who actually took part in the final approval of the 1930 Geneva Convention on bills of exchange.[70] While discussing the ambiguity of art. 17 (agir *sciemment au détriment du débiteur* ['knowingly acting to the detriment of the debtor']), Amedeo Giannini, the Italian delegate to the conference, asked his colleagues: "êtes-vous contents de cette formule? Non. Lui donnez-vous votre vote? Oui. Je lui donne mon vote parce que personne n'est content. Cela veut dire que c'est l'unique formule qui puisse rallier tous les suffrages. [Are you pleased with this formula? No. Do you give it your vote? Yes. I'll give it my vote since nobody's happy. This means that that is the only formula that may collect all votes].[71]"

When considering the workings of the European legislator one must observe that "the Community legislative process is characterized by the political input and the fact that it sometimes appears that the need to have a text prevails over the actual content of the act, although efforts to improve that situation have been visible more recently. One consequence is a lack of clarity, whether conscious or unconscious.[72]"

The distribution of legislative texts between opening recitals ("whereas") and specific rules ("articles") does not necessarily help in the interpretation process, as sometimes some premises are not transformed into specific articles and it is not always clear how much interpreters should consider themselves bound by considerations only quoted in the preamble. The strategy of leaving unsettled matters as opening considerations at the beginning of the document does not help in terms of clarity.

---

[69] Eörsi, Gyula. 1977. Unifying the Law. (A Play in One Act, with a Song). *American Journal of Comparative Law* 25 (4). 658–662.
[70] The League of Nations. 1930. Convention Providing a Uniform Law For Bills of Exchange and Promissory Notes. Geneva: SiSU.
http://www.jus.uio.no/lm/bills.of.exchange.and.promissory.notes.convention.1930/portrait.pdf (accessed November 9, 2017).
[71] *Rapport du Comité de rédaction,* in *Comptes-rendus,* Geneva. 1930. 293.
[72] Jacobs, Francis. 2003. How to interpret legislation which is equally authentic in twenty languages. Lecture at European Commission, seminars on quality of legislation, Legal Revisers Group, Brussels. 20 October.

In a well-known case, IATA and ELAA judgment (Case C-344/04), the European Court of Justice specified that:

> (76) However, it must be stated with regard to those submissions, first, that while the preamble to a Community measure may explain the latter's content (see *Alliance for Natural Health*, paragraph 91), it cannot be relied upon as a ground for derogating from the actual provisions of the measure in question (Case C-162/97 Nilsson and Others [1998] ECR I-7477, paragraph 54, and Case C-136/04 Deutsches Milch-Kontor [2005] ECR I-0000, paragraph 32).

9 Conclusions: predictability

To conclude on the expectation to predict how the European Court of Justice will interpret a legal provision of European law, criticisms according to which the interpretation by reference to systemic and teleological considerations is contrary to the principle of legal certainty should be considered, especially those that are contrary to the predictability of enforcement. According to this view, teleological interpretation, disregarding the wording of a rule, means that adjudication within the context of EU law is particularly unpredictable.

Eliminating linguistic discrepancies by way of interpretation may be argued to run contrary to the principle of legal certainty given that one or more language versions may have to be interpreted in a manner that is not in accordance with the ordinary usage of words (...) the Court has stated that it is appropriate to reach a solution that does not prefer any one of the language versions. To do so, the Court resorts to the teleological method of interpretation that takes as its starting point the *telos*; that is, the purpose and objectives of the rule in question as well as contextual and systemic considerations[73] (Paunio 2013 and Rasmussen 1992).

To counterbalance this accusation we should consider that, when confronted with texts expressed in many languages, interpreters (and especially the European Court of Justice) have to reconcile several concerns. The final result is the product of a very complex web of conditions.

First of all, primary sources must be respected: no legal provision may be read outside of the European institutional framework. The literal meaning may have to give way to a presumption of conformity with the general framework. So that for example, the principle of equality may take precedence over the explicit expression used in a regulation or a directive.

Secondly, when facing problems of interpretation, the concern to safeguard the validity of EU acts whenever possible, rather than invalidating them, plays its role.

---

[73] Paunio, Elina. 2013. *Legal Certainty in Multilingual EU Law*, Language, *Discourse and Reasoning at the European Court of Justice*. Ashgate: Routledge. 1–51. Previously: Rasmussen, Jalte H. 1992. Towards a Normative Theory of Interpretation of Community Law. *University of Chicago Legal Forum* 7 (1). 135–178.

This concern is not so strongly felt at the domestic level of the member States, except perhaps when constitutional provisions are involved. At the national level one can reasonably expect that the Parliament will find the opportunity to correct a rule that has proved to be defective when actually implemented and submitted to judicial review. Given the very complex and time-consuming process by which legislative acts are approved at the European level, it is not surprising that interpreters try hard to reconcile differences between several languages rather than surrendering to the fact that the legislation is too vague to be implemented.

Other concerns that may affect the final understanding of a rule depend on the need to harmonize, where possible, European law with the national law of the member States, while trying to avoid open clashes that would cause conflict with lawyers educated in their own tradition. This explains why the European Court of Justice, when confronted with a flexible definition, or an undefined legal institution, often refers to a comparative interpretation. As an example we may quote the situation involving the so called lawyer-client privilege (legal professional privilege)[74]: in one instance the European Court of Justice had to decide whether the protection of communications between a party and his/her lawyer could also include in-house lawyers, that is to say, lawyers employed by a firm rather than self-employed. As no express definition was included in the European sources nor could a common agreement be found in the States' legal systems, the Court had to embark both on a comparative examination of the prevailing trend and consider the meaning of the requirement of "independence" that should qualify the position of a lawyer in front of his client.[75] Similarly the notion of "family member" in the law pertaining to immigration and asylum seekers was enlarged to include other "relatives" (such as grandchildren) on the basis of "humanitarian" grounds taking into account the differences between the scope of the words used (for example) in the English version of a regulation.[76]

In conclusion, it must be recognised that the Court does not have many other strategies at hand if not to attempt to harmonize the various versions of a text by looking to the aim of the legislator. A different notion of legal predictability emerges at the EU level: "legal certainty is also said to exist when judicial decision-making is

---

[74] European Court of Justice. Case C-550/07. Akzo Nobel Chemicals Ltd and Akcros Chemicals Ltd v European Commission.
http://curia.europa.eu/juris/liste.jsf?language=it&num=C-550/07.

[75] Opinion of the Advocate General Kokott. In European Court of Justice. Case C-583/11. Inuit Tapiriit Kanatami and Others v European Parliament and Council of the European Union. Paragraph 61 was especially explicit on the importance of guaranteeing the lawyer's autonomy advising a client.
https://eur-lex.europa.eu/legal-content/EN/TXT/?uri=CELEX%3A62011CJ0583.

[76] European Court of Justice. Case C-245/11. K v Bundesasylamt. Paragraphs 39-41-42. http://curia.europa.eu/juris/liste.jsf?num=C-245/11&language=EN.

acceptable, consequently fulfilling the imperatives of rationality and moral acceptability[77]" (Paunio 2013).

The effort by the European Court of Justice to regularly quote precedents shows a certain degree of care in making decisions predictable. The way in which precedents are recalled may seem unfamiliar to common law lawyers as the Court tends to refer to the most recent affirmation of a certain trend, rather than going back to the first episode in which a certain principle has been upheld, as would be most obvious in a common law setting. It is rather in the literature that we read comments retracing recent cases to famous leading cases such as Costa, Ratti or Francovich and so on. This may be a disadvantage as it is not always easy to initially distinguish whether a certain interpretative trend is recent or long established. The varying level of acuity in comments on the predictability of the European Court of Justice case law depends partly on the different expectations that lawyers belonging to various legal traditions have in relation to judicial review. Some continental Constitutional courts engage in interpretations of the legislation that fill incomplete provisions (in light of the Constitution). This experience may affect the lawyers' reactions also in the face of "creative" readings by international courts, making them seem less shocking for civil lawyers than for common lawyers.

References

Bajčić, Marina. Challenges of translating EU terminology. In Maurizio Gotti & William Cristopher. 2010. *Legal discourse across languages and culture*. Bern: Peter Lang AG.
Brady, Hugo. 2014. Twelve things everyone should know about the European court of justice: *The ECJ thinks in French*. Center for European Reform. 35. http://www.cer.eu/publications/archive/report/2014/twelve-things-everyone-should-know-about-european-court-justice (accessed November 10, 2017).
Carnimeo, Nicolò. 2013. Passengers protection: Development and analysis. *Aviation Space Journal* 12 (1). 2–10. http://www.ingfo.unibo.it/servizi/rivista/The_Aviation_Space_Journal_n%201_2013.pdf (accessed November 10, 2017).
Derlén, Mattias. 2007. *A castle in the air*: Practical problems of the multilingual interpretation of European community law. *Umeå Studies in Law* 16. 678.
Edward, David. 1995. How the court of justice works. *European Law Review*. 539–546.
Eörsi, Gyula. 1977. Unifying the law: (A play in one act, with a song). *American Journal of Comparative Law* 25 (4). 658–662.
Government of Canada, Privy Council Office. 2001. *Guide to making Federal Acts and Regulations* (2nd edn.). Part II, Making Acts.
Heinkelmann, Bärbel. 2014. Scope and limits of comprehensibility in the drafting process: The European commission as an example. Second European symposium on improving the

---

[77] Paunio, Elina. 2013. *Legal Certainty in Multilingual EU Law*, Language, *Discourse and Reasoning at the European Court of Justice*. Ashgate: Routledge. 101.

comprehensibility of legal provisions. Berlin. November 11. http://www.bmjv.de/SharedDocs/Kurzmeldungen/DE/2014/20141112_Symposium_Verst%C3%A4ndlichkeit_Rechtsvorschriften.html. (deleted, November 10, 2017; see: http://www.bmjv.de/DE/Themen/Rechtssetzung Buerokratieabbau/Sprachberatung/EUSymposium2014.html).

International Institute for the Unification of Private Law. 2010. Art. 1.6 (2) UNIDROIT Principles. Rome. http://www.unilex.info/dynasite.cfm?dssid=2377&dsmid=14311 (accessed November 10, 2017).

Jacobs, Francis. 2003. How to interpret legislation which is equally authentic in twenty languages. Lecture at European commission, seminars on quality of legislation. Legal Revisers Group, Brussels. October 20. http://ec.europa.eu/dgs/legal_service/seminars/agjacobs_summary.pdf (accessed November 10, 2017).

Jeckel, Sebastian. 2014. An overview of the EU legislative process: Scope and limits of comprehensibility in the drafting process, intervention. The *Second European Symposium on Improving the Comprehensibility of Legal Provisions*, Berlin, November 11, 2014. http://www.bmjv.de/DE/Themen/RechtssetzungBuerokratieabbau/Sprachberatung/EUSymposium2014.html.

Le Bot, F. 2013. La protection des passagers aériens dans l'Union Européenne. *Revue trimestrielle droit européen* 49. 753–771.

Lemarié, Alexis. 2012. *La force majeure en droit du contrat de transport maritime*. Sarrebruck : Editions Universitaires Européennes.

Maalouf Report. 2008. *A rewarding challenge: How the multiplicity of languages could strengthen Europe*. http://www.poliglotti4.eu/docs/a_rewarding_challenge.pdf. (accessed 15 June 2016); https://ec.europa.eu/education/sites/education/files/rewarding-challenge-report_en.pdf (accessed November 10, 2017).

Malenovský, Jiří. 2014. EU Passenger Rights. Conference EU Law in the Member States. Air Passenger Rights, 10 Years on. Collège d'Europe, Bruges. September 26–27.

https://www.coleurope.eu/events/conference-eu-law-member-states-air-passenger-rights-10-years (accessed November 10, 2017).

Manifeste pour le français, langue juridique de l'Europe, 2004.

http://www.francophonie-avenir.com/Index_MD_Manifeste-Druon_pour_que_le_francais_soit_la_langue_juridique_de_1%27Europe.html; http://www.institut-idef.org/Manifeste-en-faveur-de-la-langue.html (accessed November 10, 2017).

Mann, A. Francis. 1983. Uniform statutes in English law. *Law Quarterly Review* 99 (3). 376–406.

Marí, Isidor & Miquel Strubell. 2017. The linguistic regime of the European Union: Prospects in the face of enlargement. www.europadiversa.org/eng/pdf/strubell_mari_eng.doc (accessed November 10, 2017).

Paunio, Elina. 2013. *Legal certainty in multilingual EU Law, language, discourse and reasoning at the European court of justice*. London: Routledge.

Pescatore, Pierre. 1983. The doctrine of "direct effect": An infant disease of community law. *European Law Review* (8). 155–169.

Pozzo, Barbara & Valentina Jacometti (eds.). 2006. *Le politiche linguistiche delle istituzioni comunitarie dopo l'allargamento*. Milan: Giuffré.

Rasmussen,H. Jalte. 1992. Towards a normative theory of interpretation of community law. *University of Chicago Legal Forum* 7 (1). 135–178.

Report of the Directorate General for Translation. *Languages and Translation* 4 (1).

http://ec.europa.eu/dgs/translation/publications/magazines/languagestranslation/documents/issue_01_en.pdf.

Šarčević, Susan. 2001. *Legal translation: Preparation for accession to the European Union*. Reijeka: Faculty of law, University of Reijeka.

Šarčević, Susan (ed.). 2013. *Language and culture in EU law: multidisciplinary perspectives*. London: Ashgate.

Sir Schiemann, Konrad. 2013. The advantages of obscurity: The drafting of EU legislation and judgments. Seminar at the Institute of Advanced Legal Studies, International Association of Legislation. London. October 7.
http://www.ial-online.org/2013/10/recording-the-advantages-of-obscurity-the-drafting-of-eu-legislation-and-judgments/ (accessed November 10, 2017)
Schübel-Pfister, Isabel. 2005. Enjeux et perspectives du multilinguisme dans l'Union Européenne: après l'élargissement, la "babelisation". *Revue du Marché Commun et de L'Union Européenne* 332.
Solan, M. Lawrence. 2008. The interpretation of multilingual statutes by the ECJ. *Brooklyn Journal of International Law* 34 (9). 276.
Solan, Lawrence. 2007. Statutory interpretation in the EU: The Augustinian approach. *Brooklyn Law School Research Papers* 78. http:/ssrn.com/abstract=998167 (accessed March 3, 2015).
Stotz, Rüdiger. 2014. *The interpretation of legal texts by the court of justice of the European Union*. Second European Symposium on Improving the Comprehensibility of Legal Provisions. Federal Ministry of Justice and Consumer Protection, Berlin. November 11.
http://www.bmjv.de/DE/Themen/RechtssetzungBuerokratieabbau/Sprachberatung/EUSymposium2014.html (accessed November 10, 2017)
Swedish Language Council. 1998. Draft Action Programme for the Promotion of the Swedish Language. http://www.spraknamnden.se/SSN/handleng.htm (not available on November 10, 2017; see: https://aiic.net/page/286/swedish-in-sweden-and-in-the-european-union/lang/1, accessed November 10, 2017)
The European Consumers' Centre Network. 2005. Air passenger rights: Consumer complaints 2005. A Summary & Analysis of Consumer Complaints reported to the European Consumer Centre Network. http://ec.europa.eu/consumers/archive/topics/air_passenger_complaints2005.pdf (accessed November 10, 2017).
The League of Nations. 1930. Convention providing a uniform law for bills of exchange and promissory notes. Geneva: SiSU.
http://www.jus.uio.no/lm/bills.of.exchange.and.promissory.notes.convention.1930/portrait.pdf (accessed November 9, 2017).
Tiersma, Peter & Solan, Lawrence (eds). 2012. *The Oxford handbook of language and law*. Oxford: Oxford University Press.
Twining, William & David Miers. 1999. *How to do things with rules* (4th edn.). London: Butterworths.
Wellington, M. Louise. 2001. *Bijuralism in Canada: Harmonization methodology and terminology*. Canada Department of Justice. http://www.justice.gc.ca/eng/rp-pr/csj-sjc/harmonization/hfl-hlf/b4-f4/bf4.pdf (accessed November 10, 2017).
Zweigert, Konrad & Hein Kötz. 1998. *An introduction to comparative law* (3rd edn). Oxford: Clarendon Press.

Cases

England and Wales Court of Appeal. Civil Case 14/1974. H.P. Bulmer v. J Bollinger SA. http://www.bailii.org/cgi-bin/markup.cgi?doc=/ew/cases/EWCA/Civ/1974/14.html&query=Bulmer+and+v+and+Bollinger+and+%281974%29&method=boolean.
European Court of Justice. Case C-550/07. Akzo Nobel Chemicals Ltd and Akcros Chemicals Ltd v European Commission. http://curia.europa.eu/juris/liste.jsf?language=it&num=C-550/07.
European Court of Justice. Case C-372/88. Cricket St Thomas.
European Court of Justice. Case 29/69. Erich Stauder v. City of Ulm. http://eur-lex.europa.eu/legal-content/EN/TXT/HTML/?uri=CELEX:61969CJ0029&from=EN.

Europen Court of Justice. Case C-451/08. Helmut Müller GmbH v Bundesanstalt für Immobilienaufgaben. http://curia.europa.eu/juris/liste.jsf?language=en&num=C-451/08.
European Court of Justice. Case C-344/04. IATA and Elfaa. http://curia.europa.eu/juris/document/document.jsf?text=&docid=57285&pageIndex=0&doclang=EN&mode=lst&dir=&occ=first&part=1&cid=593132.
European Court of Justice. Case C-445/09. IMC Securities BV v Stichting Autoriteit Financiële Markten. http://curia.europa.eu/juris/document/document.jsf?text=&docid=107264&pageIndex=0&doclang=EN&mode=lst&dir=&occ=first&part=1&cid=84038#Footnote*.
European Court of Justice. Case C-429/07. Inspecteur van de Belastingdienst v X BV. http://curia.europa.eu/juris/liste.jsf?language=en&num=C-429/07.
European Court of Justice. Case C-149/97. Institute of the Motor Industry.
European Court of Justice. Case C-245/11. K v Bundesasylamt. http://curia.europa.eu/juris/liste.jsf?num=C-245/11&language=EN.
Europea Court of Justice. Case C-64/95. Lubella v. Hauptzollamt Cottbus.
European Court of Justice. Case C-506/06. Mayr v. Bäkerei und Conditorei Gerhard Floeckner. http://curia.europa.eu/juris/liste.jsf?language=it&num=C-506/06.
European Court of Justice. Case C-12/11. McDonagh v. Ryanair.
European Court of Justice. Case C-119/05. Ministero dell'Industria, del Commercio e dell'Artigianato v *Lucchini*. http://curia.europa.eu/juris/document/document.jsf?text=&docid=62742&pageIndex=0&doclang=EN&mode=lst&dir=&occ=first&part=1&cid=112127.
European Court of Justice. Joined Cases C-581/10 & C-629/10. Nelson and Others v Deutsche Lufthansa AG & TUI Travel and Others v Civil Aviation Authority. http://curia.europa.eu/juris/document/document.jsf?text=&docid=128861&pageIndex=0&doclang=EN&mode=lst&dir=&occ=first&part=1&cid=253017.
European Court of Justice. Case C-240/98. Océano Grupo Editorial SA contro Roció Murciano Quintero. http://curia.europa.eu/juris/liste.jsf?num=C-240/98.
European Court of Justice. Case C-239/07. Sabatauskas and Others .
European Court of Justice. C-161/06. Skoma-Lux sro v Celní ředitelství Olomouc. https://eur-lex.europa.eu/legal-content/EN/TXT/?uri=CELEX%3A62006CJ0161.
*European Court of Justice. Case 283/81. Srl Cilfit and Lanificio di Gavardo SpA v Ministry of Health.*http://eur-lex.europa.eu/legal-content/EN/TXT/PDF/?uri=CELEX:61981CJ0283&from=EN.
European Court of Justice. Joined Cases C-402/07 & C-432/07. Sturgeon and Others. http://curia.europa.eu/juris/liste.jsf?language=en&num=C-402/07.
European Court of Justice. Case C-292/89. The Queen and The Immigration Appeal Tribunal, ex parte Gustaff Desiderius. Antonissen. http://curia.europa.eu/juris/showPdf.jsf?text=&docid=96732&pageIndex=0&doclang=EN&mode=lst&dir=&occ=first&part=1&cid=114059.
European Court of Justice. Case C-58/08. Vodafone Ltd et al. V Secretary of State for Business, Enterprise and Regulatory Reform. http://curia.europa.eu/juris/document/document.jsf?text=&docid=79665&pageIndex=0&doclang=EN&mode=lst&dir=&occ=first&part=1&cid=115728.
European Court of Justice. Case C-487/12. Vueling Airlines SA v Instituto Galego de Consumo de la Xunta de Galicia.
Opinion of the Advocate General Jacobs. In European Court of Justice. Case C-292/00. Davidoff & Cie SA v Gofkid Ltd. http://curia.europa.eu/juris/document/document.jsftext=&docid=47256&pageIndex=0&doclang=EN&mode=lst&dir=&occ=first&part=1&cid=56345.
Opinion of the Advocate General Kokott. In European Court of Justice. Case C-583/11. Inuit Tapiriit Kanatami and Others v European Parliament and Council of the European Union. https://eur-lex.europa.eu/legal-content/EN/TXT/?uri=CELEX%3A62011CJ0583.

Opinion of the Advocate General Shrapston. In European Court of Justice. Case C-396/06. Kramme. http://curia.europa.eu/juris/document/document.jsf?text=&docid=63514&pageIndex=0&doclang=EN&mode=lst&dir=&occ=first&part=1&cid=599820#.

Opinion of Advocate General Sharpston. In European Court of Justice. Joined Cases C-402/07 & C-432/07. Sturgeon v Condor Flugdienst GmbH and others. http://curia.europa.eu/juris/documenti.jsf?text=&docid=76092&pageIndex=0&doclang=EN&mode=req&dir=&occ=first&part=1&cid=597895.

United Kingdom House of Lords. Appeal Case 593/1992. Pepper (inspector of taxes) v. Hart. http://www.bailii.org/uk/cases/UKHL/1992/3.html.

United Kingdom Supreme Court. Case 59/12. X v. Mid Sussex Citizens Advice Bureau.

Laws, Regulations and Directives

http://europa.eu/legislation_summaries/institutional_affairs/institutions_bodies_and_agencies/ai0049_en.htm.

http://ec.europa.eu/transport/themes/passengers/air/doc/neb-extraordinary-circumstances-list.pdf.

Conclusions on language competences to enhance mobility of the Council of the EU. 2011. http://www.consilium.europa.eu/uedocs/cms_data/docs/pressdata/en/educ/126373.pdf.

Directive 1995/46 EC of the European Parliament and the Council on data protection. http://www.dataprotection.ie/viewdoc.asp?DocID=91&m=

Directive 2004/18/EC of the European Parliament and of the Council of 31 March 2004 on the coordination of procedures for the award of public works contracts, public supply contracts and public service contracts. *Official Journal* (L134). 114.

Directive 2013/48 EU of the European Parliament and of the Council of 22 October 2013 on the right of access to a lawyer in criminal proceedings (...) and in European arrest warrant and on the right to have a third party informed upon deprivation of liberty and to communicate with third persons and with consular authorities while deprived of liberty.

Document quality control in public administrations and international organisations. July 14, 2013. http://bookshop.europa.eu/is-bin/INTERSHOP.enfinity/WFS/EU-Bookshop-Site/en_GB/-/EUR/ViewPublication-Start?PublicationKey=HC0113339.

Explanatory memorandum to the original Commission proposal (COM [2001]) 784 final) of the Commission of the European Communities. 2001.

Barcelona European Council, 15 AND 16 March 2002,C/02/930, Presidency Conclusions, Par. 44, Pdf Annexed to http://europa.eu/rapid/press-release_PRES-02-930_en.htm (accessed November 10, 2017).

Marina Timoteo
15 Contemporary Chinese law: a linguistic perspective

1 Introduction

Within the framework of the formation of a modern legal system in China, in the second half of nineteenth century, a new intimate connection between language and law was established, mainly through a huge work of legal translation that was a fundamental part of a process of reception of Western legal models. To introduce these models, coming from afar to provide a key to enter modernity, a fundamental preliminary work had to be done to create the necessary linguistic premises for the reception of models that were extraneous at all for Chinese legal environment. Thus, a preliminary passage to enter into the sphere of the contemporary Chinese legal language is understanding of this work of legal translation, mainly based on the creation of neologisms introduced into the legal language for the specific purpose of translating foreign legal concepts. This kind of work represents a sort of "guaranteed translation", where correspondences with the foreign translated words are ensured through the official creation of a new word in the language of the receiving country (Sacco 2005: 16). However, even if guaranteed, these practices of translation do not eliminate risks and problems at both linguistic and legal levels. The first part of this essay has, thus, been dedicated to this first stage of the translation process and to its most critical aspects.

Translations and processes of innovation of legal language also remain a core aspect of the functional relationship between language and law in contemporary China. Thanks to the great elasticity of the Chinese language, to its capacity to capture the most essential elements of concepts and render them through the semantic transparency of its writing system, legal changes in China have been constantly accompanied by an intense process of linguistic change that did not end with the introduction of a new set of vocabulary at the beginning of the modern law reforms. Especially the last few decades, marked by a great acceleration of the Chinese economic and legal reforms, have been times of huge changes in legal language trends and times of great challenges for translators. With regard to these last developments, two main aspects are taken in due consideration in the following part of paper: the new word-level issues of translation that have been emerging, and the growing uncertainties of Chinese legal language, especially at the legislative and regulatory levels, as a result of the functional interactions of Chinese language and law reforms in times of rapid and profound changes.

In the aforementioned context, in the last few years, a new critical aspect has been emerging in the perspective of work with Chinese law and language, i.e. problems of uncertainties associated to the categories used in legal discourses, in connection with the intensifying intersections of legal models and concepts. Currently, over the past few decades, the strongly renewed stress on legal transplants and the new interactions of different "legal Chineses" – after the re-opening of channels of dialogue with Taiwanese law scholars, and the return of the British Crown Colony of Hong Kong to China – contributed to a growing complexity of the Chinese language of the law. The result of this evolution is the urgent need to work with the terms expressing legal concepts that, as comparative lawyers have clearly shown, have the main function of creating boundaries of meaning and demarcating legal facts (Gambaro 2003: 772). A process of re-conceptualization is highly needed in several fields of the Chinese legal system, also in order to render more efficient the translations of Chinese laws into Western legal languages, mainly into English. The final part of this essay is dedicated to these emergent critical aspects, which are capable of conditioning the future relation between language and law in China.

2 Legal transplants and the creation of a new legal vocabulary in modern China

Modern Chinese legal language is largely a translated language, as a result of a massive process of modernization through legal transplants in various law fields, which is intimately connected to the creation of new law taxonomies.[1] This process started in the second half of nineteenth century, within a historical context in which the key to entering the modern world was the introduction in the country of Western legal models, and was assisted by the medium of the work already done by the Japanese who created a new Western-style legal system and a new Japanese legal language during the Meiji period (1868–1914). The most relevant part of that process was represented by the practice of *yijie* 義解, which literally means *"translation and introduction or introduction through translation"* (Cao 2004: 162), that was necessary instrumental in constructing the modern Chinese Law.

From a linguistic point of view, the assimilation of words coming from the vocabulary of different Western Laws has followed, mainly, the strategy of semantic loans, creating neologisms in the Chinese legal language. Even when the neologisms were formed through graphic loans, that is introducing the Japanese characters in which Western legal concepts and categories had already been translated, behind the imported compounds there normally were operations of semantic lending (Masini 1993: 42–47). Following this method, at the time of the approval of the first modern

---

[1] For a general overview of the legal transplant literature, with a focus on the Chinese legal modernization process, see Perenboom (2006: 823–871) and Chen (2011: 389–432).

codes, under the Nationalist government of Jiang Jieshi, the taxonomic, conceptual and lexical framework of the Chinese Law had been completely rewritten, giving new meanings to existing characters or combination of characters: for example, the Constitution was named *xianfa* 憲法 (simplified Chinese 宪法)[2] where *xian* means "decree" or "primary law" and *fa* means "law"; the "people" (*min*) associated with the "law" (*fa*) had given rise to *minfa* 民法, the civil law; the legal act was conveyed as *falu xingwei* 法律 行為 (法律 行为) where *falu* stands for "legal" and *xingwei* is "act"; the notion of legal person had been translated *faren* 法人, where *fa*, intended as the law, joins the *ren*, which means "person", while the concept of legal duty was made as *yiwu* 義務 (义务), compound formed by *yi* of "justice" and *wu* to "engage".

Sometimes, the terms imported from Japan belonged to the category of return loans, that is an operation of restitution of previous Chinese loans to Japan, with renewed meanings, as in the case of the word "democracy" expressed by the Chinese characters 民主 (*minzhu*), formed by *min*, "people", and *zhu*, "master", which originally meant "lord of the people".[3]

Only a few words were handed down intact from the Imperial law to the Republic's law: *qiyue* 契约 "contract", *jicheng* 继承 "succession", *hunyin* 婚姻 "marriage", were among them. Their meaning, however, was bound to change under the new regulatory framework and taxonomy.

The creation of this new legal vocabulary, mostly made giving a new meaning to an existing character or combination of characters, has highlighted the limits and the dangers of a process of translation between languages and legal cultures which were extremely distant from each other (Cao 2004: 162). In this process, the outcome of the operation of the transfer of meaning could appear entirely inadequate, to the point of almost being non-sense, as in the case of the quadrisyllabic term "*quanli nengli*" 權利 能力 (权利 能力), coined to translate the notion of legal capacity, whose literal translation reads: "power-interest-capacity-ability" (Pazzaglini 1991: 53–54).

We could also face the danger of a radical transformation of meanings. In this regard, the most classic reference is to the neologism which has attracted the attention of those Western scholars who have dealt with the first phase of the modernization of the legal Chinese: that neologism was created to translate into Chinese the English word "right", 權利 *quanli* (权利), which is the first part of the aforementioned quadrisyllabic compound employed to translate the concept of the legal capacity.

---

[2] Chinese writing underwent a process of simplification involving its characters, between 1956 and 1964. In this paragraph we report, to quote the first generation of legal neologisms with simplified characters, the traditional version and in brackets the simplified one, which took over late.

[3] The word "revolution", *geming* 革命, that would mark the main historical passages of modern China, was the return of a previous loan from China to Japan. At the time of the original broadcast *geming* was the meaning of "withdrawing the mandate of Heaven" (i.e. de-legitimizing the government of the sovereign). On these back loans see Abbiati (2008: 110).

The creation of the compound *quanli* is traced back to the Chinese translation of the well-known handbook by Henry Wheaton, "Elements of International Law",⁴ published in 1864 in Beijing, in classical Chinese with the title *Wangguo gongfa* 萬國 公法 (万国 公法 literally "Public Law of ten-thousand countries").⁵ The translator, William A.P. Martin, an American missionary in charge of the translation by Prince Gong and joined in this job by four Chinese scholars, construed the word "*quanli*" from the combination of two compounds: *quanli* 權力 (权力 "authority" and "power") and *liyi* 利益 ("profit").⁶ So the term "*quanli*" – destined to become a key term of the new Chinese legal vocabulary, forming, with the first part of the compound, *quan*, the words with which we call subjective rights⁷ – was semantically related to an idea of domination that seemed far removed from that associated with the original "right".

However, we cannot say for sure if the translation was born due to a misunderstanding or, conversely, as a sign of clear understanding of reality. As has been observed by Linda Liu:

This is not to say that the translators were incapable of comprehending the true meaning of "right". On the contrary, the "excess" signification seems to heed the historical message of "rights" discourse in the *practice* of international law only too well, because it registers the fact that the idea had been brought into China by the nineteenth-century representatives of European international law who had asserted their "trade rights" and the "right" to invade, plunder, and attack the country (Liu 2004: 131).

3 Chinese legal developments in the XXI century and the evolution of the legal terminology

The aforementioned massive experience of legal transplants and the contextual creation of a new legal language were the starting point of a complex process of legal modernization, which passed through several epoch-making historical transitions: the fall of the Empire (1911) and the creation of a modern system inspired by civil law models in the Republican period (1927–1949), the foundation of the People's Republic of China (1949) and the influence of the soviet legal models in 1960s, the wave of legal

---

4 Published in 1836, and becoming one of the most popular manuals of International Law of the nineteenth century, it was translated into French, Spanish, Italian, as well as the Chinese language.
5 At the time, the expression for "International Law" had been created with the term *wangguogongfa* that would later be replaced with the word, derived from Japanese, and still in use, *guojifa*, 国际法.
6 Svarverud (2001: 130) identified a precedent with respect to the work of Martin, in the translation of Murray's Cyclopedia of Geography, carried out by Wei Yuan, which to translate the word "right" into Chinese used the character *quan* 权.
7 For example "credit right" is translated into *zhaiquan* 债权, "property right" into *suoyouquan* 所有权.

nihilism under the late leadership of Mao Zedong, the huge economic and legal reform process started after Mao's death (1976). Since the third plenum of the eleventh Central Committee of the Chinese Communist Party, in 1978, China has entered a new stage of its legal modernization within a new transitional phase of the country's history. This phase, labelled under the policy of "opening up and reform" (*gaige kaifang* 改革开放), was marked by both a radical economic reform leading to the creation of a socialist market economy (*shehuizhuyi shichang jingji* 社会主义市场经济) and a process of strong rehabilitation of law. The latter had its watershed in the 1999 incorporation of the principle of "ruling the country in accordance with law, establishing a socialist rule of law country" (*yifa zhiguo, jianshe shehui zhuyi fazhi guojia* 依法治国, 建设社会主义法治国家) into the Constitution.[8]

The last few decades, following these developments, with the acceleration of the market reforms, have been times of huge changes in the legal language trends and times of great challenges for translators. We witnessed the continuous evolution of concepts and taxonomical frameworks.

Let's take the example of the Western law concept of "natural person". From the legal point of view, persons were classified into "natural persons" and "legal persons" (*ziranren* 自然人 and *faren* 法人) in the 1929 Civil Code. The concept of natural person disappeared in socialist China, when it was substituted by the public law concept of *gongmin* 公民, "citizen". We still find the reference to *gongmin* 公民 even in the General Principles of Civil Law which, in 1987, rewrote the basic principles of the new Chinese civil law for the innovative age of legal and economic reforms.[9] The second chapter of General Principles of Civil Law, is titled "Citizens", but, just after the word *gongmin* 公民, the expression *ziran ren* 自然人 is placed in brackets, as indication of a reform process in progress. The final act of the transition from the public concept of "citizen" to the private law concept of "natural person" took place in 1999, when the Contract Law,[10] the first of the fundamental laws that have re-shaped civil law in contemporary China according to the new system of socialist market economy, referred to *natural person* freeing it from brackets. According to Article 2 (1) of the 1999 Contract Law, a contract is an agreement between *"natural persons"* (*ziranren* 自然人), *"legal persons or other organizations"* acting as *"equal parties"* to *"establish, modify and extinguish relationship of civil rights and duties"*.

A further step in this legal and linguistic evolution, strictly linked to the process of economic reforms, has been made with the introduction of a new concept that

---

8 On the shaping of the 'rule of law' in the Chinese experience, see Perenboom (2002: 1–598).
9 General Principles of Civil Law (中华人民共和国民法通则, *Zhonghua renmin gongheguo minfa tongze*), issued on April 12th 1986 and entered into force on January 1st 1987, is accessible at http://www.npc.gov.cn/wxzl/wxzl/2000-12/06/content_4470.htm (accessed 20 December 2015).
10 Contract Law (中华人民共和国合同法, *Zhonghua renmin gongheguo hetong fa*), issued on March 15th 1999, accessible at http://www.gov.cn/banshi/2005-07/11/content_13695.htm (accessed 20 December 2015).

refers to natural persons with regard to the aspect of the entitlement to ownership of assets, the concept expressed with the compound *siren* 私人. Here, the fundamental step is the admission in the official legal vocabulary of the character *si* 私 ("private"), bearing an original negative meaning and thus banned from the lexicon of socialist era (Zanier 2008: 9). If, with regard to the aspect of the entitlement to ownership of assets, we still find, in the General Principles of Civil Law, the reference to "the assets of the citizen" (*gongming de hefa caichan* 公民的合法财产), the 2007 Law on Real Rights,[11] another epoch-making law of the new post-Maoist China, which filled in the country's "legal blank" with regard to property law, introduced the new term *siren* 私人 next to the word "ownership right". In the title of chapter five of part two of the law (*guojia suoyouquan he jiti suoyouquan, siren suoyouquan* 国家所有权和集体所有权、私人所有权), *siren suoyouquan* 私人所有权, i.e. the "ownership rights of the private", is put at the same level of the "ownership rights of the State" (*guojia suoyouquan* 国家所有权) and "ownership rights of Collectives" (*jiti suoyouquan* 集体所有权) i.e. the two classical components of public ownership of the socialist State.

Starting from the new legal word for "private", *siren* 私人, a new trisyllabic compound has been created to express the concept of "privatization", through the combination with the suffix *hua* 化.[12]

However, we should note that the legal concept expressed in English with the word "privatization" is not only rendered into Chinese with the compound *sirenhua* 私人化. There is, at least, another new word that should be taken into consideration from the legal point of view, which is the word *siyouhua* 私有化 (See Zhao 2007: 90–94; Meng 2010). As can be observed, the two trisyllabic compounds share the first and the third character and differ only in the character at the centre: *ren* 人 (which, as we have already seen, means "person") in the first, *you* 有 (meaning "to have") in the second. Thus, the "individual" is at the centre of the first compound created to express the concept of privatization, while "having", "possessing", is at the centre of the second. A first glimpse to these words allows the inference of the difference in meaning of the two compounds: the former embodies a concept that refers to the individual sphere, while the latter refers to the sphere of capital. As a matter of fact, *siyouhua* 私有化 is the trisyllabic compound coined to define the epoch-making process of privatization

---

11 Real Rights Law (中华人民共和国物权法, *Zhonghua renmin gongheguo wuquanfa*) issued on March 16th 2007, accessible at http://www.gov.cn/flfg/2007-03/19/content_554452.htm (accessed 20 December 2015).

12 Many of the neologisms created in the last few decades are trisyllabic compounds that end with the suffix *hua* 化, a character which expresses the idea of a transformation process. The character is composed of two parts, or rather by two images which are combined to determine a meaning: on the reader's left there is the image of a man (another way of drawing a man, even more stylized than what we have seen above), on the right there is the representation of a ladle. *Man* plus *ladle* suggests "alchemy" and, indeed, *hua* 化 means to transmute, to change. *Hua* 化 is the character used to define the science of chemistry. See McNaugthon (1987: 165).

of state enterprises, those enterprises that until the Nineties had been the pillar of the Chinese socialist economic system and that have undergone a dismantling process in the transition to the "socialist market economy".[13]

Thus, in the last few decades, in the fast-moving global world, new word-level issues of translation have emerged, in connection with both the huge legal changes which took place in China and the capacity of Chinese characters to follow this evolution, also defining nuances of meanings, as the example of *sirenhua* and *siyouhua* has shown. In this context, translators to and from legal Chinese have to keep abreast of the great and continuous change in language trends and be fully aware of the several possibilities and problems of variations connected to these trends.

4 Linguistic and legal uncertainties in Chinese law

4.1 Written law and language

The aforementioned example of terminological evolution shows not only the rebirth of a legal vocabulary that had been erased under Mao's era, but also the great flexibility of the Chinese language, its capacity to capture the most essential elements of concepts and render them through the semantic transparency of its writing system. However, this capacity is more of a literary nature, resulting in the outlining of shades of meanings and does not have anything to do with the technicalities of the Western legal languages. As a matter of fact, according to several prominent scholars working on the topic of Chinese law and language, problems of linguistic uncertainty represent a critical marking point of both written and spoken legal Chinese (Lubman 2006: 36).

These problems are connected, first of all, to those that are considered inherent features of uncertainties in the Chinese language, a contextual oriented language, more than a sentence oriented one (DeFrancis 1984: 50). In particular, Debora Cao indicates two features of linguistic uncertainty highlighted, for classical Chinese, by the well reputed sinologist Derk Bodde and still valid in modern Chinese: "the absence of inflection, that is words can assume a variety of grammatical functions without morphological change, and the 'rule of economy', that is writers can choose to eliminate, if they wish, grammatically significant indicators" (Cao 2004: 162).

Another relevant feature of uncertainty is the high percentage of polysemic words that are frequently present in Chinese legal texts, in particular in Chinese legislation.

---

13 As explained by Zanier (2008: 8), the compound expresses the concept of "denationalization", "a complex process consisting in non-state enterprises replacing, taking over, or merging with SOEs, whereas SOEs are being converted into privately-managed joint ventures with either domestic or foreign partners, or are being reorganized into privately-managed joint-stock companies".

This feature creates problems in working with legal concepts, as it blurs distinctions between concepts and categories. We can find several cases of concepts that are differentiated in Western legal models for which a single legal term is used in Chinese: this is the case, for example, of the concepts of "voidability" and "revocation" of contracts that, in the 1999 text of Contract law, share the same term in Chinese, *chexiao* 撤销 (Art. 48 and 54). In the same law, the concepts of void and non-effective contracts are also expressed with the same word, *wuxiao* 无效.[14] In 1999, the Supreme People's Court (SPC), in its Interpretation on the Implementation of Contract Law, introduced a new term to express non-effectiveness, i.e. *wei shengxiao*, 未生效.[15] However, several scholars have continued to use *wuxiao*, 无效 to express both concepts (Han 2004: 45; Ma 2004: 28). Even the administrative regulations[16] issued by the State Council after the SPC Interpretation continued to use the undifferentiated term of "(无效) *wuxiao*". Several years later it was, again, the Supreme People's Court, through new judicial interpretation of the law, who stressed the differentiation of the two concepts[17] of non-effective contract *he tong wei sheng xiao* 合同未生效 and void contract *he tong wu xiao* 合同无效.

Other sources of ambiguity and uncertainty in Chinese law deriving from language are to be found in a legislative drafting style in which general clauses and non-technical language are preferred. This also happens when the rules are strict

---

14 The Contract Law of 1999 中华人民共和国合同法 (*Zhonghua renmin gongheguo hetong fa*) only refers to *youxiao* (effective contracts) (art. 44) and *wuxiao* (void contracts) (art. 52).
15 See "最高人民法院关于适用《中华人民共和国合同法》若干问题的解释 (*Zuigao renmin fayuan guanyu shiyong "zhonghua renmin gongheguo hetong fa" ruogan wenti de jieshi*") [Supreme People's Court Interpretation on some questions about the application of the Contract Law of the People's Republic of China], [Fa shi (1999) Di 19 hao], entered into force on 29 December 1999, whose article 9 distinguishes between "*wuxiao*" and "*wei shengxiao*".
16 See, for example, 中华人民共和国中外合资经营企业法实施条例 (*Zhonghua renmin gongheguo zhongwai hezijingying qiyefa shishitiaoli*) [Implementing Regulations of Foreign Joint Ventures Law of PRC] issued by the State Council on July 22th 2001, at article 20.
17 In particular, in the Interpretations of the Supreme People's Court on Certain Issues Concerning the Applicability of the Arbitration Law in 2006, in the Provisions of the Supreme People's Court on Several Issues Concerning the Hearing of Cases about Disputes Involving Foreign-funded Enterprises (I) in 2010, and in the Interpretations of the Supreme People's Court on Issues Concerning the Application of Law for the Trial of Cases Involving Disputes over Sale and Purchase Contracts in 2012: see, respectively, 最高人民法院关于适用〈中华人民共和国仲裁法〉若干问题的解释 (*Zuigao renmin fayuan guanyushiyong zhonghua renmin gongheguo zhongcaifa ruogan wenti de jieshi*), issued on 23th August 2006, accessible at http://www.court.gov.cn/fabu-xiangqing-1053.html (accessed 15 December 2015). 最高人民法院关于审理外商投资企业纠纷 案件若干问题的规定（一）(*Zuigao renmin fayuan guanyushenli waishang touziqiye jiufenanjian ruoganwenti de guiding* (I), issued on 5th august 2010, accessible at Xinhua net http://news.xinhuanet.com/legal/2010-08/16/c_12451286.htm (accessed 15 December 2015). 最高人民法院关于审理买卖合同纠纷案件适用法律问题的解释 (*Zuigao renmin fayuan guanyushenli maimaihetong jiufenanjian shiyongfalv wenti de jieshi*), issued on 10th May 2012, is accessible at http://www.chinacourt.org/law/detail/2012/05/id/145832.shtml (accessed 15 December 2015).

reproduction of foreign models. Western scholars have shown several examples in Chinese laws of this aspect (Perenboom 2002: 147; Lubman 1999: 391). I will quote here a more recent example that I have been able to examine studying the rules on liability for environmental pollution provided for in the 2009 Tort law.[18] Article 66 of his law adopts, as a unified rule, the shift in the burden of proof in causation that applies to all environmental tort liability cases, laying down in this regard that: *"Where any dispute arises over an environmental pollution, the polluter shall assume the burden to prove that it should not be liable or its liability could be mitigated under certain circumstances as provided for by law or to prove that there is no causation between its conduct and the harm"*. This rule goes in the direction of expanding liability for environmental pollution following a solution that can be found in Japanese and German laws. In the book edited by the Legislative Affairs Commission of the Standing Committee of the National People's Congress after the enactment of the Tort Law, the first of the three foreign statutory models quoted in reference to Article 66 of the Chinese tort law is the German Act, and in particular Articles 6 and 7 thereof. However, several linguistic problems surrounded the borrowing of this rule: first of all, we find in the Legislative Commission's book a very inaccurate (and problematic to read) translation of the German reference rule into the Chinese language. In addition to (and, probably, as a consequence of) this, the Chinese Tort law is more vague in its language than the German law taken as model and, due to the many difficulties of proving causation and damages in pollution related compensation claims, art. 66 gave rise to different interpretations with different solutions about the distribution of the burden of proof: some authors have considered this rule an expression of the principle of "causality presumption" (*yinguo guanxi tuiding* 因果关系推定), according to which the plaintiff is requested to provide some preliminary evidence regarding the causation, while other interpreters found in art. 66 the stricter principle of "reversal of the burden of the proof" (*juzheng zeren daozhi* 举证责任倒置) under which the defendant is in any case called upon to give evidence excluding the causal link between the damage and his conduct. The application of the two interpretations by Chinese judges results in different outcomes in environmental tort law cases (Timoteo 2015: 121–133). The uncertainty determined by the vague law provision was solved, in June 2014, by the Supreme People's Court of China in its "Opinions on Strengthening the Judicial Work and Providing Judicial Support for Promoting the Ecological Civilization Construction".[19] In chapter 8, which provides for the trial of civil environmental disputes,

---

18 The Tort Law of the People's Republic of China 中华人民共和国侵权责任法 (*Zhonghua renmin gongheguo qinquan zeren fa*), promulgated by the Standing Committee National People's Congress, December 26, 2009, available at <www.gov.cn/flfg/2009-12/26/content_1497435.htm> (accessed 7 May 2015), translated in LAWINFOCHINA, <www.lawinfochina.com/Display.aspx?Lib=law&Id=7846&keyword> (accessed 7 May 2015).
19 最高人民法院关于全面加强环境资源审判工作为推进生态文明建设提供有力司法保障的意见 (法发 (2014) 11号) (*Zuigao renmin fayuan guanyu quamian jiaiang huanjing ziyuan shenpan gongzuo*

the Opinions state that "[...] *the plaintiff* shall provide [...] *preliminary evidences* for the potential causality between the pollution and damage, while *the polluter* shall assume the *burden to prove that it should not be liable or its liability could be mitigated under certain circumstances as provided for by law or to prove that there is no causation between its conduct and the harm.*"

Thus, the Supreme People's Court, with its Interpretation of the law, has been assuming an increasingly relevant role towards the reduction of the uncertainties created by Chinese legislators (Cui 2007: 35; Wu 2013: 98). However, the work to be done is even greater, as the use of words with uncertain meanings is a common usage of Chinese legislators also in non-technical parts of the discourse. One of the most commonly used words is *deng* 等, a linguistic element that "can indicate both open-endedness when listing things and can also be used to end a listing, a closure, to be all inclusive, depending on actual use and context" (Cao 2004: 102).

We face continuous problems of interpretation on the word "等" within both public and private legal documents.[20] In order to understand the difficulties of working on this word in legal texts we can take the example of article 42 of the Law on Administrative Penalties which contains a list of three administrative penalties, i.e. order of the suspension of production or of business, revocation of a business permit or a license and imposition of the heavy fine, putting at the end of the list the word "等".[21] In the local implementing regulations on the Law of Administrative Penalties we find different approaches with regard to article 42: some of them repeat exactly the same words of article 42, some of them list additional administrative penalties, some of them limit the types of administrative penalties to three.[22]

---

wei tuijin shengtai wenming jianshe tigong youli sifa baozhang de yijan.) The text is available at: http://www.chinacourt.org/law/detail/2014/06/id/147914.shtml (accessed 10 October 2015).

[20] With regard to Laws see, for example, (Jian, Cao, and Zhang 2013); with regard to private legal documents there are several disputes about wills and contracts: see for example 秦大科与悦达咖世家(上海)餐饮管理有限公司租赁合同纠纷 (*Qindake yue da ka shijia (shanghai) canyin guanli youxian gongsi zulin hetong jiufen*) [Dispute of Lease Contract between Dake Qin and Yue Da Ka Shi Jia (Shanghai) Can Yin Guan Li Ltd] and 龚某、杨甲诉杨乙法定继承纠纷 (*Gong mu Yang jia su yang yi fading jicheng jiufen*) [Yang Jia Vs. Yang Yi over Statutory Succession Dispute].
http://www.court.gov.cn/zgcpwsw/sh/shsdezjrmfy/ms/201411/t20141126_4352514.htm (Accessed 07 December 2014).

[21] Law of Administrative Penalties (中华人民共和国行政处罚法 *Zonghua renmin gongheguo xingzheng chufa fa*), adopted by the National People's Congress, March 17, 1996. The full text of the Chinese version of the Law is available at: http://www.npc.gov.cn/wxzl/wxzl/2008-12/15/content_1462070.htm (accessed at 1 Jan. 2016); the English version, at http://www.npc.gov.cn/englishnpc/Law/2007-12/11/content_1383613.htm (accessed at 1 Jan. 2016);

[22] See, for the three different approaches: Article 2, 1997, 海南省行政处罚听证程序规定 (*Hainan sheng xing zheng chu fa ting zheng cheng xu gui ding*) [Hearing Procedures of Administrative Penalties in Hainan Province].

4.2 Spoken law and language

Another element of linguistic ambiguity deserving mention is the recurrence of homophones, which is normal in a language where there are only about 1.200 syllables for a number of distinct characters reaching into tens of thousands. With regard to the phenomenon of homophones the classical example is that of the aforesaid word for right, *quanli*, which is the identical pronunciation of two compounds that have completely different meanings. The two compounds share the first character, *quan* 权, while the second part of the compounds, pronounced *li*, is written with two characters having different meanings. The first *quanli* 权力, having the meaning of power, is made by *quan* 权, "power" and *li* 力, "strength"; in the second *quanli* 权利, which means right, after the *quan* 权 we find a *li* that means "profit, "interest" 利. The two *quanli* are identical in speech and only distinguishable by context and in the written language.

A further source of linguistic and legal confusion at the phonetic level is that of the assonances occurring when we have terms that have a similar, but not identical, pronunciation. A case of similarity is found, for example, in terms of "well-known trademarks", one of the crucial issues in the current framework of trademark protection in the Chinese legal system. The "well-known trademarks", *chiming shangbiao* 驰名商标, are recognized by the Chinese Trademark law.[23] The "well-known trademark" (*chiming shangbiao* 驰名商标) status can be granted through either administrative or judicial procedures. The Beijing Trademark Office and the Trademark Review and Adjudication Board can make decisions on the recognition of well-known trademarks during the course of trademark administrative proceedings or when dealing with trademark disputes. The judicial recognition of well-known trademarks is rendered by the People's Courts at all levels, i.e. at one of the four levels of the court system which comprehend Basic courts, Intermediate courts, Provincial High courts and the Supreme People's court. The courts will, depending on the facts and the necessity of such a recognition to the outcome of the case, determine whether a trademark should be granted the status of "well-known" (Jing and Shubha 2009: 119–161).

Article 3, 1997, 深圳经济特区行政处罚听证程序试行规定 (*Shenzhen jing ji te qu xing zheng chu fa ting zheng cheng xu shi xing gui ding*) [Provisional rules on hearing procedures of administrative penalties in Shenzhen Special Economic Zone].
Article 2, 1997, 山东省行政处罚听证程序实施办法 (*Shandong sheng xing zheng chu fa ting zheng cheng xu shi shi ban fa*) [Measures for implementation on hearing procedures of administrative Penalties in Shandong Province].
23 Article 13 of the Trademark Law of the People's Republic of China, 中华人民共和国商标法 (*Zhonghua renmin gongheguo shangbiao fa*) [People's Republic of China Trademark law] Adopted by the Standing Committee of the Fifth National People 's Congress on August 23, 1982, last amended on August 30, 2013). http://www.wipo.int/edocs/lexdocs/laws/en/cn/cn195en.pdf (accessed at 15 Dec. 2015).

In the context of a policy of economic development which has also relied on the geographical diversification of development strategies and on the initiative of provincial governments in stimulating the growth of local businesses, many Chinese provinces and municipalities have been recognized the autonomy to enact local rules in the field of intellectual property law. Many provincial and municipal governments (such as those of Guangdong, Beijing and Tianjin) have thus issued Regulations on the determination (by the local government itself) and protection of provincially well-known brands.[24] In these cases, the Chinese expression used to refer to the reputation is different from what we find in national legislation: in the latter, we find the expression *chiming shangbiao* 驰名商标, while the former adopt, respectively, the expressions *zhuming shangbiao* 著名商标 and *zhiming shangbiao* 知名商标, both expressions that in the common language mean "well-known trademark". *Zhuming shangbiao* 著名商标 and *zhiming shangbiao* 知名商标, while presenting a close phonetic similarity with the word used in the Trademark Law to define the "well known trademark", differs in the first character. The slight linguistic difference, almost imperceptible by a non-Chinese ear, shows the diversity of legal concepts, which are the expression of categories that have different territorial scope of application and that are subject to different procedures to obtain the legal status of "well-known" (Timoteo [2010] 2014: 39).

5 The growing complexity of the language of law in China: legal taxonomies and concepts overlapping

The examples illustrated in the previous paragraphs outline a picture of growing complexity of language problems in the Chinese contemporary legal system, in a context where the number of norm-creating actors and of sources of law is rising.

Another factor of increasing complexity of the contemporary Chinese legal language is the dramatic change in the practices of legal transplants that have been taking on a different guise since the very beginning of the Chinese legal reforms started in 1978. During this stage, Chinese legal texts and discourses have been enriched (and made more complicated) by a huge circulation of foreign legal models and an increasingly complex amalgam of patterns coming from other systems. In this context, a first source of complexity has derived from the contamination between civil law and common law models. While in the first stage of modernization European civil law systems offered the main reference models, in the last few decades a

---

24 See, for example, 北京市著名商标认定和保护办法 (*Beijing shi zhuming shangbiao rending he baohu banfa*) [Rules on the determination and protection of well-known brands in the city of Beijing], into force from Jan. 1st, 2002; 天津市著名商标认定和保护办法 (*Tianjin shi zhuming shangbiao rending he baohu banfa*) [Rules on the determination and protection of well-known brands in the city of Tianjin], entered into force from Feb. 1st, 2007.

growing number of scholars received their foreign education in the USA and, given also the central role of common law legal models in the setting of contemporary global law, one of the most relevant facts of the last decades of reform has been the arrival in the Chinese legal system of common law models. For example, in the making of the 2009 Tort law, the drafting group worked on the basis of "大陆法为体，英美法为用", which means "grounding on civil law while absorbing common law" (Yang 2002).[25] In the legislation, common law concepts such as punitive damages were actually inserted within a taxonomy based on civil law models. The same happens in the 1999 Contract Law, which has been influenced by common law, civil law and uniform law tools.

To this strategy, which led to the coexistence of concepts coming from different traditions, other elements of complexity are added by the renewed influence of legal language and taxonomies introduced during the period of Republic of China. This phenomenon results in the emersion of frequent problems in working with the terms expressing legal concepts. An illustrative example of this can be found in the evolution of one of the core concepts of civil law, i.e. the concept of fault for tortious liability. It was rendered in the Nationalistic Civil code with the compound *guoshi*, 过失, denoting negligent wrongdoing. This concept, in the code, was distinguished by *guyi*, 故意, denoting intentional wrongdoing (Art. 184 Nationalistic Code). In the post 1978 legal reforms, the element of wrongfulness was embedded within the unique concept of *guocuo* 过错, denoting both negligent and intentional wrongdoing without distinction. *Guocuo* 过错 was featured in the provisions of Article 106 of the General Principles of Civil Law as the subjective element of liability.[26] In the 2009 Tort Law (*Qinquan zeren fa*, 侵权责任法), under Article 6 the *guocuo* 过错 principle was confirmed.[27] However, in the last few decades the influence of Taiwanese scholars resulted in the reintroduction, in scholars' writings, of *guoshi*, 过失. Thus, when, with the progression of the reforms, the common law concept of "comparative fault" entered Chinese legal discourses and had to be translated into Chinese, some scholars referenced to *guoshi* 过失, while others resorted to *guocuo* 过错. The result of this duality was the overlapping of different expressions, used in an interchangeable way, which in turn caused linguistic and legal uncertainties (Xu 2013).

---

25 www.civillaw.com.cn/qqf/weizhang.asp?id=10588 (accessed 15 December 2015).
26 According to Article 106, GPCL: "公民、法人由于过错侵害国家的、集体的财产，侵害他人财产、人身的，应当承担民事责任" (*Gongmin, faren youyu guocuo qinhai guojia de, jiti de caichan, qinhai taren caichan, renshen de, yingdang chengdan minshi zeren*) [Citizens and legal persons who through their fault violate state or collective property or the property or person of other people shall bear civil liability.]
27 Art. 6 of Tort Law reads as follows: "行为人因过错侵害他人民事权益，应当承担侵权责任" (*Xingwei ren yin guocuo qinhai taren minshi quanyi, yingdang chengdan qinquan zeren.*) [Who is at fault for infringement upon a civil right or interest of another person shall be subject to the tort liability.]

The multiple affiliations of the contemporary Chinese legal language have found new expressions, and provoked new research works, in connection with the growing diversification of three legal systems using Chinese characters, i.e. People Republic of China (PRC), Republic of China (ROC) and Hong Kong Special Administrative Region. Let us take the example of the concept of contract. Contract was expressed by the term *qiyue* 契约 in the Republic of China civil code (art. 153). *Qiyue* 契约 is a word that also existed in Imperial times.[28] In the People's Republic of China, in the initial regulatory framework for various types of economic contracts enacted since 1950, two different words, i.e. *hetong* 合同[29] and *heyue* 合约,[30] were used to refer to the concept of contract during that period. Then, from 1981, *heyue* 合约 was nailed down as the only official legal term to represent the concept of contract, connoting both written and oral agreements. *Hetong* 合同 as a legal concept was explicitly defined in the aforementioned art. 2 of the 1999 Contract law.

However, the word *heyue* 合约 was chosen in Hong Kong to translate the English word "contract" in local Chinese. While *hetong* 合同 represents the idea of unity of the concerned parties (which is often echoed by the clause usually inserted in contracts according to which "in case of dispute the parties should first resolve their dispute through friendly consultation"), *heyue* 合约 stresses more the idea of obligation and duties arising from mutual consensus.[31]

The existence of different Chinese words defining the same concept can be a source of confusion if we consider that, within the same legal system, we can find their use at the same time. For example even if in mainland China *hetong* 合同 is the word used in statutory law, several scholars use the word *qiyue* 契约 in their writings. When the Italian civil code was translated into Chinese, the authors decided to use the word *qiyue* 契约 (Fei and Ding 1997).

---

28 In Chinese, it basically refers to the contract in written form, with *qi* "契" meaning engrave as expressed by the figure of knife (刀), *yue* "约" meaning restrain, and here is the figure of string(丝) that suggests the meaning.
29 The figures of two words, he 合 and tong 同 are very similar, both composed by *yi* 一 ("one") and *kou* 口("mouth"). Therefore "合" implies that the contract is made by an offer (the words spoken by one party of the contract) plus an acceptance (the words from the other party). At the same time, the contents of the offer and the acceptance should draw together and bind the parties, which is the signification of 同. Hence, the legal term 合同 stands for a legally binding promise or agreement, where two or more persons declare their consent as to any act or thing.
30 While *hetong* 合同 represents the idea of unity of the concerned parties (which is often echoed by the clause usually inserted in contracts according to which "in case of dispute the parties should first resolve their dispute through friendly consultation"), *heyue* 合约 stresses more the idea of obligation and duties arising from mutual consensus.
31 On the linguistic evolution described in the text see (Ni, Cheng, and Sin 2010: 159–180).

6 The emergence of China as a global actor: law and language implications

The aforesaid difficulties of maintaining, especially in a world of increasing legal contaminations, the precision of legal concepts and taxonomies which frame the rules in a given system, are amongst the main challenges of the contemporary stage of the Chinese legal reforms. It is a challenge, first of all, for the process of codification of civil law, that was officially resumed with the approval of the *Resolution of the CPC Central Committee on Certain Major Issues Concerning Comprehensively Advancing the Law-Based Governance of China*,[32] at the end of the Fourth Plenary Session of the 18th Central Committee of the Communist Party of China, held in Beijing from October 20 to 23, 2014. According to this document, after several years in which the matter of civil codification receded in the background, the Civil Code once again became a fundamental part of the political agenda[33] for the XXI century China, in connection with efforts to strengthen the rule of law and bring forwards the economic reforms. On 15 March 2017, the first book of the Code, ie tha *People's Republic of China General Civil Law Rules* (中华人民共和国民法总则), were formally adopted at the Fifth Session of the Twelfth National People's Congress. They entered into force on 1 October 2017.

Facing this new stage of the process of civil codification, the aforementioned growing complexity of the conceptual and linguistic frameworks of the Chinese legal system represents a crucial issue. Law is a cognitive institution. As such, new laws need to be connected to other rules, institutions, legal categories and taxonomies. This connection role is a typical role that Chinese lawmakers still assign to a civil code. As a result, for China, the current process of civil codification should open the way to the process of re-conceptualization that is highly needed in several fields of its private law system.

Moreover, this work should also be extremely important for the creation of a standard frame of reference for English translations of Chinese laws, another crucial field affected by the growing complexity of language problems in the Chinese legal system.

---

32 中共中央关于全面推进依法治国若干重大问题的决定 (*Zhonggong zhongyang guanyu quanmian tuijin yifa zhiguo ruogan zhongda wenti de jueding*) [Resolution of the CPC Central Committee on Certain Major Issues Concerning Comprehensively Advancing the Law-Based Governance of China], 30 October 2014.
33 We should remember that the history of the making of a civil code in contemporary China is a long one, starting in the first years of the People's Republic's foundation and yet moving towards a still to be attained landing place. Up to now, the only Civil Code enacted in modern China, remains that of the Nationalistic government, abrogated in 1949 with the plan of drafting a new civil code, as a socialist milestone along the road to legal modernisation. However, notwithstanding the fact that the Chinese legislature has repeatedly engaged in the codification of the civil law, this plan was never implemented.

Nowadays, most of Chinese legislative initiatives are becoming very important for the entire globalized world. Let us think, for example of the crucial field of environmental protection and climate change laws, where it is difficult to imagine anything relevant at global level without the participation of China.

For these reasons, it will be increasingly important and even necessary to have access to Chinese legislation in English.

I will here quote an example which is illustrative of the problems that, in absence of translation enjoying binding legal force in China,[34] we can meet in this field. This example refers to the rule dealing with the issue of the liability of multiple tortfeasors in environmental torts (Articles 12 and 76 of tort law) and to a comment that well-known European environmental law scholar made when she analysed the English version of these rules. The comment, quoted verbatim, reads as follows:

Amongst these rules the provision contained in Article 12 seems to be particularly intricate and complicated to understand, one of the reasons being the English translation currently available. [...] The second part of article 12 is the most difficult to unravel, given that the same words in English employed in the translation of the rule do not have a well-established or clear technical meaning, but must be understood in that specific context. The rule states: *'if the seriousness of liability of each tortfeasor is hard to be determined, the tortfeasors shall evenly assume the compensatory liability'*.

In this provision, the word *'evenly'*, means *'the same share, the same amount'* and *'compensatory liability'* is the liability for paying the compensation, independently of any consideration as far as the fault is concerned. In other words, where it is difficult to ascertain the contribution of each tortfeasor, liability for compensation will be divided by the number of the tortfeasors and each tortfeasor will bear the same share of liability. While the word evenly is an expression that does not have a clear technical meaning, as far as the meaning of the term *'compensatory liability'* is concerned, this is a concept that rarely features in traditional textbooks on tort law. It is nonetheless a term that has acquired a specific meaning in some special statutes, such as those governing environmental issues, e.g. the American Oil Pollution Act (Pozzo 2012: 304).

Problems of both linguistic uncertainties and reconstruction of meaning and operative boundaries of legal concepts are core problems in English translations of Chinese legislations. Nowadays, within the current process of global legal integration, China has adopted a major position in the international rulemaking arena and it is necessary to guarantee foreigners who are not able to read Chinese reliable access

---

34 The situation is still the same described by Cao in Translating Law (2007, 103), "There are many different translated versions of various Chinese laws, official and non-official. For instance, the Chinese government in recent years has been behind translating and publishing various English translations of all the major Chinese laws in its efforts of integration into the international community. There are private translations such as law publishers and legal academic research bodies as well. But none of such translations enjoys binding legal force in the Chinese or any other jurisdictions".

to Chinese legislation. English translations must be as accurate as possible and this opens the way to a few reflections on the perspective of having some sort of standardized English specific to translating from Chinese.

Up until now, in China, only two official works have been discovered that can be used as reference material for the translation of Chinese laws and regulations into English, i.e. a handbook of "Chinese-English terminology for Laws and Regulations" issued in 1998 by the State Council Legislative Affair Office and a handbook for legal translations issued in 2005 by the same office, the latter only for internal use. However, the two works mainly concentrate on public and administrative law, while for civil law there is no analogous work. A growing interest in perceiving the need for a more comprehensive reference tool to translate Chinese law into English can be observed in China (Qu 2013).[35]

7 Conclusive remarks: linking the present to the past

This work has framed, from a comparative law perspective, the most crucial issues of the relation between law and language in modern and contemporary China. Amongst these issues, problems associated with legal translations – traditionally the first concern for those (law drafters, scholars, lawyers) who work with foreign laws – maintain a central role. From this first analysis, it is evident that both in translations of law rules and legal concepts from foreign languages into Chinese and in translations between legal Chinese and legal English, the work of negotiation between law and its verbalizations needs to be further perfected.

Legal translations and the choice of words need to be supervised with accurate studies of the characters and the evolution of the legal vocabulary and languages involved, using tools established by comparative scholars for dealing with legal translation problems. As we have seen, the precision of legal concepts can first be blurred and then be lost on the way of legal transfers and legal translations. This risk is particularly high in the current global framework of increasing legal contaminations.

Within the complex passages of the Chinese legal modernization a trans-lingual story has been written. This story speaks (of) several legal languages: the conceptual language of civil law, which dominated the formation of the Chinese modern legal system and left profound traces both in the laws of Republic of China and People's Republic of China; the language of the common law, mostly of American derivation,

---

[35] gov.cn/fzbChinese/page/lawtranslation/lawtranslation/22901.htm (accessed 12 December 2015). A forthcoming work is "法学名词" (*Faxue mingci*) [Legal Terms] by Legal Terms Editing Committee at China National Committee for Terms in Sciences and Technologies. http://www.cnctst.cn/Organ/SubCommittee?id=20 (accessed 20 January 2016).

that has highly influenced the last few decades of Chinese legal development; the language of the new legal English emerging as lingua franca or as vehicle language at both the international and supra-national levels.

Dealing with this trans-lingual story we must not forget that in China, Chinese is spoken and written. Language is part of the Chinese cultural heritage and civilization, a strong link between the present and the past, crossing and shaping this trans-lingual story. In order to add a last piece to the complex puzzle that makes up the contemporary language of the law in China, I would thus like to conclude this essay quoting the case of a key legal concept of contemporary Chinese legal language that represents a keyword of the Chinese cultural code. The concept is that of *heli* 合理 translated into English as reasonable, reasonableness. These English words, as it is well known, are hallmarks of the Anglo-American legal culture and in the last few decades have known a supranational diffusion, mainly through the vehicle of international legal instruments[36] also exerting a remarkable influence in the Chinese statutory law where we find them translated into the aforementioned compound *heli* 合理. However, if we look beyond the surface of the statutory rule reproducing foreign and supranational law models, we find that a local line of development of the legal concept of *heli* is already embedded in a long historical line, that of the Chinese legal tradition. The world *heli* consists of two Chinese characters: (*he* 合) meaning to 'suit', 'agree', 'join'; and (*li* 理) meaning 'reason', 'principle'. This last character, that is the main part of the compound, was commonly used in the legal discourses of the Imperial legal system, in connection with the character *qing* 情, translated as 'human feelings' or 'circumstances'. Thus *heli* 合理 represented a well-rooted balancing standard for settling legal decisions founded on the evaluation of the specific circumstances of each case, in the respect of human feelings. (Bourgon 2002)

This legal concept, having been first of all used, as a non-expressed but latent legal pattern, in the first decade of the post-Mao legal reforms to balance law and circumstances within the context of an incomplete, fragmented formal legal system, then reappeared, as explicitly stated rule, in judicial discourses and in legislation, often in association with the word *gongping* 公平 The latter compound consists of the character *gong* 公, meaning 'public', 'common', 'equitable' and of the character *ping* 平 which means 'fair', 'equal'. The expression *gongping heli (de)* 公平合理 (的) is usually translated as "reasonable and fair" or reasonably fair. In these most recent judicial and statutory uses, *heli* 合理 usually in association with *gongping* 公平 works as a balancing standard[37] that often goes well beyond the scope of meaning of the concept of reasonable imported from abroad. (Timoteo 2010)

---

36 For example, in international rules governing contract law issues, such as the Vienna Convention on International Sale of Goods (CISG) and the International Institute for the Unification of Private Law (UNIDROIT) Principles for International Commercial Contracts.
37 For example in cases dealing with change of circumstances in contracts and in determination of the amounts of damages in contract and tort law cases.

One of the most recent and debated use of the concepts *gongping heli* 公平合理 is in the General part of civil law, within the Chapter on civil rights, under Article 117, concerning compensation for expropriation for public interest. Procedures of expropriation of land and buildings are one of the most critical issues of the Chinese economic and legal reform, giving rise to several episodes of social unrest and a huge number of lawsuits mostly reletated to compensation: with the last intervention on this crucial matter, judges were handed over, by Chinese lawmakers, a hermeneutical key full of meanings, whose linguistic and legal boundaries are marked by borrowings, contaminations, adaptations, and underlying cultural patterns that will impinge on the operative aspects of the statutory rules.

From this example, we should once again recognize that a new era has started for Chinese legal development, an era in which for both Chinese and foreign legal actors, the language factor and its multiple intricate connections with the Chinese legal system can no longer be underestimated.

In this direction, we should simply follow the lesson of Master Confucius on the Rectification of Names:

The Master said (...): If names be not correct, language is not in accordance with the truth of things. If language be not in accordance with the truth of things, affairs cannot be carried on to success.

When affairs cannot be carried on to success, proprieties and music will not flourish. When proprieties and music do not flourish, punishments will not be properly awarded. When punishments are not properly awarded, the people do not know how to move hand or foot.

Therefore a superior man considers it necessary that the names he uses may be spoken appropriately, and also that what he speaks may be carried out appropriately. What the superior man requires is just that in his words there may be nothing incorrect.[38]

References

Abbiati, Magda. 2008. *Guida alla lingua Cinese*. Roma: Carocci.
Beauprè, Micheal, Ichiro Kitamura, Gérard-René De Groot & Rodolfo Sacco. 1987. La traduction juridique. *Les Cahiers du Droit* 28 (4). 735–859.
Bourgon, Jérome. 2002. Uncivil dialogue : Law and custom did not merge into civil law under the Qing. *Late Imperial China* 23 (1). 50–90.
Cao, Deborah. 2004. *Chinese law – A language perspective*. Aldershot: Ashgate Publishing Limited.
Cao, Deborah & Xingmin Zhao (eds.). 2006. *Lianhe guowenjian fanyi* (Translation at the United Nations). Beijing: China Translation and Publishing Corporation.
Cao, Deborah. 2007. *Translating law*. Clevedon, Buffalo & Toronto: Multilingual Matters.

---

38 See Legge (1861: 128), English translation of Confucius, *Analects*, Book XIII, Chapter 3, verses 5–7.

Chen, Tsung-fu. 2011. Transplant of civil code in Japan, Taiwan, and China: With the focus of legal evolution. *National Taiwan University Law Review* 6 (1). 389–432.

Cui, Jianyuan. 2007. Woguo hetong xiaoli zhidu de yanbian [Evolution of contract effectiveness in China] *Henansheng zhengfa guanli ganbu xueyuan xuebao* [Journal of Henan Administrative Institute of Politics and Law] 2.

DeFrancis, John. 1984. *The Chinese language: fact and fantasy*. Honolulu: University of Hawaii Press.

Fei, Anling & Mei Ding. 2004 [1997]. *Yidaly minfadian/codice civile Italiano*. [Italian civil code]. Transl. into Chinese. Beijing: CUPL Press.

Gambaro, Antonio. 2003. The plan d'action of the European commission – A comment. *European Review of Private Law* 11 (6). 768–781.

Han, Shiyuan. 2004. *Hetong fa zong lun* [Fundamentals of contract law]. Beijing: Beijing Law Press.

Jian, Chao Li, Hongjun Cao & Fukui Zhang. 2013. Xiugai hou xing su fa zhong de "deng" zi jiedu, renmin jiancha [Analysis on the character Deng in the revised criminal procedure law]. *People's Procuratorial Semimonthly* 11.

Jing, "Brad" Luo & Ghosh Shubha. 2009. Protection and enforcement of well-known mark rights in China: History, theory and future. *Northwestern Journal of Technology and Intellectual Property* (7). 2.

Legge, James. 1861. The Chinese classics. Vol I. Confucian analects, the great learning, and the doctrine of the mean. In James Legge (ed.), *The Chinese classics: With a translation, critical and exegetical notes, prolegomena, and copious indexes* [English translation of Confucius, analects, Book XIII, Chapter 3, verses 5–7]. Hong Kong & London: Trübner & Co.

Li, Xia. 2015. *Gongsi hezuo hetong* [Public-private partnership contract]. *Huadong zhengfa daxue xuebao (ECUPL Journal)* 3. 139.

Liu, Lydia. 2004. *The clash of empires: the invention of China in modern world making*. Cambridge: Harvard University Press.

Lubman, Stanley. 1999. Bird in a cage: Chinese law reform after twenty years. *Journal of International Law & Business, Berkeley Law Scholarship Repository* 20. 391.

Lubman, Stanley. 2006. Looking for law in China. *Columbia Journal of Asian Law* 20. 1. http://scholarship.law.berkeley.edu/cgi/viewcontent.cgi?article=1444&context=facpubs (accessed 5 December 2015).

Ma, Qiang. 2004. Wuxiao hetong ruogan wenti yanjiu (Several issues on the void contract) *Hetongfa pinglun (Contract law review)*. Beijing: Renminfayuan Press.

Masini, Federico. 1993. The formation of Modern Chinese lexicon and its evolution towards a national language: the period from 1840 to 1898 (English translation). *Journal of Chinese Linguistics monograph series* 6.

McNaugthon, William. 1987. *Reading and writing Chinese*. Tokyo: Charles E. Tuttle Company Inc. Rutland.

Meng, Qinguo. 2010. Jiekai zhongguo tudi siyouhua kun de miansha [Piercing the veil of the theory of land privatization in China]. *Beifang faxue (Northern Legal Science)* 1.

Ni, Shifeng Cheng Le & Sin King Kui. 2010. Terminology evolution and legal development: A case study of Chinese legal terminology. *Terminology* 16 (2). 159–180.

Pazzaglini, Hermes. 1991. La recezione del diritto civile nella Cina del nostro secolo. *Mondo Cinese*. 49–66.

Perenboom, Randall. 2002. *China's long march towards the rule of law*. Cambridge: Cambridge University Press.

Peerenboom, Randall. 2006. What have we learned about law and development? Describing, predicting and assessing legal reforms in China. *Michigan Journal of International Law* 27. 823–871.

Poon Wai Yee, Emily 2005. Cultural transfer in legal translation. *International Journal for the Semiotics of Law* 18 (2–3). 307–323.

Pozzo, Barbara. 2012. Liability for environmental harm: The uncertain path of legal transplants and legal translation between China and Europe. In Marina Timoteo (ed.), *Environemntal law in action – EU and China perspectives*, 299–315. Bologna: Bononia University Press.

Qu, Wensheng. 2013. Zhongguo falu shuyu duiwai fanyi mianlin de wenti yu chengyin fansi [The problems in translations of Chinese legal terms and their causes]. *Fagui fanyi*. [Translation of regulations]. www.shanghailaw.gov.cn (accessed 12 December 2015).

Sacco, Rodolfo. 2000. Traduzione giuridica. *Digesto delle discipline privatistiche, Aggiornamento*. Torino: Utet.

Sacco, Rodolfo. 2005. Language and law. In Barbara Pozzo (ed.), *Ordinary language and legal language*, 1–21. Milan: Giuffrè Editore.

Svarverud, Rune. 2001. The notions of 'power' and 'rights' in Chinese political discourse. In Michael Lackner, Iwo Amelung & Joachim Kurtz (eds.), *New terms for new ideas: Western knowledge and lexical change in late imperial China*, 125–144. Leiden, Boston & Köln: Brill. http://www.wsc.uni-erlangen.de/pdf/svarverud.pdf (accessed 20 December 2015).

Timoteo, Marina. 2010. Vague notions in Chinese contract law: The case of Heli. *European Review of Private Law* 5. 939–951.

Timoteo, Marina. 2014 [2010]. *La difesa di marchi e brevetti in Cina*, 2nd edn. Torino: Giappichelli.

Timoteo, Marina. 2015. Law and language: issues related to legal translation and interpretation of Chinese rules on tortious liability of environmental pollution. *China-EU Law Journal* 4. 121–133.

Wang, Li & Jia You. 2015. Tudi zhengzhi zhong zhaijidi de tuichu jili jizhi [Research on the exit incentive mechanism of the homestead in land consolidation and improvement]. *Zhengfa luntan* [Tribunal of Political Science and Law] 4. 149.

Wu, Guangrong. 2013. Xingzheng shenpi dui hetong xiaoli de yingxiang [Influence of the administrative approval on the contract effectiveness]. *Faxuejia (Jurists)* 1.

Xu, Chuanxi. 2013. Zhongguo qinquan fa xianzhuang: kaocha yu pinglun [The current situation of Chinese tort law: observation and comment]. *China Civil and Law Review*. http://www.civillaw.com.cn/article/default.asp?id=7789 (accessed 27 August 2015).

Yang, Lixin. 2002. Zhonghua renmin gongheguo qinquan xingwei fa bian qicao shuoming, [The clarification of the drafting of Chinese tort law]. *Zhongguo min shang falu wang (Civil Law)*. www.civillaw.com.cn/qqf/weizhang.asp?id=10588 (accessed 15 December 2015).

Zanier, Valeria. 2008. The Chinese economic language: Issues in translation. In Valerie Pellatt & Elena Minelli (eds.), *Proceedings of the bath symposium*, 2–12. Cambridge: Cambridge Scholars Publishing. http://www.cambridgescholars.com/download/sample/60085 (accessed 20 December 2015).

Zhao, Xiaojun. 2007. Dui tudi siyouhua zhi pipan [Criticism on the land privatization]. *Hebei faxue (Hebei Law Science)* 1. 90–94.

Roberta Aluffi
16 Unity and varieties of Arabic as a legal language: practices of interpretation and translation

1 Introduction

Arabic is, at the same time, unitary and diverse. This is specifically true for Arabic legal language.

Literary Arabic includes classical Arabic, rooted in the language of the Qur'ān, and modern standard Arabic, the language presently used for written and oral formal communication. A substantial continuity characterizes the development of literary Arabic over the span of fourteen centuries. The unity and temporal continuity of literary Arabic are greatly due to its role as the religious language of 1.5 billion Muslims. As to Arabic-speakers, they are much less numerous and make use of a large series of dialects, or spoken varieties of Arabic.

The tension between unity and plurality, and between a high language with universal aspirations and a low local variety leaves its distinctive mark on the life of the law and on the activity of legislators, judges, lawyers and law professors.

Arabic is the language of *fiqh*, the Islamic legal doctrine whose first basis is the the Qur'ān. The vocabulary of *fiqh* was developed by legal scholars over centuries, but retains its importance in the religious field to this day.

Building on the linguistic heritage of the Islamic legal doctrine, modern national states shape their official legal languages. A linguistic drift of the multiple national legal languages may appear, due to different external influences or to specific internal options. At the same time, the role played by Arabic as an official language in a number of international organisations pushes towards the harmonisation of the national varieties of legal Arabic.

Arabic is not always the only language used for legal purposes in an Arab state. Other languages can compete with it, both in the legislature and in the courtrooms, although multilingualism is rarely officially recognized.

2 Arabic and *fiqh*

Arabic is the language of *fiqh*, the Islamic jurisprudence. Like the other religious sciences, *fiqh* is firmly based on the Qur'ān, which contains the very word of God, expressed in Arabic (*Qur'ān*, XLIII, 3). Qur'ān is miraculous and inimitable and cannot be translated for liturgical or scientific purposes. Translations simply allow non-Arabic-speaking Muslims to grasp the meanings of the Sacred Text, but the text itself cannot be transposed into another language. Because of its deep relationship to religion, Arabic has spread throughout the regions converted to Islam and has become the common language of the religious *élites*.

To this day, Islam ensures the prestige of Arabic; it probably contributes to the opposition between formal written Arabic and its spoken varieties, while, at the same time, allowing Arabs to claim to speak one and the same language.

A *fiqh* scholar must be proficient in classical Arabic, whatever his mother tongue. Arabic classical legal terminology influences the major languages of the Islamic civilization, like Ottoman Turkish (*lisān-ı Osmānī*) and Persian,[1] and easily reaches the farthest borders of the Islamic world. It can even go beyond them. A number of Arabic legal terms have smoothly acclimatized to European legal languages, particularly in the field of trade law, which tends to flourish irrespective of religious or political borders. *Douane/dogana/aduana* come from the Arabic term *dīwān* (Colin, 1977) meaning 'office' in general. No doubt that, in European traders' experience, the best known office was the *dīwān al-malāzim*, where taxes on the imported products were levied, and which became the *dīwān par excellence* for them. An Arabic etymology is also proposed for cheque/*chèque*/*Scheck*: these terms would come from the Arabic *ṣakk* (through the Persian *čak*), meaning "document" (Littmann, 1920). Similarly, *aval/avallo* (endorsement) would to be linked to the Islamic *ḥawāla* (Badr, 1978).

3 Arabic and state law

The linguistic heritage of *fiqh* was the basis for modern national states to develop and shape their official legal languages, under the influence of European models.[2]

The adaptation of the legal language to the new needs precedes the modernization of Arabic language in general.[3] In 1919, when the first Arab Academy (*al-maǧmaᶜ al-ᶜilmī al-ᶜarabī*) started working on scientific terminology in Damascus (Hamzaoui

---

[1] The Arabic term for *right* (*haqq*) is to be found both in Persian, and in Modern Turkish (*hak*).
[2] In fact, European influence plays a double role in the shaping of Arabic into the legal language of the state: on the one hand, the process is fuelled by the spread of European cultural models; on the other, it may be hindered by the relations of political and financial dependence. In Egypt, for instance, a substantial contact with the European legal models was provided by the Mixed Courts, created in 1876 by the Egyptian state, with the agreement of the capitulary powers. Those Courts were mostly staffed with European judges, applying codes written in French, and using French, and later English, as their working languages. Significantly, the first judicial decision ever published in Arabic in Egypt dates back to 1937, the year the Convention of Montreux opens the way to a transition period towards the abolition of the Mixed Courts (Brinton, 1968; Brown, 1993; Gérard, 1996).
[3] The profound changes undergone by the Egyptian legal language as a semiotic system are closely analysed by G. Parolin (Parolin, 2015).

1965), the modernization of the legal language was already under way. Language schools paved the way for institutions for legal education and the training of civil servants. In Egypt, a School of Public Administration and Languages was founded in 1868. In a short time, the school split into two departments, and in 1886 the Department for Public Administration took the name of *Madrasat al-ḥuqūq al-ḥidīwiyya* (Khedivial Law School), which represents the origin of the Law Faculty of the University of Cairo.

The rich and sophisticated Arabic terminology of *fiqh* smoothed the great difficulties sometimes experienced by non-Western legal translators faced with European legal texts in the C19th. A term as essential for the Western legal discourse as *right* is not a challenge in Arabic, unlike Chinese. An unambiguous translation is available: *ḥaqq* (pl. *ḥuqūq*). Moreover, *ḥaqq* is not a marginal nor a neglected term for Muslim legal scholars. It is the tool they use to structure the whole legal field, which is dominated by the opposition between the rights of God (*ḥuqūq Allāh*), and the rights of men (*al-ḥuqūq al-adamiyya* o *ḥuqūq al ᶜibād*) corresponding to the distinction between public and private interests (Johansen, 1981; Gellner and Vatin, 1981; Gellner, 1999; Weiss, 1998; Emon, 2006).[4]

On the contrary, it is not possible to find an exact equivalent for the term *law* in Arabic. In the Arab countries, Law School or Law Faculty correspond to *madrasat al-ḥuqūq* and *kulliyat al-ḥuqūq*, respectively. When one tries to literally re-translate these expressions into English, the result sounds quite strange: Faculty of Rights, School of Rights. No Arabic term has the same comprehensive meaning as the English *law*. Arabic has three different terms to indicate separately the Sacred Law (*šarīᶜa* or *šarᶜ*), the law enacted by the ruler (*qānūn*)[5] and the customary law (*ᶜurf* or *ᶜādāt*). They represent three separate, non-homogeneous domains, whose rules are different in nature. In Arabic, no term refers to a comprehensive category, integrating the Sacred Law, statutory law and customary law. The unresolved difficulty involved in translating the word *law* into Arabic is evident in the expression *al-qānūn al-ṭabīᶜī*[6] used as an equivalent of natural law, but literally corresponding to a quite oxymoric "natural statutory law".

Conversely, this lack of direct correspondence between the term *law*, and the various Arabic words relating to the same semantic field, may lead to major ambiguities in the translation of legal texts from Arabic. If the translated text is a statutory

---

4 The word *ḥaqq* links its specific legal technical meaning to a vast set of concepts, which are distinct and, at the same time, subtly intertwined. It refers to truth, reality, that is, to God. "Like God, *ḥaqq* is a deeply moralized, active and demanding real... Thus besides "real", and more profoundly, *ḥaqq* means "right", "correct", "obligatory", "necessary", "just", "lawful", "legitimate", "merited", "authentic", and therefore "a right, title or claim to do something", "rightful possession", "property", "one's due" (Geertz, Geertz and Rosen 1979).

5 The Arabic term *qānūn* clearly comes from the Greek κανών, and shares this root with Canon law. This distant common origin makes them in a way false friends: while in the Christian tradition Canon law is the law of the Church, and therefore imbued with religion, the Arabic *qānūn* refers to the law enacted by the ruler, distinct from the Sacred Law, and sometimes conflicting with it.

6 This expression can be found, for instance, in art. 2 of the Egyptian Civil Code (1948).

provision admitting "any *legal* mode of proof", it is crucial to know whether the original in Arabic refers to the modes of proof regulated by the Islamic *šarīʿa*, or by statute. Thus, the reader may discover that the rebuttal of the presumption of paternity is possible exclusively by means of an archaic *šarʿī* procedure, the oath of *liʿān*: a DNA test would be of no use.

To meet the expressive needs of the new legal discourse, Arabic can follow four different paths. Old terms can be retrieved or reinvented, by the method called *istinbāṭ*. In 1861, Tunisia adopted the first constitution of the Arab world and called it *dustūr*, which is the term commonly used to this day. In the past, *dustūr*, a word of Persian origin, was used to indicate a person exerting an authority, a counsellor, and eventually a rule or regulation, especially within a guild.

A second path makes use of the generative potentialities of Arabic. New terms are created from existing consonantal roots. To indicate the new idea of citizenship, the relationship of the individual to the state, Ottoman statutes coin the term *ǧinsiyya*, coming from *ǧins*, genus, race, species (from the Greek γένος), whereas to indicate the citizen, slightly later sources derive the word *muwāṭin* from *waṭan*, the place of birth or residence. Presently, a new abstract term *muwāṭana* is developing, as a competitor of the older *ǧinsiyya* (Parolin, 2007).

An important role in adapting the legal terminology to the new needs is played by loan words, called intruding words in Arabic (*kalimāt daḫīla*). A word can be borrowed from another language, and adapted to Arabic phonetics and the writing system. Innumerable examples of this phenomenon can be cited, involving Italian words: (*būlīṣa*) for policy; (*būrūtistū*) for protest; (*kāmbiāla*) for bill of exchange.

Another type of loan-words is a *calque*: phrases are borrowed from another language by a word-for-word translation. For instance, the expression *statut personnel* becomes *al-aḥwāl al-šaḫṣiyya* in Arabic, by literally translating the two components of the French phrase. This expression, which was created in Egypt by Muhammad Qadrī Bāšā in 1875, has successfully imposed itself in all Arab countries. It originally referred to family and inheritance law, as well as to the law of charitable foundations, due to their religious character, that made these norms only applicable to Muslims, to the exclusion of the adherents to any other religion. However, in a number of countries, the expression has been retained even after the unification of the law at the national level and the overcoming of the personal law system: in Tunisia, for instance, the family code, which is applicable to all the nationals, irrespective to their religious affiliation, is called *Maǧallat al-aḥwāl al-šaḫṣiyya*.

Arabic legal terminology evolves spontaneously. Changes take place mostly at the national level, since the state has established itself as the main source of legal rules. A linguistic drift of the multiple national legal languages has appeared, due to different external influences or to specific internal options.

This drift is built upon the traditional divergences in terminology existing among the different legal schools of *fiqh* (*maḏāhib*): the *waqf*, or 'charitable foundation', is called *ḥabūs* by the Malikis, and the term is maintained in the national legal lexicon by states where the Maliki tradition spread. The same is true for the word *ṣadāq*, another peculiarity of the Maliki terminology, used to indicate what the other schools call *mahr* (dower).

The linguistic drift may be reinforced by the specific choices of the various national legislators: each one picks its favourite solution among the different possibilities offered by the Arabic lexicon, renowned for its richness. The *relation juridique*, is normally translated as *ᶜalāqa qānūniyya*, but in Morocco it may also be referred to as *rābiṭa qānūniyya*.

The possible extent of the drift between different national varieties of Arabic is particularly evident when a text written in a foreign language is officially translated into Arabic by two states (Sacco 2008). This was the case, for example, of the text drafted in French by a Franco-Tunisian commission led by David Santillana (1855–1931), and promulgated as the *Code des obligations et contrats* in both Tunisia (1906) and Morocco (1913). After independence, when the *Code* was translated into Arabic, two considerably different versions came to light. The intent/*volonté* becomes *irāda* in Morocco, and *riḍā'* in Tunisia; deceit is translated by the term *taġrīr* in Tunisia, and by the more traditional *tadlīs* in Morocco; the *cause illicite* of the contract is the *sabab ġayr ğā'iz* in Tunisia, and the *sabab ġayr mašrūᶜ* in Morocco; the *délits et quasi-délits* are the *ğunaḥ wa šibh al-ğunaḥ* in Tunisia, and the *ğarā'im wa ašbāh al-ğarā'im* in Morocco; the *cas fortuit* is the *ḥādiṯ fuğā'ī* in Tunisia, and the *amr ṭāri'* in Morocco; the annulment is *fasḫ* in Tunisia, and *ibṭāl* in Morocco; the *paiement* is the *adā'* in Tunisia, and the *wafā'* in Morocco; the *prescription* is the *murūr al-zamān* in Tunisia, and the *taqādum* in Morocco. The list of the terminological differences could well become an endless one, proving the extreme richness of the Arabic lexicon, and revealing a relative inclination of the Moroccan official translator for more traditional terminological choices, drawn from the technical legal heritage of *fiqh*.

The linguistic drift between national legal languages normally consists in the use of different terms for the same meaning; but it may also follow a gradual divergence between the meanings of the same term. The term *kafāla* is an excellent example of this kind of phenomenon. Across the Arab world, the term *kafāla* refers to a specific type of warrant, thoroughly regulated by *fiqh*. But alongside this main meaning, the word has acquired new ones. In the Gulf states, as well as in some countries of the Levant, *kafāla* refers to sponsorship in the field of immigration, whereby the employer is responsible for the foreign labourer's visa and legal status. By contrast, in the countries of the Maghreb, *kafāla* has taken another meaning, referring to a specific form of child protection which does not contrast with the ban on adoption. This ban finds its source in the Qur'ān, and is implemented in almost all the Muslim states. In this specific meaning, *kafāla* has reached global fame, as it is internationally recognised as an institution of Islamic law by art. 21, n. 3 of the *Convention on the Rights of the Child* (1989), and by art. 3(e) of the *Hague Convention on Jurisdiction, Applicable Law, Recognition, Enforcement and Co-operation in Respect of Parental Responsibility and Measures for the Protection of Children* (1996).

Another factor favouring the nationalisation of the legal terminology is the organisation of state bureaucracies: new functions are regulated by national rules, with no significant link with the century-long tradition of *fiqh*, and which may therefore easily drift apart. The establishment of a modern system of civil registration and the issue of identity documents offer a good example of how new sets of legal terms are generated at the national level for administrative purposes.

A modern system of civil registration requires that names be standardised. Most of the Arab states opted for the western solution, based on the couple formed by first name and surname, or family name. The first element, the first name, invariably corresponds to the classical Arabic *ism*, while for the surname, coming from an alien culture and devoid of precedent for the Arabs, the solutions vary from country to country: Morocco makes use of the *calque ism al-ᶜāila* (*nom de famille*); Lebanon adopted the word *šuhra*; Algeria, Tunisia and Iraq preferred *laqab*, a classical term indicating an honorific title. Another group of countries, notably in the Gulf, stick to the traditional tripartite name system (*al-ism al-ṯulāṯī*), comprising the name the person is given at birth, his/her father's name and his/her paternal grandfather's name, with no family name. In Saudi Arabia and Oman, the father's and grandfather's names are preceded by the word *ibn*, meaning *son of* … ; while in other countries, like Somalia, the three names are simply juxtaposed, respecting the order of the generations. The tripartite name, linking the person to a specific lineage (*nasab*), is assigned in strict compliance with *šarīᶜa* rules, and makes clear the inequality of the maternal and paternal descent. On the contrary, the family name refers to a vaguely defined group and, as it is normally very common, cannot, on its own, clearly indicate the person's descent. It is artificial and bureaucratic and it is consequently given in accordance to the regulations adopted by the state, sometimes to protect vulnerable persons, like children born outside of wedlock or abandoned children. The implications of the national choice between the binary and the tripartite name systems will unavoidably influence the way the interpreter thinks about the individual, as well as his/her understanding of many legal provisions in different fields.

Finally, the drift of national legal languages may be partly due to the foreign languages of reference that lawyers use, along with Arabic, in education and communication. Each language conveys not only its own terms, but also its specific concepts and categories. In every state, at a given point in history, a foreign language of reference normally exists, which is shared by the majority of lawyers. The language of reference may change, though, and sometimes two languages may co-exist, sharing the national community of lawyers according to their generational profiles. A small detail indicating the decline of French as the most important language of reference in the Arab world is the way lawyers talk of comparative law: *al-qānūn al-muqāran* is being replaced by *al-qānūn al-muqārin*. A simple vowel, not even registered in the writing system of Arabic, shifts the sense of the word from the passive, as in *droit comparé*, to a more active one, as in *comparative law*.

4 Arabic and its competitors

Arabic as a national legal language is permeable to the influences coming from outside the boundaries of the state. Within the state, it frequently coexists and competes with other languages.

Arabic was declared the official language of the States on their independence. Nevertheless, in a number of them, a French version of the 'Journal Officiel' is still published alongside the Arabic one. While in some sub-Saharan countries[7] the two versions have formally the same importance, in North Africa (Algeria, Morocco and Tunisia) the Arabic text is to be considered as the original, always prevailing over the French text (Charfi, 1997). A Tunisian statute defines the French version as a mere translation, intended to inform the non-Arabic-speaking public (art. 1, l. n. 64 of 5 July 1993).

Nowadays, the non-Arabic-speaking public mainly consists of European or other Western lawyers and judges. In fact, the French version of the Arabic 'Journal Officiel' serves sometimes to exhibit the merits of the new pieces of legislation, and the translation is intended to prevent any biased misunderstanding of the Arabic text. In 2004, the French translation of the new Moroccan Family Code carefully avoided the word *répudiation* to translate the Arabic *talāq*, well realizing the rejection it would unleash in European readers. Paradoxically, this choice makes the French text ambiguous and allows some undesired results in the application of the Code by foreign courts (Aluffi, 2015).

In the past, a substantive number of non-Arabic-speaking readers of the 'Journal Officiel' were to be found in the Arab states themselves. At independence, it seemed unlikely that the French version of the 'Journal Officiel' would lose its operative importance all at once. In the event, it has taken independent states a long time to fully Arabise their legal and judicial systems. In Algeria, for example, the process was started in 1963, by the decree replacing the obligation to translate decisions in Arabic into French, with that of translating French language decisions into Arabic, but only if they were "addressed to Muslims". Arabisation accelerated during the 1970s, involving both the judiciary and the academic staff of the Law Faculties (Bentoumi 2010). Nevertheless, it seems that the French version could still exert some influence on the interpretation of the statutes well into the 1990s. This influence could explain the hesitation shown by the Cour Suprême in interpreting art. 169 of the *Algerian Family Code*. This article deals with *tanzīl*, a statutory institute which remedies the lack of representation in Islamic inheritance law, by providing a kind of *ex lege* bequest in favour of the orphaned grandchildren (*aḥfād*). The problem is how to interpret the Arabic word *aḥfād*: does it mean only the grandchildren born to a son, or the grandchildren born

---

[7] This is the case for Chad and Djibouti. In Sudan, Arabic plays the role of official language alongside English; in Somalia with Somali.

either to a son or a daughter? At first, the Cour preferred the stricter interpretation, which can be supported by the French version of the Code. In French, art. 169 mentions the *descendants du fils*, while other articles (art. 170–171) explicitly refer to *petits-fils et petites filles*, irrespective of the sex of their predeceased parent. More recently, this decision has been overruled: the Cour Suprême sees no reason to give different interpretations to the same Arabic word used in the three provisions, and concludes that *aḥfād* has a clear meaning in Arabic, including all the grandchildren, without considering the sex of their predeceased parent (Mahieddin, 2016).

Statutes are passed by parliaments and promulgated by the heads of State in the Arabic version. However, at least in Morocco, the draft legislation is prepared in French, with the only exception of the texts relating to family law, charitable foundations, traditional justice (for example, rules governing the activity of *ᶜudūl*, the religious notary witnesses) and religious matters. In Algeria, French is still used as the working language of the government and the ministries, and consequently it is the language of draft legislation. Texts published in French on the 'Journal Officiel' are not legally binding, but are frequently taken as a reference by legal professionals in order to dispel their doubts. Moreover, if the French text dates back to the colonial period, it is preferred to its Arabic translation, which is sometimes mistrusted.

All the judgments, as well as police records, are written in standard Arabic. In Morocco, the religious notary witnesses make use of Arabic, contrary to modern notary witnesses, whose documents need to be translated into Arabic if it is necessary to produce them in judicial proceedings. In court hearings, colloquial Arabic is used. As a large part of the Moroccan population speaks Tamazight, judges would admit its use well before the constitutional amendment of 2011, which declared it the second official language of the Kingdom. Tamazight-speaking people are numerous in Algeria, too, and they have the right to translation, when the court does not understand their language.

In Iraq, the constitution of 2005 recognises Kurdish, along with Arabic, as an official language, and provides for the use of both languages in great detail (art. 4). Nevertheless, the place of Arabic is strengthened compared with Kurdish, by the mention of the role of Iraq as a founding member of the Arab League and by the reassertion of the state's commitment to the Charter of that organisation.

In multilingual states, Arabic plays the major role, because of its prestigious literary tradition, its relationship to Islam and the number of Arabic-speaking nationals. An exception exists: Israel. In 1948, upon independence, all provisions in the law allowing the use of the English language, but not Arabic, were repealed. Hence, the provision prescribing the use of Arabic and Hebrew for all ordinances, official notes and official forms of the government, and allowing it in debates in the legislative Council, in Government offices and in courts is still formally in force (*Palestine Order-in-Council*, 1922, art. 82). Nevertheless, practice is unilingual, and Arabic is used only by the Arab local authorities (Saban and Amara, 2002).

5 Factors favouring the harmonisation of legal Arabic

The drift of the different national legal languages is counteracted by some factors favouring improved coordination and harmonisation of Arabic legal terminology.

During the process of Arabisation of legal and judicial systems that followed independence, Arab lawyers would move from country to country, enhancing the dissemination of pieces of legislation,[8] judgements and scholarly legal literature.

Secondly, Arabic plays a major role as an international language (Lutz, 1996, 1998). It is, quite obviously, the only official language of the League of Arab States,[9] of the Arab Maghreb Union,[10] and of the Cooperation Council for the Arab States of the Gulf.[11] In 1973, the UN added Arabic to the existing list of five official languages (Chinese, French, English, Russian and Spanish).[12] Arabic is one of the working languages of the African Union, side by side with the African languages and English, French and Portuguese.[13] As the Islamic language *par excellence*, Arabic has been chosen as the official language of the Organisation of Islamic Cooperation, together with English and French.[14]

International organisations, when sufficiently determined and provided with financial resources, can very effectively support and spread a uniform legal terminology. In the late 1980s, the UN started to develop a series of linguistic tools, including UNTERM, a database used to translate the terminology of the six official languages.[15] As regards Arabic, some Arab national academies and the Department for Arabisation of the League of Arab States give their contribution to this project (Boella, 2008).

---

8 The Egyptian Civil Code of 1948, drafted by the Egyptian lawyer ʿAbd al-Razzāq al-Sanhūrī (1895–1971), is the most notable example of a legislative text largely circulating in the Arab world. Different versions of it were adopted in Syria (1949), Iraq (1953), Libya (1954), Algeria (1975), and Jordan (1977). Its provisions regulating obligations were incorporated in the Commercial Code of Kuwait (1980) (Castro, 1985; Salih, 1993; Bechor, 2007).
9 Formed in 1945, the organisation has currently 22 members (www.lasportal.org).
10 The Arab Maghreb Union, created in 1989, comprises five states: Algeria, Libya, Mauritania, Morocco and Tunisia.
11 Originally named the Gulf Cooperation Council, this regional organisation was established in 1981 and comprises Bahrein, Kuwait, Oman, Qatar, Saudi Arabia and the United Arab Emirates: all the Arab countries of the Gulf, with the exception of Iraq.
12 Already before that date, Arabic was a working language in some specialized agencies of the UN. In 1973 it was included among the official and working languages of the General Assembly, and subsequently of the subsidiary organs of the General Assembly (1980), and of the Economic and Social Council and of the Security Council (1982).
13 Constitutive Act of the African Union (2000), art. 25.
14 Charter of the Organisation of Islamic Cooperation (2008), art. 38. The arrangement about languages is qualified as transitional. The Organisation, established in 1969, presently consists of 57 States.
15 http://unterm.un.org/UNTERM (accessed 10 November 2017).

At around the same time, the League of Arab States undertook a number of ambitious projects, within the organisational framework of the Arab Centre for Legal and Judicial Research, based in Rabat. They include the drafting of a series of Arab Uniform Codes, alongside the necessary development of an Arabic uniform legal lexicon.[16] The semi-paralysis presently affecting the Arab League is hindering the success of these initiatives.

It must be acknowledged that terminological choices made by the international organisations in their treaties and conventions find it difficult to spread and influence the different national varieties of legal Arabic. To this end, it would be necessary for legal scholars, across the different Arab states, to comment on these texts using uniform terms, which is not yet the case (Castellani, 2011).

In addition, some international terminological choices are ignored simply because they involve highly sensitive cultural issues, difficult to agree on. This kind of cultural uneasiness may result in different terms being used in Arabic to translate the same expression in international documents. To cite just one instance, the prohibition of discrimination for reason of birth poses a major challenge to the translator. In the Arabic version of the Universal Declaration of Human Rights (art. 2), the term used for birth is *nasab*. *Nasab* indicates the link to the male ascendants, that allows the inclusion of a person in the agnatic kinship and finds its immediate expression in the patronymic (*ibn...*/son of; *bint...*/daughter of). The choice of the term takes us back to an old controversy concerning the Islamic community: whether all Muslims are equal because of their faith, or whether Arabs are to be distinguished from other Muslims, the members of the Prophet's tribe from other Arabs, and the members of the family of the Prophet from all others. The *Universal Declaration* takes an egalitarian stand on this issue, but at the same time risks opening the way for another discrimination: actually, there are persons without *nasab*, notably children born outside wedlock. In order to avoid this embarrassing conclusion, in the *Convention on the Rights of the Child* 'birth' is translated with the Arabic term *mawlid*, referring to the birth as a simple natural fact. The *Convention on the Rights of the Child* is the only UN convention signed by all the Arab states, none of which has expressed any reservation on art. 2. Notwithstanding the commitment of the states to take appropriate measures to ensure the protection of the rights set forth in the convention, they have not reduced discrimination against children born outside wedlock. Nor has the term become of common use in the legal discourses advocating non-discrimination against illegitimate children.

---

16 Succinct reports about the work of the Commission charged with the unification of the Arabic legal terminology were published in the journal *al-Maǧalla al-ᶜarabiyya lil-fiqh wa'l-qaḍā'* [Arab Journal for *fiqh* and case law] issued by the General Secretariat of the Council of the Arab Ministries of Justice.

6 Conclusions

Legal Arabic is a multiform language; translation of legal texts from and into Arabic is a multiform task.

A legal scholar whose article is translated into Arabic gains a vast transnational readership, at least potentially. If the legal text is a contract, where every single word has to be weighed, it is wise to translate it into that specific variety of legal Arabic in use in the country of the performance of the contract, or whose law is chosen to govern the contract: Saudi legal Arabic is not Tunisian legal Arabic.

Important tools exist to assist the translator: there are well-known legal dictionaries (Faruqi 1972, 1980; Al-Wahhab 1988; Guinchard and Montagnier 2010),[17] and countless legal lexicons, printed or electronic, established by universities, courts, international organisations and various institutions, normally focusing on specific legal fields. Translation of legal texts from Arabic into English is beginning to be investigated as a scientific issue (Emery 1989; Alwazna 2013, 2014; Husni and Newman 2015; El-Farahaty 2016). But undoubtedly, the tools developed by comparative lawyers to deal with the transposition of legal texts from one linguistic and cultural environment to another may also be useful to the translator facing such a huge and fascinating challenge as the legal translation from and into Arabic.

References

Aluffi, Roberta. 2015. Interpréter et traduire l'arabe, langue des droits. *Droit de la famille* 20(9). 28–29.
Al-Wahhab, I Ibrahim. 1988. *Law dictionary (English-Arabic)*. Beirut: Librairie du Liban.
Alwazna, Y. Rafat. 2013. Testing the precision of legal translation: the case of translating Islamic legal terms into English. *International Journal for the Semiotic of Law – Revue Internationale de sémiotique juridique* 26(4). 897–907.
Alwazna, Y Rafat. 2014. Important translation strategies used in legal translation: Examples of Hooper's translation of the Ottoman Majalla into English. In Le Cheng, King Kui Sin & Anne Wagner (eds.) *The Ashgate handbook of legal translation*, 237–254. London & New York: Routledge.
Badr, Gamal Moursi. 1978. Islamic law: Its relations to other legal systems. *American Journal of Comparative Law* 26(2). 187–198.
Bechor, Guy. 1993. *The Sanhuri code, and the emergence of modern Arab civil law (1932 to 1949)*. Leiden: Brill.
Bentoumi, Amar. 2010. *Naissance de la justice algérienne*. Alger: Casbah Editions.
Boella, Marco. 2008. L'arabo lingua delle Nazioni Unite: Una risorsa per la glottodidattica? In Alessandro Monti (ed.), *Essays in honour of Fabrizio Pennacchietti*, 67–88. Alessandria: Edizioni dell'Orso.
Brinton, J. Y. 1968. *The mixed courts of Egypt*. New Haven & London: Yale University Press.

---

17 Faruqi's law dictionaries are available online.

Brown, J. Nathan. 1993. The precarious life and slow death of the mixed courts of Egypt. *International Journal of Middle Eastern Studies* 25(1). 33–52.
Castellani, Luca. 2011. Diritto del commercio internazionale e paesi Islamici: brevi considerazioni. In Massimo Papa, Gian Maria Piccinelli & Deborah Scolart (eds.), *Il libro e la bilancia: Studi in memoria di Francesco Castro. vol. II – La Bilancia*, 573–579. Napoli: Edizioni Scientifiche Italiane.
Castro, Francesco. 1985. La codificazione del diritto privato negli Stati Arabi contemporanei. *Rivista di Diritto Civile* 31(4). 387–447.
Charfi, Mohamed 1997. *Introduction à l'étude du droit*. Tunis: Cérès Editions.
Colin, Georges Séraphin. 1977. DĪWĀN – Occident Musulman. *Encyclopédie de l'Islam*, 2nd edn. (2)341. Leyde-Paris: Brill-Maisonneuve & Larose S. A.
Emery, G. Peter. 1989. Legal Arabic texts: implications for translation. *Babel* 35(1). 1–11.
Emon, E. Anver. 2006. A legal heuristic for a natural rights regime. *Islamic Law and Society* 13(3). 325–391.
El-Farahaty, Hanem. 2016. Translating lexical legal terms between English and Arabic. *International Journal for the Semiotic of Law – Revue Internationale de Sémiotique Juridique* 29(2). 473–493.
Faruqi, Harith Faruqi. 1972. *Faruqi's law dictionary: Arabic-English*. Beirut: Librairie du Liban.
Faruqi, Harith Suleiman. 1980. *Faruqi's law dictionary: English-Arabic*, 3rd edn. Beirut: Librairie du Liban.
Gérard, Delphine. 1996. Le choix culturel de la langue en Égypte : La langue française en Égypte dans l'entre-deux-guerres. *Égypte/Monde arabe* 27–28. 253–284.
Geertz, Clifford, Hildred Geertz & Lawrence Rosen. 1979. *Meaning and order in Moroccan society: Three essays in cultural analysis*. Cambridge: Cambridge University Press.
Guinchard, Serge & Gabriel Montagnier. 2010. *Lexique des termes juridiques. Français – Arabe – Anglais*. Paris: Coédition Dalloz – Hachette A. Antoine.
Hamzaoui, Rached. 1965. *L'académie Arabe de Damas et le problème de la modernisation de la langue Arabe*. Leiden: Brill.
Husni, Ronak & Daniel Newman. 2015. *Arabic-English-Arabic translation: Issues and strategies*. London: Routledge.
Johansen, Baber. 1981. Secular and religious elements in Hanafite law: function and limits of the absolute character of government authority. In Ernest Gellner & Jean-Claude Vatin (eds.), *Islam et politique au Maghreb*, 281–303. Paris: Editions du CNRS.
Johansen, Baber. 1999, *Contingency in a sacred law: Legal and ethical norms in the Muslim Fiqh*. Leiden: Brill.
Littmann, Enno. 1920. *Morgenländischer wörter im Deutschen*. Berlin: Curtius Verlag.
Lutz, Edzard. 1996. Stylistic elements in the use of Arabic as language in diplomacy: Recent developments in United Nations context. *Die Welt des Islams* 36(1). 25–58.
Lutz, Edzard. 1998. *Language as a medium of legal norms: Implications of the use of Arabic as a language in the United Nations system*. Berlin: Duncker & Humblot.
Mahieddin, M. Nahas. 2016. Le droit patrimonial de la famille dans la legislation Algérienne. *Les cahiers du LANDREN* 7. 19–90.
Parolin, P. Gianluca. 2007. *Dimensioni dell'appartenenza e cittadinanza nel mondo Arabo*. Napoli: Jovene Editore. Parolin, Gianluca. 2015. Comment parle-t-on du droit en Egypte. *Études Arabes* 112. 1–22.
Saban, Ilan & Mohammed Amara. 2002. The status of Arabic in Israel: reflections on the power of law to produce social change. *Israel Law Review* 36(2). 5–39.
Sacco, Rodolfo. 2008. Dall'interpretazione alla traduzione. In Elena Ioriatti Ferrari, *Interpretazione e traduzione del diritto*, 3–11. Padova: CEDAM.
Salih, Nabil. 1993. Civil codes of Arab countries: The Sanhuri codes. *Arab Law Quarterly* 8(2). 161–167.
Weiss, J. Bernard. 1998. *The spirit of Islamic law*. Athens & London: University of Georgia Press.

Domenico Francavilla
17 Law, language and communication in the Indian context

1 Introduction

The linguistic complexity and stratification existing since ancient times in the Indian subcontinent have had many manifestations in the field of law. The view according to which the language of classical Indian law is Sanskrit and that of modern law is English, although useful at a general level of analysis, is a simplified one that does not take into account the complex dynamics between different languages in the Indian context. In the course of the entire legal history of India, the language of law has been at the center of competing phenomena of uniformisation and pluralization. Even more significantly, language issues have been a manifestation of the relationship between different political, cultural and legal systems that have played a role in the historical development of Indian law as a whole.[1]

Bearing in mind this general perspective, one can understand the relationship between language and law in contemporary India, starting with the Constitution of 1949, which came into force in 1950, three years after Independence. Some of the forces that have driven the evolution of the relationship between language and law in India continue today and make the linguistic issue, in general and specifically in the legal field, an open-ended issue that still has not found a stable balance.

The new Indian Republic had the opportunity to overcome its colonial heritage also through the adoption of an Indian language, instead of English, as an official language, and in particular as the language of law. The choice made by the Constituent Assembly was characterised by a remarkable pragmatism and the promotion of Indian languages, especially of Hindi, did not lead to a complete rejection of the English language.

To understand this point, the great linguistic diversity that has always characterized the Indian subcontinent should be taken into account. In fact, there is not an "Indian" language as such, but many Indian languages spoken in different parts of the country. These languages may differ deeply and belong to four main language families. The two most important are the Indoaryan family and the Dravidian family.[2]

---

[1] For an introduction to the Indian legal system, see Menski (2006), Francavilla (2010) and Choudhry, Khosla and Mehta (2016). On legal language in precolonial India, see Lubin (2013).
[2] Other important linguistic families are Austroasiatic languages, particularly Munda languages, and Tibeto-Burman languages. Remarkably, Indian languages also adopt different writing systems. For instance, Hindi uses the Devanagari script, used also in classical Sanskrit, while Dravidian languages use different systems.

This lack of linguistic homogeneity has the important consequence of the difficulty of communication between Indians themselves from different parts of the country.[3]

In this context, when the Indian Constituent Assembly had to decide on official languages, the majority opinion was that, while recognizing constitutionally a plurality of languages, and while adequately protecting linguistic minorities, it was necessary to choose *one* Indian language as the official language of the Union. This language could only be the Hindi language, that is the language spoken by the majority of the population; but Hindi speakers account for little more than fifty percent of the population. In addition, it is a language concentrated in the North of the country.[4] Indian nationals who did not speak Hindi but other languages, such as Bengali or Tamil, which in some cases are very different from Hindi, had their reasons to protest at the prospect of Hindi being the official language of the Union. From the outset, many saw in English a *lingua franca* with many advantages, since it did not introduce privileged positions among Indian languages and so among Indian citizens. For example, a Tamil-speaking South Indian person would perceive the use of English as less discriminatory than the use of Hindi.

The next section provides an analysis of constitutional rules on languages and of policies adopted in the following years, in order to provide the general framework of the issue. This framework is organised on the distinction between the Union and State levels, on the use of English as a subsidiary language for official purposes, on the recognition of regional languages, and on the specific rules devoted to the language of the law.

Sections 3–4 are more specifically devoted to issues related to legal language. We will see that many legal reasons explain the fact that English is the main language in law. Among them, the most significant seems to be that many Indian jurists consider the use of English as essential in legal practice. In fact, law, as a specialised field, requires perfect command of legal terminology and interpretive doubts are to be addressed within a tradition where English terms and embodied categories have been used since long to frame legal issues. We will also analyse some aspects of the parallel development of Indian languages, particularly Hindi, as legal languages. This is a very interesting process that shows the effort put into the creation of a standard legal terminology, assuring consistent translations, which is seen as necessary for the functioning of Indian legal multilingualism.

---

[3] According to Census India 1961, the languages spoken in India, including those that did not have their origin in the subcontinent, were 1.652; in 1991 1.576 mother tongues have been reported; in 2001 29 languages have more than a million of native speakers, 60 languages more than 100.000 and 122 more than 10.000 speakers.

[4] It is worth reminding that Hindi has a standard form coexisting with several variations constituting a dialect continuum. According to Census 2001, more than 422 millions of persons (41.03 percent of the total population) returned Hindi as their mother tongue.

As a conclusion, we will highlight that linguistic issues in the Indian legal system show a peculiar attitude to avoid clearcut solutions and rather search for viable, even though demanding, accommodations in order to suit the needs of the country.

2 A difficult balance: the language of the law in a multilingual and multicultural context

Language issues were widely debated in the Constituent Assembly of India. The extreme variety of languages spoken in different parts of India, their connection with cultural identity, the difficult issue of defining the borders of States taking part in the Union, and, more generally, the fears related to possible imbalances in Indian federalism, required an extraordinary effort to find a suitable balance between competing forces. These issues were not new and the Constitution did not resolve them in a definitive way. Nonetheless, it managed to find a method of dealing with linguistic diversity.[5]

The Indian Constitution adopted Hindi as the official language of the Union, and, at the same time, English as a subsidiary language for official purposes. In addition, it recognized officially several regional languages and provided for official languages at the State level.

The basic choice was to make Hindi the official language of the Union.[6] The Constitution does not speak of a national language. However, the choice of the official language is not a neutral issue and easily becomes charged with political meaning. It is no coincidence that on this point there have been conflicts between different communities in India and several States have loudly called for protection of the languages spoken in their territory. Citizens of some States consider Hindi to be almost a foreign language and its choice as the Union's official language is often perceived as an imposition by the central government in Delhi. In this field, besides cultural and identity factors, practical reasons, such as possible advantages in education and employment for Hindi speakers, also have an important role.

The choice of Hindi as the official language of the Union required a very complex transitional regime. Article 343(2) of the Constitution provides that for a period of fifteen years after the entry into force of the Constitution, the English language would continue to be used for all official purposes of the Union for which it was used

---

[5] For a comprehensive analysis of linguistic nationalism and constitutional design, see Choudhry (2009), King (2009), and Austin (1966).
[6] The Indian Constitution deals with language in the XVII part and in several other provisions from other parties. Part XVII, entitled "Official language", consists of four chapters. The first is devoted to the Union's language, the second to the regional languages, the third to the higher courts' language, while the fourth contains some heterogeneous provisions.

immediately before its commencement. This provision makes clear the need for continuity and the constraints of path-dependency. According to the Constitution, when the period of fifteen years expired, the Parliament could provide by law for the use of the English language for some specific purposes.

Remarkably, article 346 establishes that: "The language for the time being authorised for use in the Union for official purposes shall be the official language for communication between one State and another State and between a State and the Union: Provided that if two or more States agree that the Hindi language should be the official language for communication between such States, that language may be used for such communication".

Article 344 introduces a Commission and a parliamentary Committee for promoting progressive use of Hindi.[7] Article 351 establishes that the Union has a duty "to promote the spread of the Hindi language, to develop it so that it may serve as a medium of expression for all the elements of the composite culture of India and to secure its enrichment by assimilating without interfering with its genius, the forms, style and expressions used in Hindustani and in the other languages of India specified in the Eight Schedule, and by drawing, wherever necessary or desirable, for its vocabulary primarily on Sanskrit and secondarily on other languages".

Schedule Eight of the Constitution, amended several times, last in 2003, provides special recognition to twenty-two of the many languages spoken in India.[8] They were chosen not only on the basis of the number of speakers, since there are some regional languages not included in the list that are more widely spoken than some of those included, but also according to their cultural importance, their being national languages of some Indian States, and the need for recognition of minority language groups. Interestingly, the list also includes Sanskrit, which only about 15,000 persons consider their mother tongue, according to Census 2011. The inclusion of Sanskrit depends on historical and cultural reasons; as the main Indian classical language, it has had and continues to have great cultural and liturgical importance. In this regard, it is worth highlighting that the Constitution also gives Sanskrit the role of being the first source for the elaboration of modern Hindi vocabulary.

Inclusion in the list means that representatives of these languages take part in the Commission established according to article 344 of the Constitution, which has the duty to make recommendations to the President of the Union as regards the progressive use of Hindi for official purposes of the Union. Secondly, as mentioned, according to article 351, the development of Hindi as "a mediun of expression for all the elements of the composite culture of India" has to take these languages into account.

---

[7] Art. 344 provides for a Commission and a Parliamentary Committee on official languages, both refererring to the President of the Union of India.
[8] The languages included in the Eight Schedule are Assamese, Bengali, Bodo, Dogri, Gujarati, Hindi, Kannada, Kashmiri, Konkani, Maithili, Malayalam, Manipuri, Marathi, Nepali, Oriya, Punjabi, Sanskrit, Santhali, Sindhi, Tamil, Telugu, Urdu.

A balance between unity and diversity is reached in the Constitution through the distinction between the Union and the States. Although Hindi is the official language of the Union, individual States may have their own official language, or their own official languages, which of course may be different from State to State.[9]

A transitional regime of fifteen years was envisaged, during which English would have been used in all cases in which it was used prior to the commencement of the Constitution and Hindi would have been in the meanwhile joined to English gradually. Immediately after Independence it was necessary to ensure continuity with the colonial period, if only for practical reasons, but clearly a choice was made in favor of Hindi replacing English by providing for a gradual path to assess the feasibility of this substitution and also to develop Hindi, particularly as regards technical legal terms.

As noted by Jain (2004) three phases were prefigured: in the first one, there was the prevalence of English and parallel use of Hindi; in the second, prevalence of Hindi and parallel use of English; finally, complete replacement of English with Hindi.

Even at the State level, the Constitution (art. 345) provided for the use of English in all cases in which it was used at the time prior to the entry into force of the Constitution until otherwise decided by the State parliaments.

If the above is true in general for official languages, the most interesting rules are those relating specifically to the language of the law. Article 348(1) provides that, regardless of the general provisions, until a decision is made in this area by Parliament, all the proceedings of the Supreme Court and of all the High Courts, and all the legislation of Union and States Parliaments must be in English. Even the ordinances of the President or of the Governors of the States, and orders, rules, regulations and bye-laws adopted under the Constitution or under any Act of Parliament or the Legislature of a State must be in English.

Article 348(2) provides that the Governor of a State may, with the prior consent of the President, authorize the use of Hindi or any other language used for the official purposes of the State in the proceedings of the High Court, it being understood that this clause does not apply to judgments, decrees or orders, which must be in English. Clause 3 also provides that for Bills, Acts and Ordinances enacted at the State level in a regional language, an official English translation should be published.

Another element of complexification emerges from linguistic issues in the work of Parliament. In fact, art. 120(1) of the Constitution provides that regardless of the provisions in Part XVII, but subject to the provisions of article 348, concerning the

---

[9] For instance, the official language of Maharashtra is Marathi, the official language of Panjab is Panjabi; Kannada is the official language of Karnataka, and Telugu of Andhra Pradesh. Bengali is the official language of West Bengal. The official language of Tamil Nadu is Tamil and the official language of Kerala is Malayalam; in both State English is a co-official language. Hindi is the official language, or a co-official language, of several States and Union Territories, such as, for instance, Uttar Pradesh, Bihar, Jharkhand, Uttarakhand, Madhya Pradesh, Rajasthan, Chattisgarh, Himachal Pradesh, Haryana and Delhi territory.

language of Bills and Acts, Parliament's work must be in Hindi or English. The presidents of the two Chambers (Chairman of the Rajya Sabha and Speaker of Lok Sabha) may authorize any member of Parliament to address the Assembly in their own language if he or she is not able to speak adequately in Hindi or English.[10] According to the same article, after fifteen years from the entry into force of the Constitution, Parliament's ability to work in English should cease, unless Parliament provides otherwise by law.

At the expiring of the transition period, the Official Languages Act of 1963 was enacted and amended in 1967. The use of English was confirmed and it continues to be considered as an additional official language. Hindi has gained more space. In particular, Union legislation has to be published in an official English version and in an official Hindi version. The Official Languages Act has also provided the opportunity for the Governor of a State to authorize the use of Hindi, or even of another Indian official language, in the High Courts' judgments, decrees and orders, although official translation in English is obligatory. The Official Languages Act confirmed the possibility of conducting parliamentary work in English. Lok Sabha's debates are published in three versions, the English one, the Hindi one, and the one called original, which contains debates and speeches in English and in Hindi, and English and Hindi translations of debates and speeches made using regional languages.

The Official Languages Act also established that where English or Hindi are used for communication between Ministries, Departments, offices, and companies owned or controlled by the Government, a translation into the other language shall be provided.

Finally, it establishes that "English language shall be used for purposes of communication between the Union and a State which has not adopted Hindi as its Official Language". When Hindi is used in communication between two States, and one of them has not adopted Hindi as its official language, there shall be a translation into English. A State that has not adopted Hindi as its official language can nonetheless choose to adopt Hindi for communication with the Union or a State adopting Hindi as an official language, and, in these cases, a translation into English will not be obligatory.

As we have seen, the choice made by the Constituent Assembly to retain English for an interim period was a pragmatic choice. Only in theory would a clear break with the colonial period have been possible, because such a break would have in fact created enormous problems both in the functioning of the institutions and in the relations between different parts of the country. In other words, regardless of any other consideration, at the dawn of Independence it was impossible to do without English. A stance in favor of the Hindi language as a complete replacement of English

---

10 For State Parliaments there is a twin norm, article 210(1), which of course adds the official languages of the State to Hindi and English.

was clear.[11] However, the replacement of English proved to be unfeasible and India has since then elaborated an articulate view of multilingualism in the legal system.

3 Legal English in India

Even though Hindi has gained importance and is increasingly used as the official language of the Union, English remains the main language of legislation and of judgments, and this is demonstrated by the fact that the Supreme Court must always "speak" in English. To understand the reasons for this situation one must consider the factors in favor of the continuing use of English, and the competing factors in favor of the promotion of Hindi and other Indian languages. Some of these factors are specifically legal and related to the legacy of common law in India, to the work of judges and lawyers, legal education, and access to justice. Others reflect more general issues relating to culture and politics, and more specifically to the composite nature of Indian culture along regional divides.

In order to describe the current situation, one has to distinguish between Union language and language of the States. In addition, one has to consider that there may be differences between the language of legislation and of the courts, and between the language of lower courts and of higher courts. The picture is thus very varied, but the general terms of the question can be analyzed through a report published by the Law Commission of India in 2008, significantly titled *Non-feasability of introduction of Hindi as compulsory language in the Supreme Court of India (216th Report)* (Law Commission of India 2008). This report follows a proposal for the introduction of the use of Hindi instead of English in the Supreme Court. The report reviews the constitutional provisions on the point, and includes a series of views of eminent Indian jurists, in particular judges and senior advocates. A brief account of some of these opinions can give a sense of the points of view of Indian jurists. The report refers to the language of the Supreme Court and the arguments are not automatically applicable to all contexts, but they may be seen as having a general scope, considering the importance of the Supreme Court and the kind of issues that arise.

Among these opinions, a remarkable one is that by Iyer, a former judge of the Supreme Court. Iyer's main argument is the need for a balance between the different Indian languages. In his view, Hindi chauvinism is not pragmatic. In fact, acceptance

---

11 In the Constituent Assembly debate (meeting of 17 September 1949) about the need for a Hindi official version of the Constitution, one of the arguments used against the English draft is that it meant to hold English on the same pedestal that has occupied during the time of "slavery". The relationship with the English is part of the larger problem of the relationship with the colonial legacy. English was the first language of the colonial administration, and as such can have a negative emotional meaning. As with individuals, the language one speaks is to a large extent a matter of identity.

of Hindi as an official language is not widespread, and citizens of southern States like Tamil Nadu would never accept the idea that in the Supreme Court Hindi has a leading position. Iyer makes explicit reference to Tamil Nadu, but the same may be repeated for other States, such as Maharashtra or West Bengal, where Marathi and Bengali are official languages. In fact, this would make knowledge of Hindi mandatory and would constitute in his view a case of imperialism of the language of a part of India on the others. On the other hand, the status of English as the language of law is problematic, particularly as the judgments of the Supreme Court, the Acts of the federal Parliament and other regulatory documents written in English are not fully accessible to all Indian citizens. In this context, the solution Iyer suggests is the adoption of a trilingual system in which official Acts, including judgments of the Supreme Court, should be published in three versions, namely in English, Hindi and at least one regional language. A solution of this kind undoubtedly presents many difficulties of implementation, but it has the merit of not sacrificing any of the interests involved, and from this point of view seems to be the solution that is most consistent with Indian multilingualism.

Shrikrishna, former judge of the Supreme Court, raises another interesting argument: the introduction of Hindi as a compulsory language in the Supreme Court would be self-harming. In fact, not all Indian lawyers are able to express themselves in Hindi and its introduction as a compulsory language would inevitably produce a dysfunction in the legal system. It would take at least two generations of lawyers educated in Hindi in order to make the Court function in an effective way (Law Commission of India 2008: 20).

According to Shetty, former judge of the Supreme Court (Law Commission of India 2008: 21), English should not be regarded as a foreign language in India. English is now widely used and accepted in India, to the point that there is an Indian English. In addition, the privileged position of English in India is actually an asset, because it enables Indians to take part in a global culture that expresses itself in English.

Furthermore, Paripoornan, former judge of the Supreme Court, has argued that Indian law has "imbibed English common law" (Law Commission of India 2008: 29). Some concepts, such as the rule of law, acquire a meaning in India only in the perspective of the common law. The fact that higher courts' judgments are written in English is also important to put Indian Courts in communication with other common law courts, encouraging circulation of legal knowledge. This argument, however, acquires all its force in connection with the observation by Malimath, former Chief Justice of Karnataka High Court and Kerala High Court, that Indian jurists used English for centuries and this has had considerable effect on their own way of thinking (Law Commission of India 2008: 36). Therefore, it is valuable that lawyers can take care of legal issues in the language that is most natural for them. Ensuring all Indians are able to understand judgments, as well as other sources, can be achieved through translation into Hindi and other Indian languages, conducted by specialized staff. Hindi native speakers themselves would actually find it difficult to write judgments in

Hindi, because law is a special field. A related argument is that the use of English facilitates movement of lawyers in the country, between High Courts and to the Supreme Court. Furthermore, English is the language of legal education, of legal handbooks and doctrinal works, and of training as an advocate, as highlighted by Datar, Senior Advocate (Law Commission of India 2008: 46). Remarkably, legal publishing in Hindi is developing and some courses in law are taught in Hindi or regional languages.

The views of Indian jurists considered in the Report and the opinion of the Law Commission are thus against adopting Hindi as a compulsory language in the Supreme Court. We can summarize three arguments. The first is the chaos that would ensue. Given that not all judges know Hindi and that even Hindi native speakers have been educated in English and accustomed to reasoning and interpretation on English texts, the adoption of Hindi would cause serious trouble. A reform of the entire legal education system would be needed and it would take generations to make it function well. The second argument, linked to the first, is the connection between language and legal system. It is not clear why it would be useful to abandon English as the language of a legal system belonging, albeit with strong specificity, to the family of common law, which uses conceptual categories mediated by the English language. The English language also makes possible the circulation of legal knowledge and can increase the role of India on the international legal scene. A third argument, which summarizes the previous ones and answers the objection that English is a foreign and colonial language, is that the English language and the common law are now part of Indian culture in all respects.

Of the above arguments, we can further highlight some aspects related to the so-called indigenisation of the English language. At present India is the second country in the world in terms of the number of English speakers, considering also those who speak it as a second or third language. The indigenisation process of the English language, as well as that of the common law model, involves change and adaptation in the new context. Indian English has acquired its own autonomy as happened with American English. Indian English presents some features that can become significant at a deep level of linguistic analysis.[12] The point that is worth highlighting here is that, as well as literary texts in Indian English being full of untranslatable terms belonging to Hindi or other Indian languages, and often stemming from linguistic practice, the legislation itself, and consequently judgments, while in English, may contain a number of terms in Hindi or other Indian languages. For this reason, federal legislation in English is not necessarily fully understandable to a non-Indian. Some key terms are in Indian languages and they may be either general terms or specialist technical terms.

We must also consider that Indians normally learn the English language as a second or third language. The Census of Inda 2011 records approximately only

---

[12] On Indian English, see, for instance, Sailaja (2009).

225,000 persons describing themselves as speaking English as their mother tongue, even though English may become the first language in use. Therefore, an Indian who uses English as the language of the law also speaks another language, an Indian language. This simple observation shows that the apparent legal monolingualism is an insufficient paradigm even at this level of analysis, given that English is used in a multilingual environment. The Indian jurist who speaks Hindi or Tamil does not translate into English or from English when in his or her professional context. This situation can be described as a situation of bilingualism, where speakers switch from a communicative context to another without having to translate and have adequate expertise in both contexts. It should not be forgotten that a judge who writes a decision in English may not speak English outside his or her professional context, but, for example, Hindi, and there may be many interconnections between the work environment and other communicative contexts, and these in fact may also influence the professional context.

4 Hindi legal language

Even though English still resists as a co-official language, particularly for Union legislation and judgments of the higher courts, the "movement" for Hindi is not exhausted and public policies support it. In addition, a movement for the development of other Indian languages as legal languages is emerging. In this section, we will focus on the development of legal Hindi, which is particularly important at the Union's level, but similar issues could be analysed with reference to other Indian languages.

Members of the Constituent Assembly took into account the reasons in favor of Hindi as the language of the Indian Union, namely the importance for democracy that the law is expressed in an Indian language. As the knowledge of English is not widespread, especially among the most disadvantaged sections of the population, this is not a trivial matter. Several actors, including State governments and civil society, actively pursue legal literacy programs. In this context, language issues may be an additional hurdle.[13]

As a result, the proliferation of translations of normative documents into Hindi and other regional languages is inevitable. Translation of English Acts into Hindi or other Indian languages produces two official versions, raising some issues on interpretation that we will see below. Besides official translations, translation is also

---

[13] It could be noted that even if the judgments of the Supreme Court were available in Hindi not much would change, since in many cases the root problem is illiteracy, not to mention the fact that a very small percentage of people, even in Europe and even in Law Schools, have read a judgment of a superior court. In other words, if access to knowledge of rights is important, it is realistic to believe that this knowledge should be usually mediated.

involved in disseminating legal knowledge. In all cases, a prominent issue is the establishment of standard legal terminology for Hindi and other Indian languages.

At the Ministry of Justice, the Official Languages Wing has a statutory mandate primarily for translations. We must not forget that it is the Constitution itself that provides for the promotion and development of Hindi as a language capable of fully expressing the modern technical lexicon, including the legal one.[14] The basic idea is that it is appropriate to build on Hindi, as the language spoken by the majority of the population, adapting it as regards both syntactic structures and lexicon, based primarily on Sanskrit and secondarily on other Indian languages.

Therefore, even if the Indian attitude is remarkably pragmatic and English is still used as the language of law, we must not underestimate other aspects related to the development of legal Hindi. From a political point of view, no one has decided that Hindi will never be used and, on the contrary, the tendency towards an increased use of Hindi has strengthened in recent years. Furthermore, the issue is especially interesting from a theoretical point of view. One can question whether it is even possible for Hindi to express an adequate legal vocabulary and similar objections regard regional legal languages. A linguistic factory is therefore at work and it can provide some interesting indications for legal translation studies and for cross-cultural analysis of legal concepts.

The lexical problem is the most important. Hindi vocabulary is mainly derived from Sanskrit. For this reason, it can continue to draw from classical Sanskrit for the expression of a substantial part of the legal lexicon. In the event that Hindi does not already have an appropriate term, this is sought primarily in Sanskrit. The Hindi legal lexicon is composed partly by terms already existing in legal Sanskrit and partly by neologisms built by drawing from Sanskrit terms.

It is possible to sketch a taxonomy of Hindi legal terms, taking into account some key terms as examples. One may first consider two very general terms as *vidhi* (विधि) and *adhikāra* (अधिकार). The first is the Hindi word for "law", while the second is the Hindi word for "right". Both are terms that come directly from the Sanskrit legal lexicon. In classical Sanskrit, the word *vidhi* brings a prescriptive charge and was originally referred to the prescriptive parts of the Vedas (Francavilla 2006). *Vidhi* is now the general term that is used for "law" in Hindi versions of Indian legal texts, including the Constitution. Significantly the term *dharma* is not used: it is the fundamental normative concept in the Hindu legal tradition and refers to an order inherent in the cosmos and society, while the term *vidhi* more clearly conveys a conception of law as authority and command.[15]

---

14 One of the duties of the Official Languages Wing at the Ministry of Justice is the creation of the standard legal Hindi lexicon, which has to be elaborated having in mind its translatability into regional languages.
15 For an extensive analysis of the concept of *dharma*, see Menski (2003).

Adhikāra is a key term in the sphere of ritual. In the structure of sacrifice, all is about *adhikāra*: one's position, what one can do, the things one is entitled to do. *Adhikāra* does not necessarily have a positive connotation, since it can also be a privilege. This term becomes the term for right when the language of liberal rights enters into Indian legal culture. In the Constitution, fundamental rights are *mulādhikāra*, and human rights are *mānavādhikāra*.[16] It is interesting that in the Indian Constitution the term used to refer to the fundamental rights is a term that for centuries has been crucial to explain the idea that the Brahmins, placed at the top of the social hierarchy, can do things that the *śūdras*, belonging to the lowest castes, cannot do.

If we consider other general legal terms, the corresponding Hindi terms derive directly from Sanskrit. Contract becomes *anubandha* (अनुबन्ध) or *sanvidā* (संविदा).[17] Breach of contract becomes *sanvidā bhanga*; voidable agreement becomes *śūn'yakaraṇīya anubandha*, literally an agreement that is made void, and void is *śūn'ya*, which means empty and indicates the numeral zero. The fact that the concept of contract in classical Hindu law can be different from the concept of contract in common law is not so important. The terms used are general enough to convey the basic concept.

A term like marriage does not raise translation problems. Marriage is *vivāha* (विवाह), a Sanskrit term adopted in Hindi. Nonetheless, but this is a more complex discourse, the concept of *vivāha* is more extensive and includes a number of very different relationships provided for in traditional Hindu law, some of which are not included in the Western concept of marriage. In current Hindu family law, some of these types of *vivāha* are no longer recognized, but it is not necessary to find a new term.

Some more specific English terms, for example, patent or trademark, are simply transliterated into the Devanagari alphabet used for Hindi. License agreement becomes *lā'isēnsa anubandha* (लाइसेंस अनुबंध), in which only a portion is actually translated.

Moreover, in Hindi legal texts one can often find transliterated English words, even when a Hindi term is available. Similarly, in English texts one can find transliterated Hindi terms. Transliteration is not a translation but the adoption of a different writing system, the term remaining the same, sometimes with some phonetic changes. Examples are such terms as *pañcāyat* (पंचायत), a traditional council, *sapiṇḍa* (सपिण्ड), a form of ritual kinship, *saptapadī* (सप्तपदी), a term that refers to the seven steps taken in the most important form of marriage celebration, and *jūrī* (जुरी), jury.

Pañcāyat is a term that refers to a traditional council, an assembly. The literal translation would be the council of five, because originally five people took part in it, but also in Hindi the original meaning is now lost, and it refers to a council, regardless of the number of components. The term *pañcāyat* is not translated. The Indian Constitution itself devotes a whole section to the *pañcāyat* retaining the original term.

---

16 On the relationship between *adhikāra* and rights, see Singh (2003).
17 As an example of the diversity among Indian languages, the Tamil term for contract is *oppantam*.

The term is not translated because, while referring to an institution of the genus of council or assembly, it has a more profound meaning, even from an emotional point of view, because it is an expression of a policy of reappraisal of traditional institutions for the promotion of self-government that originated with Gandhi.

A similar example is provided by the term *sapiṇḍa*, which is relevant in family law, and expresses a certain category of kinship based on ritual connections. Literally the term means "riceballs fellows", referring to the joint participation in some rituals where little rice balls are used. Belonging to the same category, the term *saptapadī*, literally seven steps, refers to a specific form of marriage celebration consisting in the seven steps the bride and bridegroom take before the sacred fire; it is not translated in the Hindu Marriage Act of 1955.[18] Another very interesting term is jury, which becomes *jūrī*, or even *pañcāyat*; thus, it is either a transliteration of an English term or the somewhat ambiguous adaptation of a traditional term.

The use of Hindi terms in the English versions may make it difficult for a non-Indian lawyer in some cases to understand Indian legislation. The same problem may also arise for terms that by themselves are unproblematic, such as *crore* and *lakh*, which simply indicate ten million and one hundred thousand, but that for a non-Indian are not immediately clear. In general, translation requires not so much a dictionary as an encyclopedia, and interpretation of Indian legal texts, even in the English version, in many cases will require extensive knowledge of the specific cultural context.

The spread of Hindi official versions alongside the English ones causes also in India some issues raised by the interpretation of multilingual texts, widely studied in the European context.[19] Interpretation may have to deal with legal or common terms. The existence of official Hindi versions of legislation poses a problem of interpretation. In case of conflict, the English version prevails, but, if there is conflict, the Hindi version can be used in order to ascertain whether a particular English word should be interpreted as referring to a specific object.[20]

5 Conclusion

At the end of this analysis, the oversimplification inherent in the statement that English is the language of Indian law should be apparent. The Union's legislation is in English but an official translation into Hindi and in many cases into other Indian languages is available. Similarly, State legislation is available in English and in regional

---

18 The Hindu Marriage Act 1955 offers a legal definition of *saptapadī*, but does not translate the word.
19 See, among others, Pozzo and Jacometti (2006) and Ferreri et al. (2013).
20 An important case in this regard is *Park leather industry (p) Ltd. & anr. vs. State of Uttar Pradesh & ors.*, Supreme Court of India (2001).

languages. The Supreme Court's language is always English. The language of proceedings of High Courts such as, for instance, the Rajasthan High Court is Hindi, and also judgments and decrees can be written in Hindi, as an option, even though an official translation into English must be provided. The lower courts' language is increasingly a regional language.

If one considers that, in a trial, witnesses and documentary evidence may be taken in a language other than that of the Court, that the rules to be applied in a particular case may be partly found in English texts and partly in texts written in Hindi or another language, and that a judgment of the Supreme Court, necessarily in English, will be based on legal texts or documents, for instance contracts, originally produced in another language, not only Hindi, we can conclude that in the Indian legal system, as a whole, many languages interact in different ways.

The Indian legal system is therefore a multilingual one, even though at a certain level of analysis English can still appear to be the only language of the law, as it is still the main language. Furthermore, the concrete life of Indian law takes place within a general context of multilingualism. An important point in this regard is that, although many languages are officially recognized, these are still few to represent Indian general multilingualism. Secondly, rules governing language in the legal contexts are followed within an environment where other languages are spoken in different societal and personal settings.

In this regard, one could synthetically define Indian legal multiligualism as an imperfect and vertical one. It is imperfect because, notwithstanding all the efforts, it hardly mirrors Indian linguistic complexity as a whole, and it is vertical in the sense that several languages are involved, but to a different extent depending on specific legal contexts, from trials in lower courts to parliamentary proceedings. A third keyword may be added: disaggregation. Choudry (2009: 608) highlights the "disaggregation of official-language status into a series of discrete institutional choices". For instance, "article 348 disaggregates the question of the official language of court proceedings into the language of *deliberation* and the language of *outcomes* or decisions. The former can be multilingual while the latter, for the sake of the unity of the judicial system, cannot" (Choudhry 2009: 607). This tendency towards a disaggregated system may be seen as the outcome of an effort to find suitable solutions in context. At a more general level, including also, for example, the need for a huge translation machinery, the Indian experience shows a remarkable refusal of oversimplification and the willingness to bear the costs of complexity in order to protect fundamental needs and values.

References

Austin, Granville. 1966. *The Indian Constitution: cornerstone of a nation*. Oxford: Clarendon Press.
Choudhry, Sujit. 2009. Managing linguistic nationalism through constitutional design: lessons from South Asia. *International Journal of Constitutional Law* 7(4). 577–618.

Choudhry, Sujit, Madhav Khosla & Pratap Bhanu Mehta (eds.). 2016. *The Oxford handbook of the Indian Constitution*. Oxford: Oxford University Press.

Ferreri, Silvia et al. 2013. *Document quality control in public administrations and international organisations: a study*. Luxembourg: Publications Office of the European Union.

Francavilla, Domenico. 2006. *The roots of Hindu jurisprudence*. Torino: Corpus Iuris Sanscriticum.

Francavilla, Domenico. 2010. *Il diritto nell'India contemporanea. Sistemi tradizionali, modelli occidentali e globalizzazione*. Torino: Giappichelli.

Jain, M.P. 2004. *Indian constitutional law*. New Delhi: Wadhwa.

King, Robert D. 1997. *Nehru and the language politics of India*. Delhi: Oxford University Press.

Law Commission of India. 2008. *Non-feasability of introduction of Hindi as compulsory language in the Supreme Court of India (216th Report)*. http://lawcommissionofindia.nic.in/reports/report216.pdf

Lubin, Timothy. 2013. Legal diglossia: Modeling discursive practices in premodern Indic law. In Vincenzo Vergiani and Whitney (eds.), *Bilingual discourse and cross-cultural fertilisation: Sanskrit and Tamil in medieval India*. Pondicherry: Institut Français de Pondichéry – École Française d'Extrême-Orient.

Menski, Werner F. 2003. *Hindu law: Beyond tradition and modernity*. Delhi: Oxford University Press.

Menski, Werner F. 2006. *Comparative law in a global context: the legal systems of Asia and Africa*, 2nd edn. Cambridge: Cambridge University Press.

Pozzo, Barbara and Valentina Jacometti (eds). 2006. *Multilingualism and the harmonization of European law*. Boston/Dordrecht: Kluwer Law International.

Sailaja, Pingali. 2009. *Indian English*. Edinburgh: Edinburgh University Press.

Singh, Mahendra Pal. 2003. Human rights in the Indian tradition: Alternatives in the understanding and realization of the human rights regime. *Heidelberg Journal of International Law* 63. 551–584.

Andrea Ortolani
18 The many languages of Japanese legal language

1 Introduction

Historically, Japan has been fairly receptive to foreign cultural models, which influenced heavily its language and other aspects of its culture. Such influences had a significant effect upon the legal system.

The first wave of reception of laws dates back to the eighth century, when the Japanese sovereigns introduced in their domains the Chinese collections of regulations known in Japan as *ritsu-ryo*. These were documents quite advanced for the time, and contributed to shaping the legal mentality of Japan. With the modernization of the country in the nineteenth century, the source of inspiration switched from China to the West. Japan introduced a Constitution several, codes and built a legal system following the European models of the time. The evolution of language went in parallel with the changes in the legal system. From this perspective, the last century saw many deep changes in the language spoken by the legislator, by the government and by legal scholars.

This chapter analyses the birth and evolution of legal language in Japan. In the first part, I will introduce the main features of the Japanese writing system, focusing in particular on the problems related to the reception of the Chinese writing system and on the consequences it entailed.

The second part of the chapter will outline the modern language policy of Japan and the effect such a policy had on the legislation. Between 1868 and 1898, Japan endeavoured to enact a Constitution a civil code and several statutes in all fields of law. These achievements were the result of the zealous effort of the intellectuals of the time, who studied the Western legal systems and translated their statutes and legal literature. In this way, they created a new Japanese legal terminology and made possible the establishment of a modern legal system on par with the Western ones.

The final part analyses how the reception of foreign law is mirrored in the present style of the legislation, and how recent sociolinguistic changes are affecting the language of the law. Such an analysis will shed light on some recurring patterns underlying the Japanese reception of foreign law, and how they shaped the modern legal system as a complex structure made of multilingual and multicultural bricks.

Note: In this chapter Japanese is romanized according to the revised Hepburn system. Long vowels, however, are not marked. All names are written according to the Western order, i.e. first name followed by surname.

2 Language in Japan

2.1 The languages of the archipelago: hidden multilingualism

Japanese is the primary and official language spoken by the 127 million inhabitants of the archipelago.[1] Japanese ranks as the 9th world language for number of native speakers (Simons and Fennig 2018). In 2012, approximately 3.6 million people were studying Japanese outside of Japan (The Japan Foundation 2017) and it is a recognized language in the Republic of Palau, an island state in the Western Pacific Ocean. The standard modern Japanese (*hyojungo*) is based on the Edo dialect of Tokyo, (Hasegawa 2015: 14) but many other dialects are spoken in the Japanese archipelago. Differences among them can sometimes be substantial, and there are mutually unintelligible dialects (Hasegawa 2015: 17; Tsujimura 2014: 403).

Some other languages are spoken in Japan; for example, Ainu and the Ryukyuan languages spoken in the Southern prefecture of Okinawa. Ainu is spoken in the northern island of Hokkaido (Tamura 2000), and it has been recognized as a language by Japan in Act 52 of 1997 on the promotion of the Ainu culture (*Ainu bunka no shinko narabini Ainu no dento to ni kansuru chishiki no fukyu oyobi keihatsu ni kansuru horitsu*). The Act mentions the "Ainu language" (*Ainugo*) in art. 2 as a part of the Ainu culture. The Ryukyuan languages are not officially recognized by legislative acts, and remain part of a political debate. Recent studies list them as dialects of Japan (Hasegawa 2015: 18; Tsujimura 2014: 405). UNESCO lists six languages spoken in Okinawa as endangered (Moseley 2010), while *The Ethnologue* lists 11 languages under the category "Ryukyuan" (Simons and Fennig 2018). The politically charged question whether Okinawan is a language, a dialect, or a group of languages or dialects, is therefore still open to debate.[2]

Korean and Chinese are spoken by the communities of immigrants who settled mainly in the large cities of the Tokyo-Yokohama area, in Kansai and in parts of the southern island of Kyushu (Maher and Yashiro 1995). In addition there are pockets of immigrants or returnees from Brazil who settled in the archipelago especially in the late twentieth century, where Portuguese is spoken (Tsuda 2003).[3]

English is widely studied, is spoken by immigrants from English-speaking countries and is the standard language for international communication, sometimes

---

[1] As of June 2015, the population of Japan was 126,929,347 (Somusho tokeikyoku 2015)
[2] For a brief historical introduction to the problem see Shibatani (1990: 189–196).
[3] The Brazilians settled mainly in the Aichi and Shizuoka prefectures. In the Nagoya subways, announcements are made also in Portuguese. According to the latest statistics by the Ministry of Justice, Brazilians are the fifth largest group of foreign residents in Japan, after the Chinese, Koreans, Filipinos and Vietnamese. As of June 2017 there more than 187,000 registered residents, totalling about 6.2% of all foreign residents (Seifu tokei no sogo madoguchi 2017).

together with Chinese and Korean.[4] A number of prominent companies have recently adopted English as the official language for meetings and internal communication even in purely domestic contexts among Japanese employees.[5]

The influence of other languages upon Japanese is moderate. Older loanwords tend to originate from Portuguese or Dutch, as those were the first Western countries having official commercial relations with Japan (Irwin 2011; Frellesvig 2010: 404–6). More recent loanwords do not follow well-defined patterns, except in some cases where the country of origin is particularly linked with certain fields or specialized languages: for example, Italian loanwords abound in music, French in fashion, while the lexicons of medicine, philosophy and alpinism have many German loanwords (Irwin 2011: 23–69; Shibatani 1990: 149).

Thus, while the linguistic landscape of Japan may at first sight appear substantially uniform, it is in fact quite complex and faceted.

2.2 The Japanese language

The Japanese language shows several aspects common to many languages. Its subject-object-verb word order is the same as about half of the world languages. Its phonetic and syllabic structures do not differ sharply from those of many other languages (Shibatani 1990: 90–93).

However, contrary to most of the major modern languages, which developed through evolution and differentiation from ancestral languages, Japanese is the result of a series of linguistic contacts (Shibatani 1990: 89–118; Loveday 1996). This is the reason of the particular complexity of the writing system and of the ubiquitous presence in it of elements of Chinese and, in more recent times, of English and other foreign languages, now rooted permanently in the language.

In 1859, words of Chinese origin, or *kango*, made-up about 60% of the lexicon of Japanese, loanwords from other languages 1.4%, and native words accounted for the remaining 38.6% (Shibatani 2009: 746). More recent studies have found that the proportion of non-Chinese foreign words is steadily increasing. For example a study of popular magazines published in 1994 found 41.6% of native Japanese vocabulary, 45.9% of Sino-Japanese words, 10.5% of non-Chinese loanwords and 2% of hybrid terms (Hasegawa 2015: 63).

---

[4] As of June 2017, there were 105,189 persons from the US, 24,026 from the UK, and 16,798 from Canada. (Seifu tokei no sogo madoguchi 2017)
[5] Some examples of companies who adopted the policy of using English for internal communication include Rakuten, the Japanese e-commerce giant; Fast Retailing, the parent company of the apparel chain Uniqlo; and the world-famous tire producer Bridgestone.

The writing system of modern Japanese is based on Chinese characters and two sets of syllabaries used only in Japanese: the *hiragana* and the *katakana*. Latin alphabet and Arabic numerals are also widely used.

The Chinese characters, called *kanji* in Japanese, first appeared on the archipelago around the fourth century, and spread around the seventh and eighth century (Hasegawa 2015: 43–57; Seeley 1991; Shibatani 1990: 125). These *kanji* were the first signs used to write the Japanese language, which previously had only been spoken. For this reason, most *kanji* acquired two or more readings: one or more phonetic readings (in Japanese *on'yomi)*, derived from the pronunciation of the character in the Chinese language, and a "Japanese" reading, or native reading (*kun'yomi*), corresponding to the Japanese word indicated by the character. These two readings, radically different, were and still are used alternatively, according to rules abundant in exceptions. In addition, since Japan was exposed to Chinese culture in different periods, when the pronunciation on the continent followed different patterns, some *kanji* were associated with different readings. For example, the *kanji* for the English word 'under' may be read in the Chinese way as *ka* or *ge*, besides the many Japanese readings *shita*, *shimo*, *moto* and as a verbal root *sa-, kuda-, o-*.

Because of the limited use of tones in the Japanese language, the phonetic structure of the Chinese characters was almost completely lost in the process of reception, and this resulted in a large number of homophones in the Japanese language. For example, the sound *ko* (with a long vowel O) is a reading of more than 170 characters; the word *seika* can be written in more than ten combinations of different characters, each conveying a distinct meaning.

Two sets of phonetic characters were developed through simplification of the Chinese characters: the *hiragana* (plain *kana*) and the *katakana* (fragmentary *kana*) (Seeley 1991: 59–76). Both sets include the five vowels *a, i, o, e, u,* and their combinations with nine consonants, plus the letter *n*. In theory, the combinations are 50 plus the *n*, but the syllables used in modern Japanese are only 46 as certain combinations have become obsolete. Through diacritic signs that modify the pronunciation of certain syllables the combinations were increased of 25 syllables for a total of 71.[6]

The characters of the *hiragana* sillabary derived from the cursive writing of *kanji* and can be considered the "connective tissue" of the Japanese language. Today *hiragana* characters are used mainly to write verb endings, particles of grammar and syntax, or to write words in which *kanji* are too complex, obsolete or not appropriate to the context. *Katakana* derived from simplified parts of *kanji*. This form of script is currently used mainly to write onomatopoeia, foreign names and loanwords.

---

[6] For example, the *k* in *ka* becomes *g*, giving the syllable *ga*, and *gi, gu, ge, go* when combined with the other vowels; the *h* in *ha* becomes *b* or *p* depending on the diacritic sign added, giving the series of syllables *ba, bi, bu, be, bo* or *pa, pi, pu, pe, po*.

The Latin alphabet (*romaji*, literally 'Roman characters') is widespread in many levels of society as a sign that conveys modernity. It is used to write short acronyms, or sometimes foreign terms. In exceptional cases, mostly related to art, entertainment or advertising, it is used to write Japanese words or names.

Besides this, an important role of the Latin alphabet is found in the urban environment: traffic signs, train stations, but also signs for shops and restaurants. Furthermore, an increasing number of public services display some form of English translation. Latin letters are also on the keyboards of personal computers, where Japanese text is typed in *via* its romanization, and software systems assist the user in choosing the right *kanji*. Virtual keyboards such as those commonly used on smartphones and tablets may also have layouts based on the Japanese *kana*.

The most used systems for transliterating Japanese words in Latin alphabet are the Hepburn and the Kunrei systems (Hasegawa 2015: 55). The first, invented by American missionary James Curtis Hepburn, is based on English writing conventions for consonants, while the vowels generally sound similar to Italian. The Kunrei system was sanctioned by a cabinet ordinance of 1937 as the system of transliteration of the Japanese into Latin characters. Nonetheless, the Hepburn system is still widely used in official documents such as passports and on traffic signs and train stations.

In sum, the same Japanese word can be written, at least in theory, in four ways: in *kanji, hiragana, katakana* or *romaji*. For example, '*horitsu*' (act, statute) is normally written with *kanji*: the first character '*ho*' can mean 'law' or 'method', and the second '*ritsu*' can stand for 'rule', 'regulation'; 'rhythm' or 'pitch'. The writing in *hiragana* can respond to certain stylistic choices; for example it can be used by children or those who do not know how to write the two (not particularly complex) *kanji*.[7] *Katakana* can be used to highlight the term, and in this case it is equivalent to the use of graphical styles such as the upper case or the underlined in English. *Romaji* may be used in special situations, such as on book covers, on signs, logos or other situations where a particular visual impact is looked for.

The use of Chinese numbers survives in formal settings or in situations where the writer wants to convey the image of the old and traditional Japan. In all other situations they have been supplanted by Arabic numerals.

Along with the Western Gregorian calendar, Japan adopts a modified version of it in which the number of the year is expressed counting the year of reign of the Emperor. Dates of statutes and other official documents use this Japanese calendar. Therefore, the Meiji Emperor began his reign according to the Gregorian calendar

---

[7] The first kanji '*ho*' is taught in the fourth year of elementary school, but the second character '*ritsu*' is not taught until the sixth year. Therefore, children under 11 years of age may not know how to write *horitsu* correctly in *kanji*, although they can always use the *hiragana* signs.

system in 1868, but in Japan this would be referred to as Meiji 1 (*Meiji gannen*). The Constitution of the Empire of Japan was promulgated in 1889 or Meiji 22, World War II ended in 1945 or Showa 20 and the Fukushima-1 nuclear accident happened on March 11 of 2011, or Heisei 23.

The listing of items, including official documents such as statutes, can reflect the order of the phonetic syllabaries, or the alphabetical order based on the romanization of the Japanese word. Bulleted items in lists can be marked through numbers, Latin letters, Latin numbers and other graphic conventions. In some cases, especially in older texts, lists follow the *i-ro-ha* order, based on a traditional rhyme that contains the entire syllabary.[8] Many lists in statutes and other legal documents follow this *i-ro-ha* order.

2.3 The Japanese language, Japan's non-official language

While Japanese is spoken in the courts and in Parliament, is the language of laws and rulings, and is the first language taught in schools, there is no legislation that designates it as the official language of Japan (Saito: 2006). Within legal texts it is possible to find the term *kokugo* (national language), which is universally understood as a synonym for the Japanese language.[9] Article 21, Paragraph 5, of the School Education Act (Act No. 26 of 1947) states that among the objectives of the mandatory schooling is "making [students] familiar with reading, and develop the fundamental skills needed to understand and correctly use the national language (*kokugo*) necessary for the requirements of daily life". Furthermore, the Nationality Act of 1950 contains no provisions requiring an adequate knowledge of the Japanese language as conditions to meet in order to obtain the Japanese nationality (Nationality Act, act no. 147 of 1950, art. 5). However, as a matter of fact, officials of the Ministry of Legal Affairs carry out procedures to assess the Japanese proficiency of applicants seeking naturalization, within the ample discretionary powers they enjoy (Gottlieb 2012: 7).

---

8 A traditional rhyme is used to teach this sequence. It reads as follows: '*i-ro-ha-ni-ho-he-to-chi-ri-nu-ru-yo-wa-ka-yo-ta-re-so-tsu-ne-na-ra-mu-u-wi-no-o-ku-ya-ma-ke-fu-ko-e-te-a-sa-ki-yu-me-mi-shi-we-hi-mo-se-su*'. Therefore, item number 1 on the list is marked as "i", item number 2 as "ro", item number 3 as "ha" and so on. Among the most recent statutes using this way of numbering lists, the Companies Act (*Kaisha ho*, Act 86 of 26 July 2005). E.g., articles 48 and 107 have a complex structure with subdivisions in paragraphs, subparagraphs marked in Chinese numbers and sub-sub paragraphs marked with *i-ro-ha* signs.
9 On the distinction between *kokugo* (national language) and *nihongo* (Japanese language), its ideological roots and its consequences, see Burgess (2012).

In 1999, the Parliament defined the provisions for two symbols intimately connected with national identity: the national flag and the national anthem. The *Kokki oyobi kokka ni kan suru horitsu* (Act on national flag and anthem) reads as follows:

> Article 1. The national flag is the *Nisshoki*. The form of the *Nisshoki* is as defined in attachment 1.
>
> Article 2. The national anthem is the *Kimigayo*. The lyrics and the tune of the *Kimigayo* are as defined in attachment 2.

The act did not introduce any changes in what were the *de facto* national flag and anthem since the Meiji period. No law has been enacted to define the official language. Therefore, there are currently no provisions defining Japanese as the official language of Japan. Some texts, however, make explicit reference to the Japanese language (*nihongo*). For example, Article 74 of the Court Act (Act No. 59 of April 16, 1947) provides that "In the court, the Japanese language shall be used".

Provisions on language in the codes of civil and criminal procedure follow different terminological choices, that reflect the different legislative styles and sociolinguistic sensibilities of the periods in which the codes were drafted.

In particular, provisions on language are found in articles dealing with court interpreters. The Code of Criminal Procedure, which went into effect in 1948, uses the more antiquated term *kokugo* to define the national language. Article 175 states that "When the court has a person who is not proficient in the national language make a statement, it shall have an interpreter interpret it". Art. 177 notes that "The court may have letters or marks written in languages other than the national language translated".[10] Thus, the judges decide on the necessity of interpreting, and there are no clear guidelines on what is meant by "not proficient in the national language". The wording of the code mandates the presence of an interpreter only when the defendant needs to make a statement and nothing is said about the right of the defendant to understand the proceeding. However, as a signatory to the International Covenant on Civil and Political rights, Japan provides the right to everyone to "be informed promptly and in detail in a language which he understands of the nature and cause of the charge against him (ICCPR art. 14.3.a)" and to "have the free assistance of an interpreter if he cannot understand or speak the language used in court (ICCPR art. 14.3.f)" (Nakane 2012: 156).

The more recent Code of Civil Procedure, promulgated in 1996, states in Article 154: "If a person who participates in oral argument is unable to communicate in Japanese, or unable to hear or speak, an interpreter shall attend the oral argument; provided, however, that in the case of a person who is unable to hear or speak, it shall be permissible to ask questions of him/her or have him/her make statements by means of writing". The need for interpreters seems to be less pressing in civil

---

[10] The translations quoted here are those provided by the Japanese Law Translation Database System of the Ministry of Legal Affairs, at http://www.japaneselawtranslation.go.jp/ (see par. 5 in this chapter)

proceedings; however there can be cases in some areas, e.g. those related to family matters, where if a party is not fluent in Japanese, the attendance of an interpreter would be extremely important.

2.4 Japanese language policy: an overview

The decision to avoid intervening in the matter of making Japanese the official language does not necessarily mean that the government is disinclined to deal with this question or to formulate a policy. A glance at the evolution of Japanese language policy over the past 150 years shows that since the Meiji period, numerous reform proposals have taken aim at the Japanese language explicitly stating that Japanese is the national language (Lee 2010). Extreme proposals, such as those considering the elimination of Japanese and the adoption of another language, were never acted upon, but more moderate reforms were adopted with respect to various aspects of Japanese language and writing. The language spoken in Japan today is in part the result of the language policy measures summarized below.[11]

The period in which the debate was the most heated was the second half of the nineteenth century, and in particular the years immediately following the Meiji Restoration.

The first modern proposal on language policy was presented in 1866, when a noted translator of the time, Hisoka Maejima, put forward in his writing "*Kanji gohaishi no gi* ('Proposal for the abolition of the Chinese characters)" a policy suggestion addressed to Shogun Yoshinobu Tokugawa (Griolet 1985: 15). Maejima proposed the outright elimination of the Chinese characters from the Japanese writing. He was driven by the conviction that such a change would achieve the highly desirable goal of saving time in children's education, giving them the opportunity to enrich their knowledge in other fields (Maejima 1899: 6–24). Maejima wrote three other short essays in 1869 restating this idea (Griolet 1985: 31) and advocating the use of the colloquial style in writing. These proposals, written using the very *kanji* Maejima intended to eliminate, had a certain following and were taken up again in the years to come by other intellectuals of the time. For example, Uesaburo Shimizu wrote an article in 1874 entitled *The theory of hiragana* for the journal *Meiroku Zasshi* in which he advocated the elimination of *kanji* in favour of the *hiragana* syllabary. Shimizu published an introductory book to chemistry which used many *hiragana* terms showing that it was possible to substitute terminology that used Sino-Japanese compounds with more colloquial terms even in technical fields (Griolet 1985: 37).

During this period newspapers and magazines written entirely in *hiragana* appeared, such as the *Iroha Shinbun*, as well as publications in which the pronunciation of

---

[11] On early modern Japanese language policy, see also Lee (2010).

the *kanji* script was also printed in *hiragana* and was positioned just above the Sino-Japanese characters (Griolet 2002: 35). Between 1881 and 1883, a number of associations were founded with the aim of revolutionizing the Japanese script by abolishing *kanji*. The *Kana no tomo* (The friends of *kana*) in 1881, for example, counted among its founders the diplomat Shigetoshi Yoshihara, the poet Masakaze Takasaki, Takami Monozume, professor of literature at the University of Tokyo, and the famous linguist Fumihiko Otsuki (Griolet 1985: 38). In 1882, the naval engineer Hamagoro Hida, the physicist Goto Makita, the historian Yonekichi Miyake, together with a group of alumni of Keio University including Shogoro Atano and Hikoichi Motoyama, founded the *Kanabunkai* (Association for writing in *kana*) (Griolet 1985: 38). These two groups merged in 1883 as the *Kana no kai* (The *Kana* Association), an association for the abolition of *kanji* in favor of *kana*, headed by Prince Takehito Arisugawa and counting up to 10.000 members. Over the course of a few years, the association lost momentum, split into two groups as a consequence of internal dissent over questions related to such things as the choice of the pronunciation to be used for the transliteration of the Sino-Japanese characters into *kana*, and other issues related to orthography (Griolet 1985: 39).

More extreme was the 1869 proposal put forward by Yoshikazu Nanbu, who suggested that both *kanji* and *kana* be abandoned and the Latin alphabet alone be adopted. His proposal, written in the antiquated *kanbun* style, was presented as a strategy for preserving the Japanese language from the risk of disappearing because of the possible encroachment of Western languages (Griolet 2002: 157). The intellectual Amane Nishi supported this idea as well and in 1873, he wrote in the first issue of *Meiroku Zasshi* a long and passionate article arguing for the use of the Latin alphabet: *Yoji o motte kokugo o shosuru no ron* (On writing the national language using the Western characters) (Griolet 1985: 50–60). Like the supporters of the introduction of *kana*, Nishi was not concerned about the loss deriving from this radical linguistic switch. On the contrary, he viewed the use of the Latin alphabet as a last-resort measure to prevent what seemed a possible, and far more disastrous risk at the time, that is, the complete loss of the Japanese language in favour of the adoption of a Western language (Griolet 1985: 64–68).

In 1885, the *Romaji kai* (Latin Characters Association) was founded (Griolet 1985: 72), but this movement soon split as well, following disagreements over fundamental issues such as which register to base the language on and which transliteration method to use. The association ceased its activities in 1892, but it left an important mark on the evolution of the Japanese language, as it contributed to the adoption of punctuation marks in writing. Until this time, there was no consistent use of punctuation marks in Japanese writing.

In this period, Arinori Mori proposed the most radical approach to the issue of the modernization of the Japanese language. Mori had been a diplomat and statesman of the early Meiji period and was a founder of the Japanese educational system. In 1872, Mori wrote a letter to American professor William Dwight Whitney asking advice on the idea of using English as the language of education in order to improve the education system of the country (Lee 2010: 9–14). This gives an idea of the wide range of choices that reformers of the period were ready to pursue.

Leading public intellectuals such as Yukichi Fukuzawa and Fumio Yano advanced more pragmatic proposals.[12] Fukuzawa stated his position on the issue of writing reform in *Moji no oshie* (Elementary reader for children) believing that while it might be desirable to abandon the Chinese characters, it would be difficult to achieve in a short period. Therefore, he proposed that the right policy would be to select some 2.000 to 3.000 characters to use in everyday language. Yano and other intellectuals, including Setsurei Miyake and Takashi Hara, who would become Prime Minister of Japan from 1918 to 1921, advanced similar policies (Griolet 1985: 88–92). This turned out to be the acceptable compromise between tradition and modernization, that would inspire all future methods of political intervention in language reform in the country (Griolet 2002: 178).

The lists of Sino-Japanese characters approved in the past and still in force, with some modifications, have the objective of creating a standard to be followed in compulsory education, of being a reference for the communication needs of social life, and of regulating and standardizing the writing of characters and their admitted readings. The most recent list are the 1,850 "*Kanji* for General Use" ("*Toyo kanji*") of 1946, replaced in 1981 by the 1,945 "*Kanji* for regular use" ("*Joyo kanji*"). The list continues to be revised from time to time by the Ministry of Education, Culture, Sports, Science and Technology. It was last modified in 2010. The characters in the latest version of the list are now 2,136. They have been taught in schools since 2012, and high schools and universities started using these *kanji* within the entrance examinations that started in 2015.

These *kanji* are therefore considered the practical standard of the Japanese language and constitute the basis of the language taught in compulsory education. Since 2010, the Agency for Cultural Affairs has advised publishers, broadcasters, and all authors of public documents against using *kanji* not appearing on the list. When absolutely necessary, the Agency encourages indicating the pronunciation in *hiragana* (Agency for Cultural Affairs, 2010).

3 Legal Japanese

3.1 The style of the legal language

The analysis of the Japanese legal language can be carried out on two levels. The first is represented by the problems related to the translation of Western law and

---

12 The digital reproduction of the original version is available at the Digital Gallery of Rare Books and Special Collections of Keio University http://project.lib.keio.ac.jp/dg_kul/fukuzawa_title.php?id=73

jurisprudence into Japanese, and the creation of the legal terminology in the Meiji period. It is not possible to present in detail here this complex history, but some recent examples relating to the creation of neologisms, and other terminology problems will be examined. Another line of inquiry focuses on the sociolinguistic evolution of the Japanese language and its repercussions on legal language in Japan. The most important example of change in the language of the law in recent times is the linguistic reform of the civil code.

Since the Meiji Restoration, the style of legislation and other legal texts has undergone a radical evolution. Statutes and other binding acts prior to World War II were written in an extremely formal style. In some respects, that style was already antiquated at the time of the promulgation of those statutes. This style of prose, called *katakana-bungotai*, makes use of extremely formal syntactic structures, and presents all the "connective tissue" of the Japanese language, i.e. verbal suffixes, prepositions and other particles, written in the *katakana* sillabary. In addition, some *kanji* appear in classical, antiquated forms, barely recognizable to the contemporary untrained reader. This combination of grammatical, syntactic, and graphic features makes such texts quite difficult to understand for the layman. The style adopted by legislation was in turn adopted by judgements and used by legal scholars in their writings. A turning point can be identified in the current Constitution.

3.2 The post-war Constitution of Japan

The promulgation of the current Constitution in 1946 brought a dramatic change. This was the first legal text written in the less formal style called *kogotai*, or literally "colloquial style," in which Sino-Japanese characters are mixed with *hiragana* characters, with the adoption of a style closer to the everyday language. In addition, the text of the Constitution included punctuation marks.

The first draft of the Constitution was written in the traditional *katakana-bungotai* style. However, General MacArthur refused this text and in February of 1946 took the initiative to draft the new Constitution of Japan. This draft, produced by the occupation forces, was then, with some changes, translated into Japanese.

The unprecedented switch to the colloquial style was due to several factors. First, several members of the Cabinet Legislation Bureau and members of the occupying forces entrusted with the drafting of the Constitution, wanted a text more easily understood. Second, the Association for People's Language Movement (*Kokumin no kokugo undo renmei*) submitted a series of recommendations, advocating for a switch to a less formal, more modern language, for the use of *hiragana* instead of *katakana*, and for the introduction of punctuation marks and other widely used conventions (Inoue 1991: 29–30).

Finally, the forces in the government supporting the use of a more formal language realized that they would not have enough time to draft a document in classic

Japanese, with a stylistic refinement worthy of the role that the fundamental charter of the nation would play. Eventually, they reluctantly agreed to have the charter written in the colloquial style. The draft of the revised Japanese Constitution was published on 17 April 1946, one week after the first general elections in post-war Japan. In line with the tradition of Japanese collective responsibility, the choice of adopting the colloquial style was not attributed to any particular individual (Inoue 1991: 29–31; Koseki 1997: 133–137).

Writing the Constitution in colloquial Japanese was "a revolution in legal texts" (Koseki 1997: 133). The colloquial style was an extremely important factor in popularizing the contents and the role of the Constitution for the new Japan. In addition, the less formal style helped to conceal the feeling of translation deriving from the fact that the draft of the Constitution presented to the Parliament was the Japanese version of a draft of the Supreme Command for the Allied Powers (SCAP). As a consequence of the choice the new style, the text of the current Constitution is less vague than the text previously written in classical Japanese (Koseki 1997: 133).

This change in style brought about another important consequence. Since the fundamental charter of the nation was written in the colloquial style, then all legislation had to adapt to and follow this style. All subsequent legislation adopted the *hiragana-kogotai* style even though there is no formal or explicit provision sanctioning this change. It looks as if social dynamics related to different registers were transferred in the abstract world of the law and applied to the relation between the Constitution and ordinary statutes. Just as in everyday life the use of a higher register signals the higher status of the speaker, if an ordinary statute were to adopt a more formal language than the Constitution, this would be considered odd, if not an impertinence.

After 1946, all laws were therefore written in the colloquial style. This shift created a gap in the legislation. Since the laws prior to the Constitution were not automatically abrogated but continued to be in force, the result was the coexistence in the legal system, and in particular in the body of legislation, of two different styles. For instance, the reform of family law of 1946 modified several provisions of books IV and V of the civil code, and as a result they were re-written entirely in *hiragana-kogotai*. Books I, II and III, dedicated to general provisions, property (real rights), and obligations, remained untouched and were written in *katakana-bungotai* until 2005. Other examples of laws in force still written in *katakana-bungotai* include the laws on debt securities and parts of the Commerce Code. As for the Civil Code, Japan remedied this stylistic schism with the language reform of 2004, which is described in greater detail below.

3.3 The Civil Code language reform of 2004

The law of 2004 that amended parts of the Civil Code was, until the reform of the law of obligations of 2017, the most important change to the Japanese Civil Code after the occupation period. The Act intervened on two aspects of the Japanese Civil Code.[13] First, it reorganized Article 446 *et seq.* on guarantee obligations. More importantly, the reform rewrote the articles of the first three books in modern, colloquial Japanese and created a heading for each article while reorganizing the numbering and the subdivisions of the paragraphs of the entire code (Nakata 2005).

The five books of the Japanese Civil Code were originally approved by the Japanese Parliament in two stages over the two-year period 1896–1898.[14] The Civil Code therefore went into effect on July 16, 1898, on the basis of decree (*sokurei*) no. 123. In more than 100 years of life, the Civil Code has undergone numerous reforms, but the main modifications of its first 100 years date back to the Act 222 of 1947 which completely reformed books 4 and 5 on family law and successions. The style used by the reform was the modern colloquial *hiragana-kogotai* style. The reform also targeted some parts of the first three books, but since the modified parts were so few, the drafters chose not to tackle issues related to the old style. These modified sections were written following the old *katakana-bungotai* style. The stylistic split between the two parts of the code remained unchanged until the act of 2004.

The contrast between laws written in the old, formal style and laws written in the modern style is not limited to the Civil Code. As mentioned earlier, the style adopted by the Constitution of 1946 determined the change of the legislative style, but of course this change did not affect the entire legislation. In principle, acts prior to 1946, being outside the scope of reform, remained in effect even under the new Constitution.

Rewriting all acts in force and translating them from the classical style to the modern would have been an extremely complex and time-consuming task. In 1990, a debate over language modernization arose in academic circles.[15] Until the early 1990s, among the basic statutes and codes, the code of civil procedure, and the penal code were a written in the old *katakana-bungotai*. In 1995 the penal code was rewritten in the modern language (Act 91 of 1995) and in 1996 a new code of civil procedure was promulgated and written in *hiragana-kogotai* (Act 109 of 1996).

As for private law, the Ministry of Legal Affairs instituted the "Committee to study the modernization of the Civil Code language" (*Minpoten gendaigoka kenkyukai*) in 1991. The committee was headed by University of Tokyo professor emeritus Eiichi Hoshino, and included seven members from some of the most prestigious universities of the country along with some ministry officials.[16] It began its works in July 1991. The

---

13 *Minpo no ichibu wo kaisei suru horitsu* (Act reforming a part of the Civil code), Act no. 147 of 1 December 2004.
14 In particular, the first three books (I: general provisions (*sosoku*); II: real rights (*bukken*); III: claims (*saiken*)), were promulgated by Act 89 of 1896, books IV and V (relatives (*shinzoku*) and inheritance (*sozoku*)) were promulgated by Act 8 of 1898.
15 Some of the proposals can be seen in Kagayama (1990a) Kagayama (1990b); Hoshino (1992).
16 The legal scholars of the commission were (in parentheses the affiliation at the start of the works): Masao Ikeda (Keio University), Kiyoe Kado (Rikkyo University), Hiroyasu Nakata (Hitotsubashi

first period was spent discussing whether or not using this opportunity to bring also substantial changes in the civil code. The committee was faced with three options. The first would have been for the committee to limit itself to "translating" the code without carrying out any substantial modifications. A second approach would have been to make minimal changes beyond the work of modernizing the language, where the provisions of the code were conclusively deemed to be obsolete and no longer in accordance with well-established case law. A third option would have been a broader intervention, not exclusively limited to those changes required to adapt the letter of the law to the established court precedents, but including innovative amendments which would influence the overall structure of the code.

The committee chose the second option, giving priority to rewriting and transposing well-established doctrines, leaving further innovative changes for a later time. The work was then divided among the members, who worked in pairs consisting of one academic and one ministry official. After 17 plenary sessions, the committee presented its draft to the Ministry of Legal Affairs on 7 January 1994, but the corrections and amendments went on until 25 June 1996, when chairman Hoshino presented the draft in its final version to the ministry. Beyond modernizing the language, the committee added a heading to each article, a numbering for the paragraphs of most of the articles, and carried out substantial changes to the letter of the law, in order to have it reflect well-established doctrine, in 14 articles. The reform however lost momentum and for years it was taken off the government's agenda.

In August 2004, the Ministry of Legal Affairs posted a draft on their homepage that included changes beyond those carried out by the committee. Out-dated provisions were eliminated or rewritten, and all the provisions, not only from the first three books but also those of the last two, were reorganized and coordinated. The draft was open to public discussion so that people and institutions could submit comments and opinions. In the period from 4 August to 3 September, the public offered 52 opinions: 42 were from individuals and 10 from groups. Although the language modernization sparked mostly favourable feedback, there was criticism of other aspects of the proposals. In particular, some of the opinions raised doubts about the fact that the theories that were intended to be incorporated were truly well established. Other opinions voiced scepticism about the advisability of inserting into a document such as the Civil Code definitions of terms in a way resembling those found in contracts. As a result of this criticism, along with the anxiety expressed by ministry officials, according to whom the addition of definitions would create substantial changes in the code for which there was no mandate, the committee almost completely abandoned introducing articles containing legislative definitions.

University), Tadashi Otsuka (Waseda University), Nobuhisa Segawa (Hokkaido University), Makoto Takahashi (Osaka City University) and Seiichi Yamada (Kobe University).

The draft was then presented first to the House of Councillors on 12 October, then to the House of Representatives on 12 November. The legislative process ended without complications on 25 November, and the statute was promulgated on 1 December 2004. The reform included five fundamental changes in the civil code.

The first change was the rationalization of the formal source of the books of the Civil Code. Until the reform, the Civil Code found its source in two different statutes. One enacted the first three books, another the last two books. Through the amendment of the title and the heading of Act 89 of 1986, which originally enacted the first three books of the code, this Act of 1896 became the formal source of the entire Civil Code.

The second change was the new numbering of the articles. The text remained divided into five books, but the reform changed the numbering of the chapters and articles, and closed the gaps left by repealed articles. In addition, parts of those articles that were previously only separated by a change in paragraph were now given numbers. By making several adjustments, the committee managed to leave unchanged the numbering of key articles, with which Japanese jurists were familiar.

The addition of a heading (*midashi*) to each article was the third modification. While in most cases the creation of a heading did not cause big problems, in other cases it provoked debate over which term should be used, and if it was suitable to use legal terminology not present in the code. The solution that was adopted in some cases favoured certain formalism, out of respect to the original terminology and to cross-references within the code. Thus, in Article 192 instead of the modern legal expression *zen'i shutoku* (on acquisition in good faith), the expression *sokuji shutoku* was preferred, since the word *sokuji* (immediate) is used in the same article as an attribute of the acquisition. Article 413 on the default of a creditor was given the heading *juryo chitai* (delayed acceptance), for the same reasons of internal cross-referencing, not the more common legal expression *saikensha chitai* (creditor's delay). Nevertheless, there are many examples where terms and expressions that were not present in the code, but commonly used by Japanese jurists, were introduced. Nakata (2005: 92) cites more than 40 examples. Some of the most important are *kiken futan* (assumption of risk), *daisansha no tame ni suru keiyaku* (contracts for the benefit of third parties), *shi'in zoyo* (gifts on donor's death), and *seito boei* (self-defense).

Still, the main point of the reform was to modernize the language, working on two levels: a technical-legislative update combined with a purely linguistic modernization. The Japan's Cabinet Legislation Bureau was the main proponent of the first type of change, since the reform had to to harmonize the terminology and style of the Civil Code with other laws. Therefore, the well-known *tadashigaki*, that is, the exceptions to the rules introduced by the adversative conjunction *tadashi* written with implicit and concise sentences, were paraphrased and expressed with explicit sentences that are more easily understandable. The use of *toki* (when), *baai* (in the case in which), *tekiyo* (application (of a regulation)), and *jun'yo* (application (of a regulation) mutatis mutandis) was harmonized and rationalized.

Another important point of the reform related to definitions. However, since the draft submitted for public comment drew criticism on this point, they were almost completely eliminated. First, in some cases definitional expressions analogous to those that might be found in contract law were introduced. For example, Article 10, which discusses the term of guardianship, reads as follows: "[...] the guardian (hereinafter referring to the guardian of a minor and the guardian of an adult) [...]." In other cases the definition was inserted in order to remove tedious repetition from the text. Thus, Article 25 reads: "In cases where any person who has left his/her domicile or residence (hereinafter referred to as 'absentee') did not appoint an administrator of his/her property (hereinafter in this Section referred to simply as 'administrator'), the family court may [...]". Article 85 is even more explicit: "Article 85. Definition. The term 'Things' as used in this Code shall mean tangible thing." Finally, a third method of technical modernization consisted of inserting references to other laws in the body of the code. For example, Article 13: "Acts requiring the consent of curator," Paragraph 1, Item 5, mentions "make a gift, make any settlement, or agree to arbitrate (referring to the agreement to arbitrate as provided in paragraph (1), Article 2 of the Arbitration Act (Act No. 138 of 2003))".

The purely linguistic modernization was carried out on at least three levels. First, terms and expressions typical of the *bungotai* style were translated into corresponding terms or expressions of the *kogotai* style. For example, the expression *seki ni makasu* was changed to *sekinin o ou* (to assume responsibility) as found in many articles. The many recurrences of the verb *nasu* (to do), written with the *kanji* of the verbal root *na-* and the *katakana* ending *-su*, were replaced with the modern synonym *suru* written entirely in *hiragana*.

Second, complex or obsolete terms were replaced with modern synonyms. For example, the antiquated *kison* (damage) has given way in almost every case to *sonsho*; *shinshaku* (*suru*) (take into consideration) has been replaced by *koryo* (*suru*); *kenketsu* (lack/shortage) was replaced by *fusonzai*. In certain cases, however, where the legal connotation of particular terms was regarded as indispensable, such terms have been preserved. This is the case of *kashi* (defect, as in articles 101, 120, 187 and many more), for which no *kanji* does appear on the *joyo kanji* list, but were kept into the code anyway. This was also true for *kison*, which is commonly used in the expression *meiyo kison* (defamation) and was maintained in Article 723 on recovery in defamation.

It was also decided to introduce corrections necessitated by the change in lifestyle and material conditions of Japan in the 2000s. For example, the term *kidosen*, (which is written with the *kanji* of wood, door and coin) that was used to mean the cost of admission to shows, was replaced by the modern *nyujoryo*, which means admission charge (Art. 174). Also, *bokuhi* (servant) and *shintan'yu* (a term that connects the *kanji* for *takigi/maki* (wood for burning), *sumi* (coal), and *abura* (oil/fat) were replaced respectively with *kaji shiyojin* (domestic servants) and *nenryo oyobi denki* (fuel and electricity, Art. 310). In Article 638, which dealt with warranty related to immovable property, the term *renga* (bricks) was rewritten in *hiragana*, since the two *kanji* that compose it do not appear on the list of *joyo kanji*, and the term *conkuriito* (concrete) was added.

The reform was not just a work of intralinguistic translation, however. The committee took advantage of the opportunity to refine technical terminology that was imprecise or ambiguous. The most important example was the substitution of *torikeshi* (annulment) with *tekkai* (revocation), as since the latter was regarded as more appropriate in the subsection on contract formation (Article 521). In addition, eleven provisions that became obsolete because of the evolution of case law were reformed in order to make the text of the law reflect the law in action.[17] In the draft submitted for public comment, there were three more articles subject to modification due to case law evolution. However, given the large amount of criticism received, these modifications were not approved in the final draft.[18]

Finally, the reform abrogated some obsolete dispositions. For example, the former Article 35 on legal entities pursuing commercial activity was abrogated because it was considered analogous to Article 52 of the Commercial Code. Also abrogated were Article 98 on public offering, and the articles previously numbered 311 and 320c on the responsibility of public officials.

4 Terminological problems: homophones, recent neologisms and *gairaigo*

4.1 Homophones

As previously mentioned, one of the main problems affecting oral comprehension of the Japanese language is the high number of homophones. This problem does not affect terms of Japanese origin as much as words composed of multiple *kanji*, which are usually pronounced according to their *on* (Chinese) pronunciation. Usually the context helps identify the correct term, but if speakers want to reduce the risk of misunderstanding, they might resort to pronouncing each *kanji* in isolation, i.e. pronouncing the *kun* reading of the character that might cause misunderstanding.

---

17 These provisions are: art. 108 on self-contract and representation of both parties; art. 109 on apparent authority due to manifestation of grant of authority of agency; art. 151 on filing for settlement and conciliation; art. 153 on demand; art. 162 on acquisitive prescription of ownership; art. 192 on immediate acquisition; art. 478 on performance to a holder of quasi-possession of claim; art. 513 on novation; art. 660 on obligation of depositary to give notice; art. 709 on damages in torts and art. 720 on self-defense and aversion of present danger.
18 The provisions were art. 415 on damages due to default, art. 541 on right to cancel for delayed performance and art. 711 on compensation for damages to next of kin.

Legal language is no exception, as it contains many homophones as well. Sometimes these can be understood thanks to their context, but in certain cases they can only be identified by pronouncing the characters individually. One of the most recurring examples in the field of Japanese law is *shiho*, which means 'private law' (*watakushi-ho*), or 'administration of justice' (*tsukasa-ho*), depending on the characters by which it is written. Another example is *shinpan* which can be associated with at least five common meanings: 1) 'judge, referee' or 'trial, decision, hearing'; 2) 'ordeal, divine judgment'; 3) 'intrusion, encroachment, criminal violence', 4) 'sales on credit' and 5) 'new edition'. Of course the context can help eliminate unlikely meanings and avoid misunderstandings, but when speaking it is sometimes necessary to refer to the written characters for clarification.

An example of an even more delicate problem is presented by the term *ishi* which, among its various meanings based on the ways it can be written, includes 'will/volition'. This is a word made of two characters. The two characters used in ordinary language are the *kanji* read as *i* and corresponding to 'mind, meaning' and *shi* corresponding to 'intent, ambition'. However, when the word 'will/volition' is used in the legal context, in expressions such as *ishi hyoji* ('manifestation of intention', as used for example in articles 91–101 of the civil code) it has the same pronunciation *ishi*, but the character *shi* is not the *shi* ('intent, ambition') used in the common language but is the *shi* corresponding to 'to think' (*kun* reading: *omou*).

Similar problems arise from other readings used distinctively in the legal terminology. For example, the term that translates as 'will/testament', according to the common rules and to the most frequent readings of its components, can be pronounced *igen*, but the correct reading in the legal context is *igon* or *yuigon*.

4.2 Recent neologisms

The golden age for the creation of current Japanese legal lexicon was the second half of the nineteenth century, when Japanese legal scholars had to create the words that were necessary to translate Western law. Much of the legal terminology was created before the end of the nineteenth century, but disputes over translation choices continued until the 1920s.

Even today, neologisms may be coined to cater for new linguistic needs. An important and recent example can be found in the introduction of a system of public participation in the criminal justice in the early 2000s. The Japanese language had a term to indicate the institution of the jury which was *baishin*. This term was coined in the Meiji period and was formed with two *kanji*. The first, *bai*, means to accompany a superior, and the second is the character *shin* of judgment, trial. The term is also used in the common parlance, thanks to Hollywood movies and foreign news. *Baishin* normally refers to the Anglo-American jury (Ortolani 2010).

Therefore, the term *baishin* is not completely foreign to the Japanese legal lexicon. In the 1920s, Japan introduced a system of public participation in criminal trials. Serious crimes were to be tried by a jury based loosely on the American model, with important modifications that limited its power and independence. The life of the *baishin* system was short and unfortunate because the number of defendants who opted for the jury trial declined year after year. In 1942, only one jury trial was held in the entire country, and in 1943 the system was suspended indefinitely. The jury trial was not restored in the immediate post-war period and attempts to revive it were unsuccessful, until the late 1990s.

An alternative concept to *baishin* is the word *sanshin*; a term that is used to indicate a type of popular participation in the trial. The second character '*shin*' is the same as in *baishin*, while the first is '*san*' meaning 'to participate, to visit'. *Sanshin* is the legal term closely related to the so-called "mixed jury" found in the French *Cour d'Assises*, or in the German or Scandinavian systems, where professional judges sit together with lay judges, to decide on questions of facts and deliberate on sentencing. A third common legal term is *juzai'in*, which literally means 'court of serious crimes' and it is the established translation of the French *Cour d'Assises* or of the Italian *Corte d'Assise*.

The debate over the reintroduction of juries in Japan flared up again in the 1980s, with the first concrete proposals put forward in the 1990s. Proposals fluctuated between introducing a '*baishin*', that is, a jury that would rule only on the facts and would give a verdict of guilty or not guilty, and introducing a '*sanshin (seido)*', or a mixed jury system, that would rule on questions of fact and on the sentencing. After a long tug-of-war between the Supreme Court of Japan, the Ministry of Legal Affairs and the Japan Federation of Bar Associations, the law passed in 2004 provided for a body of six lay assessors and three professional judges who would decide, by majority vote, on matters of fact and on sentencing. From this point of view, this institution would fit with the characteristics of the *sanshin* system, being closer to the civil law rather than the common law models.

The drafters of the act intended to dissociate this institution from its Anglo-American and continental antecedents. This Japanese "jury" is neither a *baishin* nor a "court of serious offenses" (the above-mentioned *juzai'in*), even if its authority is limited to the most serious offenses. During the drafting of the bill, the expression that would eventually be adopted by the act and that would then become the name of the current Japanese jury was found: this was "*saiban'in seido.*" While the second term *seido* (system, institution) poses no problems, the first, *saiban'in*, is a quasi-neologism in Japanese law.[19] It links the two *kanji* of 'judgment' (*saiban*), to the character '*in*' which means 'member'.

---

19 The Judge Impeachment Act uses the word *saiban'in* with a completely different meaning (Saibankan dangai ho, Act 137 of 1947). In this act, the *saiban'in* are the members of the parliament who

The adoption of a neologism to indicate the new institution initially created translation problems. It cannot be translated as 'Court of assizes', as such choice would overstate its connection with the European models, nor is it correct to translate it simply as 'jury', because this choice would pose a risk of confusion with the Anglo-American model. Therefore, the English literature on this topic employs different expressions such as 'mixed jury', 'quasi-jury', or borrows the original term *saiban'in* as a loanword in order to underline the Japanese peculiarity.

The choice of using the neologism *saiban-in* was partly aimed at avoiding confusion with the institution Japan introduced in the 1920s. On the other hand, it resulted from a clash between the voices, prevalently among lawyers, who called for the introduction of a jury inspired by the Anglo-American model, and those who strenuously resisted the introduction of any form of public participation in the criminal trial. The choice of adopting a mixed system in which professional judges sit next to ordinary citizens in deciding a criminal case represented a compromise. However, the creation of a neologism was surely also a symbolic gesture, as it suggested that the new system was an original institution, different from the American jury as well as from the European models, made to order for the Japanese society (Ortolani 2010).

4.3 *Gairaigo*: words from abroad

The creation of *kanji* neologisms is uncommon in modern Japan, in particular as far as specialized language is concerned. Most neologisms are based on transliteration of loanwords in *katakana* characters. In rare cases, Latin letters, sometimes side by side with Sino-Japanese characters may be used. These words are called *gairaigo,* which means "words coming from the outside". *Gairaigo* abound in everyday Japanese life. In fields more open to foreign influences like the arts, fashion, music and technology, *katakana* signs and words of foreign origin are a very common sight.

There have been attempts to regulate the use of foreign expressions in the Japanese language. For example, the Ministry of Health and Welfare in 1997 published guidelines (communication 89 of 10 September 1997) on the correct use of words in *katakana* in the documents of the Ministry. In 2005, the Ministry of Education published a short glossary of loanwords in *katakana* with their suggested equivalent term in Japanese *kanji*.[20] These documents did not prohibit the use of the *katakana* terms but simply promoted the use of the Japanese expressions in order to pursue greater clarity.

---

decide on the impeachment of judges. However, such usage is little known, even among legal professionals. In general jurists and laymen perceive the term *saiban'in* as a neologism.
20 The list is available at http://www.mext.go.jp/b_menu/hakusho/html/hpba200501/shiryo/017.htm

Despite these calls to the use of the Japanese language, *gairaigo* and *katakana* expressions made their way also into the legal field. The examples abound and may be divided into many categories as laws sometimes need to refer to non-technical terms of everyday life. For example, the City Planning Act (Act no. 100 of 1968) refers to concrete plants and golf courses using the *katakana* transliteration: *conkuriitopuranto* and *gorufukoosu*. Such everyday language expressions may be composed of two words, and may therefore mix a loanword and a Japanese term in *kanji*. For example, radio broadcast is called "*rajio* (in *katakana*) *hoso* (in *kanji*)"; the Japanese for videogame console puts together the false English loanword "*terebigeemu* (from 'televi(sion) game')" with the word "*ki*" ('machine, device'), to form the expression "*terebigeemuki*". Sometimes the *katakana* loanword appears in the very title of the act as in "*supootsu*" found in the Sport Promotion Act, "*enerugii*" in the Act on the Rational Use of Energy, "*supaikutaiyaa* (spike tires)" in the Studded Tires Regulation Act (Tajima 2001: 120).

In some cases the creation of new expressions in the legal lexicon is made through mixing loanwords and Japanese words. This is the case, for example, of the Japanese translation of "insider trading" rendered with the mixed expression "*insaidaa torihiki*." Next to the *kanji* term "*torihiki*," which means 'commercial transaction' is the transcription of the English term 'insider' which is expressed by "*insaidaa*" in *katakana*.[21] This makes the reference to the foreign expression very clear to legal scholars. The cost of this terminological choice is the loss of the information that the Sino-Japanese characters convey. The *katakana* transcription of foreign terms is just a sound without the meaning conveyed by *kanji*, and it tells nothing to those who are not already familiar with the original expression.

Mixed expressions can also contain Latin letters, as happens in the case of the act on domestic violence. Its official name is "*Haigusha kara no boryoku no boshi oyobi higaisha no hogo ni kansuru horitsu* (Act on the Prevention of Spousal Violence and the Protection of Victims)" which is regularly referred to as "*DV boshiho*" where DV is the abbreviation of the English expression 'domestic violence'.

Another pattern of creating Japanese equivalents of foreign expressions entails abbreviating and rearranging the original expression, preferably into terms of four syllables, which present a metric and musicality familiar to the Japanese ear. For example, this is the case for the word *sekuhara*, which corresponds to 'sexual harassment'. The expression has a wide meaning and includes cases of criminal offense and lighter cases where the offending party is liable only for a monetary compensation based on tort. Recently a series of words linked to various types of harassment have been created with the suffix "*–hara*": *pawahara* (power harassment) that is harassment by superiors at the workplace, *akahara* (academic harassment) for cases occurring

---

21 Molteni (2001) has analyzed many examples of neolgisms and loanwords in the field of economics.

between students and professors, or even *aruhara*, the contraction of 'alcohol harassment', that is inciting others to binge drink.

In some cases, the *katakana* loanword is introduced in the legislation as a consequence of a change of the language spoken in the common parlance. For example, Article 73 of the National Public Service Act listed, among the programs to improve the efficiency of the public service, actions in the area of recreation for public officials. In the original version of the law, enacted in 1947, the expression used was made with four *kanji*: *genki kaifuku*. When the law was amended in 1965, the expression was considered to be out of touch with modern parlance and therefore it was substituted with a *katakana* loanword: *rikurieeshon* (Tajima 2001: 122).

In general, the use of *katakana* or the Latin alphabet, along with the practice of abbreviating or contracting foreign terms achieves three effects. First, it masks the content and softens the impact of terms that could be uncomfortable or embarrassing for the speaker or for the audience. This is clearly the case of *DV* or *sekuhara*. Texts or discourses containing expressions such as 'domestic violence' or 'spousal abuse', 'rape', especially if expressed in *kanji*, may be perceived as too heavy or embarrassing both for the source and for the receiver of the communication.[22] The use of euphemistical loanwords aims at avoiding these problems by an anesthetization of the discourse.

The second effect of this use of loanwords is the increase in the obscure nature of the discourse. Due to the speed with which the Japanese language has evolved and engulfed foreign expressions, it is not always easy to figure out and trace back the original inspiration behind a term in *katakana* or a *romaji* abbreviation, especially when those expressions belong to specialized languages. The original terms are clear only to persons belonging to a certain group or with expertise in the relevant area who are familiar with the meaning behind the abbreviation or new *katakana* term.[23]

Finally, the use of *katakana* reveals very clearly the foreign models of influence. The analysis of the origins of the loanwords reveals what models scholars are using as a reference at a certain point in time. For example, the terminology related to environmental damage and pollution problems include Sino-Japanese terms in *kanji*, as well as terms in *katakana*. Each notion conveys different nuances of meaning and reveals different origins. Thus, the term *kogai*, composed of two Sino-Japanese characters, indicates widespread environmental damage, generally related to commercial activities, and a corresponding protection which is not only of a private nature but also involves aspects of public law. The doctrine of *kogai* developed in Japan in the twentieth century, as a response to problems of environmental pollution, environmental damage and mass tort.

---

22 A common expression in *kanji* for "domestic violence" is *kateinai boryoku*, literally "violence in (within) the family". A common *kanji* equivalent of "rape", and the term used to define the crime of rape in the Penal code (art. 177) is *"gokan"*.
23 For a general discussion of the functions of Japanese Anglicisms, see Scherling (2012: 123–136).

Being an original development, the translation of the term *kogai* in English or other languages poses some problems: sometimes it can be translated as environmental pollution, sometimes as mass pollution, sometimes mass tort or in other more specific contexts with even more specific expressions, such as noise pollution in case of "airport *kogai*". In the same field, the *katakana* terms *"immisshon"* and *"nyuusansu"* refer respectively to the German word *"immission"* and the English "nuisance", revealing the source of the doctrinal construction taken as example. Besides these expressions, '*kinrin bogai*' is the more or less literal translation of the French '*troubles de voisinage*'. '*Kankyo higai*' and '*kankyo songai*' are functional translations of the expression 'environmental damage' as it emerged in Western legal scholarship since the 1970s.

Thus, through the choice of terminology, the Japanese jurist implicitly transmits a signal of affiliation to a school of thought and a foreign model of prestige.

5 Japanese law translated

During the allied occupation of Japan after the World War II, newly promulgated acts and other legal documents were published in the *Official Gazette of Japan* in English and Japanese. With the end of the occupation in 1952, as a consequence of the full sovereignty regained by Japan, new statutes and other legal texts were published in the *Official Gazette* only in the Japanese language.[24]

In 1956, the private publisher *Eibun-Horei-Sha* started publishing English translations of Japanese statutes. In 2008, the entire collection of English translations included some 330 translations of Japanese laws, published in binders and updated when necessary. Until the mid 2000s, the collection of *Eibun-Horei-Sha* has been the largest collection of English translations of Japanese law.

In the early 2000s, the Japanese government embarked on an ambitious program to modernize and improve the transparency of the legal system (Kashiwagi 2007). Action was taken to focus on the translation of Japanese laws and regulations in foreign language and in particular in English, in order to promote international trade, foreign investment, and general knowledge of the Japanese legal system abroad.

By the end of 2004, the Cabinet Office established the "Study Council for Promoting Translation of Japanese Laws and Regulations into Foreign Languages", which held its first meeting on 2 February 2005. The mission of the council involved discussing numerous points:
"(i) the basic principles of translation,
(ii) how translation should be promoted (what laws and regulations are to be translated, and the method of translation),

---

24 From the homepage of *Eibun-Horei-Sha*, https://www.eibun-horei-sha.co.jp/inf.php?v_id=70

(iii) development of a framework for facilitating access to the translations of laws and regulations, and
(iv) development of a framework for continuous maintenance of the translations, such as responding to legal amendments, with respect to development of the foundation for promoting the translation of Japanese laws and regulations into foreign languages. At the same time, the Study Council would
(v) compile a standard bilingual dictionary [...] and
(vi) translate some of the laws and regulations in the later-mentioned working group" (Study Council 2006: 2).

In 2009, the Ministry of Legal Affairs launched the Japanese Law Translation Database System, a website that publishes English translations of Japan's most important statutes and the Standard Legal Terms Dictionary, which is periodically updated (Takeda & Sekine 2014: 226). Any person can freely access and download English translations of statutes as well as the legal dictionary, and search keywords in context. A disclaimer warns the users that all translations are unofficial and are to be used solely as reference materials, and that the government of Japan is not responsible for the accuracy of the translation.[25] In general, the quality of the translations is acceptable though mistakes have been pointed out.[26]

Among the translated acts are the Antitrust Act, the Companies Act, the Court Act, the Civil code, the Code of Civil Procedure, the Code of Criminal Procedure, the Penal Code, the State Redress Act and many more.[27] Another section of the website offers a list of English translations of the names of government bodies, ministry agencies, departments and positions. These translations are submitted by ministries themselves and are updated periodically. The number of acts, ordinances and other official documents translated as of April 2018 was more than 700.

The website of the Supreme Court of Japan also offers translations of some of its judgments. In this case too the usual disclaimer, warning readers that translations are not official, appears in the search page: "All of the translations of judgments on this

---

25 See http://www.japaneselawtranslation.go.jp/
26 Takeda and Sekine (2014: 228) classify the problems of the into three categories: translation errors, careless mistakes, and inconsistent translations. The first mistakes are often due to the translator's lack of familiarity with the specificity of legal language, while careless mistakes (e.g. those related to numbering format) and lack of consistency in the terminology can be ascribed to the fact that agencies and ministries in the government outsource the translation of the laws in the area of their competence to different private contractors.
27 The most frequently accessed laws are those related to business and finance, such as the Commodity Exchange Act, the Companies Act, the Civil Rehabilitation Act, and the Banking Act (Takeda and Sekine 2014: 228) and the Small and Medium-Sized Enterprise Cooperatives Act.

website are unofficial. The Supreme Court of Japan assumes no responsibility for the accuracy of the translations.[28]"

6 Conclusion

What general conclusions about the Japanese legal system can a comparative law scholar draw from the analysis of the Japanese legal language? The first phenomenon worth mentioning is the evolution of the treasure box effect associated with the Japanese words coined as translations of foreign legal terms. In the Meiji period, the old *kanji* used in a creative manner had a meaning behind their signifier that only the initiated could decipher. However, since the *kanji* neologisms were, at first sight, graphically no different from other words, they blended in with the rest of the language. Their aspect was that of words that belonged naturally to the Japanese language.

Since Japan was the first East Asian country to modernize its legal system and its jurisprudence, neighbouring countries were eager to replicate its success and sent their students to the archipelago to study law. The neologisms created by the Japanese therefore spread into the region, being adopted also in the modern Chinese legal language. In this way, the Chinese characters used as components of the neologisms of the Japanese legal science returned on the continent that they left several centuries before, bearing new meanings and new knowledge.

In modern times, *kanji* neologisms have become rarer and rarer. Neologisms are regularly made using *katakana* signs. The use of *katakana* makes explicit the presence of a foreign word as the source of the notion. *Katakana* may therefore work as an explicit signal, alerting the reader that the word comes from the outside, and that an original meaning should be looked for into the legal system of origin.

However, this is not the only effect of the use of *katakana* in Japanese. In some instances, instead of helping the reader it may work, paradoxically, in the opposite direction, as a strategy to obfuscate the meaning of a word, making it accessible only to specialists. In this case, the choice of using *katakana* may create terms with different meanings for the non-initiated reader who receives a superficial, sometimes misleading message, while the specialists understands the deeper meaning with reference to the original word and concept behind the *kana*.

For the comparative law scholar analysing legal transplants and influences between legal models, the information carried by *katakana* can be very important, as it lays bare the origins of a word, and helps track its system of provenance and the legal framework and doctrines surrounding it. At the same time, the success of *katakana* may undermine the prestige of Japanese legal science, since with *katakana*

---

28 http://www.courts.go.jp/app/hanrei_en/search?

neologisms the foreign origin of the words and of the related doctrines is revealed, and makes it easier to bypass the Japanese sources.

References

Agency for cultural affairs. 2010. Government of Japan, *Joyo kanjihyo* (*Kanji* for regular use), http://www.bunka.go.jp/kokugo_nihongo/sisaku/joho/joho/kijun/naikaku/kanji/index.html.
Beyer, Vicki & Keld Conradsen. 1995. Translating Japanese legal documents into English: A short course. In Marshall Morris (ed.), *Translation and the law* (American Translators Association Scholarly Monograph Series – Volume VIII 1995), 145–177. Amsterdam & Philadelphia: John Benjamins.
Burgess, Chris. 2012. 'It's better if they speak broken Japanese': Language as a pathway or an obstacle to citizenship in Japan? In Nanette Gottlieb (ed.), *Language and citizenship in Japan*, 37–57. New York and Abingdon: Routledge.
Coulmas, Florian. 1991. *The writing systems of the world*. Oxford, UK and Cambridge, MA: Blackwell.
Frellesvig, Bjarke. 2010. *A history of the Japanese language*. Cambridge: Cambridge University Press.
Fujii, Yasunari. 2013. The translation of legal agreements and contracts from Japanese into English: The case for a free approach. *Babel* 59(4). 421–444.
Gary F. Simons and Charles D. Fennig (eds.). 2018. *Ethnologue: Languages of the World, Twenty-first edition*. Dallas: SIL International. http://www.ethnologue.com.
Gottlieb, Nanette. 2012. Language, citizenship and identity in Japan. In Nanette Gottlieb (ed.), *Language and citizenship in Japan*, 1–18. New York and Abingdon : Routledge.
Griolet, Pascal. 1985. *La modernisation du Japon et la réforme de son écriture*. Publications orientalistes de France.
Griolet, Pascal. 2002. Langue, écriture et modernité, in Cipango. n. hors-série, 2002.
Hasegawa, Yoko. 2015. *Japanese – a linguistic introduction*. Cambridge: Cambridge University Press.
Hayashi, Ooki & Jun'ichi Aomi (ed.). 1981. *Ho to nihongo* [Law and Japanese language]. Tokyo: Yuhikaku.
Heinrich, Patrick. 2007. The debate on English as an official language in Japan. In Florian Coulmas (ed.), *Language regimes in transformation: future prospects for German and Japanese in science, economy, and politics*. Berlin: Mouton de Gruyter.
Henderson, Dan Fenno. 1983. Japanese law in English: some thoughts on scope and method. *Vanderbilt Journal of Transnational Law* 16. 601–620.
Hoshino, Eiichi; Koya Matsuo; Shizuo Mizutani & Machi Tawara. 1992. *Zadankai – Horitsu no gendaigoka wo megutte* [Round table – On the linguistic modernization of legal language] in Jurisuto (994). 10–29.
Howland, Douglas. 2002. *Translating the west: language and political reason in nineteenth-century Japan*. Honolulu: University of Hawai'i Press.
Kagayama, Shigeru. 1990a. *Minpo zaisanhen no kogoka soan (shian)* 1 [Draft for the transformation in vernacular language of the books on patrimonial rights of the Civil code (private proposal) 1] in Osaka hogaku (155). 185–244.
Kagayama, Shigeru. 1990b *Minpo zaisanhen no kogoka soan (shian)* 2 [Draft for the transformation in vernacular language of the books on patrimonial rights of the Civil code (private proposal) 2] in Osaka hogaku (156). 495–574.

Kashiwagi, Noboru. 2007. Translation of Japanese statutes into English. *Journal of Japanese Law* 23. 221–226.
Lawson, Carol. 2007. Found in translation: The 'transparency of Japanese law project' in context. *Journal of Japanese Law* 24. 187–199.
Lee, Yeonsuk. 2010. *The ideology of Kokugo*. Honolulu: University of Hawai'i Press.
Levy, Indra (ed.). 2011. *Translation in Modern Japan*. London and New York: Routledge.
Loveday, Leo J. 1996. *Language contact in Japan: a socio-linguistic history*. Oxford: New York: Clarendon Press.
Irwin, Mark. 2011. *Loanwords in Japanese*. Amsterdam: John Benjamins.
Maejima, Hisoka. 1899. *Kokuji kokubun kairyo kengisho*, Shueikai, Tokyo. Electronic copy at the National Diet Library Digital Collection http://dl.ndl.go.jp/info:ndljp/pid/992770
Maher, John C. & Kyoko Yashiro (eds.). 1995. *Multilingual Japan*. Exeter: Short Run Press.
Maher, John C. & Yumiko Kawanishi. 1995. On being there: Koreans in Japan, in John C., Maher and Kyoko Yashiro (eds.), *Multilingual Japan*, 87–101. Exeter: Short Run Press.
Maher, John C. 1995. The *Kakyo*: Chinese in Japan. In John C. Maher and Kyoko Yashiro (eds.), *Multilingual Japan*, 125–138. Exeter: Short Run Press.
Molteni, Corrado. 2001. *Analisi dei nuovi termini economici relativi alle bolle speculative e alle crisi finanziarie* [Analysis of the new terms in economics related to speculative bubbles and financial crises,] in *Il Giappone verso il terzo millennio: radici e prospettive: Atti del XXIII Convegno di Studi sul Giappone*. Repubblica di San Marino, 23–25 settembre 1999, Rimini, Il Cerchio.
Moseley, Christopher (ed.). 2010. *Atlas of the world's languages in danger, 3rd edn.* Paris: UNESCO Publishing. http://www.unesco.org/culture/en/endangeredlanguages/atlas
Nakane, Ikuko. 2012. Language rights of non-Japanese defendants in Japanese criminal courts. In Nanette Gottlieb (ed.), *Language and citizenship in Japan*, 155–174. New York and Abingdon: Routledge.
Nakata, Hiroyasu. 2005. *Minpoten no gendaigoka* [The linguistic modernization of the Civil code] in Juristo 1283. 86.
Ortolani, Andrea. 2010. Reflections on citizen participation in criminal justice in Japan: jury, saiban'in system and legal reform. *Journal of Japanese Law* 15. 153–176.
Saito, Akio. 2006. *Horitsu to kokugo – Nihongo. Rippo to chosa* 2006/7. 257.
Scherling, Johannes. 2012. *Japanizing English: anglicism and their impact on Japanese*. Tübingen: Narr.
Seeley, Christopher. 2000. *A history of writing in Japan*. Honolulu: University of Hawai'i Press.
Seifu tokei no sogo madoguchi [Portal site of official statistics of Japan)]. 2017. *Zairyu gaikokujin tokei* 17-06-01-2 (Statistics on foreign residents as of June 2017). http://www.e-stat.go.jp/SG1/estat/List.do?lid=000001196143 (accessed 5 May 2018).
Shibatani, Masayoshi. 1990. *The languages of Japan*. Cambridge: Cambridge University Press.
Shibatani, Masayoshi. 2009. Japanese. In Bernard Comrie (ed.) *The world's major languages* (2nd edn.). London and New York: Routledge.
Somusho tokeikyoku [Statistics Bureau of the Ministry of Internal Affairs and Communications]. 2015. Jinko suikei Heisei 27 nen 11 gatsu ho (Population estimates, November 2015 report). http://www.stat.go.jp/data/jinsui/pdf/201511.pdf (accessed 5 February, 2016)
Takeda, Kayoko & Yasuhiro Sekine. 2014. Translation of Japanese laws and regulations. In Le Cheng, King Kui Sin & Anne Wagner (eds.), *The Ashgate handbook of legal translation*, 223–236. Farnham: Ashgate.
Tamura, Suzuko. 2000. *The Ainu language*. Tokyo: Sanseido.

The Japan Foundation. 2017. *Survey report on Japanese-language education abroad 2015*. Tokyo: The Japan Foundation.

Tsuda, Takeyuki. 2003. *Strangers in the ethnic homeland: Japanese Brazilian return migration in transnational perspective*. New York: Columbia University Press.

Tsujimura, Natsuko. 2014. *An introduction to Japanese linguistics* (3rd edn.). Chichester: John Wiley & Sons.

Biographical notes

Tommaso Agnoloni received a master's degree in Computer Science Engineering from the University of Florence in 1998 and PhD in Systems Engineering and Computer Science in 2002 at the Computer Science Department (DSI), University of Florence. In 2005 he joined the Italian National Research Council at the Institute of Legal Information Theory and Technologies (CNR-ITTIG), where currently he is a Researcher. He is responsible for scientific collaborations with the Italian Senate, Ministry of Justice, Supreme Court of Cassation. He has been involved in several national and European projects on eGovernment, eJustice, eParticipation. He is lecturer in Semantic Resources for Legal Texts Annotation at the International Summer School LEX on Legislative XML and for the joint doctoral programme LAST-JD. He his coordinator of the development and author of several software projects including xmLegesEditor an open source visual XML editor for the adoption of legal national standards (www.xmleges.org). Currently he is involved in the implementation of open standards, annotation vocabularies and information extraction tools for the interconnection of open legal datasets towards the creation of a linked legal data cloud.

Roberta Aluffi is Associate Professor of Comparative Law at the Law department of the University of Turin. Her main research interests focus on family law in the Arab Countries, and the challenges faced by the European legal systems in dealing with Islamic normativity.

Jennifer Davis is a lawyer and member of the Centre for Intellectual Property and Information Law at the Faculty of Law, University of Cambridge, as well as an Emeritus Fellow of Wolfson College Cambridge. Before joining the Cambridge Law Faculty, she practiced in the field of intellectual property litigation. She has lectured and published on a number of areas of intellectual property law, including the law relating to confidence and privacy and the international protection of intellectual property, but has a particular interest in trade marks and unfair competition. An influential early example of her work on trade marks is "Locating the average consumer: his judicial origins, intellectual influences and current role in European trade mark law" (2005) *Intellectual Property Quarterly*, Issue 2. A number of her publications have adopted an interdisciplinary approach, including *Trade Marks and Brands* (Cambridge University Press 2008) and *Copyright and Piracy* (Cambridge University Press 2010), both co-edited with Lionel Bently and Jane Ginsburg.

Alan Durant is Professor of Communication in the School of Law at Middlesex University, London. In the course of his career, he has held chairs in two UK English departments, a university business school, and a law school, and was formerly Head of English at Goldsmiths' College, University of London, and previously Director of the Programme in Literary Linguistics, University of Strathclyde. Recent publications include a collection of essays on topics in law, linguistics and anthropology (co-edited with Janny HC Leung), *Meaning and Power in the Language of Law* (Cambridge University Press 2018) and the monograph *Meaning in the Media: Discourse, Controversy and Debate* (Cambridge University Press 2010). He is also co-author of the interdisciplinary textbooks *Language and Law* (co-written with Janny HC Leung, Routledge 2016) and *Language and Media* (co-written with Marina Lambrou, Routledge 2009).

Sabine Ehrhardt studied English and German linguistics at the University of Jena/Germany. She received a bachelor's degree in English for International Business from the University of Central Lancashire and in 1999 completed her master's degree in English and German Linguistics. She finished her PhD thesis on the use of dialogue forms in language teaching in Renaissance England and graduated as Dr. phil. at the University of Jena in 2004. In 2004 Sabine joined the Forensic

Science Institute of the German Bundeskriminalamt (BKA)in Wiesbaden. Since then she is an expert for Forensic Linguistics, analyzing texts of disputed authorship on request of the German police, prosecution and the courts. Besides her expert work, she lectured on forensic linguistics at the University of Frankfurt from 2009 to 2011. In 2013, Sabine became the head of the forensic linguistics department at the BKA. She is responsible for quality management within the forensic linguistics department and she works as auditor within the BKA Forensic Science Institute. To complement her expert wort, she undertakes research on related topics such as empirical studies on linguistic manipulation, typologies of forensically relevant texts and quality assurance measures in forensic linguistics. Lately, her research interest shifted to automated approaches to linguistic analyses and she carried out several research projects on automatic text comparison systems.

Silvia Ferreri is full professor of Comparative Law at the Law Department, University of Turin, Italy. Previously she held academic positions at the Università Bocconi, in Milan; Università Ca' Foscari in Venice; and Università Amedeo Avogadro, Eastern Piedmont, in Alessandria. She has cooperated in many international research projects, notably in connection with the process of integration within the European Union (Acquis Group – European Research Group on Existing EC Private Law, "Acquis group. Org"). She was visiting professor at Louisiana State University Law School (2008) and in London within the CTLS, the international program run by Georgetown University together with several other universities belonging to different countries. She is an "expert linguist" of the REI (network for the excellence of institutional Italian, EU Commission, DGT, Italian Department). She is a member of the SIRD (Società Italiana Ricerca in Diritto Comparato), the French-based Association Henri Capitant des amis de la culture française, as well as member of the International Academy of Comparative Law and fellow of ELI (European Law Institute).

Domenico Francavilla is Associate Professor of Comparative Law at the Department of Law, University of Torino, where he teaches Comparative Legal Systems and Indian law. He holds a Laurea in Giurisprudenza (Catholic University, Milan) and a PhD in Legal Theory (University of Padova). He was Early Career Visiting Fellow at the Department of Law, Queen Mary University of London, and a Research Associate at the School of Law at SOAS. His main areas of interest are Indian law, Hindu law, law and culture and methodology of comparative law. He has published two books (*The Roots of Hindu Jurisprudence*, Corpus Iuris Sanscriticum et Fontes Iuris Asia Meridianae et Centralis, Torino, 2006; *Il diritto nell'India contemporanea. Sistemi tradizionali, modelli occidentali e globalizzazione*, Giappichelli, Torino, 2010) and several articles in the field of comparative law. He also contributed to the *OUP Encyclopedia of Legal History* and *Sage Encyclopedia of Law and Society*.

Chris Heffer is Director of MA Programmes, including the MA in Forensic Linguistics, in the Centre for Language and Communication Research at Cardiff University and co-founder of Cardiff Language and Law (CaLL). He has published articles in linguistic and legal journals on various theoretical and communicational aspects of the trial process and is the author of *The Language of Jury Trial: A Corpus-aided Analysis of Legal-Lay Discourse* (Palgrave 2005), Simulating Truth: Lying, Bullshit and the Analysis of Untruthfulness (Oxford University Press 2018) and co-editor of *Legal-Lay Communication: Textual Travels in the Law* (Oxford University Press 2013). He has a particular interest in both forensic narrative and forensic voice. He sits on the Editorial Board of the OUP Language and Law series.

Georgina Heydon is an Associate Professor of Criminology and Justice Studies at the Royal Melbourne Institute of Technology (RMIT University) and President of the International Association of Forensic Linguists. Her work focuses on the discourse and conversational structures of police interviews and other forms of crime reporting and she is an internationally recognised expert in the field of forensic linguistics and investigative interviewing. Prof Heydon has published numerous academic papers and a book, 'The Language of Police Interviewing: A Critical Analysis'

(2005, Palgrave Macmillan), on the topic of interviewing and information. As a forensic linguist, she provides expert evidence on authorship attribution, threat identification and in commercial trademark cases. She has delivered interviewing training and advice to police and legal professionals in Australia, Sweden, Belgium, Indonesia, Mozambique and Canada, and to members of Australian judicial colleges and tribunals as well as lawyers and corporate clients.

Michael Jessen works as expert for forensic speech and audio analysis at the National Forensic Science Institute of the German Bundeskriminalamt (BKA) in Wiesbaden since 2001. He received his MA in linguistics from Universität Bielefeld, Germany, in 1989 and his PhD in linguistics from Cornell University in 1996. From 1993 until 2001 he was lecturer for phonetics and linguistics at the Natural Language Processing Department of Universität Stuttgart, Germany. In 1998/99 he carried out post-doctoral research on the phonetics of Xhosa at the Research Unit for Experimental Phonology of University of Stellenbosch, South Africa. He was chair of an EU-funded research project on forensic voice comparison in 2008 to 2010. Since 2009 he is co-editor of the *International Journal of Speech, Language and the Law*. He is one of the main authors of *Methodological guidelines for best practice in forensic semiautomatic and automatic speaker recognition* [2015] – the first international guideline on Likelihood Ratio-based forensic voice comparison. His current research focuses on exploring the speaker discriminatory performance of automatic speaker recognition systems under forensically realistic conditions and how the results from these systems complement information derived from phonetic/linguistic analysis.

Janny HC Leung is Associate Professor of English and Programme Director of Law and Literary Studies (BA & LLB) at The University of Hong Kong. She obtained her M Phil and PhD in English and Applied Linguistics from the University of Cambridge, an LLB from the University of London, and an LLM from Yale Law School. In 2013–2014, she was a Visiting Scholar at the Harvard Yenching Institute, Harvard University. Her current research interest lies in the interdisciplinary area of language and law, with a particular focus on challenges, ideologies and paradoxes in multilingual legal practice. She has written about language rights, legal interpretation, unrepresented litigation, courtroom discourse, legal translation, representations of law in the media, and the evolution of law in the modern communication environment. Her articles have appeared in journals including *Semiotica, International Journal of Speech, Language and Law, Journal of Legal Pluralism, Journal of Multilingual and Multicultural Development, International Journal of the Semiotics of Law, Law and Humanities,* and *Law Text Culture.* With Alan Durant, she has co-authored the book *Language and Law: A Resource Book for Students* (Routledge 2016) and co-edited the volume *Meaning and Power in the Language of Law* (Cambridge University Press 2017). Her monograph, entitled *Shallow Equality and Symbolic Jurisprudence in Multilingual Legal Orders*, is forthcoming with Oxford University Press (2018).

Lucia Morra lectures on Logic and Philosophy of Science at the School of Medicine of the University of Turin. Her research revolves around the pragmatics of legal linguistic practices; she wrote extensively on legal metaphors and their role in legal interpretation, and together with Barbara Pasa edited a collection of essays on legal translation (*Translating the DCFR and Drafting the CESL: A Pragmatic Perspective,* Sellier 2014). More recently she worked on the functions of implicatures and presuppositions in legal texts, and in 2015 edited with Barbara Pasa Questioni di genere nel diritto. Impliciti e crittotipi (Giappichelli 2015), a collection of essays in which pragmatic tools for the extraction of implicit information are applied to gender issues.

Andrea Ortolani is Assistant Professor at the Faculty of law, Keio University (Tokyo). He graduated in law from the University of Torino in 2001 and earned a PhD in comparative private law at the University of Trento in 2005 with a dissertation on the reception of Western law and legal jargon in

Japan. He lives in Tokyo since 2003, and he earned a PhD in law at the University of Tokyo in 2017, with a dissertation on the assignment of contract in Italy and Japan. His current research focuses on legal transplants in the Japanese legal system. He has also written on the introduction of the mixed jury system in Japan (the *saiban'in* trial). He is co-founder and the current secretary of the Italo-Japanese Association for Comparative Law.

Barbara Pasa is Associate Professor of Comparative Private Law at the Iuav University of Venice, Department of Design and Planning in Complex Environments. She is research fellow at the SSST, an institution of excellence and higher education for the University of Turin, where she teaches Law, Politics and Globalization. Her research interests lie in the field of comparative law, European private law, contract law and intellectual property rights, legal translation, and cultural and linguistic pluralism.

Richard Powell has held the post of professor at Nihon University in Tokyo for over a decade, where he teaches courses on English language and on language and human rights. He has a BA in history from Cambridge University, an MSc in politics from London University's SOAS, an MA in linguistics from Macquarie University, and a PhD in education and law from Melbourne University, and he passed the England and Wales Solicitor's Final Examination after spending several years as a legal clerk and trainee solicitor working in criminal and civil rights law. Richard's research interests include language and law, forensic linguistics, legal education, bilingualism, language planning and cross-cultural pragmatics. He has written several books, book chapters and articles in these areas and his book entitled *Language choice in postcolonial law: Lessons from Malaysia* is due to be published by Springer in 2018. He frequently conducts research in East Asia (especially Japan), Southeast Asia (especially Malaysia), South Asia and East Africa and regularly gives conference presentations at the International Association of Forensic Linguists, the Law and Society Association and the Asian Law and Society Association. Richard sits on the editorial committee of a number of international journals and is the book review editor of the *International Journal of Speech, Language and the Law* and a director and steering committee member of the Japan Association of Law and Language. He is also a founding member of the Malaysian Association of Applied Linguistics.

Peter Robson has an LLB from St. Andrews University and a PhD from Strathclyde University. He is a solicitor and sits as a judge in the Appeals Services dealing with disability issues. He has been Professor of Social Welfare Law in the University of Strathclyde since 1992. He works and advises on housing law and is the author of *Homelessness and the Law* (3rd edn. 1996), *Housing Law in Scotland* (2010) and *Residential Tenancies* (3rd edn 2012). He has written widely on law, film and television in journals and edited collections including co-editing *Law and Film* (with Stefan Machura) in 2001. His most recent film work (with Steve Greenfield and Guy Osborn) *Film and the Law: The Cinema of Justice* was published in 2010 and updates the influential 1st edition. He is co-editor with Jessica Silbey of *Law and Justice on the Small Screen* (2012). He is the author of essays on British lawyers on TV and is co-editor with Jennifer Schulz and author of a global TV lawyers project – *A Transnational Study of Law and Justice on TV* (2016). His latest work is on the development of Scottish Court architecture, funded by the Royal Society of Edinburgh. The book, with Johnny Rodger, is entitled *The Spaces of Justice: The Architecture of the Scottish Court* (Fairleigh Dickinson 2018).

Roger W. Shuy, Distinguished Research Professor of Linguistics, Emeritus, Georgetown University, in 1968 founded and headed Georgetown's Sociolinguistics program and served a term as chair of Georgetown's Department of Linguistics. Professor Shuy was one of the co-founders of The American Association of Applied Linguistics in which he has served as a term as its president and has received its Award for Distinguished Scholarship. He also co-founded the sociolinguistics conference, New Ways of Analyzing Variation, where in 2001 he received its award for Distinguished Service and Pioneering Efforts in Sociolinguistics. In 2009 he was elected Fellow of the Linguistic Society of America where he also was awarded the Victoria Fromkin Distinguished Service Award in 2017. He has published over 200 articles in various academic journals along with 24 books about sociolinguistics and 15 about language and law. His books in the area of language and law include: *Language Crimes: The Use and Abuse of Language Evidence in the Courtroom* (1993), *The Language of Confession, Interrogation and Deception* (1996), *Bureaucratic Language in Government and Business* (1998), *Linguistic Battles in Trademark Disputes* (2002), *Creating Language Crimes: How Law Enforcement Uses (and Misuses) Language* (2005), *Linguistics in the Courtroom: A Practical Guide* (2006), *Fighting Over Words: Language in Civil Law Cases* (2008), *The Language of Defamation Cases* (2010), *The Language of Perjury Cases* (2011), *The Language of Sexual Misconduct Cases* (2012), *The Language of Bribery Cases* (2013), *The Language of Murder Cases* (2014), *Speaking of Language and Law* [co-edited with Lawrence Solan and Janet Ainsworth] 2015), *The Language of Fraud Cases* (2016), *Deceptive Ambiguity by Police and Prosecutors* (2017).

Lawrence M. Solan is the Don Forchelli Professor of Law and Director of the Center for the Study of Law, Language and Cognition, and Director of Graduate Education at Brooklyn Law School. He holds a PhD in Linguistics from the University of Massachusetts and a JD from Harvard Law School. Much of his writing is about the interpretation of statutes and contracts. His books include *The Language of Judges*, *Speaking of Crime* (with Peter Tiersma) and *The Language of Statutes: Laws and their Interpretation*, all published by the University of Chicago Press. He and Peter Tiersma co-edited *The Oxford Handbook of Language and Law* (2012), and he co-edited the 2015 volume, *Speaking of Language and Law: Conversations on the Work of Peter Tiersma*, with Janet Ainsworth and Roger Shuy, also published by Oxford. Solan has been a visiting professor at the Yale Law School, and in the Psychology Department and Humanities Council at Princeton University.

Marina Timoteo is full professor of Comparative Private Law at the Department of Legal Studies, University of Bologna, where she also teaches Asian Countries Law and Law and Business in China. She has been visiting professor at the Renmin University and Beijing University (Beijing, China) and Chuo University (Tokyo, Japan). Since 2015 she is the Director of the Italian University Consortium AlmaLaurea and since 2012 she is an internal member of the Board of Directors of the University of Bologna. She is one of the founding members of the European Association for Chinese Law Studies (ECLS) and she is member of the International Academy of Comparative Law and the board of the *Società Italiana per la Ricerca nel Diritto Comparato* (Italian Association for research in Comparative Law). She has been involved in several EU-China projects of legal cooperation, having being appointed in 2010 and 2011 as senior expert for the *"EU-China Project for the Protection of Intellectual Property Rights/IPR 2"* and, since 2008, is a delegate of the University of Bologna at the General Assembly of the China-Europe School of Law. She has written 3 monographs, more than 50 articles and papers and is the founder of the book series Chinese law in action published by Bononia University Press.

Giulia Venturi received a PhD in Computational Linguistics from the University of Torino (Italy) in 2011 with a dissertation entitled "Language and law: a computational linguistics perspective" aimed at detecting and measuring differences and similarities between the language of law and the ordinary language with a view to adapt Natural Language Processing (NLP) techniques to the peculiarities of legal language. She currently has a Postdoctoral Fellowship at the Institute of Computational Linguistics "Antonio Zampolli" (ILC) of the National Research Council (CNR) in Pisa and she is member of the ItaliaNLP Laboratory (www.italianlp.it). Her main research interests include the extraction of linguistic and extra-linguistic knowledge from domain-specific corpora and its organization into Knowledge Organization Systems such as domain ontologies or knowledge graphs with a specific view to the semantic processing of legal texts. She is currently involved in the development of NLP-based methodologies to assess the level of linguistic complexity and readability across different textual genres and domains. In line with her interests in the study of sublanguages, she is part of a wide project aimed at exploiting state-of-the-art NLP tools and Information Extraction technologies to classify, organize and semantically index the content of different typologies of documents which are relevant in the educational domain.

Christopher Williams is full professor of English at the Department of Law of the University of Foggia, Italy, where he is also Head of the University Language Centre. His main area of research is in legal English, in particular with reference to the changes that have taken place in legal English as a result of the pressure of the Plain language movement. His publications include the volume *Tradition and Change in Legal English: Verbal Constructions in Prescriptive Texts* (Peter Lang 2005) as well as a number of articles including publications that have appeared in *Statute Law Review* (2008), *Modality in English: Theory and Description* (Mouton De Gruyter 2009), *The Verb Phrase in English: Investigating Recent Language Change with Corpora* (Cambridge University Press 2013), *Canadian Journal of Linguistics* (2013), *Interpersonality in Legal Genres* (Peter Lang 2014), *ASp* (2016) and *Alicante Journal of English Studies* (2016). He is Chief Editor of the journal *ESP Across Cultures*.

Index

Accommodation 269–271, 276, 281
Account 201–203, 209, 210, 212, 213, 215
Adjacency pairs 206
Admissibility 171, 182, 196, 202–204, 215–216, 257, 266, 274, 296
Adversarial 256, 257, 261, 264, 346
Ambiguity 36, 42, 46, 48, 70, 83, 96, 102, 157, 172, 324, 385, 394, 409, 412
Animating 269, 271
Anonymity 169, 190, 191
AnoText corpus 190–195
Argumentation 109–111, 113, 146, 149–150, 257, 265, 266
Articulation rate 221–226, 228, 230
Attic oration 257, 265
Auditory voice quality 225– 226, 228, 230
Authentic language 374, 379, 380, 382, 385, 394
Authorship/authorizing 265, 269, 270, 275, 281
– attribution 169–171, 173, 177, 180, 184, 185, 195
– profiling 169, 173, 174–176
Automated approach 169, 178, 182, 184–186, 189, 219, 232

Bayesian approach 173, 231–234, 239
Bilingualism 8, 77, 87, 90, 92, 98, 100–102, 444
Borrowing 410, 420
Bridge-languages (langues pivot) 375
Bungotai 460–462, 465

Calibration 241–242, 246–247
Calque 426, 428
Centring 269–270
Cepstral coefficients 225, 237–243, 248
Chain rule 204, 206–210
Character navigation 256–268, 279–280
Chinese legal modernization 403–406, 413, 418
Closing arguments 257, 261–262, 264–268, 272–273, 278, 280
Co-drafting of legislation/parallel drafting in different languages 378
Coherence 50, 152, 161
Collaborative authorship 170, 181

Common law 50, 51, 91, 93, 100, 339, 343, 384, 385, 392, 397, 413, 418, 468
– system 13–15, 18–20, 22, 33, 151, 441–443, 446
Confession 193, 202, 204, 206, 214
Constitutional norms 51–52
Contract drafting 14, 16, 18, 20, 22–29, 33
Converging 269, 271
Conversation analysis 204, 205, 215
Conversation management (CA) 202, 206
Conveyed meaning 322, 325, 326, 335, 337
Corpus, corpora 42–45, 85, 94–97, 99–101, 120, 126–127, 132, 178–179, 247, 261, 316
– analysis 42–45
Corpus of Contemporary American English (COCA) 43–44, 307
Courtroom 67, 84, 87, 94, 97, 100, 203, 280, 296, 298, 322, 363, 423
Courtroom discourse (similarity: language of the Courts) 256, 261, 262, 280, 437, 439–442, 448
Cross-examination 257, 261–262, 266–267, 271, 273, 277–280
Cryptotype 141, 143–146, 150, 151, 153, 162
Customary law 145

Defamation 83, 191–192, 321–337, 465
– in British law 321
– in US law 321
Demystification 351
Dictionaries 40–44, 228, 298–299, 433
Deixis 323
Direct method [for semi- or automatic speaker recognition] 239, 241
Discourse framing 324, 331–333
Discourse structure 260–261, 321, 322, 324, 337
Discriminatory power 186–188, 220, 222
Domain adaptation 113, 114

Equal Error Rate 186, 247
Error analysis 183, 184
Error rate 186, 196

Escapism 363–364
Evaluation of evidence 172–174, 178, 180, 181, 186, 187–189
Evidence 38, 52, 99, 171, 182, 195, 201–204, 210, 213–216, 222–224, 231–237, 247, 256, 262, 270, 295–303, 315–318, 321–326, 337, 353, 410, 448
Evidential value 171, 172, 187, 188
Extortion letter 179, 189, 191, 192

Fair notice 36, 48
False consensus bias 40
Filled pauses 228, 276
Film studies focus 347
Focussing 269–270, 273, 279
Forensic 256–257, 263–265, 267, 271–272, 281
– discourse 257, 265
– linguistics 169–172, 177, 179, 182, 189, 190, 195, 196, 287
– rhetoric 256, 265, 267, 271–272, 281
– rhetorical situation 263–265, 267, 271
– text comparison 171, 176–178, 181, 185, 186
Formant frequencies 225–227, 230, 236–239, 242–244, 246
Framing 269–270, 272–274, 278
Fundamental frequency 221–222, 224–227, 230, 234, 237–239, 243

Gairaigo 466, 469–470
Gaussian Mixture Model 232, 234, 236, 238–240, 243–244
GMM-UBM approach 244, 246
Grammatical referencing 321, 322, 333–335, 337

Harmonisation 208, 423, 431
Highlighting 270, 273, 277
Hindi 93, 94, 435–438
Human rights 54, 56, 58–62, 64–69, 71, 73–78, 87, 376, 432, 446

Identity 54, 58, 61, 74, 144, 163, 266, 269, 357, 437, 456
Ideology 92, 142
Idiolect 169–170, 226, 228
Implicature 141, 148, 149, 151, 152, 157, 161, 162, 323
Implicit information 150, 162
Indexing 269–270, 272–274, 278

Indian English 442–443
Innuendo 325, 326
Insinuation 326, 328
Institutional discourse 256–257, 263–266, 268, 270–271, 281–282
Intentionality 144, 322, 324, 326
Inter/intra individual variation 187, 188, 220–222, 227, 236, 247
Inter-/intra-author variation 187, 188
International language 56, 78, 377, 431
Intralinguistic translation 464–466
Intuition 39–40
I-vector approach 242

Japanese Civil Code 461–466
Japanese Constitution 460–461
Japanese language, Japanese law 450–475
Japanese language policy 457–459
Joyo kanji 459, 465–466

Katakana loanwords 469–472
Kogotai 460–462, 465

Language modernization 458–459, 462–464
Law 54–82
– and film 345–347
– and literature 342–345
– and TV 348–349
Lawyer portrayals 356–362
Lawyer-client privilege 396
Legal certainty 97, 313, 374, 395, 396
Legal communication 83, 95, 100–102, 141, 142, 143, 147
Legal discourse 90, 95, 350, 403, 414, 426, 432
Legal drafting 13–16, 19, 20, 22, 24–26, 28–31, 33–35
Legal education (similarity legal training) 84, 91, 97, 98, 340–343, 350, 357, 441, 425, 443
Legal knowledge extraction 109, 112, 119, 125, 126, 128
Legal language processing 109–111, 118, 122, 125, 130
Legal lexicon (similarity: legal terminology) 84, 89, 95, 96, 122, 123, 131–133, 436, 445, 467, 470
Legal models 402, 403, 405, 409, 410, 413, 414, 419, 424, 474

Legal neologisms 102, 392, 402–404, 407, 445, 460, 467, 474
Legal semantics modeling 112, 115, 130
Legal translation (similarity: translation) 84, 87–91, 101, 112, 317, 375, 402, 403–405, 408, 410, 416–418, 420–426, 436, 448, 439–440, 442, 444–448, 459, 468–470, 474
Legal transplants 403, 405, 413, 472, 475
Legal/statutory interpretation 16, 20, 36, 39, 47–50, 52, 109, 143, 148, 384, 443, 447
Legislation 84, 91–94, 96, 97
Legislative drafting 14, 16–18, 20–23, 95, 131, 409
Legislative preparatory works 383, 385, 389, 390
Libel 192, 323, 325
Lie detection 202
Likelihood ratio 173, 178, 185, 186, 188, 189, 219, 231–233, 239, 241–242, 244, 246, 248
Linguistic diversity 56–57, 60–61, 67, 69, 72, 76–77, 79, 435, 437, 439
Linguistic drift 423, 426, 427
Linguistic manipulation 174, 184, 191
Linguistic nationalism 55, 78, 437
Local jurisdiction focus 354–356

Malicious language 321, 322, 325, 335–337
Media impact 346–347
Metalanguage (differences between legal and linguistic) 287, 311
Minority language 55–61, 63, 65–73, 77–79, 438
Mismatched conditions 220, 241
Mixed jury 403–404, 445, 460, 468–469
Multidimensionality [of speaker characteristics] 224
Multilingual state 378, 430, 435–436, 439, 442, 448
Multilingualism 60, 77, 85, 99, 112, 373, 375, 399, 436–437, 441–444, 447–448
Multivariate Kernel Density method [for semiautomatic speaker recognition] 244
Mute law 144

Narrative 202, 212–215, 256–281
– anti-narrative 256–257, 260–261
– employment 256, 264–268, 272–274
– evaluation 258, 260–262, 265, 276
– forensic narration 256–258, 260–261, 264–268, 270–272, 275–278, 280–281
– inequality 256–266, 271–272, 275, 277–278, 280–281
– master 265–266, 271
– navigation 256, 265–268, 272, 280–281
– paradox 256, 258
– personal experience 258–261
– practices 256–281
– story vs. discourse 261–262
Narrativity 256, 258, 261–263, 267–268, 280
National language 54–57, 72, 78, 83–84, 90–91, 94, 98, 100–101, 437–438, 455–458
Neologisms 102, 192, 307, 308, 310, 313, 315, 392, 402, 404, 467–469

Official languages 17, 62, 72, 78, 84, 92, 121, 317, 423, 429, 430, 431, 435–441, 445
– of EU 373, 376, 377, 382
Ontologies 109, 111, 115, 116, 118, 123–125, 131
Opening statement 257, 261–262, 264–268, 277
Ordinary meaning 36, 39–52, 151, 158
Ordinary reader 326

Passing off 289
PEACE model 202, 210
Persuasion 257, 264–265, 269, 271, 276
Pet fish problem 49
Police and Criminal Evidence Act 201, 202
Polysemy 408
Population-level data 173, 182, 186, 189
Pragmatic inference 37–38, 145
Pragmatics 145, 146, 150, 162, 262, 323
Precedent 20–22, 51, 91, 100, 142, 145, 158, 384, 397, 463
Presupposition 148, 149, 151, 152, 155, 157, 160, 162, 170, 181
Probability 172, 173, 178, 188, 192, 233–235
Purposive interpretation 382, 383, 385, 386

Qualitative approach 169, 178, 182–184
Questioned speaker 219–220, 222–224, 229–230, 233–236, 239–242

Rapport 201–204, 206, 210, 211, 214, 216, 388
Reception 450, 453

Reception of Western legal models 402, 410, 413, 414
Reid Method 202, 216
Relevant population 223–224, 229–230, 233–235, 239–240
Responsibility claim 171, 179, 193, 194
Roman law 13, 37, 50–52

Sanskrit 435, 438, 445–446
Schemas 329
Scoring method [for semi-or automatic speaker recognition] 241
Semantic resources 109, 111, 112, 115, 119, 120, 122, 123, 130
Single film analysis 352–353
Social realism 363–364
Social themes 353–354
Spanish Civil Code 37
Speaker characteristics 220–222, 225–227, 229–231, 233, 244, 248
Speaker-discriminatory power 220, 222
Speech acts 140, 191, 193, 259, 321–323, 326–330, 334, 337
Standard Arabic 423, 430
Standard Hindi 436
Standard legal terminology (similarity: uniform terminology) 431, 436, 445
Statutes' recitals 391, 394
Storytelling 350–351
Strength of the evidence 182, 219, 223, 231, 232, 234
Styling 269–270, 273, 276–277, 280
Stylistic analysis 183
Suspect [suspected speaker] 171, 177, 202, 207, 211, 219–220, 222–224, 226, 229–230, 233–242, 281

Tamil 87, 89, 90, 93, 95, 99, 436, 444, 446
Text as offence 169, 191–193
Tippett plot 186, 245–247
Topic analysis 331, 337
Trade marks 287–302, 318
– Abercrombie scale 309–311
– average consumer 292–295, 300, 301, 313–316, 317–318
– blurring 287, 295, 299, 307
– characteristics of signs used as 287, 291–294, 297–311
– commercial functions served by 290–291, 293, 303, 305, 316
– dilution 287, 294–295, 299, 303, 306
– forensic linguistic contribution to analysing 287, 296–302
– infringement 293, 296, 298, 303, 311, 312, 317
– relative grounds for refusal to register 293, 317
– semiotic approach to analysing 303–306, 312
– similarity between signs claimed as 293–295, 297–302, 306–313, 316, 317
– tarnishment 287, 295, 299, 306
– treatment of marks with a reputation 294–295
Training for police interviewers 201
Translation (of the Qur'an) 423
Trial discourse 256–281
Truth or falsity 323, 327
Typicality 178, 183, 185, 187, 188, 222–224, 229–231, 234–236, 244, 248

Uncertainty 37, 241, 246, 375, 408, 409, 410
UNIDROIT Principles of international commercial contracts 393, 419
Universal Background Model 239

Vagueness 36, 48–49
Voice 256, 258, 265, 268–272, 280–281
– loss of 256, 268, 271–272, 280–281
– projection 256, 258, 265, 268–271, 280–281

Whole act rule 36
Whole code rule 36
Witness examination 257, 259, 261, 266–268, 271, 273, 277–281
Working language 84, 373, 375, 376, 378, 424, 430, 431

Zeitgeist 350

Bei Fragen zur Produktsicherheit wenden Sie sich bitte an:
If you have any questions regarding product safety,
please contact:

Walter de Gruyter GmbH
Genthiner Straße 13
10785 Berlin
productsafety@degruyterbrill.com